HANDBOOK
OF THE
LINGUISTIC GEOGRAPHY
OF
NEW ENGLAND

LINGUISTIC ATLAS OF NEW ENGLAND

BY

HANS KURATH

Director and Editor

WITH THE COLLABORATION OF

MILES L. HANLEY
Associate Director

BERNARD BLOCH
Assistant Editor

GUY S. LOWMAN, JR.
Principal Field Investigator

†MARCUS L. HANSEN
Historian

Three Volumes and a Handbook

SPONSORED BY THE AMERICAN COUNCIL OF LEARNED SOCIETIES

AND ASSISTED BY UNIVERSITIES AND COLLEGES IN NEW ENGLAND

AMERICAN COUNCIL OF LEARNED SOCIETIES

HANDBOOK
OF THE
LINGUISTIC GEOGRAPHY
OF
NEW ENGLAND

BY

HANS KURATH

WITH THE COLLABORATION OF

†MARCUS L. HANSEN   JULIA BLOCH

BERNARD BLOCH

AMERICAN COUNCIL OF LEARNED SOCIETIES
1219 Sixteenth Street, N. W.
Washington 6, D. C.

COMPOSED, PRINTED AND BOUND BY
THE GEORGE BANTA PUBLISHING COMPANY, MENASHA, WISCONSIN

PHOTOLITHOPRINTED IN THE UNITED STATES OF AMERICA BY
CUSHING - MALLOY, INC., ANN ARBOR, MICHIGAN, 1954

COMMITTEE IN CHARGE

HANS KURATH, Brown University, *Chairman*

LEONARD BLOOMFIELD, University of Chicago

CARL BRIDENBAUGH, Brown University

C. H. CARRUTHERS, McGill University

CHARLES H. GRANDGENT, Harvard University

MILES L. HANLEY, University of Wisconsin

†MARCUS L. HANSEN, University of Illinois

ARCHIBALD A. HILL, University of Virginia

JOHN S. KENYON, Hiram College

†GEORGE P. KRAPP, Columbia University

KEMP MALONE, The Johns Hopkins University

†EDUARD PROKOSCH, Yale University

WILLIAM A. READ, Louisiana State University

G. OSCAR RUSSELL, Ohio State University

STAFF

HANS KURATH, Brown University, *Director*

MILES L. HANLEY, University of Wisconsin, *Associate Director*

BERNARD BLOCH, Brown University

JULIA BLOCH

MARGUERITE CHAPALLAZ

†MARCUS L. HANSEN, University of Illinois

RACHEL S. HARRIS

LEE S. HULTZÉN, University of California at Los Angeles

MARTIN JOOS, University of Toronto

GUY S. LOWMAN, JR.

HERBERT PENZL, University of Illinois

CASSIL REYNARD

v

TABLE OF CONTENTS

PREFACE

I

The *Handbook* has a double purpose. It presents a concise outline of the regional and social dialects of New England, and it provides the apparatus for the critical evaluation and the historical interpretation of the materials contained in the *Linguistic Atlas of New England*.

The two major dialect areas of New England and their sub-divisions are described in Chapter I, *The Dialect Areas of New England*. It was not the intention to treat a large body of material in this chapter, but rather to show the dialectal structure of New England by means of clear and striking examples and to relate this regionalism in the speech of New England to the more tangible factors of the population history, such as the early settlement and the dissemination of the population in the 17th and 18th centuries, the population shifts resulting from the rise of the industries, the development of cultural and economic centers, of trade areas, of education, etc. The linguistic facts are presented in simple, non-technical form so that they may be readily understood not only by linguists, but also by historians, geographers, sociologists and others interested in the social and cultural history of New England.

Chapter III, *The Settlement of New England*, with a bibliography of New England regional and local history, is intended primarily for linguistic scholars who want to familiarize themselves with the history of the New England population as a background for the historical interpretation of New England speech. However, the skillful presentation of the subject by Marcus L. Hansen should make this chapter valuable to the historian as well. Since the original settlement, the 'land taking,' is without doubt the most important single factor in the genesis of the dialect regions of New England, it has been convenient to make the organization of Chapters I and III parallel. Historians and geographers will welcome this clear and striking demonstration of the coincidence of speech areas with settlement areas and culture areas (Chapter I); linguists, on the other hand, will see that a realistic interpretation and a true understanding of local, regional and social 'dialects'—including the 'dialects' of the cultured, the regional standard languages—cannot be attained without a thorough knowledge of the population history.

In Chapter II, *Methodology*, brief consideration is given to the organization of the field work (the selection of communities and informants, the qualifications of the field workers, the conduct of the interviews) and to editorial procedure (the evaluation of the field records, the make-up of the maps and commentaries). This chapter also contains a bibliography of selected studies in linguistic geography.

The tools of the language geographer, the phonetic alphabet and the work sheets, are presented in Chapters IV and V; the description of communities and informants (the case histories) in Chapter VI.

The *Handbook* was planned by the director and he assumes responsibility for its organization. However, a considerable part of the book was written or edited by his collaborators and there is no chapter in which he has not had their willing and generous help.

Chapter III, *The Settlement of New England*, was written by the late Professor Marcus L. Hansen of the University of Illinois, historical advisor to the Linguistic Atlas, whose early death is a great loss to the staff. Mr. Hansen approved of certain rearrangements made in the chapter, which were designed to facilitate the use of the historical material in the interpretation of the linguistic data. The historical bibliography was compiled under my direction by Margaret Chase George from a great many sources, but Mr. Hansen supplied the main stock of items. Professor Carl Bridenbaugh of Brown University has read the entire chapter and has made several important additions to the bibliography as well as a number of factual corrections in the text, for which grateful acknowledgment is made herewith.

The original short draft of the phonetic alphabet for the guidance of the field workers was made by the director and later revised in consultation with the members of the staff. In its present form, Chapter IV, *The Phonetic Alphabet*, is the work of Bernard Bloch. It has seemed better to include a full and detailed account of the phonetic notation of the Atlas than to limit this chapter to a statement of deviations from the accepted practice of the International Phonetic Association. The notes on the peculiarities in notation of the several field workers, printed in smaller type, are based on observations made during six years of editorial work, on transcription tests and on statements made by the field workers at the invitation of the director.

The work sheets (Chapter V) were compiled by the director and edited for the *Handbook* by Mr. Bloch.

The long and laborious task of compiling and editing Chapter VI, *Communities and Informants*, was performed by Julia Bloch. The histories of the towns are based largely on notes made by Mr. Hansen, and on the description of their present character by the field workers; the population figures have been taken directly from the Census of the United States and the various colonial and state censuses. Many other sources have been consulted in assembling and checking the data. The lives of the informants give in briefest form all the essential information supplied by the field workers. In many cases several pages of interesting and pertinent notes had to be reduced to a dozen short lines. If the case histories are trustworthy, as I believe them to be, and convey a wealth of information, short as they are, Mrs. Bloch's skill and meticulous care deserve a large measure of the credit.

It is not possible to name here the hundreds of informants from every walk of life who allowed themselves to be interviewed and who spent from six to twenty hours answering the field workers' questions, often with visible enjoyment of the mental exercise and the memories of bygone days which these evoked, sometimes from a sheer sense of duty toward their community, so characteristic of New England, or out of respect for the university or college with which the investigator was associated. The number of persons who helped us to select the informants is even larger: town clerks, who often know most of the families in the town; local historians, genealogists and antiquarians, whose advice was invaluable in selecting informants; college professors whose work or family connections had put them in touch with leading men in their state or section; librarians, businessmen, bankers and many a chance acquaintance. To all these willing informants and consultants the Atlas staff is most grateful.

The continued progress of the Linguistic Atlas is in no small measure due to the unflagging interest and the resourcefulness of Dr. Waldo G. Leland, historian and Director of the American Council of Learned Societies. In broad questions of policy as well as in practical matters his advice and help were always cordially given.

Further acknowledgments are made below in the historical sketch of the Atlas project.

II

The Linguistic Atlas project was initiated by members of the Modern Language Association of America and of the Linguistic Society of America.

From the time of its organization in 1921 until the actual launching of the Atlas project, the Research Group of the MLA for Present-Day English devoted much thought and discussion to the question of a survey of American English. Many scholars participated in this early exploration of the problem: Harry Morgan Ayres of Columbia, James L. Barker of Utah, William Frank Bryan of Northwestern, Sir William Craigie of Oxford and Chicago, Charles C. Fries of Michigan, Charles Hall Grandgent of Harvard, William Cabell Greet of Columbia, Miles L. Hanley of Wisconsin, John S. Kenyon of Hiram, George Philip Krapp of Columbia, Hans Kurath, then of Ohio State, John Matthews Manly of Chicago, Samuel Moore of Michigan, Allen Walker Read, then of Missouri, now of Chicago, James Finch Royster of North Carolina, and Fred Newton Scott of Michigan.

The first formal proposal to consider the making of a Linguistic Atlas of the United States was made in the Present-Day English Group of the Modern Language Association in December, 1928, and a committee, consisting of Charles C. Fries (chairman), William F. Bryan, Cabell Greet, John S. Kenyon, Hans Kurath and Allen Walker Read, was appointed to study the matter. In January, 1929, without being aware of the existence of this committee, E. H. Sturtevant of Yale, delegate of the Linguistic Society to the American Council of Learned Societies, following up a suggestion made by Edward Sapir of Yale, had brought to the attention of the Council the desirability of making a systematic survey of American English. The president of the Council at this time was Edward C. Armstrong of Princeton, a scholar conscious of the importance of linguistic geography.

On February 22–23, 1929, C. C. Fries arranged a meeting of the MLA Committee in Cleveland and invited E. H. Sturtevant to attend. The cost of this meeting was borne by the National Council of Teachers of English, who recognized the importance of this project for any study of the English language in America.

In March, 1929, a definite proposal, formulated at the Cleveland meeting, was presented by E. H. Sturtevant to the Executive Committee of the American Council of Learned Societies, which authorized the organization of a conference to discuss the proposal, and made an appropriation for the purpose. Preparations for this conference on a Linguistic Atlas of the United States and Canada were made by E. H. Sturtevant, who had been officially designated by the chairman of the MLA committee as his representative to arrange for the conference. The conference, attended by fifty scholars, Karl Young presiding, was held at Yale University on August 2–3, 1929, as a part of the summer Linguistic Institute of the Linguistic Society of America. A full report has been published in *Bulletin No. 4* of the Linguistic Society.

As a result of the conference, the Executive Committee of the American Council of Learned Societies authorized (August 31, 1929) the appointment of a committee to prepare and submit to the Council a budgeted plan for a Linguistic Atlas of the United States and Canada. This committee consisted of the following: Hans Kurath (chairman), Leonard Bloomfield of Chicago, C. H. Carruthers of McGill, C. H. Grandgent of Harvard, Miles L. Hanley of Wisconsin, Marcus L. Hansen of Illinois, John S. Kenyon of Hiram, George P. Krapp of Columbia, Eduard Prokosch of Yale and G. Oscar Russell of Ohio State. Subsequently William A. Read of Louisiana, Archibald A. Hill of Virginia and Kemp Malone of the Johns Hopkins were appointed to the committee. The committee estimated the total cost of a comprehensive Atlas of the speech of the United States at $664,000. The Council, at its annual meeting on January 31, 1930, endorsed the plan in principle, but requested the committee to consider the possibility of 'conducting an experimental investigation over a restricted geographical area, to serve as a demonstration of the method to be followed, and as a basis for further estimates of the requirements of the undertaking.'

The committee accordingly drew up plans for a New England Atlas and secured the promise of the coöperation of Yale University in case the plan should be accepted. The Executive Committee of the Council approved the plan for the New England study and authorized the committee to make arrangements for the coöperation of New England universities and colleges. At the annual meeting of the Council in January, 1931, the Executive Committee was authorized 'to enter, in the name of the Council, into such arrangements with institutions, organizations and individuals as may be necessary for the execution of the plans for a study of New England speech,' and an appropriation was made available as a contribution to the expenses of the study.

There followed a period of active preparation for the beginning of the work. A staff was organized, with Hans Kurath, then of Ohio State, now of Brown University, as director, and Miles L. Hanley of the University of Wisconsin as associate director. Yale University agreed to furnish, without charge, offices for the headquarters of the project, to contribute half the salary of the associate director, and to provide a Sterling Fellowship for one of the field workers. Other members of the staff were to be supported in part by fellowships provided by Brown University (1931–33) and the University of Vermont (1932–33).

In July, 1931, the staff was brought together for a final training period of six weeks in connection with the Linguistic Institute. The process of training was greatly facilitated by Professor Jakob Jud of the University of Zürich and by Dr. Paul Scheuermeier of Bern, who, on the basis of their experiences in speech mapping in Italy and Switzerland, discussed the aims of linguistic geography and demonstrated methods of field work.

During the first summer (1931) Marcus L. Hansen of the University of Illinois made a careful study of the history of the population of New England in order to furnish a background for the selection of the communities in which field work was to be carried on.

After these preliminaries, the field work was commenced and continued actively until its completion in September, 1933, within the period of 25 months that had been allotted to it. (The names of the field workers and an indication of their shares in the field work appear in the upper left corner of the maps.)

During the second year of field work (1932–33) Harvard University provided half the salary of the associate director. Harvard made a similar provision also for the following year (1933–34) as a contribution toward the phonographic recording of New England speech.

The editing of the New England Atlas was begun in the spring of 1933. Volumes I and II have been fully edited and Volume III will be completed shortly.

The support of the *Linguistic Atlas of New England* has been assured by appropriations from the American Council of Learned Societies by a special grant from the Rockefeller Foundation and by very substantial assistance from universities and colleges in New England. This has consisted of fellowships at Brown University, Yale University and the University of Vermont; of part-time faculty arrangements at Yale University, Harvard University and Brown University, and at Mount Holyoke College and Dartmouth College; and of the providing of offices by Yale University for one year and by Brown University during the last seven years. The New England Atlas may be regarded, therefore, as a cooperative enterprise in which American scholarship in general is represented by the American Council of Learned Societies, and in which several of the institutions of higher learning in New England have participated.

HANS KURATH
Director of the Linguistic Atlas

April 2, 1939

HANDBOOK
OF THE
LINGUISTIC GEOGRAPHY
OF
NEW ENGLAND

HANDBOOK
OF THE
LINGUISTIC GEOGRAPHY
OF
NEW ENGLAND

CHAPTER I

THE DIALECT AREAS OF NEW ENGLAND*

[Italic numbers preceding italic words refer to maps in the Atlas; numbers preceding or following place names or standing alone refer to communities represented on the maps.]

INTRODUCTORY

The brief outline presented here of the dialect areas of New England and of the trends in New England speech is intended primarily to stimulate investigation of the many problems in the development of New England speech, its relation to the speech of England, and its contribution to the speech of the northern United States and of Canada. Many of the views expressed here are obviously tentative; they will be modified and replaced by sounder ones as the wealth of material presented in the *Linguistic Atlas of New England* is interpreted map by map, item by item. Much work lies ahead for those who want to arrive at a realistic conception of the origin of this type—or rather of two distinct types—of American English.

Since the speech of the Hudson Valley and of the vast and populous areas beyond is known only very vaguely, it is not yet possible to visualize New England speech in the perspective of its national setting. But the internal regional structure of the New England Area is tolerably clear.

Regional differences within New England, as elsewhere, are greater in the homely vocabulary of the family and the farm than in the vocabulary of 'society' and of urban areas. Hence most of the illustrations given are humble words. Such words reflect most clearly the regional pattern of pre-industrial New England, which must be reconstructed as well as possible if we would understand fully the present speech areas and trace the sources of New England speech back to the dialects of England.

INNOVATIONS

Innovations arise in New England in several ways. Many are derived from the literary language, which is almost universally known and is spread through the printed page, through the schools and through contact with the well-read upper classes of society. From the very beginning of the settlement most towns supported a minister who also taught the young, and many had a schoolmaster or a schoolma'am as well. The Bible was read in

---

* Various items briefly dealt with in this chapter have been more fully treated by members of the Atlas staff and by some of my students. The titles of these papers are given in the Bibliography of Linguistic Geography in Chapter II: 56, 57 Bloch, 70 Daddow, 108 Hanley, 109 Harris, 132, 134 Kurath, 154 Penzl. To these must be added Margaret T. Chase, *The Derivatives of Middle English ŏ in New England Speech;* Master's Thesis, Brown University, 1936 (in typescript).

For information concerning the speech of the Hudson Valley I am indebted to Miss Jane E. Daddow, now engaged in a survey of that important area; for the distribution of dialectal pronunciations in England, to Guy S. Lowman, Jr., who made a preliminary survey of the folk speech of southern England in 1937–38. The materials gathered by Lowman for the *Linguistic Atlas of the South Atlantic States*, now nearly complete but as yet unedited, have been invaluable in correcting my perspective. The charts in this chapter were drawn by Bernard Bloch.

I gratefully acknowledge my indebtedness to all of them.—H.K.

many homes, and reading soon became a habit in New England. A high regard for learning and for literature culminated in the nineteenth century in a distinctive and varied literature that found many readers. Compulsory education, introduced in the 1860's, brought every child into contact with the printed page. All these cultural influences resulted in a wide-spread knowledge of the literary language and opened the way for the replacement of local terms and pronunciations by standard forms.

Innovations originating in the written language and disseminated by the schools appear simultaneously at many points, but spread more rapidly and more widely in urbanized areas than in rural sections. For this reason the Boston Area and the thickly populated tract extending from 1 Stamford to 26 New Haven and from there northward to 224 Springfield (see map on page 7) often lack local dialect forms that are still current in the 'back country' of these two urbanized areas.

The acceptance of such innovations in the Boston Area not infrequently produces a breach in the coastal dialect area. Thus *262 spindle out* 'tassel out' (see Chart 7), and *553 butcher* with the vowel of *boot*, are current north and south of Boston, but—except for sporadic instances—not in the Boston Area.

When a dialect feature now occurs only north of Boston, or even when it is now confined to coastal Maine, the presumption is that it was formerly also used in the Boston Area, the heart of the Massachusetts Bay Colony.

The following appear to be rather recent innovations:

236 earthworm, still restricted largely to the better educated in the cities (cf. 26 New Haven, 224 Springfield, 60 Newport, 80 Providence, 150 Boston, 205 Worcester). On New Hampshire Bay (194, 196, 302) *earthworm* may be old, as it doubtless is in the Tidewater region of the South Atlantic States. *Earthworm* is encroaching upon *angleworm*, which in turn has replaced or competes with the more local terms *angledog, eaceworm, fishworm* and *mudworm* (see Chart 23).

145 funnel (for pouring liquids) is still rather a city word even in southern New England. In northern New England *tunnel* is in general use (cf. 280 Burlington, 360 Portland); in southern New England the country people use *tunnel* predominantly, and older city dwellers have as yet not given it up (cf. 26 New Haven, 38 Middletown, 224 Springfield, 32 New London, 80 Providence, 103 Fall River, 150 Boston).

577 seesaw is encroaching upon *teeter (board)* and the more local terms *teeter-totter, tinter, dandle, tilt(er), teedle* everywhere in New England, especially in the south, but the older terms are still vigorous. In the Plymouth Area the transition appears to be directly from *tilt, tilting board* to *seesaw*, and in western Rhode Island from *dandle* to *seesaw*. In other areas the local term was first replaced by *teeter (board)*: thus *tilter* on Casco Bay, Maine, *teedle* in Essex County, Massachusetts, and probably also *tinter* in New Haven County and the Lower Connecticut Valley.

Other terms that have gained a foothold and have spread more or less widely are:

299 cottage cheese, for various older terms (see Chart 14);

351 porch, for earlier *piazza;*

349 gutter, for *eavespout* and *eavestrough;*

355 apartment, for *tenement;*

344 pantry, for *buttery, buttry* (see Chart 4);

338 clothes closet, for *clothes press;*

175 near horse, for *nigh horse* (mostly in Western New England);

554 shopping, for *trading*;

403 at home, for *to home*;

289 griddle cake, for *fritter* (in Eastern New England).

In some instances the older expressions are now rustic or old-fashioned or have the character of relics, as in *313 het over*, replaced by *warmed over*.

Striking changes are in progress in the pronunciation of some vowels and diphthongs: [o] as in *road, stone, home;* [u] before labials, as in *room, hoop;* [ɒ] as in *rod, John, crop;* [a] as in *glass, after, dance;* [u] as in *new, student, due;* [aɪ] as in *nine, spider;* [aʊ] as in *mountain, towel, owl*. The precise manner in which new pronunciations are being accepted can be worked out in detail on the basis of the materials of the Atlas with due regard for regional differences, social groups, age groups, and the family background of the informants. Here only rough generalizations can be offered regarding these innovations.

The so-called 'New England short *o*' in words like *361B coat, 43 road, 403 home*, varying from fronted [oᵉ] to fronted [ɔ] and [ʌ], is receding throughout New England (see Chart 1). It has almost completely disappeared in Western New England and the southern part of the Eastern Margin (except for *634 whole*) and has lost much ground in southeastern New England as well, including the Boston Area. The newer sound, a prolonged [o] or an up-gliding diphthong [oʊ], appears first in bookish words where the school influence is strong, and persists longest in 'homely' words, especially in farm words. Thus many New Englanders who have the modern vowel in *35 stone, 232 toad, 43 road* still use the 'short *o*' in *159 whetstone, 160 grindstone, 119 stone wall, 168 stone boat, 280 toadstool, 44 back road*.

A down-gliding diphthongal vowel [oᵉ] in words like *coat, road, home* is in general use in the Charleston Area of South Carolina and in the greater part of rural England south of the Wash, excepting the counties surrounding London.

Both [ʊ] and [u] are current in words like *337 room, 155 broom, 348 roof, 147 hoop* and *248 root*. In *room* and *broom* the long [u·] is gaining ground in southern and western New England, but in the northeast the short [ʊ] is still general. The trends in *roof, hoop* and *root* are confused and need to be studied in detail.

The rounded vowel [ɒ] of Eastern New England in words like *45 rod, 286 johnnycake* and *124 crop* is losing ground. It is most consistently used in the northeast, but has been extensively replaced by an unrounded variety in the Eastern Margin and in such cities as *80 Providence* in the Eastern Focal Area. The fully rounded and raised variety [ɔ] is now regarded as rustic. As the result of this trend, some Easterners now have distinct phonemes in *rod, crop* and in *724 off, 550 law, 291 salt*.

In words of the type of *75 afternoon, 311 glass, 114 pasture, 410 dance*, the low-front vowel [a] appears to be gaining ground among the better educated in the cities of Southern New England, but losing ground in the countryside. It is significant that both the social shibboleth *695 can't* and the rustic *114 pasture* have [a] more widely than other words of this type and that the rather recently introduced term *524 casket* (for older *coffin*) almost universally has the vowel [æ] of *cat*. As a result of antagonistic and shifting trends, usage is much confused in Eastern New England at the present time and few persons in this area have a fixed pattern.

Words of the type of *186 tube, 563 due, 361A new*, have the simple vowel [u] in most of Eastern New England, in both cultivated and rustic speech. In Western New England [u] is widely used, but a falling diphthong [ɪu] is also common (see Chart 17). The rising diphthong [ju], so common in Southern speech, is rare in New England, but appears to be making headway among the better educated in Western New England. Pronunciations of the type of [u] and [ɪu] are common in the folk speech of eastern England to this day although Standard British English has [ju].

The diphthong [aɪ] as in *55 nine, 132 spider, 87 nice* usually begins low-front, less commonly low-central, and the tongue glides up to high position. An older pronunciation of the diphthong with a raised low-central beginning, [ɐɪ], or even a mid-central beginning, [əɪ], and a swift up-glide is still fairly common among older speakers, notably in rural areas, but is vanishing rapidly. In England this type is now current in the folk speech of East Anglia and the southwestern counties, as well as Oxford and Hampshire.

The situation is rather different in the diphthong [aʊ] as in *39 mountain, 191 cow, 142 towel* (see Chart 2). The modern diphthong [aʊ], beginning low-front, less often low-central, is gaining ground rapidly and has nearly eliminated older types of pronunciation in the urbanized areas of southern New England. In the Upper Connecticut Valley, in eastern New Hampshire and in the adjoining part of Maine, however, the older type [æʊ], with a raised low-front beginning (even [ɛʊ], with a mid-front beginning) is still widely current, though not as common as in the South Atlantic States. A very different old-fashioned diphthong, [ɐʊ], with a lowered mid-central beginning, is also occasionally encountered in all parts of New England, notably in the coast towns from *302 Seabrook, New Hampshire,* to *406 Gouldsboro, Maine,* where [æʊ] is rare. At present [æʊ, ɛʊ] is characteristic of the folk speech of most of eastern England, including the London area, and [ɐʊ, əʊ] of East Anglia and the southwestern counties.

The older diphthong [aɪ] in words like *294 boiled, 251 poison, 491 joint* is remembered by many but little used now.

In the folk speech of New England, standard pronunciations are now encroaching upon such older forms as *33 loam* [lum], still common; *585 goal* [gul], still common in children's games; *296 yolk* [jɛlk, jɔlk], still common (see Chart 3); *262 tassel* [tɔsl], still common; *633 nothing* [nɑθɪn]; *487 gums* [gʊmz, gumz]; *266 tomato* [təmætə], now mostly [təmetə] with the vowel of *make,* but [təmatə] with the vowel of *father* is not uncommon; *136 china* [tʃaɪni], now uncommon; *435 Daniel* [dænəl], still predominant; *208 trough* [trɔθ], still common; *265 muskmelon* [mʌʃmɛlən]; *279 mushroom* [mʌʃərun].

Some dialectal past tense forms are strongly entrenched in folk speech but are gradually yielding to the standard forms, e.g., *645 rung* to *rang, 658 run* to *ran, 640 come* to *came, 665 tore up* to *torn up, 480 wore out* to *worn out, 649 give* to *gave, 646 eat* and *et* to *ate. 580 dove* is the usual form on all social levels, but *dived* is advancing.

RELICS

Many features of folk speech are rapidly disappearing in New England; some are nearly extinct and many others have been entirely abandoned. The rural northern states, especially New Hampshire and Maine, have preserved local dialect features much more extensively than the industrialized southern section of New England. In southern New England relics of older usage are apt to be found on the islands (52 Block Island, 122 Martha's Vineyard, 124 Nantucket), on points of land (120 Cape Cod, 200 Cape Ann), and in quiescent coast towns (28 Guilford-Madison, 30 Saybrook, 56 Narragansett, 102 Westport, 180 Marblehead).

When relics of a dialect feature appear in Western as well as in Eastern New England, it is to be assumed that it was formerly current among certain social groups or families in all parts of New England. This is clearly the case in the uninflected plural of nouns of measure, *46 nine foot, 45 ten rod, 45 ten mile, 83 three year*; in *73 sunup* 'sunrise'; in *217 foddering time* 'chore time, feeding time'; in *642 clum* and *clim* 'climbed'; and probably also in *198 nicker* 'whinny'. The pronunciation of *490 palm* (of the hand), *528 psalm* and *478 calm* to rhyme with *lamb*, now rare even in folk speech except for the northeast, must once have been rather common everywhere; and *151 hammer* formerly had the same vowel as *harm* in the speech of many New Englanders, both east and west.

When an expression, a grammatical form or a pronunciation is now confined to the folk speech of eastern or northeastern New England, it may or may not have been current formerly also in Western New England. Since Western New England has been more hospitable to innovations than the secluded Eastern Area, features that are now encountered only in the east may be relics of usage now abandoned in the west. Written records of an early date may help us in such cases to arrive at a decision.

Eastern relics are numerous and only a few can be mentioned here. Most of them are now restricted to the area north of Boston.

The following are some of the terms that have survived more or less extensively in eastern folk speech:

89 fairing, fairing up, fairing off, fairing away 'clearing up (of the weather)', in scattered points;

90 smurring up 'clouding up' and *88 smurry* 'cloudy,' only on the seaboard;

352 porch '(kitchen) ell', on the seaboard;

410 (kitchen) break-down 'kitchen dance,' in New Hampshire and Maine;

381 grandsir [grænsə] 'grandfather,' north of Boston;

299 curd cheese, curd 'cottage cheese,' in Maine and in scattered points in the Boston Area;

38 nubble 'knoll (in a field),' in Maine.

The following verb forms are now largely restricted to rustic speech of the older generation in northeastern New England:

riz 'rose,' recorded in the phrase *657 the sun rose*;

riz 'risen,' in the expression *281 riz bread* 'raised bread';

driv 'drove' and *driv* 'driven,' recorded in the phrases *645 I drove a nail* and *I have driven many nails*;

580 div in 'dived in.'

The postvocalic *r* in words like *101 barn, 488 beard, 325 chair*, and the *r*-vowel in words like *59 thirty, 377 girl* and *70 Saturday, 370 father* is now rarely heard from the old stock in Eastern New England, except on *122 Martha's Vineyard* and in *180 Marblehead* and *200 Rockport*; even in the Scotch-Irish towns *324 Antrim*, New Hampshire, and *294 Ryegate*, Vermont, it is disappearing fast. Traces of it have survived, however, especially on Narragansett Bay and in the Plymouth Area and in scattered points on the coast of Maine (*384, 400, 407*). In northern Maine (*420–424*) the *r* in such words was introduced from New Brunswick (*426–431*), where it is in regular use. This feature doubtless was formerly more common in Eastern New England.

In the folk speech of northeastern New England *304 sausage* not infrequently has the vowel [æ] as in *sap* or [a] as in the eastern pronunciation of *glass*. The vowel [a] appears here also in *376 daughter* beside the more common [ɒ] of *dot*. In the rather widely used rustic *253 (garden) sauce* 'vegetables' both [æ] and [a] occur more extensively, the former also in Western New England.

Other relic pronunciations are:

31 marsh homonymous with *mash*, observed in many communities on the seaboard from eastern Long Island (51) to New Brunswick (429); and *488 beard* rhyming with *aired*, in Maine.

Expressions and pronunciations now so rare that they have been encountered by the Atlas staff only in a few communities remind us of the fate that has overtaken countless dialect features brought to the New World from virtually all the counties of England, Scotland and Ireland. The great majority of the early settlers, if not the leading personalities, must have spoken the various local dialects, modified in some cases by contact with a provincial center in England. Unless a large or influential element in a town came from the same county in England, or from neighboring counties with similar speech, dialectal terms were abandoned in favor of literary expressions. This process has continued through the centuries.

The list of relics given below contains only features that are still used in the natural speech of one or more of our informants, and only spontaneously offered forms are cited. Most of these features are remembered by a large number of informants as belonging to the speech of a bygone generation.

395 fetched up 'brought up, reared,' in northern New Hampshire (342, 344) and Maine (366, 376, 408);

381 granther [grænθə] 'grandfather,' in New Hampshire (310, 348) and Maine (392);

288 squeal 'corn mush served with pork fat,' only in 302 Seabrook, New Hampshire;

267 cleave-stone peach 'freestone peach,' on Long Island (51), Block Island (52) and lower Cape Cod (118–120);

102 on the great-beams 'in the loft,' in scattered communities from Long Island northward to New Hampshire (51, 219, 214, 334, 348), pronounced [ˈgrɛtbimz] in 51 (see Chart 24);

236 rainworm 'earthworm' (cf. Old English *regnwyrm*), in two widely separated points: 102 Westport in the Narragansett Bay Area, and 384 Waldoboro on the coast of Maine (settled by Germans; cf. *Regenwurm*);

110 hogboist [hɔgbaɪst] 'hog house,' in two communities on Long Island Sound: 28 Madison, settled largely from Kent and Surrey in England, where *boist* 'hut' was still current in the nineteenth century (see NED under *boist*), and 56 Narragansett;

576 belly-cachunk 'belly-bump,' only in 32 New London;

642 clum 'climbed,' in scattered points (28, 29; 106, 113; 310; 372, 380, 394, 407, 408; 426, 430, 431);

376 daughter pronounced with the vowel [æ] of *hat*, in three Old New Hampshire settlements (310, 316, 368);

151 hammer beginning like *hum*, in 200 Rockport on Cape Ann and in two Old New Hampshire settlements (304, 312);

435 Daniel pronounced with the vowel [a] of *darn*, only in 362 Standish, Maine;

337 chamber with the vowel [æ] of *hat*, in scattered communities (33, 44, 272, 310), a pronunciation still widely current in New England c. 1850.

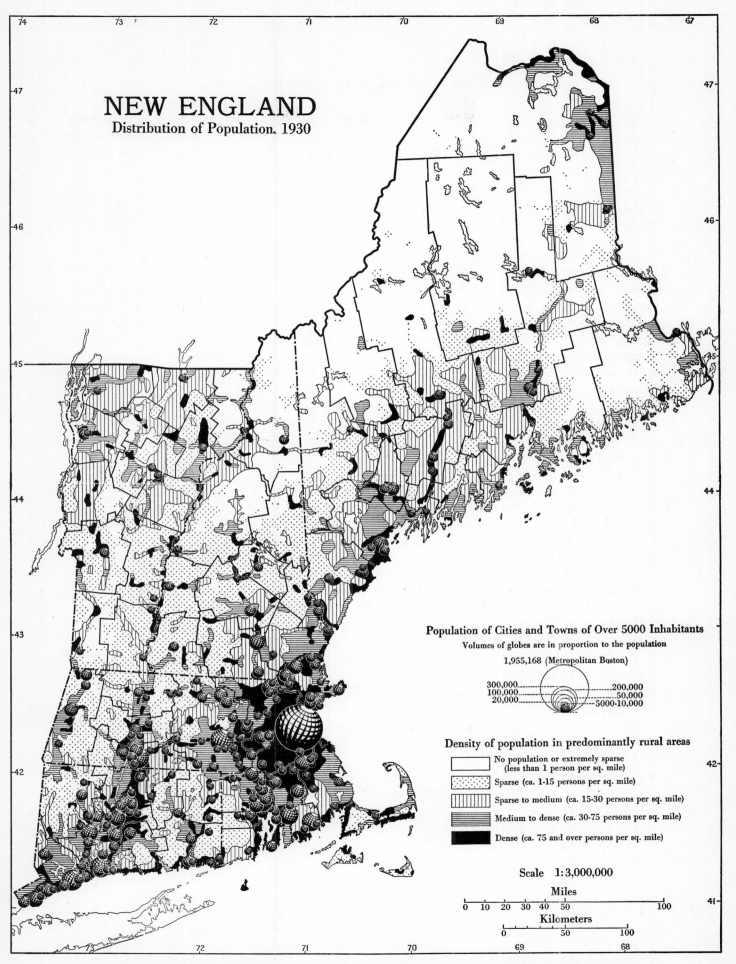

NEW ENGLAND

Distribution of Population, 1930

Population of Cities and Towns of Over 5000 Inhabitants

Volumes of globes are in proportion to the population

1,955,168 (Metropolitan Boston)

300,000 · · · · · · · · · · 200,000
100,000 · · · · · · · · · · 50,000
20,000 · · · · · · · · · · 5000·10,000

Density of population in predominantly rural areas

No population or extremely sparse
(less than 1 person per sq. mile)

Sparse (ca. 1-15 persons per sq. mile)

Sparse to medium (ca. 15-30 persons per sq. mile)

Medium to dense (ca. 30-75 persons per sq. mile)

Dense (ca. 75 and over persons per sq. mile)

Scale   1:3,000,000

Miles

0 10 20 30 40 50   100

Kilometers

0   50   100

From John K. Wright, *Regions and Landscapes of New England,* in *New England's Prospect: 1933.*
American Geographical Society, Special Publication No. 16. New York, 1933.

EASTERN NEW ENGLAND

New England has two major dialect areas, an Eastern and a Western. The Eastern Area corresponds roughly to the section of New England occupied in gradual expansion from the Atlantic seaboard; the Western, to the area settled from the Lower Connecticut Valley and from Long Island Sound west of the Connecticut River. The 'seam' between these two settlement areas runs straight north from the mouth of the Connecticut River (between 30 and 31) through Connecticut and Massachusetts to the southern boundary of Franklin County (212), where it swerves west and follows the southern boundary of Franklin County to the Berkshires (232). Here it turns north again and runs along the crest of the Green Mountains to the northern boundary of Vermont (between 286 and 288).

The eastern settlements on the Atlantic seaboard, Massachusetts Bay, Plymouth, Narragansett Bay and New London, expanded very slowly after 1640. Except for the tenuous link on Long Island Sound, the eastern settlements did not establish contact with the settlements on the Connecticut River for several generations. In Connecticut the gap was bridged by about 1700, in Massachusetts not until about 1735. (See Plates 1 and 2 in the back of the book.)

The 'seam' between the two major areas of settlement runs through the hill country of eastern Connecticut and central Massachusetts, which has always been sparsely populated; the population center of Greater Boston is separated to this day from the population centers of the Lower Connecticut Valley and Long Island Sound by a wide agricultural belt that has helped to preserve in large measure the dialectal differences between Eastern and Western New England. (See the accompanying population map.)

It is convenient to divide the Eastern section into a Focal Area comprising all the early settlements on the Atlantic seaboard except New London, and a Marginal Area including the primary settlement of New London and the secondary settlements of Windham County in Connecticut, Worcester and Franklin Counties in Massachusetts, the counties in New Hampshire and Vermont adjoining the Connecticut River, and the north-central counties of Vermont (Washington, Lamoille and Orleans).

The subdivisions of the Eastern Focal Area are, from south to north: (1) Narragansett Bay (Rhode Island, 52–82), (2) the Plymouth Area (the Old Colony, Martha's Vineyard, Nantucket, 102–125), (3) the Boston Area (the Massachusetts Bay Colony exclusive of Essex County, 140–160, 203, 211), (4) Essex County (180–200), (5) the Merrimack Valley in New Hampshire (314, 315, 318–324, 333, 338), (6) Eastern New Hampshire ('Old New Hampshire,' 308–312, 316, 348), (7) York County, Maine (352–358), (8) Maine (Casco Bay, 359–392; Penobscot Bay, 394–404, 416; Eastern Maine, 406–412, 418; Northern Maine, 420–424).

The Eastern Margin has three subareas: (1) the New London Area, a primary settlement (31–34, 43, 48), (2) the Worcester Area, which includes the northern part of Windham County, Connecticut (49; 201, 202, 204–210, 212, 218, 222), (3) the Upper Connecticut Valley from Franklin County, Massachusetts, north to Canada (214, 228, 230; 254–259, 266–272, 282, 284, 288–296; 328–332, 334–337, 340–344).

Among features of pronunciation current in the entire Eastern Area, or a large part of it, and lacking or rare in Western New England, may be mentioned:

The loss of r unless it is followed by a vowel in the same word or stress group, as in 101 *barn, 488 beard* and in *54 four, 325 chair* (at the end of a stress group or when followed by a word beginning with a consonant). See Chart 16.

The loss of 'retroflection' or *r*-color in the stressed vowel of words like *377 girl, 59 thirty* and the unstressed vowel of words like *370 father, 75 afternoon* (see Chart 8).

The use of the low-front vowel [a] in *192 calf, 80 half* and other words in which an *l* preceding the *f* has been lost (see Chart 8).

The [a] is restricted to a much smaller area in words like *75 afternoon, 311 glass, 114 pasture* (see Charts 8 and 15). It is common only in the Boston Area, in Essex County and in Maine from Casco Bay east (359—); elsewhere in the Eastern Area it appears sporadically either as an old-fashioned pronunciation or as a feature of cultivated speech. In the Lower Connecticut Valley it is almost invariably a feature of cultivated speech.

The low-back vowel [ɒ], more or less rounded, in words like *45 rod, 286 johnnycake, 537 college, 124 crop, 35 rock,* where Western New England has the low-central vowel [ɑ] (see Chart 8).

The low-back vowel [ɒ], more or less rounded, in words like *550 law, 724 off, 291 salt,* where Western New England has the raised and well-rounded low-back vowel [ɔ].

The high-central vowel [ɪ] in the unstressed syllable of *142 towel, 229 squirrel.* (In *343 kitchen, 39 mountain* this high vowel is common in the folk speech of Western New England as well.)

274 strawberry and *540 library* are often pronounced in two syllables as [strɒbri] and [laɪbri] and *525 cemetery* in three syllables as [sɛmɪtri]; or else the *r* of the last syllable is preceded by the obscure vowel [ə] instead of [ɛ]. Such pronunciations have limited currency also in the Lower Connecticut Valley.

553 butcher has the close vowel [u] of *boot* in the folk speech of the greater part of the Eastern Focal Area, which was formerly doubtless in common use also in the 150 Boston and the 60 Newport Areas and in the Eastern Margin. This pronunciation has survived also in Hartford County, Connecticut (21–24, 40–41), and in scattered points of Western New England. In this instance, as in many others, a feature once common in all of New England has been preserved more fully in Eastern New England, especially in the rural northeast.

The loss of [h] in *163 wheelbarrow, 159 whetstone,* etc., is common on the coast from 180 Marblehead to 408 Machias, and occurs in scattered points elsewhere (especially in 51 on Eastern Long Island and on 52 Block Island). In *183 wharf,* a seashore term, the loss of [h] is much more widespread. It seems that the conservative coast towns from Long Island Sound to New Brunswick have preserved in this word a type of pronunciation that was widely current in New England in Colonial times and that this coastal pronunciation has been retained in the upland through contact with the seashore.

The number of words that are found only in Eastern New England is considerable. Some are current in the entire area, but often less common in the Margin; some are confined to the Eastern Focal Area; others are now restricted to a region north of Boston or to the conservative coast towns or islands, or have survived only in scattered communities.

Among the expressions that are used in all or most of the Eastern Area, at least in folk speech, are the following:

298 bonny-clapper, bonny-clabber 'thick sour milk,' excepting Rhode Island west of the Bay and the greater part of the Upper Connecticut Valley west of the River (see Charts 7 and 13);

281 white-bread 'wheat bread' (stressed on the first syllable), excepting eastern Connecticut (see Chart 7);

342 comforter 'a thick quilt,' also scattered instances in Western New England, beside the usual *comfortable* (see Chart 7);

244 buttonwood 'sycamore, plane tree,' rare in eastern Connecticut, current also in western Vermont (see Chart 12);

168 (stone) drag 'stone boat, for hauling stones from the field' (see Chart 7);

110 (pig) sty 'pig pen, hog pen,' excepting most of the Upper Connecticut Valley (scattered instances occur in the Lower Connecticut Valley);

576 belly-bump(er) and *belly-bunt* 'face-down on a sled,' the latter variant in the Worcester Area and in the Upper Connecticut Valley as well as in western Vermont.

The following expressions are common in the Eastern Focal Area but are not widely used in the Margin or are lacking there altogether:

262 spindle out 'tassel out,' now lost in the Boston Area and not found in the Margin (see Chart 7);

334 funnel 'stove pipe,' essentially a Massachusetts Bay word, rare in Rhode Island and the Plymouth Area and not common in the Worcester Area and the Upper Connecticut Valley (see Chart 7);

108 lean-to and *tie-up* 'cow stable,' rare in Rhode Island and the Upper Connecticut Valley;

305 hog's head cheese 'head cheese,' not found in Rhode Island and rare in the Worcester Area;

292 apple dowdy 'deep-dish apple pie,' rare in Rhode Island and the Worcester Area and not used in eastern Connecticut;

299 sour-milk cheese 'cottage cheese,' not used in the Eastern Margin (see Chart 14);

289 fritter 'griddle cake,' not found in the Plymouth Area and Rhode Island or in the Margin (see Chart 7);

209 harslet, hasslet 'liver and lights,' not current in Rhode Island and the southern part of the Margin, and uncommon in the Upper Connecticut Valley (relics are found in the Lower Valley west of the River);

233 pogy 'a herring,' known only along the shore; and *233 scup* 'a sea fish, related to the sheepshead' (the fish is rare north of Cape Cod);

349 gutter (on the roof), current also in southwestern New England as a rather recent innovation (see Chart 7);

577 tilt, tilting board and *tilter, tiltering board* 'seesaw,' the former widely used in the Plymouth Area and on Aquidneck (60–64), the latter on Casco Bay (356–364), with relics elsewhere on the coast (see Chart 18);

346 culch, sculch 'rubbish, trash,' confined to the northern part of the Focal Area, with some instances in the northern section of the Plymouth Area, which often shows Massachusetts Bay influence;

218–219 co! and *coaf!*, calls to cows, used beside the widespread *co boss!* and *come boss!*; rare in the Margin; found also as a relic on Long Island Sound (1, 4, 28–30, 50–51);

195 blart 'blat, bawl (of a calf),' rare in Rhode Island west of the Bay and in the Margin (excepting the 228 Deerfield Area), and lacking in eastern New Hampshire and York County, Maine, where *blare* is current.

EASTERN WORDS AND PRONUNCIATIONS

x = in general use / = fairly common . = rare	Focal Area							Margin			West	
	Maine	Eastern New Hampshire	Essex County	Merrimack Valley	Boston Area	Plymouth Area	Rhode Island	Worcester Area	Upper Connecticut Valley	Eastern Connecticut	Lower Connecticut Valley	Western Vermont
101 [r] lost in *barn*	x	x	/	x	x	/	x	x	x	x	/	
59 [ʒ] in *thirty*	x	x	/	x	x	/	/	/	/	/		
192 [a] in *calf*	x	x	x	x	x	x	/	x	x	.	.	.
311 [a] in *glass*	x	/	x	.	x	.	/	.	.	.	.	.
45 [ɒ] in *rod*	x	x	x	x	x	x	x	x	/	x	.	
550 [ɒ] in *law*	x	x	x	x	x	x	x	.	/	/		.
142 [ɪ] in *towel*	x	x	x	x	x	x	x	/	x	x	/	.
553 [u] in *butcher*	x	x	x	x	.	x	x	.	.	/	.	.
298 bonny-clapper	x	x	x	x	x	x	x	x	/	x	/	
281 white-bread	x	x	x	x	x	x	x	x	x			
342 comforter	x	x	x	x	x	x	x	x	x	/		/
244 buttonwood	x	x	.	x	x	x	x	x	x	/		x
168 (stone) drag	x	x	x	x	x	x	x	/	/	x	.	
110 (pig) sty	/	/	x	/	x	x	x	x	.	/	.	
576 belly-bump(er)	x	x	x	x	x	x	x	/	/	x	.	
262 spindle (out)	x	x	x	/		x	x					
334 funnel 'stove pipe'	x	x	x	x	x	/	.	/	/			
108 lean-to, tie-up	x	x	x	x	x	x		/	.			
305 hog's head cheese	x	x	x	x	x	/		/				
292 apple dowdy	x	x	x	x	x	/	.	/				
299 sour-milk cheese	x	x	x	x	/	x	/					
289 fritter 'griddle cake'	x	x	x	x	/			.				
209 harslet	x	x	x	/	/	/		.				
233 pogy 'a herring'	x	.	/		/	x	/				.	
312 tonic	/	x	x	x	x	x	.	/	.			
349 gutter	x	x	x	x	x	x	/	/	/		/	
577 tilt, tilter	/	.	.		.	x	. - /					
346 (s)culch	x	/	x	x	x	.			/			
218–219 co!, coaf!	x	x	x	/	/	x	/	.	.		.	
195 blart	/		x	.	x	x	.	.		.		

THE BOSTON AREA

Boston has remained the dominant center of Eastern New England through the centuries. The history of innovations in the speech of Eastern New England is in large measure the history of the influence of Boston upper-class speech on the dialect of the seaboard from Cape Cod to Maine. This influence of Greater Boston extends at times as far west as the Connecticut River Valley in Massachusetts (especially along the old route to 224 Springfield by way of 205 Worcester and 220 Palmer), but rarely to 40 Hartford, Connecticut. The clearest case of Boston influence on the speech of the Lower Connecticut Valley is the low-front vowel [a] in words like *glass, afternoon* in the speech of the better educated (see Chart 15).

Generally speaking, the entire Eastern Area of New England is oriented in cultural matters toward Boston and hence receptive to Boston speech. To what extent this attitude unified the Eastern Area linguistically and prevented the encroachment of western forms remains to be determined. It may well be that some of the eastern features treated in the preceding section have spread from Boston rather recently and do not represent old usage as determined by the original settlement.

An interesting case of recent spreading from Boston is *312 tonic* 'soda water,' presented on Chart 5.

THE PLYMOUTH AREA

The Plymouth Area has few unique features. It has preserved some dialectal words and pronunciations that have survived also on Narragansett Bay or in northeastern New England, and others that appear in Western New England. The area has never had a prominent center and has never been an important independent economic unit such as Massachusetts Bay or Narragansett Bay; it has rather been dominated by these neighboring centers.

This situation is reflected in the spreading of Narragansett Bay features to Buzzards Bay and to Cape Cod, and in the importation of Massachusetts Bay features into Plymouth County and the Cape. The lower Cape (118–120) has been less exposed to such influences than the rest of this section.

The rather marked differences in speech between the Plymouth Area and the Massachusetts Bay Area to the north are largely due to the elimination of old local features in the urbanized area around Boston; on the other hand, the present differences between Plymouth and Rhode Island, especially Rhode Island west of Narragansett Bay, are to be attributed mostly to original differences in dialect.

Among the few unique features of Plymouth speech may be mentioned *292 apple grunt* 'a deep-dish apple pie' and *267 cleave-stone peach* 'freestone peach'; perhaps also *103 ground mow* '(hay) bay.'

Apple grunt is now practically confined to Cape Cod and Martha's Vineyard, but scattered instances have been recorded elsewhere (see Chart 18); *cleave-stone peach* appears only on the lower Cape (118–120), on 52 Block Island, on 51 Long Island and in 252 Bennington, Vermont. Both terms must formerly have been used much more widely.

Ground mow is current in the greater part of the Plymouth Area and in coastal Maine (see Chart 18). It is entirely unknown on Massachusetts Bay, including conservative Essex County, where only *bay* appears to be in use. Unless one is willing to grant that the use of *ground mow* arose independently on Casco Bay, one must assume that the Plymouth term spread to the coast towns on Casco Bay from the Plymouth settlements in the upland. These settlements were established 1770–80 and extended from Lake Sebago northward to the Androscoggin River (including 366 Casco, 377 Turner). Eastern Maine, from 396 Frankfort—a Cape Cod settlement on the Penobscot—eastward, derives *ground mow* partly from Casco Bay, partly direct from Plymouth, as both these areas contributed to the population.

A similar distribution appears in the case of *198 whicker* 'whinny,' as far as the eastern seaboard is concerned (see Chart 18).

The Plymouth Area shares some features with other conservative sections on the coast from Essex County northeastward.

577 tilt, tilting board 'seesaw,' current from Aquidneck (60–64) to Cape Cod and on Martha's Vineyard (122–123) and Nantucket (124), has survived also in scattered points north of Boston, notably 180 Marblehead (see Chart 18). The related *tilter, tiltering board*, which is practically confined to Casco Bay (356 Biddeford to 382 Harpswell) and its derivative towns beyond the Penobscot, was certainly not imported from the Plymouth Area, since it is entirely lacking there and does not appear in the Maine towns settled predominantly from Plymouth and Cape Cod. It is noteworthy that the general New England term *teeter, teeter board* has never struck root in the Plymouth Area or on Martha's Vineyard and Nantucket. *Tilt* is here being replaced directly by the literary *seesaw*, while on Casco Bay *tilter* is yielding ground to *teeter* and *teeter* in turn to *seesaw*.

The Plymouth Area and the Narragansett Bay Area have the following features in common:

94 tempest 'storm' (see Chart 19);

235 quahog [kwɒhɒg], beside the Massachusetts Bay *cohog* [ko-] and the blend *quohog* [kwo-] (see Chart 6).

It is of interest to observe that in the Plymouth Area the village green is usually called the *546 green* rather than the *common*, whereas the latter term is in general use in the Boston Area and the rest of Massachusetts, as well as in northern New England. *Green* also predominates in Rhode Island and is the only term current in Connecticut.

Narragansett Bay terms have spread into the Plymouth Area:

292 apple slump 'deep apple pie' and *289 johnnycake* 'corn griddle cake' are now used in Bristol County (102–106) and on the islands (122–124); *202 cade* has spread to upper Cape Cod (116, 117) and to Nantucket (124); *305 head cheese* has replaced *hog's head cheese* on Buzzards Bay (113, 114) and is competing with it on the upper Cape (116) and on the islands (122–124). See Charts 19 and 20.

From the Boston Area have been introduced:

235 cohog [kohɒg], for the older *quahog* [kwɒhɒg] 'round clam';

the low-front vowel [a] before voiceless fricatives as in *80 past, 142 bath*, which is still rather rare on Buzzards Bay, the Cape and the islands.

The Narragansett Bay Area

The Narragansett Bay Area, including Rhode Island and the adjoining counties of Connecticut (Windham and especially New London) and Bristol County, Massachusetts, stands out as a distinctive dialect center within the Eastern Area. Here expressions are current that have not been encountered elsewhere in southern New England. Some of these are confined to small districts, others are known on both sides of the Bay, and some have spread to Buzzards Bay, to Martha's Vineyard and Nantucket, to Cape Cod and to the New London Area.

To Rhode Island west of the Bay are confined *577 dandle (board)* 'seesaw,' *240–241 shacket* 'yellow jacket (a hornet),' *236 eaceworm* 'earthworm,' and the pronunciation of *235 quahog* [kwəˈhɒg] with end stress (see Chart 21).

Eaceworm is lacking in conservative Washington County; it appears to be a Providence Plantation term which has spread up the Blackstone Valley to 201 Uxbridge-Mendon. In the Rhode Island settlement 246 Cheshire in the Berkshires, this distinctive term has survived to the present.

The term *409 horning* 'serenade' is current on Aquidneck (62 Middletown) as well as west of the Bay. *Horning* in the Berkshires and in southwestern Vermont was almost certainly introduced by Rhode Island settlers, since it does not seem to be current in the Hudson Valley.

The island of Aquidneck (60, 62, 64), the old Rhode Island Plantation, has preserved a number of terms not found elsewhere in New England: *209 (pig's) squin* 'pluck (heart, liver and lungs of a pig),' on the island and in 102 Westport, Massachusetts, on the peninsula between Narragansett Bay and Buzzards Bay; *292 cob pie*, beside the general Narragansett Bay term *apple slump* 'deep-dish apple pie' (see Chart 21).

Aquidneck is frequently differentiated from Rhode Island west of the Bay by Plymouth Colony words (see Chart 18). On the other hand, western Rhode Island has accepted Long Island Sound words more widely than has Aquidneck (see Charts 6 and 11).

Block Island is linguistically part of the Narragansett Bay Area, but it has been exposed rather more than the Rhode Island coast to Long Island Sound influence. On Block Island two terms that do not appear elsewhere have been observed:

132 fryer 'frying pan,' as distinct from *fry pan*. *Fry pan* is current on Narragansett Bay and Nantucket and in a completely separated area, New Hampshire Bay and the Merrimack Valley (see Chart 19). The general New England term *spider* and the Long Island Sound term *skillet* are also current on Block Island, and probably older.

577 tippety-bounce 'seesaw,' the only term offered by three of the informants on the island; the fourth uses also the Plymouth Colony term *tilting board*.

The entire Narragansett Bay Area is well set off by the following dialect features (see Charts 19 and 20):

344 closet or *kitchen closet* 'pantry,' not used elsewhere in New England except for the southwestern tip of Connecticut, which has doubtless received it from the Hudson Valley. This term is in use, beside *buttery*, also on Martha's Vineyard and Nantucket, probably because of the influence of Narragansett Bay rather than of the New York Area. The modern *pantry* is gaining ground, and it is very significant that *buttery*, the old-fashioned term so widely used or remembered in all other parts of New England, does not occur at all on Narragansett Bay (see Chart 4).

As the term *closet* was preempted to denote the pantry, the clothes closet continues to be called *338 clothes press* much more widely on Narragansett Bay than elsewhere in southern New England. Persons who now use *clothes closet* are apt to prefer the distinctive terms *kitchen closet, dish closet, cold closet* or *pantry* to the older *closet*.

106 corn crib appears to be the only term for a building intended for storing Indian corn. East, north and west of the Narragansett Bay Area, either *corn house* or *corn barn* is in use beside *corn crib*, but not in Rhode Island; and it is only in Rhode Island that the simplex *crib* is common.

A hay mow over the cow stalls, open to the aisle, is called *mow* on nearly the entire seaboard from Long Island Sound to New Hampshire, including the coast towns of Rhode Island (elsewhere usually *scaffold*). Besides this term, Narragansett Bay has also the word *102 loft* in this specific sense, a term that in other coastal communities refers mostly to the sail loft. The wide currency of this term in the northern Berkshires (242, 246, 248) is probably to be attributed largely to the Rhode Island settlers.

In all of New England a lamb brought up by hand, a pet lamb, is called a *cosset*, except for the Narragansett Bay Area, where *202 cade* is current. *Cade* is the only term known to our rural informants in Rhode Island; from Rhode Island it spread eastward into Bristol County, Massachusetts (102, 103, 104), to Buzzards Bay (114), to Cape Cod (116, 117), to Nantucket (124) and westward to 34 Stonington, Connecticut (see Chart 19). The corresponding call to sheep in the pasture, *225 cade!*, is confined to the central part of this area.

The limits of Narragansett Bay influence in southern New England are clearly reflected in the two culinary terms *289 johnnycake* 'corn griddle cake' and *292 apple slump* 'deep-dish apple pie,' both of which are concentrated around the Bay, but occur also in Eastern Connecticut and in Bristol County, Massachusetts (see Chart 20).

Apple slump is used also on the eastern tip of Long Island (51) and on Martha's Vineyard (122, 123) and Nantucket (124). Scattered instances of *apple slump* on Massachusetts Bay (146, 150, 156, 158) and in New Hampshire (328, 324) and Maine (357, 394, 406) may point to a wider use of the term in the Massachusetts Bay Colony during Colonial days, but the Plymouth Colony almost certainly had a different term, *apple grunt*, which is preserved on Cape Cod and on Martha's Vineyard (122).

Johnnycake, as the name for a griddle cake made of parched corn meal, a popular specialty of Rhode Island, has spread to eastern Connecticut together with the thing itself, and is specifically designated as *Rhode Island johnnycake* on the western fringe of its area (31, 43, 46) to distinguish it from the general New England term *johnnycake* 'corn bread,' for which the Rhode Islander uses the term *286 corn bread*.

Rhode Island and the Plymouth Colony, together with the islands off-shore, sometimes form a block contrasting with the Massachusetts Bay Colony to the north and Connecticut to the west; eastern Connecticut, especially New London County, is occasionally a part of this block. In some cases we are dealing with the preservation of common Colonial usage; in others, with the dissemination of Plymouth terms, following the westward progress of the Pilgrim settlers to Narragansett Bay; in still others, with the coastwise spreading of Rhode Island terms to Buzzards Bay and Cape Cod.

A striking instance of common preservation is the word *94 tempest* 'thunder storm' (see Chart 19), now current from Cape Cod and Nantucket to 52 Block Island and 34 Stonington, and as far north as 49 Woodstock, 201 Uxbridge, and 146 Cohasset on the seaboard. One of our five informants in 150 Boston, a well-read man, and an elderly woman in 152 Weston are the only informants north of this area who use the term. The complete lack of examples in conservative Essex County and 'down East' clearly points to an early loss of the term on Massachusetts Bay, if indeed it ever was widely current there.

Another case of common preservation is *235 quahog* (ˈkwɒhɒg], whose area extends from lower Cape Cod (119, 120) and Nantucket (124) to the eastern counties of Connecticut (see Chart 6). The Massachusetts Bay form *cohog* [ˈkohɒg] and a blend of the two, *quohog* [ˈkwohɒg], have spread to the coastal area of Plymouth but have not invaded Rhode Island nor as yet reached the lower Cape.

NEW HAMPSHIRE BAY AND THE MERRIMACK VALLEY

The coastal plain extending from Cape Ann (200) in Massachusetts to the mouth of the Saco River (356) in Maine and the Merrimack Valley in New Hampshire forms a rather well-defined dialect area in which many old local features have been preserved. The area comprises (1) Essex County in Massachusetts, whose inhabitants gradually advanced up the valley of the Merrimack River and its tributaries during the 17th and 18th centuries and from there across into the Upper Connecticut Valley to 340 Haverhill and beyond; (2) the New Hampshire coast, the settlements around Lake Winnepesaukee and north of it to 346 Shelburne; (3) York County, Maine, with a number of old towns along the coast, and New Hampshire settlements in the upland.

The southern part of Essex County has been so much influenced by the Boston Area that at present the south shore and the north shore are rather distinct. However, 180 Marblehead and 200 Rockport on Cape Ann have been very conservative and have remained strikingly individual in speech.

Although the Merrimack Valley was largely settled from Essex County, it has also extensive Middlesex County settlements, which have contributed many features to the speech of the Valley.

While there are no clear lines of demarcation between the Essex settlements and the 'Old New Hampshire' settlements, there are some differences between them, as indicated below.

The entire area is conservative as compared with the Boston Area to the south; it is largely the preservation of old speech forms that makes it distinctive. There are a number of expressions current, however, especially in the old coast towns, that were probably never widely used elsewhere in New England and do not appear on the conservative Maine coast from Casco Bay eastward. Some of these can be traced to the western counties of England.

The extent of the expansion from the Essex County towns up the Merrimack River and its tributaries is reflected in the area at present occupied by *236 mudworm* 'earthworm' (see Charts 22 and 23). This term was recorded in 200 Rockport on Cape Ann, in 190 Haverhill on the lower Merrimack River, and from there northwestward as far distant as 340 Haverhill, New Hampshire, and 294 Ryegate, Vermont, in the Upper Connecticut Valley. The general New England term *angleworm* competes with the more local word and has replaced it in the greater part of Essex County.

The area of *195 blare* 'blat, cry (of a calf)' is somewhat more restricted in New Hampshire, but has a similar outline (see Chart 22). Relics of this term are found also on the southern shore of New England from 1 Greenwich, Connecticut, to Cape Cod (117–118).

A fairly large area is occupied by *132 fry pan* 'frying pan,' which has survived also on Narragansett Bay, on Nantucket, and in Maine beyond the Penobscot (see Chart 19).

132 fry kettle 'a deep kettle for frying (doughnuts) in deep fat' is more restricted geographically, being confined to the area largely populated from the coast towns of New Hampshire and York County, Maine, with scattered relics in Rhode Island.

240–241 white-arsed hornet, striped-arsed hornet and *white-tailed hornet* occupy an even smaller district in New Hampshire and York County (see Chart 22).

The expression *How be you?*—presumably of West Country origin—is concentrated in the 'Old New Hampshire' settlements (306 to 312 and 333) as distinct from the Massachusetts settlements in the Merrimack Valley; survivals of this form are also common in the Green Mountains and scattered instances are found elsewhere in New England (see Chart 22).

The extent of the Middlesex County influence in the Merrimack Valley can be seen in the present spread of *249 spoonhaunch, spoonhunt* 'mountain laurel,' which is current as far north as 310 Belmont, 314 Webster, and as far west as 328 Keene. In urbanized southern Middlesex County it has been given up, and it is rapidly being replaced elsewhere by *mountain laurel.*

In Essex County (180–200) some pronunciations and expressions have survived that one now encounters elsewhere only in western Connecticut, except for scattered relics on the Atlantic seaboard, especially on Narragansett Bay, Martha's Vineyard, Nantucket and Cape Cod. Thus *198 whinnering* for *whinnying*, and *218–219 come boss!* beside the general eastern cow calls *co, co, co!* and *coaf, coaf, coaf!*

Relics abound in Essex County and the New Hampshire coast towns. The *r* is still pronounced in words like *69 Thursday, 377 girl, 488 beard* and *101 barn* in 180 Marblehead and (less widely) in 200 Rockport, and traces of it were encountered in 182 Beverly and 198 Essex (see Chart 16). *135 orts* 'garbage' has survived in Marblehead and Rockport; *125 rowet* in 194 Newbury and 302 Seabrook, New Hampshire, beside the common eastern *fog grass, old fog; 132 creeper* 'frying pan' in 180 Marblehead (also 112 Plymouth); *262 top* and *top out* from 180 Marblehead to 304 Rye, New Hampshire, beside the usual eastern *spindle* and *spindle out* (of a corn stalk); *342 spread* 'quilt' from 198 Essex to 304 Rye; *576 belly-bumper* from 180 Marblehead to 196 Rowley, beside the usual eastern *belly-bump*.

MAINE

Maine and New Hampshire are the most conservative parts of New England. Both are rural and remote from the great population centers, with large areas that are sparsely settled and have been losing population for several decades. As a result, Maine and New Hampshire preserve many dialectal features lost in the southern part of the Eastern Area; and they still use currently other features now rare in eastern Massachusetts or losing ground in the Boston Area. In reconstructing the speech of an earlier period, Maine and New Hampshire usage of the present day will play an important rôle.

Most of the early population of Maine came from the Massachusetts Bay and the Plymouth Areas. The Massachusetts Bay settlers occupied a large tract of the Maine coast to Penobscot Bay; the Plymouth element is concentrated in the western upland from Lake Sebago (near 366) to the Kennebec River (near 388).

Since Plymouth speech differs little from Massachusetts Bay speech, Plymouth influence on the speech of Maine is hard to identify without detailed analysis. The following features, among others, appear to have been brought to Maine by Plymouth and Cape Cod settlers: *198 whicker* 'whinny' (see Chart 18); *103 ground mow* 'hay bay' (see Chart 18); perhaps also the diphthong in words like *563 due* [dɪu], *67 Tuesday* [tɪuzdi], *361A new*, where Massachusetts Bay has the simple vowel [u].

Northern Maine (420–424) is quite distinct in speech from the Maine coast. It belongs to the St. John River Area, New Brunswick, which was settled by Loyalists from New York, New Jersey and western Connecticut. Many of the western dialect features treated below are current here.

THE NEW LONDON AREA

The New London Area, settled largely from 32 New London and 33 Norwich by expansion northward along the Thames River and its tributaries, has few distinctive dialect features. The area clearly belongs to Eastern New England, although western features have been introduced through spreading on Long Island Sound. Often New London is part of a conservative block extending from the Connecticut River to Cape Cod. Some dialect features have been brought in from Narragansett Bay, especially into 34 Stonington.

The New London Area contributed a large element to the population of the Upper Connecticut Valley and the northern Berkshires, and at least one of the distinctive New London words has survived there.

Among the few terms that are characteristic of New London are the following:

576 belly-cachunk [ˈbɛli kəˈtʃʌŋk], encountered nowhere else in New England, was offered by both informants in 32 New London; an echo of it may be observed in the *belly-cabumǝ* of 31 East Lyme. The remainder of the New London Area has the Narragansett Bay word *belly-bumper.*

292 apple jonathan 'deep-dish apple pie' was recorded in a few communities along the coast: 31 East Lyme, 32 New London, 34 Stonington, 54 Richmond, Rhode Island (see Chart 21). Although three of these communities are in New London County, the term probably comes from Washington County, Rhode Island; its occurrence in the Berkshires (236, 246, 248) rather definitely points to Rhode Island. *Apple jonathan* has obviously been yielding ground to the Narragansett Bay term *apple slump* (see Chart 20) and to the western *apple dumpling.*

Worcester County and the Upper Connecticut Valley

The greater part of the Eastern Margin, comprising Worcester and Franklin Counties, Massachusetts, and the Upper Connecticut Valley, is an area of secondary settlement. The greater part of Worcester County was occupied c. 1715–35, largely from the Massachusetts Bay Area; but settlers came also from the Plymouth Area and from northern Ireland. Shortly before 1750 the westward thrust from the Massachusetts coast had reached the Connecticut River settlements and was deflected northward into the Upper Connecticut Valley. The path of this expansion can be seen in the present spread of certain dialect features.

236 fishworm 'earthworm' reflects this trek (see Charts 23 and 24). The term is current in Norfolk and Middlesex Counties (140–158), in all of Worcester County (201–210), in northern Windham County, Connecticut (49), and in the greater part of the Upper Connecticut Valley in New Hampshire and Vermont. It has even crossed the Green Mountains to 262 West Rutland and 274 Cornwall.

A similar distribution pattern is found in *576 belly-bunt* as distinct from the eastern *belly-bump*, except that *belly-bunt* has survived also in Maine between the Androscoggin and the Penobscot Rivers (364–404), an entirely detached area (see Chart 24).

Fishworm and *belly-bunt* must formerly have been current in eastern Massachusetts (note the relics in 116, 108, 184, 190); *angleworm* and *belly-bump*, respectively, have replaced them.

The phrases *102 on the high-beams* and *on the great-beams* for 'in the loft' are confined to a narrower tract which, however, extends all the way from southeastern Worcester County (204 Shrewsbury) to the very head of the Connecticut Valley (344 Columbia). Relics of these expressions are found in northeastern New England (346, 348, 368, 373; 354, 391), and *great-beams* appears also on Long Island (51). See Chart 24.

Some eastern words have maintained themselves only in smaller sections of the Eastern Margin:

195 blart 'cry (of a calf),' common on the eastern seaboard, is current in the Deerfield Area (214, 228, 230, 256), and scattered instances were recorded in the Worcester Area (49, 207) and in Vermont (260, 268, 286).

Some Worcester County features have not survived in the Upper Connecticut Valley, where they had to compete with Connecticut and New Hampshire terms; thus *249 spoonwood* 'mountain laurel,' related to the Middlesex County terms *spoonhaunch, spoonhunt*.

On the other hand, *190 toro*, a euphemism for 'bull,' is widely current in the dairy country of northern Vermont and the adjoining counties of New Hampshire, but it is now exceedingly rare in Eastern New England (only 206, 320, 310, 316, 362.)

Relics of terms current among the settlers from Connecticut are found in the Upper Connecticut Valley, among them *236 angledog* 'earthworm,' a Windsor Colony word, in 336 Hanover; *249 ivy* 'mountain laurel' in 332 Newport; *409 callathump* 'serenade,' a New Haven County term, in 268 Windsor (see Charts 9 and 23).

The rather more common occurrence of an *r*-vowel in the Upper Connecticut Valley than in other parts of the Eastern Margin may be due to settlers from the Lower Valley, but on the other hand this feature has almost certainly lost ground in Worcester County. 294 Ryegate, settled 1773 from Glasgow in Scotland, has a strong *r* to this day in words like *Thursday* and *barn* (see Chart 16).

Features in which the Eastern Margin now differs from the Eastern Focal Area and agrees with Western New England are in part to be attributed to the loss of these features along the seaboard and in part to importation from the west. In the Upper Connecticut Valley western speech forms were introduced during the period of settlement (1750–85), but in Worcester County, which did not receive any settlers from the Connecticut Valley, such speech forms must have been imported during the 19th and 20th centuries.

In any given case one may be in doubt whether the feature represents old local usage or whether it was imported from the west. *351 stoop* and *299 Dutch cheese* clearly came from the west (see Charts 10 and 14); but *168 stone boat* and *349 eavestrough* may be survivals of terms formerly also current on the coast.

WESTERN NEW ENGLAND

Western New England has contributed more to the speech of the northern United States (from the Hudson Valley west) than has Eastern New England. For this reason the dialect spoken here impresses most Americans as less distinctive than that of the seaboard.

The most distinctive feature in the pronunciation of this area is the rather general use of *r* in all positions, contrasting with the eastern habit of pronouncing *r* only when followed by a vowel, as in Standard British English.

The postvocalic *r* as in *101 barn, 488 beard, 54 four, 325 chair* is current in the Western Fringe and in the Lower Connecticut Valley as far north as 225 Southampton. East of the Connecticut River it appears only sporadically (see Chart 16). It is most fully established in western Connecticut and in the basin of Lake Champlain (274 Cornwall to 286 Enosburg), areas that have intimate contacts with the Hudson Valley, where the postvocalic *r* is in general use, except for New York City. In the Berkshires and in southestern Vermont usage varies greatly, probably on account of the large eastern element in the population and the double relation of the trading area of 242 Pittsfield to Springfield-Boston and to the Hudson Valley. In the New Haven Area and the Lower Connecticut Valley it is noteworthy (1) that the postvocalic *r* is rather uncommon in the cities (26 New Haven, 38 Middletown, 40 Hartford, 224 Springfield, 226 Northampton) and (2) that it is so little used east of the River in towns that otherwise have Valley forms (41 Glastonbury, 42 Hebron, 46 Tolland, 219 Granby). These facts point to a rather recent spreading of the postvocalic *r* into New Haven and the Lower Connecticut Valley which the cities as cultural centers have resisted. Usage must have been divided on this point from the very beginning of the settlements, since the postvocalic *r* is regularly used even today in the English dialects of the western part of England from the Bristol Channel to the very doors of London (including the county of Buckingham and the western parts of Middlesex, Hertford and Northampton). The fact that in New Haven County conservative Milford (6) lacks the *r* and conservative Guilford (28) has it leads to the same conclusion.

Words current in all or part of Western New England are treated in the following sections; others are mentioned incidentally in the section devoted to Eastern New England.

THE LOWER CONNECTICUT VALLEY

The Lower Connecticut Valley includes the counties of Hartford and Tolland, the larger part of Litchfield County and northern Middlesex County in Connecticut, and the counties of Hampden and Hampshire in Massachusetts—an area settled by expansion from the early towns of 38 Middletown, Wethersfield, 40 Hartford, Windsor, 224 Springfield and 226 Northampton. Linguistically this area is set off rather clearly from the Eastern Margin (the counties of New London, Windham and Worcester), which was settled from Eastern New England (see Plate 1). The boundary is more definite in Connecticut than in Massachusetts, where eastern speech forms have been introduced by way of the old route 150 Boston - 205 Worcester - Brookfield - 220 Palmer - 224 Springfield. The western boundary is less clearly defined, partly because Valley forms were carried up into the southern Berkshires by early settlers (cf. *236 angledog*, Chart 23) or spread westward after the settlement of the Western Fringe; partly because the Valley, as well as the Fringe, have been hospitable to Hudson Valley forms, and because local expressions and pronunciations have been given up for literary terms and 'standard' pronunciations more readily than in the isolated eastern part of New England, where local dialect usage has been supported by the dominant cultural center of Boston.

To the north the boundary is fairly sharp, but features of Valley speech have been carried northward into the Deerfield Area and into the Upper Connecticut Valley, where they compete with eastern forms.

The line between the Valley settlements and the New Haven Area has been largely obliterated, but some differences persist and others have developed through the incursion of Hudson Valley and Long Island Sound features into New Haven County.

As long as the usage of the Hudson Valley, and especially of Greater New York, is no better known than at present, it will be difficult to determine the source of certain dialectal features now shared by the Lower Connecticut Valley, New Haven and the Western Fringe of Connecticut and Massachusetts. These may represent old local usage that may or may not have spread to the Hudson Valley, or may have been imported from the Hudson Area.

Some of the features found only in the Lower Connecticut Valley and New Haven are discussed below.

249 ivy in the sense of 'mountain laurel' (the state flower of Connecticut) is current, though rapidly losing ground, from 6 Milford to 31 East Lyme on Long Island Sound, and northward to 235 Granville (near 224 Springfield) and 238 Egremont in the Berkshires. In the cities (26 New Haven, 38 Middletown, 40 Hartford, 224 Springfield) it is no longer familiar. See Chart 9.

577 tinter, teenter, beside the now more common *teeter, teeter board* and *seesaw,* is found in New Haven County (6 Milford, 26 New Haven, 28 Madison, 36 Wallingford) and in the Lower Connecticut Valley settlements east of the River, from 41 Glastonbury, Connecticut, to 219 Granby, Massachusetts; also in two derivative towns, 248 Williamstown, Massachusetts, and 260 Pawlet, Vermont. See Chart 9.

Beside the widely used *262 tassel, tossel,* denoting the blossoming top of a corn stalk, the word *top* and the corresponding verb *top out* are current in the counties of New Haven and Hartford, while the synonymous *topgallant* and *topgallant out* are confined to the adjoining county of Fairfield. Outside of Hartford and New Haven, *top* and *top out* appear only in a completely detached small area north of Boston, from 180 Marblehead to 304 Rye on the New Hampshire coast. See Chart 9.

The Lower Connecticut Valley has preserved some features of pronunciation that have been lost in southeastern New England, for example, the vowel [ɑ] in *167 harrow,* pronounced like the vowel in *car* (widely current in the folk speech of England west and north of the London area); and the vowel [u] in *553 butcher,* pronounced like the vowel in *boot.*

There is at least one word that is characteristic of New Haven County: *409 callathump* 'a noisy mock-serenade,' once popular at Yale College (cf. the quotations in the *Century Dictionary* and the *Dictionary of American English*). Outside of New Haven County the term was observed in 12 New Milford, 16 Litchfield, 20 Farmington—adjoining communities to the north; in 268 Windsor, Vermont, settled from 20 Farmington; in the speech of one informant in 190 Haverhill, Massachusetts, whose parents came from the vicinity of 334 Canaan, New Hampshire, a Connecticut settlement; and in 431 Woodstock, New Brunswick, in the speech of both informants, who are of New York and Connecticut Loyalist ancestry. See Chart 9. The term was perhaps coined at Yale.

On the other hand, there are several expressions in Hartford County and derivative areas that do not occur in the New Haven Area:

236 angledog 'earthworm' (see Chart 23) is current in northern Hartford County (21, 23, 24, 45), in northern Tolland County (44, 46), and in a number of communities which are known to have been settled in part from this area: 33 Norwich and 22 Winchester in Connecticut; 236 New Marlborough, 239 Alford and 225 Southampton in Massachusetts; and 336 Hanover, New Hampshire. This term, imported from the western counties of England (according to J. Wright, *English Dialect Dictionary,* it is now found only in Devonshire, beside *angletwitch*), may have been also current formerly in the Hartford and Wethersfield section of Hartford County, or it may always have been confined to the Windsor section of the county.

The term *576 belly-whop, belly-whopper* 'face-down on a sled' also seems to be restricted to the Valley settlements, whereas *belly-flop, belly-flopper* appears both in Hartford and New Haven Counties. The synonymous term *belly-whack, belly-whacker* is restricted in Connecticut to the eastern fringe of New Haven County (28 Madison, 36 Wallingford), but appears also in 112 Plymouth, Massachusetts. It will be observed that neither the western *belly-gut, belly-gutter* (see Chart 10) nor the eastern *belly-bump, belly-bumper* has as yet replaced the old New Haven and Hartford County terms; in the Connecticut Valley in Massachusetts, on the other hand, the Valley terms have been given up.

Fairfield County and the Lower Housatonic Valley form a rather definite speech area in Connecticut. The line separating it from the New Haven area is sometimes rather sharp;

whether there is any linguistic boundary between Fairfield County and Westchester County, New York, remains to be determined. Fairfield County has been demonstrably hospitable to Hudson Valley words; some of these have penetrated into New Haven County, others have not. When an expression or a feature of pronunciation that is not found in New England beyond the boundaries of Fairfield County is current in the Loyalist settlements of western New Brunswick, it is probably safe to assume that Fairfield County agrees with the Hudson Valley; when New Brunswick lacks the feature, it may be confined to Fairfield County.

409 skimilton, skimiton 'a noisy mock-serenade' has so far been encountered only in 1 Stamford, 4 Weston, 8 Danbury, 11 New Fairfield (see Chart 9).

262 topgallant and *topgallant out* are found only in Fairfield County and the derivative 10 Southbury and 12 New Milford (see Chart 9). They are presumably local terms, but an investigation of Westchester County, New York, may reveal a different situation.

Among the terms and pronunciations that appear to be characteristic of Fairfield County and occur also in western New Brunswick may be mentioned:

299 pot cheese 'cottage cheese,' a Hudson Valley term (probably patterned on a Dutch word) that has been carried to the eastern end of Long Island (50, 51) and introduced into the Upper Housatonic Valley (18 Sharon, 19 Cornwall, 239 Alford) as well (see Chart 14); *577 teeter-totter* 'seesaw,' which has also reached the eastern point of Long Island (50), and has entered the Upper Housatonic Valley (242 Pittsfield) and southwestern Vermont (260 Pawlet, 262 West Rutland) from the Albany region (see Chart 9);

167 harrow pronounced with [ɛ] as in *hen*, contrasting with the common Connecticut Valley type with [ɑ] as in *car*.

SPREADING ON LONG ISLAND SOUND

Some forms—phonetic, morphological and especially lexical—have a distribution pattern completely at variance with the settlement pattern, often cutting across the major settlement boundaries. These patterns arise in one of several ways.

1. Through the recession of forms once current over a large area—sometimes all of New England:

(a) The seaboard preserves forms that are given up in the upland; hence Long Island Sound and the southern seaboard to Cape Cod sometimes have the same form as the eastern seaboard, with a break in the Boston Area.

(b) Northern New England from Vermont to eastern Maine (as well as Litchfield County, Connecticut) preserves forms once current in all of New England. The result is a north-south distribution cutting across the east-west distribution produced by the settlement.

2. Through the spreading of innovations:

(a) in an easterly direction on Long Island Sound to Narragansett Bay and sometimes beyond to Cape Cod, Martha's Vineyard and Nantucket, thus obliterating the east-west distribution produced by the settlement;

(b) from Narragansett Bay eastward to Buzzards Bay and westward to New London;

(c) from Long Island Sound (Greater New York) to the population centers in the Lower Connecticut Valley (38 Middletown, 40 Hartford, 224 Springfield);

(d) from the Hudson Valley into the Western Fringe of New England (western Connecticut, the Berkshires and western Vermont) and sometimes beyond into the Lower Connecticut Valley and the Eastern Fringe, and even into the Eastern Focal Area;

(e) from the Boston Area along the coast to Cape Cod and 'down East,' and into the Eastern Margin—sometimes (sporadically) even to the Lower Connecticut Valley in Massachusetts and beyond into the Berkshires (rarely to the Connecticut Valley in Connecticut).

Forms that have spread eastward from Long Island Sound along the southern seaboard of New England into the eastern area of settlement (Narragansett Bay, Buzzards Bay, Martha's Vineyard, Nantucket and Cape Cod) can usually be distinguished without difficulty from coastal survivals. The conservative coastal communities north of Boston preserve old forms so faithfully that forms occurring only on the southern seaboard may be assumed to have been always confined to it.

The normal distribution pattern of coastal survivals can be observed in the pronunciation of 183 *wharf* as *warf* [wɔrf], which is found along the Connecticut shore, on Long Island and Block Island and on Narragansett Bay, as well as on lower Cape Cod and the entire eastern seaboard to New Brunswick. This pronunciation of *wharf* is especially common in the conservative counties along the coast from Cape Ann (200) to New Brunswick, where *w* for *wh* in stressed syllables, as in *163 wheelbarrow* and *159 whetstone*, is fairly common, although it is rare on the southern coast of New England. A similar distribution pattern appears in the cow calls *218–219 coaf!* and *co!* [koʊ, koə]. *Coaf!* occurs in the coast towns from Long Island Sound to Cape Cod and again from Cape Ann to Great Bay, New Hampshire; *co!* in scattered points on Long Island Sound and in a rather wide belt along the eastern seaboard (excepting the urbanized area around Boston) all the way to New Brunswick. Receding forms showing a coastwise distribution may thus be expected to have a wider currency from Cape Ann northeastward than on the southern seaboard of New England, and to be more widely used from Narragansett Bay eastward than on Long Island Sound.

Innovations spreading coastwise from Greater New York eastward on Long Island Sound and beyond have a characteristic distribution pattern which may be illustrated by *235 round clam* (see Chart 6). This term is now in general use in western Connecticut, where it has rather recently replaced the older *quohog* [kwohɔg], *cohog* [ko-], and has spread up the Connecticut Valley as far as 224 Springfield; east of the Connecticut River, however, this commercial competitor of the old local *quahog* [kwɔhɔg] has become established only in points along the coast as far as 80 Providence. The characteristic shape of this distribution pattern is a triangle with a broad base in western Connecticut, tapering off in an easterly direction, the tip extending to Narragansett Bay, to Buzzards Bay, or to Cape Cod and the islands south of it.

This type of distribution appears, with variations, in *233 porgy, poggy* = eastern *scup* (both from *scuppaug*, Stenotomos argyrops) and in *233 menhaden* = eastern *pogy* [pogi] (Brevoortia tyrannus). *Porgy* [pɔrgi], *poggy* [pɑgi, pɒgi] is current on Long Island and throughout Connecticut except the northeastern corner of the state; in the Lower Connecticut Valley it is known as far north as 226 Northampton, and in Rhode Island it is familiar to some of our informants on 52 Block Island, on Aquidneck (62 Middletown, 64 Portsmouth) and in Washington County (54 Wyoming) beside the usual word *scup*. The eastward progress has doubtless been retarded by the fact that *poggy* sounds so much like *pogy* = *menhaden*. *Menhaden* has penetrated much farther east; it is the only term in Rhode Island west of Narragansett Bay, and competes with the older eastern *pogy* [pogi, poəgi] east of the Bay, on Block Island, Aquidneck, Martha's Vineyard, Nantucket and Cape Cod. See Chart 11.

The close relation of the fisheries to the New York market serves to spread the New York terms on the southern coast of New England.

Some terms are confined to the coast towns on Long Island Sound and the islands:

235 hard clam (=*round clam*), on Long Island Sound (1, 3, 30, 33; 50, 51) and on 52 Block Island, 123 Martha's Vineyard, 124 Nantucket (see Chart 11).

234 mummichug, mummichog (=*saltwater minnow*), from the Connecticut River (30) to Buzzards Bay (102, 113), including Narragansett Bay (56, 62, 64, 81, 104); west of the Connecticut River (1, 6, 28, 29) a word of Dutch origin—*killifish, kellie*—seems to have taken the place of the older Indian word (see Chart 11).

132 skillet 'frying pan' appears to be in use only in a number of points on the shore from the mouth of the Connecticut River eastward (30, 34, 51, 52, 124, 125). Does contact with the southern ports during the seafaring days account for this distribution?

104 Dutch cap, hay cap, denoting a square haystack with a roof sliding on four corner posts (said to be common in the Hudson Valley), has been observed only in a small area east of Narragansett Bay (81, 102, 103, 104, 114). See Chart 11.

95 spitting 'sleeting, drizzling,' observed at several points in southwestern New England (1, 18, 235, 28), is current also in scattered points from New London to Buzzards Bay (32, 54, 64, 102).

Spreading from the Hudson Valley

Few features of Hudson Valley speech have spread beyond the Connecticut Valley Area in southern New England except along the shore, where coastwise communication has carried New York terms farther east. In northern New England such features rarely cross the Green Mountains.

The Dutch word *351 stoop*, denoting a porch of varying construction, was probably introduced into New England with the covered porch itself, which is lacking on older New England houses. This Dutch term is rather widely used in the Western Fringe and the Connecticut Valley, except for the northernmost part, and has been carried eastward through Massachusetts (along the Albany-Boston road) to the outskirts of Boston and northward into the Merrimack Valley (see Chart 10). From eastern Connecticut to Cape Cod *stoop* is rare; it is unknown on Martha's Vineyard and Nantucket, and nearly so in Maine and New Brunswick. *Stoop* may have reached the Boston Area by the time of the Revolution.

299 Dutch cheese 'cottage cheese,' a term coined by the English neighbors of the Dutch in the Hudson Valley, has spread eastward almost to the Atlantic coast (see Chart 14). On Narragansett Bay, on Martha's Vineyard and Nantucket, and from Cape Cod northward to Casco Bay, the eastern term *sour-milk cheese* continues in use; in Maine from Casco Bay eastward *curd cheese* predominates. In addition to these terms the modern *cottage cheese* is now current throughout New England, less widely in northwestern Vermont than elsewhere.

298 loppered milk 'thick sour milk' is characteristic of Western New England, including the Lower Connecticut Valley to 228 Deerfield and Vermont west of the Green Mountains (see Chart 13). The eastern boundary of *loppered milk* closely follows the 'seam' between the eastern and western settlement areas. In eastern Connecticut and Rhode Island, in the northern Berkshires (232, 246, 248, 252), and in the Upper Connecticut Valley from 214 Northfield to 294 Ryegate, Vermont, the phonetically similar term *lobbered milk* (rarely *labbered milk*) is in use; it appears also in Fairfield County (1, 3, 4) and in New Brunswick. Usage in the Hudson Valley must be established before an interpretation of the relationship between *loppered* and *lobbered* can be given. It may well be that *loppered* has spread at the expense of *lobbered*.

342 comfortable 'a heavy quilt,' is used in all of southwestern New England, including the Connecticut Valley, as far north as 256 Brattleboro and 328 Keene. In eastern Connecticut and in Rhode Island west of the Bay *comfortable* competes with the eastern *comforter*, which has limited currency also in central and western Massachusetts.

175 near horse is replacing the older *nigh horse* in Western New England, including the Lower Connecticut Valley, and has penetrated into the Eastern Margin, especially Worcester County. The term is now also current on Cape Cod and Nantucket, but is still rare in the Narragansett Bay Area.

305 head cheese is current in Western New England and the entire Eastern Margin as well as in the Narragansett Bay Area. From there it has spread to Buzzards Bay, to Martha's Vineyard and to Nantucket, but not to lower Cape Cod. The eastern *hog's head cheese* is now confined to the Eastern Focal Area except for a number of instances in the Upper Connecticut Valley. New Brunswick agrees with Western New England, and the western *head cheese* is not uncommon in Maine west of the Kennebec River. One can hardly escape the conclusion that Worcester County once had the eastern term, as the Upper Connecticut Valley still has in part.

576 belly-gut, belly-gutter (see Chart 10) occurs in the Western Fringe from Long Island Sound to 252 Bennington, Vermont, and from the Berkshires eastward to the Connecticut River (224 Springfield to 230 Colrain). In Connecticut it is confined to the Western Fringe except for scattered instances on or near Long Island Sound (26 New Haven, 38 Middletown, 33 Norwich, 34 Stonington). *Belly-gut* was introduced into the Berkshires from the Albany Area and spread from there eastward to the Connecticut River, but not beyond; *belly-gutter* spread from the New York Area eastward on Long Island Sound and beyond to Martha's Vineyard, but it did not become established in the Hartford Area, where the old local *belly-whop(per)* and *belly-flop(per)* have survived.

Of the various pronunciations of *350 clapboard*, the type of [klæboəd, klæbord] is found everywhere in New England. In southern New England the spelling pronunciation [klæpboəd] is now widely current, especially in the Narragansett Bay Area. On the other hand, the type of [klæbrd, klæbəd], an old compound with unstressed second element, has survived quite extensively in Connecticut west of the River, especially in New Haven and Middlesex Counties. Scattered instances of this type in the Upper Connecticut Valley and in eastern Massachusetts point to a much wider use in former times. It is probable that in the Narragansett Bay Area [klæbəd] rather than [klæboəd] was the predecessor of the spelling pronunciation [klæpboəd].

Sheep calls containing the element *225 nan(nie)* are used (or remembered) in two widely separated sections of New England: (1) [næn(i)] in Connecticut west of the River (as against the [kəˈde] of the eastern part of the state), and (2) [kənæn(i)] in northern New England from the Connecticut River eastward. The shorter [næn(i)] of western Connecticut occurs also on Long Island (51) and Nantucket (124), in New Brunswick (428–431) and in northern Maine (416–420, 424). This distribution points to Long Island Sound and the Hudson Valley as centers of dissemination.

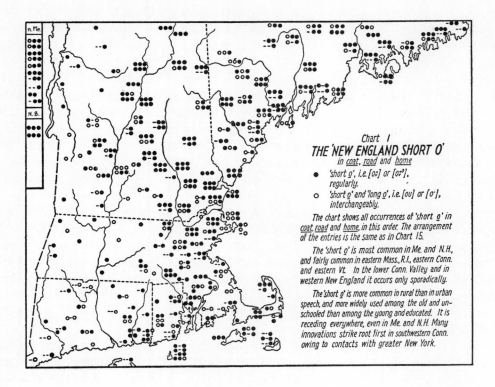

Chart 1

THE 'NEW ENGLAND SHORT O'
in <u>coat</u>, <u>road</u> and <u>home</u>

● 'short o̧', i.e. [o:] or [o:ᵊ], regularly.

○ 'short o̧' and 'long o̧', i.e. [ou] or [o·], interchangeably.

The chart shows all occurrences of 'short o̧' in <u>coat</u>, <u>road</u> and <u>home</u>, in this order. The arrangement of the entries is the same as in Chart 15.

The 'short o̧' is most common in Me. and N.H., and fairly common in eastern Mass., R.I., eastern Conn. and eastern Vt. In the lower Conn. Valley and in western New England it occurs only sporadically.

The 'short o̧' is more common in rural than in urban speech, and more widely used among the old and un-schooled than among the young and educated. It is receding everywhere, even in Me. and N.H. Many innovations strike root first in southwestern Conn. owing to contacts with greater New York.

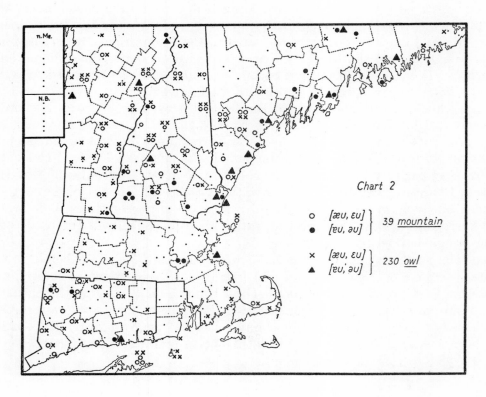

Chart 2

○ [æu, ɛu] ⎫
● [ɐu, əu] ⎬ 39 <u>mountain</u>

✕ [æu, ɛu] ⎫
▲ [ɐu,' əu] ⎬ 230 <u>owl</u>

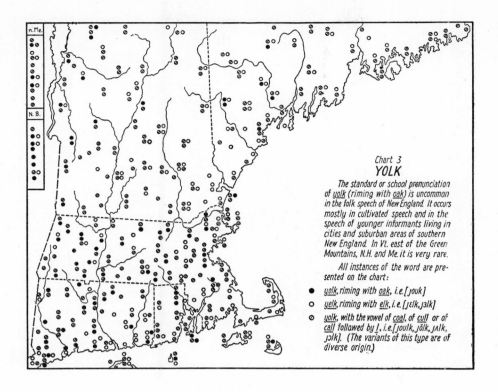

Chart 3
YOLK

The standard or school pronunciation of *yolk* (riming with *oak*) is uncommon in the folk speech of New England. It occurs mostly in cultivated speech and in the speech of younger informants living in cities and suburban areas of southern New England. In Vt. east of the Green Mountains, N.H. and Me. it is very rare.

All instances of the word are presented on the chart:

● *yolk,* riming with *oak, i.e.* [ɹouk]

○ *yelk,* riming with *elk, i.e.* [ɹɛlk, ɹɜlk]

◉ *yolk,* with the vowel of *coal,* of *cull* or of *call* followed by *l, i.e.* [ɹoulk, ɹõlk, ɹʌlk, ɹɔlk]. *(The variants of this type are of diverse origin.)*

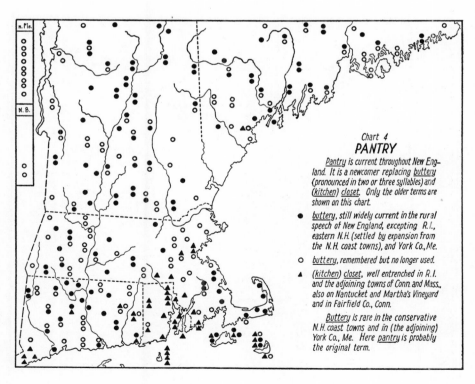

Chart 4
PANTRY

Pantry is current throughout New England. It is a newcomer replacing *buttery* (pronounced in two or three syllables) and *(kitchen) closet.* Only the older terms are shown on this chart.

● *buttery,* still widely current in the rural speech of New England, excepting R.I., eastern N.H. (settled by expansion from the N.H. coast towns), and York Co., Me.

○ *buttery,* remembered but no longer used.

▲ *(kitchen) closet,* well entrenched in R.I. and the adjoining towns of Conn. and Mass., also on Nantucket and Martha's Vineyard and in Fairfield Co., Conn.

Buttery is rare in the conservative N.H. coast towns and in (the adjoining) York Co., Me. Here *pantry* is probably the original term.

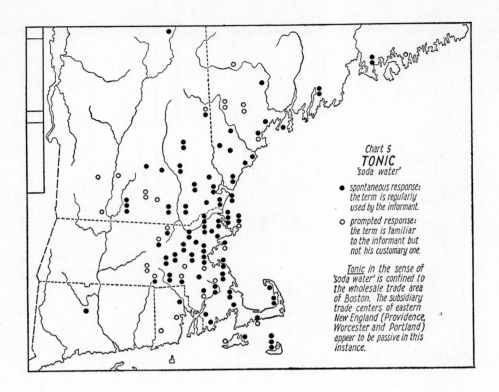

Chart 5
TONIC
'soda water'

● spontaneous response:
  the term is regularly
  used by the informant.

○ prompted response:
  the term is familiar
  to the informant but
  not his customary one.

Tonic in the sense of
'soda water' is confined to
the wholesale trade area
of Boston. The subsidiary
trade centers of eastern
New England (Providence,
Worcester and Portland)
appear to be passive in this
instance.

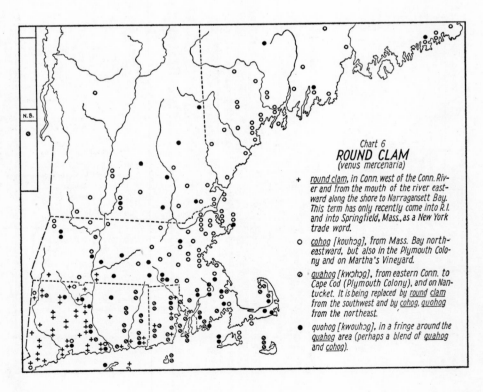

Chart 6
ROUND CLAM
(venus mercenaria)

+ *round clam*, in Conn. west of the Conn. River and from the mouth of the river eastward along the shore to Narragansett Bay.
  This term has only recently come into R.I.
  and into Springfield, Mass., as a New York
  trade word.

○ *cohog* [kouhɔg], from Mass. Bay northeastward, but also in the Plymouth Colony and on Martha's Vineyard.

◉ *quahog* [kwɔhɔg], from eastern Conn. to
  Cape Cod (Plymouth Colony), and on Nantucket. It is being replaced by *round clam*
  from the southwest and by *cohog*, *quahog*
  from the northeast.

● *quahog* [kwouhɔg], in a fringe around the
  quahog area (perhaps a blend of *quahog*
  and *cohog*).

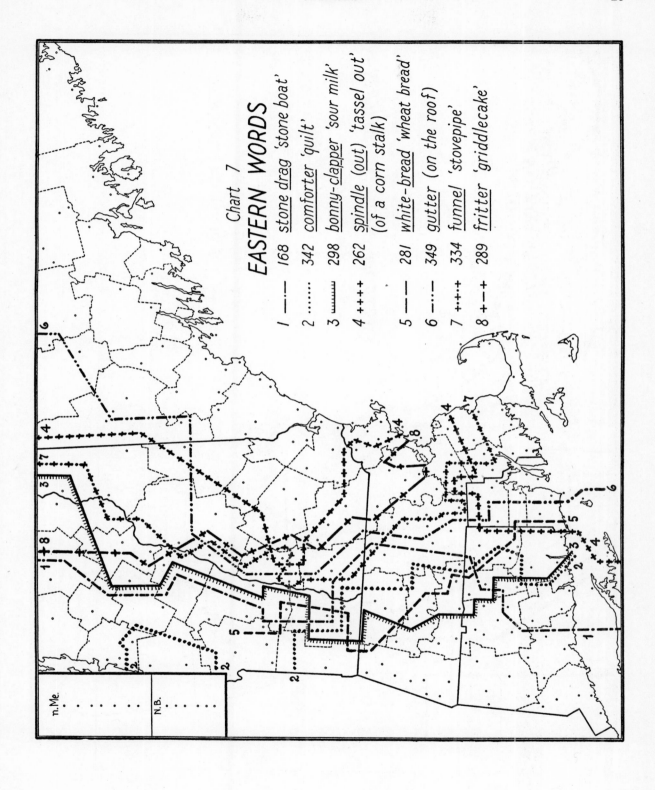

Chart 7
EASTERN WORDS

1 —— 168 *stone drag* 'stone boat'
2 ········· 342 *comforter* 'quilt'
3 +—+—+ 298 *bonny-clapper* 'sour milk'
4 ++++ 262 *spindle* (*out*) 'tassel out'
   (of a corn stalk)
5 ——— 281 *white-bread* 'wheat bread'
6 —··—·· 349 *gutter* (on the roof)
7 ++++ 334 *funnel* 'stovepipe'
8 +—··—+ 289 *fritter* 'griddlecake'

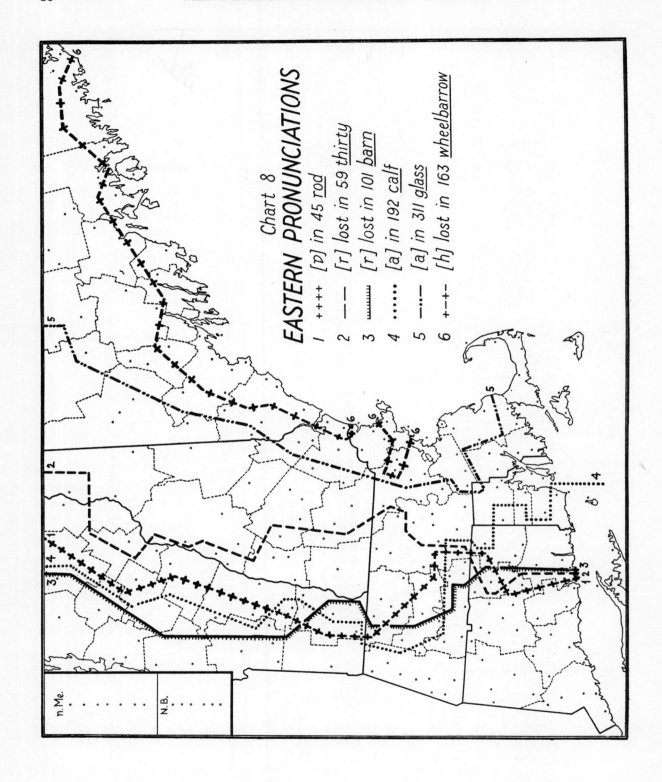

Chart 8

EASTERN PRONUNCIATIONS

1 + + + +   [ɒ] in 45 *rod*
2 ——   [r] lost in 59 *thirty*
3 ⊢⊢⊢⊢   [r] lost in 101 *barn*
4 ·······   [a] in 192 *calf*
5 —··—   [a] in 311 *glass*
6 + · + ·   [h] lost in 163 *wheelbarrow*

n. Me. · · · · · · · ·
N.B.   · · · · · · · ·

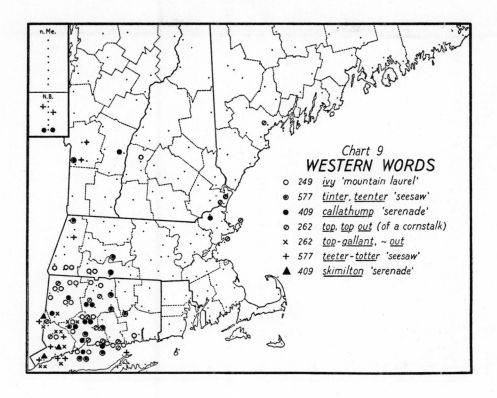

Chart 9
WESTERN WORDS

○ 249 *ivy* 'mountain laurel'
◉ 577 *tinter*, *teenter* 'seesaw'
● 409 *callathump* 'serenade'
⊘ 262 *top*, *top out* (of a cornstalk)
✕ 262 *top-gallant*, ~ *out*
✛ 577 *teeter-totter* 'seesaw'
▲ 409 *skimilton* 'serenade'

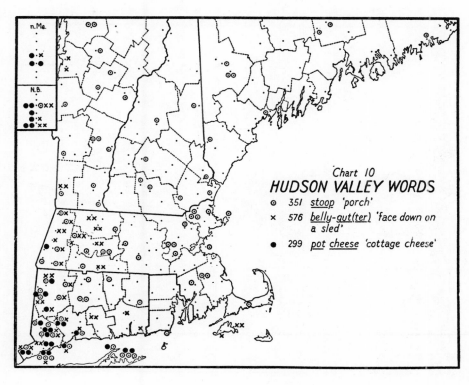

Chart 10
HUDSON VALLEY WORDS

⊙ 351 *stoop* 'porch'
✕ 576 *belly-gut(ter)* 'face down on a sled'
● 299 *pot cheese* 'cottage cheese'

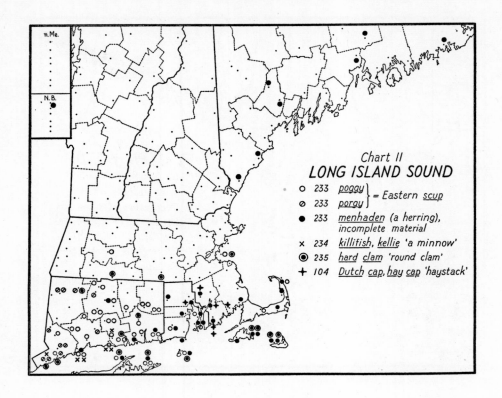

Chart II
LONG ISLAND SOUND

- ○   233   *poggy* ⎫
- ◑   233   *porgy* ⎭ = Eastern *scup*
- ●   233   *menhaden (a herring)*, incomplete material
- ✕   234   *killifish*, *kellie* 'a minnow'
- ◉   235   *hard clam* 'round clam'
- ✚   104   *Dutch cap*, *hay cap* 'haystack'

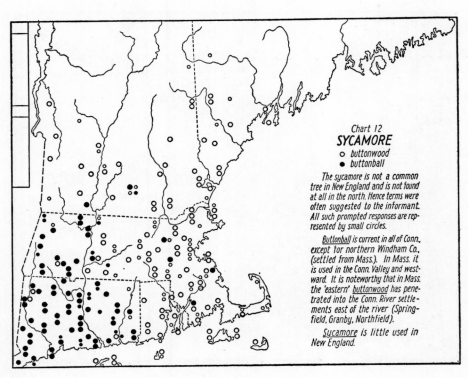

Chart 12
SYCAMORE

- ○   buttonwood
- ●   buttonball

The sycamore is not a common tree in New England and is not found at all in the north. Hence terms were often suggested to the informant. All such prompted responses are represented by small circles.

Buttonball is current in all of Conn. except for northern Windham Co., (settled from Mass.). In Mass. it is used in the Conn. Valley and westward. It is noteworthy that in Mass. the 'eastern' *buttonwood* has penetrated into the Conn. River settlements east of the river (Springfield, Granby, Northfield).

Sycamore is little used in New England.

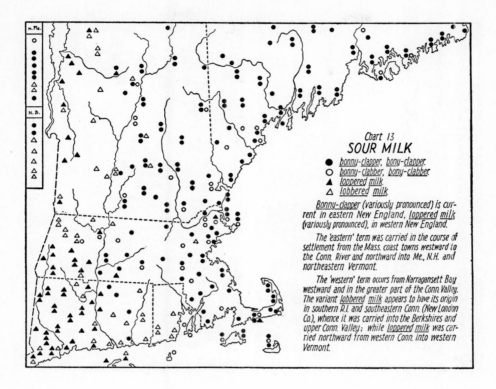

Chart 13
SOUR MILK

● *bonny-clapper, bony-clapper.*
○ *bonny-clabber, bony-clabber.*
▲ *loppered milk.*
△ *lobbered milk.*

Bonny-clapper (variously pronounced) is current in eastern New England, loppered milk (variously pronounced), in western New England.

The 'eastern' term was carried in the course of settlement from the Mass. coast towns westward to the Conn. River and northward into Me., N.H. and northeastern Vermont.

The 'western' term occurs from Narragansett Bay westward and in the greater part of the Conn. Valley. The variant lobbered milk appears to have its origin in southern R.I. and southeastern Conn. (New London Co.), whence it was carried into the Berkshires and upper Conn. Valley; while loppered milk was carried northward from western Conn. into western Vermont.

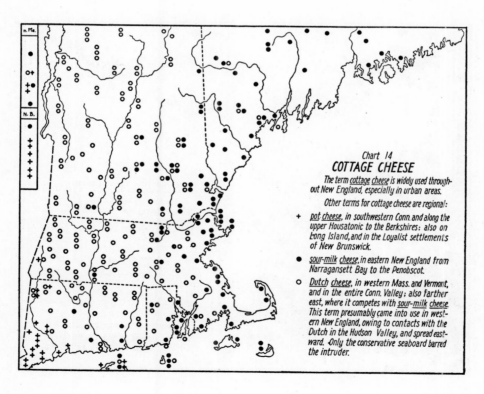

Chart 14
COTTAGE CHEESE

The term cottage cheese is widely used throughout New England, especially in urban areas.

Other terms for cottage cheese are regional:

+ *pot cheese, in southwestern Conn. and along the upper Housatonic to the Berkshires; also on Long Island, and in the Loyalist settlements of New Brunswick.*

● *sour-milk cheese, in eastern New England from Narragansett Bay to the Penobscot.*

○ *Dutch cheese, in western Mass. and Vermont, and in the entire Conn. Valley; also farther east, where it competes with sour-milk cheese. This term presumably came into use in western New England, owing to contacts with the Dutch in the Hudson Valley, and spread eastward. Only the conservative seaboard barred the intruder.*

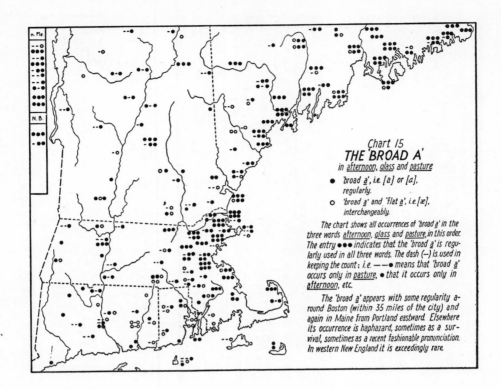

Chart 15
THE 'BROAD A'
in *afternoon*, *glass* and *pasture*

● 'broad *a*', i.e. [a] or [ɑ], regularly.

○ 'broad *a*' and 'flat *a*', i.e. [æ], interchangeably.

The chart shows all occurrences of 'broad *a*' in the three words *afternoon*, *glass* and *pasture*, in this order. The entry ●●● indicates that the 'broad *a*' is regularly used in all three words. The dash (—) is used in keeping the count; i.e. ——● means that 'broad *a*' occurs only in *pasture*, ●—— that it occurs only in *afternoon*, etc.

The 'broad *a*' appears with some regularity around Boston (within 35 miles of the city) and again in Maine from Portland eastward. Elsewhere its occurrence is haphazard, sometimes as a survival, sometimes as a recent fashionable pronunciation. In western New England it is exceedingly rare.

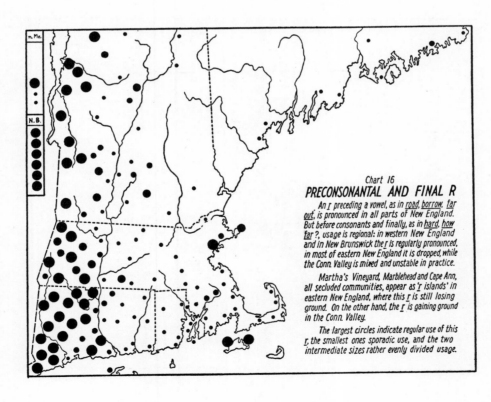

Chart 16
PRECONSONANTAL AND FINAL R

An *r* preceding a vowel, as in *road*, *borrow*, *far out*, is pronounced in all parts of New England. But before consonants and finally, as in *hard*, *how far* ?, usage is regional: in western New England and in New Brunswick the *r* is regularly pronounced, in most of eastern New England it is dropped, while the Conn. Valley is mixed and unstable in practice.

Martha's Vineyard, Marblehead and Cape Ann, all secluded communities, appear as '*r* islands' in eastern New England, where this *r* is still losing ground. On the other hand, the *r* is gaining ground in the Conn. Valley.

The largest circles indicate regular use of this *r*, the smallest ones sporadic use, and the two intermediate sizes rather evenly divided usage.

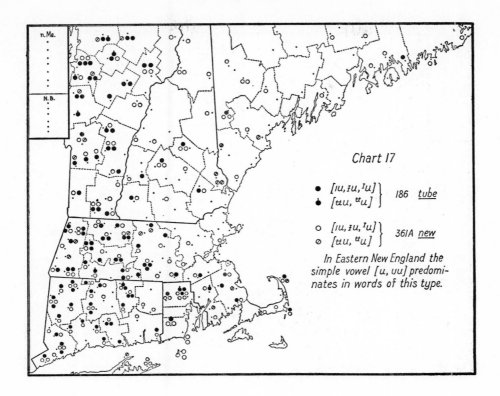

Chart 17

● [ɪu, ɨu, ᶤu] ⎫
                ⎬ 186 _tube_
◗ [ʉu, ᵘu] ⎭

○ [ɪu, ɨu, ᶤu] ⎫
                ⎬ 361A _new_
◒ [ʉu, ᵘu] ⎭

In Eastern New England the
simple vowel [u, uu] predominates in words of this type.

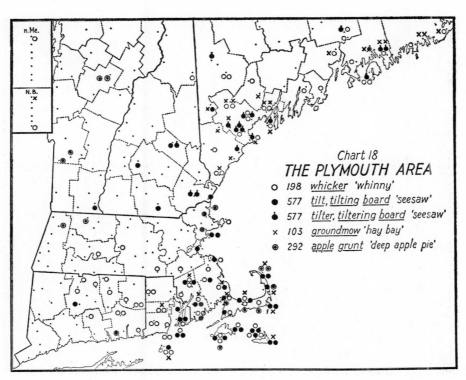

Chart 18
THE PLYMOUTH AREA
○ 198 _whicker_ 'whinny'
● 577 _tilt_, _tilting_ _board_ 'seesaw'
◖ 577 _tilter_, _tiltering_ _board_ 'seesaw'
× 103 _groundmow_ 'hay bay'
◉ 292 _apple_ _grunt_ 'deep apple pie'

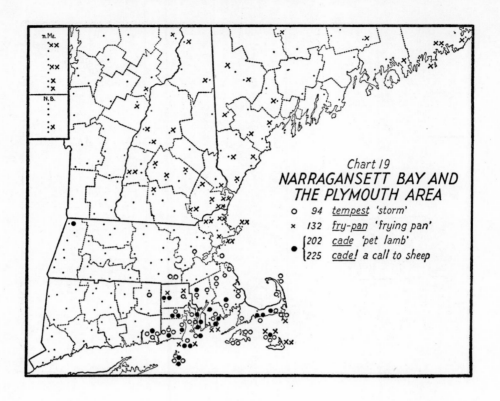

Chart 19
NARRAGANSETT BAY AND
THE PLYMOUTH AREA

o   94   *tempest* 'storm'
×   132   *fry-pan* 'frying pan'
[202   *cade* 'pet lamb'
●[225   *cade!* a call to sheep

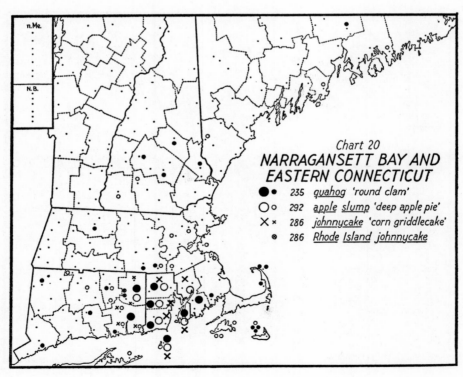

Chart 20
NARRAGANSETT BAY AND
EASTERN CONNECTICUT

●●   235   *quahog* 'round clam'
○○   292   *apple* *slump* 'deep apple pie'
×✕   286   *johnnycake* 'corn griddlecake'
⊙   286   *Rhode* *Island* *johnnycake*

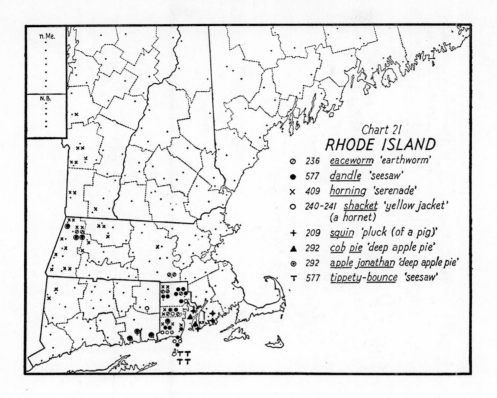

Chart 21
RHODE ISLAND

⊘ 236 *eaceworm* 'earthworm'
● 577 *dandle* 'seesaw'
× 409 *horning* 'serenade'
○ 240-241 *shacket* 'yellow jacket'
        (a hornet)
+ 209 *squin* 'pluck (of a pig)'
▲ 292 *cob pie* 'deep apple pie'
⊙ 292 *apple jonathan* 'deep apple pie'
T 577 *tippety-bounce* 'seesaw'

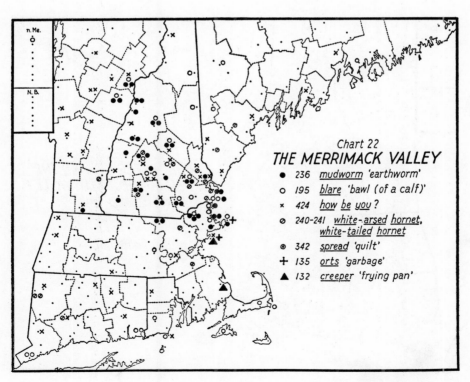

Chart 22
THE MERRIMACK VALLEY

● 236 *mudworm* 'earthworm'
○ 195 *blare* 'bawl (of a calf)'
× 424 *how be you* ?
⊘ 240-241 *white-arsed hornet*,
        white-tailed hornet
⊙ 342 *spread* 'quilt'
+ 135 *orts* 'garbage'
▲ 132 *creeper* 'frying pan'

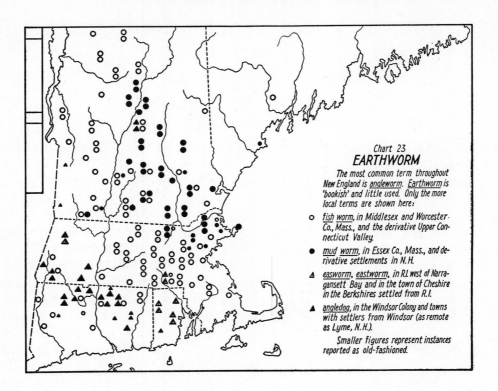

Chart 23
EARTHWORM

The most common term throughout New England is *angleworm*. *Earthworm* is 'bookish' and little used. Only the more local terms are shown here:

○ *fish worm*, in Middlesex and Worcester Co., Mass., and the derivative Upper Connecticut Valley.

● *mud worm*, in Essex Co., Mass., and derivative settlements in N.H.

△ *easworm*, *eastworm*, in R.I. west of Narragansett Bay and in the town of Cheshire in the Berkshires settled from R.I.

▲ *angledog*, in the Windsor Colony and towns with settlers from Windsor (as remote as Lyme, N.H.).

Smaller figures represent instances reported as old-fashioned.

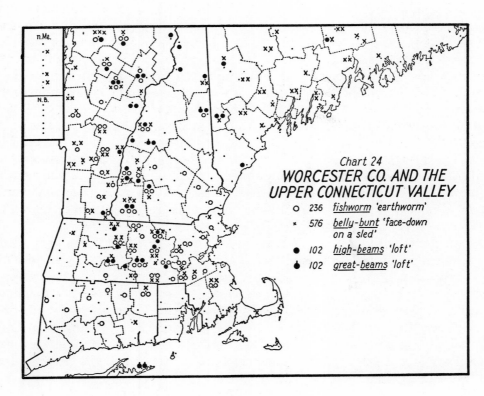

Chart 24
WORCESTER CO. AND THE UPPER CONNECTICUT VALLEY

○ 236 *fishworm* 'earthworm'

× 576 *belly-bunt* 'face-down on a sled'

● 102 *high-beams* 'loft'

◗ 102 *great-beams* 'loft'

CHAPTER II

METHODOLOGY

THE SELECTION OF COMMUNITIES

A tentative selection of communities in New England was made in August 1931 with the help of Marcus L. Hansen's historical outlines. After several months of field work, when the New England work sheets had been put into final shape, and the number of records to be expected monthly from each field worker had been approximately determined, the total number of informants for the *Linguistic Atlas of New England* was fixed, for practical reasons, at about 400 (the actual number is 416) and the number of communities at approximately 200 (actually 213, including 2 on Long Island and 6 in New Brunswick). An earlier plan of having three or more informants in each community was abandoned in order that a larger number of communities might be included. In southern New England and in coastal New Hampshire and Maine, areas which were settled early and from which the gradual occupation of the upland proceeded, the points selected are about 15 miles apart; in the upland of northern New England, an area of secondary settlement, the points are farther apart and, because of the topography and the large unpopulated districts, less evenly spaced.

In selecting the communities, consideration was given to the original settlements, as well as to later shifts in population resulting from the development of commercial centers along the seaboard and the growth of industrial centers during the 19th century. Some attention was paid also to evenness of distribution, so that there might be no serious gaps. Nearly all the old centers along the Atlantic seaboard, on Long Island Sound and on the lower Connecticut River have found a place in the Atlas, and the more important centers of secondary settlement in the upland are well represented. Care was taken to include not only representative flourishing towns and cities, and stable towns, but also towns that have been going down hill for a century or more because of the exhaustion of the soil, the rise of industrial centers and the opening of the West. The population figures given in the brief historical sketches of the towns in Chapter VI tell the story. We feel rather confident that the Atlas has not overlooked any provincial center of importance and that rural as well as urban types of communities are well represented. It is readily granted, of course, that some highly individual towns deserving special study have been omitted—for the very reason that they are not representative of a larger district.

The responsibility for selecting the communities is the director's. He gave to each field worker a plan prepared with the aid of M. L. Hansen's historical outlines and with his advice. The investigation of some communities was made obligatory; in other cases the field worker was given a choice of two or three neighboring towns of apparently equal importance, or of towns settled more or less as a unit. In such instances, the field worker's final choice was made after a visit to the area and was prompted largely by his success in finding suitable informants. Some changes in the original selection of communities were introduced on the advice of the field workers, especially in areas for which the published historical material was inadequate.

39

The accompanying sketch map shows the towns (townships) in which informants were interviewed. On the maps of the Atlas, two adjacent towns are occasionally treated as one 'community' (see Chapter VI).

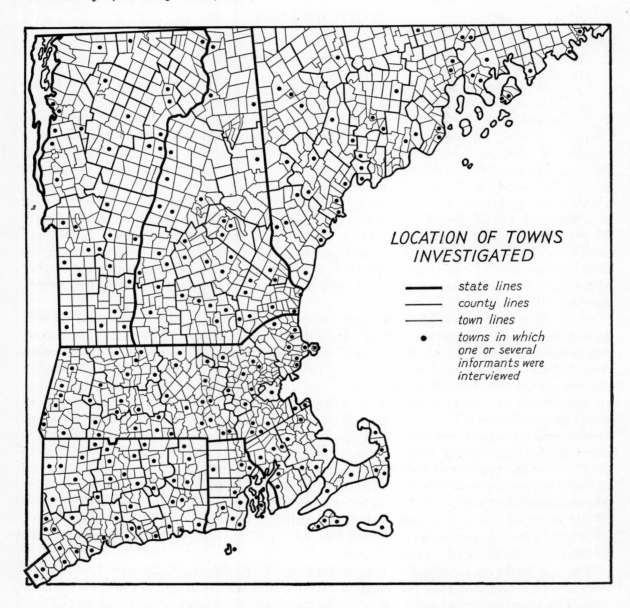

LOCATION OF TOWNS INVESTIGATED

— state lines
— county lines
— town lines
• towns in which one or several informants were interviewed

The communities investigated by the several field workers are here summarized. Where two informants in the same community were interviewed by different field workers, the community number is followed after a period by the number of the informant (e.g., 296.2 = the second informant in community 296):

Miles L. Hanley: 1–24, 141–146, 150.1,2,4, 152, 180–182, 236. (45 records.)

Hans Kurath: 26–30, 36–41. (15 records.)

Rachel Sargent Harris: 31–34, 42–43, 48–49, 52–102, 103.1, 104, 140, 201–202. (49 records.)

Bernard Bloch: 44–46, 150.3,5, 154, 203–225, 238–239, 242–254, 260–265, 271–288, 296.1. (87 records.)

Guy S. Lowman, Jr.: 50–51, 122–125, 156–160, 184–200, 256–259, 290–294, 296.2, 302–308, 310.2, 312.1, 314.2, 316.1, 318, 322.1, 324, 330.1, 333.2, 334, 338–431. (158 records.)

Cassil Reynard: 103.2, 106–120. (22 records.)

Martin Joos: 226–235, 240–241. (16 records.)

Lee S. Hultzén: 266–268, 331–332, 335–337. (11 records.)

Marguerite Chapallaz: 310.1, 312.2, 314.1, 315, 316.2, 320, 322.2, 328, 330.2, 333.1. (13 records.)

This summary appears on each map of the Atlas.

The Selection of Informants

The selection of the informants devolved largely upon the field workers. After the period of preliminary field work it was decided that three types of informants should be represented in the New England Atlas, and the field workers were given directions accordingly:

(1) In every community selected for study an elderly descendant of an old local family was to be included: a simple but intelligent farmer or farmer's wife in rural districts, a workingman, tradesman or shopkeeper in larger villages and in cities. It was regarded as important to record this old-fashioned and most definitely local type in every community, in order that the earlier regional pattern might be accurately delineated and the oldest living forms of speech preserved as fully as possible for the historian of New England speech. Since most informants of this type are over 70 and not a few over 80, it would seem that we shall be able to establish the regionalism of the pre-industrial era of New England in considerable detail, with the possible exception of the highly urbanized area around Boston.

(2) The second informant in each community was to be a middle-aged man or woman, native to the community, who had received better schooling (high school or academy in addition to grammar school), read more widely or enjoyed contacts with the better educated. This type is represented in about four-fifths of the communities. In the others, more or less cultured informants were selected instead.

(3) Cultured informants, with a college education or the equivalent, were to be chosen in most of the larger cities, including all the older cultural centers, and in a number of smaller communities. This type is represented in approximately one-fifth of the communities (38); three-fourths of these are in urbanized southern New England, one-fourth in the largely rural north. Since the speech of the cultured is less local than that of the common man, it would seem that regional differences in cultivated speech are quite adequately exhibited in the New England Atlas. It will be observed that two cultured informants were interviewed in each of four cities: Boston (150), Providence (80), Newport (60) and Springfield (224).

The field workers tried to find these types but did not always succeed equally well. In some communities the two representatives turned out to be rather alike, in others they form sharp contrasts. Moreover, the several field workers put somewhat different interpretations on the inevitably rather vague definition of types, and showed a preference for the interesting old-fashioned local type (so L in New Hampshire) or for the quicker middle-aged type

I A	I B	II A	II B	III A	III B
		1, 1			
		3	3		**3**
	4^2	4^1			
		6			**6**
8, 8					**8**
10			10		
11 −					
				12	
		14	14		
16				**16**	
18				**18**	
19				19	
	20			**20**	
		21			
22 +			22		
23					
		24 +			
		26			**26**
		28			**28**
		29			
30			30		
31					
		32		32 −	
33 −		33			
34 +	34	34			
36					
		38	38 +	**38**	
		40	40	**40**	
		41			
42 +					
43				**43**	
44	44				
45 +	45				
46 +			46		
	48	48			
		49		49	
	50				
51 −, 51		51			
52		52	52, 52		
	54	54	54 +		
56		56			
			57		
		58	58		
				60	**60**
		62	62		
64					
80 +	80				**80, 80**
81 +					
82		82			
102		102			
		103	103		
104 +					
106 +	106				
		108 +	108 +		**108**
110 +			110 +		
112 −					**112**
113					
				114	

I A	I B	II A	II B	III A	III B
115					
116 +				**116**	
		117			
118 +	118				
119			119		
120		120 +			
		122 −			**122**
123		123 −			
124		124, 124			
140			140		
141					
			142		
146		146			
150, 150 −			150	**150**	**150**
		152	152		
		154, 154			
156		156			
158					
160					**160**
180		180			
182				**182**	
			184		
190	190	190	190		
		194	194	**194**	
		196	196		
198					
200		200	200		
		201	201		
		202	202		
		203 −	203		
		204	204 +		
				205	
206		206 +	206 +		
		207, 207			
208					
209	209 +				
	210^2	$210 -^1$			
211			211 +		
		212	212		
		214		214 −	
		218, 218			
		219 −		**219**	
				220 −	
221 +					
			222		
224, 224 +				**224**	**224**
	225				
			226 +		**226**
228				**228 −**	
		$230 +^2$	230^1		
		$232^1, 232^3$	232^2		
		233			
		234	234		
235 +			235		
236		236			
		238 −			
		239			
		240			

I		II		III	
A	B	A	B	A	B
		241			
242				242—	
		246	246		
248	248+				
	252	252+			
		254	254—		
		256—			
		257			
				258	
		259			
		260	260, 260		
262			262		
		264			
	265				
		266	266		
		268	268		
271	271				
272		272			
		274	274		
		276+, 276			
278	278				
280	280			280	
		281			
282		282			
284		284	284		
	286²	286¹	286³		
288			288		
			290		
292		292			
		294	294		
296—		296			
		302	302		
304, 304					
306			306		
		307			
		308, 308			
310		310			
		312, 312			
314		314			
				315	
316		316			
318		318+			
320		320			
322		322+			
324		324			
		328		328, 328	
330	330				
			331		
		332			
333		333			
334		334			
335					
		336	336		
338+			338		
340		340+			
342				342—	
344					
346+		346			
348+		348			

I		II		III	
A	B	A	B	A	B
	352		352		
	354				
356					
		357			
358					
		359			
360+		360		360	
362					
			363		
364		364			
		366	366		
368		368			
370+		370			
				372	
		373—			
		374			
		376+			376
377		377			
378+			378		
380+		380			
		382			
		384—		384	
386		386			
		388	388+		
			390	390—	
		391	391		
	392²	392¹			
394+			394		
396—		396			
398			398		
400+		400			
402		402			
		403			
				404	
		406	406		
407			407		
	408			408	
		410+			
411					
		412	412+		
416			416		
418					
		420	420		
422+		422			
		423			
			424		
426+					
427					
	428		428		
429					
430+					
		431	431		

Total Number of Informants by Types					
I		II		III	
A	B	A	B	A	B
120	28	139	75	34	17

(so B and J in Massachusetts, 203–241). For any treatment of social differences in speech and for any attempt to determine trends of change, the lives of the informants (Chapter VI) must be consulted. For ready reference, the accompanying rough tabulation of all informants by types should prove serviceable.

Table of Informants by Types

Type I: Little formal education, little reading and restricted social contacts.

Type II: Better formal education (usually high school) and/or wider reading and social contacts.

Type III: Superior education (usually college), cultured background, wide reading and/or extensive social contacts.

Type A: Aged, and/or regarded by the field worker as old-fashioned.

Type B: Middle-aged or younger, and/or regarded by the field worker as more modern.

Formal education and self-education through reading and association with others are more significant for the character of the informants' speech than mere age. In other words, the difference between social groups is usually greater than between successive generations of the same social group. For this reason, the age groups are treated as subclasses of the social groups.

For each informant the community number is entered in the appropriate column. When there are two or more informants in the same community, the order shown in the table (from left to right) regularly coincides with the established order in the vitae (Chapter VI) and on the maps. In the six instances where the order in the table does not coincide with the established order (4, 210, 230, 232, 286, 392), the order of the entries on the maps is indicated by superior figures following the community numbers. This divergence in the order of informants in the table and on the maps results from a different 'weighting' of the age factor and of education.

Informants designated in the vitae and on the maps as 'cultured' are represented in the table by **bold-faced** numbers. It will be observed that some informants of type III are not regarded as 'cultured' (3, 12, 19, 49, 194, 214, 220, 258, 328, 372, 390); and that conversely several informants of type II (57, 58, 428) have been designated as 'cultured.' Most of these are borderline cases. The 'cultured' informants of type II have less formal education than some informants of type III but speak a cultivated type of speech because of family background or self-education; on the other hand, the informants of type III who are not regarded as 'cultured' readjusted themselves to the common speech of the community after attending college (engineers, lawyers, one-time teachers, etc.).

A plus sign after a number indicates that the informant is better educated than most others in the same column; a minus sign, that he is less well educated.

Auxiliary informants are not included in this tabulation. On the other hand, all main informants are included, even those from whom only a few pages were recorded (except 125.1,2 and 337, for whom information is lacking).

EVALUATION OF THE FIELD RECORDS AND EDITORIAL PROCEDURE

The character of the material presented in the Linguistic Atlas of New England, as in any linguistic atlas, is conditioned by the method employed in gathering the facts. Preparatory to editing the material, careful consideration was given to all factors resulting from the method used, so that the subjective and the accidental features of the material might be identified and thus the scientific validity of the material established as clearly as possible.

The factors conditioning the character of the material are (1) the field worker's training, his personality and his approach; (2) the informant's personality, his fund of information and his attitude during the interview; (3) the character of the work sheets, such as the arrangement of the items, the verbal context and the definitions provided for the guidance of the field worker; (4) the linguistic character of the items: phonetic, lexical or syntactic; (5) the 'thing-meant': concrete or abstract, familiar or unfamiliar, etc. Information concerning these factors is conveyed partly by labels prefixed to entries on the maps and by observations in the commentaries to the maps, partly in the following chapters of this book. A brief general consideration of all such matters is given below.

Normally, the informant offered his expressions in response to the field worker's inquiry concerning the subject matter; the informant 'spontaneously' named the thing or action described by the field worker. The topical arrangement of the work sheets served to direct the informant's attention to the things themselves, so that he was usually off-guard concerning his linguistic usage. When a response was not secured in this manner, i.e., the *normal* manner, or when the informant expressed or assumed a peculiar attitude towards the thing or the expression, the particular circumstances were noted.

The following abbreviations and signs serve to describe the method by which a response was secured or the manner in which it was offered. (For a fuller treatment see Chapter IV.)

c., conversational form, obtained without direct inquiry;

r., repeated at the request of the field worker;

s., suggested by the field worker and acknowledged as natural by the informant, whether actually used by the informant at present, used by him formerly, or heard from others;

f., forced response, secured by pressing for an answer;

cr., corrected spontaneously by the informant;

:, hesitation on the part of the informant, for whatever reason;

!, amusement on the part of the informant, either at the word or pronunciation, or at the subject matter;

?, prefixed to a form, uncertainty or doubt as to its genuineness on the part of the informant or the field worker. (Queries of the editors appear only in the commentaries and are labeled *Ed.*)

⊥, expression heard from others in the community or, in the past, from a bygone generation.

Conversational forms are especially valuable in the case of the inflectional and syntactical features. They are also of great importance for normally unstressed words and unstressed syllables, as well as for certain sounds and words on which the schools and the educated or would-be educated have focused their attention and which therefore pass as social shibboleths. In such cases direct inquiry may put the informant on guard and lead him to use the 'better' pronunciation instead of his natural and habitual one.

HY, HS, K offer many conversational forms; L very few, since in his interviews he pressed forward energetically and rarely permitted the informants to expatiate or to drift into story telling and anecdote. Many of the forms which L describes as 'fast' or 'natural' are doubtless habitual conversational forms.

Conversational forms are not always identified on the maps. However, the label *c.* has always been retained (a) if the conversational form differs from the direct response of the informant, (b) if it is rather widely regarded as low-class or is rejected by the informant himself even though he uses it in unguarded moments, or (c) if it is in any way peculiar (archaic, slurred, etc.). Substandard grammatical forms, constructions and idioms taken down from the unguarded conversation of the informant always have the appropriate label, unless they predominate in folk speech.

All *suggested responses* are identified on the maps. They were of course taken down in the informant's pronunciation and insofar as the field worker could determine are actually used by the informant. Such responses must be viewed with skepticism, since memory, politeness and the desire to appear to best advantage play tricks with informants, especially with older people. Sometimes an affirmative answer is given to a suggestion merely to get the matter out of the way, and the field worker is left in doubt.

Among the 'suggested' expressions will be found (a) such as are actually used by the informant, (b) some that are recognized by him but only heard from others, and (c) some that are remembered from earlier days. A convenient check on 'suggested' expressions is provided by the responses secured from other informants in the same community or in the vicinity. Expressions or pronunciations reported as 'heard' in the speech of others must be accepted with caution. We may assume that in most cases the informant knows that they are or have been in use in his community or the immediate neighborhood. Not infrequently further information is given by the addition of such remarks as 'among the lower classes,' 'the old folks say,' 'father said,' etc. In some cases, however, the informant may rely on vague impressions and recollections, or have in mind the usage of a chance acquaintance. 'Heard' expressions are at times really obsolete expressions. In evaluating them, the general status of the item in New England should be considered.

Some informants naturally speak *fast*, others *slowly*. Most of them talk naturally when interviewed, but some take pains to speak more distinctly and slowly than usual, 'for the benefit' of the field worker. The field worker may encourage a normal tempo; but he may unintentionally encourage slow and distinct utterance if he hesitates or deliberates while recording or asks the informant too frequently to repeat utterances.

Some expressions have more or less standardized slow and fast forms, for instance *Saturday, tomorrow, afternoon*, which may have only two syllables in rapid speech or in long phrases such as *Saturday afternoon*.

Tempo is a largely uncontrolled variable. L often records both the slow and the fast form. If only the fast form is recorded, it does not necessarily mean that the informant never uses the slow form, and vice versa. The field workers often identify over-careful and emphatic utterances by stress marks or by a comment in the margin.

The informant's responses are colored by his personality, his attitude toward the interviewer, his attitude toward language, and the extent of his knowledge as determined by his occupation, his social contacts, his reading and his intellectual curiosity. He may be responsive or reticent, trusting or wary, talkative or taciturn, elusive and drifting or to the point, imaginative or matter-of-fact, friendly and open or suspicious and retiring, emotional or cold, immersed in the present or fond of 'olden days.' He may be natural, unaffected and unconcerned about 'correctness,' or else on guard, affected, conscious of 'improvements' and eager to speak 'correctly.' He may be naïve and set in his speech or vary his style with the circumstances. Some pay no attention to the speech of others, some again are observant and can report reliably the usage of relatives, neighbors and strangers. In native intelligence and in the fund of information at their disposal they are no less diverse—some highly intelligent and well-informed, others slow-witted, with limited interests. In the lives of the informants (Chapter VI) such traits are pointed out and must be duly considered in dealing with the facts presented by the Atlas.

The field worker's method of interviewing also affects the informant's responses. If older expressions and pronunciations are more or less regularly demanded or suggested, the informant falls into the habit of reporting them fully or even of offering them before he gives his natural usage; on the other hand, if the field worker is content with the first response, the informant may pass over in silence older words or pronunciations which he knows, has used or still uses, and so may drift into a 'modernizing' tendency in the course of the interview.

L and HY are inclined to direct the informant's attention to the past, B to the present. The geographical distribution of old-fashioned expressions and pronunciations in the Atlas and their relative frequency is determined in part by these personal tendencies of the field workers.

The field worker's approach to the individual items in the work sheets is reflected in the definitions he records, in the comments of the informants, in the order of the variants recorded and in the copiousness of the information obtained. Field workers differ considerably in their efforts to record synonyms and semantically related terms. Some are content with the first response (B); others suggest additional terms rather freely (L); others again secure additional terms by talking about the subject matter (HY, HS). Moreover, the field workers' practice varies from item to item. Similar differences in procedure are observable in matters of pronunciation. The paucity of synonyms and the seeming uniformity or stability of pronunciation in certain sections must not always be taken at face value, but must sometimes be interpreted in the light of observations made by the editors in the commentary.

The wording of the items in the work sheets, especially also the variants listed in the work sheets, to some extent determined the method of inquiry and hence also, in a measure, the response. Although the field workers were directed to record the expressions for certain 'things' and not the local equivalents of literary 'expressions,' the thing was doubtless occasionally suggested by means of the literary expression. L is more inclined to suggest expressions in this manner than the other field workers. However, the degree to which the individual field workers are 'bound' by the formulation of the work sheets varies from item to item. All distortions of the material due to the formulation of the item are scrupulously noted in the commentaries.

Definitions and opinions regarding the meaning and currency of expressions offered by the informants are reproduced in the commentaries either verbatim (between quotes) or in summary, even though they reflect only the informants' personal views and may be erroneous. Such remarks must not be mistaken for comments of the field workers or the editors.

Comments of the informants are usually reproduced in conventional spelling, except when they contain interesting phonetic features.

The views of the informants must be accepted with caution, but they are significant even when they are wrong. Lack of familiarity with a subject or lack of interest in it leads to vague or even erroneous conceptions and to distorted pronunciations. The occupation of the informant, his training and his personality (for which see Chapter VI) will often throw light on his comments. Men often have little knowledge of cooking, city dwellers are apt to have only the vaguest notions of farming, the younger generation lack knowledge of old-fashioned dishes, utensils and institutions, and the changing fashions in furniture and architecture have produced much confusion and uncertainty in terminology. Appropriate comments on such matters are given in the introductory statement of the commentaries, partly based upon the field workers' comments and partly derived from an analysis of the material by the editors.

INSTRUCTIONS FOR FIELD WORK

The field workers were provided with a set of instructions concerning field practice, which are here reproduced in full, even though some points may be trite or trivial. Users of the Atlas should know exactly how the material was secured, in order that they may form as clear a conception as possible of the character of the facts presented on the maps. Some of the practical hints will probably prove helpful to those who may wish to do field work of their own.

I

1. Beware of preconceived notions. Do not be misled by what you know, but trust your ear and eye. Rejoice in discovering new facts, and in having your expectations disappointed. Alertness and keenness of perception are the important factors in this work.

2. The investigator must take care to secure natural, unguarded responses. Slow and emphatic utterance differs from normal speech, especially in the treatment of syllables usually weak. For this reason the interview should be carried on as far as possible in the form of a conversation. If the desired expression is first uttered in isolation, the informant should be led or directed to utter it in context, under normal stress and at the usual speed. A question such as: 'How would you say it if you were talking to your wife or a neighbor?' often sets the informant right.

3. If the isolated form and the form in context differ, the context should be written down either in phonetic notation or in conventional spelling whenever it deviates from that given in the work sheets. Phonetic notation should be used if the pronunciation of the desired expression seems to be influenced by the surrounding sounds.

4. Never urge your informant to speak plainly. If the first response is not caught on the wing and you must ask for a repetition of the utterance, make sure whether the response is natural, or emphatic and over-careful. The natural response should be secured either by a direct request (i.e., by asking, 'How would you say it if you were talking to your wife or a neighbor?') or by leading up to it from a new angle. In certain cases it will be better to drop the matter temporarily and to take it up at a later interview.

5. Do not suggest a response by asking, 'Do you say so-and-so?' until all other methods are exhausted. If the response is secured by direct suggestion, prefix *sug.* to it. The approach should be indirect, i.e., through the idea.

Do not press too hard for an answer. If the informant lacks the information, ask someone else in the house or in the community. *All responses secured from an auxiliary informant must be starred*, and the informant should be identified in the right-hand column.

6. Do not explain to your informant during the interview in what respects his pronunciation differs from yours or someone else's, since to do so may lead to conscious avoidance of normal speech. Defer all explanations until the entire interview has been completed. A courteous promise to answer his questions later should satisfy the informant and serve to hold his interest.

7. The careful selection of informants from the various generations and from diverse social and racial elements is of supreme importance.

A representative of the oldest local families must be secured in all communities, preferably a middle-aged or an aged person.

In all communities a relatively uneducated informant must be studied: in rural communities a simple but intelligent farmer, in urban communities a workingman or a storekeeper.

The middle-aged generation (40–60) must be represented in all communities. If either the older or the younger generation differs markedly from the middle-aged generation, for whatever reason, it must be represented in our survey.

The pronunciation of 'old-timers' is of the greatest interest. Your informants will often tell you how their parents used to speak, or what new expressions their children use. All such information must be put down. It is very valuable.

8. Persons who have traveled a good deal or have attended college outside their section of the country must be avoided.

Persons who speak two dialects (say, an urban and a rustic dialect) may furnish important leads, but they are not desirable informants unless they command both dialects equally well and are in the habit of setting off one against the other. They are apt to be opinionated. The ideal informant is one who cannot help talking the way he does.

II

The following information should be secured concerning informants and communities:

1. The names of the village, town, county and state, as well as the full name of the informant, entered both in conventional spelling and in phonetic notation.

2. Education: formal schooling and extent of reading (newspapers, periodicals, fiction, scientific and technical literature).

3. Social contacts: working companions, business contacts, intimate friends; membership in church, club and other organizations; travel.

4. Family history: birthplace of father and mother, cultural and social standing, ancestry. If the family history has been published or is accessible in manuscript, give bibliographical information.

5. Character sketch: alertness and intelligence, extent and accuracy of information, attitude toward the investigator and his task, naturalness or guardedness in utterance, interest in 'improving' the language.

6. General character of the community: number of inhabitants; racial elements with an estimate of their size; industrial, residential or rural; historical or antiquarian society, library, schools.

III

1. All records must be made in duplicate in special blank books of bond paper. Use only first-class thin carbon paper, so that the carbon copy will be absolutely clear and easy to read.

2. The left-hand column in the blank book is for the phonetic record, the right-hand column for comments and definitions.

3. Number the pages in accordance with the work sheets.

4. In order to speed up the interview and to avoid irritation on the part of the informant, it will be well for you to go over the parts of the work sheets that are to be handled in a particular session with great care before confronting the informant. After the first interview you will know him well enough to be able to formulate your questions beforehand so as to secure the desired responses in the quickest and surest way. Many of your informants will be busy men and women and will have little patience with 'floundering.' Moreover, our time and our man-power are limited and we must strive to make the best of them. After each interview the record should be checked over as soon as possible so that errors may be detected and incomplete responses singled out for further inquiry and definition. If the record seems unsatisfactory, the informant's usage should be verified during the following interview. *However, the original record must not be changed;* corrections and explanations should be entered in the right-hand column.

5. It is of the greatest importance to record the informant's attitude (hesitation, doubt, amusement, etc.) as well as illuminating comments offered by him. The observer's reaction is of equal importance: uncertainty of perception, doubt concerning the genuineness of the response, certainty in the perception of surprising responses, etc. The signs to be used for this purpose are listed on a separate sheet [see Chapter IV].

6. A journal is indispensable. A loose-leaf booklet which can be conveniently carried in the coat pocket will best serve the purpose. One section should be used for notes on the speech and the personality of the informant. Entries concerning the personal history, the family history and the nature of the community should be made day by day; a summary of the most important facts should be entered in the field record when the interviews have been completed. Another section should be reserved for recording engagements: to prevent loss of time and to avoid confusion and annoyance, it is important to make appointments with informants in advance. A third section should contain a separate leaf for each tentatively selected community, on which you may enter the names and addresses of consultants and possible informants, and information concerning them or the community.

DIFFERENCES BETWEEN FIELD WORKERS IN PHONETIC RECORDING

These have been noted in detail in Chapter IV, *The Phonetic Alphabet.* A brief discussion of the sources of such 'subjective' variations and of the means of identifying them will aid in the interpretation of the maps.

The problem of handling 'subjective' factors would seem to be more difficult when more than one field worker is employed, but the reverse is true. When all the field work is done by one investigator, as for the *Atlas linguistique de la France*, his personal slant—an inevitable consequence of his hearing, his habits of systematization and his training—is an unknown quantity until others go over the same ground. When several field workers record in adjoining areas, the 'personal boundaries' furnish a valuable clue to the bias of each one of the observers, and it becomes possible to gauge the accuracy of their observations and to identify specific tendencies and weaknesses. No observer is perfect or equally reliable in every respect. Although well-trained observers rarely diverge very seriously from each other, there are differences between them that must be taken into account in establishing the objective value of their records. With this purpose in mind the following observations concerning phonetic variations are presented.

1. Regional variations in pronunciation are most clearly shown *within* the area of a single field worker. Serious confusion of dialect boundaries with 'personal' boundaries is hardly to be expected: the probability that regional and 'personal' boundaries will coincide is very slight.

2. Social variations and differences between age groups are in part determined by the choice of informants, by the field workers' practice of suggesting old-fashioned pronunciations, and by the tempo of the interview. Unless the informant is given time to talk freely, his natural pronunciation of certain words may occasionally escape the field workers' attention.

3. Variations within the phonemes of the informants, both qualitative and quantitative, depend upon (1) sentence stress and intonation, (2) the speed of utterance, either as a personal or regional characteristic or as determined by the length of the stress-group, (3) the phonetic context, i.e., the formation of preceding and especially following sounds and initial and final position in the stress-group, (4) the presence of two or more dialectal types in the home or the community of the speaker. In addition to these 'objective' variations there are 'subjective' variations resulting (5) from the field worker's tendency toward a broader or narrower notation. Broad notation disregards variations within the phonemes, narrow notation identifies them. No field worker's notation is equally narrow or broad in all parts of the 'vowel spectrum.'

4. Some subjective variations are due to differences in hearing. Such auditory differences cannot be disentangled from differences in notation that are due to divergent analyses of the 'vowel spectrum,' i.e., varying delimitations of the range of the symbols. Fortunately there is no practical need of distinguishing these two subjective factors. Both appear as regular and constant deviations in the use of the symbols, which can be inferred from the presence of 'personal boundaries' on the maps.

5. Other 'subjective' variations result from the divergent use of symbols, which depends (1) on the field worker's dialect, i.e., his own phonemic system, (2) on his training, i.e., the systematic grouping of phones under a limited number of symbols acquired from someone else, (3) on the adaptation of a system of notation to a particular dialect. The phonemic structure of any particular dialect makes for a special definition of the range of the symbols. If the same system of symbols is later applied to another dialect there is almost inevitably a a carry-over.

The naïve speaker hears a whole group of similar or at times rather different sounds as one and the same 'sound,' i.e., as one phoneme. A phoneme is a functional phonetic unit whose range is determined by its place in a particular phonemic pattern. All the infinite variety of phones in a given language are subjectively grouped into a comparatively small number of phonemes. This grouping is unique for each language or dialect. Persons speaking only one language or dialect can observe the variations within their phonemes only after intensive training; they refer all sounds in related dialects and in foreign languages to the phonemes of their native dialect, i.e., they classify foreign phones under one of their habitual phonemes. They are phoneme-bound. Training in the analysis of one's own phonemes, and still more in the analysis of the phonemic structure of foreign dialects and languages, breaks the spell of the unanalysed native phonemes and makes possible (within limits) the observation of phones without regard to their phonemic affiliations. This ability is never fully attained; the tyranny of the native phonemes is never completely escaped. Hence, the use of the phonetic symbols by the several field workers is inevitably influenced more or less by the phonemic structure of their own language (i.e., the systematization of the phones in their own speech). Field workers whose native dialects differ will therefore exhibit more or less constant divergent tendencies in the use of symbols; and field workers of different training and varying powers of analysis will also, within certain limits, differ in the use of symbols. Such differences are apt to be constant and can be singled out because they produce 'personal boundaries' on the maps. That these divergencies cannot be separated from the constant variations originating in individual peculiarities of hearing is of no practical consequence, since both are subjective.

The phonemic structure of the dialect under observation is also a determining factor in the use of symbols, i.e., in the subsuming of phones under various heads. Unless the observer maintains extreme vigilance, his systematization of the sounds of one dialect may in part be carried over into another dialect and cause inaccuracies. This carry-over can hardly be entirely avoided. The results are difficult to detect on the maps and no effective method of identifying them is at hand except independent investigation *sur lieu* or phonographic recording.

RANKING OF THE FIELD WORKERS

An attempt is made here at a rough ranking of the field workers according to their phonetic accuracy, their fullness and accuracy in recording vocabulary, and their practice of giving information on the currency and social status of pronunciations, words and grammatical forms. In the course of editing the Atlas the editors have examined the performance of the field workers in great detail, and feel that the readers should know both the stronger and the weaker points of the investigators to gauge the reliability of the linguistic record. The field worker's personality, his interests, the intimacy of his contact with the informants, his hearing, his training in phonetics and in general linguistics, the character of his own speech and some other factors are inevitably reflected in the records he makes. A common training period of six weeks in the summer of 1931 did much to standardize the practice of the field workers, but it would be wrong to assume that earlier habits of observation and notation and the effects of earlier differences in training were actually eliminated. Moreover, a good field man will develop his own technique as the result of his experience in the field—a technique that suits his personality and the nature of the terrain in which he is working.

Since the two editors had also acted as field workers, they were obliged to rank themselves as well as the others. The difficulty arising from this fact was at least in part overcome by first making independent ratings, each editor ranking all collaborators, including himself, on the several counts, and by then adjusting the differences in rating. The results of this attempt are given below.*

1. Minuteness in phonetic recording:
   B, L; C, K; J, HY; HN, HS, R.

* B = Bloch, C = Chapallaz, HN = Hultzén, HS = Harris, HY = Hanley, J = Joos, K = Kurath, L = Lowman, R = Reynard. The field workers are arranged in groups, divided by semicolons; within each group the order is alphabetical. The superior group is in each case given first.

2. Freedom from systematization according to the phonemic system of the field worker's own speech:

     L; B, C, K; HN, HY, J, R; HS.

3. Freedom from systematization according to the phonemic system of the informant:

     B, HN, HY, J, K; C, HS, L, R.

4. Avoidance of over-transcription (i.e., exaggeration of phonetic differences):

     B, C, HS, K, L; HN, J; HY, R.

5. Accuracy in recording quantity and stress:

     B, C, K, L; HY, J; HN, HS, R.

6. Observation of lexical variants:

     HS, HY, K; C, L; B, HN, J, R.

7. Definition of the meanings of words (accuracy and fullness):

     B, HN, HS, K, R; C, HY, J, L.

8. Definition of the currency of expressions and pronunciations by social and age groups:

     B, HN, J, K, L; C, HS, HY, R.

9. Fullness of notes taken down from free conversation of the informant:

     B, HS, HY, K; HN, J, R; C, L.

THE MAKE-UP OF THE MAPS

Each map presents, in principle, the usage of all the informants on one particular point: either the terms used for one and the same thing (lexical maps) or the varying pronunciations of one and the same word (phonetic maps) or else the grammatical forms or constructions employed in a given situation (morphological maps). Lexical and morphological maps present invariably also valuable phonetic features, since all responses of the informants were recorded in phonetic notation.

The location of the communities is indicated on the base map by numbers; those representing communities in which a cultured informant was interviewed are boxed. In each community a separate line is assigned to each informant, the most old-fashioned informant coming first, the better educated second, the cultured last. The order of the informants is the same on all maps. Materials from the communities in northern Maine and in New Brunswick are given in a column in the upper left-hand corner. The location of these communities is indicated in the insert on the first map of the *Linguistic Atlas of New England*.

The names of the field workers and the numbers of the communities for which they are responsible are presented on each map for the convenience of readers.

With each map a commentary is provided. If necessary, the method of asking the question, the range of meanings of the terms, and the character of the object denoted are briefly described. Definitions and significant comments by informants and field workers concerning the currency and the social status of words, forms, pronunciations and constructions are reproduced, sometimes verbatim, sometimes in summary.

In general, each map is a unit in itself. Occasionally certain expressions that should appear on the map proper had to be put into the commentary to avoid congestion. In a few instances the commentary is continued on the following (or preceding) map.

Expressions for a related subject, recorded incidentally, are sometimes given in a separate section of the commentary.

In a number of cases the wealth of material for one item was so great that it had to be presented on two (or three) successive maps. On the other hand, two (or three) separate items have sometimes been put on one map for the sake of economy.

An informant often spontaneously gives several different terms for one and the same thing or several pronunciations of one and the same word, or several variants of a grammatical form; in addition, he may report the usage of other persons in the community or region, or that of an older or younger generation. Moreover, he often recognizes as his own an expression suggested by the field worker. All these variants are presented on the map if space permits; otherwise the entry is continued in the commentary. In presenting the responses the following sequence is observed:

1. Spontaneous responses: a. *current forms,* including responses labeled as conversational (*c.*), repeated (*r.*), hesitating (*:*), amusing (*!*) and forced (*f.*); b. forms reported as *heard* from others (⊥); c. *obsolescent* and *obsolete* forms (†).
2. Suggested responses (*s.*), in the same order as above.
3. Responses of an auxiliary informant (*), in the same order as above.

The very fact that each map contains full material implies that the investigation of any one feature of pronunciation, of vocabulary, of morphology or of syntax requires the preparation of separate charts. Such charts can be made in ten to fifteen minutes on a lithoprinted base map showing the community numbers and the state and county lines, which the Atlas is prepared to furnish at cost ($1.25 a hundred).

A heavy line in red, green or blue crayon under the community number for each 'spontaneous' occurrence of the feature often answers the purpose. Prompted, reported and obsolete or obsolescent forms can conveniently be set off from spontaneous forms by using less conspicuous symbols for them, such as outline circles or triangles, while representing spontaneous forms by solid figures.

Geographically or socially complementary forms are best presented in contrasting colors, but figures of different shapes or solid and outline figures such as appear on the charts in Chapter I provide sufficient contrast for a clear and immediate perception of regional distribution or of dissemination by types of informants.

The time devoted to the charting of dialectal features is well spent. Correlations of dialect areas with settlement areas and other phases of population history cannot be easily visualized in any other way.

Bibliography of Linguistic Geography

A bibliography of selected books and papers in linguistic geography and dialectology is offered here as a convenience to scholars in the English field who wish to familiarize themselves with the aims and methods and with some of the results of the investigations undertaken in other countries during the last sixty years. In Germany and France, and more recently in nearly all the European countries from Scandinavia and the Netherlands to Catalonia and Rumania, more or less extensive surveys of the folk speech have been undertaken and published in the form of atlases and monographs. With the collection of the materials there has been going on a vigorous discussion of field technique, of editorial procedure, of methods of historical interpretation, and of the contribution of linguistic geography to the understanding of the history of standard languages and to the elucidation of the central problem of linguistic change in its relation to migrations and to cultural, economic and political history. In this literature, scholars who wish to familiarize themselves with the technique of linguistic geography and to form a critical opinion of its merits and limitations will find much that will help them to deal with the materials presented in the New England Atlas more effectively than they otherwise could. New types of materials and problems call for new methods of research.

The bibliography here presented includes (1) the chief bibliographies, (2) the more important journals (some of which publish reviews and annual bibliographies) and serials, (3) the linguistic atlases published or in process of publication (unpublished and projected atlases are described in J. Schrijnen's bibliography), and (4) a selection of books and articles by individual authors, especially contributions by leading scholars in the field of German, French and Italian dialectology. Works dealing with the aims, the technique and the general problems of linguistic geography and of dialectology have been freely admitted to the list, even if they run to only a few pages. The choice of treatises and monographs was a more difficult task: they were included, most of them at least, if they were thought to furnish models for various types of investigations.

As a convenience to the reader, a rough list of titles arranged by subjects is given at the end of the bibliography.

It has not been thought necessary to list in this bibliography individual works in English and American dialectology because they are conveniently presented in A. G. Kennedy's excellent and exhaustive *Bibliography of Writings on the English Language* (to 1922). The more recent titles will be found in the current bibliographies.

BIBLIOGRAPHIES

1. American Bibliography, published annually by A. C. Baugh, G. Paine and others in Publications of the Modern Language Association of America, Supplement. New York City.

2. Annual Bibliography of English Language and Literature. Edited for the Modern Humanities Research Association by Mary S. Serjeantson and L. N. Broughton. Cambridge, 1921–.

3. Bibliography in American Speech. Formerly by A. G. Kennedy, now by A. L. Hench. 1925–.

4. Gauchat, L., Jeanjaquet, J., Tappolet, E. Bibliographie linguistique de la suisse romande. Neuchâtel, 1912–19.

5. Indogermanisches Jahrbuch. Edited by A. Debrunner and W. Porzig. Berlin and Leipzig, 1914–.

6. Jahresberichte über die Erscheinungen auf dem Gebiete der germanischen Philologie. Publ. by the Gesellschaft für deutsche Philologie in Berlin. Berlin, 1880–.

7. Kennedy, A. G. A Bibliography of Writings on the English Language. Cambridge and New Haven, 1927.

8. Kurath, H. A Bibliography of American Pronunciation, 1888–1928. Language 5, 155–162 (1929).

9. Mentz, F. Bibliographie der deutschen Mundartenforschung . . . bis 1889. Leipzig, 1892.

10. Martin, B. Bibliographie zur deutschen Mundartenforschung in den Jahren 1921–6. Teuth., Beiheft 2 (1929).

11. Roedder, E. C. Linguistic Geography. Germanic Review 1, 251–308 (1926).

12. Roques, M. Bibliographie des travaux de J. Gilliéron (Société de Publications Romanes et Françaises, No. 1). Paris, 1930.

13. Schrijnen, J. Essai de bibliographie de géographie linguistique générale. Nimègue, 1933.

15. Year's Work in Modern Language Studies. Edited for the Modern Humanities Research Association by W. J. Entwistle. London, 1931–.

16. Zeitschrift f. deutsche Mundarten (1915–24), Teuthonista (1924–34), Zeitschrift für Mundartforschung (1935–). Annual bibliography of German dialectology.

JOURNALS AND SERIALS

17. **American Speech,** a quarterly of linguistic usage. Ed. by L. Pound, K. Malone, A. G. Kennedy and J. S. Kenyon. Baltimore, 1925–32.—Ed. by W. C. Greet and others. New York (Columbia University Press), 1933–.

18. **Bulletin de dialectologie romane.** Société inter-

nationale de dialectologie romane. Cöthen (Anhalt), 1909–15.

19. Bulletin de la Société de Linguistique de Paris. Paris, 1871–.

20. Deutsche Dialektgeographie. Berichte und Studien über G. Wenkers Sprachatlas des Deutschen Reichs. Ed. by F. Wrede. 38 vols. to date. Marburg, 1908–.

21. Dialect Notes. Published by the American Dialect Society, ed. by the successive secretaries of the Society (by M. L. Hanley since 1930). Norwood, Mass., 1890–99; New Haven, 1900–.

22. English Dialect Society. Glossaries, grammars, and bibliographies. No's. 1–80. London, 1873–1896.

23. L'Italia dialettale: rivista di dialettologia italiana. Ed. by C. Merlo. Pisa, 1924–.

24. Noord- en Zuid-nederlandsche Dialectbiblio-

theek. Ed. by L. Grootaers and G. G. Kloeke. The Hague, 1926–.

25. Revue de dialectologie romane. Ed. by B. Schädel. Cöthen (Anhalt), 1909–15.

26. Revue des patois gallo-romans. Ed. by J. Gilliéron and L'abbé Rousselot. 5 vols. Paris, 1887–93.

28. Teuthonista, Zeitschrift für deutsche Dialektforschung und Sprachgeschichte. Ed. by H. Teuchert and others. 8 vols. Bonn and Leipzig, 1924–28; Berlin, 1928–29; Halle, 1930–34.

29. Vox Romanica. Ed. by J. Jud. Zürich, 1936–.

30. Zeitschrift für (hoch)deutsche Mundarten. Ed. by O. Heilig and P. Lenz 1900–1912; by O. Heilig and H. Teuchert 1913–18; by H. Teuchert 1919–24. Heidelberg, 1900–05; Berlin, 1906–24.

31. Zeitschrift für Mundartforschung [continuing Teuthonista]. Ed. by W. Mitzka. Halle, 1935.

Linguistic Atlases

32. Bartoli, M. and **Bertoni, G.** Atlante linguistico italiano. In preparation.

33. Blancquaert, E. Dialect-atlas van Klein-Brabant (150 maps). Antwerp, 1926.

34. Blancquaert, E. and **Vangassen, H.** Dialect-atlas van Zuid-Oost-Vlaanderen I, II. Antwerp, 1931.

35. Bloch, O. Atlas linguistique des Vosges méridionales. Paris, 1917.

36. Bottiglioni, G. Atlante linguistico etnografico italiano della Corsica. Pisa, 1932–.

37. Gilliéron, J. Petit atlas phonétique du Valais roman (Sud du Rhône). Paris, 1881.

38. Gilliéron, J. and **Edmont, E.** Atlas linguistique de la France. Paris, 1902–1910. Supplément, vol. 1. Paris, 1920.

39. Gilliéron, J. and **Edmont, E.** Atlas linguistique de la Corse. Paris, 1914.

40. Griera, A. Atlas linguistic de Catalunya. Barcelona, 1923–.

41. Grootaers, L. and **Kloecke, G. G.** Taalatlas van Noord- en Zuid-Nederland. Leyden, 1939–.

42. Jaberg, K. and **Jud, J.** Sprach- und Sachatlas Italiens und der Südschweiz. Zofingen, 1928–.

43. Leroux, P. Atlas linguistique de la Basse-Bretagne. Paris, 1924–.

44. Millardet, G. Petit atlas linguistique d'une région des Landes. Paris, 1909.

45. Puscariu, S., Pop, S. and **Petrovici, E.** Atlas linguistique roumain [to consist of 10 vols.]. 1937–.

46a. Weigand, C. Linguistischer Atlas des Dacorumänischen Sprachgebietes. Leipzig, 1898–1909.

46b. Wirth, Paul. Beiträge zum sorbischen (wendischen) Sprachatlas. Kartenband, instalment 1 (46 maps); Textband, instalment 1. Leipzig, 1933.

47. Wrede, F. Deutscher Sprachatlas, auf Grund des von Georg Wenker begründeten Sprachatlas des deutschen Reichs. Marburg, 1926–.

Individual Works

48a. Ayres, H. M. American Speech Records at Columbia University. American Speech 5, 334–58 (1930).

48b. Bach, A. Deutsche Mundartforschung. Heidelberg, 1934.

49. Bartoli, M. Introduzione alla neolinguistica (=Bibl. dell'Arch. Rom. II, vol. 12). Geneva, 1925.

50. Bayot, A. La géographie linguistique. Bull. du dict. wall. VI, 65 (1911).

51. Bennicke, V. and **Kristensen, M.** Kort over de danske folkemål. Pp. 188 and 104 maps. Copen-

hagen, 1898–1912.

52. Berthold, L. Die wortgeographische Forderung und die Programme der modernen deutschen Mundartwörterbücher. Teuth. 1, 222.

53. Bertoni, G. A proposito di geografia linguistica. Modena, 1911.

54. Bertoni, G. Italia dialettale. Milan, 1916.

55. Bloch, B. Interviewing for the Linguistic Atlas. American Speech 10, 3–9 (1935).

56. Bloch, B. Post-vocalic *r* in New England. Diss. Brown Univ. (typescript), 1935.

57. Bloch, B. Postvolcalic *r* in New England Speech. Actes du IVe congrès international de linguistes, 195–99. Copenhagen, 1938.

58. Bloomfield, L. Language, chaps. 5 and 19. New York, 1933.

59. Bohnenberger, K. Sprachgeschichte und politische Geschichte. Zs. f. hochdeut. Mundarten 3, 321–6.

60. Bohnenberger, K. Die Ostgrenze des Alemannischen. PBB 52, 217–291 (esp. 249–).

61. Bohnenberger, K. Zur Mundart im Südosten des Bodensees. Teuth. 7, 1–41 (1931).

62a. Bottiglioni, G. Come si preparano e come si studiano gli atlanti linguistici. Annali della R. Scuolo Normale Superiore di Pisa, Series II, vol. 2, 1–14 (1933).

62b. Braune, W. Althochdeutsch und Angelsächsisch. PBB 43, 361 (1918).

63. Bremer, O. Beiträge zur Geographie der deutschen Mundarten in Form einer Kritik des Wenkerschen Sprachatlas (=Sammlung Kurzer Grammatiken deutscher Mundarten, vol. 3). Leipzig, 1895.

64. Bremer, O. Zur Kritik des Sprachatlas. PBB 21, 27– (1896).

65. Bremer, O. Politische Geschichte und Sprachgeschichte. Hist. Vierteljahrsschrift 5, 315–46 (1902).

66. Bretschneider, A. Sprachkarte und Sprachgeschichte. Idg. Forsch. 48, 181 (1930).

67. Brøndum-Nielsen, J. Dialekter og dialektforskning. Copenhagen, 1927.

68. Bruneau, C. Enquête linguistique sur les patois d'Ardenne. Paris, 1914–26.

69. Caffee, N. The speech of Charlottesville, Va. Diss. Univ. Va. (typescript), 1935.

70. Daddow, J. The Speech of Chepachet, R. I. Master's Thesis, Brown Univ. (typescript), 1935.

71. Dauzat, A. Essais de géographie linguistique. Paris, 1921.—Series 2: 1929.

72. Dauzat, A. La géographie linguistique. Paris, 1922.

73. Dauzat, A. Les patois; évolution, classification, étude. Paris, 1927.

74a. Doroszewski, W. Pour une représentation statistique des isoglosses. Bull. de la Société linguistique de Paris 36, 28–42 (1935).

74b. Ellis, A. J. Early English Pronunciation, Part V. London, 1889.

75. Fletcher, H. Speech and Hearing. New York, 1929.

76. Frings, T. Die deutsche Sprachwissenschaft und die deutsche Mundartforschung. Zs. f. deutsche Ma. 16, 2–12.

77. Frings, T. Rheinische Sprachgeschichte. Essen, 1924.

78. Frings, T. Sprachgeographie und Kulturgeographie. Zs. f. Deutschkunde 1930, 564.

79. Frings, T. and Tille, E. Kulturmorphologie. Teuth. 2, 1–18.

80. Frings, T. Sprache und Siedlung im mitteldeutschen Osten (=Berichte d. Sächs. Ak., phil.-hist. Kl. 84, heft 6). Leipzig, 1932.

81. Frings, T. Germania Romana (=Mitteldeutsche Studien, heft 2). Halle, 1932.

82. Frings, T. Die Grundlagen des Meissnischen Deutsch. Halle, 1936.

83. Gamillscheg, E. Die Sprachgeographie und ihre Ergebnisse für die allgemeine Sprachwissenschaft. Neuphilologische Handbibliothek 2. Bielefeld and Leipzig, 1928.

84. Gamillscheg, E. Zur sprachlichen Gliederung Frankreichs. Becker Festschrift 50–74. Heidelberg, 1922.

85. Gamillscheg, E. Romania Germanica. 3 vols. Berlin and Leipzig, 1934–6.

86. Gauchat, L. Gibt es Mundartgrenzen? Arch. f. d. Stud. d. neueren Sprachen 111, 365–403 (1904).

87. Gauchat, L. L'unité phonétique dans les patois d'une commune. Festschr. Morf 175–232.

88. Gauchat, L. Sprachforschung im Terrain. Bull. de dial. romane 2, 93.

89. Gauchat, L. Über die Bedeutung der Wortzonen. Basel, 1907.

90. Gauchat, L., Jeanjaquet, J. and Tappolet, E. Tableaux phonétiques des patois suisses romands. Neuchâtel, 1925. [Introduction has important discussion of method.]

91. Gilliéron, J. Petit atlas phonétique du Valais Roman (Sud de Rhône). Paris, 1884.

92. Gilliéron, J. L'Aire clavellus d'après l'atlas linguistique de la France. Résumé des conférences faites a l'école pratique des hautes études en 1912. Neuveville, 1912.

93. Gilliéron, J. Généalogie des mots qui ont désigné l'abeille. Paris, 1918.

94. Gilliéron, J. La faillité de l'étymologie phonétique. Paris, 1919.

95. Gilliéron, J. Étude de géographie linguistique. Pathologie et thérapeutique verbales. Paris, 1921.

96. Gilliéron, J. Thaumaturgie linguistique. Paris, 1923.

97. Gilliéron, J. and Mongin, J. Étude de géographie linguistique. Scier dans la Gaule romane du Sud et de l'Est. Paris, 1905.

98. Gilliéron, J. and Roques, M. Études de géographie linguistique. Paris, 1912.

99. Gilliéron, J. and **Roques, M.** Mirages phonétiques. Rev. de phil. franç. 21, 118.

100. Grant, W. Plans of the Committee on Scottish Dialect. Pamphlet of the English Association, no. 11. Oxford, 1909.

101. Green, B. Word-book of Virginia Folk-speech. Richmond, 1889.

102. Grootaers, L. and **Kloeke, G. G.** Handleiding bij het Noord- en Zuid-Nederlandsch dialectonderzoek (= Dialectbibliotheek, vol. 1). The Hague, 1926.

103. Haag, K. Drei Wege der Mundartforschung. Germ. Rom. Mon. 16, 165 (1928).

104. Haag, K. Sieben Sätze über Sprachbewegung. Zschr. f. hochdeutsche Mundarten 1, 138 (1900).

105. Haag, K. Sprachwandel im Lichte der Mundartgrenzen. Teuth. 6, 1–34 (1929).

106. Hajek, L. Das Phonogrammarchiv der Akademie der Wiss. in Wien von seiner Gründung bis zur Neueinrichtung im Jahre 1927. Sb. Ak. 207, 3. Abhandlung (1928).

107. Hanley, M. L. Technique of Phonographic Recording. R. C. Binkley, Manual on Methods of Reproducing Research Materials, 177–82. Ann Arbor, 1936.

108. Hanley, M. L. 'Serenade' in New England. American Speech 8, 24–26 (1933).

109a. Harris, R. S. New England Words for the Earthworm. American Speech 8, 12–17 (1933).

109b. Harris, R. S. The Speech of Rhode Island. Diss. Brown University (typescript), 1937.

110a. Hempl, G. Language Rivalry and Speech Differentiation in the Case of Race Mixture. TPAPA 29, 31–48.

110b. Hempl, G. Grease and Greasy. Dialect Notes 1, 438–44 (1896).

110c. Hempl, G. Stovepipes and Funnels. Dialect Notes 2, 250–6 (1902).

111. Hof, J. J. Friesche Dialectgeographie (= Dialectbibliotheek, vol. 3). The Hague, 1933.

112. Huber, J. Sprachgeographie, ein Rückblick und Ausblick. Bull. de dial. rom. 1, 89.

113. Hübner, A. Die Mundart der Heimat. Breslau, 1925.

115. Jaberg, K. Sprachgeographie. Beitrag zum Verständnis des Atlas linguistique de la France. Aarau, 1908.

116. Jaberg, K. Aspects géographiques du langage. Paris, 1936.

117. Jaberg, K. and **Jud, J.** Der Sprach- und Sachatlas Italiens und der Südschweiz und die Bezeichnungsgeschichte des Begriffes 'anfangen.' Rev. de ling. rom. 1, 114 (1925).

118. Jaberg, K. and **Jud, J.** Der Sprachatlas als Forschungsinstrument. Kritische Grundlegung und Einführung in den Sprach- und Sachatlas Italiens und der Südschweiz. Halle, 1928.

119. Jaberg, K. and **Jud. J.** Ein neuer Sprachatlas. Idg. Jahrbuch 9, 1–12 (1924).

121. Jaberg, K. and **Jud, J.** Transkriptionsverfahren, Aussprache- und Gehörsschwankungen bei Mundartenaufnahme. Zschr. f. Rom. Phil. 47, 171–218 (1927).

122. Jud, J. Problèmes de géographie linguistique romane. Rev. de ling. rom. 1, 181 (1925).

123. Jud, J. Le valeur documentaire de l'atlas linguistique de l'Italie et de la Suisse méridionale. Rev. de ling. rom. 5, 251 (1928).

124. Karg, F. Mundartengeographie. Archiv f. Kulturgeschichte 20, 222–38 (1930).

125. Kauffmann, F. Zur Frage nach der Altersbestimmung der Dialektgrenzen. Zs. f. deutsche Phil. 39, 145 (1907).

126a. Kloeke, G. G. Die niederländische Mundartenforschung. Zs. f. deutsche Mundarten 15, 80–92 (1920).

126b. Kloeke, G. G. De hollandsche Expansie in de 16. en 17. eeuw . . . The Hague, 1927.

127a. Kretschmer, P. Wortgeographie der hochdeutschen Umgangssprache. Göttingen, 1918.

127b. Krohn, Kaarle. Die folkloristische Arbeitsmethode. Oslo, 1926.

128a. Kurath, H. The Origin of Dialectal Differences in American English. Mod. Phil. 25, 385–95 (1928).

128b. Kurath, H. American Pronunciation. Society for Pure English, Tract 30. Oxford, 1928.

129a. Kurath, H. Report of the Conference on a Linguistic Atlas of the United States and Canada. Bulletin No. 4, Linguistic Society of America, 20–47. Baltimore, 1929.

129b. Kurath, H. The Linguistic Atlas of the United States and Canada. Annual reports of progress, beginning 1931, in the *Bulletin* of the American Council of Learned Societies, Washington, D. C.

130. Kurath, H. and **Hanley, M. L.** Progress of the Linguistic Atlas of the United States and Canada. Annual reports, beginning 1930, in *Dialect Notes*.

131. Kurath, H. The Linguistic Atlas of the U. S. and Canada, in Essai de bibliographie de géographie linguistique générale, ed. by Joseph Schrijnen for the Comité International Permanent des Linguistes. Nimègue, 1933.

132. Kurath, H. The Linguistic Atlas of New England. Proceedings of the American Philosophical Society 74, 227–43. Philadelphia, 1934.

133. Kurath, H. The Linguistic Atlas of the U. S. and Canada. Proceedings of the International Congress of Phonetic Sciences (London, 1935) 19–22. Cambridge, 1936.

134. Kurath, H. New England Words for the Seesaw. American Speech 8, 14–18 (1933).

135. Lerch, E. Über das sprachliche Verhältnis von Ober- zu Unterschicht. Jb. f. Phil. 1, 70–124.

136a. Martin, R. Untersuchungen zur rheinmoselfränkischen Dialektgrenze (= Deutsche Dialektgeogr., vol. 11a). Marburg, 1922.

136b. Martin, B. and others. Von Wenker zu Wrede (Deutsche Dialektgeographie, heft 21). Marburg, 1933.

137. Maurer, F. Sprachschranken, Sprachräume, und Sprachbewegungen im Hessischen. Giessen, 1930.

138. Maurer, F. Der deutsche Sprachatlas. Eine Kritische Würdigung . . . Zs. f. Deutschkunde 41, heft 9 (1927).

139. Maurer, F. Sprachräume und Sprachbewegungen im deutschen Mittelalter. Monatsschrift für höhere Schulen 37, 289–307 (1938).

140. Mawer, A. Problems of Place-Name Study. Cambridge, 1929.

141. Meillet, A. J. Gilliéron et l'influence de l'étude des parlers sur le développement du romanisme, in Linguistique historique et linguistique générale, 2. ed., 305. Paris, 1926.

142. Meillet, A. [Concerning the Atlas linguistique de la France] BSL. 1913, 284; 1915, 65; 1921, 70, 228; 20, 93.

143a. Menner, R. J. Linguistic Geography and the American Atlas. American Speech 8, 3–7 (1933).

143b. Meyer-Lübke, W. Aufgaben der Wortforschung. Germ.-Rom. Monatsschrift 1, 643.

144. Millardet, G. Linguistique et dialectologie romanes. Paris, 1923.

145. Millet, A. L'oreille et les sons du langage d'après l'abbé Rousselot. Paris, 1926.

146. Mitzka, W. Sprachausgleich in den deutschen Mundarten bei Danzig (= Königsberger Deutsche Forschungen, heft 2). Königsberg, 1928.

147. Mitzka, W. Grundzüge nordostdeutscher Sprachgeschichte. Halle, 1937.

148. Morf, H. Mundartforschung und Geschichte auf romanischem Gebiet. Bull. dial. rom. 1, 1 (1909); 2, 163 (1910).

149. Morf, H. Zur sprachlichen Gliederung Frankreichs. Abh. preuss. Ak. d. Wiss., phil.-hist. kl., Abh. 2. 1911.

150. Naumann, H. Über das sprachliche Verhältnis von Ober- zu Unterschicht. Jb. f. Phil. 1, 55–69.

151. Orbeck, Anders. Early New England Pronunciation. Ann Arbor, 1927.

152. Paris, Gaston. Les parlers de France. Revue des patois gallo-romans 2, 161–75 (1888).

153. Penzl, H. New England Terms for 'Poached Eggs.' American Speech 9, 90–95 (1934).

154. Penzl, H. The Development of ME *a* in New England Speech. Diss. Univ. Vienna (typescript), 1934.

155. Pessler, W. Deutsche Volkstumsgeographie. Braunschweig and Berlin, 1931.

156. Pessler, W. Deutsche Wortgeographie. Wörter und Sachen 15, 1 (1932).

157. Pessler, W. Grundzüge zu einer Sachgeographie der deutschen Volkskunst. Jb. f. hist. Volkskunst 2, 44.

158. Pessler, W. Grundbegriffe volkstumskundlicher Landkarten. Volk und Rasse 1926 (heft 1).

159. Pfalz, A. Grundsätzliches zur deutschen Mundartenforschung (Germ. Forschungen). Vienna, 1925.

160. Pollak, H. W. Das Phonogrammarchiv der Kais. Ak. der Wissenschaften in Wien. Germ.-Rom. Monatsschrift 6, 257 (1914).

161. Pop, S. Buts et méthodes des enquêtes dialectales. Paris, 1927.

162. Puscariu, S. Der rumänische Sprachatlas. Arch. f. vergleich. Phonetik 2, 107–118 (1938).

163. Roedder, E. C. Linguistic Geography. Germanic Review 1, 251–308.

164. Rousselot, L'abbé. Les modifications phonétiques du langage étudiées dans le patois d'une famille de Cellefrouin (Charente). Revue des patois gallo-romans 4, 65–208; 5, 209–434 (1891–2).

165. Sapir, E. La réalité psychologique des phonèmes. Jour. de Psych. 30, 247–265 (1933).

166. Schädel, B. Über Schwankungen und Fehlergrenzen beim phonetischen Notieren. Bull. de dial. rom. 2, 1.

168. Scheuermeier, P. Observations et expériences personnelles faites au cours de mon enquête pour L'atlas linguistique . . . de l'Italie . . . Bull. de la Soc. Ling. de Paris 33, 93–110 (1932).

169. Scheuermeier, P. Wasser- und Weingefässe im heutigen Italien. Sachkundliche Darstellung auf Grund der Materialien des Sprach- und Sachatlas Italiens . . . Bern, 1934.

170. Scheuermeier, P. Methoden der Sachforschung. Vox Romanica 1, 334–369 (1936).

171. Schuchardt, H. Über die Klassifikation der

romanischen Mundarten. [Graz, 1900]. Reprinted in Schuchardt-Brevier (ed. L. Spitzer), 166.

172. **Skeat, W. W.** English Dialects from the Eighth Century to the Present Day. Cambridge, 1912.

173. **Sommerfelt, A.** Sur la propagation des changements phonétiques. Norsk Tidsskrift for Sprogvidenskab 4, 76 (1930).

174. **Spitzer, L.** Die Sprachgeographie (1909–1914). Kritische Zusammenfassung. Rev. de dial. rom. 6, 318.

175. **Stroh, F.** Hessische Forschung. Von Sinn und Leistung des Südhessischen Wörterbuchs (= Mitteilungen des Oberhessischen Geschichtsvereins 32, 8–35). 1934.

176. **Streitberg, W.** and **Michels, V.** Die Erforschung der indogerm. Sprachen: Germanisch, 144–177 (= Grundriss der idg. Sprach- und Altertumskunde II, 2, 1. lieferung). Berlin, 1927.

177. **Swadesh, M.** A Method for Phonetic Accuracy and Speed. Amer. Anthropologist 39, 4 (1937).

178. **Tappolet, E.** Neuere Aufgaben der Wortforschung. Germ.-Rom. Monatsschrift 12, 130.

179. **Tappolet, E.** Über die Bedeutung der Sprachgeographie, mit besonderer Berücksichtigung der französischen Mundarten. Festgabe Morf, 385. Halle, 1905.

180. **Terracher, A.** Les aires morphologiques dans les parlers populaires du nord-ouest de l'Angoumois (1800–1900). Paris, 1912–14.

181. **Terracher, A.** Autour de L'atlas linguistic de Catalunya. Rev. de ling. rom. 1, 440 (1925).

182. **Terracher, A.** L'histoire des langues et la géographie linguistique. Oxford, 1929.

183. **Teuchert, H.** Grundsätzliches über die Untersuchung von Siedlungsmundarten. Zs. f. deutsche Mundarten 10, 409 (1915).

184. **Tourtoulon, C.** and **Bringuier, O.** Étude sur la limite géographique de la langue d'oc et de la langue d'oïl. Paris, 1876.

185. **Trubetzkoy, N.** Phonologie und Sprachgeographie. Travaux du cercle ling. de Prague 4, 228 (1931).

186a. **Trubetzkoy, N.** Anleitung zu phonologischen Beschreibungen. Ass. internationale pour les études phonologiques. Brno, 1935.

186b. **Trubetzkoy, N.** Grundzüge der Phonologie. Cercle Linguistique de Prague. Prague, 1939.

187. **Vidossi, G.** L'atlante linguistico italiano; questione di metodo e di fini. Boll. dell'atl. ling. it., no. 1 (1933).

188. **Wagner, K.** Deutsche Sprachlandschaften (Deutsche Dialektgeographie, heft 23). Marburg, 1927.

189. **Wagner, M. L.** Die Beziehungen zwischen Wort- und Sachforschung. Germ.-Rom. Mon. 8, 45.

190. **Wartburg, W. von.** Die Ausgliederung der romanischen Sprachräume. Zs. f. rom. Phil. 56, 1–48 (1936).

191. **Wegener, P.** Die Bearbeitung der lebenden Mundarten. Grundriss der germanischen Philologie (2. ed.) 1, 1465–82. Strassburg, 1901.

192. **Wegener, P.** Über deutsche Dialektforschung. Zs. f. deut. Philologie 11, 450.

193. **Weisgerber, L.** Zur Erforschung des Sprachwandels. Idg. Forsch. 48, 26–45.

194. **Wenker, G.** and **Wrede, F.** Der Sprachatlas des deutschen Reiches, Dichtung und Wahrheit: I. Herrn Bremers Kritik des Sprachatlas; II. Über die richtige Interpretation der Sprachatlaskarten. Marburg, 1895.

195. **Wenzel, W.** Wortatlas des Kreises Wetzlar . . . [including an atlas of 104 maps] (= Deutsche Dialektgeographie, heft 28). Marburg, 1930.

196. **Wrede, F.** Ethnographie und Dialektwissenschaft. Hist. Zeitschrift 88, 22–43 (1902).

197. **Wrede, F.** [Reports on the progress of the Sprachatlas.] Anz. f. d. deut. Alt. 18, 406; 19, 100; 20, 211; 22, 334; 24, 116. Zs. f. d. deut. Alt. 37, 288; 39, 226.

198. **Wrede, F.** Über den Sprachatlas des deutschen Reichs. Arch. f. d. Stud. d. neueren Sprachen 111, 365.

199. **Wrede, F.** Die Diminutiva im Deutschen. Deutsche Dialektgeographie, heft 1, 71–144. Marburg, 1908.

200. **Wrede, F.** Zur Entstehungsgeschichte der deutschen Mundartforschung. Zs. f. deut. Mundarten 14, 3–18 (1919).

201. **Wrede, F.** Sprachliche Adoptivformen. Behagel Festschrift 83–91. Heidelberg, 1924.

202. **Wrede, F.** Ingwäonisch und Westgermanisch. Zs. f. deut. Mundarten 19, 270–84 (1924).

203. **Wright, J.** English Dialect Dictionary. London, 1898–1905.

204. **Wright, J.** English Dialect Grammar. Oxford, 1905.

Subject Index to the Bibliography

1. **Bibliographies:** 1–16.

2. **Journals and Serials:** 17–31.

3. **Linguistic Atlases:** 32–47.

4. **Aims, Methods and Results of Linguistic Geography (General):** 48 Bach, 58 Bloomfield, 62 Bottiglioni, 63, 64 Bremer, 66 Bretschneider, 67 Brøndum-Nielsen, 71, 72, 73 Dauzat, 86 Gauchat, 103, 105 Haag, 112 Huber, 115, 116 Jaberg, 117, 118, 119 Jaberg and Jud, 122, 123 Jud, 126a Kloeke, 128, 132 Kurath, 136b Martin, 138 Maurer, 142 Meillet, 152 Paris, 159 Pfalz, 161 Pop, 163 Roedder, 174 Spitzer, 175 Stroh, 176 Streitberg, 178, 179 Tappolet, 181 Terracher, 183 Teuchert, 187 Vidossi, 191 Wegener, 194 Wenker, 200, 201 Wrede.

5. **Model Treatises:** 68 Bruneau, 77, 81, 82 Frings, 87, 90 Gauchat, 93, 95 Gilliéron, 126b Kloeke, 127a Kretschmer, 136a Martin, 149 Morf, 164 Rousselot, 180 Terracher, 184 Tourtoulon, 188 Wagner, 190 Wartburg, 191 Wegener, 195 Wenzel, 199 Wrede.

6. **Dialect Boundaries and Social Stratification:** 48 Bach, 60 Bohnenberger, 74 Ellis, 86, 87, 89 Gauchat, 104 Haag, 123 Kauffmann, 135 Lerch, 137 Maurer, 150 Naumann, 173 Sommerfelt.

7. **Dialects and Population History:** 48 Bach, 59 Bohnenberger, 65 Bremer. 80, 81 Frings, 85 Gamillscheg, 110a Hempl, 147 Mitzka, 148 Morf, 196 Wrede.

8. **Dialectology and Historical Grammar:** 66 Bretschneider, 76 Frings, 83 Gamillscheg, 94, 99 Gilliéron, 139 Maurer, 141 Meillet, 144 Millardet, 182 Terracher, 202 Wrede.

9. **Dialectology and the Study of Folk Culture:** 48 Bach, 78, 79 Frings, 113 Hübner, 127b Krohn, 155, 157, 158 Pessler, 169, 170 Scheuermeier, 189 Wagner.

10. **Field Recording; the Work Sheets (Questionnaire):** 48 Bach, 55 Bloch, 74 Ellis, 88 Gauchat, 102 Grootaers, 114 Institut d'Ethnologie, 168 Scheuermeier.

11. **Phonetic Recording; Phonemics; Phonographic recording:** 58 Bloomfield, 75 Fletcher, 90 Gauchat, 106 Hajek, 107 Hanley, 121 Jaberg and Jud, 145 Millet, 160 Pollak, 165 Sapir, 166 Schädel, 177 Swadesh, 185, 186 Trubetzkoy.

12. **Studies in the Linguistic Geography of New England:** 48a Ayres, 56, 57 Bloch, 70 Daddow, 108 Hanley, 109a, b Harris, 110b, 110c Hempl, 128a, 128b, 131, 132, 133, 134 Kurath, 143a. Menner 151 Orbeck, 153, 154 Penzl.

CHAPTER III

THE SETTLEMENT OF NEW ENGLAND*

I. *EASTERN NEW ENGLAND*

1. THE COAST

The Massachusetts Bay Colony

Boston Bay: 150 Boston, 152 Weston, 154 Sherborn, 156 Concord, 158 Burlington, 160 Billerica, 203 Marlborough, 211 Groton.

North Shore: 180 Marblehead, 182 Beverly, 184 Topsfield, 190 Haverhill, 194 Newbury, 196 Rowley, 198 Essex, 200 Rockport.

South Shore: 140 Norfolk-Wrentham, 141 Foxborough, 142 Sharon, 146 Cohasset-Hingham.

'The Great Migration'

The Colonial population of New England derives very largely from that group of Puritans and their associates who settled about Massachusetts Bay in the years between 1628 and 1640. The tide of migration began to flow when the Massachusetts Bay Company undertook the colonization of its lands; it came to an abrupt end when the troubles that were to culminate in the Puritan Revolution attracted the attention of the leaders to affairs within England. In the century and a half after 1640, new blood was constantly coming into New England, but the influx was usually rather small, and the larger groups, such as the Scotch-Irish, settled upon the frontier. In the Boston area, the stock provided by the original 'planting' determined social customs and intellectual standards, which were accepted by later additions to the population. It is true that as a seaport the city had also a floating population of sailors, adventurers and immigrants on their way to a permanent location; but this class was transitory and there is no evidence that it was ever large enough to develop distinctive features of life to be handed down from generation to generation.

It is unfortunate that so little is known about the people of the 'great migration.' Most of the records kept at ports of embarkation have been lost, and on the American side there were few contemporary documents. No early census enumerates the inhabitants present when the immigration came to an end. Churches and towns differ so widely in their interpretations of the words 'inhabitants,' 'Freemen' and 'sojourners' that whatever figures remain cannot be used to determine the number in each class. It is quite possible that the land records extant in most of the towns might reveal the amount of land occupied at any given time, and that these facts might yield reasonable estimates regarding the population; but no one has thus far ventured upon a task involving so much labor.

Very early in the history of New England the tradition arose that the 'great migration' had brought to the Bay four thousand families, consisting of twenty thousand persons. This generalization has never been seriously questioned, and enumerations of the population at later dates present figures which are consistent with an original stock of that size; but this unanimity of opinion does not extend to other matters associated with the settlers. Their motives, geographical origin, mental traits and social standing have all been variously

* See Plates 1 and 2 at the back of the book.

appraised. Contemporary historical scholarship seems to be agreed upon certain funda-
mentals: that if not all of them were Puritans whose religion was the cause of their de-
parture, at least they came from that class in rural England from which the constituency
of the independent churches was principally recruited; that the majority originated either
in the eastern and southern counties of England, where Puritanism and agricultural change
were in the air, or else in the western counties, where fishing and shipping were important
occupations; and that most of them, far from belonging to the vagrant or unlanded classes,
were rather above the average in education, material resources and physical stamina. An
important feature was the cohesion within groups, which persisted from the original up-
rooting to the final location. Many churches in eastern Massachusetts had been founded
on the other side of the Atlantic; the members sailed together to the new world, and ultimately settled as neighbors in the center of a township, of which the uncleared lands were
gradually occupied by their descendants for two or three generations. Few strangers came
in from the outside to modify the characteristics stamped upon the community by the
original pioneers.

Occupation of the Shores of Boston Bay

The patent granted to the Massachusetts Bay Company determined the general area of
settlement. The rocky promontory of Cape Ann was well known to navigators along the
coast, and fishing stations were established there soon after 1620. It was only natural,
therefore, that the first companies of Puritans should settle upon the shores of its inlets,
where their predecessors had temporarily camped, and where an acquaintance with the
waters made navigation less hazardous. But the immediate hinterland was rather forbidding; and as ships brought successive groups of colonists, each group, instead of pushing
inland, established itself at the western fringe of the settlement along the peninsula until
the mouth of the Charles River in Boston Bay was reached.

Boston Harbor in the 1620's was a tangle of islands and peninsulas. The sea was rapidly
eating away the coast. The islands had recently been peninsulas, and the peninsulas were
prevented from becoming islands only by the colonists' exertions. Still, the region presented
some evident advantages. It lay at the mouth of the Charles River, a stream which was
navigable for a dozen miles inland for the ocean-going vessels of the 17th century. Beyond,
it led into the Indian country, from which the settlers, who had exaggerated notions regarding the number of the Indians and the resources of the forest, expected to draw a trade that
would yield an immediate profit. Fifteen years before, a pestilence had swept away the tribes
inhabiting these islands and peninsulas. There were no natives left to dispute the ownership
of the first comers, and the fields which the Indians had cleared could be prepared for the
plough without much labor.

The first point on the Charles River to be occupied was Charlestown. It commanded the
entrance to the river, and could be reached by land from the villages up the Cape. Here, it
was expected, would be the seat of government and the commercial center of the scattered
'plantations.' But since Charlestown obtained its drinking water from the river, and since
the first families to settle there suffered (apparently as a consequence) more sickness than
was usual even among pioneers, it was felt that the lack of springs would always make the
place unhealthful. A migration across the bay was soon in progress; and later comers, taking
the advice offered them, settled on the southern and western points projecting into the
harbor.

Boston, Roxbury and Dorchester were the towns thus founded. Each location was protected by its semi-detachment from the mainland. Salt marshes provided good pasturage for the cattle; fish and clams abounded in the surrounding waters; the soil was fertile and the springs were plentiful. But only a limited agricultural population could be supported here, and after the first year or two there was no more room for permanent settlers. The original home lots had been small, the supply of timber was by now exhausted, the herds of cattle multiplied rapidly, and almost every vessel with immigrants brought additions to the livestock. Expansion was therefore inevitable. Those who pushed farther into the wilderness were usually not the latest comers but the first pioneers, who had learned the methods of settlement and were willing to start anew, selling their houses and lots to those who arrived from England for gold and for supplies. This is an important fact to be kept in mind in tracing the social and cultural development of these communities: that the first company of settlers was often not the permanent company.

The first expansion was naturally up the banks of the Charles. Cambridge, Watertown, Waltham, Newton and other towns were settled shortly after 1630. Before the middle of the decade it was necessary to pass beyond the inlets of the sea. The most noteworthy of these 'second migrations' was that which led to the planting of the towns of Windsor, Wethersfield and Hartford on the Connecticut River. But at the same time expansion was proceeding in three rather clearly defined movements to the north, south and west—a quiet and unobtrusive growth that was to continue for almost a century, until the 'Boston area' was peopled with as large a population as its agricultural resources could support.

Settlement of the North Shore

The term 'North Shore' is applied generally to the area north and east of Boston. Settlement did not proceed along the coast line but pushed into the interior from the temporary locations about Boston, attracted by the natural resources of the region, including its nearness to the shore. The area so occupied corresponds roughly to the present Essex County.

Essex County is well watered. The Saugus River flows to the south, the Ipswich and Parker Rivers northward through the central part; the Merrimack River, with numerous small tributaries, drains the north. The first settlers found so many springs that each home could be within easy distance of pure water. The surface is rolling, hilly in parts; and the soil is of the type called stony—not particularly fertile but yielding satisfactory crops to consistent labor decade after decade. Most valuable of all to the colonists were the extensive salt marshes along the shore. The meadows and swamps along the rivers offered pasturage in the summer, the luxuriant growth of the marshes provided an almost unlimited supply of hay for the long winter. Every farmer acquired his acre or two of marsh to assure him fodder, and there was a surplus which in later years was sent in boats around to Boston or up the Merrimack to inland settlements. When the first years had passed, all fear of famine vanished; and the development of a homogeneous native population became merely a matter of time.

Settlement proceeded in two regions. From the early towns on the south shore of Cape Ann it progressed gradually northward. Although originally not adapted to agriculture, the fields, when fertilized with fish and intensively cultivated, yielded satisfactory crops, for which a market was at hand in the maritime towns of Salem and Gloucester. Their population, employed upon the sea, had to be fed from the adjacent land. Many settlers combined farming with fishing or with service as sailors on ships bound for the West Indies.

North of this southern tier of towns the dispersion of the population proceeded from three inland centers: Ipswich, Rowley and Newbury. These settlements had been planted early, each in the center of an extensive area which it took almost a hundred years to fill. This slow rate of expansion was due only in part to emigrations to other towns. More important was the compactness of the settlements. The farms were comparatively small, but since there were marshes to provide hay, it was possible to cultivate them more fully than elsewhere. Shipbuilding was an important seasonal occupation; shoemaking and nail-making became household industries in almost every home; and many of the inhabitants owned interests in vessels trading along the coast or across the Atlantic. Thus the settlers did not depend entirely upon the soil.

Between these two regions of Essex County there were marked contrasts. The villages on the shore provided a temporary home for companies of settlers, who tarried a few months or perhaps years and then went on to Boston Bay or the Connecticut shore. Each company left a residue; and this, together with individual adventurers, provided the original stock. The resultant variety, existing from the first, was increased by the influx of stray individuals from the many points on the Atlantic visited by the fishing and trading vessels. Diversity of blood, language, customs and ideals overshadowed all other factors. In the interior, on the other hand, uniformity prevailed at the beginning and its persistence was fostered by the conditions of growth. Whatever variety existed was due to the different English origin of each of the three groups that founded the original towns of Ipswich, Rowley and Newbury.

Settlement of the South Shore

The shape of Boston Harbor has been compared to an irregular letter 'C' with the open side facing the northeast. It was from this direction that settlement approached, and the occupation of the southern shore of the bay proper followed in due time. But this stretch of the coast line did not possess a hinterland corresponding to Essex County in the north, and the major advance from Boston and its immediate neighbors was therefore more directly west, either to the valley of the Connecticut or to the outposts established at Dedham, Sudbury and Concord.

The Neponset River, flowing into the harbor from the south, did not invite early settlement along its course. It was bordered by extensive meadows, but these were low. Heavy rains and spring freshets transformed them into swamps that often ruined the season's labor and polluted the air with malaria. Even in the latter part of the 19th century the river constituted a drainage and sanitation problem that left its banks unpeopled. Along this river lay the lands of Dorchester, then a town extending far to the southwest and including what are now parts of Milton, Stoughton, Sharon, Canton and Foxborough. The mother town disposed of these lands only slowly, prudently leaving them as an inheritance for the settlers' children and grandchildren. Stoughton, Sharon, Canton and Foxborough were not settled until 1700; and for about two generations this region, held in reserve, constituted a wilderness wedged between the population on the coast and that which grew southwestwardly from Dedham.

This coastal area possessed decided advantages. The Indians had withdrawn to the interior. The soil was light and sandy, but the seaweed and kelp washed up on the beach by every winter gale made a good fertilizer; there were few pastures, but salt marshes provided sufficient fodder. Within a short time agriculture ceased to be the principal occupation. The waters of the Bay abounded with fish, and after the fishing season the vessels transported grain and fish to the West Indies, or carried wood from the forests adjoining the coast to Boston, which had early exhausted its own supply of timber. This growing commerce absorbed the rising generations. It was easier to find a living upon the sea than in the rocky Blue Hills region to the west. In short, isolation was the most important factor shaping social life in Dorchester. An early 19th-century description emphasizes this homogeneity: 'Their marriages were generally among themselves; so that a large portion of the members became connected by blood; and continue so, in an uncommon degree, to the present day.'[1] And when Timothy Dwight passed through a short time later he commented on the fact that 'The whole region wears remarkably the appearance of stillness and retirement; and the inhabitants seem to be separated, in a great measure, from all active intercourse with their country.'[2]

Expansion into the Interior

When immigration ceased about 1640, expansion into the interior became a slow process dependent upon the natural growth of population. The occupation of the soil did not come to an end until over a century after the 'first planting.' The advance, however, was not a westward movement along a definite frontier line. Almost at the beginning of colonization certain desirable points were seized, families were established and government was organized. Three of these towns, Dedham, Concord and Sudbury, appear so early that they must be considered 'original settlements.' They were located in the 1630's upon fertile meadows bordering sluggish streams. The territory surrounding each was hilly, stony and rather sterile.

The first comers thought that population would be restricted to the valley meadows; but as families grew, sons withdrew from the centers, gradually working their way into the hills until finally the circles of expansion from one center met those from another, and the territories of the ancient towns were divided into several jurisdictions. The history of this expansion can be studied in the genealogies of the 'mother towns.' Groton, founded a generation later (1660) on the banks of the Nashua River, occupied a similar position in the extreme northwestern corner of the area.

The Plymouth Colony

Plymouth Area: 102 Westport, 103 Fall River, 108 Bridgewater, 110 Hanover, 112 Plymouth, 113 Wareham, 114 Rochester.

Cape Cod: 115 Falmouth, 116 Barnstable, 117 Harwich, 118 Chatham, 119 Eastham, 120 Truro.

Taunton Area: 104 Rehoboth, 106 Raynham-Taunton.

Martha's Vineyard: 122 West Tisbury - Chilmark, 123 Edgartown.

Nantucket: 124, 125 Nantucket.

Topography and Soils

The 'Old Colony' or 'Plymouth Colony' is often treated as if it were merely a group of

[1] *Massachusetts Historical Collections*, Series III, vol. II, p. 85.
[2] Dwight, *Travels in New England and New York*, vol. III, p. 120.

settlements which, owing to the earlier planting of Plymouth, were not included within the bounds of its stronger neighbor, the Massachusetts Bay Colony, until 1691. But there was, in fact, a certain unity in the colonization of the Plymouth area and its later history which probably would have resulted in a marked individuality even if there had been no political separation from the Bay Colony in the beginning.

This unity has its foundation in the geographical conditions. The topography of the Old Colony is essentially different from that which characterizes the northern part of eastern Massachusetts. The ridge of high land which reaches its greatest elevation in the Blue Hills of Norfolk County marks the southern boundary of the Bay region. Below this range the surface slopes to the south. Originally it was a more elevated plain extending farther into the Atlantic, consistently level with the exception of an extensive terminal moraine shaped like a horeshoe, which occupied its eastern half. As this plain, in the course of the well-known geological evolution of New England, was tilted towards the southeast, the waters of the Atlantic submerged its eastern half, the moraine alone protruding above sea level. The eastern arm and the southern base of the elevation form what is now Cape Cod, the western arm is apparent in the range of hills along the western coast of Cape Cod Bay north and south of Plymouth.

The western half of the plain is cut by numerous meandering streams flowing towards the south and emptying into either Narragansett Bay or Buzzards Bay, indentations which also resulted from the historic submergence. The rivers flowing into Buzzards Bay are comparatively short and navigable only in the tidal zone; but the Taunton River, which drains the central and western parts of the plain and empties into Narragansett Bay, was navigable for a considerable distance up its course for sea-going ships of colonial days.

The features peculiar to the Cape are discussed in more detail below. In the rest of the region nature has not been generous. The soil is gravelly and stony. The natural meadows, even along the larger streams, are not extensive. In parts of the interior the drainage is poor, and there are swamps and bogs grown here and there with pitch pine. But along the coast and the Taunton River the settlers found marshes of coarse grass that could be readily improved, and seaweed and fish that could be used as fertilizer. Thus constant labor could produce good crops which the soil alone would not have yielded.

Plymouth and Its Expansion

Chance and haziness about the extent of land patents were responsible for the coming of the 'Pilgrims' to the vicinity of Cape Cod. They were induced to settle on the particular spot which became Plymouth by the presence of a hill commanding a view in all directions, a brook of clear water, a protected harbor and lands which the Indians had cleared, but which the pestilence of preceding years had left unoccupied.

The vicinity offered little opportunity for expansion into the immediate neighborhood. Directly behind it was some of the most worthless land in the colony. There were no inland meadows, and the terminal moraine to the north and south evidently could not produce crops many years in succession.

The dominant place occupied in the history of Plymouth by the *Mayflower* episode makes it difficult to realize that most of the Plymouth colonizers never saw that vessel. During the first winter the mortality among *Mayflower* passengers was heavy. Of the 102 *Mayflower* Pilgrims, only 25 are known to have had descendants. The following year came the *Fortune* with 35 colonists, of whom Bradford wrote, 'Most of them were lusty young men, and many of them wild enough.' Two years later two more vessels arrived, 60 persons in one and an unknown number in the other. Since the original hill at Plymouth could not hold all of them, homesteads were taken up towards the west and along 'Jones River' in the present town of Kingston.

The colonization of Massachusetts Bay began in 1628, and within twelve years the 'great migration' had brought twenty thousand inhabitants to the environs of Boston. Most of these found their homes in the towns established around Massachusetts Bay, but some, not relishing the pioneer conditions, passed on to Plymouth. All had heard of the Plymouth settlement: Bradford and Winslow had been vigorous advertisers, praising the resources of the soil beyond its due. The newcomers, many of whom had money, gave impetus to an agricultural expansion which could not be accommodated on the original grants. Duxbury and Marshfield were settled on the coast to the north; and even in the wilderness of Carver at the rear adventurous men found it profitable to establish themselves and to combine with farming the manufacture of tar from the pines in the swamps, for which the building of small vessels used in coastal traffic opened a market.

This renewed immigration was also the immediate reason for the colonization of the Cape; but before discussing this process, the later Plymouth extension inland must be briefly mentioned. From an early day the Plymouth residents had been accustomed to herd their cattle during the winter on the natural meadows skirting Buzzards Bay; and in 1680 or shortly thereafter a permanent settlement was established here which took the name Wareham. Previously, in 1651, a group from Scituate, passing around the Cape, had planted themselves upon the lowlands of Rochester on Buzzards Bay; and small colonies of sons and grandsons of Plymouth settlers had pushed to the west and northwest to Middleborough and Bridgewater, outposts where the land was only gradually put under cultivation. However, parts of these towns, as well as of the earlier established Carver, never ceased to be wilderness.

Although Plymouth men were leaders and Plymouth influence was predominant in the settlement of these areas, others had a part. In the northern tip of the 'Old Colony' were Weymouth and Hingham, peopled by the great migration to Massachusetts Bay. Residents of these Bay Colony settlements founded the adjoining towns of the Plymouth Colony. How extensive this southern drift from the Bay Colony was, it is impossible to say.

The Settlement of Cape Cod

The men of Plymouth always looked with favor upon the rather unpromising lands of Cape Cod. Their first stop in the new world had been in Provincetown harbor; and from the first many had argued that their permanent home should be established somewhere upon its sands. This was due in part to fear of the forests and the Indians that hemmed them in on the mainland; in part to the lure of the more open vegetation and the less boggy soil on the Cape; and in part to a persistent belief that the economic future of the colony rested not upon agriculture but upon fishing. As soon as Plymouth began to swarm, many families moved eastward instead of west or south.

In the three years from 1637 to 1640 settlements were founded in most of the desirable locations on the inner side of the Cape. Cape Cod Bay became a Plymouth lake, across whose waters communication was quicker and perhaps safer than travel inland. That the colony suffered no political weakening by the dispersion of its inhabitants is the more remarkable since the infusion from non-Plymouth sources was great. From the Bay Colony towns of Hingham and Weymouth, and from the more distant settlements on Cape Ann, came individuals and even organized congregations which quickly lost their identity in mingling with the children of the Pilgrims. It may be that they had not remained in the Bay Colony long enough to become part of its life, and it is likely that the strict supervision to which they were subjected by the Puritan magistrates caused them to welcome the milder rule of Plymouth.

After the planting of these original towns the complete occupation of the Cape followed as a matter of course. The growth of the population was steady. The Indians were few and peaceable; the climate was moderate; the liberal use of natural fertilizers, seaweed and fish, ensured abundant crops; cod and whales provided commerce with the outside world. By the close of the seventeenth century, all but the extreme tip of the Cape was settled, and even there it is probable that fishing stations had been erected which during the season contained a semi-permanent population.

This prosperity continued through the eighteenth century. Local industries resulted from the fishing enterprises. A large part of the Cape was originally heavily, if not densely, forested and the building of smacks and small schooners kept pace with the extension of the fishing interests. Many were employed in the making of casks for the packing of the hauls; others in the manufacture of salt from the waters of the bay and inlets. The life of the Cape became in fact so maritime that farming was recognized as an employment reserved for boys and old men. But even these trades did not reach their maximum development until the early part of the nineteenth century. There were occasional depressions, as when wars made the seas unsafe or closed to the colonists markets in which they usually disposed of their fish. It was only during these periods that the inhabitants of Cape Cod became interested in emigration and sent out groups of their young people to pioneer in the hills of western and northern New England.

Expansion from Massachusetts: Taunton and Rehoboth

In the first decades of its history the government of Massachusetts Bay was decidedly imperialistic. It extended itself northward to New Hampshire and eastward to Maine, and cast glances to the south, seeking an outlet upon Narragansett Bay. More and more the coasting trade along the shores of the colonies was growing, and to take part in this trade the merchants of Boston were obliged to send their ships out into the Atlantic, where many of them disappeared in rounding the dangerous shoals that lined Cape Cod. If they had an outlet to the southwest, the protected passage of Long Island Sound would bring their cargoes safely to New York; and if these cargoes were destined for points farther south, the ships could strike boldly into the safe Atlantic waters from Narragansett Bay.

There is no evidence that the Bay Colony government as such took part in the settlement of the western parts of the Old Colony. But it did not hinder schemes planned by its inhabitants; and in its claims before the British government concerning unsettled boundary lines it did not hestitate to cite these private ventures as arguments in its favor. The Taunton River was the natural location of such advances, and as early as 1638–39 Massachusetts men established themselves at Taunton, the head of navigation on the river, built shipyards, worked the iron ore from the bogs and gradually drained the marshes. The town of Taunton enjoyed a prosperous existence and its population spread to half a dozen neighboring towns.

Some distance to the westward another group, whose religious ideas did not find complete favor in the eyes of Bay ministers, settled upon the Indian fields at Rehoboth and set up the pioneer Baptist congregation in Massachusetts. Rehoboth itself was never an extensive plantation. The fields bought from the Indians had already lost their fertility (probably the first example of soil exhaustion in New England), compelling many of the original settlers and most of their children to seek homes in the neighboring towns of Rhode Island.

South of Taunton, bordering the outward extension of Buzzards Bay, arose some towns of obscure origin. Dartmouth and its neighbors were part of the Plymouth government, and names prominent in Pilgrim history are found on the early town rolls. But there is evidence that the majority of the people, among them many Quakers, were emigrants from Rhode Island. On this point the testimony of students of architectural history is enlightening: among the old houses erected before 1700 in Freetown and Rochester the Plymouth style of architecture prevails, but in the triangle between these towns (Dartmouth, etc.) Rhode Island influence is predominant. (H. B. Worth, 'Ten Ancient Homes' in *Old Dartmouth Historical Sketches*, No. 3.)

Popular Characteristics

Although much has been written about Plymouth Colony, the bulk of this literature concerns the 'Pilgrim Fathers' and is highly eulogistic and theoretical in its approach. Little attention is paid to the diverse elements that shared with the Pilgrims the task of colonization; how the original ideals and institutions were changed by the environment in which they were established is a subject which has never been investigated.

By the close of the Colonial period, to be 'an Old Colony man' meant to be something distinct. This individuality can best be delineated in comparison with the characteristics that stamped society about Massachusetts Bay.

In the life of the Old Colony the church was a less vital matter than in the Bay Colony. Quakers and Baptists lived as peaceful neighbors of 'Separatists' from Plymouth and Puritans from Boston. The theological wranglings and the church secessions which confused politics in many parts of Massachusetts (and also of Connecticut) do not figure upon the pages of local church history. Even the Unitarian movement of the early nineteenth century had no severe effect upon the congregations. The clergy, as a class, did not have an overwhelming leadership in politics. But while there was toleration, there was not the liberty found in Rhode Island. Church and state were united; the colony insisted upon respectable behavior and discouraged religious enthusiasm of any kind.

There was a pronounced economic and social democracy. The Pilgrims had, at the beginning, attempted communism in worldly goods; and though they soon gave up this practice, the idea of social equality persisted because economic conditions fostered it. The Massachusetts Bay towns developed two closely allied aristocracies—commercial and governmental. The Old Colony, however, enjoyed no commercial development. Its only traders were the local merchants; its farmers occupied homesteads of moderate size; every fisherman's family sailed its own boat, which was no larger or smaller than that of the neighbors. Uniformity in resources and opportunities kept all on the same plane.

But this plane, although uniform, was comparatively high. All travelers through the region, before the agricultural decline began, comment upon the well-kept lands, the fat stock and the comfortable homes of the inhabitants. Intellectually they were also comfortable. Common school education flourished, but beyond that no encouragement was offered to learning. Massachusetts Bay established Harvard College in its early days, Connecticut founded Yale, Rhode Island founded Brown. Although it was first among the colonies, the Old Colony did not create a single institution of higher learning. Aside from the early annalists, it produced no literary men. In religious developments its ministers exerted no leadership, and none of the Revolutionary statesmen came from its soil. It was probably too content with the prevalent distribution of comfort to seek any fundamental change.

Nineteenth Century Changes

Until the close of the Civil War the core of the Old Colony continued on its normal way. But on the fringe there were great changes. The Cape, after reaching its height of prosperity in the first third of the nineteenth century, suddenly declined. Capital entered fishing and the independent fisherman-farmer could not compete; salt manufacturing did not pay when the salt wells of New York began to produce; agriculture fell off when the local market was lost; whales no longer frequented the coasts. An exodus began which depleted the villages of young people, and within a generation the Cape was growing up into scrub oak and underbrush.

The decline of the Cape was not as amazing as the maritime development of the towns on Buzzards Bay and Narragansett Bay. New Bedford and Fall River grew from flourishing villages to flourishing cities. Their ships followed the whales to the Pacific and the Antarctic, their commercial vessels controlled much of the coasting trade at a time when communication between the North and the South was principally by water. Capital earned in these enterprises was invested in the shipping lines between New York and Europe, and the aristocracy they produced, though short-lived, was brilliant and influential.

On the western fringe industrial development was pronounced. Fall River, already a commerical center, became the center of textile manufacturing; and in the towns toward the north (Taunton, Mansfield, Easton, Norton, etc.) simple industries which had been conducted for two or three generations in households now expanded to a factory scale and dislocated the population in the surrounding countryside.

It was this attraction of the industrial centers, not any loss of market or depletion of soil, that led to the abandonment of the comfortable farms of the Old Colony. When no hands were left to till them, the acres reclaimed with so much labor from the forest and the swamp quickly returned to their primitive state. During the last quarter of the century the agricultural regions were the scene of almost complete desolation; but the attraction of the mills which had depopulated them ultimately caused their re-population. Since local labor could not satisfy the demand, French, Swedes, 'Black Portuguese' and Finns thronged into the factories. But factory life was not the ultimate ambition of these immigrants: one by one they reclaimed the abandoned farms. A new industry turned the swamps that had been unused for three centuries into cranberry bogs; drier lands were converted to the cultivation of strawberries. This was a type of agriculture to which the immigrant and his family could be easily adjusted, and Boston opened a market for all vegetables and fruit. In no other part of New England has the composition of rural population changed so completely as here, where in 50 years a dozen nationalities replaced the uniform American population of the preceding centuries.

Rhode Island

Providence Area: 80 Providence, 81 East Providence, 82 Foster, 58 East Greenwich-North Kingstown.

Newport Area: 54 Richmond, 56 South Kingstown - Narragansett, 57 South Kingstown, 60 Newport, 62 Middletown, 64 Portsmouth.

Block Island: 52 New Shoreham.

Geographical Features

The two important geographical features that influenced the growth and expansion of the Rhode Island population are Narragansett Bay and the glacial action in the surrounding territory. The bay with its numerous inlets, marshes, tidal rivers and islands offered what the settlers desired: easy communication with neighbors, salt marshes for their cattle, deep-sea fishing, clams and oysters. The problems of transportation and food and, to some extent, of protection were readily solved. When therefore colonization was once undertaken it proceeded rapidly until the coast was fringed with settlements that grew toward one another instead of inland. In one other respect the bay fostered the growth of population. Its waters exerted an equalizing influence upon the climate—the winters were not so cold, the summers not so hot as in Massachusetts and Connecticut; and Englishmen who found it a severe strain to accommodate themselves to the yearly New England range of temperature were spared this weakening of their health if they settled upon Rhode Island shores. Rhode Islanders were not subject to the epidemics that offset to some extent the high birth rate in neighboring colonies. As a result, the native growth of population was rapid and there was no need of immigration to ensure the speedy occupation of the soil.

The glacial action had determined the river system. In southern New England drainage is normally provided by parallel streams flowing due south. This was probably the original situation in Rhode Island also; but the retreat of the glacier left a terminal moraine extending across the mainland from the northern part of the town of Westerly northeastward. The streams in the upper two-thirds of the state, diverted from their course, flowed eastward instead of into the Sound. This moraine and the resulting river systems divided the mainland into two parts—a southern plain along the coast with an unusually fertile soil deposited by the retreating glacier, and a northern upland of rather rough and stony hills which occasionally rise to a height of 800 feet. The interior is cut by numerous small rivers, whose steep slopes offer little inducement for agriculture; and though the surrounding territory is in general a level and elevated plain, the soil is poor and rocky. These two regions were populated from different directions and under different conditions, and the society that developed in each possessed economic and social characteristics that left an impress upon politics, religion and architecture.

Indian Occupation

The natural advantages offered by the Bay and its shore line are illustrated by the Indian occupation. Figures regarding the native population are more often exaggerated than minimized, but among the contemporary estimates that of Roger Williams was conservative. The Narragansetts who inhabited the region could put into the field, he wrote, five thousand warriors, representing a total population of approximately twenty thousand. Among all the clans in New England this was not only the largest but also the most powerful, the best organized and the most commercial. Their largest villages were on the bay around the present village of Wickford, and from these their trails led northward to the tribes of central Massachusetts and southwestward along the shore of the Sound to the Hudson.

The presence of such a powerful Indian nation would normally have been an effective barrier to English colonization, but it was offset here by two circumstances. Unable to foresee the agricultural nature of the colony, the Indians welcomed the first whites as traders to whom they could sell the furs which they obtained from the interior. A still more influential factor was Indian politics. For a generation the supremacy of the Narragansetts had been threatened by the Pequots, a tribe of uncertain origin which had pushed its way down from central New England, had occupied the Sound coast about New London, and was cutting off communication between the Rhode Island Indians and their hunting and trading grounds to the north and west. As the Pequots were irreconcilably opposed to the white invasion and as hostility between them and the English was chronic, the Narragansetts welcomed Williams and his associates as allies. In the Pequot War of 1637 they aided the whites in a campaign that resulted in the crushing of the Connecticut tribe. Well pleased by this turn in their fortunes, they were naturally cordial in their relations with the colonizers, and when at last they understood what the logical result of that colonization would be and accordingly joined in the uprising under King Philip, the English were so well established that the extermination of the Indians (in 1675) was inevitable.

English Colonization

The first English communities took advantage of the natural opportunities of the region. Providence at the head of the bay had an easy outlet to the south. The Pawtuxet River and its tributaries gave direct access to the northwestern part of Rhode Island and the central area of Massachusetts. The Narragansett trail led straight to Boston and Massachusetts Bay. Directly to the east lay the Old Colony, now almost twenty years old. Trade and population might be drawn along each of these routes. Newport, at the southern tip of the island of Aquidneck, dominated the entrance to the bay, had access to rich fishing grounds, and was well located for the trade on the Sound, which was rapidly gaining in importance as a result of the colonization of Long Island and the establishment of commercial relations with the Dutch on the Hudson. The third original settlement, that at Portsmouth, in spite of its agricultural resources did not offer so much for the future. The majority of those who first located here moved on to Newport, and although the population of Portsmouth did expand towards the east and the west, this settlement never became a prominent center of dispersion, in part because its original population was small, in part because its lands on the island available for cultivation were extensive.

Although these three original settlements were founded between 1638 and 1639, colonization did not end with the first influx as in many New England communities. The motley nature of the original stock made an exclusive policy impossible. Though there is no evidence of a large influx of settlers directly from England, it is clear that many individuals who were unwelcome to the Puritans because of their unacceptable political and religious ideas were constantly entering Rhode Island from neighboring colonies. The land policy, moreover, was not as illiberal here as elsewhere and anyone who was willing to undergo the rigors of pioneering usually found it possible to secure land without being obliged to become a member of a rather close corporation of 'land proprietors.'

A considerable part of the shore line was taken up before 1650. The remainder was occupied in the next twenty-five years with the exception of the easternmost part, where settlement was delayed by uncertainty as to political jurisdiction (see Paullin and Wright, *Atlas of Historical Geography*, Plate 97C) and by the menacing attitude of the Indian tribes separated from the Narragansetts by the wedge of white population down the bay.

During this period (1650–75) Providence also was cramped. It could not expand eastward because Massachusetts Bay had already planted settlers at Rehoboth; in the north and west it already pressed upon the Indian lands. However, in 1675–76 the situation was completely changed. King Philip's War produced massacres on three sides, but it crushed the Indians of eastern New England. The warriors retreated to join tribes farther inland, the women and children were killed or enslaved. A surviving remnant was restricted to certain localities.

With the successful conclusion of the war a new era of expansion began. During the succeeding quarter of a century the lands on the bay were completely occupied and Providence extended rapidly into the hinterland. The movement was continued until 1725, when the only part of Rhode Island not yet settled was the extreme northwest corner. This area, the least desirable agriculturally, was occupied by 1750.

Routes of Dispersion

The regions into which the two larger original settlements expanded are rather clearly defined. Newport population (and with it Newport institutions and culture) took possession of the coast of the Bay and the Sound to the west. In general its boundary was the terminal moraine already mentioned. Westerly, which in turn became a center of 'secondary dispersion,' was originally settled from Newport, but also drew population from the Connecticut towns on the Sound, and had easy access directly to the north along the valley of the Pawcatuck River, which brought the current of settlers into a region distinctly different from the coastal plain. Warwick was established early as a trading post in the heart of the Narragansett Indian country. With a stock of people originally small it could do no more than take possession of the lands to the west.

The course of Providence expansion is logical. The river valleys in the up-country may not have been desirable places for settlement, but they did provide trails for communication. As Providence became more and more a commercial city after 1730, it provided a market for neighboring farmers; and although the soil was not fertile, many preferred to farm poor soil with a market at their door instead of trekking to the interior, where the valleys were more fertile but no market was at hand.

Population came into the colony from two outside centers. Rehoboth, planted in 1644 from Massachusetts Bay, was a prolific hive, sending out swarms to take possession of the coast regions adjacent to its borders: the present towns of East Providence (a part of Massachusetts until 1861), Barrington, Warren and Bristol. The Old Colony (Plymouth and its tributaries) was moving consistently to the south and west, and from this source the towns of Tiverton and Little Compton, which belong to that region geographically and were attached to it for a while politically, drew a large part of their pioneers.

Population Growth in the Eighteenth Century

Throughout the colonies in the eighteenth century there was an increasing number of non-British settlers. With liberal religious and social ideas prevailing in Rhode Island, it seems logical that many of these immigrants should find homes within its borders; but that was not the case. There was little influx and the population of the colony was knit together into clans and groups descended from the original planters. A few diverse elements, however, must be mentioned.

A colony of French Huguenots, established late in the seventeenth century in the town of

East Greenwich, had only a short life. Its members dispersed, but many of them remained within the bounds of Rhode Island and became allied with some of the most prominent families. Trade with the West Indies brought in a sprinkling from the French islands which it is impossible to disentangle from the Huguenots already settled in the cities. Jews came from Curaçao and Brazil as early as 1658. A century later a considerable number of Portuguese Jews established themselves in Newport, where they became prominent figures in the financial and social world. Irishmen who had sought to make a fortune in Jamaica and other British possessions to the south, disappointed in their hopes, found ready passage to the temperate regions of the American continent in the constant succession of trading vessels sailing for Newport and Providence. But these foreign elements quickly lost their identity in the prevailing dominant class of the Rhode Island population.

During the century emigration was a more prominent feature than immigration. Only a part of the natural growth was absorbed by the increasing commercial activities. When the agricultural population had occupied the last corner of the colony, it advanced across the borders. Connecticut had little adjacent land to offer; Massachusetts had some but not much. Rhode Islanders were accordingly forced to emigrate and establish colonies remote from their 'mother country.' Early in the century a considerable number moved across the Sound to Long Island and some established themselves in New Jersey. About 1760 a large colony was planted in Nova Scotia, taking over the lands vacated by the expulsion of the Acadians. Later many of these Rhode Island Nova Scotians moved down the coast into the state of Maine. At the close of the war with France in 1763 there was a movement to the Berkshires which continued until about 1790, when more promising areas became available in Vermont and New Hampshire and in the valleys of central New York. All commentators emphasize the cohesion retained by these emigrating groups. Where they located they planted the political institutions and the churches to which they had been accustomed and which had become a part of their community life during more than a hundred and fifty years of development. (There were eight Baptist churches in Berkshire County, Massachusetts, in 1775–76; see *Atlas of Historical Geography*, Plate 82D.)

Characteristics of the Population

Even in as small an area as Rhode Island it is impossible to generalize about popular characteristics. There are, in fact, three distinct regions corresponding to the three spheres of population expansion and growth.

The first of these is the Newport sphere. Its individuality has long been recognized; it has passed into literature as the 'Narragansett Country,' the 'South County' or the 'King's Province.' It differed essentially from anything existing elsewhere in New England. The fertile soil of the coast plains, the milder climate, and the wealth of the Newport merchants who established themselves as country gentlemen gave rise to a plantation type of agriculture. Commercial relations with the West Indies naturally led to the importation of negro slaves, who added another distinct touch of plantation atmosphere to the large estates. With these developments the entire complexion of social life was changed. Horse racing produced the 'Narragansett Pacer'; wealth and relations with the West Indies substituted the Episcopal Church for Baptist churches and Quaker meetings; and Newport became the center of an intellectual circle which perhaps had no counterpart in the colonies. Although the Revolution destroyed much of this prosperity and culture, the individuality of the Narragansett Country is still apparent.

The second region is that of the traditional Rhode Island type which prevailed in the northern two-thirds of the colony. The farms were small and the families large. Individuality was pronounced, and expressed itself in religion and politics. There was much religious speculation, with sects dividing and subdividing on every controversial point. 'A Baptist and a Democrat' was the usual description of a man. The style of living was plain, the architecture of the homes simple: architects find a clear dividing line running through Wickford which separates the northern style of dwellings from the southern. Common school education was slow in appearing and the proportion of those who 'made their mark' on documents is higher than in other regions of eastern New England.

The third region, comprising the towns east of the Bay, is easily overlooked. Into this narrow strip, bordering on the rest of Rhode Island as well as on the Old Colony, came families from both areas. It is a transition ground between the highly developed community organization of the Massachusetts Bay settlement and the pronounced individualism of Rhode Island.

Nineteenth Century Changes

The main lines of the development of Rhode Island economic life in the nineteenth century are clear. From agricultural and commercial it became industrial, and at the same time the old 'Narragansett Country' developed so great a summer trade that the life of that section was profoundly affected.

The industrial evolution in the northern part of the state caused important population changes. The first result was a demand for labor that the surrounding countryside could not satisfy. In the two decades 1840–60, therefore, Irishmen went from the canals and railroads into the mills. After the Civil War there was an influx of English textile operatives; but as their ideas respecting labor organization were obnoxious to the employers, they were gradually replaced by French-Canadians. More recently Italians and Portuguese have begun to predominate in some sections, and Poles and Scandinavians (especially Swedes) are becoming numerous.

These stocks are not uniformly distributed. Racial cohesion is an important factor and each of the industrial centers has its own dominant nationality. To present this distribution is a rather difficult matter because the figures of the United States census are printed only for counties, units too large to be of significance.

Attention is directed to the following features:

The large English element. Immigrants from England soon lose themselves in the mass, but many (perhaps most) of them are workers in the textile mills, where they come in daily contact with foreigners learning the English language and thus may influence the speech of a large element in the population.

The large number of Italians. Those of Italian birth outnumber those of French-Canadian birth, although the French 'stock' is still the greater. Much less is heard of the Italians than of the French—perhaps an indication of more rapid Americanization.

The concentration of the foreign stocks in the industrial centers. In the rural regions 'Americans' still predominate; the tendency of the foreign-born to take up land in abandoned farming regions, such an important feature in other parts of New England, seems to be small in Rhode Island. More recent developments may make a modification of this generalization necessary.

Eastern New Hampshire

Old New Hampshire: 302 Seabrook, 304 Rye, 306 Lee, 307 Barrington, 308 Kingston, 310 Loudon-Belmont, 312 Gilford-Laconia, 316 Deerfield-Candia, 348 Conway.

The Merrimack Valley:

Scotch-Irish Settlements: 318 Derry-Londonderry, 322 Francestown - New Boston, 324 Antrim.

Massachusetts Settlements: 314 Webster, 315 Concord, 320 Bedford-Amherst, 333 Wilmot-Sutton, 338 Plymouth.

This area includes New Hampshire east of the divide separating the valley of the Connecticut River from that of the Merrimack River. It comprises the valleys of the Merrimack and the Piscataqua, the coastal plain between them, and the headwaters of the Saco and the Androscoggin Rivers, which flow down through Maine to the sea. The area has a certain geographical unity, which was strengthened by the historical developments.

Original New Hampshire Settlements

The lands bordering Great Bay, the estuary of the Piscataqua River were first occupied (chiefly for fishing purposes) in the early 1620's, before the founding of the Massachusetts Bay Colony. The population in these settlements was probably transitory. In the latter part of the next decade (from 1635 on), several congregations left the Bay Colony because of religious difficulties and founded compact agricultural towns along the coast and some few miles inland, in the region between the Merrimack and the Piscataqua Rivers. In the course of the next century these settlements received few additions to the population from outside. Jurisdiction and land titles were in dispute, and Indian dangers frightened away prospective settlers. These same conditions caused the colonists already established to hug the coast, and as a result of their isolation they developed a marked individuality. The English origin of these people calls for more investigation.

Expansion from Essex County, Massachusetts

Essex County, adjoining New Hampshire on the south, was early settled and well peopled. Agricultural expansion to the westward was forestalled by the towns in the Boston area, whose lands extended inland to the north and west of the Bay. A considerable amount of the population increase of this county was absorbed by the development of maritime interests (Newburyport, Salem, etc.), but the surplus of the farming population had to look for farms to the valley of the Merrimack. During the late 17th and early 18th centuries the north side of this valley, as far west as the great bend, was generally occupied by the Essex County people; and in the second quarter of the 18th century they began to advance northward in the valley on a rather broad front, establishing some outposts like Concord and Boscawen higher up the river for purposes of Indian trade. In the meantime the Scotch-Irish at Londonderry (see below) were moving directly westward, and when the Essex County pioneers reached this 'wedge' they had to jump over it into Merrimack County. There the Essex County stock predominated, but it was joined by a considerable admixture of population from the northern towns of Middlesex County, Massachusetts.

The Scotch-Irish

Several hundred Scotchmen from Northern Ireland were planted at Londonderry in the years 1718–20. Their first experiences in the wilderness were not encouraging, but in the course of the next generation they developed into ideal pioneers. The Indian danger to the north prevented the natural movement up the valley of the Merrimack; they advanced therefore towards the west, forming the wedge mentioned above. In 1775 there were more than twenty Presbyterian churches in this part of the state, of which only four survived until 1860 (*Atlas of Historical Geography*, Plates 82B and 84G). The next generation contributed greatly to the peopling of northern New Hampshire and Vermont. The Scotch-Irish were never made to feel at home in New England, and in New Hampshire, as elsewhere in the region, they developed a social clannishness which contributed certain distinct characteristics to the towns in which they lived.

Expansion of the Original New Hampshire Settlements

The danger from Indians and from the French in Canada made any advance up the valleys of the Piscataqua and the Salmon Falls Rivers a cautious movement. During the first century the descendants of the colonists did little more than occupy the territory adjacent to the estuary of the river and the 'Great Bay.' Shipbuilding and seasonal fishing probably accommodated a population that agriculture alone could not have supported. It was not until after the defeat of the French and the Indians, and the Peace of 1763, that the normal line of growth could be followed; the date of settlement and the extent of territory indicated on Plate 2 are evidence of the great migration that followed the conclusion of that war. Posts had been established in the lakes region of Belknap County before that time, but these were primarily commercial and military stations.

Maine

The Coast:

York County: 352 York, 354 Kennebunkport, 356 Biddeford, 357 Acton, 358 Shapleigh, 363 Limington.

Casco Bay: 359 Cape Elizabeth, 360 Portland, 362 Standish, 364 Yarmouth, 382 Harpswell.

The Kennebec Area: 378 Webster, 380 Brunswick-Topsham, 384 Waldoboro-Nobleboro, 386 Pittston-Farmingdale.

The Penobscot Area: 394 Owls Head - Rockland, 396 Frankfort-Searsport, 398 Bluehill, 403 Holden, 404 Brewer.

The Extreme East: 400 Tremont - Southwest Harbor, 402 Penobscot-Ellsworth, 406 Gouldsboro, 407 Jonesport, 408 Roque Bluffs - Machias, 410 Lubec, 411 Perry.

The Inland:

The Androscoggin and the Kennebec Rivers: 346 Shelburne, 366 Casco, 368 Denmark, 370 Woodstock, 372 Hanover, 373 Newry, 374 New Portland, 376 Farmington, 377 Turner, 388 China, 390 Norridgewock-Skowhegan.

The Penobscot River: 391 Newport, 392 Dover-Foxcroft, 416 Lincoln-Lee.

The St. Croix and the St. John Rivers: 412 Calais, 418 Waite, 420 Houlton, 422 Fort Fairfield, 423 Ashland, 424 Fort Kent.

Original Coast Settlements

The first attempts at colonization in New England were made along the Maine coast. Some of these trading and fishing posts may have continued as permanent establishments, but their history is unknown. The same movement which led to the settlement of the Old

Colony and the Massachusetts Bay region resulted in the planting of colonies of traders and fishermen to the northeast, and by 1640, the end of the period of active New England colonization, six points had been occupied. Two of these—York and Kittery—were located in what is now York County; two were in the vicinity of Cape Elizabeth—Scarboro on the inlet south of the Cape, and Casco (Portland) on the inlet north of the Cape; a fifth post was founded on the lower Androscoggin and a sixth on the lower Kennebec. This remained the extent of settlement for approximately a century. Many attempts were made farther to the east, but the hostility of the Indians and the claims of the French (which extended westward to the Penobscot) prevented their success. Whatever natural growth the population enjoyed was accommodated in the vicinity of the centers named or was employed in trading and fishing.

During this century the population of Maine (excepting York County) was most unstable. At any given time many of the inhabitants were residents of Cape Ann, Cape Cod, or the west of England, temporarily engaged in fishing, lumbering, or the Indian trade. Representatives of most of the maritime nations of Europe were to be found at one time or another on the shores of Maine. The original stratum of the population was therefore probably more varied than that of any other seventeenth-century American community, with the possible exception of the city of New York.

The Land Policy

This original cosmopolitan population gave promise of being further diversified by the process of disposing of the land. In the other New England colonies land was closely associated with social ideas: townships were granted after a fixed pattern that guaranteed the growth of a homogeneous community. The Maine lands were thought of only as potential wealth, to be used for discharging obligations or for bringing an income to defray the cost of frontier protection. The first grants were made by the king of England to individuals of wealth or political influence in the kingdom. By 1674 all of these rights had come into the hands of the Province of Massachusetts. In general, the sub-grants made by the former proprietors were recognized if some steps had been taken to actually occupy the soil. One of these grants had been taken up by the so-called 'Plymouth Company,' a group of the leading men of the Old Colony. Their lands were located in the present counties of Kennebec and Somerset, and the recognition of their title probably accounts in large measure for the extensive migration from the Plymouth area and Cape Cod into Maine—undoubtedly the largest single element in the composition of the pioneer stock.

In the second third of the eighteenth century the desire of the Province to erect a bulwark of people in the east for the protection of the frontier led to an extensive grant along Penobscot Bay to General Samuel Waldo. It was a time when the surplus population of southern New England still found possibilities for taking up lands in the older regions; but it was also a time when Scotch, Scotch-Irish and Germans were beginning to move in large numbers to America. These currents General Waldo tried to turn to his grant. To some extent he was successful, and a dozen pioneer coast towns of Maine in the counties of Sagadahoc, Lincoln, Knox and Hancock have borne distinct traces of the presence of these non-English settlers.

With the coming of peace in 1763 Massachusetts entered upon a more rapid distribution of her territory. In the next twenty years approximately half a million acres were granted to individuals and groups, principally as compensation or indemnity for losses in other areas where disputed titles had not been successfully maintained. This in itself would not have led to settlement, as such grants were usually held off the market for speculative purposes. After 1783, however, a more democratic policy prevailed. Opportunities were advertised, a land office was opened, and comparatively liberal terms (150 acres at $1 per acre) were offered to any individual. This policy led to the extensive colonization of Maine which took place in the next twenty-five years.

When the State of Maine was created in 1820, the Act of Separation provided for an equal division of the remaining public lands between Maine and Massachusetts. This joint ownership lasted until 1853, when Maine finally acquired the titles to those areas still in the possession of the mother state.

The Eastward Movement in Maine

Much of the original population in the lands east of the Androscoggin came from the older parts of Maine. The movement did not get under way until more than a century after the planting of these older communities, which were now (like the other ancient settlements in New England) ready to swarm.

This trek was a coastal movement resulting in an almost solid Maine fringe along the shores of Hancock and Washington Counties. The other Maine patch seems to be located inland, but is in fact upon the banks of the Kennebec River and its navigable tributaries. Economic life in the older areas had centered about fishing, lumbering, shipbuilding and quarrying. The coast and the river offered the same resources, and in the years that followed the Peace of 1763, when the whole colonial world was going through an era of development requiring ships, lumber and stone for houses, and fish for food, many families moved to the east to supply the demands of the market. Drought and fires in the years 1761 and 1762, together with the natural aftermath of war, had created many debtors who were eager to begin anew in a place offering better prospects of wealth.

New Hampshire and Massachusetts Elements in the Population

The towns settled by emigrants from New Hampshire are few and form no distinct group. Since the coast line of this province was short, there were not many maritime interests to contribute fishermen or sailors. The agricultural population could secure more fertile lands from their own government. The Maine towns peopled by New Hampshire stock were probably those in which the proprietors either were New Hampshire men or had family or business connections with New Hampshire.

On the other hand, all parts of eastern Massachusetts contributed to Maine's settlement. Essex County was maritime-agricultural. Its sons had adjusted themselves to serve on both land and sea, a combination they could continue in Maine. Towns with a large Essex contingent are scattered from York County eastward as far as Hancock County. In the Plymouth area farmers were predominant, and its emigrants settled in the more distinctly agricultural areas in the counties of Oxford, Androscoggin, Kennebec, Penobscot and Hancock. From Cape Cod the movement was extensive, especially in the years during and immediately after the Revolution, when the fishing and trading activities of the Cape were completely ruined. This Cape Cod element was probably much larger than the provenience of the first settlers might suggest, since local history indicates that in many of the towns founded by Maine men it was the families from Cape Cod who left the most numerous descendants.

2. THE INLAND

Eastern Connecticut

(The Counties of New London and Windham and Part of Tolland County)

New London Area: 31 East Lyme, 32 New London, 33 Bozrah-Norwich, 34 Stonington. Massachusetts Settlements: 43 Windham, 48 Canterbury, 49 Woodstock-Pomfret.

Eastern Connecticut is rather well defined geographically. It is that part of the state drained by the Quinebaug and the Shetucket, which join north of Norwich to form the Thames River. In the east it is set off from Rhode Island by sparsely settled hill country, and in the west from the Connecticut Valley area by a range of hills forming the backbone of Tolland County. It is open to the north, where it communicates with the Worcester area, and along the Sound.

The Pequot War

The Pequot War is the event with which the history of eastern Connecticut begins. The origin of the Pequots is obscure; they were evidently not an old New England tribe. According to tradition, they were invaders from the northwest, who in the sixteenth century had fought their way from western Massachusetts into central Massachusetts and then down into Connecticut, finally establishing themselves on Long Island Sound with their principal villages about the mouth of the Thames River—first called by the whites the Pequot River. From here they ruled the Sound from the lands of the Narragansetts west to the Quinnipiac River; inland their jurisdiction extended up the Connecticut to Windsor. The Sound itself was generally recognized as theirs and the Indians upon Long Island were subject to them. Though this was the extent of their actual jurisdiction, all neighboring tribes lived in such fear as to be practically vassals.

From the beginning the Pequots were hostile to the whites. They killed English traders and threatened frontier settlements. To anticipate massacre, combined forces from Massachusetts and Connecticut, aided by contingents from all the non-Pequot Indians, fell upon the Pequot villages in 1637, destroyed them and the year's crops, and pursued the warriors westward along the Sound until they were completely scattered. This was the end of the political and military power of the Pequots. All the Indians who had seen the destruction were so impressed with the English thoroughness that there was no rising until a new generation appeared in 1675. The end of the Pequot War guaranteed peace for three decades and opened up by conquest the area which formerly had been the seat of Pequot authority.

The settlement of this area proceeded from a number of early centers: New London and Norwich in the south; Woodstock, Windham and Plainfield in the north. The southern half of New London County was taken up from New London, the northern half from Norwich. The northern part of Windham County was settled from Woodstock (a Bay Colony town), and by immigrants coming directly from eastern Massachusetts; the southern part from Windham and Plainfield (which in turn had been occupied jointly by Bay Colony and Norwich families). In Windham County only the towns of Plainfield, Canterbury and Windham, along the southern boundary, appear to have had a considerable Norwich element.

The Founding of New London and Norwich

The successful outcome of the Pequot War and the publicity attending it naturally gave rise to projects of settlement upon the conquered lands. But settlement was hindered by two factors. The first was the nature of the territory itself. Its outward appearance (described in more detail below) was not promising, for its broken surface and narrow valleys did not offer the 'meadows' that the English of the time considered the necessary center of any colonizing venture.

The second factor was the question of jurisdiction. Boundary lines had not yet been drawn and the Massachusetts charter was unclear. Both the Bay Colony and the Connecticut settlements claimed ownership of the soil by right of conquest from the Pequots. The first to take the risk of planting a colony in this area was John Winthrop the Younger, whose father was Governor of Massachusetts Bay and had been associated also with the Connecticut planting. He had friends in both governments and might hope for generous treatment from both. In 1645–46, with a company drawn from Massachusetts Bay and the Connecticut River (especially from Cape Ann and Wethersfield), he established himself at the mouth of the Thames and founded the town of New London. It is probable that Winthrop was thinking more of trade than of agriculture, because everyone predicted a great commercial development on Long Island Sound. The early population was therefore rather transitory; many came, but many went when their hopes did not quickly materialize. Thus from the beginning New London was more cosmopolitan in origin than any other Connecticut settlement. In 1650 arrived what was known as the 'Welsh Company,' from which many of the leading families of colonial New London were descended. The problem of jurisdiction was simplified in 1650 when Winthrop accepted a commission as magistrate from the Connecticut government.

New London was at the mouth of the Thames. Fourteen miles up, on navigable water, was another desirable location, which came to be occupied by emigrants from Saybrook. Saybrook, founded in 1635, had been feeling more and more the hopelessness of its position; and in 1660, under the leadership of their minister, the Reverend John Fitch, a large number of the inhabitants migrated in a body to this desirable spot and organized the town of Norwich. The town also attracted a considerable number of adventurers, but these in time moved on, and Norwich, like New London, settled down to steady growth as an agricultural community, cherishing hopes for commercial riches which were not to be realized until more than a century after the founding. The first occupation was the easier because of the existence of Pequot fields ready for the hoe; the growth inland, however, involved difficulties that were only slowly overcome.

The Settlement of the Sound and the Movement Inland

The settling of the coast towns of eastern Connecticut and the agricultural advance inland from the Sound were almost entirely the results of the natural growth of the New London and Norwich population. The uninviting appearance of the landscape discouraged immigration. Back from the narrow coastal plain the surface is hilly and rugged, and the banks of the rivers and brooks are so steep as to be almost gorges. There are some patches of gently rolling hills, but the soil is stony and hard to cultivate: experience alone taught its use.

The expansion along the Sound and inland is so logical that it calls for little comment. Residents of New London early discovered the small meadows and Indian fields at Groton and Stonington and established themselves there; and for the next century children, grandchildren and great-grandchildren moved with a certain regularity to the north, east and west from the center at New London and its environs. Few New Londoners advanced beyond the southern boundary of Norwich, nor was there any migration southward from Norwich into the New London area.

Norwich grew up the valleys of the Quinebaug and Shetucket Rivers, which unite above Norwich to form the Thames. Expansion to the west would probably have been more pronounced had it not been retarded by the so-called 'Mason Claim' put forward by the heirs of Captain John Mason of Pequot War fame. The Mason heirs declared that a large part of the region rightfully belonged to them and was not vested in the General Court of the colony. Final decision by the British Crown was not made until 1767; judgment was in favor of the colony, which had for some time been granting titles to those who would risk settlement.

Although most of the increase in population resulted from internal growth, certain groups of settlers came from Essex County towards the close of the seventeenth century. They had been driven from their first home, it is reported, by the intolerance of the witchcraft delusion. How extensive this immigration was, and what influence it exerted upon society, history does not record.

The northernmost towns settled in part from Norwich (Plainfield, Canterbury and Windham) contributed largely to the population of their neighbors and in the middle of the eighteenth century sent out numerous colonists to take up lands in northwestern Connecticut, in the Berkshires of western Massachusetts and in the Connecticut Valley in Vermont and New Hampshire.

The Movement Southward from Massachusetts

Uncertainty about the exact location of the northern boundary of Connecticut resulted in the establishment of rather extensive Massachusetts settlements in Windham County, the northeastern corner of the colony. The occupation of this region came comparatively late because of the topography and the bad reputation of the soil. The 'Connecticut Path' ran directly through what was later to become the town of Woodstock, and the Bay emigrants and officials in their travels were able to observe the possibilities and the drawbacks of the region. Among the drawbacks was the presence of Indians—the Nipmucks—who had not joined in the Pequot War and had been allowed to remain. These Nipmucks were a special object of concern to the Bay Colony. The 'Apostle Eliot' made some progress in Christianizing them; after King Philip's War, when all Indians were subjected to rigorous treatment, Eliot became minister of the church at Roxbury, Massachusetts, and soon interested the leading citizens of that town in colonizing their sons upon the lands at Woodstock. At first named New Roxbury, it was founded in 1686 by representatives of the leading families of the old town; and until the boundary line was definitely drawn in 1755, all the relations of the town were with the Bay settlements. In time Woodstock extended its population into the surrounding hills.

Two other towns from which settlement proceeded in the following decades were established in Windham County in the 1680's: Windham and Plainfield. The former was granted to Norwich men, but most of the settlers were from Massachusetts Bay; the latter was planted by emigrants from Chelmsford and other towns in eastern Massachusetts, who were joined in their enterprise by Connecticut families from Stonington, New London and Norwich.

Windham County, with its large Massachusetts population and its intimate relations with Massachusetts, thus represents a distinct area in the state of Connecticut.

Another early Massachusetts settlement was Enfield on the Connecticut River. Before the boundary between Massachusetts and Connecticut was established, the lands on the river were the possession of Springfield, which in 1681 granted them to a colony from Salem. Enfield's original stock was small, but grew steadily and advanced into the disputed lands towards the east, creating the towns of Somers and Stafford. Lying between the spheres of Enfield and Woodstock was the hilly town of Union, not settled until after 1725. Its pioneer settlers were from the Scotch-Irish colony of Worcester County, but later others came in from the neighboring towns.

Characteristics of the Colonial Population

The eastern half of Connecticut has not received the attention given to the rest of the state, where politics, religion and education were centered. Generalizations about its characteristics must therefore be tentative.

It is comparatively safe to say, however, that an important feature was the social and political influence of the clergy. Dissenters were originally few; there was religious solidarity within the community, and provision was made in the distribution of lands for the support of the ministers on a scale that at once put them upon a high economic level. All things were carried on with decorum (it was reported), and the general tone of society was probably closest to that which prevailed in the Connecticut River towns and their hinterland. The solidarity was based to some extent on a universal tie—family connections. It is said of the town of Windham, for example: 'The young people remained at home, marrying mostly among their own townspeople, till, in process of years, nearly the whole population were knit together in one great family circle.' (Ellen D. Larned, *History of Windham County*, vol. I, p. 92.)

Exceptions to this solidarity do occur. The Massachusetts area was a rather distinct unit, but its ideals were similar to Connecticut ideals. Besides, the people were generally drawn from the Bay region, not from the Plymouth area where more diversity was apparent in personal and communal life.

Scotch-Irish were present in appreciable numbers in three towns—Voluntown, Union and Ellington. Their clannishness kept them together and in rather close touch with the Scotch-Irish settlements of Massachusetts; but the Yankees of Connecticut, though they commented on the clannishness, had nothing but praise for the industry and morals of the Scotch. To the Rhode Islanders who drifted over the border they were not so generous. These invaders they considered 'lawless Rhode Island borderers' with whose politics and religion they had little sympathy and for whose company they expressed little desire.

In the middle of the eighteenth century emigration was an important fact in the economic and social life of eastern Connecticut. First the northwestern part of the state, then western Massachusetts and finally the upper Connecticut Valley were the regions favored for new settlements; in the decade 1750–60 emigration to the lands on the Susquehanna in Pennsylvania was a topic that absorbed much thought and energy. Eastern Connecticut was little disturbed by the events of the Revolution, and at the beginning of the nineteenth century it still retained most of those characteristics which had been bred into it in a century and a half.

Nineteenth Century Changes

The first change was the commercialization which came over New London and Norwich in the great period of American expansion upon the sea in the first third of the century. This attracted to the cities many sons of the farm, and farming began to decline not so much because of competition (there being as yet little competition for the city markets) as because of the greater attractions of commerce. The depletion of farm population was continued when industry invaded the hills to make use of the narrow valleys and swift currents of the many rivers. Since it was impossible to operate the new labor-saving farm machines upon the rough terrain, farms were abandoned and agricultural life became secondary in society for lack of man-power.

Industrial labor was recruited from foreign sources when after the Civil War the countryside had no more children to contribute. Most important among these new elements were the French-Canadians, but the Irish, Swedes and Poles were numerous also. During the last three decades the immigrants have been moving back to the farms, clearing away the forests again and reëstablishing country life on a new basis.

Central Massachusetts

(Worcester County and the Adjoining Parts of the Counties of Hampshire and Franklin)

Expansion from Massachusetts Bay: 201 Uxbridge-Mendon, 202 Oxford-Charlton, 204 Shrewsbury, 205 Worcester, 206 Spencer, 207 Sterling, 209 Lunenburg, 222 Holland. Mixed Area: 208 Templeton, 210 Winchendon, 212 New Salem, 218 Hardwick.

The area designated here as Central Massachusetts includes the hill country of Worcester County and the eastern fringe of the counties of Hampshire and Franklin. It is flanked in the east by the region settled through gradual expansion from Massachusetts Bay and in the west by the region settled largely from the Connecticut Valley.

Physical Features

The most important topographical feature of this section is visible to geologists only. A line of hills (Tatnuck, Wachusett, Watatic, etc.) extends towards the north from eastern Connecticut, and finally ends in New Hampshire in the outstanding landmark, Mount Monadnock. Although at present these hills are detached and isolated, they are the remnants of a 'Blue Ridge' which once formed the backbone of Worcester County. Like the Blue Ridge of the South it was probably a series of parallel ridges with intervening parallel valleys, each ridge towards the east and towards the west being lower than its neighbor towards the center, sloping down to the Atlantic on one side and the Connecticut River on the other. This provided a simple drainage system of rivers leading southward to the Sound, of which the Quinebaug and the Blackstone alone remain. In the process of submergence and erosion this simple outline of surface had been destroyed, ranges had been cut through and valleys had been blocked, until, when the Englishmen came, central Massachusetts was a maze of hills which formed a natural barrier to trade east and west, north and south. There were many rivers, but not one was navigable; there were valleys, but they had little relationship to one another.

The approaches to this highland, so important in the process of settlement, were clearly marked. On the west Miller's River, the Chicopee River and their branches led inland from the Connecticut River; on the east the Nashua River and its many tributaries, the Blackstone River and its headwaters, and (to a smaller extent) the upper branches of the Concord and the Charles provided natural routes from the older towns. These valleys, however, grew narrow, and the meadows skirting the streams were few and small; the winters were long and the snowfall heavy, making more difficult the ever-present problem of providing winter fodder for cattle. The soil was fertile but heavily wooded, from the water's edge in the valleys up the hillsides and along the tops of the 'mountains,' which in many places flattened out into extensive plateaus. One fact was clear: the region could support a large population, but the task of agricultural occupation was so great that it would be a last choice.

The topography of a region may be a barrier to population movement, however, without making the region actually impenetrable. There were few places on the continent of North America through which a man on foot or on horseback could not force his way, though in many places the journey was so difficult and tiresome that residence there meant almost complete isolation from the group from which the settlers had come. This was the condition of central Massachusetts for almost a century after its first crossing by the whites. Indians had already prepared a thoroughfare: a trail, or more precisely a succession of trails, united the Connecticut River with Massachusetts Bay. This primitive route, which figures in the early history of almost every town in Worcester County, was known by two names—a fact confusing to investigators. Those who lived in the vicinity of Boston called it the 'Connecticut Path' because it led to the settlements in the colony of Connecticut; the inhabitants of the latter colony naturally called it the 'Bay Path' because it led to the metropolis of New England. It is impossible to trace its course with certainty. Almost every local historian endeavors to prove that this early line of communication crossed the lands in his own town, and in many cases the boast is well-founded, since there were alternative routes for wet seasons and dry seasons, for winter and for summer. The line shifted also from year to year and from decade to decade according to the friendliness or hostility of the Indian tribes that hunted, fished and lived in the surrounding hills. Only the trend and certain junction points are definitely established, and these, with other considerations, determined the location of the first English settlements in the central area.

Early Occupation

Perhaps even before 1630 traders and trappers from the coast traveled over the Connecticut Path. When the river towns were established in the middle of the decade 1630–40, it assumed an important place in the political and social but not in the economic life of both groups of settlements. Every year it was crossed and recrossed by emigrants, ministers, commissioners of the New England Confederation and deputies to the Massachusetts General Court. Little of what they saw encouraged them to advise permanent settlement, but the few places which offered natural advantages and contributed to convenience in travel were settled between 1643 and 1667. These places were the outposts which in the following century gradually extended themselves into the surrounding territory.

The first of these outposts was Lancaster. Its significance can be understood only in the light of what was happening in that part of New England which later became New Hampshire. The Merrimack River was a great highway into the Indian country to the north, and moreover possessed in the Nashua River a tributary leading to the southwest. By this route the hills of Worcester County could be reached by water, and here—at the point where trails to the interior, connecting with the Connecticut Path, crossed the Nashua River—a trading post was established in 1643. In the vicinity were meadows, and soon trading became subsidiary to farming. The river lost its importance as a line of communication when roads were laid out to tie up with the roads of Middlesex County, and within a few years Lancaster ceased to be primarily a center of Indian trade and became an agricultural outpost on the frontier of Massachusetts Bay.

Marlborough is not in Worcester County but adjoins it on the east, and its development is closely associated with the settlement of the central area. Lying upon tributaries of the Sudbury River, with meadow lands and swamps that could be easily drained, it soon attracted colonists; by 1657 settlement was under way.

The third opening wedge on the east was Mendon. Through its central part the Blackstone River flows to the southeast toward Narragansett Bay; in its eastern part are the headwaters of the Charles River, which empties into Boston Bay. The town was situated, therefore, upon a natural line of communication between Massachusetts and Rhode Island, and in 1660 families from Braintree and Weymouth established themselves upon the lands. But the soil was stony and the surface rough; Mendon never flourished as an agricultural community. This very fact encouraged emigration to the towns that arose on its western border.

An important station on the Connecticut Path was called by the Indians Quabaug. Here a branch trail known as the 'Hadley Path' struck out across country to Old Hadley and Northampton, where a considerable tract of land was almost completely cleared of forests. Such a location could not long remain merely a resting place on the 'Path'; in 1660 adventurers from Ipswich planted the town of Brookfield. Brookfield was more than an outpost, it was a settlement in the heart of the wilderness. For two generations all it could do was to hold its own against the Indians, the French and the natural disadvantages which hemmed it in on all sides.

With four settlements founded before 1670, the subsequent tardy development of the area calls for some explanation. It is to be found in the Indian wars which began in 1675 and continued under one guise or another until the 1720's. In King Philip's War all these plantations suffered; in the war at the close of the century the French and their Indian allies stopped the colonists' plans for the erection of about a dozen new towns. Although there was renewed activity after 1713, the real influx of settlers was postponed until the year 1726 brought peace among the Indians in Maine and New Hampshire. Thereafter settlement advanced rapidly and by 1763 central Massachusetts was sending out young families to pioneer upon new frontiers.

Settlement from the East

The eastern third of the area received its population from the centers of dispersion that existed at Lancaster, Marlborough and Mendon. To some extent this was due to mere proximity. The lands adjacent to the valleys and intervales which had first tempted settlement were not of the best. While prospective inhabitants from more remote sections readily saw the drawbacks of farming on elevated and thin soil, the children and grandchildren of local families were less apt to be aware of the undesirable features or were inclined to overlook them in view of the advantages involved in living near the homes of their parents and the society of which they were a part. Consequently they pushed clearings farther up the hillsides, established meeting houses of their own, created voting precincts and finally seceded from the old town politically by being incorporated into a new town. This repeated dismemberment of old towns was possible because of the great extent of the original grants. The General Court, probably in order to encourage settlement on the frontier, had been unusually generous in defining bounds, and by so doing provided not only for the original grantees but for their children as well through the third or fourth generation. These same remarks apply also to Brookfield, which, though greatly crippled by Indian depredations, sent out its families to take possession of its outlying lands.

A social consequence of this growth from within should be apparent in a striking homogeneity of the population in each of the sections. The subject has not been investigated, but it is suggested that if the original stock in each possessed certain individual traits of conduct and speech, those traits would be intensified by the intermarriage of sons and daughters and by the isolation which for more than a century and a half was characteristic of life in the hills of Worcester County.

Aside from the Brookfield expansion, which contributed largely to the population of the surrounding towns (especially Spencer, Warren and Ware), the settlement of the western section of central Massachusetts proceeded in a rather confused manner from eastern Massachusetts. By the eighteenth century the General Court of the colony had adopted the policy of granting 'townships' to groups in reward for special services or of selling them as a revenue measure. As a result the landscape was dotted with towns of diverse origin. However, a certain concentration of the various elements is apparent. In the northern part (the towns of Fitchburg, Gardner, Templeton, Phillipston and Petersham) were many colonists from the Boston area; on the southern boundary (the towns of Oxford, Dudley and Charlton) were many from the region about Salem. In the northwest (the towns of Orange, Wendell, New Salem, Preston, Hardwick and Enfield) were the children of the Old Colony; their settlement was later and their lands were farther west and poorer. All parts of eastern Massachusetts are represented in the central section except the northern half of Essex County. Emigrants from that area followed a natural and historic route, up the Merrimack into New Hampshire or along the coast into the District of Maine.

The Scotch-Irish

The population of central Massachusetts included a group which, though small, was distinctly individual. Early in the eighteenth century Ulstermen began to appear upon the shores of New England, and from 1720 on there was a steady influx centering about Londonderry in New Hampshire; they contributed appreciably to the settlement of northern New England. A few of them drifted down to Massachusetts, but the majority of those who established themselves there came directly from Ulster, usually by way of the pioneer center of Worcester. The nucleus of this center was formed by immigrants who, coming to Boston in 1718, were accommodated with lands in the then primitive region of the present city of Worcester. There were probably two hundred in this earliest group, but from time to time other individuals and families arrived.

Though the colony was small, its members undoubtedly outnumbered the New Englanders already there to such an extent that the Ulstermen could form their own society and segregate themselves from their neighbors. This segregation was apparent when, disregarding the methods by which religious parishes were formed according to Massachusetts custom, the Scotch-Irish organized themselves into a Presbyterian body and proceeded to erect a church. The structure was not completed: irate 'natives' fell upon it at night and tore down the timbers. The result was a migration from the Worcester colony. Groups went out to the rougher land in the west and northwest, especially to the towns of Palmer, Ware, Barre, Oakham, Greenwich and Pelham; others migrated southward to Connecticut; and some established themselves beyond the Connecticut River. A considerable proportion remained, however, giving a distinct flavor to the society of Worcester so long as it remained a rural, agricultural town. It is of some interest to note that there were three Presbyterian churches in central Massachusetts in 1775, but only one in 1860 (*Atlas of Historical Geography*, Plates 82B and 84G).

From time to time in the decades that followed, as emigration became general throughout the region, new companies were sent to the north and west; but these maintained a closer connection with the mother town than did most emigrating groups. Intermarriage was common, the mother town and the outposts exchanged ministers and supported political leaders (for instance Daniel Shays) in common. Though scattered, the Scotch-Irish preserved many features of community life. They are credited with introducing the cultivation of the potato and the manufacture of linen; and it is likely that along with these economic contributions they brought a certain rigidity of opinion, a stern insistence upon religious observances, and no doubt a variety of Northern English modified by residence of a century or more in the north of Ireland.

Nineteenth Century Changes

Central Massachusetts came to agricultural maturity quickly. Not until the 1720's did settlement become general, but by the time of the American Revolution there was no more room upon its hills. The labor involved in this conquest was immense. Originally the lands had been almost wholly timbered, but before the forest began to come back into its own during the nineteenth century, fully 80 or 85 percent of the surface was cleared for agriculture. During the first decades there was cereal farming even on the summit of the ranges; but deforestation dried out the soil, which had been unusually moist for such elevations, and forced a more varied arrangement. This brought on the emigration which began shortly after the Revolution and continued for fifty years. The upper lands, however, were not abandoned. Pasturage and hay fields were substituted for grain, and agriculture was prosperous until the decade beginning in 1840. Thereafter came the decline.

The decline was not caused by western competition. Rather, the population was drawn from the hills down into the neighboring valleys to provide manpower for the flourishing local manufactures. The valleys with their swift streams had come into their own. The presence of sheep stimulated the woolen industries, cattle gave an impetus to the leather trade, minerals fostered the manufacture of tools, and a constant supply of timber provided winter occupation in the fashioning of woodwork and furniture. Along even the smallest brook a series of mills extended from the mouth almost to the source; the operatives were more than a sufficient market for the neighboring farmers.

Thus far population had been rearranged but not changed. Each center drew to itself from the surrounding territory people who were essentially the same in social background. But when mills gave way to factories there came a revolution in population. The change began with the completion of the Blackstone Canal in 1828, which united Worcester with Providence. The canal opened wider markets and made location on its banks an advantage. The smaller mills were forced out and many of the larger moved to better sites. Since connection with Providence also facilitated the importation of cotton, cotton factories more and more displaced the woolen mills or encouraged their concentration. To provide the labor other sources were necessary. Irish took the place of natives; English operatives tended to replace the Irish; French-Canadians and Italians in succession replaced the English as the older group ceased to be 'cheap labor' and rose into positions of management or moved on to more individual occupations.

The history of this transition can be written only locally. Each city has its own individual industries, and each industry has its own distinct national groups of workers. But the distribution of the original American stock in the population, though covered with successive layers of immigrants, has been little disturbed, and undoubtedly retains to the present day the characteristics peculiar to the first group of pioneers.

The Upper Connecticut Valley

(The Western Counties of New Hampshire, and the Eastern
and North-central Counties of Vermont)

Southern Subarea: 230 Colrain; 254 Wilmington, 256 Brattleboro, 257 Newfane, 258 Rockingham, 259 Andover, 266 Plymouth; 328 Keene-Marlow.

Central Subarea: 268 Windsor, 271 Stockbridge, 272 Northfield, 296 Topsham-Newbury; 330 Charlestown, 331 Goshen, 332 Newport, 334 Canaan, 335 Hanover, 336 Lyme, 337 Orford.

Northern Subarea: 282 Calais, 284 Johnson, 288 Troy, 290 Lemington, 292 Saint Johnsbury - Lyndon, 294 Ryegate; 340 Haverhill, 342 Lancaster, 344 Columbia.

Physical Factors

This area is well defined topographically, bounded on the east by the hills and mountains which form the watershed between the Connecticut and the Merrimack Rivers, on the west by the Green Mountains. Down its entire length runs the narrow winding valley of the Connecticut River, widening here and there, especially at the mouths of its tributaries. It was along this valley that the first settlements were planted, progressing northward from Massachusetts. The range of hills in the east is broken through at several points, providing ready access from that direction. Through these approaches came many early settlers from eastern New Hampshire and eastern Massachusetts. The Green Mountains in the west are more formidable, especially in southern Vermont: not many settlers came into the valley from the west.

The occupation of the Upper Valley of the Connecticut proceeded, on the one hand, in a northerly direction from the older valley towns in Massachusetts and Connecticut; and, on the other, in a northwesterly direction across the watershed of the Merrimack Valley from the older parts of eastern New England, and from the secondary settlements of Worcester County (Massachusetts) and eastern Connecticut. The traditional ties of the Upper Valley with the Lower Valley and especially with eastern New England have never been lost, despite the incorporation of the counties west of the River into the state of Vermont (1791).

Historical Factors

The Upper Valley was settled comparatively late because of the menace offered by the French in Canada until 1760. Only the southernmost part was settled before the defeat of the French. Some of the earlier establishments were more military than agricultural, and the earlier dates of settlement must be interpreted with caution. With the exception of distinctly mountainous towns, the occupation of this area was completed by 1790.

Settlement was further retarded by the disputes regarding the jurisdiction of the region, which were not settled until the creation of the State of Vermont and its admission to the Union in 1791. New Hampshire claimed the lands as far west as the present western boundary of Vermont and made grants; New York extended its claims eastward to the Connecticut River and also made grants; Massachusetts claimed a line considerably to the north of her present boundary. There were, accordingly, some towns which were granted from three different sources. As a result, much of the early population was migratory, and stability began only when the land titles in any particular town were finally adjusted.

Composition of the Population

The Upper Valley is an area of secondary and tertiary settlements and its population a mixture of earlier mixtures. All of the older sections of New England excepting the western third of Connecticut, Berkshire County (Massachusetts) and Vermont west of the Green Mountains had an appreciable share in settling this area, and hardly a town in the Upper Valley did not draw upon several sources.

Much work in local history and in genealogy must be done before the composition of the population will be adequately known. On the basis of fragmentary and very uneven information only tentative generalizations can be made concerning the provenience of the population. The following statements must be regarded in this light.

The Upper Valley can be divided into a southern, a middle and a northern part. These subareas are fairly distinct in date of settlement and in the character of the population mixture.

(1) The southern part, including Cheshire County, New Hampshire, and Windham County together with the southwestern half of Windsor County, Vermont, was settled largely from Massachusetts. This subarea comprises in addition to the Connecticut Valley proper the valleys of three tributaries, the Ashuelot River in New Hampshire and the West and Williams Rivers in Vermont.

On the New Hampshire side the settlement began in 1740 (Swanzey, 1740; Winchester, 1745; Keene, c. 1746); on the Vermont side, in the 1750's (Brattleboro, 1754; Bellows Falls, c. 1760); the more fertile lands were taken up before the French and Indian War (1763). Many of the settlers on the New Hampshire side of the Connecticut River came from the Bay Colony (especially also from eastern Worcester County); some came from the Plymouth Colony (Rehoboth, Taunton), from Rhode Island (Smithfield), and from eastern Connecticut. The Merrimack Valley contributed its share, especially to the eastern fringe of towns in Cheshire County. Settlers from the Connecticut Valley in Massachusetts were not numerous, except in the towns adjoining the river. On the Vermont side, especially in Putney and Westminster, the Valley element (from Northfield, Amherst, Hadley, Springfield, Windsor, Hartford and Middletown) was larger, but the great majority of the settlers appear to have come from eastern Massachusetts, with some from the Merrimack Valley. Essex County and New Hampshire settlers are numerous in Bellows Falls and in the towns along the Saxtons River.

It is worthy of note that Windham County, Vermont, is part of the wholesale marketing area of Keene, New Hampshire, which in turn belongs to the major trading area of Boston.

(2) The middle part of the Upper Valley, including Sullivan County and the southwestern part of Grafton County in New Hampshire and the northeastern half of Windsor County and Orange County in Vermont, was settled largely from eastern Connecticut. It comprises the Connecticut Valley proper from the mouth of the Sugar River (Claremont, New Hampshire) to the mouth of the Waits River (Bradford, Vermont), the valleys of the Sugar and Mascoma Rivers in New Hampshire, and the valleys of the Ottauquechee River

(Woodstock), the White River and its many tributaries (White River Junction, Bethel), and the Waits River in Vermont, all tributaries of the Connecticut River.

This part of the Upper Valley was settled after the defeat of the French in 1760, and all except the mountainous parts were occupied by the beginning of the Revolution in 1776. Most of the settlers were emigrants from eastern Connecticut, especially from the counties of Windham and Tolland and from the adjoining towns in the counties of New London (Norwich, Lebanon, Colchester), Middlesex (Middletown) and Hartford (East Hartford, East Windsor, Enfield). Many a town in the middle part of the Upper Valley is named for its mother town in Connecticut. The Connecticut element appears to be especially strong in the valleys, which of course were taken up first. In the hills back from the river the admixture of settlers from eastern Massachusetts, the Merrimack Valley and eastern New Hampshire, present everywhere, is more extensive, and in some of the towns the Connecticut element is small. The settlers from eastern New Hampshire represent the southern fringe of the movement from the New Hampshire coast towns by way of Lake Winnepesaukee and the Pemigewasset River (the northern branch of the Merrimack) into the Upper Connecticut Valley.

The infiltration of families from the recently settled southern part of the Upper Valley must not be forgotten in any treatment of the middle and the northern parts. It should be noted that at present Windsor County and southern Orange County belong to the Rutland trading area, whereas the New Hampshire towns along the river are oriented toward the east.

(3) The northern part of the Upper Connecticut Valley, including the northwestern third of Grafton County and the western half of Coos County, New Hampshire, and the counties of Caledonia, Essex, Orleans, Lamoille and Washington in Vermont, is a patchwork of towns of diverse origin. This area comprises (a) the Connecticut Valley proper and the valleys of its tributaries—the Bakers River (Haverhill), the Ammonoosuc River (Woodsville, Littleton) and the Israel River (Lancaster) in New Hampshire, the Wells River (Ryegate) and the Passumpsic River (St. Johnsbury) in Vermont; (b) the upper reaches of the Winooski River (Montpelier) and its tributaries and of the Lamoille River, which flow westward into Lake Champlain. Both the Winooski and the Lamoille Rivers are easily approached from the Connecticut Valley, the first by way of the Wells River, the second from the Passumpsic.

As far north as Guildhall, the towns bordering on the Connecticut River were settled between 1764 and the beginning of the Revolution, but the greater part of this area was not taken up until after the end of the war in 1783. The more desirable lands along the Winooski and Lamoille Rivers were occupied before 1790 (Montpelier and Hyde Park, 1787), the remainder in the following decade (Newport, 1800).

The settlers of this northern subarea came in considerable numbers from the older parts of New Hampshire and from Vermont east of the crest of the Green Mountains. (In the western part of the counties of Washington and Lamoille, they derive also from the southwestern part of Vermont and from western Connecticut.) Others came from Worcester County, Massachusetts, from Rhode Island and from eastern Connecticut. The population of most of the towns is thoroughly mixed, but areas can be pointed out where certain elements are concentrated: families from eastern Connecticut are numerous in the towns adjoining the Connecticut River in the counties of Essex and Coos, Rhode Islanders along the Passumpsic River (St. Johnsbury, Lyndon), and New Hampshire families on the upper Lamoille River. The towns of Barnet and Ryegate in Caledonia County were settled directly from Scotland.

II. *WESTERN NEW ENGLAND*

1. THE LOWER CONNECTICUT VALLEY AND NEW HAVEN

The New Haven Area: 26 New Haven, 28 Madison-Guilford, 29 Killingworth, 30 Old Saybrook, 36 Wallingford.

The Hartford Area: 14 Wolcott, 16 Litchfield, 20 Farmington, 38 Middletown, 40 Hartford, 41 Glastonbury, 42 Hebron.

The Windsor Area: 21 Hartland, 22 Winchester, 23 Granby, 24 Simsbury, 44 Somers, 45 East Windsor, 46 Tolland.

The Springfield Area: 220 Palmer, 221 Monson, 224 Springfield, 235 Granville.

The Northampton and Deerfield Area: 214 Gill-Northfield, 219 Granby, 225 Southampton, 226 Northampton, 228 Deerfield.

The south-central section of New England comprises (1) the Lower Connecticut Valley, which was settled by gradual expansion in all directions from the 'River Towns' of Wethersfield, Hartford, Windsor and Springfield, situated on the fertile bottom lands of New England's largest river, and from Saybrook at the mouth of the river; (2) the New Haven area, which was occupied from New Haven, Branford and Guilford in slow expansion northward from Long Island Sound.

This section holds a large population concentrated in a belt extending from New Haven northward through Waterbury, Meriden, Middletown, New Britain, Hartford, Springfield and Holyoke to Northampton. Both east and west it is flanked by thinly settled farm lands and hills, the Berkshires and the Litchfield Hills on the west, and the hills of Worcester County, Massachusetts, and Tolland County, Connecticut, on the east. From New Haven the belt of concentration runs southwest along the Sound to Greater New York. Both topographically and demographically the Lower Valley of the Connecticut is linked, by way of New Haven, with the New York area.

The Connecticut River Settlements

As the Connecticut River Valley dominates the physical geography of the state, so the communities established within its bounds dominated the settlement of the regions both east and west. A variety of motives led to the emigration of four groups from the Massachusetts Bay Colony in the middle of the 1630's. Religious differences played a part in these migrations; but the settlers were also influenced, they said, by the 'straitness of the territory' available about the Bay, which made it difficult for them to secure sufficient pasturage for their cattle. This factor determined their location within the Valley. In general the flood plain of the Connecticut River is narrow, but occasionally it broadens out into natural meadows extending back five miles or more towards the hills. Such meadows the English named 'intervales' and upon them they pitched. These meadows provided pasturage in the summer and fodder for the winter; and fertile fields for growing Indian corn could be secured without the strenuous labor which attended later pioneering. It must be remembered that the early settlers of New England had not yet learned how to handle the ax.

The four initial communities, Windsor (1633), Wethersfield (1634), Hartford (1635) and Springfield (1636), were located upon such intervales, and for approximately a generation the growing families found accommodation upon the undivided common adjacent to the villages. For the first generation these river settlements were isolated except for their communication with each other. Because of developments in England, there was no further immigration from the mother country after 1640, and the Bay Colony deliberately prevented further secession from its ranks by a liberal land policy that tended to keep new swarms settled within its jurisdiction. In this period (until the union of all the Connecticut settlements in the Charter of 1662) the river towns below Springfield evolved a society, a religion and a political policy which were to become characteristic of much of the State of Connecticut in later years.

From the beginning Springfield possessed some features which distinguished it from its neighbors to the south. Its site was not the most desirable. There is evidence that some of those who made their homes farther down the river had originally contemplated establishing themselves upon these upper fields or meadows, but that they were persuaded to pass on because navigation on the Connecticut was interrupted by the falls at Enfield, and river trade was the only tie that bound them to the outside world.

In the opinion of William Pyncheon and his associates in Roxbury, this disadvantage was balanced by a strategic location. The Springfield meadows lay at the meeting of the trails. The northern part of the river was here divided from the southern; a path or succession of paths led overland to the Bay; the Longmeadow Path skirted the river down to Windsor; and the Westfield River and its valley marked the route into the Indian country to the west. For men who had fur trading in mind the location was ideal, and in 1636 Pyncheon's company occupied the fields, built a warehouse and planned to begin operations in the valleys and hills about them. This emphasis upon the commercial character of the venture is necessary to explain the slow expansion of the upper settlement as compared with its three contemporaries to the south. Planters were not urged to join the company; agriculture was at first carried on only to the extent necessary to provide food; and projects for occupying favorable locations to the north, east and west were not encouraged.

In one other respect Springfield followed an evolution that set it off from its neighbors. Politically it became part of Massachusetts, although in 1636 its standing with respect to the Bay was the same as that of the three lower towns. This divergence was of gradual growth. It began in the Pequot War of 1637 when Springfield's failure to coöperate with Hartford, Windsor and Wethersfield, caused these latter to accuse Pyncheon of bad faith. It was intensified by a dispute over the right of one community to levy a tax upon trade passing down the river from above. Perhaps the unecclesiastical nature of the Springfield undertaking automatically put it in disfavor with the ministers below. At any rate, in 1639, when the three towns joined together in the 'Fundamental Orders' from which the government of Connecticut grew, Springfield was not a party to the agreement. Left to itself, its affections naturally turned toward the east. But the Bay was in no hurry to take the frontier outpost under its protection and to be responsible for quarrels that its extending trade might engender: it was not until 1649 that deputies from the river were admitted to the General Court of Massachusetts and the annexation was complete.

Contemporaneous with these first settlements, another point on the river was occupied. At the mouth of the river, an ambitious project led to the founding of Saybrook in 1636.

Planned and peopled from England, its objectives were fundamentally different from those of its neighbors to the north. Its object was trade; meadows meant nothing. Great cities, it was argued, were located at the mouths of rivers, and therefore a great city would naturally arise where the Connecticut emptied into the Sound. But as Saybrook had no thriving hinterland from which to draw its commerce, its ambitions soon faded. Much of its original population went east and planted Norwich (1660) on the Thames River above New London; and those who remained only slowly filled in the lands to the immediate west and north.

Within a few years one more point on the river was occupied: Middletown (1640). In the subsequent spread of Connecticut's population this town was of little importance and few colonies were sent out from it to people the interior. The explanation is simple. As it was located at the southern end of the fertile Connecticut Valley and accessible to the ocean-going vessels of the time, Middletown fell heir to the commerce of which Saybrook had dreamed. It became the great shipping center of the colony, absorbing all the natural increase of its inhabitants. Until shortly before the Revolution it was superior to all other Connecticut cities in wealth and population.

New Haven and the Adjoining Settlements on Long Island Sound

While this planting of the valley was still under way, a second line of advance upon the wilderness of western Connecticut was being established. Before 1650, colonists had located themselves at a dozen points on the shore of Long Island Sound from Saybrook west to the dominions of the Dutch in New Netherland. The topography of the coastal plain reveals a score of rivers, most of them small, flowing into the Sound. The mouth of almost every one of these streams was soon in the possession of Englishmen, the site being determined not so much by any possibility of trade offered by communication with the interior as by the fact that these rivers, broadening out by the sea, created meadows and marshes which provided the same kind of pasturage and arable fields which the river settlers had sought. The exception was New Haven. Like Saybrook it planned a commercial future; but the disasters that attended the early ventures ruined these prospects, and finally its attention was turned from commercial expansion upon the sea to agricultural expansion inland.

The people who settled upon the coast were derived from numerous sources. Those at New Haven (1638) came almost directly from England. Those at Milford (1639) and Guilford (1639) were also recent immigrants who had tarried only a few months at New Haven. Branford (1640), Stratford (1639), Fairfield (1644), Norwalk (c. 1651) and Stamford (1641) received a more motley population, many of whom had spent a few seasons at the river towns or in the Bay Colony but had been unable or unwilling to establish themselves there permanently. In any case they still retained the characteristics which they had brought with them from England.

Another source of population, apt to be overlooked, is Long Island, which is the more important because it continued to contribute its people long after the other sources had run dry. For the colonizing dissenters of eastern New England, Long Island held great attractions: its climate was mild, its soil apparently fertile, its government non-existent. Several plantations on the Island were founded early but did not thrive. The soil was too sandy and porous for the type of agriculture that the colonists were obliged to practice. Thus the reports from the northern side of the Sound lured many away. The extent of this movement can be realized only from the genealogies of the shore towns of Connecticut. When Long Island became English territory by the conquest of New Netherland in 1664, another motive for emigration appeared. The royal government of New York adopted a strict church and land policy which forced away many who had previously been content to stay. This then was a further element added to the already rather diverse composition of the population that was to approach the Connecticut interior from the Sound.

The advance northward was at first slight. The group in each of the original towns was comparatively small and for two generations the cause of interior colonization was not so much the pressure of population as religious dissension and the promising opportunities for Indian trade.

Of the original settlements along the Sound west of the mouth of the Connecticut River, Saybrook, Guilford, Branford and New Haven are here treated as belonging to the south-central area, while the settlements to the west of New Haven constitute the nucleus of the southern subarea of western New England. This procedure is partly a matter of convenience, but it may be justified on the ground that the New Haven area, though originally quite distinct, has enjoyed intimate relations with the Valley for a century or more, while southwestern Connecticut has been oriented toward New York from the very beginning.

The First Interior Settlements

The first interior settlement was one destined to play an important rôle in the process of population distribution. Farmington was founded by Hartford families in 1640 near the southern bend of the Farmington River, at a spot where there were meadows equal to the Connecticut River intervales in fertility though not in size. This was, moreover, a favorable place for the Indian trade, and the settlement was encouraged in the hope that influence might be exerted on the Indian tribes to the northwest. Farmington was well located for communication with the interior. It sent out colony after colony from its own family stock and also became a focus where individuals and families from the eastern parts gathered and prepared for their advance into the up-country.

At a date almost as early as the founding of Farmington it was planned to establish a similar post near the northern bend of the Farmington River where valleys and trails from the northern part of the colony met. But the natural advantages were slighter and the Indian danger was greater, so that it was not until 1664 that Windsor men settled there permanently. This post was named Simsbury. Like its southern neighbor, during the next century it contributed largely to the peopling of the neighboring hills.

The first 'colony' for which Springfield was directly responsible was not founded for more than twenty years after its own planting, while the trade in furs was still the dominating motive of Springfield life. From year to year the importance of the Westfield River was demonstrated, and in the course of time competitors appeared upon its upper waters. Not all the inhabitants of Connecticut were willing to devote their undivided attention to farming the meadows. Some were jealous of the ready wealth which the Indians were sending through the Massachusetts town. The resources of the forests that stretched towards the northwest belonged as much to them as to Pyncheon and his associates in Springfield, they argued, and plans were made to divert part of the riches into their own warehouses. Their activities were naturally secret and history has not been able to reveal what steps they actually took. In any case, an undertaking was begun which would have resulted and possibly did result in the establishment of a Connecticut station upon the Westfield River at some point where communication by the interior valleys of western Connecticut would not be too difficult.

To prevent the competition from becoming too strong and perhaps to anticipate the occupation by their rivals, Springfield men located themselves, about 1660, nine miles up the Westfield River upon a meadow called Woronoco. Here they combined farming with trading. They were incorporated as the town of Westfield; and in time, when the furs ceased to come down from the mountains, Westfield became the opening wedge in the agricultural advance upon the Berkshires.

Before this maneuvering was accomplished, Springfield had ceased to be the northern frontier. The Connecticut Valley in Massachusetts is divided into two parts by the range of hills that reaches its highest altitude in Mount Tom and Mount Holyoke. North of this barrier the valley widens again. Here there were meadows and intervales, navigable waters and Indian fields. In the first settlement of the valley these sites, if they were known, were passed over as being too remote. But by 1653 this had ceased to be unknown ground; and since there had been no Indian disturbances for more than a decade, men were now willing to settle here. In that year inhabitants of Hartford and Windsor bought from the Indians the lands at Nonotuck; the following spring they founded the town of Northampton. Five years later, a group of Hartford families seceded from the local church because of religious differences and located upon the meadows across the river from Northampton, where they organized the town of Hadley (1659). Within a few years settlers a little to the north organized Hatfield, and three thriving agricultural communities began to grow.

It may seem strange that Springfield influence did not prevent these intrusions from Connecticut. Springfield evidently concurred in them, since trading with the Indians was not the motive of these planters, and her settlers welcomed neighbors whom they had no reason to fear. For a century Northampton and Hadley remained frontier towns. The new generations crowded upon the lands about their parents' homesteads or moved to the south to participate in the colonization of the interior parts of Connecticut. Settlement to the north and the west was prevented by the Indian danger.

Northampton and Hatfield are the northernmost towns settled by direct expansion from the valley towns in the south. The land to the north on either side of the Deerfield River was occupied by Dedham families in 1672 and organized as the town of Deerfield. This, the extreme outpost of settlement in the Connecticut Valley for three-quarters of a century, suffered severely from Indian massacres until the end of Queen Anne's War in 1713. It must be remembered that Deerfield was an independent settlement from Massachusetts Bay, established a generation later than the first settlements in the Valley, and not like Northampton an offshoot of these early towns. However, such contacts as it had during its early history (until c. 1750) were with the valley towns south of it.

The first interior settlement planted from New Haven was Wallingford. Although New Haven and the Connecticut Valley remained separate governments until 1662, communication between them naturally arose early—not by the roundabout water route of River and Sound, but directly up and down the lowlands extending northward from New Haven along the course of the Quinnipiac River. Near the northern boundary of the New Haven jurisdiction lay an extensive plain. Its advantages in agriculture and trade were obvious, and before 1670 New Haven families had planted themselves there. It was this community which later became the town of Wallingford, and from which in turn parts of the towns of Meriden and Cheshire were settled.

Later Expansion

Expansion from the early centers progressed very slowly. In 1700 an uninterrupted string of settlements extended from the mouth of the Connecticut River to Northampton and Hadley in Massachusetts; further up the valley was the detached frontier town of Deerfield (including Greenfield). Few families at this time lived more than ten miles from the river.

Nearly a century elapsed before contact was established with settlements in the east. In Connecticut this contact was made by 1725, in Massachusetts one to three decades later. Expansion westward was even slower, the greater part of the area taken up by expansion from the river towns being occupied between 1725 and 1750.

Although many of the later towns were settled by families from several of the older communities, settlers from one of these usually predominated in any one town. Most of southern Hartford County and the adjoining parts of the counties of Tolland, New London, Middlesex (Middletown), New Haven (Waterbury) and Litchfield were taken up from Hartford-Farmington and from Wethersfield; the northern half of Hartford County and the adjoining parts of Tolland and Litchfield, largely from Windsor-Simsbury. In Massachusetts nearly all of Hampden County was taken up from Springfield-Westfield, the central part of Hampshire County from Northampton-Hadley, and the central part of Franklin County from Deerfield-Greenfield.

The area of the Valley settlements is about 50 miles wide in Connecticut; in Massachusetts it tapers off rather sharply north of Springfield. Here expansion from the east anticipated expansion from the Valley or else was contemporaneous with it, with the result that the population is more mixed in the upland parts of Hampshire and Franklin Counties.

The Expansion Policy of Connecticut

A vital consideration that must be kept in mind in dealing with the growth of Connecticut is the colony's land policy. If left entirely to itself the expansion probably would have been more logical (as in Rhode Island), but in Connecticut the movement was held firmly in check by control of the public lands. In earlier times a few grants were made to individuals in reward for special services; but it ultimately became the rule to dispose of the domain by the granting of towns to proprietors who undertook to settle a part of the grant within a specified time, to open roads and build bridges, to maintain mills, and to establish a church and support a 'Godly and learned' minister within its bounds. But when the requisite number of families had been planted (either by the proprietors or by those whom they induced to become the actual settlers), only a fraction of the town lands was occupied. The proprietors were in no hurry to complete the process. Land was wealth and time increased its value. They retained the unoccupied portion as a heritage for their children or even great-grandchildren. At intervals the proprietors divided among themselves parts of the remaining common, and settled these possessions upon their heirs or sold them to landless people.

This explains the irregular chronology of settlement. New Haven was founded in 1638. Hamden, at its rear, was not settled until the 1730's—a century later. The rougher terrain accounts in part for the delay, but the principal explanation is the fact that the lands which became Hamden were owned by New Haven and reserved for coming generations. Most of the older communities were flanked by reserves of this kind.

The social and cultural consequence of this policy was a pronounced provincialism. Population was not invited into established towns, and if it appeared it was not encouraged to remain. The numbers steadily grew but they grew from within, not from without. Thus every community had a solidarity in families, religion and culture which could trace a direct descent from the characteristics developed by the original founders.

Nineteenth Century Changes

The first third of the nineteenth century was marked by a decline in agricultural population and prosperity, the second third by the foundation of numerous industries in almost all parts of the western half of the state and a new rearrangement of the native population around these industries, the last third by a large influx of immigrants from abroad.

Unfortunately the State of Connecticut takes no census and the Federal returns deal with counties, not towns. It is therefore impossible to present data regarding the distribution of nationalities except so broadly as to offer nothing of significance. But the predominant nationality in foreign groups may readily be observed in the cities, and for the open country a study conducted by the Storrs Agricultural Experiment Station (Davis and Hendrickson, Bulletin No. 127) tabulates the number and variety of foreign-born farmers in every town in the state. These tables give minute data regarding every rural community, and make it possible to generalize to the extent of saying that Italian farmers are concentrated in a triangular area with its apex about twenty miles north of New Haven; that there are extensive Irish colonies in Hartford and Fairfield Counties; and that the town of Monroe is the seat of a Jewish colony, while scattered Jewish farmers are found in parts of Hartford County.

2. THE WESTERN FRINGE

Western Connecticut: 1 Stamford-Greenwich, 3 Westport-Bridgeport, 4 Weston, 6 Milford, 8 Bethel-Danbury, 10 Southbury, 11 New Fairfield, 12 New Milford.

Western Massachusetts: 18 Cornwall, 19 Sharon; 232 Cummington, 233 Middlefield, 234 Blandford, 236 New Marlborough, 238 Egremont, 239 Alford, 240 Stockbridge, 241 Lenox, 242 Pittsfield, 246 Cheshire, 248 Williamstown; 252 Shaftsbury-Bennington.

Western Vermont: 260 Pawlet-Dorset, 262 West Rutland - Castleton, 264 Wallingford, 265 Mount Holly, 274 Cornwall, 276 Ferrisburg, 278 Huntington, 280 Burlington-Charlotte, 281 South Burlington, 286 Enosburg.

Three subareas are to be distinguished along the western border of New England:

1. Western Connecticut, including the towns along the Sound from Milford (east of the mouth of the Housatonic River) to the New York State line, and the hill country on the lower Housatonic and its tributaries. This area was occupied between 1640 and 1730 by gradual expansion northward from the Sound.

2. Western Massachusetts, with the valleys of the upper Housatonic and the Hoosic (including a number of towns in Connecticut and in Vermont), settled by diverse elements between 1730 and 1770.

3. Western Vermont, occupied in northward progression predominantly by Connecticut families between the end of the French and Indian Wars (1763) and 1790.

Western New England possesses no focal area such as we find in Eastern New England and in the Lower Connecticut Valley. The three subareas are rather independent of each other, but are nevertheless loosely linked together by family ties and cultural traditions, as well as by a common orientation toward the focal area of the Hudson Valley rather than the Connecticut Valley. This latter fact makes for a rather ready acceptance of speech forms current west of New England.

Western Connecticut

(Fairfield County and the Adjoining Sections of New Haven and Litchfield Counties)

The settlement of the coast towns from the mouth of the Housatonic westward is part of the movement that led to the settlement of the Sound from New Haven eastward to the mouth of the Connecticut River. The occupation of the Sound (1638–45) began only a few years after the planting of the river towns of Windsor, Wethersfield and Hartford (1633–35), and lagged hardly more than a decade behind the settlement of Massachusetts Bay. Aside from a small number of Dutchmen, all the early settlers of the Connecticut towns on Long Island Sound were born in England. Some of these Englishmen came to the Sound directly from England; others had stayed a number of years in Wethersfield, as did the settlers of Stratford (1639) and Stamford (1641), or in the Massachusetts Bay Colony, as in the case of Fairfield (1639), or else on Long Island, as did many early families of Greenwich (1640).

Expansion inland from the Sound was exceedingly slow. The first inland town was Derby, planted in the 1650's by Milford men at the point where the Naugatuck flows into the Housatonic. Derby, being situated on navigable waters less than ten miles from the Sound, devoted itself to trade and played only an indirect part in the later settlement of the towns along the Housatonic and the Naugatuck. No further expansion inland occurred until a new generation had grown up in the towns bordering on the Sound.

The two points taken up in the interior in the last decades of the seventeenth century are Woodbury, organized in 1673 by Stratford families, and Danbury, settled in 1685 from Norwalk. Woodbury (first called Pomperaug) comprised a large tract of land north of the Housatonic including the valleys of the Pomperaug and the Shepaug Rivers, from which the towns of Southbury and Roxbury were set off at a later date. The occasion for the settlement was a bitter quarrel in the church of Stratford, which prompted the emigration of one of the factions.

For another generation no further towns were organized. During this period Woodbury and Danbury, on opposite sides of the Housatonic, formed an island separated by a strip of unsettled broken hill country (the later towns of Oxford, Newtown, Redding and Ridgefield) from the towns along the Sound and by a similar tract from their neighbors to the east and west. To the north lay the wilderness. Between 1710 and 1725 contact was established on all sides except the north.

The population of southwestern Connecticut is largely derived from the original settlements along the Sound. New land was taken up whenever the old towns could no longer accommodate their offspring or when dissent within the church caused one of the factions to emigrate.

After western Connecticut had been completely occupied, families from the southwestern section of the state played an important part in the settlement of the Berkshires and of western Vermont.

Western Massachusetts

(Berkshire County and the Adjoining Parts of Hampshire and Hampden Counties, Massachusetts; Northwestern Litchfield County, Connecticut; and Southern Bennington County, Vermont)

The principal features of the physical geography of this area are two parallel ranges of mountains: the Berkshires, forming the western wall of the Connecticut Valley, and the Taconic Range, forming the eastern wall of the Hudson Valley. Between the two ranges lie the valley of the Housatonic, flowing southward through Connecticut into the Sound, and the valley of the Hoosic, flowing northward through the southern corner of Vermont and then westward into the Hudson River above Troy. Both river valleys offered ready access to this region. Up the Housatonic came the first settlers of Berkshire County (c. 1730), mostly of Connecticut ancestry, while the Hoosic was followed by Dutch families who settled in and about Bennington, Vermont (c. 1760). Some of the Rhode Islanders also used this approach, embarking in Narragansett Bay and landing near Albany on their way to northern Berkshire County (1760–70).

The Berkshires were not easily entered from the Connecticut Valley. The valleys of the Farmington, Westfield and Deerfield Rivers, which drain the eastern slope of the Berkshires, are gorge-like near the crest, and the height of land is reached only with difficulty. Moreover, the slopes and many of the summits of the Berkshires were heavily wooded and had to be cleared with much labor. Here and there, to be sure, were natural meadows, and many of the mountains were topped with small plateaus accommodating several farms. Such broad summits could be more readily occupied, but settlement there meant complete isolation in a region infested with hostile Indians and Frenchmen until 1760. For these reasons the occupation of the eastern slope of the Berkshires was long delayed.

Compared with southwestern Connecticut (the southern subarea of Western New England), the population of western Massachusetts is very complex in its origin. In nearly every town were settlers from all the older parts of southern New England; yet in most of the towns one element predominated. Using the rather scanty historical evidence that has been assembled, the following tentative generalizations can be made:

(1) Southern Berkshire County was occupied between 1730 and 1760 by emigrants from Connecticut. This was natural: for a decade or two the whole trend of expansion in that colony had been up the Housatonic, Naugatuck and Farmington Rivers into the hills of Litchfield County, and when these lands were filled the tide flowed northward into Massachusetts and branched off into the spurs leading to the mountain ranges. Some of these settlers came from the Connecticut Valley, others from the lower Housatonic and the Sound, others from eastern Connecticut.

(2) Most of northern Berkshire County and the western fringe of the counties of Hampshire and Franklin, as well as the Bennington area in Vermont, were taken up by settlers from eastern Massachusetts between 1760 and 1770, after the end of the French and Indian Wars. Only after a detailed study of genealogy could one be more specific about the origin of these people. A preliminary survey suggests that the Plymouth area, Norfolk County and the older parts of Worcester County contributed the largest share. Inhabitants of the Connecticut Valley were more inclined to follow the river up into Vermont and western New Hampshire, while families living in the Boston area and in Essex County turned towards eastern New Hampshire and Maine.

(3) Rhode Islanders were scattered through most of the towns in the northern Berkshires, and in the towns of Adams (c. 1770) and Cheshire (1767) they appear to have been rather numerous. It is noteworthy that there were eight or nine Baptist churches in the northern Berkshires in 1775 (*Atlas of Historical Geography*, Plate 82D). These Rhode Island settlements are practically contemporaneous with the Rhode Island settlements in the Hudson Valley and in Rutland County, Vermont. It is known that the Rhode Islanders who settled in the Hudson Valley traveled by water through Long Island Sound and up the Hudson River; hence it is probable that the Berkshire settlers from Narragansett Bay came by the same route rather than overland.

In some of the towns along the New York boundary (especially in Egremont, Great Barrington and Bennington), Dutch settlers had established themselves before the arrival of the English, but they have left few descendants.

A peculiar feature of the settlement of the Berkshires was the emigration which began almost as soon as the colonization was complete, about 1790, and continued for about two decades. It can be explained by the conditions under which the immigration had taken place: the rush had been so great that it had resulted in over-population. To encourage the influx of inhabitants, speculators had disposed of lands in lots that were economically too small, often containing only fifty acres. Fifty acres might support a family in Rhode Island or on Cape Cod, but not in the hills. This was a lesson soon learned. Those who could buy from neighbors increased their holdings by purchase, and the sellers moved on to Vermont or New York. The adjustment was accomplished in a few years, after which western Massachusetts settled down to a stable population and a satisfactory economic society until about 1870.

Features of the Society

In the course of several decades the diverse elements that had entered into the population were fitted to a more or less common pattern characteristic as being 'from the hills.' But in the earlier years the differences were marked. The 'Dutch' (who were probably Germans) had brought in a distinct civilization which was doomed to disappear because of the overwhelming numbers of English-speaking settlers. The Rhode Islanders did not accept gracefully the Massachusetts ideas regarding the relation of church and state; but they were unorganized. Many of them had been squeezed out in the readjustment of population, and the church to which they belonged gave them little assistance.

The most powerful non-Massachusetts elements were the Connecticut people. They had settled mostly in groups of families or of old neighbors. Even where they were in the minority, superior cohesion or church leadership enabled them to elect candidates to local offices and thus to control town affairs. Their Connecticut origin was not forgotten. It was kept alive by the natural route of trade and intelligence leading to the south. The political questions of western Massachusetts were thrashed out in the pages of the *Hartford Courant*, the common vehicle for news west of the Berkshires; and the churches looked to Yale for their supply of ministers.

The Massachusetts men were typical of the time and remained so. If half a century later they differed from their relatives in the east, the relatives had changed as much as they, perhaps more. When they emigrated in 1760 they brought the church and society that they knew, and these institutions were little influenced by the social and religious innovations that accompanied and followed the American Revolution in the older communities. The

Unitarian movement made no progress among the churches in the hills, and the Episcopal Church was confined to those towns where New Yorkers had established a congregation. Eighteenth century orthodoxy persisted until the society itself began to decline.

The Nineteenth Century

When this society began to decline, its fall was so rapid that one may have difficulty in realizing that for almost a century the towns in the hills had been prosperous and the people progressive. Almost self-sufficing at the beginning, they gradually specialized in those occupations which yielded satisfactory returns. There was pasturage on the hillsides for sheep, and woolen mills arose in the valleys. The forests provided bark for tanning, and the leather industry prospered. The forests were never denuded, and the lumber trade and cabinet-making developed as improving communication brought markets within reach. There was a constant emigration of young people who could not be accommodated with farms or in professions or trades, but although the population remained stationary, it was not stagnant.

Intellectual activity was, in fact, unusually brisk. Williams College had been founded when western Massachusetts was still a pioneer community, and many preparatory schools (academies and seminaries) were established shortly thereafter. The newspaper press was vigorous and exhibited a pronounced literary bent. Private circulating libraries existed in even the most remote communities.

The reasons for the agricultural decline of western Massachusetts shortly after the Civil War are well known. The competition of the West deprived the people of local markets that had hitherto been theirs. With the loss of agriculture, local industry also felt the depression, and this in turn reacted upon the remaining residents. For thirty years the process of abandoning farms continued; it was halted at last not by the return of farmers but by the influx of summer visitors.

Scattered among the hills, which had been primarily agricultural, were several small cities whose industries had resisted the general decline. Having survived the crisis, Pittsfield and North Adams have followed a course of evolution which has turned them into modern industrial cities with a large foreign population. They have little in common with the frontier communities out of which they arose. But the rural parts, except in the valley, are still peopled by the descendants of the first pioneers and probably retain more of the old hill characteristics than a cursory inspection would suggest.

Western Vermont

(The Counties of Bennington, Rutland, Addison, Chittenden and Franklin)

Geographically western Vermont is rather effectively separated from the eastern part of the state by the Green Mountains. In the north, to be sure, there are the transverse valleys of the Winooski and Lamoille Rivers, affording convenient routes to the upper Connecticut Valley. But in the southern part of the state the Connecticut River could be reached only by crossing the high crest of the Green Mountains. The earliest route here was the Old Military Road, constructed shortly before 1760, from Charlestown, New Hampshire, along the Black River up to the present town of Ludlow, and from there across the crest to Rutland.

Western Vermont is open to the west. The Hoosic River and the Batten Kill, draining Bennington County, empty into the Hudson River; the other rivers flow into Lake Champlain. Otter Creek, flowing northward through the counties of Rutland and Addison, was the avenue of approach from the south to the lowlands of the Lake Champlain basin.

The present western boundary of Vermont was first proposed in 1781 by the Continental Congress and was accepted by New York and Vermont in 1790. From 1749 until 1789 New York had claimed the entire present area of Vermont as its own, and this claim had been confirmed in 1764 by an Order of the King in Council. Grants were made to New York families, but the number of such families was not large and many were driven out later by the New England settlers.

The occupation of western Vermont begins with the defeat of the French at Quebec in 1760. Before this date individual families had established themselves in Bennington County, but the danger from the Indian attacks instigated by the French had discouraged any extensive settlement of the land. When this danger was removed, settlers from all the older parts of New England rushed into the newly opened area in such numbers that by the beginning of the Revolutionary War, despite conflicting claims of jurisdiction, the better lands in the three southern counties of Bennington, Rutland and Addison had been taken up. In the War, when a British expedition pushing southward from Canada through the Champlain basin attempted to cut New England off from the other colonies by joining another army pressing northward along the Hudson, western Vermont became a battleground. But within a few years after the conclusion of the War the two remaining counties in the northern part of the state, Chittenden and Franklin, had been settled, and in 1791 Vermont was received into the Union as a separate state.

Although the settlers of western Vermont had come from various parts of older New England, in most of this area the Connecticut element was numerically the strongest and politically and culturally the most influential. The political leaders in the early history of the state—Governor Chittenden and the Allen brothers—were Connecticut born. All parts of Connecticut contributed to the early population of Vermont, but the contributions of the eastern part of the state (Norwich, Windham, Canterbury, Plainfield) and of Fairfield and Litchfield Counties seem to have been especially large. An admixture of settlers from the lower Connecticut Valley and from eastern New England is found in all the counties west of the Green Mountains. Only a detailed study of family histories would enable one to point out the various towns in which such elements are concentrated. However, two such areas can be pointed out here: a cluster of Rhode Island towns in southwestern Rutland County (Wallingford, Shrewsbury, Mount Holly, etc.) and the New Hampshire towns in Franklin County. Most of the Rhode Island settlers appear to have come from the hilly western part of the state adjoining that section of Connecticut which contributed so generously to the population of Vermont.

The New Hampshire men who took up land in Franklin County represent the vanguard of the movement from the Merrimack Valley across the upper Connecticut River into the valley of the Lamoille. In this northernmost part of Vermont there is probably no such distinct cultural and linguistic line of demarcation between the western and the eastern parts of the state as farther south, where no convenient gateways existed to lure settlers from eastern New England.

HISTORICAL BIBLIOGRAPHY

Books and papers dealing with all of New England or a large section of it are given in part I, under the following headings: 1. Bibliographies, 2. General Histories, 3. Geology and Physiography, 4. Population History, 5. Agriculture, 6. Commerce, Industries and Transportation, 7. Political History, 8. Social and Cultural History.

Works on the individual states and their counties are presented in parts II–VII. Each state bibliography has three subheads: 1. Bibliographies, 2. State and County Histories, 3. Special Studies (comprising subheads 3–8 of part I).

Bibliographical notes on the towns investigated for the New England Atlas will be found in Chapter VI.

For Long Island and western New Brunswick a number of bibliographical references have been inserted in Chapter VI, preceding communities 50 and 426, respectively.

This bibliography is far from being exhaustive. It will fulfill its purpose if it lightens the work of linguists in search of historical explanations for the speech of New England.

I. NEW ENGLAND

1. *Bibliographies*

Bradford, T. L. and **Henkels, S. V., eds.** Bibliographer's Manual of American History, containing an Account of All State, Territory, Town and County Histories. 4 vols. and index vol. Philadelphia, 1907–10.

Buck, Morison, Merk and **Schlesinger.** The Harvard Guide to American History [rev. ed. of Channing, Hart and Turner's Guide . . .]. In prep.

Channing, E., Hart, A. B. and **Turner, F. J.** Guide to the Study and Reading of American History. Boston, 1912.

Columbia University Library. Bulletin no. 2, Books on Education. New York, 1901.

Edwards, E. E. A Bibliography of the History of Agriculture in the United States. U. S. Department of Agriculture, Miscellaneous Publication no. 84. Washington, 1930.

Evans, Charles. American Bibliography: a Chronological Dictionary of All Books, Pamphlets and Periodical Publications printed in the U. S. A. from the genesis of printing in 1639 down to and including the year 1820. Chicago, 1903–34.

Flagg, Charles A. and **Jennings, Judson T.** Bibliography of New York Colonial History. New York State Library Bulletin 56. Albany, 1901.

Greene, Evarts B. and **Morris, Richard B.** A Guide to the Principal Sources for Early American History (1600–1800) in the City of New York. New York, 1929.

Griffin, G. G. Writings on American History: A Bibliography of Books and Articles on United States and Canadian History. Washington, 1908–.

Hasse, A. R. Materials for a Bibliography of the

Public Archives of the 13 Original States, covering the Colonial Period and the State Period to 1789. Am. Hist. Assoc., Annual Report 1906, vol. 2, 239–572. Washington, 1908.

Journal of American Folk-lore. Index to vols. 1–40. (Memoirs of the American Folk-lore Society, vol. 14.) New York, 1930.

New England Quarterly. Annual Bibliography of New England History. Baltimore, 1928–.

Nichols, Charles L., comp. Checklist of Maine, New Hampshire and Vermont Almanacs. Proceedings of the American Antiquarian Society, N.S. 38, 63–163. Worcester, 1929.

Perkins, F. B., comp. Check List for American Local History. Boston, 1876.

Sabin, Joseph, ed. Bibliotheca Americana. A Dictionary of Books relating to America. 29 vols. New York, 1868–1936.

Turner, Frederick J. and **Merk, Frederick.** List of References on the History of the West, revised edition. Cambridge, 1922.

Wright, J. K. Aids to Geographical Research. American Geographical Society Research Series no. 10. New York, 1923.

Wright, J. K., ed. New England's Prospect: 1933 (by 27 scholars). American Geographical Society, Special Publication no. 16. New York, 1933.

2. *General Histories*

Adams, Henry. History of the United States. 9 vols. New York, 1889–91.

Adams, James T. The Founding of New England. Boston, 1921.

Adams, James T. Revolutionary New England, 1691–1776. Boston, 1923.

Adams, James T. New England in the Republic, 1776–1850. Boston, 1926.

Andrews, C. M. The Fathers of New England. New Haven, 1921.

Andrews, Charles M. The Colonial Period of American History. 4 vols. to date. New Haven, 1934–38.

Avery, E. M. A History of the United States and its People from their Earliest Records to the Present Time. 7 vols. Cleveland, 1904–10. Index. Tarrytown, N. Y., 1915.

Bailey, W. B. Urban and Rural New England. Publications of the American Statistical Association 8, 345–88 (1903).

Brigham, Albert P. Geographic Influences in American History. New York, 1903.

Brigham, Albert P. The United States of America: studies in physical, regional, industrial and human geography. London, 1927.

Brown, John. The Pilgrim Fathers of New England and their Puritan Successors. New York, 1896.

Coolidge, A. J. and **Mansfield, J. B.** History and Description of New England, General and Local. Boston, 1859.

Dixon, Roland B. The Early Migrations of the Indians of New England and the Maritime Provinces. Proceedings of the American Antiquarian Society, N.S. 24, 65–76 (1914).

Eggleston, Edward. The Transit of Civilization from England to America. New York, 1901.

Eggleston, Edward. The Beginners of a Nation. New York, 1896.

Egleston, Melville. The Land System of the New England Colonies. Johns Hopkins Studies in Historical and Political Science, Fourth Series xi, xii. 1880.

Ellis, G. W. and **Morris, J. E.** King Philip's War. New York, 1906.

Greene, E. B. Provincial America, 1690–1740. New York, 1905.

Hawthorne, Hildegarde. Old Seaport Towns of New England. New York, 1916.

Hayward, John. The New England Gazetteer; Containing Descriptions of All the States, Counties and Towns in New England. Boston, 1857.

Johnson, Allen, ed. Chronicles of America. New Haven, 1918–21.

McMaster, J. B. A History of the People of the United States, from the Revolution to the Civil War. 8 vols. New York, 1883–1913.

Nettels, Curtis P. The Roots of American Civilization. New York, 1938.

Palfrey, John G. History of New England. 5 vols. Boston, 1858–90.

Paullin, Charles O. (Wright, John K., ed.) Atlas of the Historical Geography of the United States. Washington and New York, 1932.

Sargent, Porter E. A Handbook of New England. Boston, 1916, 1921.

Semple, Ellen C. American History and its Geographic Conditions. Boston, 1903.

Statistical Atlas of the United States. 1874, 1898, 1902, 1914, 1925.

Sylvester, Herbert M. Indian Wars of New England. Boston, 1910.

de Tocqueville, Alexis. Democracy in America. Translated by Henry Reeve. London, 1862.

Turner, Frederick J. The Frontier in American History. New York, 1920.

Turner, Frederick J. Greater New England in the Middle of the Nineteenth Century. Proceedings of of the American Antiquarian Society, N.S. 29, 222–41 (1919).

Turner, Frederick J. The United States, 1830–50. New York, 1935.

United States Department of Commerce and Labor, Bureau of the Census. A Century of Population Growth, from the first census of the U. S. to the twelfth, 1790–1900. Washington, 1909.

United States Department of Commerce and Labor, Bureau of the Census. Fifteenth Census of the United States: 1930. Washington, 1933.

Weeden, W. B. Economic and Social History of New England, 1620–1789. 2 vols. Boston, 1890.

Weeden, W. B. Three Commonwealths: Massachusetts, Connecticut, Rhode Island; their Early Development. Proceedings of the American Antiquarian Society. N.S. 15, 130–64. Worcester, 1904.

Wilson, Harold F. The Hill Country of Northern New England. New York, 1936.

Wright, John K., ed. New England's Prospect: 1933 (by 27 scholars). American Geographical Society, Special Publication no. 16. New York, 1933.

3. *Geology and Physiography*

Davis, W. M. The Physical Geography of Southern New England. National Geographic Monthly 1, 269–304 (1895).

Emerson, Philip. The Geography of New England. New York, 1922.

Fenneman, N. M. Physiographic Divisions of the United States. Annals of the Association of American Geographers 18, 261–353 (1928).

James, P. E. The Blackstone Valley: A Study in Chorography in Southern New England. Annals of the Association of American Geographers 19, 67–109 (1929).

Wright, John K. Regions and Landscapes of New England. New England's Prospect: 1933, 14–49.

4. *Population History*

Adams, William F. Ireland and Irish Emigration to the New World from 1815 to the Famine. Yale Historical Publications. New Haven, 1932.

Bailey, W. B. Urban and Rural New England. Publications of the American Statistical Association 8, 345–88 (1903).

Baird, Charles W. History of the Huguenot Emigration to America. 2 vols. New York, [c. 1885].

Banks, Charles E. English Sources of Emigration to the New England Colonies in the Seventeenth Century. Proceedings of the Massachusetts Historical Society 60, 366–73 (1927).

Banks, Charles E. Scotch Prisoners deported to New England by Cromwell, 1651–52. Proceedings of the Massachusetts Historical Society 61, 4–29 (1927–28).

Baxter, James P. The Pioneers of New France in New England. Albany, 1894.

Bidwell, Percy W. Population Growth in Southern New England, 1810–1860. Publications of the American Statistical Association 15, 813–39 (1917).

Bolton, Charles K. Scotch-Irish Pioneers in Ulster and America. Boston, 1910.

Bolton, Charles K. The Real Founders of New England. Boston, 1929.

Bolton, H. E. and **Marshall, T. M.** The Colonization of North America, 1492–1783. New York, 1922.

Brewer, Daniel C. The Conquest of New England by the Immigrant. New York, 1926.

Byrne, Stephen. Irish Emigration to the United States. New York, 1873.

Cance, A. E. The Decline of the Rural Population in New England. Publications of the American Statistical Association 13, 96–101 (1912).

Coolidge, Ruth D. The Scotch-Irish in New England. New England Magazine 42, 747–50 (1910).

Desmond, H. J. A Century of Irish Immigration. American Catholic Quarterly Review 25, 528.

Dexter, Franklin B. Estimates of Population in the American Colonies. Proceedings of the American Antiquarian Society, N.S. 5, 22–50 (1887–88).

Dodge, Stanley D. A Study of Population Regions in New England on a New Basis. Annals of the Association of American Geographers 25, no. 4 (Dec. 1935).

Eno, Joel N. Highland Scottish Clans, Sub-Clans and Families Represented in America. Americana 18, 313–27 (1924).

Faust, Albert B. The German Element in the United States (vol. 1, 247–62). Boston and N. Y., 1909.

Ford, H. J. The Scotch-Irish in America. Princeton, 1915.

Gordon, John C. The Scot in New England. Americana 6, 32–41; 143–50 (1911).

Greene, Evarts B. and **Harrington, Virginia D.** American Population before the Federal Census of 1790. New York, 1932.

Hale, Edward E. Letters on Irish Emigration. Boston, 1852.

Hall, Edward A. The Irish Pioneers of the Connecticut Valley. Papers and Proceedings of the Connecticut Valley Historical Society 2, 175–213 (1904).

Hansen, Marcus L. The Second Colonization of New England. New England Quarterly 2, 539–60 (1929).

Hansen, Marcus L. (Schlesinger, A. M., ed.) A history of American immigration to 1860. MS, to be published by the Harvard University Press, 1939.

Hansen, Marcus L. and **Brebner, J. Bartlet.** The Mingling of the Canadian and American Peoples. Vol. 1: Historical. New Haven, 1939.

Hoar, G. F. Obligations of New England to the County of Kent. Proceedings of the American Antiquarian Society, N.S. 3, 345–71 (1884–85).

Hulbert, Archer B. Soil: Its Influence on the History of the United States. New Haven, 1930.

Hypes, J. L. Recent Immigrant Stocks in New England Agriculture. New England's Prospect: 1933, 189–205.

Mathews, Lois M. The Expansion of New England. Boston and New York, 1909.

New England Historical and Genealogical Register. List of Emigrants to America from Liverpool, 1697–1707. Vol. 64, 158–66; 252–63; 336–46 (1910).

O'Brien, Michael J. Irish Pioneers in New England. Journal of the American Irish Historical Society 18, 110–44 (1919).

Perry, Arthur L. The Scotch-Irish of New England. The Scotch-Irish in America; Proceedings and Addresses 2, 107–44 (1890).

Sainsbury, W. Noel. The British Public Record Office and the Materials in it for Early American History. Proceedings of the American Antiquarian Society, N.S. 8, 376–89 (1892–93).

Schoff, Wilfred H. The German Immigration into Colonial New England. Pennsylvania-German 12, 395–402; 517–22 (1911).

Scofield, Edna. The Origin of Settlement Patterns in Rural New England. Geographical Review 28, 652–63 (1938).

Shipton, Clifford K. Immigration to New England, 1680–1740. Journal of Political Economy 44, 225–39 (1936).

Smyth, George H. The Scotch-Irish in New England. Magazine of American History 9, 153–67 (1883).

Spengler, J. J. Has the Native Population of New England been Dying Out? Journal of Economics 44, 639–62 (1930).

Sutherland, Stella H. Population Distribution in Colonial America. New York, 1936.

Thornthwaite, C. Warren. Internal Migration in the United States. Philadelphia, 1934.

5. *Agriculture*

Anonymous. American Husbandry. London, 1776. [Best contemporary account.]

Bidwell, Percy W. The Agricultural Revolution in New England. American Historical Review 26, 683–702 (1921).

Bidwell, Percy W. Rural Economy in New England at the Beginning of the Nineteenth Century. Trans. Conn. Acad. of Arts and Sciences 20, 241–399.

Carrier, Lyman. The Beginnings of Agriculture in America. New York, 1923.

Davis, I. G. Agricultural Production in New England. New England's Prospect: 1933, 118–67.

Deane, Samuel. The New England Farmer; or Georgical Dictionary. 3. ed. Boston, 1822.

Eliot, Jared. Essays upon Field Husbandry [1760]. Reprinted in Columbia University Studies in History of Agriculture. New York, 1934.

Sanborn, A. F. The Problem of Rural New England. The Atlantic 79, 577–98 (1897).

United States Department of Agriculture. Farming in New England, 1850–1870. Yearbook 1870, 250–67.

Wilson, Harold F. The Hill Country of Northern New England. New York, 1936. [Good bibliography.]

6. *Commerce, Industry and Transportation*

Appleton, Nathan. Introduction of the Power Loom, and Origin of Lowell. Lowell, 1858.

Artman, C. E., ed. Commercial Survey of New England. Domestic Commerce Series of the U. S. Department of Commerce, Bureau of Foreign and Domestic Commerce. Washington, 1929–30.

Artman, C. E. Industrial Structure of New England. Commercial Survey of New England, part 1. Washington, 1930.

Artman, C. E. and Reed, S. H. Foreign Trade Survey of New England. Bureau of Foreign and Domestic Commerce. Washington, 1931.

Batchelder, Samuel. Introduction and Early Progress of Cotton Manufacture in the United States. Boston, 1863.

Bishop, J. L. History of American Manufactures from 1608 to 1860. Philadelphia, 1861–66.

Burgy, J. H. The New England Cotton Textile Industry: A Study in Industrial Geography. Baltimore, 1932.

Clark, V. S. History of Manufactures in the United States. New York, 1929.

Cole, A. H. The American Wool Manufacture. Cambridge, 1926.

Copeland, M. T. The Cotton Manufacturing Industry of the United States. Cambridge, 1912.

Cunningham, W. J. The Railroads of New England. New England's Prospect: 1933, 344–61.

Dean, Arthur W. The Highways of New England. New England's Prospect: 1933, 362–71.

Dodge, Stanley D. The Geography of the Codfishing Industry in Colonial New England. Bulletin of the Geographical Society of Philadelphia 25, 43–50 (1927).

Gerish, Edward F. Commercial Structure of New England. (Commercial Survey of New England, part 2.) Domestic Commerce Series, no. 26, of the U. S. Department of Commerce. Washington, 1929.

Gerish, Edward F. Market Data Handbook of New England. (Commercial Survey of New England, part 3.) Domestic Commerce Series, no. 24, of the U. S. Department of Commerce. Washington, 1929.

Gerish, E. F. The Trading Areas of New England. New England's Prospect: 1933, 393–404.

Hazard, Blanche E. Organization of the Boot and Shoe Industry in Massachusetts before 1875. Harvard Economic Studies, vol. 23. Cambridge, 1921.

Hulbert, Archer B. Historic Highways of America. Cleveland, 1902–05.

Johnson, E. R., Van Metre, T. W., Huebner, G. G. and Hanchett, D. S. History of Domestic and Foreign Commerce of the United States. Washington, 1915.

Keir, John S. New England's Manufactures. New England's Prospect: 1933, 322–43.

McFarland, Raymond. A History of the New England Fisheries. New York, 1911.

Meyer, B. H. and MacGill, C. E. History of Transportation . . . before 1860. Washington, 1917.

Millard, J. W. Atlas of Wholesale Grocery Territories. Bureau of Foreign and Domestic Commerce. Washington, 1927.

Radcliffe, Lewis and **Fitzgerald, G. A.** The Fisheries of New England. New England's Prospect: 1933, 247–77.

Stewart, P. W. Market Data Handbook of the United States. Bureau of Foreign and Domestic Commerce. Washington, 1929.

Taussig, F. W. The Tariff History of the United States. New York, 1888.

Ware, Caroline F. The Early New England Cotton Manufacture. Boston, 1931.

Weeden, William B. Economic and Social History of New England, 1620–1789. 2 vols. Boston, 1890.

Wood, Frederic J. The Turnpikes of New England. Boston, 1919.

7. *Political History*

Akagi, Roy H. The Town Proprietors of the New England Colonies, 1620–1770. Philadelphia, 1924.

Andrews, C. M. Colonial Self-Government, 1652–1689. New York, 1904.

Bates, F. G. Village Government in New England. American Political Science Review 6, 367–85 (1912).

Channing, Edward. Town and County Government in the English Colonies of North America. Baltimore, 1884.

Ford, Amelia C. Colonial Precedents of our National Land System. Bulletin of the University of Wisconsin, no. 352. Madison, 1910.

Lauer, Paul E. Church and State in New England. Johns Hopkins University Studies in Historical and Political Science. Baltimore, 1892.

MacLear, Anne B. Early New England Towns; a Comparative Study of their Development. New York, 1908.

Munro, William B. The Government of the United States, National, State and Local. 3. ed. New York, 1931.

Parker, Joel. The Origin, Organization and Influence of the Towns of New England. Proceedings of the Massachusetts Historical Society 9, 14–65 (1866–67).

Sly, John F. Town Government in Massachusetts (1620–1930). Cambridge, 1930.

Sly, John F. State and Local Government in New England. New England's Prospect: 1933, 415–30.

Treat, Payson J. The National Land System, 1785–1820. New York, 1910.

8. *Social and Cultural History*

Backus, Isaac. History of New England with particular reference to the Baptists. 3 vols. Newton, Mass., 1784. [Reprint, 1871.]

Benedict, David. A General History of the Baptist Denomination. New York, 1848.

Bridenbaugh, Carl. Cities in the Wilderness: the First Century of Urban Life in America, 1625–1742. New York, 1938.

Brown, Elmer E. The Making of our Middle Schools. New York, 1903.

Crane, E. B. What Our New England Forefathers Had to Read. Proceedings of the Worcester Society of Antiquity 23, 76–103 (1907).

Davis, John Russell. Diary of a Journey through Massachusetts, Vermont and Eastern New York in the Summer of 1800. Vermont Historical Society Proceedings 1919–20, 159–83.

Dexter, Edwin G. A History of Education in the United States. New York, 1904.

Dexter, Franklin B. Early Private Libraries in New England. Proceedings of the American Antiquarian Society, N.S. 18, 135–47 (1907).

Dexter, Franklin B. Influence of the English Universities in the Development of New England. Proceedings of the Massachusetts Historical Society 17, 340–52 (1879–80).

Dorchester, Daniel. Christianity in the United States. New York, 1889.

Eames, Wilberforce. Early New England Catechisms. Proceedings of the American Antiquarian Society, N.S. 12, 76–182 (1897–98).

Eggleston, Edward. The Transit of Civilization from England to America in the Seventeenth Century. New York, 1901.

Felt, Joseph B. Ecclesiastical History of New England. 2 vols. Boston, 1855–62.

Fenn, W. W. The Religious History of New England. King's Chapel Lectures, pp. 77–133. Cambridge, 1917.

Halsey, R. T. H. and **Cornelius, Charles O.** The Metropolitan Museum of Art: A Handbook of the American Wing, 5. ed. New York, 1932.

Hazard, Caroline. The Narragansett Friends' Meeting in the XVIII Century. Boston, 1899.

Hypes, J. L. Social Participation in a Rural New England Town. New York, 1927.

Jernegan, Marcus W. Laboring and Dependent Classes in Colonial America, 1607–1783. Chicago, 1931.

Jones, Howard Mumford. America and French Culture, 1750–1848. Chapel Hill, N. C., 1927.

Meriam, Rufus N. The Early History of Schools and School Books. Collections of the Worcester Society of Antiquity 9, 87–98.

Miller, Perry and **Johnson, Thomas H.** The Puritans. New York, 1938.

Morison, Samuel E. Builders of the Bay Colony. Boston, 1930.

Morison, Samuel E. The Puritan Pronaos. New York, 1936.

Morison, Samuel E. The Founding of Harvard College. Cambridge, 1935.

Morison, Samuel E. Harvard College in the Seventeenth Century. Cambridge, 1936.

Morison, Samuel E., ed. The Development of Harvard University, 1869–1929. Cambridge, 1930.

O'Donnell, James H. History of the Catholic Church in the New England States. Boston, 1899.

Odum, Howard W. Southern Regions of the United States. Chapel Hill, N. C., 1936. [Many maps include New England.]

Odum, Howard W. and Moore, Harry E. American Regionalism: A Cultural-Historical Approach to National Integration. New York, 1938.

Schlesinger, Arthur M. and Fox, Dixon R., edd. A History of American Life. 12 vols. to date. New York, 1927–.

Shelton, Jane DeF. The Salt Box House. New York, 1929.

Shipton, Clifford K. Secondary Education in the Puritan Colonies. The New England Quarterly 7, 646–61 (1934).

Shipton, Clifford K. Literary Leaven in Provincial New England. The New England Quarterly 9, 203–17 (1936).

Shipton, Clifford K. The New England Frontier. The New England Quarterly 10, 25–36 (1937).

Smith, Helen E. Colonial Days and Ways, as Gathered from Family Papers. New York, 1900.

Thwing, Charles F. A History of Higher Education in America. New York, 1906.

Tracy, Joseph. Great Awakening. Boston, 1842.

Trent, William P. and others. The Cambridge History of American Literature. New York and Cambridge, England, 1933.

Woodworth, H. C. The Yankee Community in Rural New England. New England's Prospect: 1933, 178–88.

Wright, Thomas G. Literary Culture in Early New England, 1620–1730. New Haven, 1920.

II. Connecticut

1. *Bibliographies*

Bates, Albert C. Check List of Connecticut Almanacs, 1709–1850. Proceedings of the American Antiquarian Society, N.S. 24, 93–215. Worcester, 1914.

Bates, Albert C. Connecticut Local Histories. Connecticut Historical Society Annual Report, pp. 23–38. 1895.

Bates, Albert C. Report on the Public Archives of Connecticut. Annual Report of the American Historical Association for 1900, vol. 2, 26–36. Washington, 1901.

Connecticut Historical Society. List of Family Genealogies in the Library of the Connecticut Historical Society, corrected to Aug. 31, 1911. Hartford, 1911.

Connecticut, State of. Report of the Temporary Examiner of Public Records. 1904 and 1906.

Flagg, Charles A. Reference List on Connecticut Local History. New York State Library Bulletin 53, 175–283. Albany, 1900.

Godard, G. S. History and Progress of Collecting Material for a Bibliography of Connecticut. Bibliographical Society of America, Proceedings 2, 84–94 (1908).

2. *State and County Histories*

Andrews, Charles M. The River Towns of Connecticut: a Study of Wethersfield, Hartford and Windsor. Johns Hopkins University Studies in Historical and Political Science. Baltimore, 1889.

Andrews, Charles M. Connecticut and the British Government. [First published 1915.] Connecticut Tercentenary Commission, pamphlet 1. New Haven, 1933.

Andrews, Charles M. The Beginnings of Connecticut, 1632–1662. Connecticut Tercentenary Commission, pamphlet 32. New Haven, 1934.

Andrews, Charles M. The Rise and Fall of the New Haven Colony. Connecticut Tercentenary Commission, pamphlet 48. New Haven, 1936.

Barber, J. W. Connecticut Historical Collections. New Haven, 1836.

Bates, Albert C. The Charter of Connecticut. Hartford, 1932.

Bayles, R. M. History of Windham County. New York, 1889.

Burpee, Charles W. History of Hartford County, 1633–1928. 3 vols. Hartford, 1928.

Calder, Isabel MacB. The New Haven Colony. New Haven, 1934.

Clark, George L. History of Connecticut, Its People and Institutions. New York, 1914.

Cole, J. R. History of Tolland County. New York, 1888.

Connecticut, State of. Register and Manual, 1931. Hartford, 1931.

Connecticut. A Guide to its Roads, Lore and People. Federal Writers' Project of the Works Progress Administration for the State of Connecticut. Boston, 1938.

Crofut, Florence S. M. Guide to the History and Historic Sites of Connecticut. 2 vols. New Haven, 1937.

Dakin, W. S. Geography of Connecticut. Boston, [c. 1926].

Deming, Dorothy. The Settlement of the Connecticut Towns. Connecticut Tercentenary Commission, pamphlet 6. New Haven, 1933.

Deming, Dorothy. Settlement of Litchfield County. Connecticut Tercentenary Commission, pamphlet 7. New Haven, 1933.

Harwood, Pliny L. History of Eastern Connecticut, Embracing the Counties of Tolland, Windham, Middlesex and New London. 3 vols. Chicago and New Haven, 1931–32.

Hooker, Roland M. Boundaries of Connecticut. Connecticut Tercentenary Commission, pamphlet 11. New Haven, 1933.

Hurd, D. H. History of Fairfield County. 1881.

Hurd, D. H. History of New London County. Philadelphia, 1882.

Johnston, A. Connecticut: A Study of a Commonwealth-Democracy. New ed. Boston, 1903.

Larned, Ellen D. History of Windham County. 2 vols. Worcester, 1874–80.

Larned, Ellen D. Windham County and Providence. Historic Gleanings in Windham County, Conn., 132–67. Providence, 1899.

Levermore, C. H. The Republic of New Haven; a History of Municipal Evolution. Johns Hopkins University Studies in Historical and Political Science. Baltimore, 1886.

Litchfield County, History of. Philadelphia, 1881.

Mead, N. P. Connecticut as a Corporate Colony. Lancaster, Pa., 1906.

Middlebrook, Louis F. History of Maritime Connecticut during the American Revolution, 1775–1783. 2 vols. Salem, Mass., 1925.

Middlesex County, History of. New York, 1884.

Morgan, Forrest, ed. Connecticut as a Colony and as a State, 4 vols. Hartford, 1904.

Morris, J. Statistical Account of Several Towns in the County of Litchfield. New Haven, 1815.

Morse, Jarvis M. A Neglected Period of Connecticut History: 1818–50. New Haven, 1933.

Morse, Jarvis M. Under the Constitution of 1818: the First Decade. Connecticut Tercentenary Commission, pamphlet 17. New Haven, 1933.

Osborn, N. G., ed. History of Connecticut in Monographic Form. 6 vols. New York, 1925–28.

Pease, J. C. and **Niles, J. M.** Gazetteer of the States of Connecticut and Rhode Island. Hartford, 1819.

Perry, C. E., ed. Founders and Leaders of Connecticut, 1633–1783. Boston, 1934.

Purcell, Richard J. Connecticut in Transition, 1775–1818. Washington, 1918.

Rockey, J. L. History of New Haven County. 2 vols. New York, 1892.

Stiles, H. R. The History of Ancient Wethersfield. 2 vols. New York, 1904.

Tercentenary Commission of the State of Connecticut, Committee on Historical Publications. [Pamphlets by various authors.] New Haven, 1933–.

Trumbull, B. Complete History of Connecticut, Civil and Ecclesiastical, from 1630 to 1764. 2 vols. New Haven, 1818.

Trumbull, J. H. Memorial History of Hartford County. 2 vols. Boston, 1886.

3. *Special Studies*

Archibald, Warren S. Thomas Hooker. Connecticut Tercentenary Commission, pamphlet 4. New Haven, 1933.

Atwater, E. E. History of the City of New Haven to the Present Time. New York, 1887.

Baldwin, Alice M. The Clergy of Connecticut in Revolutionary Days. Connecticut Tercentenary Commission, pamphlet 56. New Haven, 1936.

Beardsley, Eben E. The History of the Episcopal Church in Connecticut. 2 vols. New York, 1865–88.

Bradstreet, Howard. The Story of the War with the Pequots, Re-Told. Connecticut Tercentenary Commission, pamphlet 5. New Haven, 1933.

Breckenridge, Frances A. Recollections of a New England Town. Meriden, 1899.

Chandler, G. B. Industrial History. History of Connecticut, ed. N. G. Osborn, vol. 4, 1–451. New York, 1925.

Cook, Thomas A. Geology of Connecticut. Hartford, 1933.

Coons, Paul W. The Achievement of Religions Liberty in Connecticut. Connecticut Tercentenary Commission, pamphlet 60. New Haven, 1936.

Davis, I. G. and **Hendrickson, C. I.** A Description of Connecticut Agriculture. Agricultural Experiment Station Bulletin no. 127. Storrs, Conn., 1924.

Davis, I. G. and **Waugh, F. V.** Connecticut Market Demand for Vegetables. An Economic Study of the Agriculture of the Connecticut Valley. Agricultural Experiment Station Bulletin no. 138. Storrs, Conn., 1926.

Davis, Samuel. Journal of a Tour to Connecticut, Autumn of 1789. Proceedings of the Massachusetts Historical Society 2, 9–32 (1869–70).

Day, Clive. The Rise of Manufacturing in Connecticut, 1820–50. Connecticut Tercentenary Commission, pamphlet 44. New Haven, 1935.

De Forest, John W. History of the Indians of Connecticut from the Earlier and Known Period to 1850. Hartford, 1853.

Dewey, T. M. Early Navigation of the Connecticut River. Papers and Proceedings of the Connecticut Valley Historical Society 1, 114–22.

Dexter, Franklin B. The History of Connecticut as illustrated by the names of her towns. Proceedings of the American Antiquarian Society, N.S. 3, 421–45 (1884–85).

Dorsey, C. W. and **Bonsteel, J. A.** Soil Survey in the Connecticut Valley. U. S. Department of Agriculture, Field Operations of the Bureau of Soils, pp. 125–40. 1899.

Duggan, Thomas S. The Catholic Church in Connecticut. New York, 1930.

Dutcher, George Matthew. Connecticut's Tercentenary, a Retrospect of Three Centuries of Self-government and Steady Habits. Connecticut Tercentenary Commission, pamphlet 29. New Haven, 1934.

Erving, Henry W. The Connecticut River Banking Company, 1825–1925. Hartford, 1925.

French, Robert D. The Memorial Quadrangle: a Book about Yale. New Haven, 1929.

Fuller, Grace P. An Introduction to the History of Connecticut as a Manufacturing State. Northampton, Mass., 1915.

Gardner, George C. An Architectural Monograph: Massachusetts Bay Influence on Connecticut Valley Colonial. White Pine Series of Architectural Monographs, vol. 11, no. 1. New York, 1925.

Genthe, Martha K. Valley Towns of Connecticut. American Geographical Society Bulletin no. 39, 513–44 (1907).

Hall, Edward A. The Irish Pioneers of the Connecticut Valley. Papers and Proceeding of the Connecticut Valley Historical Society 2, 175–213.

Hendrickson, C. I. A History of Tobacco Production in New England: An Economic Study of the Agriculture of the Connecticut Valley. Agricultural Experiment Station Bulletin no. 174. Storrs, Conn., 1931.

Hobbs, W. H. The River System of Connecticut. Journal of Geology 9, 469–85 (1901).

Hooker, Roland M. The Colonial Trade of Connecticut. Connecticut Tercentenary Commission, pamphlet 50. New Haven, 1936.

Hoopes, Penrose R. Connecticut Clockmakers of the Eighteenth Century. New York, 1930.

Hoopes, Penrose R. Connecticut's Contribution to the Development of the Steamboat. Connecticut Tercentenary Commission, pamphlet 53. New Haven, 1936.

Hypes, J. L. The Future of the Sparsely Populated Rural Towns of Connecticut. Geographical Review 26, 293–8 (1936).

Hypes, J. L. and **Markey, J. F.** The Genesis to Farming Occupations in Connecticut. Agricultural Experiment Station Bulletin no. 161. Storrs, Conn., 1929.

Isham, N. W. and **Brown, A. F.** Early Connecticut Houses. Providence, 1900.

Jacobus, M. W. The Dutchman in Connecticut. Papers and Addresses of the Society of Colonial Wars in the State of Connecticut 2, 133–39 (1910).

Jenkins, E. H. A History of Connecticut Agriculture. New Haven, 1926.

Kelly, J. F. Early Domestic Architecture of Connecticut. New Haven, 1924.

Kelly, J. F. Early Domestic Architecture of Connecticut. Connecticut Tercentenary Commission, pamphlet 12. New Haven, 1933.

Koenig, Samuel. Immigrant Settlements in Connecticut: Their Growth and Characteristics. Federal Writers' Project. Hartford, 1938.

Lathrop, William G. The Development of the Brass Industry in Connecticut. Connecticut Tercentenary Commission, pamphlet 49. New Haven, 1936.

Love, W. DeLoss. The Navigation of the Connecticut River. Proceedings of the American Antiquarian Society, N.S. 15, 385–441 (1902–03).

Maurer, Oscar E. A Puritan Church and its Relation to Community, State and Nation. New Haven, 1938.

McDonald, Adrian F. The History of Tobacco Production in Connecticut. Connecticut Tercentenary Commission, pamphlet 52. New Haven, 1936.

Mitchell, Isabel S. Roads and Road-Making in Colonial Connecticut. Connecticut Tercentenary Commission, pamphlet 14. New Haven, 1933.

Mitchell, Mary H. The Great Awakening and Other Revivals in the Religious Life of Connecticut. Connecticut Tercentenary Commission, pamphlet 26. New Haven, 1934.

Morgan, M. F. The Soils of Connecticut. Agricultural Experiment Station Bulletin no. 320. Storrs, Conn., 1930.

Morrow, R. L. Connecticut Influences in Western Massachusetts and Vermont. Connecticut Tercentenary Commission, pamphlet 58. New Haven, 1936.

Morse, Jarvis M. Connecticut Newspapers in the Eighteenth Century. Connecticut Tercentenary Commission, pamphlet 36. New Haven, 1935.

Morse, Jarvis M. The Rise of Liberalism in Connecticut, 1828–1850. Connecticut Tercentenary Commission, pamphlet 16. New Haven, 1933.

Munich, Austin F. The Beginnings of Roman Catholicism in Connecticut. Connecticut Tercentenary Commission, pamphlet 41. New Haven, 1935.

O'Brien, M. J. Irish Settlers in Connecticut in the 17th and 18th Centuries. Journal of the American Irish Historical Society 24, 125–41 (1925).

Olson, Albert L. Agricultural Economy and the Population in Eighteenth-Century Connecticut. Connecticut Tercentenary Commission, pamphlet 40. New Haven, 1935.

Parsons, Francis. A History of Banking in Connecticut. Connecticut Tercentenary Commission, pamphlet 42. New Haven, 1935.

Peck, Epaphroditus. The Loyalists of Connecticut. Connecticut Tercentenary Commission, pamphlet 31. New Haven, 1934.

Perkins, Mary E. Old Houses of the Ancient Town of Norwich, 1660–1800. Norwich, 1895.

Phelps, Charles S. Rural Life in Litchfield County. Norfolk, Conn., 1917.

Porter, Noah. The New England Meeting House. [First published 1883.] Connecticut Tercentenary Commission, pamphlet 18. New Haven, 1933.

Price, Carl Fowler. Wesleyan's First Century. Middletown, 1932.

Ramsay, Elizabeth. History of Tobacco Production in the Connecticut Valley. Northampton, Mass., 1930.

Rice, W. N. The Physical Geography and Geology of Connecticut. Report of the Connecticut Board of Agriculture, 74–112. 1904.

Rice, W. N. and Gregory, H. E. Manual of the Geology of Connecticut. State Geological and Natural History Survey Bulletin no. 6. Hartford, 1906.

Rosenberry, Lois K. M. Migrations from Connecticut Prior to 1800. Connecticut Tercentenary Commission, pamphlet 28. New Haven, 1934.

Rosenberry, Lois K. M. Migrations from Connecticut after 1800. Connecticut Tercentenary Commission, pamphlet 54. New Haven, 1936.

Seymour, Origen S. The Beginnings of the Episcopal Church in Connecticut. Connecticut Tercentenary Commission, pamphlet 30. New Haven, 1934.

State Highway Department. Forty Years of Highway Development in Connecticut, 1895–1935. Connecticut Tercentenary Commission, pamphlet 46. New Haven, 1935.

Steiner, Bernard C. History of Education in Connecticut. Washington (Gov't. Printing Office), 1893.

Tercentenary Commission. Three Centuries of Connecticut Furniture, 1635–1935. Hartford, 1935.

Trowbridge, B. C. Old Houses of Connecticut. New Haven, 1923.

Tyler, Clarice E. Topographical Terms in the 17th Century Records of Connecticut and Rhode Island. The New England Quarterly 2, 382–401 (1929).

Waugh, F. V. Production, Supply and Consumption of Connecticut Valley Tobacco. An Economic Study of the Agriculture of the Conn. Valley. Agricultural Experiment Station Bulletin no. 134. Storrs, Conn., 1925.

Welch, Archibald A. A History of Insurance in Connecticut. Connecticut Tercentenary Commission, pamphlet 43. New Haven, 1935.

Wheeler, Grace D. The Homes of Our Ancestors in Stonington, Conn. 1903.

Withington, Sidney. The First Twenty Years of Railroads in Connecticut. Connecticut Tercentenary Commission, pamphlet 45. New Haven, 1935.

Wright, George Edward. Crossing the Connecticut; an account of the various public crossings of the Connecticut River at Hartford since the earliest times. Hartford, 1908.

Zeichner, Oscar. The Rehabilitation of Loyalists in Connecticut. The New England Quarterly 11, 308–30 (1938).

III. MAINE

1. *Bibliographies*

Boardman, Samuel L. Agricultural Bibliography of Maine. Augusta, 1893. [Prepared under the direction of the Maine Board of Agriculture.]

Hall, Drew B. Bibliography of Maine Local History. New York State Library Bulletin 63. Albany, 1901.

Huston, Almer J., comp. A Check List of Maine Local Histories. Portland, 1915.

Maine, State Library. Sources for a Maritime History of Maine. Maine Library Bulletin 17, 34–40 (1931).

University of Maine, Department of History. A Reference List of Manuscripts Relating to the History of Maine. MS. Orono, 1935.

Williamson, Joseph. A Bibliography of the State of Maine from the Earliest Period to 1891. Portland, 1896.

2. *State and County Histories*

Abbott, J. S. C. History of Maine. Augusta, 1892.

Aldrich, P. Emory. Massachusetts and Maine, their Union and Separation. Proceedings of the American Antiquarian Society 71, 43–64 (1878).

Burrage, Henry S. Beginnings of Colonial Maine. Portland, 1914.

Clayton, W. W. History of Cumberland County. Philadelphia, 1880.

Clayton, W. W. History of York County. Philadelphia, 1880.

Coe, Harrie B., ed. Maine: Resources, Attractions and Its People. 5 vols. New York, 1928–31.

Colby, G. N., & Co., publ. Atlas of the State of Maine Including Statistics and Descriptions. 2. ed. New York, [c. 1890]. (Cover title: Stuart's Atlas of Maine.)

Danforth, Thomas. Maine Province. Publications of the Colonial Society of Massachusetts 10, 108–14.

Elkins, L. Whitney. The Story of Maine: Coastal Maine. Bangor, 1924.

Greenleaf, Moses. A Survey of the State of Maine. Portland, 1829.

Hatch, Louis C., ed. Maine: A History. 5 vols. New York, 1919.

Kingsbury, H. D. and Deyo, S. L. Illustrated History of Kennebec County. 2 vols. New York, 1892.

Lincoln, Hon. General. Eastern Counties in the District of Maine. Massachusetts Historical Collections, vol. 4. 1789.

Loring, Amasa. History of Piscataquis County, Maine, from its Earliest Settlement to 1880. Portland, 1880.

Maine. A Guide 'Down East.' Federal Writers' Project of the Works Progress Administration for the State of Maine. Boston, 1937.

Maine Historical Society. Documentary History of the State of Maine. 24 vols. Portland, 1869–1916.

Maine Register, State Year-book and Legislative Manual. Published annually. Portland.

Merrill, G. D. History of Androscoggin County. Boston, 1891.

Moulton, Augustus F. Maine Historical Sketches. Lewiston, 1929.

North, J. W. History of Augusta from the Earliest Settlement to the Present Time. Augusta, 1807.

Penobscot County, History of. Cleveland, 1882.

Sewall, Rufus K. Ancient Dominions of Maine. Bath, 1859.

Starkey, Glenn W. Maine: Its History, Resources and Government. Boston, 1930.

Stetson, W. W. History and Civil Government of Maine. Chicago, 1898.

Varney, George J. Gazetteer of Maine. Boston, 1881.

Wiggin, Edward. History of Aroostook. Presque Isle, Maine, [1922].

Williamson, William D. The History of the State of Maine. 2 vols. Hallowell, 1839.

3. *Special Studies*

Bangor Historical Magazine. List of Early Maine Settlers. Vol. 1, 97.

Boardman, S. L. Agricultural Survey of Somerset County, Maine. Augusta, 1860.

Burrage, Henry S. History of the Baptists in Maine. Portland, 1904.

Chadbourne, Ava H. Beginnings of Education in Maine. New York, 1928.

Chadbourne, Ava H., comp. Readings in the History of Education in Maine. Bangor, 1932.

Chadbourne, Walter W. A History of Banking in Maine, 1799–1930. Orono, 1936.

Chase, Edward E. Maine Railroads: A History of the Development of the Railroad System. Portland, 1926.

Clark, Calvin M. History of the Congregational Churches in Maine. 2 vols. Portland, 1926.

Coffin, Robert P. Tristram. Kennebec: Cradle of Americans. New York, 1937.

Coffin, Robert P. Tristram. Lost Paradise: A Boyhood on a Maine Coast Farm. New York, 1934.

Dunnack, Henry E. Rural Life in Maine. Augusta, 1928.

Eckstorm, Fannie H., ed. Minstrelsy of Maine: Folk-Songs and Ballads of the Woods and the Coast. Boston, 1927.

Fassett, Frederick G., Jr. A History of Newspapers in the District of Maine, 1785–1820. Orono, 1932.

Greenleaf, Jonathan. Sketches of the Ecclesiastical History of the State of Maine. Portsmouth, 1821.

Griffin, Joseph. History of the Press of Maine. Brunswick, 1872.

Hormell, Orren C. Maine Towns. Brunswick, 1932.

Kidder, Frederic. The Expeditions of Captain John Lovewell. Boston, 1865.

Lawton, R. J., comp. Franco-Americans of the State of Maine. Lewiston, 1915.

Little, George T., comp. Genealogical and Family History of the State of Maine. New York, 1909.

Loomis, Charles D. Port Towns of Penobscot Bay. White Pine Series of Architectural Monographs. Saint Paul, 1922.

Maine, Survey of Higher Education. By the University of Maine, in coöperation with Bates, Bowdoin and Colby Colleges. Orono, 1931.

Packard, L. I. The Decrease of Population along the Maine Coast. Geographical Review 2, 334–41 (1916).

Parker, Arlita Dodge. A History of Pemaquid, with Sketches of Monhegan, Popham and Castine. Boston, 1925.

Ridlon, Gideon T. Saco Valley Settlements and Families; Historical, Biographical, Genealogical, Traditional and Legendary. Portland, 1895.

Rowe, William H. Shipbuilding Days in Casco Bay, 1727–1890. Yarmouth, 1929.

Spencer, Wilbur D. Pioneers on Maine Rivers. Portland, 1930.

Stetson, William W. Study of the History of Education in Maine and the Evolution of Our Present School System. Augusta, 1901.

Sylvester, Herbert M. Maine Pioneer Settlements. 5 vols. Boston, 1909.

Thomas, W. W., Jr. The Story of New Sweden. Maine Historical Society Collections, ser. 2, vol. 7, 53–85, 113–51 (1896).

Thompson, Garrett W. The Germans in Maine.

Sprague's Journal of Maine History, vol. 5, 3–4, 140–46 (1917).

Thoreau, Henry D. The Maine Woods. Boston, 1864.

Toppan, Frederick W. Geology of Maine. Schenectady, 1932.

Walker, C. Howard. Some Old Houses on the Southern Coast of Maine. White Pine Series of Architectural Monographs. Saint Paul, 1918.

Wasson, George S. Sailing Days on the Penobscot: The River and Bay as they were in the Old Days. Salem, 1932.

Williamson, J. General Samuel Waldo. Collections of the Maine Historical Society 9, 75–93 (1887).

Willis, W. The Scotch-Irish Immigration to Maine. Collections of the Maine Historical Society 6, 1–37 (1859).

Wilson, E. M. The Aroostook Valley: A Study in Potatoes. Geographical Review 16, 196–205 (1926).

Wood, Ethel M. The Maine Indians and their Relations with the White Settlers. Sprague's Journal of Maine History, vol. 10, 6–17 (1922).

Wood, Richard G. A History of Lumbering in Maine, 1820–1861. Orono, 1935.

IV. MASSACHUSETTS

1. *Bibliographies*

Boston Public Library. A Finding List of Genealogies and Town and Local Histories Containing Family Records. Boston, 1900.

Colburn, Jeremiah. Bibliography of the Local History of Massachusetts. Boston, 1871.

Davis, A. M. Report on the Public Archives of Massachusetts. Annual Report of the American Historical Association for 1900, vol. 2, 47–59. Washington, 1901.

Flagg, Charles A. A Guide to Massachusetts Local History. Salem, 1907.

Hart, Albert Bushnell, ed. Commonwealth History of Massachusetts. 5 vols. New York, 1930.

Kittredge, H. C. Cape Cod; its People and their History. Boston and N. Y., 1930.

Massachusetts, Commonwealth of. (Department of Labor and Industries.) Population and Resources of Cape Cod. 1912. [Bibliography, 106–21.]

Wright, C. D. Report on the Custody and Condition of the Public Records of Parishes, Towns and Counties. 1889.

2. *State and County Histories*

Adams, Charles Francis, Jr. Massachusetts: its Historians and its History. Boston, 1893.

Baylies, Francis. An Historical Memoir of the Colony of New Plymouth. 2 vols. Boston, 1830.

Child, H. Gazetteer of Berkshire County, 1725–1885. Syracuse, N. Y., 1885.

Clark, Arthur H. The Clipper Ship Era. New York, 1911.

Copeland, A. M. Our County and its People: A History of Hampden County. 3 vols. Boston, 1902.

Daniel, Hawthorne. The Clipper Ship. New York, 1928.

Deyo, S. L. History of Barnstable County. New York, 1890.

Drake, S. A. History of Middlesex County, Mass. 2 vols. Boston, 1880.

Durant, S. W. History of Franklin County. History of the Connecticut Valley in Massachusetts 2, 565–77 (1879).

Durant, S. W. History of Hampden County. History of the Connecticut Valley in Massachusetts 2, 794–813 (1879).

Field, D. D. A History of the County of Berkshire. Pittsfield, 1829.

Freeman, F. The History of Cape Cod. 2 vols. Boston, 1860–62.

Hart, Albert B., ed. Commonwealth History of Massachusetts. 5 vols. New York, 1930.

Holland, Josiah G. History of Western Massachusetts. 2 vols. Springfield, 1855.

Hurd, D. H. History of Bristol County. Philadelphia, 1883.

Hurd, D. H. History of Essex County, Mass. 2 vols. Philadelphia, 1888.

Hurd, D. H. History of Middlesex County, Mass. 3 vols. Philadelphia, 1890.

Hurd, D. H. History of Norfolk County, Mass. Philadelphia, 1884.

Hurd, D. H. History of Plymouth County. Philadelphia, 1884.

Lincoln, W. and **Baldwin, C. C.** History of the County of Worcester. The Worcester Magazine and Historical Journal, vols. 1, 2. Worcester, 1926.

Mack, H. History of Hampshire County. History of the Connecticut Valley in Massachusetts 1, 163–72. 1879.

Massachusetts. A Guide to its Places and People. Federal Writers' Project of the Works Progress Administration for the State of Massachusetts. Boston, 1937.

Massachusetts, Commonwealth of. (Division of Public Records.) Historical Data relating to Counties, Cities and Towns in Massachusetts. Boston, 1920.

Morison, S. E. The Maritime History of Massachusetts. Boston and N. Y., 1921.

Whitney, P. The History of the County of Worcester. Worcester, 1793.

3. *Special Studies*

Adams, Charles F. The Genesis of the Massachusetts Town. Proceedings of the Massachusetts Historical Society, 2. ser., vol. 7, 172–263 (1891–92).

Adams, Henry. The Education of Henry Adams. Boston, 1930.

Alden, W. C. The Physical Features of Central Massachusetts. U. S. Geological Survey Bulletin no. 760 B. 1924.

Baldwin, S. E. The Secession of Springfield from Boston. Publications of the Colonial Society of Massachusetts 12, 54–82 (1908–09).

Banks, Charles E. The English Ancestry and Homes of the Pilgrim Fathers. New York, 1929.

Banks, Charles E. The Planters of the Commonwealth. Boston, 1930.

Banks, Charles E. The Winthrop Fleet of 1630. Boston, 1930.

Bliss, W. R. Colonial Times on Buzzard's Bay. Boston and N. Y., 1888.

Brigham, A. P. Cape Cod and the Old Colony. New York, 1920.

Chase, L. B. The Bay Path and Along the Way. Norwood, Mass., 1919.

Colman, Henry. Second Report on the Agriculture of Massachusetts. The County of Berkshire. 1839.

Colman, H. Fourth Report on the Agriculture of Massachusetts. The Counties of Franklin and Middlesex. 1841.

Cousins, Frank and **Riley, P. M.** Colonial Architecture of Salem. Boston, 1919.

Currier, F. A. Stage Coach Days and Stage Coach Ways. Proceedings of the Fitchburg Historical Society 2, 126–92 (1894–97).

Dixon, R. B. Population and Environment in Western Massachusetts. Bulletin of the American Geographical Society 31, 60–63, 180–82 (1899).

Edwards, Agnes. The Old Coast Road from Boston to Plymouth. Boston and New York, 1920.

Felt, J. B. Statistics of Population in Massachusetts. Collections of the American Statistical Association, 1, 121–214 (1847).

Fiske, W. The Bay Path. Medford Historical Register 30, 25–31 (1927).

Folsom, Josiah G. Farm Life in Massachusetts. U. S. Department of Agriculture Bulletin no. 1220. 1921.

Hall, H. B. A Description of Rural Life and Labor in Massachusetts at Four Periods. Thesis, Harvard, 1918.

Harding, W. G. Glass Manufacture in Berkshire. Collections of the Berkshire Historical and Scientific Society, vol. 2, part 1, 29–44 (1894).

Hyde, A. Social Life and Customs of the Early Citizens of Berkshire. Collections of the Berkshire Historical and Scientific Society, vol. 3, part 1, 27–49 (1899).

Keir, R. M. Some Responses to Environment in Massachusetts. Bulletin of the Geographical Society of Philadelphia 15, 121–38, 167–85 (1917).

Kittredge, George Lyman. The Old Farmer and His Almanack. Boston, 1904.

Latimer, W. J., Martin, R. F. R. and **Lanphear, M. O.** Soil Survey of Norfolk, Bristol and Barnstable Counties, Massachusetts. U. S. Department of Agriculture, Field Operations of the Bureau of Soils, 1911, pp. 31–67. Worcester County, 1922, pp. 1531–94.

Lockwood, John H., ed. Western Massachusetts, 1636–1925: A History. 4 vols. New York, 1926.

Long, Henry F. The Salt Marshes of the Massachusetts Coast. Topsfield Historical Society Collections, 15, 105–23 (1910).

Martin, George H. The Evolution of the Massachusetts Public School System: A Historical Sketch. New York, 1915.

Massachusetts. (Bureau of Statistics of Labor.) Census of the Commonwealth of Massachusetts, 1905. 4 vols. Boston, 1908–10. [Population by towns since 1765: vol. 1, 803–902.]

Massachusetts. (Bureau of Statistics of Labor.) Twenty-Seventh Annual Report, 1–104. 1896.

Massachusetts. (Department of Labor and Industries.) Population and Resources of Cape Cod. Boston, 1922.

McLendon, W. E. and **Jones, G. B.** Soil Survey of Plymouth County, Massachusetts. U. S. Department of Agriculture, Field Operations of the Bureau of Soils, 1911, pp. 31–67.

Morison, Samuel E. Three Centuries of Harvard. Cambridge, 1936.

Park, Charles E. Friendship as a Factor in the Settlement of Massachusetts. Proceedings of the American Antiquarian Society, N.S. 28, 51–64 (1918).

Parker, S. B. History of the Episcopal Church in Berkshire County. Collections of the Berkshire Historical and Scientific Society, vol. 2, part 2, 81–92 (1895).

Perry, J. H. The Physical Geography of Worcester, Mass. Worcester, 1898.

Pope, F. L. The Western Boundary of Massachusetts, a Study of Indian and Colonial History. Collections of the Berkshire Historical and Scientific Society, vol. 1, 27–85 (1886).

Ramsay, Elizabeth. History of Tobacco Production in the Connecticut Valley. (Smith College Studies in History, vol. 15, nos. 3 and 4.) Northampton, 1930.

Rand, E. K. Plymouth Plantation and the Golden Age. Publications of the Colonial Society of Mass. 24, 182–96 (1920–22).

Russell, C. T. Agricultural Progress in Massachusetts for the Last Half Century. Boston, 1850.

Sly, John F. Town Government in Massachusetts (1620–1930). Cambridge, 1930.

Towns in Massachusetts, On the Origin of the Names of. Proceedings of the Massachusetts Historical Society 12, 393–419 (1871–73).

Usher, Roland G. The Pilgrims and Their History. New York, 1918.

Waldin, H. G. Growth of Cities in Massachusetts from 1790. American Statistical Association, N.S. 2, March 1891.

Weston, B. History of Paper Making in Berkshire County. Collections of the Berkshire Historical and Scientific Society, vol. 2, part 2, 3–23 (1895).

Wright, T. G. Literary Culture in Early New England, 1620–1730. New Haven, 1920.

V. New Hampshire

1. *Bibliographies*

Dover Public Library. A List of Books and Pamphlets in the Dover Public Library Relating to New Hampshire. Dover, 1903.

Hammond, Otis G. Checklist of New Hampshire Local History. Publication of the New Hampshire Historical Society. Concord, 1925.

2. *State and County Histories*

Belknap, Jeremy. History of New Hampshire. 3 vols. Dover, 1812.

Child, Hamilton. Gazetteer of Cheshire County, New Hampshire. Syracuse, 1885.

Child, Hamilton. Gazetteer of Grafton County, New Hampshire. Syracuse, 1886.

Coos County, History of. Syracuse, 1888.

Fogg, Alonzo J., comp. Statistics and Gazetteer of New Hampshire. Concord, 1874.

Hammond, I. W., ed. New Hampshire Town Papers, Documents Relating to Towns in New Hampshire. Concord, 1882–84.

Hazlett, Charles. History of Rockingham County, New Hampshire. Chicago, 1915.

Hurd, D. H. History of Hillsborough County, New Hampshire. Philadelphia, 1885.

Hurd, D. H. History of Merrimack and Belknap Counties, New Hampshire. Philadelphia, 1885.

Hurd, D. H. History of Rockingham and Strafford Counties, New Hampshire. Philadelphia, 1882.

Hurd, D. H. History of Cheshire and Sullivan Counties, New Hampshire. Philadelphia, 1886.

McClintock, John N. History of New Hampshire. Boston, 1888.

Meader, J. W. The Merrimack River: its Source and its Tributaries. Boston, 1869.

Merrill, Georgia D., ed. History of Carroll County, New Hampshire. Boston, 1889.

New Hampshire. A Guide to the Granite State. Federal Writers' Project of the Works Progress Administration for the State of New Hampshire. Boston, 1938.

New Hampshire. Manual for the General Court, no. 15. Department of State, Concord, 1917.

Powers, Grant. Historical Sketches of the Discovery, Settlement and Progress of Events in the Coos Country and Vicinity. Haverhill, 1880.

Rice, J. L. Dartmouth College and the State of

New Connecticut. Papers and Proceedings of the Connecticut Valley Historical Society 1, 152–206.

Rice, J. L. The New Hampshire Grants. Magazine of American History 8, 1–23 (1882).

Sanborn, Edwin D. History of New Hampshire. Manchester, 1875.

Sanborn, Frank P. The Indian Wars in New Hampshire. Manchester Historical Association Collections, vol. 4, pt. 1, 23–34 (1908).

Sanborn, Franklin B. New Hampshire, an Epitome of Popular Government. Cambridge, 1904.

Scales, John, ed. History of Strafford County, New Hampshire, and its Representative Citizens. Chicago 1914.

Stackpole, E. S. History of New Hampshire. 5 vols. New York, 1917.

Upton, Richard F. Revolutionary New Hampshire: An Account of the Social and Political Forces Underlying the Transition from Royal Province to American Commonwealth. Hanover, 1936.

3. *Special Studies*

Abram, English B. The Story of a Lost Town. New England Magazine, August 1901.

Bush, George G. History of Education in New Hampshire. Washington, 1898.

Census Statistics of Towns from 1767 to 1880. Eleventh Annual Report of the Board of Agriculture of New Hampshire, 111–42 (1881).

Conrig, Allyn A. The Birth-Rate in New Hampshire. American Statistical Association Bulletin no. 71. September 1905.

Dodge, Stanley D. A Study of the Population of Vermont and New Hampshire. Papers of the Michi-

can Academy of Science, Arts and Letters 18, 131–36 (1932).

Fassett, James H. Colonial Life in New Hampshire. Boston, 1899.

Fry, W. H. New Hampshire as a Royal Province. New York, 1908.

Hammond, O. G. The Mason Title and its Relations to New Hampshire and Massachusetts. Proceedings of the American Antiquarian Society, N.S. 26, 245–63 (1916).

Harriman, W. The Boundaries of New Hampshire. Eleventh Annual Report of the Board of Agriculture of New Hampshire, 111–42 (1881).

Harrison, J. B. The Abandoned Farms of New Hampshire. The Granite Monthly 13, 153–56 (1890).

Hazen, H. A. New Hampshire and Vermont: an Historical Study. Proceedings of the New Hampshire Historical Society 2, 265–77 (1895).

Love, W. D. The Navigation of the Connecticut River. Proceedings of the American Antiquarian Society, N.S. 15, 385–441 (1902–03).

Pope, Charles H. Pioneers of Maine and New Hampshire, 1623 to 1660. Boston, 1908.

Sheldon, G. Old-time Traffic and Travel on the Connecticut. History and Proceedings of the Pocumtuck Valley Memorial Association 3, 117–29 (1901).

Stearns, Ezra S., ed. Genealogical and Family History of the State of New Hampshire. 4 vols. New York, 1908.

Upham, G. B. The Great Road to the North through the Upper Connecticut Valley. The Granite Monthly 52, 50–56 (1920).

Walker, J. B. The Valley of the Merrimack. New Hampshire Historical Collections 7, 414–32 (1863).

VI. RHODE ISLAND

1. *Bibliographies*

Bartlett, John Russell. Bibliography of Rhode Island. Providence, 1864.

Brigham, Clarence S. Bibliography of Rhode Island History, in **Field, Edward.** State of Rhode Island and Providence Plantations, vol. 3. Boston, 1902.

Chapin, Howard M. Check List of Rhode Island Almanacs, 1643–1850. Proceedings of the American Antiquarian Society 25, 19–54 (1915).

Town Records of Rhode Island. Publications of the Rhode Island Historical Society, vol. 1, no. 2 (July 1893), 101–82. [A descriptive list of manuscripts in town archives.]

2. *State and County Histories*

Arnold, Samuel Greene. History of the State of

Rhode Island and Providence Plantations [to 1790.] 2 vols. New York, 1859–60.

Bartlett, John Russell. Records of the Colony of Rhode Island and Providence Plantations [1636–1792]. 10 vols. Providence, 1856–65.

Bayles, R. M. History of Providence County. 2 vols. 1891.

Bayles, R. M. History of Newport County, 1638–1887. 1888.

Cady, J. H. Rhode Island Boundaries, 1636–1936. R. I. State Planning Board Report 7, 1936.

Carroll, Charles. Rhode Island, Three Centuries of Democracy. 4 vols. New York, 1932.

Cole, J. R. History of Washington and Kent Counties. 1889.

Field, Edward. State of Rhode Island and Providence Plantations at the End of the Century: a History. 3 vols. Boston, 1902.

Kimball, Gertrude S. Providence in Colonial Times. Boston, 1912.

Pease, J. C. and **Niles, J. M.** Gazetteer of the States of Connecticut and Rhode Island. Hartford, 1819.

Perry, A., ed. Rhode Island State Census, 1885. Providence, 1887.

Rhode Island. A Guide to the Smallest State. Federal Writers' Project of the Works Progress Administration for the State of Rhode Island. Boston, 1937.

Richmond, I. B. Rhode Island, its Making and its Meaning. 2 vols. New York, 1902.

Weeden, W. B. Early Rhode Island: A Social History of the People. New York, 1910.

3. *Special Studies*

Bicknell, T. W. The Narragansett Trail. Americana 17, 40–63 (1923).

Bonsteel, F. E. and **Carr, E. P.** Soil Survey of Rhode Island. Washington (Government Printing Office), 1905.

Bridenbaugh, Carl. Colonial Newport as a Summer Resort. R. I. Hist. Soc. Coll. 26, 1–23 (1933).

Bronson, Walter C. The History of Brown University, 1764–1914. Providence, 1914.

Brown, N. M. Home Introduction to Regional Geography: Rhode Island. Journal of Geography 22, 41–54 (1921).

Carpenter, Esther B. South County Neighbors. Boston, [1887].

Carroll, Charles. Public Education in Rhode Island. Rhode Island Education Circulars, 1918. [Bibliography, 491–94.]

Channing, Edward. The Narragansett Planters. Johns Hopkins University Studies in Historical and Political Science. Series IV, 105–27. Baltimore, 1886.

Corbett, R. B. Rhode Island Agriculture, a Statistical Description. Bulletin of the Agricultural Experiment Station of Rhode Island State College, no. 206. 1926.

Cullen, Thomas F. The Catholic Church in Rhode Island. North Providence, 1936.

Dale, T. N. Geology of Rhode Island. American Journal of Science 127, 217–28, 282–91 (1884).

Denison, Frederic. The Israelites in Rhode Island. The Narragansett Historical Register 4, 300–27 (1885–86).

Dorr, Henry C. The Narragansetts. Rhode Island Historical Society Collections, vol. 7. Providence, 1885.

Dorr, Henry C. The Planting and Growth of Providence. Rhode Island Historical Tracts, no. 15. Providence, 1882.

Downing, Antoinette. Early Homes in Rhode Island. Richmond, Va., 1936.

Earle, Alice M. In Old Narragansett. New York, 1898.

Foster, W. E. Some Rhode Island Contributions to the Intellectual Life of the Last Century. Proceedings of the American Antiquarian Society, N.S. 8, 103–32 (1892–93).

Haley, John W. The Lower Blackstone River Valley, . . . an Historical Narrative. Pawtucket, 1936.

Hartwell, B. L. and **Smith, J. B.** Concerning Rhode Island Soils in Different Parts of the State. Bulletin of the Agricultural Experiment Station of Rhode Island State College, no. 214. June 1928.

Hazard, Caroline. The Narragansett Friends' Meeting in the 18th Century. Boston, 1899.

Hazard, Caroline. Thomas Hazard . . . Call'd College Tom: A Study of Life in Narragansett in the 18th Century. Boston, 1893.

Hazard, Thomas Robinson. The Johnny-Cake Papers of 'Shepherd Tom.' Boston, 1915.

Hoyt, D. W. The Influence of Physical Features upon the History of Rhode Island. Rhode Island Education Circulars, Historical Series, no. 4 (1918).

Isham, Norman M. Providence and Its Colonial Houses. White Pine Series of Architectural Monographs, vol. 4, no. 3 (1918).

Isham, Norman M. and **Brown, Albert F.** Early Rhode Island Houses. Providence, 1895.

Jackson, E. P. Early Uses of Land in Rhode Island. Bulletin of the Geographical Society of Philadelphia 24, 69–87 (1926).

Johnston, W. D. Slavery in Rhode Island, 1755–1776. Publications of the Rhode Island Historical Society, vol. 2, no. 2, 109–64 (1894).

Miller, William Davis. The Narragansett Planters. Reprinted from American Antiquarian Society Proceedings. Worcester, 1934.

National Society of Colonial Dames in the State of Rhode Island. Old Houses in the South County of Rhode Island. Boston, 1932.

Phelps, H. A. Significance of the Economic Classes in Rhode Island. The Journal of Social Forces 4, 620–25 (1926).

Potter, E. R. Memoir Concerning the French Settlements and French Settlers in the Colony of Rhode Island. Rhode Island Historical Tracts, no. 5 (1879).

Rhode Island Bureau of Industrial Statistics. The Foreign-born Population. 21st Annual Report, 1–199 (1907).

Rhode Island Bureau of Industrial Statistics. Race Factors. 23rd Annual Report, part 5, 219–423 (1909).

Rhode Island, State Department of Agriculture and Conservation. First Annual Report. Providence, 1935.

Rhode Island, State Department of Labor. Rhode Island Commercial Fisheries, Special Report no. 6. Rhode Island Population Trends, Special Report no. 8. Rhode Island Water Resources, Special Report no. 9. 1936.

Shaler, N. S. Geology of Narragansett Bay. American Naturalist 6, 518–28, 611–21, 751–60 (1872).

Shippee, L. B. Some Aspects of the Population of Providence. Report of the Commissioner of Labor, 1916–19, pp. 207–84.

Stockwell, T. B., ed. A History of Public Education in Rhode Island from 1636 to 1876. Providence, 1876.

Tolman, William Howe. History of Higher Education in Rhode Island. Washington, 1894.

Updike, Wilkins. History of the Episcopal Church in Narragansett, R. I. New York, 1847. 2. ed., Boston, 1907.

Weeden, W. B. Early Oriental Commerce in Providence. Proceedings of the Massachusetts Historical Society, 3. ser., vol. 1, 236–78 (1907–08).

White, George Savage. Memoir of Samuel Slater. Philadelphia, 1836.

VII. Vermont

1. *Bibliographies*

Gilman, M. D. Bibliography of Vermont. Burlington, 1897.

Vermont. A Guide to the Green Mountain State. Federal Writers' Project of the Works Progress Administration for the State of Vermont. Boston, 1937.

2. *State and County Histories*

Aldrich, L. C., ed. History of Franklin and Grand Isle Counties, Vermont. Syracuse, 1891.

Aldrich, L. C. and **Holmes, F. R., eds.** History of Windsor County, Vermont. Syracuse, 1891.

Child, H. Gazetteer and Business Directory of Addison County, Vermont. Syracuse, 1882.

Child, H. Gazetteer and Business Directory of Bennington County. Syracuse, 1882.

Child, H. Gazetteer of Caledonia and Essex Counties. Syracuse, 1887.

Child, H. Gazetteer and Business Directory of Chittenden Co. Syracuse, 1882.

Child, H. Gazetteer and Business Directory of Franklin and Grand Isle Counties. Syracuse, 1883.

Child, H. Gazetteer and Business Directory of Lamoille and Orleans Counties. Syracuse, 1883.

Child, H. Gazetteer of Orange County. Syracuse, 1888.

Child, H. Gazetteer and Business Directory of Rutland County for 1881–82. Syracuse, 1882.

Child, H. Gazetteer of Washington County. Syracuse, 1889.

Child, H. Gazetteer and Business Directory of Windham County, 1724–1884. Syracuse, 1884.

Child, H. Gazetteer and Business Directory of Windsor County. Syracuse, 1884.

Crockett, Walter H. History of Vermont. 5 vols. New York, 1921.

Crockett, Walter H. A History of Lake Champlain, 1609–1936. Burlington, 1937.

Denio, Herbert W. Massachusetts Land Grants in Vermont. Publications of the Colonial Society of Massachusetts 24, 35–59 (1920–22).

Hall, Benjamin. History of Eastern Vermont. New York, 1858.

Hall, S. R. The Geography and History of Vermont. Montpelier, 1874.

Hemenway, Abby M., comp. Vermont Historical Gazetteer. 5 vols. Burlington, 1867–90.

Orleans County. The History of Orleans County, Vt. White River Junction, 1882.

Perkins, Nathan. A Narrative of a Tour through the State of Vermont from April 27 to June 12, 1789. Woodstock, Vt., 1920.

Rann, W. S. History of Chittenden County, Vt. Syracuse, 1886.

Redington, Lyman W., comp. Rutland County Centennial Celebration, March 4, 1881. Montpelier, 1882.

Rutland County. Civil, Ecclesiastical, Biographical, Military. White River Junction, 1882.

Smith, H. P. History of Addison County, Vt. Syracuse, 1886.

Smith, H. P. and **Rann, W. S., edd.** History of Rutland County, Vt. Syracuse, 1886.

Thompson, Zadock. History of Vermont, Natural, Civil and Statistical. Burlington, 1853.

Wardner, Henry S. The Birthplace of Vermont: a History of Windsor to 1781. New York, 1927.

Williams, Samuel. The Natural and Civil History of Vermont. Burlington, 1809.

3. *Special Studies*

Andrews, Edward D. The County Grammar Schools and Academies of Vermont. Proceedings of the Vermont Historical Society, vol. 4, no. 3 (1936).

Crane, Charles E. Let Me Show You Vermont. New York, 1937.

Dodge, Stanley D. A Study of the Population of Vermont and New Hampshire. Papers of the Michigan Academy of Science, Arts and Letters 18, 131–36 (1932).

Dodge, Stanley D. The Vermont Valley: a Chorographical Study. Papers of the Michigan Academy of Science, Arts and Letters 16, 241–74 (1931).

Goodrich, J. E. Immigration to Vermont. Proceedings of the Vermont Historical Society, pp. 65–86 (1908–09).

Hayes, Lyman S. The Connecticut River Valley in Southern Vermont and New Hampshire. Rutland, 1929.

Horton, Guy B. History of the Grange in Vermont. 1926.

Lamson, G. Geographic Influences in the Early History of Vermont. Proceedings of the Vermont Historical Society, 1921–23, 74–138.

Lee, W. Storrs. Father Went to College. New York, 1936.

Mackintosh, W. A. Canada and Vermont: A Study in Historical Geography. Canadian Historical Review 8, 9–30 (1927).

Perkins, G. H. Physiography of Vermont. Report of the State Geologist 17, 1–54 (1929–30).

Robinson, Rowland E. Writings, centennial edition. 7 vols. Rutland, 1934.

Rossiter, W. S. Vermont, an Historical and Statistical Study of the Progress of the State. Quarterly Publications of the American Statistical Association, 12, 387–454 (1911).

Stilwell, Lewis D. Migration from Vermont, 1776–1860. Proceedings of the Vermont Historical Society, N.S. 5, 63–245 (1937).

Stone, Mason S. History of Education, State of Vermont. Montpelier, 1934.

Thompson, F. M. Vermont from Chaos to Statehood; New Hampshire Grants and Connecticut Equivalent Lands. Pocumtuck Valley Memorial Association Proceedings 6, 231–71 (1921).

Vermont Commission on Country Life. Rural Vermont: A Program for the Future. Burlington, 1931.

Vermont, Industrial Survey of the State of. Summary Report, 1930.

Vermont State Planning Board. Progress Report. Montpelier, 1936.

Wells, G. F. The Status of Rural Vermont. Twenty-third Vermont Agricultural Report, 61–109 (1903).

Wilbur, J. B. The making of the Republic of Vermont, the Fourteenth State. Proceedings of the American Antiquarian Society, N.S. 31, 359–76 (1921).

Chapter IV

THE PHONETIC ALPHABET
AND OTHER SYMBOLS USED ON THE MAPS

Introductory

1. In transcribing the responses of their informants, the field workers of the Linguistic Atlas used a finely graded phonetic alphabet based on that of the International Phonetic Association (IPA). The use of this alphabet is founded on the assumption that every configuration of the vocal organs produces a characteristic sound, and that every sound is determined by a characteristic configuration of the organs. (It is granted, of course, that similar acoustic effects may be produced in different ways: for example, that the effect of lip rounding may be produced not only by actual protrusion of the lips but also by retraction of the tongue.) However, although the field workers took pains to ascertain as well as they could the positions and movements of the vocal organs of their informants, they were obliged to rely largely on auditory impressions. Movements at the back of the oral cavity, in the pharynx and in the larynx cannot be observed without instruments; and even the observation of tongue movements ordinarily visible to the eye with the speaker's coöperation had often to be neglected for fear of embarrassing or offending the informant. The securing of natural responses is after all more important than minute phonetic observation.

2. The symbols of the phonetic alphabet, therefore, are to be understood as representing primarily *sounds as heard*. The field workers, in transcribing a sound, usually thought also in terms of articulation, and tried, so far as they were able, to refer their acoustic impression to the configuration of the vocal organs which produced it. But in the last analysis it is the sound itself which governed the field workers' choice of symbols.

3. The field workers' phonetic notations, which appear on the maps of the Linguistic Atlas unchanged (except as noted below), are not phonemic, but on the contrary intentionally phonic, that is *impressionistic*. The phonemic pattern of an informant's speech can be determined only after long and careful study, and only on the basis of a large body of material first recorded impressionistically—certainly not under the conditions of field-work, which require that the interviews proceed as rapidly as possible, and that the informant's first utterance be transcribed as accurately as his last.

The pronunciation of two sections, of two generations or of two individuals often differs strikingly; but in most cases the differences are without phonemic value. Thus, the difference between *faɪv* and *fɐɪv*, between *kau, kəu* and *kɛu*, between *bɔd, bɤ·d* and *bɜɪd*, etc., is nonphonemic, but of the greatest importance to linguistic geography and dialectology, and to historical grammar as well. Accordingly, the field workers were instructed to record what they heard as accurately and minutely as they could, without attempting to normalize their transcriptions or to interpret their auditory impressions in terms of a phonemic system. If two utterances of the same word by the same informant struck their ears as different —no matter how small the difference might be—, they were to write them differently. As a result, the field workers' records may well include some observations of minute phonetic detail too trivial to be of much use to the linguist. But on the other hand this procedure has several great advantages: small differences which may turn out to possess phonemic importance are not overlooked; positional and accentual variants of phonemes, required for the proper description of a dialect, are duly observed; and such nonphonemic differences in pronunciation as are characteristic of regional and social dialects automatically come to light. Moreover, the field worker is relieved of the time-consuming and hazardous task of deciding on the spot how much of his auditory impression is phonemically relevant.

Personal differences among the field workers in their use of the symbols are relatively slight, with one exception (see **15**). Most of them are of little practical importance. However, it was thought desirable in the interests of accuracy to furnish the user of the Atlas with information on all points of difference, in order that the materials presented may be properly interpreted.

Vowels and Diphthongs

General

4. The vowel symbols of the Linguistic Atlas alphabet are presented in the following diagrammatic arrangement, which differs only in detail from the diagram of the IPA. For an explanation of the general principles of this arrangement the reader is referred to various works by members of the IPA (especially Daniel Jones, *An Outline of English Phonetics*,

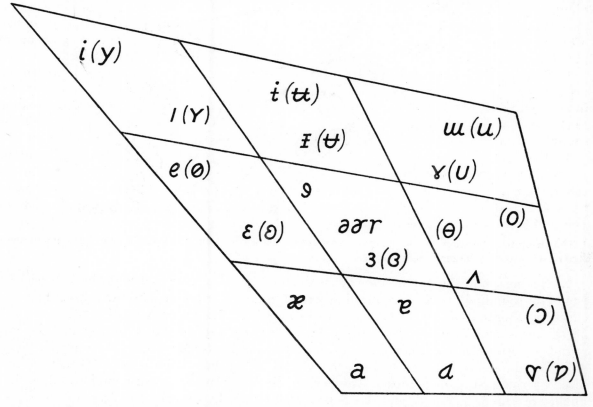

The symbol *r* is entered in this diagram as well as in the consonant table below (**43**) because it is used with a twofold value: both as a consonant symbol (see **59** and **60**) and as a vowel symbol (see **19**). The use of *r* to write syllabic sounds as in *father* faðr is parallel on the one hand to the use of *l, n* in *table, kitchen* teɪbl, kɪtʃn, and on the other hand to the use of *ə* in *sofa* soufə.

3d edition, Cambridge 1932; Daniel Jones in M. Heepe's compilation *Lautzeichen und ihre Anwendung in verschiedenen Sprachgebieten*, Berlin 1928; Ida C. Ward, *The Phonetics of English*, Cambridge 1931). It is not claimed that this diagram represents the exact physiological relation of the vowels to each other; it merely indicates for each vowel the point about which the tongue position fluctuates, and serves as a convenient scheme of reference.

5. The 'central values' of the symbols *i, ι, e, ε, æ, a, ɔ, ʌ, o, u, u* may be approximately defined as the vowels of *beat, bit, bait, bet, bat, palm, bought, but, boat, put, boot*, respectively, in the most usual pronunciation of native speakers in the north-central United States (west of the Hudson River, north of the Ohio River). This dialect was adopted as a standard of reference partly because it is spoken by the largest number of native Americans, and partly because it is the variety with which all but two of the field workers were most familiar.

The following diagram illustrates the relation of the 'central values' of certain American vowels to the 'cardinal vowels' described by Daniel Jones in *An Outline of English Phonetics*, 3d edition, Chapter VIII.

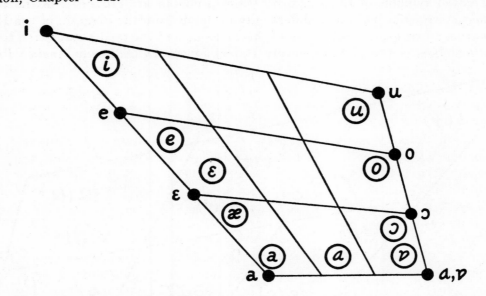

The theoretical positions of the 'cardinal vowels' are shown by solid black circles, the positions of the American vowels by larger outline circles.

6. Symbols shown in parentheses in the diagram in **4** denote vowels with the acoustic effect of lip-rounding (usually produced by actual rounding or protrusion of the lips but sometimes by other means). Of the twelve vowels so marked, nine are paired with symbols denoting the corresponding unrounded vowels: *i y, ι ʏ, e ø, ε œ, ɨ ʉ, ɪ ʊ, ɜ ɞ, ɯ u, ɤ ʊ*; three denote rounded vowels whose unrounded counterparts are not provided with special symbols: *o, ɵ, ɔ*.

7. The difference between tense (narrow) and lax (wide) vowels is not explicitly recognized by this system of notation. The basis of the notation, as already emphasized, is the quality of sounds as heard; and this is produced jointly by the size and shape of the resonance chambers (determined by the configuration of the vocal organs) and by the hardness of the surfaces which line these chambers (determined in part by muscular tension). Under the conditions of field work the two factors cannot be isolated. However, it is usually to be assumed that *i y, ɨ ʉ, ɯ u* are respectively tenser than *ɪ ʏ, ɨ ʉ, ɣ ʊ*, and *e, ɘ* tenser than *ɛ, ɜ*. Note especially that *æ, a, ɑ, ɒ, ɔ, ʌ, ɚ* may be either tense or lax.

8. Five symbols have values markedly different from those assigned to them by most users of the IPA alphabet: *ɒ* = low-back unrounded or weakly rounded, not regularly rounded (see **14**); *a* = low-central, not low-back (**15**); *ʌ* = advanced lower-mid-back, not the unrounded counterpart of *ɔ* and not the corresponding sound of standard British English (**16**); *ɘ* = advanced higher-mid-back weakly rounded, not midway between *ø* and *o* (**17**); *ɣ* = unrounded *u*, not unrounded *o* (**18**). Two vowel symbols used in the records of the Linguistic Atlas are not included in the alphabet of the IPA: *ɚ* and *r* (**19**).

Individual Vowels

9. *ɛ* denotes the vowel of *bet, men, fell*, as pronounced by the majority of speakers in the north-central United States (**5**). It is slightly lower than the corresponding sound in standard British English (written **e** by Daniel Jones in 'broad' transcription), though still considerably higher than the sound transcribed *ɛ* in French *père, bête. ɵ*, the rounded counterpart of *ɛ* (IPA **œ**), is rare, but appears sometimes as a rounded and exceptionally advanced variety of the vowel in *bird*.

10. *ɨ ʉ* denote high-central vowels, respectively unrounded and rounded, usually tense. *ɨ* occurs rarely (only in records by K, B, L, C). *ʉ* is common, especially in words like *music, beautiful, new*.

R perhaps wrote *ʉ* in some cases for an advanced but not fully centralized *u*, more accurately written *u̇* (see **22**). No change has been made in such transcriptions.*

11. *ɨ ʉ* denote lower-high-central vowels, respectively unrounded and rounded, usually lax. *ɨ* occurs very frequently in unstressed syllables of words like *habit, because, merry* and as the second element of the diphthongs in *bite, bait, boy* (see **39–40**), sometimes also as a stressed vowel in words like *will, bristles*. A lowered *ɨ* approaches *ə* in its acoustic effect.

Several field workers, especially in their earlier records, regularly wrote *ɪ* for the unstressed vowel of *habit*, etc., and for the second element of diphthongs. An *ɪ* in these positions, in early records by K, HS, B, R, J and in all records by HY, HN, is usually to be interpreted as equivalent to *ɨ*.

12. *ɜ, ɞ, ɘ* are used chiefly to write the stressed vowel of *bird* when pronounced without retroflection or 'r-color.' *ɜ* is common throughout eastern New England. It is normally somewhat higher, perhaps also somewhat farther front, than the corresponding sound in standard British English (written *ə:* by Daniel Jones in 'broad' transcription). A retracted *ɜ* approaches *ʌ* in its acoustic effect. *ɞ* denotes a fully rounded variety of *ɜ. ɘ* is used rather rarely, chiefly in eastern Massachusetts (only by HY, B, L). It denotes a mid-central vowel considerably higher and slightly more advanced than *ɜ*, usually very tense. The relation of *ɘ* to *ɜ* is roughly the same as the relation of *e* to *ɛ*.

13. *ə* denotes the common 'obscure' mid-central vowel heard in unstressed syllables of words like *about, confess, sofa*. In stressed syllables *ə* is used chiefly to write the first element of diphthongs of the type of *əɨ, əu*, rarely also a monophthong higher and more advanced than *ʌ* in words like *cut*.

Some of the field workers assign to this symbol a somewhat wider range than to those nearer the periphery of the diagram in **4**, commonly using *ə* for any unstressed vowel not distinctly high, low, front or back (thus

---

* The names of the field workers are abbreviated as follows: B = Bloch, C = Miss Chapallaz, HN = Hultzén, HS = Miss Harris, HY = Hanley, J = Joos, K = Kurath, L = Lowman, R = Reynard.

HY, R, HN). Others try to distinguish more carefully among the various shades of obscure mid-central vowels (thus K, B, L, C).

HS sometimes uses the symbol ə in positions where the other field workers write ɨ or ɪ, as for example in the unstressed syllable of *merry* and the like. HS's ə in such positions is probably to be interpreted as a high variety of ə or a low variety of ɪ.

14. ɒ usually denotes a weakly rounded low-back vowel; but several of the field workers use it also for the unrounded variety. A low-back vowel with full rounding is sometimes written ɒ (see **29**). In the later regional atlases of the United States and Canada the use of ɒ in this double function will be avoided by the addition of a new symbol: ɒ will be written only for the rounded variety, ɑ for the unrounded variety. Weak rounding will then be indicated by ɑ, over-rounding by ɒ. (The symbol ɑ is not used in the *Linguistic Atlas of New England.*)

According to their own statements, K and HN use the symbol ɒ only for rounded vowels; B uses it indifferently for rounded and unrounded vowels, provided they are heard as low-back; HY uses it chiefly for unrounded or weakly rounded vowels; HS uses it for weakly rounded vowels, writing fully rounded low-back vowels as ɒ; R uses it for unrounded vowels; L uses it for rounded vowels only, but sometimes writes ɒ˂ or ɒ˷ for unrounded vowels farther back than ɑ. For further particulars see the note to **15**.

15. a, ɑ, ɒ denote low vowels; æ, ɐ, ɔ denote higher-low vowels, that is vowels higher than those in the series a – ɒ but lower than mid position. In their use of the symbols a, ɑ, ɒ, ɔ the field workers show more disagreement than on any other point.

The following diagrams (each consisting of the lowest third of the trapezium in **4**) represent the practice of six of the field workers with respect to the low-vowel symbols. The indications of the range of values as-

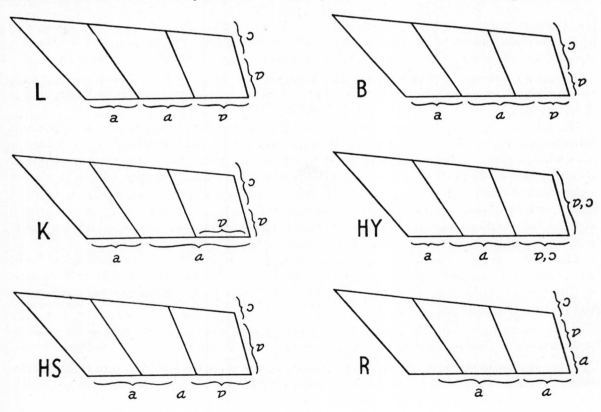

signed to each symbol by the several field workers are based partly on the reports of the field workers themselves, partly on the results of a test given them to determine their actual usage. In this test, held about one year after the beginning of the field work, HY, K, HS, B and L simultaneously transcribed a selected number of words containing low vowels in two phonograph records of American speech (Victor records of American Speech No. 68A and 69B). Their transcriptions of these words furnish a valuable check on their normal practice in field work.

As these diagrams show, L, B and K are for the most part in agreement; HY deviates from their practice especially in the treatment of low-back vowels; HS and R differ from the foregoing and from each other more seriously.

L divides the range of low vowels equally among the three symbols a, ɑ, ɒ, and the range of low-back vowels equally between the two symbols ɒ, ɔ. His practice may be taken as a standard of comparison.

B differs from L only in assigning a somewhat wider range to the symbols ɑ and ɔ, with the result that the values of these symbols in B's records overlap to some extent with the values of ɒ in L's records. For example, forms of *crop* and *frost* recorded by B show a preponderance of ɑ and ɔ respectively, while forms of these words recorded by L show in both cases a preponderance of ɒ.

K agrees with L in the treatment of ɑ and ɔ, but uses ɑ both for low-central and for low-back unrounded vowels, overlapping in the latter value with L's ɒ, which K uses for low-back rounded vowels only.

HY assigns a narrower range to ɑ and a wider range to ɑ than L, so that HY's ɑ (especially as the first element of diphthongs) may sometimes correspond to the a of other field workers. According to his own statement, he uses ɒ and ɔ for vowels articulated in the same range of positions, writing ɒ for unrounded or weakly rounded vowels, ɔ for fully rounded vowels.

HS assigns a very wide range to a and to ɒ, using ɑ but rarely (except in early records) and ɔ less commonly than the other field workers. Hence the values of a in records by HS overlap with or even include the values of ɑ in other records, and the values of her ɒ similarly extend into the range assigned by other field workers to ɔ.

R uses a for a wide range of low vowels not fully front, ɑ for low-back unrounded vowels, ɒ for rounded back vowels somewhat higher than ɑ, and ɔ for still higher back vowels (consequently for vowels slightly higher than the position indicated for ɔ in the diagram in **4**). R's a therefore overlaps with other field workers' ɑ, his ɑ with other field workers' ɒ, and his ɒ with other field workers' ɔ. See also **26** note.

J agrees in his practice with B; HN agrees with K; C agrees with L.

This disagreement in the treatment of low vowels sometimes results in the appearance of 'personal boundaries'—that is, in lines which seem to divide dialect areas with different vowels in the same or similar words, but which reflect only a difference in practice among the field workers. These isographs are easily identified and distinguished from real isophones by reference to the table appearing on each map, which lists the communities investigated by each of the several field workers. Thus, if the boundary between the types of *krɑp* and *krɒp* is discovered to coincide with the boundary between communities investigated by B and those investigated by L, the difference in the recorded forms may be assumed to be 'personal' rather than dialectal. On the other hand, if the boundary between such types does not coincide with the boundary between two field workers' areas, or if it coincides with the boundary between the areas of two field workers who treat the symbol in question in the same way, it must be interpreted as a real isophone.

ɐ is used rarely by HY and HN. HS and J use it chiefly for an open unstressed vowel in words like *sofa*; K, L and C use it chiefly for the first element of diphthongs in words like *bite, bout*; B and R use it in both these ways, and also for a stressed monophthong in words like *cut* and *crop*. In words which K, B, L and C frequently transcribe with the diphthong ɐɪ, HY often writes ɒɪ, which may indicate a diphthong of the same kind or one actually beginning near ɒ (cf. **40**).

16. ʌ denotes the vowel of *cut* as pronounced in the north-central United States. The corresponding standard British English sound (written ʌ by Daniel Jones) is considerably lower and somewhat farther advanced than the American sound. A vowel slightly lower than this American ʌ but not as low as the British variety is commonly heard in the speech of eastern New England.

HS, a native of Essex County, Mass., pronounces an exceptionally low variety of ʌ in words like *cut*. As a result, sounds which most of the other field workers would write as ʌ or even ʌˇ (see **25**) impress her as raised varieties and appear in her transcriptions as ʌˑ (**24**). R, on the other hand, a native of Ohio, pronounces a rather high variety of ʌ, and consequently writes most occurrences of this vowel in eastern Massachusetts as ʌˇ.

17. ɵ is used chiefly for an extreme variety of the so-called 'New England short *o*,' as in the rural pronunciation of words like *whole, home, coat*. It appears also (rarely except in records by L) for unstressed *o* in words like *swallow*. Less fully centralized varieties of the 'New England short *o*' are commonly written by K, HS, B, L, C as oˇ, oˢ, ɔˇ, ɔˢ or as ŏˢ, etc. (see **21** ff.).

R regularly uses ɵ̇ for all varieties of short centralized *o* in words like *whole*, etc. When the transcription of the other field workers seems to show that the vowel in question is normally less advanced than this symbol would indicate, R's ɵ has been changed to ŏˇ; but in most cases no change has been made.

HY often denotes varieties of this short centralized *o* by writing u, ɔ, ʌ, etc., or simply by writing ŏ, as in *hul, hɔm, hʌm, kŏt.*

18. ɣ denotes a somewhat advanced lower-high-back unrounded vowel, the unrounded counterpart of ʊ. It appears sometimes as a variant of ʊ in words like *good*, sometimes as a variant of ɜ in words like *bird*, sometimes as a glide before velar consonants as in *log* /lɔɣg/.

19. ɚ denotes a strongly 'retroflex' mid-central vowel, as in the most common American pronunciation of words like *bird*. The 'retroflection' or 'r-color' may be produced by actual raising and inversion of the tongue tip or by retraction and lateral contraction of the body of the tongue (cf. **31**). Most of the field workers use this symbol only for a vowel in stressed position, writing the corresponding sound in unstressed syllables and after vowels as r: thus they would write *bird, further, father, fear, cart* as bɝd, fɝðr, faðr, fir, kart. But L and C (as well as B in late records) use ɚ for a strongly 'retroflex' vowel in all positions: thus they would write these words as bɚd, fɚðɚ, faðɚ, fiɚ, kaɚt. In accordance with **31**, ʐ, ɻ denote varieties of ɚ, r in which the retroflection or 'r-color' is still stronger.

L, who discriminated more carefully among the different varieties of this sound than the other field workers, defines his use of the symbols in question as follows (May, 1935): 'I use ɚ for a vocalic sound. The tip and blade are greatly retracted; the rest of the tongue is laterally contracted and very high, so that the sides of the tongue touch the roof of the mouth in the palatal, velar and uvular sections. The raising or curling back of the tip is not essential. When this curling back is more extreme or more noticeable I use ʐ; in this case the back part of the tongue is usually lower than for ɚ. When the sound suggests a consonant I use r, or ɻ for the more extreme type, chiefly in sequences like ɜr, ɜɻ. I use ɝ for a very weakly r-colored ɚ, usually without retraction of the tongue tip. ɜ, ɝ differ from ə, ɚ chiefly in length.'

HS in early records uses a special symbol ɝ for a weakly retroflex mid-central stressed vowel. This has been changed by the editors to ɝ.

R in early records often writes ɚ for a sound which is probably more accurately denoted by ɝ. No change has been made in such transcriptions.

20. ø and ɔ are used instead of the IPA symbols ø and œ respectively, without any difference in value.

The field workers regularly write œ for the rounded counterpart of ɛ. The substitution of ɔ for œ was carried through mechanically in transferring the linguistic entries from the field records to the published maps.

HY and L often write *ɒ* for *ɒ* (the rounded counterpart of *ɜ*) without distinction of value; B in his early records writes *ɒ* for an advanced variety of *ɒ*, which has been editorially replaced by *ɒ·* (see **22**). All these deviations from standard practice have been systematically corrected.

Shift Signs

21. In order to avoid the necessity of using special symbols for the innumerable shades of sound intermediate between any two of the vowels shown in the diagram in **4**, the phonetic alphabet of the Linguistic Atlas provides shift signs in the form of small arrowheads, which are placed after a vowel symbol to indicate varieties heard as articulated in a higher, a lower, a more advanced or a more retracted position than the vowel denoted by the unmodified letter. These shift signs must be interpreted on the basis of the vowel diagram.

22. An arrowhead pointing *to the left* indicates, after a front-vowel symbol, a vowel articulated exceptionally far forward; after a central-vowel symbol, a fronted vowel (one approximating front position); after a back-vowel symbol, a centered vowel (one approximating central position). Thus *a‹*=an extremely advanced variety of *a*; *ɑ‹*=a vowel between *a* and *ɑ* but nearer to *a*; *ɒ‹*=a vowel between *ɒ* and *ɑ* but nearer to *ɒ*.

23. An arrowhead pointing *to the right* indicates, after a front-vowel symbol, a centered vowel (one approximating central position); after a central-vowel symbol, a backed vowel (one approximating back position); after a back-vowel symbol, a vowel articulated exceptionally far back. Thus *a›*=a vowel between *a* and *ɑ* but nearer to *a*; *ɑ›*=a vowel between *ɑ* and *ɒ* but nearer to *ɑ*; *ɒ›*=an extremely retracted variety of *ɒ*.

24. An arrowhead pointing *up* indicates a vowel articulated in a higher and usually also in a somewhat more advanced position: compare the sloping sides of the vowel diagram. Thus *æˆ*=a vowel between *æ* and *ɛ* but nearer to *æ*; *ɑˆ*=a vowel between *ɑ* and *ɐ* but nearer to *ɑ*; *oˆ*=a vowel between *o* and *u* but nearer to *o* (not a vowel between *o* and *ʊ*, since *ʊ* is not in the direct line of fully back vowels).

25. An arrowhead pointing *down* indicates a vowel articulated in a lower and usually also in a somewhat more retracted position: compare the sloping sides of the vowel diagram. Thus *ɛˇ*=a vowel between *ɛ* and *æ* but nearer to *ɛ*; *ɔˇ*=a vowel between *ɔ* and *ɒ* but nearer to *ɔ*; *iˇ*=a vowel between *i* and *e* but nearer to *i* (not a vowel between *i* and *ɪ*, since *ɪ* is not in the direct line of fully front vowels).

26. The varieties of unrounded high vowels, from front to back, can thus be represented by the series *i‹ - i - i› - ɨ‹ - ɨ - ɨ› - ɯ‹ - ɯ - ɯ›*. The varieties of rounded back vowels, from high to low, can be represented by the series *u‹ - u - uˇ - oˆ - o - oˇ - ɔˆ - ɔ - ɔˇ - ɒˆ - ɒ*.

HN sometimes writes *ē, ɛ̄, ō, ɔ̄* for centered vowels in unstressed syllables. These have been changed by the editors to *e›, ɛ›, o›, ɔ›* respectively.

As a result of his peculiar placing of the low-vowel symbols in the diagram (see **15** note), R habitually writes *a·* for a variety of *a* tending toward *ɒ*, and *aˆ* (especially as the first element of a diphthong) for a low-central vowel tending toward *ʌ*. R's *a·* has been changed to *a›*, and his *aˆ* to *ɐˇ* except where he has marked these transcriptions as certain (cf. **74** note).

27. Double shift signs (one pointing to the left or right, the other up or down) are used to indicate shades of sound for which single shift signs are inadequate. These combinations must be interpreted according to the statements in **22–25**. Thus *iˇ‹*=a vowel between *i* and *ɨ* and *ɪ* but nearest to *i*; *oˇ‹*=a vowel between *o* and *ɵ* and *ɔ* but nearest to *o*; *əˇ‹*=a vowel between *ə* and *ɛ* (or *e*) and *ɨ* but nearest to *ə*; *aˇ‹*=a vowel between *a* and *ɐ* but nearer to *a*.

Some of the field workers often use single shift signs where double shift signs would be more accurate. Thus they sometimes write *i·, e·, u·* for vowels tending respectively toward *ı, ɛ, ʊ* (more accurately *ıᶻ, ɛᶻ, ʊᶻ*), or inversely *ı·, ɛ·, ʊ·* for vowels tending respectively toward *i, e, u* (more accurately *ıᶻ, ɛᶻ, ʊᶻ*). No change has been made in such transcriptions.

HY and HS sometimes indicate the precise shade of a vowel by a note in the margin instead of by shift signs, writing for example 'ɛ , almost ı' or 'ı , toward ə' or 'ɚ , ı-like.' In all such cases the proper shift signs have been supplied by the editors (thus *ɛ·, ıᶻ, ɚᶻ*, etc.). HY also uses the note 'ı -like' to refer to the symbol ʒ. In accordance with his own instructions, all cases of ʒ so marked have been changed to ʚ.

HS in early records uses the symbol *ɀ* for a lowered and centralized variety of ɔ. This symbol has been replaced on the maps by ɔᶻ.

28. The following diagram will help to visualize the meaning of shift signs:

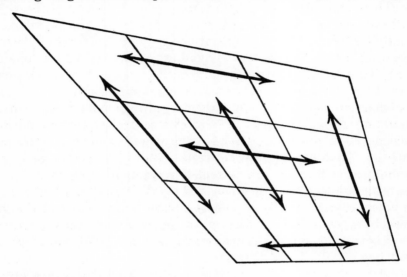

Diacritics Used with Vowel Symbols

29. The diacritic for labialization ˬ (equivalent to the IPA diacritic ˳) may be written under symbols for unrounded vowels to indicate weak rounding, as *ɯ̜*, and under symbols for rounded vowels to indicate over-rounding, as *u̜*. It is thus possible to represent four degrees of lip-rounding, as *ɯ – ɯ̜ – u – u̜*.

In the later regional atlases of the United States and Canada, a diacritic for lip-spreading ˍ will be written under symbols for rounded vowels to indicate slight unrounding, and under symbols for unrounded vowels to indicate over-spreading. It will thus be possible to represent six degrees of lip-rounding, as *ɯ̱ – ɯ – ɯ̜ – u̜ – u – u̜*.

30. The diacritic for nasalization ˜ may be written over any vowel symbol to indicate nasal resonance, produced by pronouncing the vowel with the velum relaxed so as to allow part of the air current to escape through the nose. The modification so marked may vary from a very faint nasal tinge to very strong nasality.

When the speech of a given informant is colored throughout by a 'nasal twang,' which affects all or most of his oral sounds (except stops), the nasality is usually not indicated separately for every sound, but is mentioned once and for all in the general statement characterizing the informant's speech. See Chapter VI.

31. The diacritic for 'retroflection' ˛ may be written under any vowel symbol to indicate the acoustic effect of 'r-color,' whether this is produced by actual raising and inversion of the tongue tip or by retraction and lateral contraction of the body of the tongue (cf. **19**). Thus a̠, o̠, ə̠, ɜ̠ denote retroflex or 'r-colored' a, o, ə, ɜ respectively; ɚ, ɼ denote varieties of ɚ, ɼ in which the 'retroflection' inherent in these vowels is especially strong or noticeable.

32. The diacritic for breath or devocalization ˳ may be written under any vowel symbol to indicate voicelessness. Voiceless vowels are not uncommon in unstressed syllables between voiceless consonants.

This diacritic is usually written below the symbol; but when the shape of the symbol or the presence of other inferior diacritics makes this inconvenient, it may be written above the symbol instead; thus i̥, ą̊, ə̊ but ẙ, å̧, ə̊. (No other diacritic is used like this in two different positions.)

Length Marks

33. The method used to mark vowel length (quantity) is that of the IPA, with such deviations in practice as will appear from the following statement. The rules here formulated apply to vowels in both stressed and unstressed syllables, and to both elements of a diphthong.

Some of the field workers (especially HY, HS, R, HN) were less careful to mark vowel length than to indicate vowel quality. They were especially prone to omit the length mark after long vowels in words like *beat, bait, palm, bought, boat, boot,* frequently writing these words simply as *bit, bet, pam, bɔt, bot, but.*

34. Vowels heard as neither distinctly long nor distinctly short are not specially marked. Half-long vowels are usually treated in the same way, though the remark 'half-long' is sometimes entered in the commentary when the field worker considers this degree of length for any reason worth noting.

35. Vowels which strike the field worker as distinctly long are marked with a single dot, as a·. In practice, the field workers occasionally write the single dot also to mark half-long vowels appearing in contexts where short vowels are more usual, as in *bid bi·d* with half-long *i*.

36. Vowels which strike the field worker as overlong—that is, as appreciably longer than ordinary long vowels—are marked with a colon, as a: . Overlong vowels are rare except in the speech of certain informants and in such phrases as the calls to animals. Still longer vowels, when they occur, may be marked with a double colon, as a:: .

HY very often, and B in his earliest records, use the colon to mark any vowel heard as long. Except where the field worker specifically indicates that the colon marks an overlong vowel, it has been changed to a single dot.

37. Vowels which strike the field worker as appreciably shorter than ordinary short vowels are marked with a breve, as ă. In practice, the field workers occasionally write the breve also to mark vowels of ordinary shortness appearing in contexts where long or half-long vowels are more usual, as in *home hŏm* (see **17** note).

38. Very short vowels heard as mere glides without forming the peak of a syllable are written with superior letters, as in *frost frᵛᵊst, five faⁱv, beans bᵊiˑnz, biˑⁱnz* and the like.

Some of the field workers (especially B, R, J) often write superior letters for vowels which are short but clearly syllabic, as in *because bᵊkɔz.* These have been replaced by full-sized letters marked with a breve, as in *bə̆kɔz.* R very often writes a final superior *o, u* in words like *swallow swɒlᵒ, swɒlᵘ* (changed to *swɒlŏ, swɒlŭ*). In early records R writes also a final superior *i* in words like *merry mɛrⁱ* to denote an unstressed vowel somewhat higher than *ɪ.* This has been changed to *ɩ,* as in *mɛrɩ.* Similarly, R writes a final superior *r* in words like *water wɒtʳ* to denote a weakly retroflex unstressed vowel. This has been changed to *ə,* as in *wɒtə.*

Diphthongs

39. A diphthong, definable as a vocalic sound characterized by a continuous movement of the tongue or lips resulting in a continuous audible glide, is written with two symbols (occasionally with three, when the middle part of the glide is for some reason prominent). A falling diphthong, one with decreasing stress, is written with the first symbol full-sized, the second either full-sized or superior according to the length of the glide. A rising diphthong, one with increasing stress, is written with the first symbol superior, the second full-sized. Each symbol in a diphthong may of course be modified by any of the diacritics used with vowels and may be followed by a single or a double shift sign.

40. Of the two symbols used in writing a diphthong, the first regularly denotes the acoustic impression of the glide at its beginning, interpreted as the position from which the tongue (or lip) movement starts. The second symbol may denote either (A) the position to which the articulating organ actually moves before the beginning of the next sound, or (B) the position toward which the glide tends but which the articulating organ does not actually attain before the beginning of the next sound. The exact point at which a diphthongal glide ends is often difficult to determine by ear, though sometimes the end of the glide leaves a clear auditory impression. The following transcriptions of a diphthong of the *aɪ* type will illustrate the two methods used by the field workers: (A) *aɪ, ae, aɛ, aɛ̌, aɪ*ˑ—the glide begins at *a* and appears to end respectively at *ɪ, e, ɛ, ɛ̌, ɪ*ˑ; (B) *aı, aɪ, aj*—the glide begins at *a* and moves toward some variety of high-front vowel, or generally in an upward and forward direction. (Note that *aɪ, aı* may represent either method of transcription.)

K, B, J attempt to use method (A) systematically, writing as the second element of all or most diphthongs the symbols which most accurately represent the auditory impression of the end of the glides. The other field workers generally use method (B). L in early records regularly writes the second element of the diphthongs in *bite, bait, beat, boy* as *j*, and the second element of the diphthongs in *bout, boat, boot* as *w*, thus *bajt, bejt, bijt, bɔj, bawt, bowt, buwt* and the like. Later he uses *j* and *w* only in the diphthongs in *beat* and *boot*, and writes the other diphthongs with *ɪ* and *ʊ* or *u*, thus *bijt, buwt* but *baɪt, beɪt, bɔɪ, baʊt, baut, boʊt, bout.*

41. The length of each element in a falling diphthong is marked in the usual manner. If the first element is long (that is, if the glide which characterizes the diphthong is drawled or is preceded by a momentary hold with no perceptible change in quality) it is marked with a single dot; if it is very short (that is, if the glide appears to move away from its starting position very abruptly) it is marked with a breve. The second element is treated similarly, with the added provision that if it is so faint as to be no more than a scarcely audible vanishing glide, it may be written with a superior letter. If the whole diphthong is long each element may be marked with the sign of length; if the whole diphthong is short each element may be marked with a breve. The following series illustrates various distributions of length (though by no means all possible combinations) in a diphthong of the *aɪ* type: *a:ɪˑ, aˑɪ, aɪ, aˑɪ̆, aɪ̆, ăɪ, ăɪ̆, aɪ, ăɪ.*

L sometimes writes *a͞ɪ*, etc., to indicate that the first element is longer than the second but that the whole diphthong is short. Such transcriptions have been simplified by the omission of the breve.

HY and HS often indicate a drawled pronunciation by writing *e-ɪ, e- ə, ɔ-ɪ* and the like in words like *bait, care, boil*. Such forms have been changed to *eˑɪ, eˑə, ɔˑɪ*, etc., except when it is clear from the context or from a note by the field worker that the hyphen indicates a syllabic division (see **42**).

HY and R, sometimes also HS and J, tend to write simply *e* and *o* in words like *bait, boat*, using *eɪ* and *oʊ* only for the most strikingly diphthongal varieties of these sounds. It is to be borne in mind that in records by these field workers, *e,o* in stressed syllables do not always (or even usually) denote monophthongs.

Most of the field workers generally write the vocalic sounds in *beat, boot* as monophthongs (that is, with *i, u* or *i·, u·*), disregarding the slight diphthongization often heard in such words. B regularly writes these sounds as *ii, uu*; L and C regularly write them as *ij, uw*. Both methods of transcription are intended simply to indicate a slightly diphthongal pronunciation; the difference in practice between B and L probably does not reflect any real difference in pronunciation, but only a difference in the field workers' habits of transcription.

42. When two contiguous vowel symbols are not intended to represent a diphthong, they are separated by a hyphen: thus *drawing* drɔ-ɪŋ, *real* ri-əl, when pronounced in two syllables (cf. *boil* bɔɪl, bɔ·ɪl, *fear* fiə, fi·ə). But the hyphen is not used—(A) between a stressed diphthong and a following unstressed vowel, as in *rowen* raʊɪn, raoən; (B) between an unstressed vowel and a following stressed vowel or diphthong, if the stress mark is written (see **61**), as in *piazza* pi'æzə, *create* kri'eɪt; (C) between identical vowel symbols, as in *tidying* taɪdɪɪŋ, taɪdɪɪŋ; or (D) elsewhere if no misunderstanding can arise.

CONSONANTS

General

43. The consonant symbols of the Linguistic Atlas alphabet are presented in the following tabular arrangement, which differs only in detail from the table of the IPA (see Daniel Jones

		BILABIAL	LABIODENTAL	DENTAL	ALVEOLAR	PALATALIZED ALVEOLAR	RETROFLEX	ALVEOLO-PALATAL	PALATO-ALVEOLAR	PALATAL	RETRACTED PALATAL	ADVANCED VELAR	VELAR	GLOTTAL
STOPS	55	*pb*		*t̪d̪*	*td*	*ţḑ*	*ʈɖ*			*cɟ*	*c̄ɟ̄*	*k̄ḡ*	*kg*	*ʔ*
NASALS	56	*m*	*ɱ*	*n̪*	*n*	*ny*	*ɳ*			*ɲ*	*ɲ̄*	*ŋ̄*	*ŋ*	
LATERALS	57			*l̪*	*l̹* *ƚ*	*ɭ*	*l*			*ʎ*				
FLAPS	58			*ɾ̪*	*ɾ* *ɺ*		*ɽ*							
FRICATIVES	59	*φβ*	*fv*	*s̪z̪* *θð*	*sz* *ɹ* *r* *R*	*ʂʐ* *ɭ*	*ʂʐ* *ɭ̣*	*ʃʒ* *ʃʒ*	*ɕʑ*	*çʝ*	*ç̄ʝ̄*	*x̄γ̄*	*xγ*	*hɦ* *ɦ*
FRICTIONLESS CONTINUANTS	60	*(ɥ)* *(w)*	*Fʋ*		*ɹ*		*ɽ*			*j* *ɥ*	*j̄* *ɥ̄*	*w̄*	*w*	

in Heepe, referred to in **4**). In this arrangement the symbols are largely self-explanatory.

The following deviations from the alphabet of the IPA should be noted:
(1) The symbols *ʅ* and *ɟ* have been added.
(2) The diacritics appearing in *ş, č, ğ* are not recognized in this use by the IPA.
(3) The symbols *r, ɹ* have slightly different values from those usually assigned to them by the IPA.
(4) The symbol *ʀ* has a totally different value from that assigned to it by the IPA.
(5) Several symbols are shaped somewhat differently, though without differences of value: *ʔ* = IPA *ʾ*, *φ* = IPA *ɸ*, *ß* = IPA *β*, *γ* = IPA *ɣ*.

44. The terms at the head of the columns in this table indicate the organ involved in the formation of the sounds and the point against which it articulates:

bilabial: the lower lip against the upper lip;

labiodental: the lower lip against the upper front teeth;

dental: the tip or blade of the tongue against the edge or back of the upper front teeth;

alveolar: the tip or blade of the tongue, or both, against the upper gums or the teeth-ridge, rarely just back of the teeth-ridge;

palatalized alveolar: the same, with the front of the tongue raised toward or touching the anterior or mid part of the hard palate;

retroflex: the tip (rarely the blade) of the tongue against a point back of the teeth-ridge or against the anterior part of the hard palate;

alveolo-palatal: the blade and front of the tongue against the teeth-ridge and the anterior part of the hard palate, the opening being smallest at the teeth-ridge;

palato-alveolar: the front of the tongue against the teeth-ridge and the hard palate, the opening being smallest at the hard palate;

palatal: the front of the tongue against the anterior or mid part of the hard palate;

retracted palatal: the front of the tongue against the back part of the hard palate or still farther back;

advanced velar: the back of the tongue against the anterior part of the soft palate or still farther forward;

velar: the back of the tongue against the mid (rarely the back) part of the soft palate;

glottal: formed by closure or (slight) contraction of the glottis, the configuration of the oral cavity being of only secondary importance.

(For definitions of the terms at the head of the horizontal rows in the table see **55–60**.)

45. When two symbols appear side by side in a single compartment of the table, the first denotes a voiceless, the second a voiced consonant. It is usually to be assumed that the voiceless sound is stronger (fortis) than its voiced counterpart (and in the case of stops also slightly shorter). When only one symbol appears without another beside it in the same compartment, it denotes a voiced consonant, except that *ʔ* and *ɦ* in the last column are voiceless.

46. When two or more symbols appear one below another in a single compartment of the table, they denote sounds of the same class articulated at the same point but differing in some other respect. Consult the description of the individual sounds in **57–60**.

Diacritics Used with Consonant Symbols

47. Voiceless consonants for which no separate symbols are provided are written by adding a small circle below or above the symbol for the corresponding voiced sounds, as *r̥, l̥, ŋ̊* (cf. above, **32**). When symbols for voiceless and voiced consonants exist side by side, the same diacritic may be added to the latter to indicate a voiceless sound somewhat more weakly articulated than the usual voiceless variety: thus *z̦, d̦, d̦ʒ* are respectively weaker than *s, t, tʃ* (lenis instead of fortis).

48. The diacritic for voicing ˛ may be written below symbols for voiceless consonants to indicate a voiced sound somewhat more strongly articulated (and sometimes also shorter) than the usual voiced variety: thus *ș, ț, țʃ* are respectively stronger (and shorter) than *z, d, dʒ* (fortis instead of lenis).

49. The diacritic for retroflection . is used with consonant symbols in two ways. It is written below symbols for alveolar consonants to denote the corresponding retroflex consonants: thus *ṣẓ, ʞ, ɽ*, homorganic with *tḍ, ṇ, ḷ, ł̣, ɽ*; and it is written below other consonant symbols to indicate the acoustic effect of 'r-color,' usually produced by raising and inversion of the tongue tip during the articulation of the consonant: thus *ẉ = w* with simultaneous tongue-tip action, *ʃ̣ = ʃ* with raised tongue tip, etc.

50. The diacritic for labialization ˎ may be written below any consonant symbol to indicate the acoustic effect of lip-rounding. When written below a symbol for a bilabial consonant the diacritic indicates protrusion of the lips, often resulting in a characteristic labial off-glide; when written below the symbols *w, ɥ* it indicates more than the usual degree of lip-rounding; when written below other consonant symbols, it indicates labialization (lip-rounding simultaneous with the articulation of the tongue).

51. The diacritic for nasalization ˜ may be written above any symbol denoting an oral continuant (laterals, fricatives and frictionless continuants) to indicate nasal resonance. Compare **30**; on nasalized flaps see **56, 58**.

52. Velarized consonants, that is consonants modified by raising the back of the tongue toward the soft palate, are written with the same symbols as the unmodified variety (except for *ł*, see **57**). The comment 'velarized' is entered in the commentary whenever necessary.

Velarized consonants, chiefly *r, m, b, d*, are distinguished only by B, L, C. L writes such sounds with a wavy line through the letter, as *r, m, b, d* and the like.

53. Syllabic consonants, that is consonants which form the peak of a syllable, are marked with the diacritic ˌ. But this diacritic is used only when needed for an unambiguous reading of the form. Thus in *table teɪbl̩* the diacritic is not written under the *l*, since the phonetic context shows that this must be syllabic; but in *leveling lɛvl̩ɪŋ* the diacritic is written, since in such a form the *l* may or may not be syllabic.

54. Consonants which strike the field worker as distinctly long or as 'double' are written with doubled symbols, as in *land, picture, bulge lænnd, pɪkktʃə, bʌlldʒ* or in phrases like *what time, some men, this year hwɒt taɪm, sʌm mɛn, ðɪʃ ʃiə*. But when the long consonant is the peak of a syllable it is marked with the usual sign of length, as in *wool w̩·l, sh!* (a call to animals) *ʃːˑ*.

The field workers wrote long consonants sometimes with doubled letters, sometimes with a dot to indicate the length, apparently without distinction of value: thus *lænnd* and *læn·d* indifferently. This inconsistency has been eliminated by the editors.

Consonants which strike the field worker as distinctly short, though of normal strength and audibility, may be marked with a breve, as in *three, April, glass θr̆iˑ, eɪpr̆ɪl, glæs*. Faintly articulated consonants, if they are not only short but indistinct as well, may be written with superior letters, as in *eɪpʳɪl, pɪᵏtʃə, læsᵗ*.

Consonants marked with a breve occur very rarely except in records by L. The other field workers use superior letters for all consonants which impress them as abnormally short, whether weakly audible or of normal strength and distinctness.

Individual Consonants by Classes

55. *Stops:* sounds formed by a complete stopping of the air current at some point in the larynx or mouth, the nasal passage being shut off by the velum.

p, t̯, t, ţ, ƫ, c, č, ǩ, k denote strong (fortis) voiceless stops, as a rule slightly aspirated when initial in a word or in a stressed syllable, otherwise unaspirated.

b, d̯, d, ḑ, ȡ, ɟ, ɟ̌, ǧ, g denote weak (lenis) voiced stops. When initial in a word or final in a phrase, these sounds are often partly or wholly voiceless.

HY sometimes indicates the voiceless ending of such stops in words like *rub, mud, rug* by writing b^{p}, d^{t}, g^{k}. Since he presumably does not mean to indicate that these stops are aspirated, such combinations have been changed to $b^{\mathring{b}}$, $d^{\mathring{d}}$, $g^{\mathring{g}}$. HS in similar cases frequently writes b^{h}, d^{h}, g^{h}, presumably to indicate devocalization of the end of the stop. These combinations have been simplified by deleting the superior ^{h}.

pʻ ... kʻ denote voiceless stops with exceptionally strong or noticeable aspiration, or else slightly aspirated stops in contexts where the unaspirated variety is more common.

p^{h} ... k^{h} denote voiceless stops with very striking aspiration. A still stronger degree of aspiration may be indicated by *ph ... kh*.

L and C commonly use p^{h} ... k^{h} to indicate a degree of aspiration which other field workers write as *pʻ ... kʻ*.

p^{φ}, p^{f}, t^{s}, $ǩ^{ç}$, k^{x} and the like denote affricated voiceless stops, in which the oral occlusion is broken gradually, with a resulting fricative off-glide. When this off-glide is still slower, stronger or more noticeable, the sounds may be written *pφ ... kx*. When the affrication is acoustically stronger than the stop, the stop may be written with a superior symbol, as $^{p}\varphi$ ... ^{k}x.

b^{β}, b^{v}, d^{z}, g^{γ} and the like denote affricated voiced stops. Compare the remarks in the preceding paragraph.

ˀp ... ˀk denote glottalized stops, articulated with a simultaneous glottal closure. This is usually released before the release of the oral closure, less commonly after it or at the same time.

ʻp ... ʻk denote preaspirated stops, in which the occlusion is preceded by a short but audible puff of breath.

p̬ ... k̬ denote strong (fortis) voiced stops, usually somewhat shorter as well as more energetically articulated than *b ... g*.

Some of the field workers (especially B, R, J) in early records write *d* for the short voiced fortis stop intervocalic in words like *butter, city*. This has been changed to *ţ* except where the field worker has marked his original transcription as certain.

b̥ ... g̊ denote weak (lenis) unaspirated voiceless stops, usually somewhat longer as well as less energetically articulated than *p ... k*.

HY very often writes *b̥, d̥, g̊* for unaspirated or weakly aspirated *p, t, k* initial in a word, and for the normal unaspirated stop after *s*, as in *pole, toll, coal, spill, still, skill, resting b̥ol, d̥ol, g̊ol, sb̥ɪl, sd̥ɪl, sg̊ɪl, rɛsd̥ɪŋ*. No change has been made in these transcriptions; but it is to be noted that they represent essentially the same sounds which the other field workers usually write *p, t, k* in similar contexts.

B and other field workers also use *b̥, d̥, g̊* for unaspirated voiceless stops in words like *pole, toll, coal*, but only when they are heard as distinctly weak (lenis).

t d̦ denote palatalized alveolar stops, articulated like *t d* with the tip and blade of the tongue touching the teeth-ridge (see **44**), but modified by raising the front of the tongue toward the hard palate (sometimes with actual contact) so as to produce a characteristic palatal coloring.

c ɟ denote true palatal stops, articulated with the tip of the tongue lowered and the front of the tongue touching the anterior or mid part of the hard palate.

ǩ ǧ denote velar stops articulated in a somewhat more advanced position than *k g*. In practice, the field workers use *ǩ ǧ* chiefly for advanced velar stops in contexts where the less advanced variety is more common, as in *keg, car, garden*. Velar stops contiguous to high-front vowels, as in *keep, geese, weak*, are normally more advanced than velar stops contiguous to central or back vowels, but are usually written simply as *k g*.

HY frequently writes *kᴵ gᴵ* in words like *car, garden*, presumably to denote an advanced variety of *k g* followed by a palatal off-glide. These combinations have been changed to *ǩᴵ ǧᴵ*.

HY sometimes writes *c ɟ* for sounds which are probably advanced velars rather than true palatals. When the context or the transcription of the other field workers makes it clear that HY's *c ɟ* are an overstatement of the palatal timbre, these symbols have been changed to *ǩ ǧ*.

tʃ dʒ denote the consonants in *church, judge*. These are regularly so written, though the stop element is probably often more palatalized and somewhat farther retracted than ordinary *t d*. When the palatalization is especially distinct, the sounds may be written as *tʃ dʒ* or *țʃ d̦ʒ*.

ʔ denotes a strong (but unaspirated) glottal stop. It may occur initially before a vowel in hesitating or emphatic utterance, as in *all ʔɔl*, or less commonly in final position after a vowel when the utterance is abruptly broken off, as in *whoa! hwouʔ*, or else in medial or final position as a substitute for some other stop, usually *t* or *k*, as in *little, sit, actress lıʔl, sıʔ, æʔtrɪs*. A superior *ʔ* usually marks the glottalization of an oral stop (see above), but may also be used for a weak glottal stop after a vowel, as in *say! seɪʔ*.

The field workers write an initial or medial glottal stop sometimes as *ʔ*, sometimes as *ˀ*, apparently without distinction of value. The inconsistency has been corrected by using *ʔ* in all positions except in combinations like *ˀp* and at the end of a word.

HY and R sometimes write *tˀl dˀl* in words like *class, glass*. These combinations have been changed to *tl dl*; but in a note of December 1933 (several months after the end of his field work) HY states that his *tˀl dˀl* should perhaps be interpreted as *tl̩ dl̩*. Similarly, HY sometimes writes *dˀr* in words like *grow*. This combination has been changed to *dr*.

56. *Nasals:* sounds differing from stops in that the velum is lowered to let the air current escape through the nose. The symbols in the consonant table are self-explanatory. Voiceless nasals are written by adding the diacritic for breath below or above the letter, as *m̥, n̥, ŋ̥*.

In the articulation of *m*, the tongue plays an important part. Its position (described as neutral) usually varies according to the character of the preceding or following sound. A palatalized *m*, that is one with the tongue position of a high-front vowel in contexts where other timbres are more usual, is sometimes written with the symbol *m̡*.

A flapped *n*, articulated by a quick up-and-down movement of the tongue tip with momentary contact between this and the teeth-ridge, is occasionally heard as a substitute for the combination *nt* in words like *center, into*. B and L write this sound as a nasalized flapped *r r̃* (see **58**). K sometimes writes *nr* in such words.

57. *Laterals:* sounds formed by contact of the tip (and blade) of the tongue, or of the front of the tongue, with some part of the roof of the mouth, in such a way that the air current is free to pass along one side or both sides of the tongue, usually without friction.

l usually denotes the normal, weakly velarized *l* of American English, articulated with the tip of the tongue touching the teeth-ridge in the median line. But some of the field workers (especially HS) commonly use this symbol for all varieties of *l* without distinction except in special cases:

l̦ denotes a distinctly 'clear' *l*, that is an alveolar *l* with the front of the tongue evenly rounded and the back relatively flat or sloping, so as to produce the timbre of a front vowel.

ł denotes a distinctly 'dark' (velarized) *l*, that is an alveolar *l* with the front of the tongue slightly depressed and the back raised toward the soft palate, so as to produce the timbre of a back vowel.

HN usually indicates the timbre of this *l* in words like *cattle* by writing ᵁ*l* or ᵘ*l*, thus in *kætʊl, kætᵘl*. These combinations have been replaced by the symbol *ł*, thus in *kætł*.

l̹ denotes a distinctly palatalized *l*, that is an alveolar *l* with the front of the tongue either raised toward or actually touching the anterior part of the hard palate, so as to produce a strong palatal timbre and sometimes an off-glide written as *j* or *ʲ*.

HY sometimes writes *cl̦ ɟl̦* in words like *class, glass*. Since the lateral is certainly affected by the palatal stop, these combinations have been changed to *cl̹ ɟl̹*.
L regularly and B in early records write *l̹* to denote a clear *l*. This has been changed to *l̦* in all cases except where the context makes a palatalized *l* probable, as in *glass, stallion* and the like.

ļ denotes a retroflex *l*, homorganic with *t ḍ*. It may be neutral, slightly 'dark' or slightly 'clear,' according to the phonetic context.

ɭ (used only by B) denotes a retroflex *l* with distinct velar timbre: a 'dark' retroflex *l*.

ʎ denotes a true palatal *l*, homorganic with *c ɟ*. The symbol is rarely used.

R uses this symbol, according to his own statement, to write both a 'clear' and a palatalized alveolar *l*. The proper symbol, *l̦* or *l̹*, has been substituted for his *ʎ* in all cases by reference to the context and the transcription of the other field workers.

Superior lateral symbols, especially ˡ and ˡ, denote sounds resembling true laterals but formed without actual contact between the tip of the tongue and the roof of the mouth, heard frequently in words like *will, milk*. When these sounds are heard as completely vocalized (when they are acoustically identical with vowels or vocalic glides) they are written with vowel symbols, as in *wɪᵘ, mɪɯk* and the like.

58. *Flaps* or taps: sounds formed by a single quick up-and-down movement of the tongue tip, usually but not always with momentary contact between this and some point on the roof of the mouth.

ɾ denotes an alveolar flapped *r*. It may represent a variant of the *r* phoneme, as in *three, very θɾiˑ, vɛɾɨ*, or of the *t* phoneme, as in *water, butter wɒˑɾə, bʌɾə, bʌɾɾ*. On nasalized *r̃* see **56**.

ɺ denotes a flapped *l* (which may be neutral, slightly 'clear' or slightly 'dark'), formed like *ɾ* but with lateral contraction of the tongue at the moment of contact. This sound, distinguished only by B and L, seems to be limited to the position after initial consonants, as in *blue, slow bɺuˑ, sɺou*.

ɽ denotes a retroflex flapped *r*, formed like *ɾ* but homorganic with *t ḍ*. It is usually a variant of the *r* phoneme, less commonly of the *t* phoneme.

In words like *three, throw,* when pronounced with a flapped *r,* B generally writes *ɾ,* L generally writes *ɽ.* The two field workers probably intend the same kind of sound by these transcriptions.

L very often marks the symbol *ɾ* with a breve, presumably to emphasize the momentary character of the sound.

59. *Fricatives:* sounds formed by constricting the oral or glottal passage so that the passing air current sets up more or less audible friction at the point of narrowing.

φ, f, ꞩ, θ, s, ꜱ, ʂ, ʃ, ʃ, ɕ, ç, ʄ, x̄, x, h, ɦ denote strong (fortis) voiceless fricatives. Weaker (lenis) varieties may be written by adding the diacritic for breath to the symbols for the corresponding voiced sounds.

β, v, ẕ, ð, z, ɺ, r, ʀ, ẓ, ɟ, ẕ, ɟ, ɽ, ʒ, ʒ, ʑ, j, ʝ, ɣ̃, ɣ, ɦ denote weak (lenis) voiced fricatives. When initial in a word or final in a phrase, these sounds are often partly or wholly voiceless (equivalent to β̥ ... ɣ̊). This fact is not usually indicated by the field workers unless the devocalization is complete or especially noticeable.

HY writes *ẓ* and the like in final position much more often than any other field worker, probably using this transcription even when the sound in question is not completely voiceless but only devocalized at the end.

HS sometimes writes final fricatives as *vɣ, zẓ* and the like, to indicate the unvoiced ending of these sounds. In order to avoid the implication that the sounds in question are long or double, these combinations have been changed to *vˣ, zˢ,* etc.

φ β, f v denote bilabial and labiodental fricatives respectively.

ꞩ ẕ, θ ð denote dental (rarely interdental) fricatives, distinguished from each other by different kinds of tongue contact and opening. ꞩ ẕ, like *s z,* are (in Jespersen's terminology) rill spirants, articulated so as to leave a narrow channel along the median line of the tongue; θ ð are slit spirants, articulated so as to leave a wide flat passage over a large part of the tongue.

s z, ɺ, ʀ denote alveolar fricatives, distinguished from each other by different kinds of tongue contact and opening. *s z* are rill spirants articulated by the blade of the tongue; ɺ is a strongly fricative slit spirant articulated by the tip of the tongue, often heard after alveolar stops in words like *try, dry;* ʀ is a fricative and strongly velarized slit spirant. On *r* see **60.**

ɺ is very rarely used by HS, R, J, HN, who usually write all varieties of consonantal *r* with the letter *r.*

ʀ is rarely used except by HY to denote a peculiar *r*-sound in the speech of one informant (6.1). HY defines the sound as 'a kind of velarized *r* that sounds like a uvular scrape.' In extreme cases it may be accompanied by actual friction between the back of the tongue and the soft palate.

ʃ ʒ, ɟ denote palatalized alveolar fricatives, homorganic with *ţ ɖ,* distinguished from each other in the same way as *s z, ɺ.*

ʂ ẓ, ɽ denote retroflex or retracted alveolar fricatives, homorganic with *ţ ɖ,* distinguished from each other in the same way as *s z, ɺ.* On *r* see **60.**

B and R sometimes represent a sound acoustically intermediate between *s* and ʃ by the combination ʃˢ. This has been replaced by the symbol ʂ.

ʃ ʒ, ʃ ʒ denote alveolo-palatal fricatives, as heard in *ship, leisure* and as part of the affricates in *church, judge.* ʃ ʒ are distinguished from ʃ ʒ by a palatal timbre, usually produced by advancing the front of the tongue nearer to the hard palate.

ɕ ʑ denote palato-alveolar or advanced palatal fricatives, roughly intermediate in acoustic effect between ʃ ʒ and ç ʝ, sometimes heard in phrases like *this year, these years* ðɪɕ (ʝ)iə, ðiʐ (ʝ)iəz.

ç ʝ denote palatal fricatives, as heard in German *ich, ja*. For a more common use of the symbol ʝ see **60**.

x ɣ denote velar fricatives, homorganic with k g.

L sometimes uses ɣ̇ (an advanced voiced velar fricative modified by raising of the tongue tip) to denote a peculiar kind of r-sound heard after initial g in words like *green, grow*.

ç̣ ʝ̣, x̄ ɣ̄ denote respectively retracted palatal and advanced velar fricatives, representing nuances intermediate between ç ʝ and x ɣ.

h ɦ denote the ordinary h-sounds of English, articulated with the tongue and lip position of the following sound. (Thus ha = ɑ̥a, hi = ḭi, hw = ʍw, etc.) 'Voiced h' ɦ is murmured rather than fully voiced. ɦ̡ denotes a distinctly palatalized h, that is one with front-vowel timbre in a context where central- or back-vowel timbre is more common. The symbol is rarely used; it is sometimes replaced by ɦ̵.

60. *Frictionless continuants:* sounds formed by narrowing or modifying the shape of the oral passage, but not sufficiently to make the passing air current set up audible friction.

ɥ, w are entered in the first compartment of this row within parentheses to indicate that the protrusion of the lips which characterizes these sounds is only a part of their articulation. See below. The difference between ɥ and w is exactly analogous to the difference between the vowels y and u.

ꜰ ʋ denote sounds resembling f v but with less friction and usually shorter.

r denotes the common alveolar or slightly post-alveolar frictionless r-sound of American English, as in the most usual pronunciation of *red, run, gray, arrow, far away*. Several field workers use this symbol also to denote the fricative r-sound, regularly written ɹ by B and L. (For this reason r is entered in the consonant table both as a fricative and as a frictionless continuant.) On the use of r as a vowel symbol see **19**.

If a word ending in r is recorded in a context in which it is immediately followed by a word beginning with a vowel (as *father* in the context *father and mother*), but if this following word does not appear as part of the entry on the map, a link ‿ is added after the final r to indicate prevocalic position: thus faðər‿ as compared with faðə.

ɽ denotes a sound of the same kind as r but articulated farther back. Like r, this symbol is used not only for a frictionless continuant but also for a fricative r (otherwise ɻ) and for a 'retroflex' unstressed vowel.

ʝ, ɥ denote frictionless palatal continuants, distinguished from each other by the position of the lips: for ʝ the lips are unrounded (neutral), for ɥ they are rounded and sometimes protruded. The voiceless counterparts of these sounds are written ʝ̥, ɥ̊. Observe that ʝ is used also (though rarely) for the voiced counterpart of ç. (For this reason ʝ is entered in the consonant table twice.)

w denotes a frictionless velar continuant articulated with rounded lips. The initial consonant of *white, wheel* and the like is variously written. Transcriptions range from ʍ (completely voiceless), through ʰw (voiceless at the beginning), ʰw (voiced except for a scarcely audible voiceless beginning) and ɦw (fully voiced except for a half-voiced or murmured beginning), to w (voiced throughout).

B sometimes writes w for an extremely labialized r-sound, as in *grow* gwoʊ, in which the acoustic effect of the lip-rounding predominates over the effect of the tongue-tip articulation.

ACCENTUATION

Stress

61. Word and sentence stress, the relative prominence of syllables in polysyllabic words and in groups of two or more words, is marked in accordance with the practice of the IPA. A primary stress (the chief stress in the word or word group) is indicated by a superior vertical stroke ' immediately preceding the stressed syllable; a secondary stress is indicated by an inferior vertical stroke , preceding the syllable.

62. Except when special circumstances make it necessary, stress is not indicated in the entries on the maps of the Linguistic Atlas. Since the great majority of words and phrases recorded by the field workers are pronounced by all informants with the same stress pattern, it would be superfluous to mark this separately in each entry. Instead, a concise statement in the commentary is usually sufficient to describe the distribution of stress in all forms shown on the map. On the other hand, when a word or phrase (as *automobile, how are you?*) is pronounced by different informants with different stress patterns, the position of the primary stress(es) is indicated in the entries on the map wherever the information is available.

The observation of stress (or rather of the relative prominence of syllables, produced jointly by stress, pitch and length) is beset with serious difficulties under the conditions of field work. The tendency of the informants to offer some words with an overcareful or overemphatic pronunciation, as well as their hesitation or uncertainty in pronouncing others, often produces unnatural distributions of stress in the recorded forms. The difference between primary and secondary stresses is likely to become obscured or to disappear; compounds normally pronounced with the main stress on either the first or the second member are likely to be given even stress (as |stone |wall instead of |stone wall or stone |wall); and the usual stress pattern may even be reversed when contrasting two similar expressions (as hay |stack and hay |mow instead of the normal |hay stack and |hay mow). Moreover, the degree and the distribution of stress often depend largely upon the context in which the expression happened to be uttered; but since the context was only rarely recorded, the clue to many exceptional stress phenomena has been lost.

It is well known that individuals differ greatly in their judgments of the relative stress or prominence of syllables. For this reason the marking of stress in the records of some of the field workers is less trustworthy than the indication of sound quality. HY, R, J, HN often neglect to mark the position of the primary stress in polysyllabic words and in phrases; HS, except in her latest records, rarely distinguishes between primary and secondary stress.

63. When a word or compound is described as having level stress, it is to be understood that according to circumstances either the first or the second stress may be the stronger, or that the two may be equal in force. The determining factors are usually of three kinds: sentence rhythm (cf. *he is |four|teen, he is |fourteen |years, he is |just four|teen; a |stone |wall, the |old stone |wall, the |stone wall |fell,* etc.); contrast or distinction (cf. |thirteen |fourteen |fifteen in counting; *back |porch and back |stoop, |back porch and |front porch,* etc.); or emphasis (cf. *for the |last |four|teen |years,* etc.).

Intonation

64. The intonation (rise and fall of pitch) was recorded, and is shown on the maps of the Linguistic Atlas, only in the case of certain special phrases, such as greetings and the calls to domestic animals, in which the pitch pattern is more or less fixed by habit and may be regarded as an integral part of the expression. On the maps, intonation is indicated by small letters following the linguistic form:

l = level intonation lr = level-rising intonation

r = rising intonation rf = rising-falling intonation

f = falling intonation   etc.

65. In recording these phrases, the field workers used a system of straight lines, curves and dots on a staff of three levels, usually written under the phonetic transcription. In this way the perceived intonation could be much more minutely and objectively indicated than by the use of any diacritics or of the simplified method used on the maps. In this system,

(a) the tones of stressed syllables are indicated by straight lines and curves placed on three levels for high, middle and low pitch respectively:

—　level or nearly level tone

⌣　gently rising tone

⌐　gently falling tone

⌡　sudden rise (nearly always from low to high)

⌐　sudden fall (nearly always from high to low)

⌣⌡　falling-rising tones

⌢⌐　rising-falling tones

(b) the tones of unstressed syllables are indicated by dots placed on three levels, or occasionally by curved lines when a change of tone is perceptible.

WORD DIVISION

66. When an entry on the map is a phrase containing two or more words, the words are separated by spaces for the sake of convenience in reading. This rule is observed even when the phonetic divisions between syllables do not coincide with the word divisions.

67. When a phonetic element of one symbol or more representing a complete word does not form a syllable by itself, but is part of a syllable whose peak lies in the preceding or following word, this nonsyllabic element is written separately in accordance with the rule just given, but is joined to the preceding or following word by a link ‿ : thus *here is* hɪər ɪz but *here's* hɪə‿z, *is it* ɪz ɪt but *is 't* ɪz‿t, *it is* ɪt ɪz but *'t is* t‿ɪz or *it's* ɪt‿s, *they are* (two syllables) ðe ə but *they are* (one syllable) ðe‿ə. When a nonsyllabic element representing a complete word seems to belong equally to the preceding and to the following word, it is linked to both: thus *here's your clothes* hɪə‿ʒ‿ə klouz. Occasionally a sequence of three words may form only one syllable. In that case both the nonsyllabic elements are linked to the word containing the syllabic peak: thus *what is it worth* hwɒt‿s‿t wɜ·θ, *if he's there* f‿i‿z ðɛə.

68. The rule governing the separation of words is observed also when the final consonant of one word and the initial consonant of the following word are partially assimilated: thus *this year* ðɪs jɪə, ðɪʃ jɪə, ðɪˢ ʃɪə; and even when these two sounds are completely assimilated, provided the resulting consonant is long or 'double': thus ðɪʃ ʃɪə. But when the resulting consonant is short, so that a single consonant belongs equally to both words, the words are not separated: thus ðɪʃɪə.

It is sometimes difficult or impossible to decide where the boundary between two words should be drawn. In such cases the words are usually not divided: thus *used to* ˈjuːstə.

69. In writing a phrase of two words, the field workers sometimes indicate that the stress on the second word sets in before or together with the final consonant of the first word, so that this consonant belongs phonetically to the following syllable: thus *far off* fɑˈrɔf, *New*

England nu'wiŋglənd, *post office* 'poʊs,tɒfɪs. In such cases, where the syllabic division and the word division disagree, the rule in **66** has nevertheless been observed; but a statement has been included in the commentary giving the necessary information concerning the peculiarities of the syllabic division.

Labels and Other Symbols Used on the Maps

Labels

70. Besides the linguistic forms, transcribed by the field workers in the phonetic alphabet presented above, the entries on the maps of the Linguistic Atlas sometimes contain various 'labels' to indicate (A) the manner in which the response was secured, (B) the informant's attitude toward the response, (C) the status of the form offered according to the informant's comments, and (D) doubt on the field worker's part as to the accuracy of his transcription.

71. (A) Labels indicating the manner in which the response was secured are abbreviations (small letters followed by a period) immediately preceding the form. They are used to mark all responses not secured as straightforward answers to the usual form of the question. **Each of these abbreviations except *s.* applies only to the one form to which it is prefixed.**

c. marks a form recorded from the informant's conversation, not in answer to a question. Such forms are especially valuable as samples of spontaneous, natural usage. Many of the strictly grammatical items, such as the forms of auxiliary verbs, the case forms of pronouns and double negation, were secured in this way.

cr. marks a form offered by the informant as a spontaneous correction of some other form (usually the one immediately preceding it in the entry). Such forms are often self-conscious attempts at elegance or correctness; but sometimes a conscientious informant may correct his affected first response to a more natural form.

r. marks a form repeated at the field worker's request, usually because he has not heard the first utterance clearly or is not sure that he has transcribed it correctly. The notation of the first utterance is sometimes included in the record (preceding the repeated form), sometimes omitted.

f. marks a form secured as a forced response by repeated questioning or by insisting on an answer when the informant is reluctant to give one. Such forms are to be accepted with reservations, since an informant may sometimes be forced by the field worker's persistence into offering a response which does not represent his normal usage.

s. marks a form suggested (that is, actually pronounced) by the field worker and repeated by the informant. A suggested response is of course not recorded by the field worker unless he has reason to suppose that it represents the informant's natural usage; but since this question cannot always be satisfactorily decided under the conditions of field work, forms marked as suggested are in general to be regarded as less trustworthy than responses secured in other ways. **The abbreviation *s.* applies to all the forms following it in the entry, except to forms separated from it by a semicolon or marked with an asterisk.**

Some of the field workers resorted to suggestion more freely than others. L was especially inclined to suggest forms in which he was particularly interested if his informants failed to offer them spontaneously, and in his later records systematically suggested a number of terms which he had found it difficult to secure by indirect questioning. B also resorted to suggestion instead of indirect questioning in the case of certain difficult items, but used this procedure less frequently than L.

It is of course understood that a suggested form was not entered by a field worker in his record unless the informant actually repeated it himself and signified that it was natural to him.

72. (B) Labels indicating the informant's attitude toward the response (usually toward the word or phrase offered, sometimes toward the subject-matter to which this refers) are marks of punctuation immediately preceding the form. **Each of these marks applies only to the one form to which it is prefixed.**

(:) A colon marks a hesitating response, regardless of the cause of the hesitation. This may be uncertainty on the informant's part, his inability to recall the term, or his disinclination to utter it (as in the case of words which he regards as indelicate).

(!) An exclamation point marks a form at which the informant evinces amusement, whether this is caused by the phonetic character of the term, by its meaning or connotation, or by the broader subject-matter to which it refers.

(?) A query marks a form concerning which the informant expresses doubt, whether this refers to its meaning, to its pronunciation or to its naturalness; or else (less commonly) a form which the field worker considers to be of doubtful validity as a sample of the informant's natural usage.

73. (C) Labels indicating the status of the form offered according to the comments or explicit statements of the informant are arbitrary superior symbols immediately preceding the form. **Each of these symbols applies only to the one form to which it is prefixed.**

($^{\perp}$) marks a form not used by the informant himself, but offered by him as an expression used by others. Very often this label is amplified by a statement in the commentary indicating whether the informant has heard the form in question from natives of his own community or from strangers, from educated or uneducated persons, and the like.

(†) marks a form characterized by the informant as old, obsolete, no longer used or the like, whether it is one which he himself used formerly or one which he only has heard from older people. A statement in the commentary often indicates the status of 'old' terms more precisely.

Not all the field workers were equally interested in securing reports of obsolete terms. L systematically asked for or even suggested older variants of the expressions offered by his informants; B on the other hand was usually content to record present-day usage. As a result, the maps of the Linguistic Atlas show a far greater proportion of terms marked with a dagger (†) in L's territory than elsewhere.

Forms characterized by the informants as older though still in use, or as old-fashioned but still natural, are not marked with the dagger. Instead, the status of such forms is noted in the commentary. It is often difficult to decide, from the indications given by the field workers (especially by L), whether a particular form is to be regarded as 'old' (†) or as 'older' than another term but still current; and the editors' decisions may not be in all cases correct.

($^{\rightarrow}$) marks a form characterized by the informant as recently introduced, new, used only by the younger generation or the like, especially if he states that it has come into currency since his own speech habits became fixed.

Forms characterized by the informants as modern but natural are not marked with the arrow. Instead, the status of such forms is noted in the commentary.

(*) marks a form offered not by the informant from whom the entry is usually recorded (the main informant) but by someone else (an auxiliary informant), generally a native of the same community and often a member of the main informant's immediate family. The auxiliary informant is usually identified either in the commentary or (when a considerable number of starred forms were offered by a single person) in the account of the main informant in Chapter VI.

Forms offered by an auxiliary informant are entered on the map only if they present features of special interest or if the main informant offered no response. They are of course to be disregarded in any consideration of the main informant's speech.

74. (D) The label indicating doubt on the field worker's part as to the accuracy of his transcription is a query in parentheses (?) immediately following the form. When the field worker's uncertainty refers to only one feature in the transcription (for example, to the quality of a particular vowel in the word), the reference of the label is more fully explained in the commentary.

In the actual field work, doubt as to the accuracy of a transcription was indicated by a wavy underline under the doubtful symbol or symbols. Conversely, when the field worker wished to indicate that a given transcription was to be accepted as certain (especially in the case of transcriptions which might seem to the editors to involve a slip in notation), he marked the symbol or symbols concerned with a double straight underline. This double underline has not been reproduced on the maps; but when a form so marked in the field record might appear to the reader as a mistake, the comment 'sic' has been entered in the commentary.

Forms marked by the field worker as doubtful are included in the entries on the maps only if no other form (or no other form of the same type) was recorded from the same informant.

Substitute Symbols

75. Under this head are grouped a number of signs used to avoid the repetition of identical words or parts of words in a single entry on the map, or to represent forms not given in phonetic transcription.

76. (~) The omission sign is used

to replace a word or group of words (or each of two noncontiguous words) repeated without change in a single entry: thus *hæf pæst sevən, ha·f pa·st* ~ (to repeat the word *sevən*), *hæf pæst sevən, ha·f* ~ *sɛbm* (to repeat the word *pæst*), *hæf pæst sevən,* ~ *sɛbm* (to repeat the words *hæf pæst*), *hæf pæst sevən,* ~ *æftə* ~ (to repeat the words *hæf* and *sevən*);

to replace one member of a compound repeated without change in a single entry: thus *hwiȷlbærou,* ~*barə* (to repeat the first member *hwiȷl*), *hwiȷlbærou,* ~*barə, wiȷl*~ (to repeat the first member *hwiȷl* and then the second member *bærou* or *barə*);

sometimes to represent a part of a phrase which is regularly shown on the map but which in a particular case was not recorded by the field worker: thus *hɛdz əv* ~ *heads of*, part of the expression *heads of lettuce*, where the last word of the phrase was omitted from the record.

77. (-) The hyphen is used to replace a sequence of sounds (usually a syllable or a group of syllables) repeated without change in two or more forms of the same word in a single entry: thus *ȷɛstədɨ, ȷɪstə-* (to repeat the syllable *dɨ*), *ȷɛstədɨ, ȷɪs-* (to repeat the syllables *tədɨ*), *ȷɛstədɨ, -deɨ* (to repeat the syllables *ȷɛstə*).

78. (=) The equal-sign is used after a semicolon to indicate that all the forms preceding the semicolon in the entry are to be repeated after it: thus, on the map which shows the preterite and past participle of the verb *drive*, separated by a semicolon, *drouv;* = (preterite *drove*, participle also *drove*), *drouv, drɪv;* = (preterite either *drove* or *drɪv*, participle the same), *drouv; =, drɪvən* (preterite *drove*, participle either *drove* or *driven*).

79. (?) A query standing alone (not immediately preceding or following a linguistic form, as in **73** and **74**) indicates that the informant was unable to make the proper response to the field worker's question, either because he was unfamiliar with the subject-matter involved or because the term asked for had escaped his memory.

The query is rather rarely used in this sense. In most cases the absence of a response, indicated either by a dash or by a blank line (see **80**), is not specially explained.

80. When no response was secured for a given item, either because the question was not asked or for some other reason (cf. **79**), the line on the map in which the informant's responses are usually entered is left blank. But if a form was offered by another informant in the same community, and if this other informant's responses regularly follow those of the one first mentioned, the missing entry is replaced by a dash in order to make possible the identification of the following line or lines. Thus, in a community where two informants were interviewed, if no response was obtained from the younger, the second of the two lines assigned to this community is left blank (since this does not affect the identification of the first line). If no response was obtained from the older informant, a dash is entered in the first line in order to identify the other line as the second. If no response was obtained from either informant, both lines are left blank.

81. Other symbols occasionally used on the maps—a triangle (△), numerals either standing alone or suffixed as exponents to linguistic forms, etc.—are explained in the commentary of each map on which they appear.

Miscellaneous Signs Used in the Commentaries

82. In the commentaries of the maps, when a form in phonetic transcription is given in a context of words in traditional orthography, the phonetic symbols are enclosed in square brackets [ ]. But the brackets are not used when the phonetic form is sufficiently separated from surrounding words in traditional orthography by marks of punctuation, or when no such words appear in the same entry.

83. In the commentaries, cited forms (including words and phrases quoted from the speech of the informants to illustrate their usage) are written in SMALL CAPITALS. Definitions and comments of the informants reproduced verbatim are enclosed in single quotation marks. Comments supplied by the editors are provided with the signature 'Ed.' Field workers' comments and paraphrases of informants' comments are entered with no particular distinguishing marks.

Chapter V

THE WORK SHEETS

Introductory

The items investigated for the *Linguistic Atlas of New England* are given below in the order in which they appear in the revised edition of the New England work sheets.

Page numbers of the work sheets are printed in boldface, item numbers in plain roman, and the corresponding map numbers in italics. The map number usually represents the map on which the material recorded under the item in question is published; but in some cases, where the recorded material proved to be fragmentary or untrustworthy, the number represents instead the map on which the material is summarized or otherwise referred to. Note that several items are followed by more than one map number (where the material recorded under a single item has been subdivided and presented on two or more maps), and that conversely the same map number occasionally appears after more than one item (where the material recorded under several items has been combined and presented on a single map).

For each item the key word is given, often with indications of context set off by single parentheses and with definitions or instructions enclosed in square brackets. The short selection of known variants and dialectal synonyms appended to many of the lexical items in the field workers' copy, intended to help them in their investigation, has been omitted.

The short set of work sheets used with some of the informants, instead of being printed as a separate list, is incorporated in the long or regular set, the items included in both versions being identified by an asterisk (*).

The lexical and phonetic items are arranged topically. A considerable number of morphological features, especially verb forms, have been placed in one or another of these topical groups. Verbs, verb phrases (modal and temporal), adverbs, prepositions, conjunctions, exclamations and pronouns were assembled in twelve small units and scattered through the work sheets. The intention was to avoid prolonged questioning on such abstract items at any one time for fear of discouraging the informant.

Some of the field workers asked the questions precisely in the order in which they appear in the work sheets, but others found it more convenient to begin with the terms for familiar things in and about the home (**7.7** ff.) and to defer the morphological sections to the end of the interview. This practice has the advantage that the informant is put at ease from the beginning and that the investigator has the opportunity to observe the inevitably recurring verb forms, adverbs, conjunctions, exclamations and idioms while the informant is off-guard, before questioning him directly on matters of usage which are apt to be a test of rusticity and about which the younger and the better educated are inclined to twit their elders and their country kin.

The *regular* work sheets (questionnaire) of the *Linguistic Atlas of New England* contain 814 words and phrases grouped in 711 numbered items on 103 pages; the *short* set, 421 words and phrases grouped in 388 such items. It was the task of the field workers to ascertain the usage of each informant on all these points. In general, the work sheets indicate only the information sought: words which the informants were to pronounce; objects, actions, qualities, etc. which they were to name; and grammatical expressions for which their normal usage was to be investigated. The form of the questions by which these responses were to be secured was left largely to the ingenuity of the individual field workers, although the topical setting and the context provided in the work sheets often served as pointers.

The field workers soon learned by experience how to ask for each expression so as to secure reliable responses most speedily and safely. Although no two of them used exactly the same words in phrasing their questions, the general purport of these questions was in nearly all cases the same. The relatively few instances where the field workers differ from each other in some important respect in their manner of putting the question are noted in the commentaries of the maps concerned.

The short work sheets contain about half the material of the long or regular work sheets. They were used when it was necessary to complete a record speedily, either because the field worker lacked the time or because the informant could not spare him the long hours required for a full interview. The 421 expressions selected for the short work sheets include the most important key words, providing in outline a complete body of material on the informant's pronunciation and selected features of his vocabulary and grammar.

In the account of the individual informants given in Chapter VI, the note 'short work sheets' indicates that the informant under consideration was interviewed with the reduced version of the questionnaire. By referring to Chapter VI and to the work sheets as presented below, the reader will be able to determine whether the lack of a response from a particular informant on any of the maps of the *Linguistic Atlas of New England* is due to the informant's inability to answer the field worker's question or to the fact that the question was not asked of him.

The lexical and morphological features in the work sheets are selected from an extensive collection compiled largely from the regional and local word lists in *Dialect Notes* and *American Speech;* the phonetic items are derived mostly from H. Kurath's collections and from J. S. Kenyon, *American Pronunciation* (4 ed., Ann Arbor, 1930). Most of the dialect features in G. Hempl's short list (*Dialect Notes* 1, 316–18) have been included.

Care was taken to provide sufficient material for a rather full description, both phonemic and phonic, of the pronunciation of each informant, and hence for determining the regional and social distribution of the phonic variations of all the phonemes of American English, and for establishing differences in phonemic structure.

In order to facilitate comparison with British dialects, an effort was made to include as many features as possible from A. J. Ellis' *Comparative Specimen*, his *Dialect Test*, and his *Classified Word List* (*Early English Pronunciation*, part V, pp. 7*, 8* and 25*–29*: London, 1889).

The first set of work sheets was prepared by the director in 1929–30 and tried out in Ohio. Members of the committee in charge of the Atlas, especially C. H. Grandgent, J. S. Kenyon and G. P. Krapp, criticized this set and made many helpful suggestions, as did also William Ellery Leonard and Sterling A. Leonard of the University of Wisconsin.

The field test and the criticisms so generously offered enabled the director to construct a greatly improved edition, which was used in the final training period of the field workers in the summer of 1931. This additional experience with informants from different parts of the country resulted in the elimination of less productive items, and in more accurate definition of many of the items.

The first edition of the work sheets issued to the field workers (September 1931) contained

915 expressions grouped in 807 numbered items. After the field work had been under way for four months and records had been made in various parts of New England, it was decided to drop 131 items and to add 35. Some items were omitted because many informants were unfamiliar with the subject-matter involved, some because they were difficult to secure by direct questioning, others because no significant variations had been recorded. A number of dialectal expressions that had been discovered, often by chance, during these early interviews seemed worth looking into and were at this stage incorporated into the questionnaire.

The revised version of the work sheets was issued to the field workers in January 1932. Most of the new expressions were fitted into the work sheets at appropriate places where the dropping of an old item had left a number vacant; others were grouped together on two pages (102, 103) appended to the end of the work sheets. It is this revised version which is presented below. (The gaps in the numbering of the items on many of the pages resulted from the revision.)

The responses to questions later dropped from the work sheets, which were collected during the early months of the investigation, are occasionally presented in full or summarized in the commentaries of maps showing related expressions. Thus the recorded forms of the word *July*, originally included as part of item 1.8, are listed in the commentary of Map *66 April*.

The work sheets for the Atlas of the South Atlantic States contain approximately two thirds of the items of the New England Atlas; the remaining items are concerned mostly with dialectal variations within the South. The total number is somewhat larger than in the New England set.

A reduced set of work sheets containing about 400 items taken from the New England set and the Southern set, most of them common to both sets, has been prepared more recently (1937). It is intended for wide-meshed surveys of pronunciation and vocabulary and for 'sampling' operations.*

Contents of the Work Sheets

1.1–	1.7	numerals	33.1–	39.4	domestic animals, calls to animals
1.8–	5.3	expressions of time	39.5–	40.7	*adverbs*
5.4–	7.6	the weather	41.3–	42.1	farm crops
7.7–	12.1	the dwelling	42.2–	44.2	*pronouns*
12.2–	14.1	*verb forms*	44.3–	51.6	food, cooking, mealtime
14.2–	16.7	the farm	52.1–	53.8	*pronouns*
16.8–	20.7	vessels, utensils, implements	54.1–	57.4	fruits, vegetables
20.8–	24.4	vehicles, implements	57.5–	58.7	*verb phrases*
24.6–	26.2	*verb forms*	59.1–	61.3	animals
26.5–	29.1	clothing and bedding	61.4–	62.8	trees, berries
29.3–	32.1	topography, roads	63.1–	66.5	the family
32.2–	32.7	*prepositions*			

* The reduced set was used by G. S. Lowman, Jr., in his survey of the dialects of Southern England (1937–38). It is now being used in the survey of the Great Lakes and the Ohio River area (directed by A. H. Marckwardt, University of Michigan), the survey of the Hudson Valley by Jane E. Daddow, Vassar College, and the survey of Nova Scotia and Eastern New Brunswick by H. Alexander, Queens University. Copies of the reduced work sheets can be furnished to investigators for a nominal charge.

THE WORK SHEETS

1 1 one *52;* two *53;* three *53;* *four *54.* 2 *five *55;* six *56;* seven *57;* eight *56.* 3 nine *55;* ten *56;* eleven *58;* *twelve *58.* 4 *thirteen *59;* fourteen *54;* twenty *60;* *twenty-seven *60.* 5 *thirty *59;* *forty *54;* seventy *57;* *hundred *61.* 6 the first (man *62;* the second (man *62;* *the fifth (man *63;* *the sixth (man *63.* 7 once *52;* twice *53.* 8 *January *64;* *February *65;* April *66.*

2 1 *Tuesday *67;* Wednesday *68;* Thursday *69;* *Saturday *70.* 4 *good morning! [until what time?] *77.* 5 afternoon [the part of the day before supper] *75.* 6 good day! [in meeting? in parting?] *78.* 7 evening [the part of the day after supper] *76.*

3 3 We start to work before) sunrise *73.* 4 The sun) rose (at six *657.* 5 We work until) sunset *74.* 7 *yesterday *71.*

4 2 *tomorrow *72.* 3 What time is it? [record the entire sentence] *79.* 4 *a gold) watch *157.* 5 *half past seven *80.* 6 *quarter of eleven *81.* 7 for quite a) while *85.* 8 *this year *82.*

5 1 He is) three years old *83.* 3 *a year ago *84.* 4 It's a) fine day *87.* 5 It's a) cloudy day *88.* 7 *It's) clearing up *89.* 8 The weather is) clouding up [when rain or snow is expected] *90.*

6 1 shower [heavy rain of short duration] *93.* 2 *thunder storm *94.* 3 The wind) blew (hard *637.* 5 *It's) drizzling *95.* 6 *fog *96.* 7 *foggy *96.*

7 1 drought *97.* 2 *The wind is) getting stronger *91.* 3 *The wind is) going down *92.* 4 It's a) snappy (morning *99.* 5 *We had a) frost *98.* 6 The lake) froze over (last night *648.* 7 *parlor, sitting room [where guests are entertained] *323.* 8 *The room is) nine feet high *46.*

8 2 (a) chimney *332;* (b) hearth *329.* 3 *mantel shelf *328.* 4 chimney [of an industrial plant] *333.* 5 *log *330.* 6 *soot *335.* 7 The ashes are (white *331.* 8 *chair *325.*

9 1 *sofa *326.* 2 chest of drawers [describe] *340.* 3 bureau [describe] *339.* 4 *bedroom *337.* 5 *window shades [roller shades] *327.* 6 clothes closet *338.* 7 *attic *345.* 8 *kitchen *343.*

10 1 pantry *344.* 2 rubbish [old worthless furniture and implements] *346.* 3 She cleans up (every morning *336.* 4 *The broom is behind (the door *155, 723.* 5 *Who does the) laundry? *359.* 6 I rented a room *356.* 7 *tenement *355.* 8 *porch [at front door; at back door; describe construction] *351.*

11 1 *Shut the door *347.* 2 *Who) rang (the bell? *656.* 3 *clapboards *350.* 4 I drove in (a nail *645*.   5 I have driven (many nails *645*.   6 *roof *348*.   7 *gutter(s) *349*.   8 shed, ell [for wood, tools, etc.; separate and built on] *352, 353*.

12   1 *privy [separate structure; the usual word and jocular terms] *354*.   2 I have my (troubles); you—; we—*614*.   3 I have heard it (many times); he—; they—[unstressed *have*] *683*.   4 *I haven't (done it); he—[both stressed and unstressed] *684*.   5 I haven't; he—[stressed, in answer to 'Have you seen him?'] *685*.   6 I do it (all the time); he—; we—*686*.   7 Does he do (that sort of thing? *687*.   8 He does [stressed] *687*.

13   2 *He doesn't care *688*.   3 I work (all day); we—; *they—*691*.   4 I was talking (to him); you—; we—; *they—*680*.   5 *I have been thinking (about it); we—; they—*682*. 7 People think (he did it *692*.   8 *They say (he did it *693*.

14   1 *says I; —you; —we; —they [= I said, etc.] *693*.   2 *barn [What is it used for?] *101*.   3 corn crib [building for storing corn] *106*.   4 granary [building or part of building used for storing grain] *105*.   5 loft, scaffold [upper part of barn; describe or make sketch] *102*.   6 mow, bay [place(s) in barn for hay; describe] *103*.   7 hay stack, cock [observe shape and size; out of doors or in barn?] *104*.

15   2 cow stable [shelter for cows; describe] *108*.   3 horse stable [shelter for horses; describe] *109*.   4 pig pen, hog house [shelter for pigs and hogs; describe] *110*.   5 *dairy *107*.   6 barnyard [where stock is kept or fed] *113*.   8 pasture [where cows or sheep graze] *114*.

16   1 field [the place where potatoes, cabbage, tobacco are grown] *120*.   2 *picket fence *115*.   3 pickets [pointed or not? shape in cross-section] *115*.   4 *barbed wire fence *116*. 5 rail fence [zigzag and other types] *117*.   6 posts *118*.   7 *stone wall [of loose stones] *119*. 8 tin cup [with small looped handle] *133*.

17   1 *china *136*.   2 *bucket [wooden vessel; shape and use] *129*.   3 *pail [large open tin vessel for water, milk] *129*.   4 dinner pail [small tin vessel with cover for carrying dinner] *130*.   5 *garbage pail [describe] *135*.   6 *frying pan *132*.   7 *kettle [heavy iron vessel with large opening; shape] *131*.

18   1 *I must) wash the dishes *137*.   2 *She rinses (the dishes *138*.   3 dish cloth [for washing dishes] *139*.   4 dish towel [for wiping dishes] *140*.   5 *wash cloth [for the face] *141*.   6 *bath towel *142*.   7 *faucet [on water pipe at kitchen sink] *143*.   8 *The pipe) burst (last night *639*.

19   1 *It must have) burst *639*.   2 an empty glass *311*.   3 flour sieve [for sifting flour] *134*.   4 *funnel *145*.   5 *whip, goad [for driving horses, oxen] *179*.   6 switch [for punishing children] *398*.   7 *bag [made of paper; size; record *paper—, burlap—*] *149*.   8 *sack [made of cloth; size] *150*.

20   1 *clothes basket *360*.   2 *keg *146*.   3 *hoops *147*.   4 *cork [for bottle] *144*. 5 mouth organ *413*.   6 *hammer *151*.   7 Who took (my knife? *664*.   8 (a) wagon tongue *170;* (b) shafts [of a buggy] *171*.

21   1 wagon tire [of steel or iron] *169*.   2 whiffletree *172*.   3 evener *173*.   4 *He was) hauling (wood in his wagon *180*.   5 *plow *166*.   7 harrow *167*.   8 *stone boat [for transporting stones from the field] *168*.

22   1 *sled [for children; describe the several types used] *573, 574*.   2 crowbar, lever [of steel or iron] *154.* 3 *sawhorse *162.* 4 *cog wheel *158.* 5 *brush *155.* 6 *razor strop [for sharpening razor blades] *156.* 7 cartridge *161.* 8 *seesaw *577.*

23 1 (a) coal hod *148;* (b) stovepipe *334.* 2 *wheelbarrow *163.* 3 *whetstone [for sharpening scythe] *159.* 4 grindstone *160.* 5 *Can you drive an) automobile? *185.* 7 He pleaded (guilty *654.* 8 *grease (the car *188.*

24 1 *greasy *188.* 2 *oil *187.* 3 *inner) tube *186.* 4 (a) *They are going) to launch the boat *181, 182;* (b) a launch [a boat] *182.* 6 I am going (today); we—; *they—*673.* 7 Am I going (to get some?);—they—*675.* 8 *These are (the kind I like [say cigars, apples] *620.*

25 1 Here are your clothes [mother to child] *357.* 2 *There are (many people who think so *678.* 3 *I am not (going to hurt him); he—; they—*674.* 5 *I'm right,) am I not? *676.* 6 We were (going to do it); you—; *they—*679.* 7 *Those were (the good old days *622.* 8 *No, it wasn't I *604.*

26 1 Be you going? [enter phrases like *How be you? He's busier than I be*] *677.* 2 *If I were you, (I wouldn't wait [intonation] *681.* 5 sample [of cloth] *365.* 6 *That's a) pretty (dress *457.* 7 She has a) prettier (dress *457.* 8 *apron *364.*

27 1 *coat *361B.* 2 I have) brought (your coat *638.* 3 His coat) fitted (me *647.* 4 *new suit *361A.* 5 The pockets) bulge *362.* 6 They) knitted (sweaters for the soldiers *647.* 7 *The collar) shrank *660.* 8 It has shrunk *660.*

28 1 She likes to) dress up *358.* 2 purse [for coins] *368.* 3 bracelet *369.* 4 *low shoes *366.* 6 suspenders *363.* 7 an old) umbrella *367.* 8 *bedspread *341.*

29 1 quilt *342.* 3 *loam [rich black soil] *33.* 4 fertile *34.* 5 lowland [flat low-lying land along a stream] *28.* 6 meadow, swale [low-lying grass land] *29.* 7 swamp, bog [inland] *30.* 8 salt marsh [along the sea] *31.*

30 1 *They are) draining (the marshes *32.* 2 *creek, cove, bay [shallow arm of the sea; tidal stream] *40.* 4 ravine, notch [deep, narrow valley of a small stream] *36.* 5 gully, washout [channel cut by a stream in road or field] *37.* 6 *brook [small fresh-water stream; arrange by size] *41.* 7 *[names of streams in the neighborhood] *41.* 8 *hill [small elevation; arrange by size] *38.*

31 1 *mountain *39.* 3 *wharf [where boats stop and freight is unloaded] *183.* 5 *cement road *43.* 6 [Do you still use the word 'pike' or 'turnpike'? What does it mean? Name some pikes.] *42.* 7 side road *44.*

32 1 *He threw a stone (at the dog *35, 667.* 2 *He isn't) at home *403.* 3 (a) *without (milk; (b) *with (milk [*with* followed by a voiced sound] *725.* 5 *He was coming) toward(s) me *722.* 6 I ran) across (him [=met him] *422.* 7 We named the child) after him *394.*

33 1 *dog *211.* 2 *mongrel *212.* 3 *He was) bitten (by a dog *636.* 4 bull [among farmers; in the presence of women; term used by women] *190.* 5 *cow *191.* 6 two) yokes of oxen *189.* 7 *calf: (a) female, heifer(-calf); (b) male, bull-calf; (c) altered male, steer (calf) *192.* 8 *Daisy is going to) calve *193.*

34 1 stallion [among farmers; in the presence of women; term used by women] *197.* 2 gelding *196.* 3 *horse [Do you use the word *horse* as a general term for geldings, mares and stallions?] *196.* 4 I have never) ridden (a horse *655.* 5 He fell) off (the horse *724.*

6 *horseshoes *199.*   7 *quoits [a game] *199.*   8 ram [among farmers; in the presence of women; term used by women] *200.*

35 1 (a) ewe *201;* (b) pet lamb *202.*   2 wool *203.*   3 boar [among farmers; in the presence of women; term used by women] *206.*   4 pig [how old?] *205.*   5 shote [weaned pig? how old?] *205.*   6 *hogs [male and female? old and young?] *204.*   7 *bristles *207.*   8 *trough, troughs *208.*

36 1 *castrate [horses, bull-calves, boars, cats] *210.*   2 blat [of a calf being weaned] *195.*   3 moo [during feeding time] *194.*   4 *whinny [during feeding time] *198.*   6 feed) the poultry [general term] *213.*   7 setting hen *214.*   8 *chicken coop [describe] *111, 112.*

37 2 wishbone *215.*   3 pluck, haslet, giblets [comprehensive term for edible 'insides']: (a) [of a fowl] *216;* (b) [of a pig or calf] *209.*   4 chore time *217.*   5 [calls to cows;   mark stress and intonation in all calls, note repetition]: (a) [to get them from the pasture] *218–219;* (b) [to make them stand still during milking] *220.*   6 [calls to calves] *218–219.*   7 [calls to oxen to make them go left or right in plowing] *221.*   8 [calls to horses to get them from the pasture] *222.*

38 1 *[calls to horses to urge them on] *223.*   2 *[calls to horses to stop them] *224.* 3 [calls to pigs when feeding them] *226.*   4 [calls to sheep to get them from the pasture] *225.* 5 [calls to chickens when feeding them] *227.*   6 I want to) harness (the horses *176.* 8 [What is a team?   the horses or both horse(s) and wagon?] *174.*

39 2 reins [from bit to driver] *177.*   3 *stirrups *178.*   4 the near horse [horse on left] *175.*   7 *He's feeling bad *493.*   8 *a little way (over *50–51.*

40 1 a long way (to go *50–51.*   2 *You can find that) anywhere *709.*   3 He walked) backwards *706.*   4 He fell) forwards *705.*   7 *I ain't done nothing [record other cases of double negation] *718.*

41 3 *furrows [trenches cut by plow] *123.*   4 We raised a big) crop (of wheat *124.* 5 We cleared (the land [of shrubs, trees] *122.*   6 second crop [of clover, grass] *125.*   7 sheaf (of wheat *126.*   8 *forty) bushels (of wheat *127.*

42 1 Oats are thrashed *128.*   2 *You and I (will do it *608.*   3 He and I (are coming *609.*   4 (a) *It's for) him and me *613;* (b) between) you and me *613.*   5 *You've got to do it.) I? [emphatic] *603.*   6 *It's I; *—he; *—she; *—they *603.*   8 He isn't as tall) as I *606.*

43 1 I'm not as tall) as he *606.*   2 *He can do it better) than I *607.*   4 These are) the largest (apples we have *272.*   5 Two miles is) the farthest (he can go *49.*   8 *It's yours; *—ours; *—theirs; *—his; *—hers *615, 616, 617.*

44 1 They must look out) for themselves *619.*   2 *He'd better do it) himself *618.* 3 *wheat bread [in loaves] *281.*   4 *[other kinds of bread made of flour: preparation, shape] *281.*   5 a pan of) biscuits *282.*   6 *corn bread [in large cakes] *286.*   7–8 [other kinds of bread and cake made of corn meal: preparation, shape] *287.*

45 1 homemade bread and) baker's bread *285.*   2 *sweet roll [describe] *283.*   3 *doughnut [preparation, shape] *284.*   4 *griddle cake [of wheat] *289.*   6 two pounds (of flour *556.* 7 *a cake) of yeast *290.*   8 *yolk *296.*

46 1 *boiled eggs *294.*   2 *poached eggs *295.*   3 salt pork *301.*   4 bacon rind *302.* 5 dried beef *303.*   6 *sausage *304.*   7 *butcher *553.*   8 The meat is) spoiled *306.*

47   1 head-cheese *305*.   3 *sour milk *298*.   4 *cottage cheese *299*.   5 Most cheeses are (round *300*.   6 You'd better) strain the milk *297*.   7 *apple dumpling [baked in a deep dish; preparation] *292*.

48   2 *sauce [sweet liquid served with pudding] *293*.   4 a bite [food taken between regular meals] *314*.   5 *We ate (at six o'clock [When did you eat?] *646*.   6 How often) have you eaten (today? *646*.   7 *I'm going to) make some coffee *310*.   8 *a glass of water *311*.

49   1 *I drank (a lot of it *644*.   2 *How much) have you drunk? *644*.   3 *soft drink *312*.   4 Sit down! [invitation to sit down at table: (a) addressed to relatives or intimate friends; (b) addressed to strangers] *318*.   5 *He was) sitting (at the table *324*.   6 I sat down *661*.   7 Help yourself (to potatoes! *319*.   8 *I don't care for any [when declining food: (a) to members of family; (b) to host] *320*.

50   1 warmed over [of food] *313*.   2 *chew *315*.   4 hard to) digest *317*.   5 *corn meal mush *288*.   6 fruit salad *309*.   7 *vegetables [home-grown] *253*.   8 *vegetable garden *121*.

51   2 The molasses is (thick *307*.   3 *genuine maple syrup *307, 308*.   4 Sugar is sold) in bulk *555*.   5 *salt and pepper *291*.   6 Give me an apple *270*.

52   1 these fellows *624*.   2 *those boys *625*.   3 *Those are (the fellows I mean *621*.   4 *that tree *623*.   8 What's that? [when failing to hear someone's utterance] *594*.

53   1 Whom (do you want? *627*.   2 Whom (did you talk to? *627*.   3 I don't know) whom (you mean *628*.   4 He didn't tell me) whom (he voted for *628*.   6 *A man) that's poor (has a hard life *630*.   7 *He's the man) who owns the orchard *246, 629*.   8 *He's a boy) whose father (is very rich *631*.

54   1 *stone [of a cherry] *269*.   2 pit [of a peach] *268*.   3 *clingstone peach *267*.   4 freestone peach *267*.   5 core [of an apple] *271*.   8 *walnut shell *277*.

55   1 *almonds *278*.   2 *The oranges are all gone *273, 557*.   3 *radishes *256*.   4 *tomatoes *266*.   5 *onion *257*.   6 *spring onions *258*.   7 *Those cabbages are (big *255*.   8 *to) shell beans *260*.

56   1 *Lima beans [large, yellowish, flat seeds, not pods; distinct varieties?] *259*.   2 *two) heads of lettuce *254*.   3 husks [on an ear of corn] *263*.   4 *sweet corn [served on the cob] *261*.   5 *corn tassel [top of corn stalk] *262*.   6 *pumpkin *264*.   7 *muskmelon *265*.   8 *mushroom *279*.

57   1 *toadstool *280*.   3 *He couldn't) swallow it *316*.   4 cigars and cigarettes *321–322*.   5 *She was) singing and laughing [enter other participles in -*n* or with prefix *a*-] *420, 671, 672*.   6 I didn't) get to do it *701*.   7 *I can't [stressed] *695*.   8 I done worked (all day [only emphatic?] *669*.

58   2 *You dare not go *696*.   3 *He ought not to [negative of *he ought to*] *698*.   4 *I) won't do it *702*.   6 I wish (you would come tonight *703*.   7 *We'll go hunting,) come cooler weather *100*.

59   1 screech owl *230*.   4 We used to hunt) fox(es) *228*.   5 *gray squirrel *229*.   6 red squirrel *229*.   8 porgy [a fish] *233*.

60   1 *round clam *235*.   2 *frog *231*.   3 *toad *232*.   4 *earthworm *236*.   6 *moth *237*.   7 *lightning bug *238*.   8 *wasp, hornet, yellow-jacket [describe varieties: shape, color, size; location and shape of nest; sting very painful?] *239, 240–241*.

61 2 minnows [a bait] *234*. 3 spiderweb [(a) in house; (b) in woods and fields] *242*. 4 roots *248*. 5 *elm *243*. 6 *sycamore *244*. 7 sugar maple *247*. 8 sugar maple grove *247*.

62 1 *cherry tree *245*. 2 *sumach *250*. 3 strawberries *274*. 4 hull [of a strawberry] *275*. 5 *raspberries *276*. 6 Some berries are) poisonous *251*. 8 mountain laurel *249*.

63 1 I must ask) my husband *374*. 2 I must ask) my wife *375*. 4 widow *389*. 5 *father *370*. 6 *[What do (or did) you call your father? (usual term and terms of affection)] *371*. 7 *[What do (or did) you call your mother? (usual term and terms of affection)] *372*. 8 *parents *373*.

64 1 *grandfather [usual term and terms of affection] *380, 381*. 2 *grandmother [usual term and terms of affection] *382, 383*. 3 *Our children (are still in school *378*. 6 *daughter *376*. 7 *girl *377*. 8 [pet-names for 'child'] *379*.

65 1 *She is) pregnant [terms used by women] *392*. 3 *The boy) looks like (his father *393*. 4 She has) brought up (three children *395*. 5 She has to) take care of (the baby *396*. 6 *You're going to get a) whipping [to a child] *397*. 7 Bob) grew (a lot in one year *650*. 8 You've) grown (big *650*.

66 2 *nephew *687*. 3 *orphan *390*. 4 *guardian *391*. 5 her relatives *388*.

67 1 *There's a) gentleman (at the door *438*. 2 *Mary *432*; Martha *432*; Nelly *433*; *Billy *433*; Matthew *434*. 3 *Daniel Webster *435*. 4 (a) *Mrs. Cooper; (b) *Mrs. Brown [slow and fast forms of *Mrs.*] *436*. 5 Miss Brown *437*. 6 the Reverend Mr. Simpson *439*. 7 woman schoolteacher *444*. 8 your aunt *384*.

68 1 *Aunt Sarah *385*. 2 Uncle William; Uncle John *386*. 3 General (Scott *440*. 4 Colonel (Brown *440*. 5 Captain (Smith *441*. 6 Judge (Marshall *442*. 7 *student *445*. 8 *secretary *446*.

69 1 (a) *the selectmen; (b) *He's a) selectman *443*. 2 tourist *449*. 3 *actress *448*. 4 *an American *451*. 5 *an Italian [record also nicknames] *453*. 6 *[nicknames for an Irishman] *454*. 7 *[nicknames for a Jew] *455*.

70 1 *negro [neutral and derogatory terms] *452 A, 452 B*. 3 *a rustic [neutral and derogatory terms] *450*. 4 It's) almost (midnight *714*. 5 You were not) far off [=nearly right] *48*. 6 *just a minute! *86*. 7 *How far (is it to Boston? *47*. 8 Look here! [exclamation; seriously or jestingly?] *596*.

71 1 Look) over there! *707*. 2 *How often (do you go to town? *711*. 3 *Either you or I (must do it *610*. 4 Neither you nor I (can do it *611*. 5 I'm not going to do it!—) Nor I (n)either! *612*. 6 forehead *485*. 7 the) right ear *486*. 8 beard *488*.

72 1 *gums *487*. 2 *palm (of the hand *490*. 3 *joint *491*. 4 *chest *489*. 5 shoulders *489*. 7 stout, paunchy *458*. 8 emaciated [as the result of ill health] *459*.

73 1 *strong *460*. 2 *good-natured *468*. 3 He's so) awkward [referring to physical appearance] *463*. 4 that) awkward fellow! *464*. 5 *He is quite) skillful at (plowing, carpentering, odd jobs *462*. 6 that fool! [only of men? of women?] *465*. 7 He is a) tightwad *484*.

74 1 She is) quite lively [of young people? of old people? of both?] *461*. 3 *I'm afraid *475*. 4 She) didn't use to (be afraid [negative of *used to be*] *700*. 5 *She's too) slovenly (for me *466*. 6 *careless *467*. 7 *Don't be so) obstinate *471*.

75　1 touchy [easily offended] *470*.　2 *He got awfully) angry *472*.　3 *He was as mad as) a wet hen *473*.　4 He was) all excited [with expectation] *476–477*.　5 The sea is) calm (today *478*.　6 *tired, exhausted [normal and strong terms] *479, 481, 482*.　7 He is) worn out *480*.

76　1 He) got sick *492*.　2 He is) some better *496*.　3 *He is still) in bed *495*.　4 He will be well again) by and by *712*.　6 *He) caught a cold *499*.　7 *I'm) hoarse *501*.　8 *He has a) cough *500*.

77　1 Haven't you) taken (your medicine yet? *664*.　2 *deaf *502*.　3 fever *505*.　4 [What is the ague?] *505*.　5 He sweated (hard *662*.　6 boil [discharging] *512*.　7 pus *513*.　8 *My hand) swelled up *663*.

78　1 *It is) swollen *663*.　2 (a) *inflamed wound *514;* (b) *proud flesh *515*.　3 *iodine *516*.　4 *quinine *517*.　6 He) died [neutral, veiled and crude terms] *519, 520, 521*.　7 I don't know what) he died of *519*.　8 *cemetery *525, 526*.

79　1 *coffin *524*.　2 *They are in) mourning *523*.　3 *pretty well [in response to *How are you?*] *497*.　4 Don't worry! *498*.　5 Rheumatism is (painful *506*.　6 (The) mumps is (dangerous *507*.　7 *diphtheria *508*.　8 *jaundice *511*.

80　1 *appendicitis *509*.　2 tuberculosis *510*.　3 vomit [neutral, crude and jocular terms] *504*.　4 *He is sick) to his stomach *503*.　5 He came over) to tell (me about it *572*.　7 You) ought to take (it easy *697*.

81　1 I shall be (disappointed if he doesn't come *694*.　2 *We shall be (glad to see you *694*.　5 How is it that (you are here? *595*.　6 *He is) courting her, keeping company with her *404, 405*.　7 *her boy-friend [normal and jocular terms] *399*.　8 *his girl-friend [normal and jocular terms] *400*.

82　1 his fiancée *401*.　2 She turned him down [serious and jocular terms] *406, 407 A, 407 B*.　3 He lives) up in (Boston, etc. *720*.　4 He lives) up at (the Browns' *721*.　5 *serenade [noisy burlesque serenade after a wedding; describe] *409*.　6 *married *408*.　7 big social affair *414*.　8 the whole crowd [depreciative terms] *415*.

83　1 *a dance *410*.　2 five) couples *411*.　3 School) lets out (at four o'clock *538*.　4 When does school) begin? [after a vacation] *539*.　6 *education *535*.　7 *class *536*.　8 *college *537*.

84　1 *library *540*.　2 *post office *545*.　3 *railroad station *544*.　4 *hotel *543*.　5 *theater *541*.　6 We were in a) moving picture theater *542*.　7 *hospital *518*.　8 *nurse *447*.

85　1 *public square *546*.　4 *He walked) kitty-cornered *547*.　5 *on the) trolley car *184*.　6 I) want to get off (at the next corner *699*.　7 county seat *548*.　8 the Federal) Government *549*.

86　1 *the Civil War *551*.　2 *law and order *550*.　3 The murderer was) hanged *651*.　4 He) hanged (himself *651*.　5 *New England *4;* *Connecticut *10;* *Massachusetts *8;* Rhode Island *9;* Maine *5*.　6 *New Hampshire *6;* Vermont *7;* *New York *11;* Virginia *12*.　7 *North Carolina *13;* Georgia *14;* *Florida *15;* Tennessee *16*.　8 *Missouri *17;* Texas *16;* *California *18*.

87　1 *Boston *19;* *New Haven *20;* *Springfield *21;* *Chicago *22;* *Cincinnati *23*.　2 *Ireland *24;* *France *25;* *Russia *26;* *Asia *27*.　4 ten) miles *45*.　5 *a hundred) rods (from here *45*.   6 I don't know whether I want to *733*.   7 I don't care,) just so (you get back soon *728*.   8 It seems) as if (he'll never get well *732*.

88   1 *I won't go) unless (he goes *730*.   2 instead of (helping me *726*.   3 *while I (was talking to him *727*.   4 I don't know) but that (I had better *731*.   7 I like him) because (he's so good-natured *729*.

89   2 They joined (the Church *531*.   3 *God [as pronounced in church] *527*.   4 *my God! [an oath] *527*.   5 Mass *529–530*.   6 *sermon *529–530*.   7 *psalm *528*.   8 (a) music *412*; (b) beautiful *456*.

90   1 *devil [also veiled and jocular terms] *532, 533*.   2 ghost *533*.   3 *a haunted house *534*.   4 It's) rather (cold *717*.   5 *I'd rather (not go *717*.   6 It's) awfully (cold *716*. 7 I'm mighty glad to see you! *426*.   8 I'm) good and hungry *716*.

91   1 *certainly! [strong affirmation] *590*.   2 *why yes! *589*.   3 *[Do you habitually say *yes sir* and *yes ma'am* or simply *yes*? Mark intonation and stress, both normal and emphatic] *588*.   4 a lot of fun *416*.   5 a little bit *417*.   6 *well [hesitation] *593*.   7 That's) enough *418*.   8 *Is it) really true? *715*.

92   1–2 damn (it)! [arrange oaths in order of emphasis; what expressions are peculiar to women?] *599*.   3 for the) land's sake! [ever used by men?] *601–602*.   4 shucks! [impatience] *600*.   5 *the idea! *597*.   6 why! [stressed exclamation] *589*.   8 *How are you? [to an intimate friend; intonation] *424*.

93   1 *How do you do? [to a stranger; intonation] *425*.   2 *good-bye! [only when parting for a long time?] *427*.   3 *come again! [to a visitor] *428*.   4 hurrah! *598*.   5 Merry Christmas! *430*.   6 Happy New Year! *431*.   8 Don't mention it! *429*.

94   1 *I think (I'll have time *592*.   2 grocery store *552*.   3 *I had to do some) shopping (downtown *554*.   5 How much do you charge for it? [in a store; intonation] *559, 560*. 6 (a) How much do you want? [in a private deal] *561*; (b) auction *565*.   7 *sell) at a loss *562*.   8 The bill is) due *563*.

95   1 *pay) the dues *563*.   2 *borrow *564*.   3 It isn't of much) value *558*.   4 *The boys) coast (down the hill *575*.   5 *coast) lying down flat *576*.   6 *somersault *578*. 7 *I swam across *579*.   8 *He dived in *580*.

96   1 *He was drowned *522*.   2 The baby) creeps (on the floor *582*.   4 *He climbed (up a tree *642*.   5 I have often) climbed up *642*.   6 crouch *581*.   7 *She) kneeled (down *652*. 8 *I'm going to) lie down *494*.

97   1 *He) lay (in bed all day *653*.   2 *I) dreamed (all night *643*.   3 *I woke up *668*. 4 You'd better) pitch in [i.e., start working] *567*.   5 *He ran like) a house afire *474*. 6 *stamp (on the floor *583*.   7 *May I) see you home? *402*.   8 pull *164*.

98   1 push *164*.   2 I lugged (the suitcase to the station *165*.   3 *Don't you touch it! *689*.   4 I'll have to) repair (the table, harness, etc. *152*.   5 Go bring (me a knife *153*. 7 *goal [in games] *585*.   8 *catch (the ball! *584*.

99   1 *Who) caught (it? *641*.   2 I have never) caught (it yet *641*.   3 He is) wasting time *568*.   5 *Give me another chance! *570*.   7 in good) humor *469*.   8 I want to) get rid of him *569*.

100   2 Who) swiped (my pencil? *566*.   4 *I didn't) recognize (you *423*.   5 We're going to) miss you *421*.   6 They used to) chat (for hours *419*.   7 I have) written (a letter *670*. 8 *I expect an) answer *571*.

101   1 *Who) taught (you that? *666*.   2 We) intend (to go soon *704*.   3 He queered himself (with me *483*.   4 You won't) tell on (me, will you? [terms used by adults, by children] *586*.   5 [children's nicknames for one who tattles] *587*.   6 pick flowers *252*.

102   1 *That's the one you) gave (me *649*.   2 *He) began (to talk *635*.   3 *He) ran *658*.   4 *He) came (to see me *640*.   5 *He) saw (me *659*.   6 *The road was all) torn up *665*.   7 He) did it (last night *690*.   8 (a) He put it) on; (b) He put it) on (the table *708*.

103   1 *nothing *633*.   2 *something *632*.   3 *It's) such a (good one *626*.   4 *the whole (thing *634*.   5 *always *710*.   6 *I haven't seen him) since (Monday *713*.   7 *He did it) on purpose *719*.   8 (a) *uh-huh; (b) *uh-uh [grunts of affirmation and negation; intonation] *591*.

Chapter VI

COMMUNITIES AND INFORMANTS

Introductory

The proper interpretation of the Linguistic Atlas records requires at least some knowledge of the history and character of the communities investigated, and of the life and personality of the informants interviewed. This information is presented below in a series of individual case histories. For each community and for each informant the reader will find a condensed and abbreviated account of the essential facts, together with bibliographical references intended to facilitate a more intensive study of local history.

The communities investigated for the *Linguistic Atlas of New England* are numbered from **1** to **431**: **1–49** Connecticut; **50–51** Long Island (N.Y.); **52–82** Rhode Island; **102–248** Massachusetts; **252–296** Vermont; **302–348** New Hampshire; **352–424** Maine; **426–431** New Brunswick (Canada).

Except for the New Brunswick parishes, the communities are either towns (townships) or cities. The New England settlements were usually organized as towns, and the town has remained to this day the political unit within the county. From time to time, however, towns have been incorporated into cities. In Connecticut parts of some towns have been incorporated as cities or boroughs; sometimes, for example in New Haven, the town and the city (or borough) have come to be coextensive.

In several cases two adjoining towns have been grouped together as one Atlas community, represented on the maps by a single number. Whenever two towns are thus treated as a single community, the same community number appears (in bold-face type) before the name of each in the list below. In such 'split communities' the sequence of the historical sketches and of the *vitae* depends on the order the informants have been given on the maps.

Each historical sketch in the list below presents, in principle, the following information:

(1) The name of the town (or city) and the county. The name of a particular village, section, borough or other subdivision of a town in which the informant lives is sometimes given in parentheses after the town name.

(2) The date of settlement or of incorporation or of both. This is sometimes only approximate. Historical sources do not always agree on the exact year when permanent settlement of a particular town began.

(3) Provenience of the settlers, sometimes followed by a note on the 'mother towns' from which they came. To avoid repetition of the historical notes, the names of Atlas communities incidentally cited are usually preceded or followed by their community numbers as cross references.

(4) Notes on the early history of the community. These are based on material compiled for the use of the Atlas staff by the late Professor Marcus L. Hansen, sometimes from individual town histories, sometimes from the county and state histories listed at the end of Chapter III, sometimes from other sources.

(5) A description of the present character of the community, with notes on the chief industries or agricultural pursuits, the make-up of the population and the like. This description is based chiefly on notes made by the several field workers from first-hand observation and from the reports of their consultants and informants.

159

(6) Population figures for 1790 (or 1800), 1820 (or 1830), 1850, 1880, 1910 and 1930; sometimes also population estimates of a still earlier date. The 1930 population of a particular village, borough or city within a community is sometimes added in parentheses. An asterisk (*) after a population figure indicates that the town was subdivided into two (or more) towns at some time between the date of that census and the date of the one preceding, so that the decrease in population is due not to an actual loss of population but to a reorganization of the township.

(7) Bibliographical notes on published histories of the community. No attempt has been made to offer an exhaustive bibliography, including such items as vital records, genealogies, personal reminiscences, local fiction or poetry. Much additional information will be found in the county and state histories listed in the Historical Bibliography at the end of Chapter III; for towns which have to date no published history, such works are the only available source of historical information. For an intensive study of a town or a group of towns, the various bibliographies of local history and the publications of local historical societies are especially valuable.

On some New England towns a good deal of historical material has been published in books, pamphlets, newspapers and periodicals, but not all of it may be accessible outside the town itself, and early publications may be out of print. The bibliographical notes given below include only selected items which may prove helpful to readers in search of more detailed information concerning a particular community. New local histories will appear from time to time, especially when a town celebrates an anniversary of its incorporation.

Although town histories often have long titles, they are usually cited below in full, so that the reader may have some means of judging what a particular book is likely to contain.

Each historical sketch is followed immediately by the *vita* of the informant(s) interviewed in that community. The *vitae* of informants in the same community are numbered to correspond to the order which the informants have been assigned on the maps of the Linguistic Atlas. When a community is represented by only one informant, the *vita* is not numbered.

When two or more informants were interviewed in the same community, the most old-fashioned (who is in most cases also the oldest) is entered first, the most modern (who is in most cases also the youngest) is entered last. The order depends partly on the actual age of the informants, partly on the amount of formal education they have received, partly on their general personality—their receptiveness to new ideas, their interest in the present and so on. Compare the Table of Informants by Types in Chapter II.

Each *vita* in the list below presents information on the following points, so far as it is available in the field worker's record:

(1) The informant's occupation.

(2) His age—sometimes only approximate.

(3) His birthplace. When no birthplace is mentioned, the informant was born in the community under which his *vita* appears. Note that county (and state) names are added to town names in the *vitae* only when the town referred to is outside the informant's own county (or state). Distances in miles are often cited for convenience in localizing the town referred to. Such distances are measured (approximately) from the informant's community.

(4) His residence in other parts of the same state, in other states, or abroad. If there is no specific mention of other places in which the informant has lived, it is to be assumed that he has spent all his life in his own community.

(5) The birthplace of his parents. (F = father, M = mother.)

(6) The birthplace of his ancestors. (PGF = paternal grandfather, MGF = maternal grandfather, PGM = paternal grandmother, GGF = great-grandfather, PGGF = paternal great-grandfather, etc.)

(7) His schooling: his attendance at grammar school, high school (academy) and college (seminary, normal school, university); and the extent of his reading and of other experiences or activities which may have affected his cultural level. In rural communities the grammar school attended by informants of 60 or over was very often a one-room 'district school.'

(8) His social contacts, especially with particular classes of the town's population; his church affiliation, membership in clubs and fraternal organizations and the like. The informant's church membership is not always mentioned by the field worker.

(9) His personality and character, as described by the field worker: temperament, habits, interests and the like.

(10) His speech: familiarity with dialects other than his own, attitude toward 'correctness' in speech, individual characteristics (especially such as do not appear from the individual transcriptions on the maps of the Atlas: tempo, intonation, firmness of articulation, nasality, etc.). Occasionally the field worker adds a note on local peculiarities of dialect not illustrated in the speech of the informant.

(11) Identification of incomplete records and of records based on the short work sheets (see Chapter V), where necessary.

(12) The field worker's name and the serial number of the record. B = Bloch, C = Chapallaz, HN = Hultzén, HS = Harris, HY = Hanley, J = Joos, K = Kurath, L = Lowman, R = Reynard. The serial number indicates the place of the record in the list of all records made by one field worker (e.g., HY 17 = the 17th record made by Hanley), and thus enables the reader to distinguish earlier and later records. In general, later records are more accurate than earlier ones by the same field worker.

42 informants in 38 communities are designated in the *vitae* below as CULTURED INFORMANTS. These are men and women of superior education or culture, chosen to represent the standard cultivated type of speech in their respective communities. Communities in which such informants were interviewed are identified on the maps of the Atlas by a line above and below the community number.

Some of the *vitae* mention an AUXILIARY INFORMANT, whose occasional responses are entered on the maps of the Atlas in the same line as those of the main informant, but distinguished in all cases by a prefixed asterisk.

A few records were made jointly by the main informant and a SUPPLEMENTARY INFORMANT, the latter so designated in the *vita*. (See for example 400.2, Southwest Harbor, Maine. In this record the field worker has the following note: 'The two women have been lifelong friends and insisted on answering the questions together.') The supplementary informant's contributions to the record are in every case identified as exactly as possible in the *vita;* but his responses, unlike those of an auxiliary informant, are not distinguished on the maps by an asterisk.

The *vitae* of auxiliary and supplementary informants are not separately numbered, but follow immediately after the *vitae* of the main informants in whose records their responses appear.

The informant's family name was always recorded by the field worker (both in conventional spelling and in phonetic transcription), but usually with the explicit understanding that it would not be published. A number of informants, despite their willingness to aid in the recording of New England speech, would have refused to be interviewed if the field workers had not promised that they should remain anonymous. On the other hand, many informants supplied bibliographical references to published genealogies of their families. All such information is permanently filed at the headquarters of the Linguistic Atlas.

Most of the abbreviations used are self-explanatory. Some have been noted above, a few others are added here. FW = field worker. Associations and societies: A.A.U.W. = American Association of University Women, D.A.R. = Daughters of the American Revolution, I.O.O.F. = Independent Order of Odd Fellows, W.C.T.U. = Women's Christian Temperance Union.

CONNECTICUT

1 Town of Stamford (city of Stamford), Fairfield Co.

Settled 1641 under New Haven jurisdiction by a group of Wethersfield families. (Wethersfield settled 1634–35 from Watertown, Mass.) Stamford (named 1642 from Stamford, Lincolnshire) was part of the New Haven Colony 1643–62 (see 26 New Haven).— City (inc. 1893) is rapidly growing. Manufacture of machinery, boats, hardware, rubber and brass goods, paints, clothing, etc. Many commuters to New York City.—Pop. 1774: 3563, '90: 8810 (including Norwalk), 1820: 3284*, '50: 5000, '80: 11,297, 1910: 28,836, '30: 56,765 (S. city 46,346).—Huntington, E. B. History of Stamford, from its settlement in 1641 to the present. . . . 492 p. Stamford, 1868.— *Wethersfield:* Stiles, Henry R. The history of ancient Wethersfield. . . . 2v. N.Y., 1904.

1. Wealthy farmer, 85.—F born in Greenwich; M born here.—Grammar school and some private tutoring. Reads genealogical books and local history.—Formerly Congregationalist. Lives alone, frugally; small circle of friends.—Quiet, rather distinguished. Regarded as a rich eccentric. Somewhat suspicious.—Old-fashioned speech. No attempt to conform to ideas of correctness.—HY 18.

1 Town of Greenwich (Old Greenwich), Fairfield Co.

Settled c. 1640. Land had been bought from the Indians by agents of the New Haven Colony, but was claimed by New Netherland. Boundary disputes resulted in cession to Connecticut, 1664, of all the present town of Greenwich. Some Dutch settlers; many Englishmen from Long Island.—Shipping and shipbuilding in early 19. cent. Now a fashionable residential section. Many New York people have come here.—Pop. 1774: 2776, '90: 3175, 1820: 3790, '50: 5036, '80: 7892, 1910: 16,463, '30: 33,112.—Mead, D. M. History of the town of Greenwich, Fairfield Co., with many important statistics. 318 p. N.Y., 1857. Mead, Spencer P. History of Greenwich. . . . 768 p. N.Y., 1911.

2. Oyster grower (retired), 79.—F born here; M in Pound Ridge, Westchester Co., N.Y.—Grammar school.—Congregationalist.—Shrewd, observing, industrious. Notably successful in business —No affectations. Slow tempo, with tendency to diphthongization.—HY 20.

3 Town of Westport (Greens Farms), Fairfield Co.

Set off from Fairfield, Norwalk and Weston in 1835. Fairfield settled 1639 from Windsor (see 45 East Windsor); many from Concord, Mass., in 1644, and from Watertown, Mass. Norwalk settled from Hartford (q.v., 40) and the Conn. River towns; inc. 1651. Weston (q.v., 4) set off from Fairfield in 1787. —Mainly residential. Farming and some manufacturing.—Greens Farms, originally part of the West Parish of Fairfield, has many fashionable estates. Old residents keep to themselves.—Pop. 1850: 2651, '80: 3477, 1910: 4259, '30: 6073.—Westport in Connecticut's history, 1835–1935. 126 p. Printed in Bridgeport. (Centenary souvenir book.)—*Fairfield:* Child, F. S. An old New England town; sketches of life, scenery and character. 230 p. N.Y., 1895. Schenck, Mrs. E. H. History of Fairfield, Fairfield Co. . . . 2v. New York, 1889, 1905.— *Norwalk:* Hall, Edwin. Ancient historical records of Norwalk, with a plan of the ancient settlement and of the town in 1847. 320 p. Norwalk, 1847. Weed, S. R., comp. Norwalk after 250 years. 387 p. South Norwalk, [1902].

1. Farmer, 76. Aged 10, moved to Wisconsin, where his family lived for 15 years; he returned, meanwhile, to attend school in Conn., and finally settled here.—Family influential in the county and related to many of the older families. F and M born here.—Little formal education. Wide reading, especially in American and local history.—Prominent in his church and in town government.—Strict, upright, rather stern, proud of his ancestry.—Good feeling for local usage. Still remembers expressions heard in Wisconsin shortly after the Civil War. Careful to avoid overstatement.—HY 19.

2. Stenographer, 27.—F and M born here. F's family, working people, have lived here for several generations.—High school.—Business associates include a number of New York people. Social contacts through the Congregational Church.—Pleasant, frank, intelligent.—Local speech, a good contrast to that of the older generation. A few affectations which she has been taught to consider elegant. Final consonants often omitted. Many glottal stops.—HY 17.

3 City of Bridgeport, Fairfield Co.

Settled c. 1650; inc. 1821, set off from Fairfield (see Westport, above) and Stratford; city inc. 1836. Stratford settled 1639 from Wethersfield (see 1 Stamford); Mass. families came also from Roxbury, Boston, Concord.—Whaling and seafaring until middle of 19. cent. Now manufacture of machinery, munitions, hardware, brass and steel products, electrical equipment, etc.—Many Italians, Czechs, Poles and Hungarians.—Pop. 1850: 7560, '80: 29,148, 1910: 102,054, '30: 146,716.—Orcutt, Samuel. History of the city of Bridgeport. 536 p. New Haven, 1887. Orcutt, Samuel. History of the old town of Stratford and the city of Bridgeport. 2v. 1393 p. New Haven, 1886.

3. Stenographer, 20.—F born here; PGF born in Germany; PGM in U.S.A. M born here; MGF born in Yonkers, Westchester Co., N.Y. (c. 40 m. southwest); MGM in Orange, Grafton Co., N.H.—Catholic, but did not attend parochial school. High school 3 years, night school 2 years, business college 2 months.—Social contacts with other stenographers and clerks. Lives in section with large foreign element and many factory workers.—Speech influenced by her associates and recognizable at once as a city type; strikingly different from her mother's. Pronounced drawl and nasalization. Many glottal stops. Strongly velar k.—Short work sheets.—HY 29.

4 Town of Weston, Fairfield Co.

Settled c. 1700 as part of Fairfield (see 3 Westport); inc. 1787.—Isolated agricultural community.—Pop. 1790: 2479, 1820: 2767, '50: 1056*, '80: 918, 1910: 831, '30: 670.

1. Prosperous farmer, 77. Born in Wilton, neighboring town. Has lived all his life in Weston except for recent trips to the South in winter.—Parents and grandparents born within 4 m. of present home. Ancestors came to Yarmouth, Mass., in 1639, to Fairfield, Conn., in 1660, and to Weston in 1744.—Little education. Reads a good deal.—Member of Congregational Church. One of the most influential men in his community. Former representative in State Legislature.—Alert, intelligent, well informed, scrupulously honest; independent and set in his ways. Difficult to approach, but an excellent informant.—Speech idiomatic, entirely unaffected. Rapid tempo. Clear articulation.—HY 2.

2. Farmer, 44.—Family has lived here for 4 generations.—'I can read a little, but when it comes to writing I got a pretty heavy hand.'—Few social contacts.—Proud of his Yankee ancestry. Honest and independent.—Speech distinctly local. Initial sound of cow, calf, etc. strongly aspirated and palatalized.—HY 1.

6 Town of Milford, New Haven Co.

Settled 1639 from England (Hereford, Essex, York), by way of New Haven and apparently under New Haven jurisdiction. A company from Hertfordshire is said to have come also. The first year c. 200 people arrived, a few from Wethersfield. Several of the settlers soon moved on to other towns, and in 1666 some Milford families joined the Conn. group which founded Newark, N.J.—Shellfishing from earliest times; noted for oysters and clams.—Agriculture and manufacturing: machinery, tools, etc. Many summer visitors.—Pop. 1774: 2127, '90: 2087*, 1820: 2785, '50: 2465*, '80: 3347, 1910: 4366, '30: 12,660.—Ford, George Hare, comp. Historical sketches of the town of Milford. 80 p. New Haven, 1914. Greene, M. L. Early Milford. Connecticut Magazine 5 (March, 1899), 135–46. Greene, M. L. Milford, 1689–1900. Connecticut Magazine 5 (Nov. 1899), 570–84. Labaree, Leonard W. Milford, Connecticut: the early development of a town as shown in its land records. Connecticut tercentenary commission, pamphlet 13. New Haven, 1933.

1. Fisherman, 68. Aged 15 to 17, lived one year in New Haven (c. 10 m. northeast), one year in Naugatuck (c. 20 m. north) and 6 months in Ansonia (c. 10 m. north).—F, M, PGF, PGM born here.—2 years of high school.—Spends most of his time on the water; has always been an outdoor man. Methodist.—Tall, powerful, proud of his health and strength. Stern moral principles.—Loud, penetrating, rather raucous voice. Frequently uses a velarized r which sounds like a uvular fricative.—HY 32.

2. CULTURED INFORMANT. Fruit farmer, 57. Officer of a historical association.—F born here of old local family (genealogy published). M born in Thomasville, Ga., but came here as infant; MGF born in Middlebury (northern New Haven Co.); MGM born here.—Orange District School (neighboring town); Milford Public School; Hopkins Grammar School, New Haven (5 years); Sheffield Scientific School at Yale University (1898).—Many social and business contacts. Congregational Church.—Dignified, gracious, intelligently interested in the questionnaire.—Quick, precise speech; consciously cultivated, but not affected.—Auxiliary informants: daughter (in high school) and wife.—HY 28.

8 Town of Bethel, Fairfield Co.

Set off from Danbury (q.v., below) in 1855.—Rural community, some manufacturing. Hat making since 18. cent.—Pop. 1880: 2727, 1910: 3792, '30: 3886.

1. Housewife, 78. Born a few miles east of here. Has lived c. 3 years in Danbury and some time in Redding Ridge, town of Redding, just south of here.—F born here; M in Warren, Litchfield Co. (c. 25 m. north).—Grammar school.—Episcopal Church. Physical infirmity prevents much social life.—Bright and alert.—Speech rather old-fashioned. Uses local idiom and knows no other. Quick tempo.—Auxiliary informant: husband, born here of foreign parents. His speech characteristic of the neighborhood.—HY 26.

2. Farmer, 70.—F born here, M in Redding.— Attended school, but says he has little education.— Informant and his wife Methodist; parents Episcopalian, formerly Universalist.—Strong, active, positive person, always busy.—Dental *d* and *t*. Scornful of errors in English, including his own.—Incomplete record: long work sheets pp. 6–41, short work sheets pp. 44–56, and scattered items.—HY 27.

8 Town of Danbury, Fairfield Co.

Settled 1685 by eight families, seven from Norwalk (see 3 Westport) and one from Stratford (see 3 Bridgeport).—City of Danbury (inc. 1889) a manufacturing center in an agricultural town. Since the 18. cent., when beaver hats were made here, Danbury has specialized in hats; now the majority of its mills are connected with the industry.—State Normal School.—Summer visitors.—Pop. 1774: 2526, '90: 3032, 1820: 3873, '50: 5964, '80: 11,666, 1910: 23,502, '30: 26,955 (D. city 22,261).—Bailey, J. M. History of Danbury, 1684–1896, comp. with additions by S. B. Hill. 583 p. N.Y., 1896.

3. CULTURED INFORMANT. Farmer, 47. Born in Newtown (c. 10 m. east) at grandparents' home, but was soon brought to Danbury.—F born here. His family originally from Scotland. PGF born in East Aurora, Erie Co., N.Y.; PGM and her F born in New Fairfield (adjoining town). M born in Newtown.—Mt. Hermon (preparatory school in Franklin Co., Mass.) 3 years. Harvard 4 years, A.B. 1908. Well read and well informed.—Lives just outside the city (c. 3 m. from the center); contacts are mainly with the city.—Highly intelligent.—Cultivated urban speech. No affectation; local idiom. Medium tempo, rather drawling.—Short work sheets (with some items added from long work sheets).—HY 30.

10 Town of Southbury, New Haven Co.

Set off from Woodbury in 1787. Woodbury settled 1672–74 from Stratford (see 3 Bridgeport) by a faction of the congregation.—Rural community. Agriculture, small manufactures.—Pop. 1790: 1734, 1820: 1662*, '50: 1484, '80: 1740, 1910: 1233, '30: 1134.—Cothren, William. History of ancient Woodbury, from the 1st Indian deed in 1659 to 1879, including the present towns of Washington, Southbury, Bethlehem, Roxbury and a part of Oxford and Middlebury. 3v. Waterbury, 1854–79.

1. Farmer, wood chopper, professional fox hunter, 71. Always here except for 3 years in Waterbury (c. 10 m. northeast) and 3 months in New York State.—Descended from old local stock (genealogy published).—Disliked school and left as soon as possible. Not much reading.—Few contacts. Not interested in social life or church activities.—Vigorous and independent. Can outwalk and outwork younger men. Never embarrassed or self-conscious. —Speech always natural and unguarded. Pronunciation representative of the older type in his neighborhood.—Auxiliary informant: sister.—HY 3.

2. Farmer, 59. Born in Johnson Co., Missouri, but came here when 6 months old. (Parents lived in Missouri only 2 years.) Has spent 1 year in Florida. —F born here, of prominent local family; M born near Holyoke, Hampden Co., Mass.—1 year at Oberlin College (Ohio).—Accustomed to respect. Knows everybody in his community.—Dislikes putting on airs and is almost deliberately countrified.—Quick, staccato, rather nasal speech.—HY 24.

11 Town of New Fairfield, Fairfield Co.

Settled c. 1730 (inc. 1740) from Fairfield (see 3 Westport); hostile Indians and boundary dispute with N.Y. had delayed settlement.—Rural community with decreasing population. Formerly lumbering. Many summer residents around Lake Candlewood.—Pop. 1774: 1308, '90: 1572, 1820: 788*, '50: 927, '80: 791, 1910: 551, '30: 434.

Farmer, 65. Never lived away from here until past 50; settled in Bethel (c. 10 m. southeast), his present home, 14 years ago.—F born in Plattekill, Ulster Co., N.Y. (c. 45 m. northwest); came here aged 23, to marry. PGF born in Ulster Co., N.Y. M born here on farm settled by her GGF, birthplace also of of her M and her GM. MGF born in Ulster Co., N.Y. Never went to school and never reads.— Quaker. Goes to quarterly Friends' Meetings at Chappaqua, Westchester Co., N.Y.—Sharp observer, capable.—Speech not illiterate; precise and uncolloquial, but not pedantic. Slow tempo. Uses Quaker 'thee.'—Auxiliary informant: wife.—HY 36.

12 Town of New Milford, Litchfield Co.

Settled 1707 (inc. 1712) from Milford (q.v., 6) and Woodbury (see 10 Southbury), and from Westfield, Mass.—Busy country town. Dairying, tobacco raising. Some manufacturing.—Pop. 1774: 2770, '90: 3170, 1820: 3830, '50: 4058, '80: 3907*, 1910: 5010, '30. 4700.—New Milford historical committee. Two centuries of New Milford, Conn. 307 p. New York, 1907. Orcutt, Samuel. History of the towns of New Milford and Bridgewater, 1703–1882. 909 p. Hartford, 1882.

State education official, 74. Aged 30, spent a year in Norfolk (c. 35 m. northeast).—Parents, grandparents and great-grandparents born here.—Public school.—Has visited schools all over the state.—

Intelligent.—Recognizes speech variations, but uses the idiom of his own community. Final consonants very weak, frequently omitted.—HY 23.

14 Town of Wolcott, New Haven Co.

Set off from Southington and Waterbury in 1796. Southington settled 1700–20 as part of Farmington (q.v., 20), chiefly by Farmington families; a few from Wallingford and New Haven. Waterbury settled 1674, largely from Farmington.—Rural community. Much old stock.—Pop. 1820: 943, '50: 603, '80: 493, 1910: 563, '30: 972.—Orcutt, Samuel. History of the town of Wolcott, from 1731 to 1874; with an account of the centenary meeting, Sept. 10–11, 1873, and with the genealogies of the families of the town. 608 p. Waterbury, 1874.—*Waterbury:* Bronson, Henry. History of Waterbury, the original township, embracing present Watertown and Plymouth and parts of Oxford, Wolcott, Middlebury, Prospect and Naugatuck; with an appendix of biography, genealogy and statistics. 582 p. Waterbury, 1858.

1. Joiner, retired, 73. Has built houses and worked at many trades. Born in Old Saybrook, Middlesex Co. (c. 40 m. southeast), came here as a child.—F, PGF born here. M born in Old Saybrook; her family moved here. MGGF was commander of the Saybrook fort.—Grammar school, and 'a kind of high school' in Southington, Hartford Co. (adjoining town).—Many social contacts.—Shrewd, humorous, full of vigor. Prosperous.—Speech very old-fashioned, like that of most old natives here. Deliberate, rather drawling. Articulation clear.—HY 31.

2. Dealer in farm implements, 36. Spent 1 year in Waterbury (adjoining city), as a child, and another year when he was 21. Ran a farm on shares in Middlebury (c. 10 m. southwest) for 1½ years.—F born in Bridgewater, Litchfield Co. (c. 25 m. west), came here at 20 to raise tobacco. M born in England, came to Goshen, Litchfield Co. (c. 25 m. northwest) when she was 6; married here.—Grammar school.—Holds local offices. Knows everybody in town.—Intelligent, cheerful, obliging.—Keen observer of other dialects. Speech quick, jerky, nervous. Enunciation often blurred, final consonants indistinct. Strong nasalization.—HY 35.

16 Town of Litchfield (1 Bantam; 2 Litchfield), Litchfield Co.

Settled 1720–21 by families from the river towns of Windsor, Hartford, Wethersfield, Farmington, and from Stratford and Lebanon.—Important military base during Revolution. Early industrial development: iron works, cotton mills, etc.—Now a quiet country town with many old families. Summer residents.—Bantam is a small manufacturing center. (The town of Morris, home of the auxiliary informant, was set off from Litchfield in 1859.)—Pop. 1774: 2554, 1800: 4285, '20: 4610, '50: 3953,

'80: 3410*, 1910: 3005, '30: 3574.—Kilbourne, P. K. Sketches and chronicles of the town of Litchfield, historical, biographical and statistical, together with a complete official register of the town. 264 p. Hartford, 1859. White, Alain C., comp. The history of the town of Litchfield, 1720–1920. 360 p. Litchfield, 1920. Woodruff, G. C. History of the town of Litchfield. 64 p. Litchfield, 1845.

1. Farmer, 72. F born here, M in Washington (just southwest of Litchfield).—Grammar school.—Brought up in Episcopal Church, also attends Congregational. Prominent and respected in the community.—Honest, hard-working, successful.—Extreme drawl, overlong vowels, characteristic of the neighborhood.

Auxiliary informant: farmer, 80.—Descended from original settlers.—Very little education.—Not an entirely satisfactory informant.—Some starred forms also from the wife and the sister of informant 1.—HY 13.

2. CULTURED INFORMANT. Lawyer, 75. Spent one summer in Lakeville, town of Salisbury (c. 25 m. northwest).—F born in Salisbury; PGF in New Milford (c. 20 m. southwest); PGGF in Pomfret, Windham Co. M born here.—Yale, B.A. 1880; graduated from Yale Law School, 1883.—Episcopalian.—Gentleman of good family, noted for his honesty.—Many old-fashioned forms in his speech.—Auxiliary informants: servants.—HY 14.

18 Town of Cornwall (West Cornwall), Litchfield Co.

Settled c. 1740 (inc. 1740) largely from Plainfield; others from Tolland, Colchester, Litchfield and Norwalk. Plainfield settled 1689 from northeastern Mass. (Chelmsford, Haverhill, Ipswich, Woburn, Concord) and from New London Co. (Stonington, New London, Norwich).—Rural community with decreasing population. Summer homes.—Pop. 1774: 974, '90: 1475, 1820: 1662, '50: 2041, '80: 1583, 1910: 1016, '30: 878.—Gold, T. S. Historical records of the town of Cornwall. 339 p. Hartford, 1877. Starr, Edward C. A history of Cornwall, Conn., a typical New England town. 547 p. 1926.

1. Gardener, 68. 'I've worked at most everything, exceptin' books!' At 18 went to Morris (c. 15 m. southeast) and lived there 7 years. Worked for short periods (less than a year each) in Torrington, Litchfield Co.; Thompsonville, Hartford Co.; and New Haven.—F born in Canaan (next town north); came here when 20 years old. M born in Wallingford, New Haven Co. (c. 20 m. southeast); came here early.—Grammar school.—Old-fashioned local speech.—HY 15.

2. CULTURED INFORMANT. Farmer, 69.—F born in Madison Co., N.Y.; came here when a year old. PGF born here, lived for a while in Madison Co., N.Y. Family has owned land here since the town was founded. M born in Rockville, town of Vernon, Tolland Co (c. 50 m. east).—Private tutor; Hopkins

Grammar School; Sheffield Scientific School, Yale University, 1883. Reads a good deal.—Congregationalist. Influential in town affairs.—Fine type of country landowner.—Has not tried to change his pronunciation; still uses old-fashioned forms.—HY 16.

19 Town of Sharon, Litchfield Co.

Settled 1739 (inc. 1739), largely by families from eastern Conn.: Lebanon and Colchester. Lebanon settled 1695 (inc. 1700), some coming from Norwich, others from Mass. Colchester settled 1699 from the Conn. River towns and New London.—Rural community. Communication with New York State rather than with adjoining Conn. towns. Early manufactures, now agriculture. Summer residents. —Pop. 1774: 2012, 1800: 2340, '20: 2573, '50: 2507, '80: 2580, 1910: 1880, '30: 1710.—Sedgwick, C. F. General history of the town of Sharon, Litchfield Co., from its 1st settlement. Ed. 3. 204 p. Amenia, N.Y., 1898.

1. Farmer, 81, negro. Has also lived in village of Millerton, Dutchess Co., N.Y. (c. 7 m. northwest). —F, PGF born here. M born in N.Y. State, came to Salisbury (adjoining town north) aged 2.—Grammar school.—Methodist.—Good old-fashioned representative of the 'Yankee negro.' Not very well informed, but knows local traditions.—Many archaic features of speech.—Short work sheets.—HY 9.

2. Farmer, 89.—F, PGF born in Cornwall (adjoining town east). M, MGF born here.—School here until 18; then Fort Edward Collegiate Institute, near Hudson Falls, N.Y.—Energetic, remarkably well preserved for his age; has many interests.—Rapid tempo, with a peculiar drawl at the end of the phrase. Strong nasalization.—HY 10.

20 Town of Farmington, Hartford Co.

Settled c. 1640 (inc. 1645), mainly from Hartford (q.v., 40). A number of towns were later set off from the Farmington lands.—Industrial after the Revolution through the early 19. cent.: linen, hats, leather goods.—Now a quiet, attractive residential town; some wealthy Hartford families have homes here. Dairying, farming.—Pop. 1774: 6069, '90: 2683*, 1820: 3042, '50: 2630*, '80: 3017, 1910: 3478, '30: 4548.—Blakely, Quincy. Farmington, one of the mother towns of Connecticut. Connecticut tercentenary commission, pamphlet 38. New Haven, 1935. O'Connor, Alice K., ed. Farmington papers. Hartford, 1929.

1. Teamster and farmer, 47. Lived for a short time in New Britain (adjoining town south).—F and M born here.—Grammar school. Little reading. —Not many contacts.—Speech old-fashioned, with a few touches of elegance. Strong retroflection in vowels preceding r.—Auxiliary informant: aunt. Lived several years in adjoining city of Bristol. Old-fashioned rural speech.—HY 7.

2. CULTURED INFORMANT. Civil engineer and farmer, 77. Spent 2 years in Pa., Minn. and Va.— F's family has lived on this farm since 1640. M born in Middletown, Middlesex Co. (c. 15 m. southeast); lived in Granville, Hampden Co., Mass. (c. 23 m. north), until her marriage.—Preparatory school in New Britain; Sheffield Scientific School, Yale University, 1880.—Many years in the State Legislature. Well known and respected. Prosperous.—Excellent representative of the older generation. Despite certain notions of correctness, his speech is natural and unaffected.—HY 4.

21 Town of Hartland, Hartford Co.

Settled in the 1750's (inc. 1761), chiefly from East Hartford and East Haddam. East Hartford was owned and gradually settled by Hartford (q.v., 40); more rapid expansion c. 1677. Haddam, from which East Haddam was set off in 1734, was settled in the 1660's from the old river towns to the north.— Wholly rural and, until recently, isolated. Decreasing population.—Pop. 1774: 500, 1800: 1318, '20: 1254, '50: 848, '80: 643, 1910: 544, '30: 296.—*East Hartford:* Goodwin, Joseph O. East Hartford: its history and traditions. . . . 249 p. Hartford, 1879.

Painter, 78. Lived 16 months in Waterbury, New Haven Co. (c. 33 m. south).—F born in New York State, came to Hartland Hollow as a youth and to East Hartland in 1843. M born here; her ancestors from Farmington and Hartford.—School until 15. Reads a great deal. Authority on local history, genealogy, real estate and politics.—Two terms in State Legislature. Well known.—Unusually well informed, intelligent and helpful. Remarkable memory.—Speech distinctly local; fluent and clear.— HY 6.

22 Town of Winchester (city of Winsted), Litchfield Co.

Settled c. 1758 (inc. 1771) from Farmington and Wallingford (q.v., 20, 36), Waterbury (settled 1674, largely from Farmington), Goshen (1720's from Hartford, Windsor and other Conn. towns) and Torrington (late 1730's from Windsor and Durham).—Winsted is a small manufacturing city (inc. 1917). Clocks since early 19. cent.; also, more recently, knit goods, pins, hardware, tools.—Many French-Canadians.—Pop. 1774: 339, 1800: 1371, '20: 1601, '50: 2179, '80: 5142, 1910: 8679, '30: 8674 (Winsted 7883).—Boyd, John. Annals and family records of Winchester, with exercises of the centennial celebration, 1871. 631 p. Hartford, 1873.

1. Carpenter and joiner, 92.—F born near Collinsville, town of Canton, Hartford Co. (c. 11 m. southeast). Ancestor came from England to Boston in 1631. (Surname a common one in Gloucestershire.) M born in Caledonia Co., Vt.—Grammar school; private school, conducted by an Episcopalian clergyman, for 5 or 6 years. Reads a great deal.—Many

contacts. Family is prominent and highly respected. —In spite of his age, still vigorous and clear-headed, with a lively sense of humor.—Speech natural, old-fashioned, well articulated. Unaspirated *p, t, k.*— HY 5.

2. Woman farmer, 56.—F born here; ancestor from Wethersfield, Hartford Co. (c. 25 m. southeast). M born in Palmer, Hampden Co., Mass.; came here aged 21.—Grammar school. Reads considerably.— Lives on an isolated farm (within the city limits) which has been the home of her F's family for generations. She and her sister take their produce to market once a week.—Intelligent, very willing to talk.—Rather self-conscious and eager to be correct. Responses somewhat guarded.—HY 8.

23 Town of Granby, Hartford Co.

Set off from Simsbury (q.v., 24) in 1786. Settled c. 1710 (several families here as early as 1664).— Rural community: tobacco. Brief period of manufacturing c. 1830.—Pop. 1790: 2611, 1820: 3012, '50: 2498, '80: 1340*, 1910: 1383, '30: 1388.—Phelps, N. A. History of Simsbury, Granby and Canton, from 1642 to 1845. 176 p. Hartford, 1845.

Farmer, 89. Has worked also as a joiner.—F born here, M in Granby, Hampden Co., Mass. (c. 10 m. northwest). MGGF born here.—Grammar school.— Hard of hearing. Never leaves home now and sees few people except family and neighbors.—Pleasant, kindly. Disapproves of modern ways, especially modern shiftlessness.—Speech unusually old-fashioned; that of his son almost equally so.—HY 22.

24 Town of Simsbury, Hartford Co.

Settled c. 1670, largely from Windsor (see 45 East Windsor). Temporarily abandoned after Indian attack in 1676.—Prosperous farming and manufacturing community. Copper mined in northern part of town (now East Granby) during 18. cent.; German workers from Hanover were employed here (mining and smelting).—Private schools for boys and for girls.—Pop. 1774: 3700, '90: 2679*, 1820: 1954*, '50: 2737, '80: 1830, 1910: 2537, '30: 3625.—Ellsworth, John E. Simsbury, being a brief historical sketch of ancient and modern Simsbury. 190 p. Simsbury Tercentenary Committee, 1935. Phelps, N. A. History of Simsbury, Granby and Canton, from 1642 to 1845. 176 p. Hartford, 1845.

Farmer, 81.—F born here in same house; PGF from R.I. in the 1790's; PGGF from Norwalk, Fairfield Co. M born in Suffield, Hartford Co. (c. 10 m. northeast); came here to marry.—Grammar school; Connecticut Literary Institution at Suffield (now Suffield School for boys). Has done much to educate himself. (Sent one son to Harvard and another to Yale.) Wide reading.—Respected in his community for fine character and iron determination.—HY 21.

26 City of New Haven, New Haven Co.

Settled 1638 (city inc. 1784) by an English com-pany from London (mostly merchants) under the leadership of Davenport and Eaton, including families from London and the counties of York, Hertford and Kent. (In 1639 a constitution was adopted and a governor elected for New Haven Colony. Strict Puritan government, disapproving of Quakers and Baptists. While it was still an independent unit, the Colony had come to include Stamford, Milford, Guilford, and Southold, L. I. (q.v., 1, 6, 28, 50). Union with the Colony of Conn., dating from 1662, was unwillingly accepted by the New Haven Colony in 1664).—Joint state capital with Hartford from 1701 to 1875. Trade with China and the East and West Indies during 18. cent. Shipping declined in early 19. cent. and manufacturing became important: rifles, hardware, clocks, steel supplies, etc.—Large foreign groups: Italian (since the 1870's), Irish and Jewish.—Site of Yale University.—Pop. 1774: 8295, '90: 4487*, 1820: 8327, '50: 20,345, '80: 62,882, 1910: 133,605, '30: 162,655.—Atwater, E. E. History of the city of New Haven to the present time, by an association of writers; with biographies. 702 p. N.Y., 1887. Levermore, C. H. Republic of New Haven; a history of municipal evolution. 342 p. Baltimore, 1886. (Johns Hopkins University studies in historical and political science, extra v. 1.) Levermore, C. H. Town and city government of New Haven. 103 p. Baltimore, 1886. (Johns Hopkins University studies in historical and political science, 1886.)—*New Haven Colony:* see the historical bibliography in Chapter III, under *Connecticut.*

1. Harness maker, dealer in antiques, 75. Always here except for 10 years in Mass.—F's family here for several generations.—Grammar school. Reads considerably.—Congregationalist. Formerly officer in the National Guard. Many contacts with old families.—Well informed, much interested in the old days. Somewhat reticent.—Good representative of the older middle class. Speech natural. No affectation, although his late wife (minister's daughter, born in Mass.) often corrected him. Strong nasalization, much slurring.—K 11.

2. CULTURED INFORMANT. Teacher, librarian, 45. —F born in N.Y. State, of Mass. family; died early. M born here; her ancestors from Saybrook, Middlesex Co. (c. 30 m. east).—Normal school graduate.— Usual contacts of a librarian.—K 13.

28 Town of Madison (East River), New Haven Co.

Set off from Guilford (q.v., below) in 1826. Settled c. 1645 under the direction of Guilford. Among the early settlers were families from New Haven, Middletown, Windsor, and from Long Island and England.—Rural community; farming, fishing. Many old families. Summer visitors along the shore.—Pop. 1850: 1837, '80: 1672, 1910: 1534, '30: 1918.— Steiner, B. C. History of the plantation of Menunkatuck and of the original town of Guilford, comprising the present towns of Guilford and Madison. . . . 538 p. Baltimore, 1897.

1. Farmer, timber dealer, now official of insurance company, 70.—F born here; PGGF came here from East Haven (c. 15 m. west) in 1790. M born in North Guilford (c. 10 m. northwest).—Grammar school and Lee's Academy, Madison.—Prominent in Congregational Church and in Grange. Many contacts in Madison and Guilford.—Conservative. Interested in local history. Well informed.—Fond of old expressions. Tempo rather deliberate. Intonation monotonous; articulation often slurred. Strong nasalization.—K 7.

28 Town of Guilford, New Haven Co.

Settlers came chiefly from Kent and Surrey in 1639, landing at New Haven, where they remained a short time as a distinct company (not part of the New Haven company).—Conservative rural town with many old families. Oyster culture. Some manufacturing. Many summer homes along the shore.—Pop. 1774: 2930, '90: 3439, 1820: 4131, '50: 2653*, '80: 2782, 1910: 3001, '30: 3117.—Steiner, B. C. History of the plantation of Menunkatuck and of the original town of Guilford, comprising the present towns of Guilford and Madison, written largely from the manuscript of R. D. Smyth. 538 p. Baltimore, 1897.

2. CULTURED INFORMANT. Housewife, 30. 2 years in New York City. Lives a few miles outside Guilford borough.—F's ancestor one of the first settlers. His family has been important in local government. M from Litchfield Co.—Conn. College for Women, New London (c. 30 m. east).—Many friends here and in New Haven. At home most of the time.—No effort to change her speech. Pronunciation deviates little from her father's. Natural, at times somewhat guarded. Slow tempo, prolonged vowels. Distinct nasalization. Frequent glottalization.—K 14.

29 Town of Killingworth (Killingworth), Middlesex Co.

Settled, beginning 1716, from the southern part of the old Killingworth, which was inc. 1838 as the town of Clinton. Some families came from Guilford (q.v., 28) and Saybrook (q.v., 30). The southern part of the old Killingworth was settled c. 1663 (named 1667) from the Conn. River towns of Hartford and Windsor.—Strictly rural, decreasing population; dairying, poultry. Shopping done in Clinton. Some farms taken over by Germans two generations ago.—Pop. 1774: 1990, '90: 2147, 1820: 2342, '50: 1107*, '80: 748, 1910: 660, '30: 482.—Clinton: Congregational church. 200th anniversary held in Clinton, Nov. 13, 1867. 54 p. New Haven, 1868. (Historical discourse by W. E. Brooks, pp. 11–43.)

Farmer, town officer, 79. Aged 18 to 21, worked in New Haven factory.—F's family here for generations; came from Guilford in 1689. M from Guilford.

—Grammar school.—Congregational Church. Has held local and state offices.—Unassuming, clearheaded, well informed. Little concerned with the world outside his own state.—Talked freely. Can distinguish his own usage from what he hears or reads. Local speech of older generation. Has none of the fluctuations found in Saybrook (30) and Middletown (38) informants' speech.—K 2.

30 Town of Old Saybrook, Middlesex Co.

Old Saybrook (inc. 1854) is the oldest part of the original town of Saybrook, which included besides Old Saybrook the present towns of Westbrook, Essex, Saybrook, Chester, Old Lyme and Lyme. The original Saybrook was settled 1635 from England, and the settlement gradually expanded across and up the Conn. River and along the Sound. (In 1665 the part east of the river, including the present towns of Lyme and Old Lyme, was inc. as the town of Lyme.)—The hope of the founders of Saybrook to build up a great seaport at the mouth of the river was doomed to failure.—Rural and residential community, proud of its antiquity. Much old stock; Swedes, Poles and Italians in last decades. Many summer residents.—Pop. of the original town of Saybrook (west of the Conn. River) 1774: 2687, '90: 3228, 1820: 4165.—Pop. of Old Saybrook 1880: 1302, 1910: 1516, '30: 1643.—Gates, Gilman C. Saybrook at the mouth of the Connecticut; the first 100 years. 246 p. [Orange and New Haven] 1935. Saybrook's quadrimillennial; commemoration of the 250th anniversary of the settlement of Saybrook, Nov. 27, 1885. 69 p. Hartford, 1886. (Contains a brief history of the early settlement.)

1. Farmer, 92. Taught school 1865–85. Always lived here except during the Civil War, when he ran a plantation in Louisiana for the government.—Old local family.—Grammar school. Fairly extensive reading.—Many friends. Sociable, a good story teller.—Strong character. Remarkable vigor for his age.—Speech very different from that of informant 2. Well educated type of Civil War period. Regularly uses *ain't* and double negative. Many irregularities in his verbs, although he knows standard principal parts. Pronunciation set. (Became totally deaf before the interviews could be completed. Record lacks a number of items on pp. 81–103.)—Auxiliary informant: wife, born in Wisconsin of Conn. parents; here for the last 50 years.—K 3.

2. Carpenter, town officer, 65.—From prominent, long established local families.—Grammar school and part of high school. Reads local papers and some books.—Congregational Church. Active in politics. Contacts in Middletown and Hartford.—Well informed, glad to help.—Has evidently tried to improve his speech. (Wife may have influenced him.) Some of the old-fashioned or popular expressions which he attributes to others are undoubtedly also his.—K 1.

31 Town of East Lyme (Niantic), New London Co.

Set off from Lyme and Waterford in 1839. Lyme settled as part of Saybrook (see 30 Old Saybrook), inc. 1665. Waterford settled in the 1660's as part of New London (q.v., 32), inc. 1801. Niantic is in the Waterford section of East Lyme.—Rural community with many summer homes. Scallop fisheries. —Pop. 1850: 1382, '80: 1731, 1910: 1916, '30: 2575.

Farmer, road worker, now proprietor of filling station, 69. Lived 7 years in New London (c. 8 m. east) and 1 year in Providence, R.I.—F born here; died when informant was 4. M from R.I. or N.Y.— Grammar school.—Ordinary social contacts of small farming community.—Jovial, fond of imitating old timers.—Knows what is 'proper,' but prefers his rustic speech.—Auxiliary informant: wife, born in Waterford (adjoining town); spent some time in Bozrah (c. 20 m. north of Niantic). Much younger than the informant.—HS 48.

32 City of New London, New London Co.

Settled 1645, organized 1646 (city inc. 1784). In 1650–51 a number of families from Gloucester, Mass. (several of whom are supposed to have come originally from Monmouthshire) and from Wethersfield (see 1 Stamford).—Shipping, whaling in 18. and 19. cent. Printing press, said to be the first in Conn., est. here 1709. New London an important printing center for the next 150 years.—Now shipbuilding and manufacturing: silk, clothing, machinery, etc.— U. S. Coast Guard Academy. (U. S. submarine base in Groton, adjoining town.)—Conn. College for Women.—Pop. 1774: 5888, 1800: 5150*, '20: 3330*, '50: 8991, '80: 10,537, 1910: 19,659, '30: 29,640.— Caulkins, F. M. History of New London, from the 1st survey of the coast in 1612 to 1860; with memoir of the author. 696 p. New London, 1895. Stark, Benjamin. Historical sketch of the schools of New London, 1645–1895. New London County historical Society: records and papers, 2 (1896), 113–44.

1. Retired secretary (woman), 83.—F born in Waterford, M in Montville (both towns originally part of New London).—Girls' high school.—Congregational Church. For 10 years officer of G.A.R. Auxiliary. Seldom goes out now and has always led a rather secluded life.—Slightly deaf. Shy, reticent, but intelligent and glad to help. Knows nothing of farm life.—Local city speech. Final consonants often weak.—Auxiliary informants: male cousin, born and brought up on Long Island, now living here; niece, born and brought up on a farm in Waterford.— HS 49.

2. CULTURED INFORMANT. Director of Museum, 73. Has worked in a bank. Country home in Gales Ferry, town of Ledyard (c. 8 m. north).—F's family local, formerly in Stonington (c. 12 m. east on the Sound).—High school. Extensive reading and travel. —Many social contacts.—Much interested in an-

tiques. Courteous, glad to help.—Speech typical of cultivated middle-aged people here.—HS 47.

33 Town of Bozrah, New London Co.

Settled as part of Norwich (q.v., below). Church org. in 1739; town set off in 1786.—Rural community.—Pop. 1800: 934, '20: 1083, '50: 867, '80: 1155, 1910: 861, '30: 859.

1. Farmer, 91. Has lived in Franklin (adjoining town) for the last 17 years.—F from old local family.—Grammar school.—Belongs to no societies. —Frail, but active for his years. Interested in old times. Welcomed the interviews. Mind not always keen.—Slow, nasal speech. Weak articulation. Final consonants regularly unvoiced and often dropped.— HS 26.

33 Town of Norwich (Norwichtown), New London Co.

Settled 1660 from Saybrook (see 30 Old Saybrook) by a faction of the congregation; other families from New London (q.v., 32). Some Acadians came from Nova Scotia in 1755. City of Norwich inc. 1784.— Shipbuilding and overseas trade in 18. cent.; now manufacturing: electric supplies, machinery, firearms, paper, etc.—Norwichtown is a village north of the city of Norwich.—Pop. 1774: 7327, 1800: 3476*, '20: 3634, '50: 10,265, '80: 21,143 (N. city 15,112), 1910: 28,219, '30: 32,438 (N. city 23,021).—Caulkins, F. M. History of Norwich, from its possession by the Indians to the year 1866. 704 p. N. p., 1866. Perkins, M. E. Old houses of the ancient town of Norwich, 1660–1800. . . . 621 p. Norwich, 1895.

2. Single woman, between 70 and 80. As a child spent a few years in Mass., returned here during the Civil War.—F from old local family. M born in Richmond, Va.; at age of 10 brought here by local family. MGF sea captain.—School until 14.—Very few social contacts.—Has lost comfortable home and income. Frail, sensitive. At first reticent and suspicious, but came to enjoy the interviews.—Refined (but uneducated) type of speech of the older generation. Quick, high-pitched.—HS 27.

34 Town of Stonington (1 Stonington; 2 Stonington Borough; 3 Quiambog), New London Co.

Settled c. 1650, settlers coming from New London (q.v., 32) and from the colonies of Mass. Bay (Lynn) and Plymouth (Scituate). Some later from R. I. (Westerly, Kingstown). Inc. 1658 by Mass. Jurisdiction in dispute until 1662.—Shipbuilding, whaling until c. 1850. Now mostly agricultural, with some manufacturing.—Stonington Borough (inc. 1801) is an aristocratic village on a point of land. Quiambog is a rural community.—Pop. 1774: 5412, 1800: 5437, '20: 3056*, '50: 5431, '80: 7355, 1910: 9154, '30: 11,025 (S. borough 2006).—Wheeler, Richard A. History of the town of Stonington . . . from its first settlement in 1649 to 1900. . . . 754 p. New London, 1900.

1. Farmer, 61.—Local family.—School until c. 17.—Social contacts through the Grange. Takes many short motor trips.—Lively, good natured. Recent operation had made him temporarily stop working.—Natural colloquial speech. Strong nasalization. —Auxiliary informants: wife (former schoolteacher) and hired man.—HS 25.

2. Woman storekeeper, single, 45 to 50.—F from Groton (adjoining town west).—Little education.— Probably not many social contacts. (Because of family's suspicious attitude, not much biographical information obtained.)—Unassertive, reticent. Peculiarly childlike appearance. (Mother, present at most of the interviews, was quick, nervous, with considerable initiative. Inclined to anticipate informant's replies to questions.)—Speech much like her mother's, but lazier and more nasal. Short vowels.— Auxiliary informants: mother and father.—Short work sheets.—HS 23.

3. Housewife, 76. Lived for some time in New London (c. 10 m. west).—F's ancestor came from Somersetshire to Salem, Mass., in 1630; his son the first male child born in New London.—School until c. 15.—Union Baptist Church. Active in town life.— Lively, intelligent, interested in the investigation. Likes to have people about her.—Nasal speech. Glottalization.—HS 24.

36 Town of Wallingford, New Haven Co.

Set off from New Haven (q.v., 26) in 1670; settled at this time by New Haven families.—Largely agricultural until c. 1850. Wallingford borough inc. 1853.—Now extensive manufacturing: silverware, rubber goods, hardware, tools.—Site of Choate School (preparing boys for college).—Pop. 1774: 4915, '90: 3355*, 1820: 2237*, '50: 2595, '80: 4686, 1910: 11,155, '30: 14,278 (W. borough 11,170).— Davis, C. H. S. History of Wallingford, from its settlement in 1670 to the present time. . . . 956 p. Meriden, 1870.

Farmer, 75. Lives on the outskirts of the borough. —Both parents born here.—Grammar school.— Widely acquainted and much respected.—Shrewd, well informed, coöperative. Good sense of humor. Always composed. Fairly well-to-do.—Old-fashioned speech. Medium tempo. Rather clear articulation. Not much nasalization. (Speech of his sons is very different.)—K 8.

38 City of Middletown, Middlesex Co.

Settled c. 1650 (inc. 1651) from Windsor (see 45 East Windsor), Hartford (q.v., 40) and Wethersfield (see 1 Stamford). City inc. 1784.—Formerly a shipping center surrounded by farmlands. Wealthiest town in Conn. from 1750 to 1800.—Manufacturing now: webbing (since 1840), rubber goods, tools, hardware, silverware, etc.—Site of Wesleyan University, founded 1831.—Pop. 1774: 4878, '90: 5298, 1820: 6479, '50: 8441, '80: 11,732, 1910: 20,749, '30: 24,554.—Field, D. D. Centennial address with historical sketches of Cromwell, Portland, Chatham, Middle Haddam, Middletown and its parishes. 295 p. Middletown, 1853.

1. Farmer, 68. Town officer for many years.—F born in Canterbury, Windham Co. (c. 40 m. east). M born in Pawlet, Rutland Co., Vt.—Grammar school. Considerable reading.—Intelligent and well informed.—Excellent representative of the older generation. Natural, unconcerned with grammar. Rapid tempo. A preconsonantal r appears sporadically.—Auxiliary informant: wife, born in Madison, New Haven Co. (c. 20 m. south). Former schoolteacher. Has made no attempt to 'correct' her husband's speech.—K 6.

2. Dairy farmer, 60. Lives several miles from the center of the city.—Parents born here, of prominent old local families.—High school. Wide reading. (Daughter a college graduate.)—Many contacts in the city.—Intelligent, well informed, rather highstrung.—Much on guard and anxious to be correct. Speech consequently unstable, especially in treatment of r, which he normally pronounces with strong retroflection in all positions (as his father did), but sometimes avoids before consonants and finally.—K 5.

3. CULTURED INFORMANT. Official of manufacturing company, 60.—Parents born here, of prominent cultured local stock. Informant represents the 7th generation on his F's side; family originally came from New Haven.—Boarding school in Southborough, Worcester Co., Mass., for 4 years; received engineering training in his F's plant in Middletown. Extensive reading and travel.—Well informed, keenly interested in the investigation.—Speaks with ease and assurance. Knows uncultivated local speech and can use it at will.—K 4.

40 City of Hartford, Hartford Co.

Settled 1635 from Mass. Bay (especially Cambridge) and named for Hertford, England, in 1637. Plan of government for the Connecticut Colony adopted here in 1639. City inc. 1784.—Agriculture and river trade. Shipping declined after War of 1812. Woolen mill est. 1788.—Now manufactures electrical equipment, machinery, tools, typewriters, firearms, aviation motors (chiefly in East Hartford, adjoining town), etc. Tobacco market. Center of insurance business. Large foreign element: Irish, Italian.—Capital of Conn.—Site of Trinity College (Episcopalian), est. 1823, and of Hartford Theological School (Congregational). Prominent literary center after the Revolution and in the 19. cent.—Pop. 1774: 5031, '90: 4072*, 1820: 6901, '50: 13,555, '80: 42,551, 1910: 98,915, '30: 164,072.—Andrews, C. M. The river towns of Connecticut: a study of Wethersfield, Hartford and Windsor. 126 p. Baltimore, 1889. (Johns Hopkins University studies in historical and political science, v. 7, no. 7–9.) Love, W. D. The colonial history of Hartford. Hartford, 1914.

1. Retired bookdealer, 80.—F born in East Windsor (c. 12 m. northeast), where several generations of his family had lived; came here in 1848. M born in East Windsor; came here in 1848.—Grammar school until 12. Considerable reading.—Member of historical society. On intimate terms with prominent families here. Well liked for his enthusiasm and wide interests. Contacts with many writers.—Well informed, kindly, eager to give information.—Speech entirely natural. Popular forms and survivals from boyhood used side by side with literary forms. *We was, they was,* etc. usual in conversation. Rapid tempo. Articulation never precise, often slurred and hasty. Slight nasalization.—K 9.

2. Business man, 30. Worked in New Haven a year, aged 27.—F born in Barkhamsted, Litchfield Co. (c. 20 m. northwest); came here aged 20. M (*Mayflower* descendant) born in Southwick, Hampden Co., Mass. (c. 20 m. north); came here aged 20.—Grammar school and 1 year of high school.—Congregational Church. No clubs.—Not inclined to talk.—No attempt to put on airs, but avoids ungrammatical forms. Double negative rare. Occasionally *them fellows* and similar expressions. Rapid tempo.—K 10.

3. CULTURED INFORMANT. Banker, 80. Born in Westfield, Hampden Co., Mass. (c. 30 m. north); came here aged 3.—F born in Mass. M born in Ashford, Windham Co. (c. 30 m. east). (Wife born in Fitzwilliam, Cheshire Co., N.H.)—Honorary M.A., but no college education. (Son attended Yale and Johns Hopkins.) Wide reading in literature and in Conn. history. Considerable travel.—Varied and extensive social contacts. Active member of historical society.—Many interests, pronounced opinions. Collects old furniture and utensils and rare books.—Has cultivated his speech. Admires old style of elocution. Possible Mass. influence in his staccato utterance and sharp articulation of final consonants (though this may be due to training). Marked nasalization.—Incomplete record: about 35 pages of scattered items, short work sheets.—K 12.

41 Town of Glastonbury, Hartford Co.

Settled as part of Wethersfield; inc. c. 1690. Wethersfield settled 1634–5 from Mass. Bay (Watertown).—Rural community, now developing into a residential suburb of Hartford. Onion and tobacco fields. Some manufacture: soap, silverware, leather and woolen goods.—Pop. 1774: 2071, '90: 2732, 1820: 3114, '50: 3390, '80: 3580, 1910: 4796, '30: 5783.—Chapin, A. B. Glastenbury [former spelling] for 200 years; a centennial discourse, May 18th, 1853. . . . 252 p. Hartford, 1853.—*Wethersfield:* see 1 Stamford.

Caretaker of fruit farm, 70.—Both parents born here.—Grammar school. Much reading in American history.—Few social contacts, all strictly local.—

Obliging, garrulous. Extremely well informed about farm life and local history.—Knows what is correct and avoids certain 'vulgar' pronunciations. Never uses *ain't, hain't.* Verb forms conventional. Speaks very deliberately, articulates with care.—Incomplete record: only pp. 8–51 and scattered items.—K 15.

42 Town of Hebron, Tolland Co.

Settled 1704 (inc. 1708) from Saybrook (q.v., 30), Windsor (see 45 East Windsor), Northampton, Mass. (q.v., 226) and Long Island.—Rural community with decreasing population.—Pop. 1774: 2337, '90: 2313, 1820: 2094*, '50: 1345*, '80: 1243, 1910: 894, '30: 879.

Housewife, 83. Born in Marlborough, Hartford Co. (adjoining town west). Until recently lived on back road near town line.—F born in Marlborough; PGGF from England. M born here.—Grammar school. Academy in Colchester, New London Co. (adjoining town south).—Congregational Church. Formerly member of the Grange.—Friendly, eager to help. Not very strong.—Old-fashioned rural speech. Quick and nervous. Speech habits fixed.—HS 43.

43 Town of Windham (1 Windham Center; 2 Willimantic), Windham Co.

Settled in the late 1680's (inc. 1692) from Norwich (q.v., 33); but most of those who came during the first half of the 18. cent. were from eastern Mass. (Salem, Cambridge, Charlestown, Newton, Rehoboth).—Windham Center is a residential village.—The city of Willimantic (inc. 1893) manufactures thread: the large plant of the American Thread Company is located here. Nearly half the population of the city is French-Canadian.—Pop. 1774: 3528, '90: 2764*, 1820: 2489, '50: 4503, '80: 8264 (Willimantic borough 6608), 1910: 12,604, '30: 13,773 (Willimantic 12,102).—Memorial volume of the bicentennial celebration of the town of Windham. . . . 166 p. Hartford, 1893.

1. Housekeeper, laundress, 82.—F born here. M born in Ashford (c. 15 m. north).—Little education.—Few social contacts.—Intelligent, active, independent. Still goes out occasionally to work. Extremely set in her ways.—Speech unaffected, quick, clear.—HS 46.

2. CULTURED INFORMANT. Former teacher, 58. Born in Scotland (next town east), came here aged 7. Taught 4 years in Saybrook, Middlesex Co. (c. 35 m. southwest).—Descended from old Conn. families.—High school and normal school. Reads considerably.—Usual contacts of upper middle class in church and community.—Friendly, interested in educational matters.—Speech typical of her social group. Natural, but conscious of grammatical proprieties. Glottalization. Final consonants weak.—HS 45.

44 Town of Somers (1 North Somers; 2 Somers), Tolland Co.

Settled as part of Enfield c. 1713; inc. by Mass. 1734. Enfield settled 1681 from Salem, Mass., under Mass. authority. Somers and Enfield both annexed to Conn. 1749.—Agricultural: dairy farming, tobacco. Woolen mill in Somersville. 'Going to the city' means a trip to Rockville (c. 10 m. south; city with pop. of 7445, in Vernon town), to Hartford (c. 20 m. southwest) or to Springfield, Mass. (c. 10 m. northwest).—Pop. 1774: 1027, '90: 1220, 1820: 1306, '50: 1508, '80: 1242, 1910: 1653, '30: 1917.—*Enfield:* Allen, Francis O., ed. The history of Enfield, Conn. . . . compiled from all the public records of the town. . . . 3v. Lancaster, Pa., 1900.

1. Farmer, tobacco grower, 79.—F born in the same house; his family here for 200 years. M born in Wethersfield, Hartford Co. (c. 25 m. southwest); lived in Hartford for a while, then moved here.— School until 17. (Sister was a schoolteacher.)— Selectman 3 years. Has served in the State Legislature. Used to know everybody in town.—Kindly and hospitable. Though taciturn, a very good informant. Keen-minded.—Fairly old-fashioned speech, but not uniformly so. (Daughter-in-law says he once used a good many archaisms, now lost through his contacts with younger people; but he denies this.) Rapid tempo. Clear, precise articulation. Vowels half-long to over-long.—B 82.

2. Farmer, 54. Has been garage mechanic, mill hand, carpenter.—F born here; PGF born in Stafford (next town east); PGM born here. M born in Scantic, town of East Windsor, Hartford Co. (c. 10 m. southwest), came here as a girl, died when informant was 13.—School until 17. Regrets that he did not stay longer.—Fairly wide acquaintance here. Used to take part in local social events. Too busy to go out of town often.—Suspicious of strangers, but talkative as acquaintance grows. Shrewd in business dealings. Fond of exercising his wit and humor.— Knows nothing of other dialects. Realizes that he is not always grammatical. (Frequent good-natured corrections from wife and daughters.) Rustic speech, but not of extreme type, archaic in several features of vocabulary and pronunciation. Rapid tempo. Lax articulation. Weak nasalization. Diphthongs show much variation.—B 83.

45 Town of East Windsor (1 Scantic; 2 Broad Brook), Hartford Co.

Settled as part of Windsor c. 1680 (after King Philip's War) by Windsor families, who had previously used the lands as pasture and as hayfields. Set off in 1768. Windsor settled 1633 by men from the Plymouth Colony; they sold their lands in 1637–8 to settlers from Dorchester, Mass., who had come here in 1635. The Dorchester families were largely from the counties of Devon, Dorset and Somerset.—

Extensive cultivation of tobacco throughout the town. Scantic is a rural community; Broad Brook a manufacturing village surrounded by farms. Shopping center is Hartford (c. 15 m. southwest).—Pop. 1774: 2999, '90: 2581*, 1820: 3400, '50: 2633*, '80: 3019, 1910: 3362, '30: 3815.—Stiles, H. R. History and genealogies of ancient Windsor, including East Windsor . . . 2v. Hartford, 1891–92.—*Windsor:* Andrews, C. M. The river towns of Connecticut: a study of Wethersfield, Hartford and Windsor. 126 p. Baltimore, 1889. (Johns Hopkins University studies in historical and political science, v. 7, no. 7–9.) Howard, Daniel. A new history of old Windsor, Conn. 428 p. Printed at Windsor Locks, 1935.

1. Farmer, 77.—F, PGF, PGGF born here. M born in Essex Co., New Jersey, came here aged 20.— Grammar school. Attended three academies (each for one term) in Suffield and in Easthampton and Wilbraham, Mass.—Fairly secluded life with brother and sister.—Still vigorous, strong-minded. Short-spoken, though never rude; opinionated.—Old-fashioned rustic speech, slightly above uneducated level. Knows nothing of other dialects. Tries, when on guard, to avoid improper locutions. Not always sure of his own usage. Rapid tempo. Very lax articulation, often slurred; weak final sounds. Strong nasalization. Frequent glottal stops. Rather long vowels.—B 80.

2. Farmer, 53. Born in South Windsor (adjoining town), came here as infant.—F born either here or in Somers (c. 10 m. northeast). M born here.—Grammar school until 13. Reads little except the newspapers.—Foresters of America, Masons. Knows practically everyone here.—Good-natured, but not very talkative or sociable. His chief interests are his family and the farm.—Rustic uncultivated speech. In guarded responses, avoids ungrammatical forms and careless pronunciations. Medium tempo. Slightly lax articulation; suppression of weak final sounds. Rather strong nasalization.—B 81.

46 Town of Tolland, Tolland Co.

Granted to residents of Windsor (see 45 East Windsor), who petitioned for land because of 'the numerous increase of our families'. First permanent settlement c. 1713 (inc. 1715).—Rural community. County seat. Diversified farming: market gardening, dairying, etc.—Pop. 1774: 1262, '90: 1484, 1820: 1607, '50: 1406, '80: 1169, 1910: 1126, '30: 1064.— Waldo, L. P. Early history of Tolland; an address delivered before the Tolland County historical society. 148 p. Hartford, 1861.

1. Farmer, 79.—F born in Wilbraham, Hampden Co., Mass. (c. 25 m. north), came here as a child. M born in R.I., came here as a child.—Grammar school.—Used to know everyone here. Has held many town offices. Cares little for social life.— Genial, easy-going, sturdy; grandfather of 33. Keen, quick mind; excellent memory.—Knows no dialect

other than his own; no affectations. Wife (born in Coventry, next town south) has tried to improve his speech, but he is always definite as to his own usage. Medium tempo. Extremely lax articulation, often indistinct. Fairly strong nasalization. Lengthened vowels.—B 78.

2. County Officer, formerly mail carrier, 54. Traveled while working for telephone company. Permanent residence always here.—F born in Suffield, Hartford Co. (c. 20 m. northwest), came here aged 12. M born in Coventry (next town south), came here when she married.—Grammar school. Reads magazines and newspapers.—Fish and Game Clubs. Has held town offices. Takes no part in activities of church and Grange.—Has air of superior knowledge. Experience wider than that of most rural townsmen. Knows little of farm life.—Contemporary local semi-rustic speech. Avoids ungrammatical forms, and occasionally tries to substitute literary words for his natural expressions. Medium tempo. Clear and usually careful articulation. Strong nasalization. Very long vowels and diphthongs.—B 79.

48 Town of Canterbury, Windham Co.

Settled as part of Plainfield c. 1700 (inc. 1703). Settlers came from Mass. Bay (Dorchester, Cambridge), from Norwich (q.v., 33), and presumably also from Plainfield. Plainfield was settled 1689 from northeastern Mass. (many from Chelmsford, some from Haverhill, Ipswich, Woburn, Concord). Other settlers came to Plainfield from southeastern Conn. (Norwich, New London, Stonington).—Declining rural community.—Pop. 1774: 2444, '90: 1885*, 1820: 1984, '50: 1669, '80: 1272, 1910: 868, '30: 942.

1. Former mill worker, 55. Has spent some time in Lisbon, New London Co., (next town south) and Plainfield (next town east). Lived 6 years in Oxford, Worcester Co., Mass. (c. 35 m. north).—Old local stock. F's family came to this country in 1638.—School here and for 6 weeks in Plainfield. Not much education. Some reading.—Practically no social contacts. Almost never leaves his home.—Semi-invalid since boyhood. Slightly querulous. Enjoyed the interviews.—Speech quick, high-pitched, nasal. Weak final consonants and final unstressed syllables. Glottal stops very common, especially in final position.—Auxiliary informant: mother.—HS 20.

2. Housewife, 78. Born in Jewett City borough,

town of Griswold, New London Co. (c. 10 m. south); lived in Plainfield (next town east) aged 4 to 10, and in Buffalo, N.Y., aged 14 to 15. Worked three years in Brooklyn (next town north).—Old local families.—Grammar school in Plainfield. One year of school in Buffalo.—Social contacts through Congregational Church and Grange.—Keen-minded. Glad to help.—Speech habits fixed. Strong nasalization. Glottal stops frequent. Final consonants weak, often unvoiced.—HS 21.

49 Town of Woodstock, Windham Co.

Settled 1686 (inc. 1690) by a group of prominent families from Roxbury, Mass. (now part of Boston, q.v., 150), who held the lands for their descendants. Annexed to Conn. 1749.—Rural residential community with decreasing population.—Pop. 1774: 2054, '90: 2431, 1820: 3017, '50: 3381, '80: 2639, 1910: 1849, '30: 1712.—Bowen, C. W. Woodstock; an historical sketch. 64 p. New York, 1886. Bowen, C. W. The history of Woodstock, Conn. Norwood, Mass., 1926.

1. Housewife, 86. Formerly postmistress. Has lived in Putnam (c. 5 m. southeast), and for 1 year in Los Angeles, Calif.—Old local families.—Grammar school and Woodstock Academy.—Wide social contacts.—Spry, intelligent. Much interested in the investigation.—Speech in general unaffected. Sometimes prefers expressions thought proper, but knows when they are not natural to her.—HS 44.

49 Town of Pomfret, Windham Co.

Settled c. 1700 (inc. 1713) from Roxbury, Mass. (cf. Woodstock, above). A number of Woodstock settlers moved to Pomfret.—Rural residential community. Many summer homes. Large preparatory school for boys.—Pop. 1774: 2306, '90: 1760*, 1820: 2042, '50: 1848, '80: 1470*, 1910: 1857, '30: 1617.

2. Housewife, former schoolteacher (for 12 years), c. 63. Has lived in Ashford (c. 10 m. west); spent 5 years in Boston, Mass., after she grew up. Has taught in Putnam (next town east).—Old local families.—School in Pomfret, Ashford, Putnam. Much interested in educational matters. (Daughters are college graduates.) Reads considerably.—Active in local organizations and social life.—Intelligent, rather nervous.—Very conscious of her speech. Uses dictionary to verify her pronunciation. Gave normal 'incorrect' forms, but said she avoided them.—HS 42.

LONG ISLAND, NEW YORK

[Bayles, R. M. Historical and Descriptive Sketches of Suffolk County and its Towns, Villages, . . . 424 p. Port Jefferson, 1874.

Fernow, B., ed. Documents Relating to the History of the Early Colonial Settlements, Principally on Long Island . . . 800 p. Albany, 1883.

Flint, Martha B. Early Long Island: a Colonial Study. 549 p. New York, 1896.

Furman, G. Antiquities of Long Island. 478 p. New York, 1875.

Gabriel, Ralph H. The Evolution of Long Island, a

Story of Land and Sea. (Yale Historical Publication.) 194 p. New Haven, 1921.

History of Suffolk County, N.Y. . . . New York, 1882.

Thompson, B. F. History of Long Island. . . . Ed. 2. 2v. New York, 1843.

Wood, Silas. Sketch of the First Settlement of the Several Towns on Long Island. . . . Ed. 3. 181 p. Brooklyn, 1828.

See also **Flagg, Charles A.** and **Jennings, Judson T.** Bibliography of New York Colonial History. New York State Library Bulletin 56. Albany, 1901.]

50 Town of Southold (Orient), Suffolk Co., N.Y.

Long Island was settled by the Dutch and the English. In the 1640's many New Englanders were migrating to the island. By c. 1670 it was all inhabited: several Dutch towns in the west, the remainder of the settlements English. The English towns were at first independent, governing themselves by majority vote in town meetings.—Southold settled 1640 under the direction of New Haven by a congregation from Hingham, Norfolk, England.—By 1662 the L. I. English settlements had united with either the New Haven Colony or the Conn. Colony; Southold had joined New Haven. After the New Haven and Conn. Colonies were united, Long Island finally became part of New York. Southold, however, was determined to belong to the new Colony of Conn., and submitted in 1676 to New York's jurisdiction only under protest.—Rural town in the northeastern part of the island; excellent farms, fishing. Many wealthy old families here from early times.—Pop. 1790: 3222, 1820: 2968*, '50: 4723, '80: 7267, 1910: 10,577, '30: 11,669.—Whitaker, Epher. History of Southold, L.I.; its first century. 354 p. Southold, 1881.

Farmer, Justice of the Peace, 53.—Old local families.—School until 16.—Congregational Church. Not much social life.—Intelligent, coöperative, quick-witted.—Rapid tempo. Rather short vowels. Less retroflection than some older speakers here have.—Speech of entire east end of L.I. seems mixed. FW heard postvocalic retroflection on the north side, but not on the south side. On both shores occasional speakers with no retroflection whatsoever, but they do not seem typical of the majority of old families.—L 157.

51 Town of Easthampton, Suffolk Co., N.Y.

Settled 1649 from Lynn, Mass. Several of the pioneers of Milford, Conn., (q.v., 6) moved on to Easthampton and Southampton (q.v., below). Many of the early inhabitants of Easthampton were probably Kentishmen. Newcomers to the town were voted upon after careful investigation.—Easthampton and Southampton drew up plans of government, as did Southold (q.v., 50). These three towns maintained close relations with Connecticut. In 1658 Easthampton joined the Conn. Colony; like Southold, it finally accepted New York's jurisdiction with reluctance.—Located on the southeastern shore of the island. Always a rural community, now filled with large estates.—East Hampton (sic) village inc. 1920.—Pop. 1790: 1497, 1820: 1646, '50: 2122, '80: 2515, 1910: 4722, '30: 6569 (East Hampton village 1934; Sag Harbor village in this town 989, the remainder in Southampton town 1784).—Hedges, H. P. History of the town of East Hampton, N.Y., including an address delivered . . . in 1849; introduction to the 4 printed volumes of its records and genealogical notes. 344 p. Sag Harbor, 1897.

1. Farmer, fisherman, 63. Has always lived on a backwoods road just north of the village of East Hampton.—Old local stock.—Probably illiterate. (Only 4 months of school.)—No social contacts. Leads semi-Indian life.—Thinks quickly but not clearly. Content of his speech sometimes illogical and confused.—Rapid tempo. Fairly precise articulation, without the strong N.E. stress.—Incomplete record: only pp. 7–11, 14–23, 26–82.—L 154.

3. Housewife, 80. Born and brought up in a rural section southwest of the village of East Hampton, but has lived since her marriage in the village of Bridgehampton (c. 5 m. west), town of Southampton.—Old local stock.—Grammar school. (Daughter a librarian.)—Many social contacts.—Frail health and failing memory. Not a very satisfactory informant.—Speech typical of the region.—Incomplete record: only pp. 7–11, 14–23, 26–55.

Auxiliary informant: aged carpenter of old Bridgehampton (town of Southampton) family.—Rustic nasal speech. Pp. 7–11, starred forms.—L 156.

51 Town of Southampton (Sagaponack), Suffolk Co., N.Y.

Settled 1640 from Lynn, Mass. (Cf. Easthampton, above.) Many of the early inhabitants of Southampton are said to have been Yorkshiremen. Union with Conn. Colony 1644. Whale fishing off the shore during the 17. and early 18. cent. Later shipbuilding brought prosperity.—Southampton, located on the southern shore west of Easthampton, has many large estates. Sag Harbor village began with a temporary population of fishermen and became a well established settlement c. 1730. It was the center of Southampton's shipbuilding. Sagaponack is a rural community.—Pop. 1790: 3402, 1820: 4229, '50: 6501, '80: 6352, 1910: 11,069, '30: 15,341 (Southampton village 3737; Sag Harbor village in this town 1784 and the remainder in Easthampton town 989).—Howell, George R. Early history of Southampton, Long Island. . . . Ed. 2. 473 p. Albany, 1887.

2. Farmer and carpenter, 85.—Old local families.—School until 16.—Presbyterian Church.—Intelligent; rather ponderous. Gave trustworthy information.—Deliberate tempo. Some nasalization.—L 155.

RHODE ISLAND

52 Town of New Shoreham (Block Island), Newport Co.

Granted to Gov. Endicott by the General Court of Mass. in 1658; settled 1661 by families from Braintree and Roxbury. Admitted to the Colony of Rhode Island in 1664; inc. as New Shoreham in 1672. (The island was named for Adriaen Block, a Dutch navigator, who had visited it in 1614).—Fishing, some farming. Summer colony. The island was hard to approach until Old Harbor (1878) and New Harbor (1900) were constructed.—Pop. 1774: 575, '90: 681, 1820: 955, '50: 1262, '80: 1203, 1910: 1314, '30: 1029.—Livermore, Samuel T. A history of Block Island. . . . 371 p. Hartford, Conn., 1877. Livermore, Samuel T. Block Island: (1) a map and guide, (2) a history (abridged). 125 p. Hartford, Conn., 1882. Rev. and ed. by Charles E. Perry, Providence, [1901].

1. Retired fisherman, formerly in the coast guard, 91.—Descended from first settlers here.—Grammar school.—Lives in isolated neighborhood. Practically no social contacts.—Active physically for his age; mentally keen. Slightly deaf.—Archaic vocabulary. Incomplete record: only pp. 1–11, 14–23, 26–46.—Auxiliary informant: wife, 61, born here.—HS 5.

2. Farmer and fisherman, 11 years life guard, 77. —F's family originally from Scotland, came to Providence, settled here in 17. cent.—School until 17. Reads extensively. Daughter teaches here. Both regarded by their neighbors as cultured.—Baptist Church. Lives with daughter about a mile from the road in sparsely settled farming country.—Likes to be out of doors. Interested in the investigation and eager to help.—Natural, archaic speech. Can distinguish his own usage from earlier and later forms. —Auxiliary informant: daughter.—HS 3.

3. Housewife, 66. Has run summer boarding house 45 years.—Descended from original settlers.—School until 18.—First Baptist Church, W.C.T.U., American Legion Auxiliary.—Reticent; dislikes any kind of publicity.—Fairly modern type of local speech. Slow, careful of correctness. (Probably influenced by teacher who lived with her many years.)—HS 6.

4. Housewife, 50. Has rented rooms to summer visitors for 20 years.—Descended from original settlers. (Husband born in East Greenwich, Kent Co.; brought up in North Kingstown, Washington Co.; has lived here 28 years.)—School until 17.— Baptist Church, W.C.T.U., American Legion Auxiliary.—Hard-working, cheerful, kind-hearted.— Lived as a child with her grandmother, who taught her to avoid some 'incorrect' forms, particularly *ain't*. Unaffected, rapid speech. Strong nasalization.—HS 4.

54 Town of Richmond (1 and 2 Wyoming; 3 Arcadia), Washington Co.

Settled after 1709 as part of Charlestown; set off

in 1747. (Charlestown settled c. 1669, set off from Westerly in 1738.) Early settlers from Westerly, South Kingstown and Newport.—Descendants of the old stock still farming and working in the local textile mills. Town includes a number of villages: Wyoming (settled 1758, when a Hopkinton man set up an iron works) is a farming community with a textile mill; Arcadia, formerly a mill village, is now rural.—Pop. 1774: 1257, '90: 1769, 1820: 1423, '50: 1784, '80: 1949, 1910: 1633, '30: 1535.—Irish, J. R. Historical sketch of the town of Richmond. . . . 96 p. Hope Valley, R. I., 1877.—*Charlestown:* Tucker, W. F. Historical sketch of the town of Charlestown. . . . 88 p. Westerly, 1877.—*Westerly:* Denison, Frederic. Westerly and its witnesses. . . . 314 p. Providence, 1878.

1. Widow, 92. Formerly weaver in a textile mill. Born in Plainfield, Windham Co., Conn. (c. 20 m. northwest); stayed there 6 months. Has lived 2 years in Canterbury, Conn. (next town west of Plainfield); 1 year in Sterling, Conn. (next town east of Plainfield); 1 year in West Greenwich, Kent Co. (c. 10 m. north of here); 5 years in Hopkinton (c. 7 m. southwest); 3 years in Exeter (c. 10 m. northeast); also in Carolina and Richmond, both in town of Richmond.—Ancestors came to N.E. in 17. cent.— School until 15. Local authority on genealogy.— Lives alone and has few contacts now.—Very independent; does all her own work. Mind still keen.— Used to study the dictionary. Was 'learned to pronounce words as they were spelled'; also that two negatives equal one 'positive' (but she uses the double negative).—HS 13.

2. Proprietor of tea room, former schoolteacher, 75.—Old R.I. family.—Local schools.—Lives with her sister in 18. cent. homestead.—Sensitive, well-bred, quick and active.—Seemed concerned with correctness.—Auxiliary informant: sister.—HS 9.

3. Rural letter carrier, 43. Has worked on a farm, on the railroad, in a local store, at lumbering, etc. Has frequently spent a few months in Providence (c. 30 m. northeast).—Parents born here. (Wife from Nova Scotia.)—High school for 3 years; business school in Providence. Some travel.—Baptist Church. Officer of a local band. Many contacts here.—Active, alert. Interested in the investigation.—Conscious of his speech; but would not be able to change it much, even if he wished. Describes it as 'pretty plain.' Slow, deliberate tempo. Some nasalization.— Short work sheets.—HS 11.

56 Town of South Kingstown, Washington Co.

Settled c. 1670. Early families from North Kingstown and Newport, and from Sandwich, Mass. Kingstown (inc. 1674) was divided into No. Kingstown (q.v., 58) and So. Kingstown in 1723.—Agricultural town including a number of villages: Kingston, site of R.I. State College; Peace Dale and Wakefield. Textile mills since c. 1800.—Pop. 1774: 2835, '90: 4369, 1820: 3723, '50: 3807, '80: 5114, 1910: 5176, '30: 6010.—Comstock, Charles. A history of South Kingstown . . . [published 1806]. Reprinted with a foreword by W. D. Miller. 41 p. Kingston, 1934.

1. Farmer, 73. Has also worked on the railroad. Never was outside southern R.I.—Local family.—Grammar school c. 20 months.—Few social contacts.—Gentle, cheerful, honest. Partially crippled by rheumatism. Enjoyed the interviews.—Archaic, picturesque speech, entirely unguarded. Vocabulary limited. Some malapropisms, e.g., *department house.*—Auxiliary informants: (1) daughter (speech rather similar, but modified by grammar school education); (2) native (male) of Matunuck in this town (starred forms on pp. 1–8 only).—HS 10.

56 Town of Narragansett (Point Judith), Washington Co.

Formerly part of South Kingstown (q.v., above); set apart as special district in 1888, inc. 1901.—Wealthy slave-owners farmed here in Colonial times. Now some agriculture and fishing, but chiefly a summer resort.—Pop. 1910: 1250, '30: 1258.

2. Housewife, 66.—F, PGF born here. PGGF from Jamestown, Newport Co. (on Conanicut Island). M and F were cousins.—School until 16.—Baptist Church, W.C.T.U. Contacts with local people and summer residents.—Friendly, though shy. Interested in extension work in home demonstration (U.S. Department of Agriculture).—Speaks naturally, sometimes on guard. Weak articulation of final consonants. Final voiced sounds generally unvoiced.—Auxiliary informants: husband, born in Westerly (c. 20 m. west), brought up here; their 2 daughters.—HS 2.

57 Town of South Kingstown (Wakefield), Washington Co.

See 56. Center of a rural community. Much old N.E. stock. Closely associated with Peace Dale, a mill village (c. 1 m. north).

CULTURED INFORMANT. Housewife, 56. Born in Matunuck, but educated here in Wakefield. Lived in Narragansett Pier (c. 2 m. east) until aged 22; here ever since.—F from old local family. M of Welsh and Irish stock.—Grammar and high school. (Two children are college graduates.) Has traveled along the Atlantic coast.—Fairly active in social life here.—Essentially a town woman, knowing little of farm life.—Conscious of her speech, but generally gave natural responses. Some nasalization.—HS 8.

58 Town of East Greenwich, Kent Co.

Settled 1677 by veterans of King Philip's War, presumably from Warwick (settled 1642) and Kingstown (settled 1639); some from Newport.—Formerly

many Quakers.—Pottery manufactured before the Revolution; now textiles and textile machinery. Shellfisheries, truck gardens.—Pop. 1774: 1663, '90: 1826, 1820: 1519*, '50: 2358, '80: 2887, 1910: 3420, '30: 3666.—Greene, D. H. History of the town of East Greenwich and adjacent territory, from 1677 to 1877. 263 p. Providence, 1877.

1. Farmer, 73. Born 'just over the line' in Warwick (adjoining town northeast), but came here when a few months old.—Last descendant of French Huguenot family that settled in R.I. c. 1685.—School until 20; disliked it. Never wanted to travel. —Few social contacts.—Slight, active, young in appearance. Quick wit and dry humor. Generous and hospitable. Interested in antiques; owns many which have been in his family for generations.—Unaffected, laconic. Tendency to drawl. High pitch. Monotonous intonation. Slight nasalization.—Auxiliary informant: wife, 48, her M born here, her F on Block Island.—HS 7.

58 Town of North Kingstown, Washington Co.

Settled as Wickford c. 1639; inc. as Kingstown 1674. Kingstown divided 1723. (See South Kingstown, 56.) Settlers came from Newport, Portsmouth, Providence, Warwick and Long Island.—Rural community, largely native stock. Many 18. cent. houses. State Lobster Hatchery.—Pop. 1774: 2472, '90: 2904, 1820: 3007, '50: 2971*, '80: 3949, 1910: 4048, '30: 4279.—Baker, D. S. An historical sketch of North Kingstown. 26 p. Providence, 1876. Griswold, Mrs. F. B. Old Wickford, the Venice of America. 240 p. Milwaukee, 1900.

2. Housewife, former schoolteacher, 48. Lived here until 7. In Warwick and East Greenwich, Kent Co., until 37. Last 11 years again in North Kingstown.—Parents Quakers. Ancestors have lived in Washington and Kent Counties since 1670. (Husband born in Arlington, Middlesex Co., Mass.)—Schools of Warwick and Moses Brown School (Quaker) in Providence.—Baptist Church, D.A.R., Girl Scout Council. Officer of a historical society.—Intelligent, energetic. Much interested in local history.—Knows local speech, both archaic and modern. Little knowledge of other dialects. Speaks carefully and distinctly, values correctness. Pronunciation often influenced by spelling. Prolonged vowels. Final consonants carefully articulated.—HS 1.

60 City of Newport, Newport Co.

Settled 1639 by exiles from Boston. A haven for all religious sects: Quakers and Jews are said to have come here as early as 1657–8. Many Scotch families 1746–50. Rapid growth: c. 4000 inhabitants in 1730. —First fishing and farming; later foreign commerce: fortunes built in African slave trade. Great cultural center during 18. cent.; summer resort for wealthy Southerners. Sharp decline in population during the Revolution, with slow recovery. Inc. as city 1853. Manufacturing came gradually. Since c. 1830 Newport has developed chiefly as a fashionable resort.—Now three distinct units: the old town, the army and navy reservations, and the summer colony.—Pop. 1774: 9209, '90: 6744, 1820: 7319, '50: 9563, '80: 15,693, 1910: 27,149, '30: 27,612.—Bridenbaugh, Carl. Colonial Newport as a summer resort. R.I. Historical Society Collections 26 (1933), 1–23. Cahoone, Sarah S. Sketches of Newport and its vicinity. . . . 213 p. New York, 1842. Peterson, Edward. History of R.I. and Newport. 370 p. New York, 1853.

1. CULTURED INFORMANT. Single woman, 63. Born in Haverhill, Essex Co., Mass., but has spent most of her life here.—F from Mass., died when she was 2. (Informant brought up by mother, aunts and grandmother.) MGF a clergyman from Salem, Essex Co., Mass. Other maternal ancestors of old Conn. and R.I. families, largely from Newport.—Private schools here and, from 16 to 18, in Boston. At 18 went abroad; learned French.—Aristocratic in manner. Has always associated with people of her own type. Officer of historical society.—Energetic, gracious, much interested in the investigation.—Speech typical of older educated group here, quick and nervous. Regularly says *he don't*, although younger relatives correct her.—Short work sheets.—HS 12.

2. CULTURED INFORMANT. Housewife, 51.—Descended from old R.I. families.—High and normal schools here. Did not teach. Sent her children to college. Writes magazine articles and composes music.—Belongs to a number of organizations. Many social contacts.—Energetic; much interested in American history and genealogy.—High pitched, slightly nervous speech.—Auxiliary informant: husband, a local merchant.—HS 16.

62 Town of Middletown (1 Middletown; 2 Slate Hill section), Newport Co.

Settled c. 1675 from Newport (q.v., 60) and Portsmouth (q.v., 64). Set off from Newport in 1743.—Agricultural, especially nurseries. Summer homes. The village of Middletown is on the west shore; Slate Hill on the east shore is a farming section occupied largely by native stock.—Pop. 1774: 881, '90: 840, 1820: 949, '50: 830, '80: 1139, 1910: 1708, '30: 2499.—Arnold, Samuel G. An historical sketch of Middletown, R. I., from its organization in 1743. . . . 62 p. Newport, 1876.

1. Former schoolteacher, 82. Lived 2 years in Whitinsville, Worcester Co., Mass. Taught first in Auburn, City of Cranston, Providence Co.; also 1 year in Little Compton (town across Sakonnet River east of here) and 2 terms in Jamestown, Conanicut Island (west of here). Has done sewing in Providence.—Descended from old R.I. families. PGGM and MGGM were sisters; their ancestor the first president of Newport Colony.—East Greenwich Academy 2 terms, aged 18. State Normal School in

Providence, aged 23 to 25.—Methodist Episcopal Church. Partial invalid, closely confined to the house.—Glad to act as informant. Conscious of her education.—Natural speech, less careful than she thought. Frequent glottal stops. Final consonants weak.—Auxiliary informants: sister-in-law and niece.—HS 17.

2. Housewife, 65. Visited New Jersey 2 or 3 times; never away from here more than 6 months.—Descended from old local families. F's ancestors came to Portsmouth (next town north on the island) from England early in the colonial period. (Husband born in Pennsylvania.)—School here until 17.—Episcopal Church. Not many social contacts.—Kind, friendly. Interested in genealogy and antiques. Eager to help with the investigation.—Local type of speech. Slight nasalization. Final consonants weak.—Auxiliary informant: brother.—HS 15.

64 Town of Portsmouth (Bristol Ferry section), Newport Co.

Settled 1638 by Anne Hutchinson and her fellow-exiles from Mass.—Farming and shipbuilding, then fishing. Coal mining begun c. 1800 (abandoned). Now becoming residential. Summer colony.—The Bristol Ferry, est. c. 1680, connected Portsmouth with Bristol (to the north) and was in the direct line of travel from Newport to Providence. It operated until the opening of the Mt. Hope Bridge in 1929.—Pop. 1774: 1512, '90: 1600, 1820: 1645, '50: 1833, '80: 1979, 1910: 2681, '30: 2969.—West, Edward H. Portsmouth, R.I., before 1800. N.p., n.d. [1937]. (Bound pamphlet in the library of the R.I. Historical Society. Cover title: History of Portsmouth, 1638–1936.)

Retired captain of fishing vessel, ferryman, 82.—Descended from old local families.—School here until 9. 'Took to the water' (fishing) at 11.—Not many social contacts.—Active, mentally keen. Reticent, but friendly and fond of company. Keeps everything shipshape and insists on punctuality.—Unaffected speech, strongly flavored with sea terms, e.g., *come aboard* for *come in*.—Auxiliary informants: wife (a native of this town), her sister, and his granddaughter (aged 16, from Hartford, Conn.).—HS 14.

80 City of Providence, Providence Co.

Settled 1636 (inc. as city 1831) by Roger Williams and five others from the Mass. Bay Colony. Haven of refuge for various religious sects: many Baptists, Quakers and others. Slow growth; c. 1000 inhabitants in 1676.—First agriculture, fishing and fur trade; then trade in rum, molasses and slaves (first wharf in 1680). Textile industry since 1787, initiating a rapid growth in pop.: by 1800 Providence overtook Newport. Manufacture outstripped overseas trade c. 1850. Present industries: textiles, jewelry and silverware, machines, tools, precision instruments, wire, etc.—Large Irish element since

c. 1840. Large foreign population now, c. one third of total pop. being foreign born and another third of foreign stock (mostly Italian, French-Canadian and Portuguese).—Seat of Brown University (chartered 1764, in Providence since 1770), Rhode Island School of Design, Providence College, etc.—Pop. 1774: 4321, '90: 6371, 1820: 11,767, '50: 41,513, '80: 104,857, 1910: 224,326, '30: 252,981.—Greene, W. A. The Providence plantations for 250 years. 468 p. Providence, 1886. Kimball, G. S. Providence in colonial times. 392 p. Boston, 1912.

1. Single woman, 74. Has small business. Spent most of her life here, except c. 10 years. Lived at Christian Hill near Olneyville (c. 3 m. from center of city), and recently in Wickford, town of North Kingstown, Washington Co. (c. 25 m. south).—Descended from old R.I. families; traces her ancestry to Roger Williams. F born in North Scituate, town of Scituate (c. 10 m. west). PGGGF born here; was pastor of Baptist Church. M born in Coventry, town of Coventry, Kent. Co. (c. 15 m. southwest). Her ancestors came to Newport c. 1640.—Grammar school until 12; private school 12 to 14; aged 16, had a tutor for 1 year. (Parents were teachers.) Reads considerably.—Grace Episcopal Church, D.A.R. Now living in Home for Aged Women here.—Frail in health since childhood, but has survived all her family.—Wants to know correct pronunciations and frequently consults dictionary. Knowledge of farm terms limited. Quick, high-pitched, slightly nasal speech. Final consonants generally weak.—HS 19.

2. Clerk, dressmaker, 55.—F born here; his parents from Scotland. M born here; MGF born somewhere west of Pennsylvania; MGM from Maine.—Grammar school.—Congregational Church. Several local societies.—Regrets her limited education. Tries to make the most of it; often misuses words. Certain of what she normally says. Final consonants weak. Slight nasalization.—HS 38.

3. CULTURED INFORMANT. Housewife, 63. Lived in New York City for a few years after her marriage.—F born in Mass., graduated from Brown University, died when she was 2. M from old R.I. family.—Taught at home by her mother until she was 12. Attended small private school here. Never studied formal English grammar, but learned Latin, German and French. Attended Smith College, Northampton, Mass. Travels occasionally.—Central Congregational Church, A.A.U.W., Republican clubs, Foreign Policy Ass'n. Now lives alone, in comfortable circumstances.—Active, keen-minded.—Interested in words. Sure of her own speech. Nasalization.—Short work sheets.—HS 33.

4. CULTURED INFORMANT. Librarian, 46. Lived 3 years in N.Y. City after graduating from college.—F's ancestor left Surrey, England, for Virginia c. 1630; later moved to N.Y. Providence branch of family founded before the Revolution. M lived in N.Y. State until her marriage; her parents from Cambridge, England. She had many English ways and speech habits, but has gradually lost them.—High school here and Pembroke College in Brown University. Foreign study. Authority on incunabula. Education much influenced by her F.—Episcopal Church, A.A.U.W., Bibliographical Society of America, etc.—Speaks naturally. Some nasalization. —HS 35.

81 Town of East Providence, Providence Co.

Settled 1644 as part of Rehoboth, Mass. (q.v., 104), by families from the Mass. coast towns from Boston to Duxbury. Part of Mass. until 1861; inc. as East Providence in 1862.—Suburb of Providence, residential; dairies and truck gardens; some manufacturing.—Pop. 1880: 5056, 1910: 15,808, '30: 29,995.—Bliss, George N. An historical sketch of the town of East Providence. . . . 52 p. Providence, 1876.

Housewife, 70.—F's family probably from Rehoboth (c. 7 m. east across Mass. line). M's family originally from Isle of Guernsey; came here during colonial period.—School until 17.—Baptist Church, Grange.—Small, wiry, mentally alert.—Has ideas of 'proper' English. Nasal speech.—Auxiliary informant: husband, born in Portsmouth, moved to Rehoboth, Mass., when a child.—HS 30.

82 Town of Foster (1 South Foster; 2 Foster Center), Providence Co.

Settled 1717, evidently from Providence (q.v., 80) and Glocester (adjoining town north, settled late in the 17. cent. from Providence). Set off from Scituate and inc. 1781. (Scituate, inc. 1731, had been part of the outlands of Providence; it was settled shortly before 1700 from Scituate, Mass. Later some families moved in from the Providence settlement of Smithfield.)—Scattered small farms; large tracts 'grown to brush,' as farms were abandoned from c. 1830 on. Foster Center has town office, school, general store. Decreasing population.—Pop. 1790: 2268, 1820: 2900, '50: 1932, '80: 1552, 1910: 1124, '30: 946.

1. Master mechanic, auctioneer for 30 years, town officer, 74. Has lived here all but 15 years. Spent less than a year in Mass.; worked for a time in Cranston (c. 15 m. east) and in Providence (c. 20 m. east). Now divides his time between apartment in Providence and son's house here.—Descended from old local families. Traces his ancestry to Roger Williams.—School until 17. Has always read extensively.—Baptist Church. Charter Member of the Grange. I.O.O.F., Roger Williams Association.—Lively, alert, talkative. Interested in everybody and everything.—Has consciously kept his native speech, but knows other types. Likes to use long words, often pronouncing them in his own fashion. Quick, high-pitched, nasal speech. Many glottal stops. Weak final consonants.—HS 22.

2. Housewife, 73. Lives outside the village proper

on country road.—Descended from old R.I. families. —School until 16.—Baptist Church. Several local societies. Husband was a town officer for many years.—Shy, diffident, kindly.—Could distinguish between what she naturally said and what 'some calls it.' Speech typical of this region.—HS 18.

MASSACHUSETTS

102 Town of Westport (South Westport), Bristol Co.

Settled as part of Dartmouth from Plymouth (q.v., 112), set off and inc. 1787. Dartmouth est. 1664; the land had been bought by Plymouth from the Indians. Many Quakers came here. Some Westport families were from Portsmouth, R.I. (q.v., 64).—Isolated rural community. Summer cottages along the shore. —Pop. 1790: 2463, 1820: 2633, '50: 2795, '80: 2894, 1910: 2928, '30: 4408.—Ricketson, Daniel. The history of New Bedford, including a history of the old township of Dartmouth and the present townships of Westport, Dartmouth and Fairhaven. . . . 412 p. New Bedford, 1858.

1. Farmer (raised strawberries and poultry 40 years), fisherman, carpenter, 76. When 3 or 4, went to New Bedford (c. 10 m. northeast) and spent 13 years there; has also lived 7 years in Boston (c. 60 m. north).—Parents born here. M from old local family.—School in New Bedford and 2 winters in Westport.—Social contacts through the Grange.—Active, intelligent. Keen sense of humor.—Talked freely and naturally. Rather old-fashioned speech. Does not try to be grammatical.—Approximately pp. 39–103.

Supplementary informant: inmate of Town Infirmary, 75.—Old local family.—Mind not alert.— Archaic type of speech.—Was original choice, but refused because of illness to do more than the first third of the record: approximately pp. 1–38. These entries are not starred on the maps.—HS 31.

2. Housekeeper, 62. Lives with her employer (woman aged 72), whom she used to help in managing a summer boarding house. Born here; lived 3 years in New York City and in Tuxedo Park, N.Y.— Local ancestry.—School here until 16.—Congregational Church. A few summer guests still accommodated in the house where she lives. No neighbors in winter.—Intelligent, fond of company.—Certain of her speech habits. Could generally tell how she had acquired unusual forms. Moderate tempo.—Auxiliary informants: (1) Employer. Speech somewhat affected by a throat operation. Often had difficulty in pronouncing a word until she had heard it spoken. (2) The latter's husband. (3) A visitor.—HS 28.

103 City of Fall River, Bristol Co.

Set off from Freetown in 1803; first called Troy; since 1834, Fall River; inc. as a city in 1854. Freetown, settled c. 1659 mainly from Scituate, Marshfield and Plymouth, had a pop. of 2206 in 1790.— Industrial city: textile mills. Large French and Portuguese elements.—Pop. 1820: 1594, '50: 11,524, '80: 48,961, 1910: 119,295, '30: 115,274.—Earl, H. H. A centennial history of Fall River. . . . 252 p.

New York, 1877. Fenner, H. M. History of Fall River. . . . 264 p. New York, 1906. Peck, F. M. Fall River and its industries. . . . 280 p. New York, 1877.—*Freetown:* A history of the town of Freetown. . . . 287 p. Fall River, 1902. (Sketches by various local writers.)

1. Retired florist, 72. 'Farmed it' c. 10 years, drove horse cars, worked at an amusement park. Has also lived in Norton (c. 20 m. north).—F came in 1822 from Apponaug, town of Warwick, Kent Co., R.I. His family settled in Middletown, R.I., in 17 cent. M from old R.I. family.—Graduated from high school here in 1880.—Baptist Church, I.O.O.F.— Intelligent. Sociable. Somewhat offhand in manner. Good sense of humor.—Unaffected speech, slightly nasal.—HS 32.

2. Single woman, 49. Writes for newspapers, does some handicraft work. Lived here until 19, then settled in town of Rochester, Plymouth Co. (c. 15 m. east), a rural community.—F of English stock. M born here.—High school education. Not strong enough for extensive travel, but goes about the community to get news.—Habitually notices difference between her speech and that of others. Fairly natural and unguarded. Marked diphthongization of many vowels, lax as well as tense, even in syllables not receiving primary stress.—R 9.

104 Town of Rehoboth, Bristol Co.

Settled 1644 from Weymouth in the Mass. Bay Colony. Other settlers from Boston, Dorchester, Roxbury, Dedham, Hingham, Scituate, Marshfield and Duxbury. The first Baptist congregation in Mass.—Agricultural community to this day.—Pop. 1764: 3696, '90: 4710, 1820: 2740*, '50: 2104, '80: 1891, 1910: 2001, '30: 2610.—Bliss, Leonard, Jr. The history of Rehoboth; comprising a history of the present towns of Rehoboth, Seekonk and Pawtucket, from their settlement to the present time. 294 p. Boston, 1836. Tilton, George H. A history of Rehoboth, Mass. . . . 417 p. Boston, 1918.

Retired farmer, town officer, 87. Now lives in East Providence, R.I. (c. 7 m. west).—Descended from old local families. PGGF lived in Dighton (c. 7 m. east).—Grammar school and a few weeks at a private school.—Well known locally as one of the oldest and best informed citizens. Formerly influential in town affairs. Has been a member of the State Legislature, as his F was in 1865.—Glad to talk to the FW.— Sure of his speech.—HS 29.

106 Town of Raynham, Bristol Co.

Settled c. 1650; inc. 1731, set off from Taunton (q.v.,

below).—Farming and poultry raising; formerly ship-building, flour mill, shoe factory.—Pop. 1764: 694, '90: 1095, 1820: 1071, '50: 1541, '80: 1681, 1910: 1725, '30: 2136.—Sanford, Enoch. History of Raynham from the first settlement. 51 p. Providence, R.I., 1870.

1. Farmer, 80. For 16 years inspector of cattle and slaughtering. Always traded in Taunton and now lives there every winter.—F's ancestor came from England in 17. cent. and settled here.—Two terms at Pierce Academy in Middleboro, Plymouth Co. (c. 10 m. southeast).—Well acquainted in the city and at home.—Still active. Opinionated.—Stable, well preserved speech of the older generation.—R 8.

106 City of Taunton, Bristol Co.

Settled 1638–9, mostly by families from Taunton and vicinity in Somerset, England. Some of these had spent some years in Plymouth, Dorchester, etc., before settling here. Inc. as a city in 1864.—Being located at the head of navigable water, Taunton engaged in coastwise trade and built ships. Iron works since 17. cent. Diverse manufactures now.—Pop. 1764: 2744, '90: 3804, 1820: 4520, '50: 10,441, '80: 21,213, 1910: 34,259, '30: 37,355.—Emery, S. H. History of Taunton, from its settlement to the present time. 768 +110 p. Syracuse, N.Y., 1893.

2. Captain of fire station, 62. Formerly a house painter.—F emigrated from Scotland, M from Ireland; they met and married here.—Grammar school. Travel confined to this part of Mass., except for a brief trip to New York. Well informed about the city's industrial and political history.—Knows many people here.—Forthright, practical. Never saw the value of the investigation, but understood what was wanted and talked willingly.—Speech has a few Irish characteristics, such as: 'He's just after burying his wife.' Not concerned about correctness.—Short work sheets pp. 1–84, long work sheets pp. 85–103. —R 10.

108 Town of Bridgewater, Plymouth Co.

Settled 1651 (inc. 1656) by families from Duxbury (D. settled c. 1632 from Plymouth); other settlers from Hingham and Weymouth. First interior settlement in the Old Colony.—Small industrial center surrounded by farms. Iron manufacturing in 18. cent. (cannons during Revolutionary War). Cotton gins. Normal school est. 1840. Large Italian and Portuguese elements.—Pop. 1764: 3990, '90: 4953, 1820: 5670, '50: 2790*, '80: 3620, 1910: 7688, '30: 9055.—Mitchell, Nahum. History of the early settlement of Bridgewater. 424 p. Bridgewater, 1897.

1. Retired farmer, 71.—F from Vermont. M's family here for 6 generations.—High school education. Wide reading: the Bible, history, poetry, periodicals.—Unitarian Church. Well known locally.—Keen native intelligence.—Some sounds weakly articulated.—R 2.

2. Lawyer, 39. Has lived in Newton, Middlesex Co. (c. 30 m. northwest). Away from here between the ages of 21 and 30. Taught for short periods in Southborough (c. 40 m. northwest) and Gardner (c. 70 m. northwest), Worcester Co.; in Marlborough, Middlesex Co. (c. 45 m. northwest); and in Swampscott (c. 35 m. north) and Essex (c. 50 m. northeast), Essex Co.—Parents and grandparents always lived within 30 m. of here.—Normal and business schools; Northeastern University. Reads periodicals. Speech little affected by his travels.—Active socially.—Dislikes affectation. Was perfectly natural during the interviews. Has clung to a free, idiomatic type of speech.—Rapid tempo. In careful utterance retroflection is more common than in conversation. Much fluctuation in vowels and diphthongs.—R 5.

3. CULTURED INFORMANT. Drawing teacher (24 years), housewife (2 years), 45. Taught 1 year in Pepperell, Middlesex Co. (c. 60 m. northwest), and 1 year in Dedham, Norfolk Co. (c. 25 m. northwest). —F born here. M born in Duxbury (c. 20 m. east), went to school in Boston.—High and normal schools here. Trip to Europe.—Many social contacts in her own group. Church work.—Retroflection varies considerably, is often lacking in normal conversation, and may have been increased by her education (cf. informant 2).—R 1.

110 Town of Hanover (North Hanover), Plymouth Co.

Settled 1649 (inc. 1727), largely from Scituate (according to genealogies). Scituate was settled 1633 from Kent, England.—Rural community. Considerable intermarriage.—Pop. 1790: 1084, 1820: 1211, '50: 1592, '80: 1897, 1910: 2326, '30: 2808.—Barry, John S. A historical sketch of the town of Hanover. . . . 448 p. Boston, 1853. Dwelley, Jedediah and John F. Simmons. History of the town of Hanover, Mass., with family genealogies. 291 +474 p. Pub. by town of Hanover, 1910.—*Scituate:* Deane, Samuel. History of Scituate, Mass., from its first settlement to 1831. 406 p. Boston, 1831. Pratt, Harvey H. The early planters of Scituate, a history of the town . . . to the end of the Revolutionary War. 386 p. Scituate Historical Society, 1929.

1. Retired carpenter, shoemaker, 78. Calls himself a 'knacky' man. Born in East Braintree, Norfolk Co. (c. 8 m. northwest), came here aged 6. Lived in New Hampshire aged 55 to 56.—F born in East Braintree. M born here.—Two terms of high school. Not much reading except religious works and periodicals.—Active in his church. Well acquainted here. —Phlegmatic. Endless fund of recollections, but memory sometimes fails. Knows little of farm life.—Seeks 'correct' forms now and then.—Auxiliary informant: wife.—R 6.

2. Storekeeper, postmaster, 57.—Old local family.—Graduated from Massachusetts Institute of Technology in 1896. Very little reading. Went to the

World's Fair in Chicago in 1893.—Meets all the townspeople. A few outside business contacts.—On his return from college he settled back into the ways of the community.—Normally unconscious of his speech. Tends to nasalize, to run words together and to omit vowels.—R 4.

112 Town of Plymouth, Plymouth Co.

Settled 1620 by the Pilgrims; oldest settlement in N.E.—Conservative community, dominated by the old stock, but with a large foreign population. Farming, fishing, manufactures, tourist trade. Formerly also coastwise shipping.—Pop. 1764: 2246, '90: 2995, 1820: 4348, '50: 6024, '80: 7093, 1910: 12,141, '30: 13,042.—Bradford, William. History of the Plymouth Plantation, 1606–1646. Ed. by W. T. Davis. New York, 1921. Davis, W. T. History of the town of Plymouth, with a sketch of the origin and growth of Separatism. 188 p. Philadelphia, 1885. Thacher, James. History of the town of Plymouth from its first settlement in 1620 to the present time; with a concise history of the aborigines of New England and their wars with the English, etc. . . . Ed. 2, enlarged and corrected. 401 p. Boston, 1835.

1. Gardener, handy man, 67.—Of local parentage. —Practically illiterate; never went to school.—Few social contacts.—Rather dull-witted.—Excellent representative of old-fashioned popular speech.—Auxiliary informant: wife.—R 7.

2. CULTURED INFORMANT. Official of manufacturing firm, 42. In Seattle, Washington, on business, aged 24 to 26.—Descended from Pilgrims.—Graduated from Massachusetts Institute of Technology. Well informed about current events. Makes occasional short business trips.—Wide social contacts. Wife prominent in historical and social organizations.—Level-headed, intelligent.—No striking peculiarities of speech. Retroflection usually lacking.—Auxiliary informants: wife, brought up on a farm, and their children.—R 11.

113 Town of Wareham (East Wareham), Plymouth Co.

Settled c. 1680 from Hingham, Plymouth and Sandwich; inc. 1739 from parts of Plymouth and Rochester (q.v., 112 and 114).—Rural community at head of Buzzards Bay. Center of cranberry industry. Shellfisheries. Many summer colonies. Formerly whaling and shipbuilding.—Pop. 1764: 519, '90: 854, 1820: 952, '50: 3186, '80: 2896, 1910: 4102, '30: 5686.—Bliss, W. R. Colonial times on Buzzards Bay. 252 p. Boston, 1900.

Farmer, 85; also for many years owner and navigator of coasting vessels, pleasure steamer, yachts.— Local family.—Little formal education.—Formerly had wide business contacts. Sees few people now except his workmen.—Always busy. Thought the investigation foolish.—Natural speech; no concern for correctness.—Auxiliary informant: daughter.—Long

work sheets pp. 1–78, short work sheets pp. 79–103. —R 20.

114 Town of Rochester, Plymouth Co.

Settled 1651 (inc. 1686) from Scituate (settled 1633 from Kent, England).—Small quiescent rural community. Population mainly of native stock, but Portuguese are moving in to work the cranberry bogs.—Pop. 1764: 1985, '90: 2642, 1820: 3034, '50: 3808, '80: 1043*, 1910: 1090, '30: 1141.—Bliss, W. R. Colonial times on Buzzards Bay. 252 p. Boston, 1900. Mattapoisett and old Rochester, Massachusetts. (Prepared under the direction of a committee of the town of Mattapoisett.) 424 p. New York, 1907.—*Scituate:* see 110 Hanover.

CULTURED INFORMANT. Farmer, 73. Sells insurance, has taught school. Born in New Bedford, Bristol Co. (c. 10 m. southwest), came here aged 3. Taught in Carver (c. 12 m. northeast), but kept his home here.—F from northern Vt., M from New Bedford. His ancestors have farmed for several generations.—High and normal schools. Reads constantly; interested in history and geography. Makes occasional trips to northern N.E.—Social contacts in farm, business and school life.—Speech distinctly of the upper level, with a number of popular ungrammatical expressions. Considerable difference between his bound and isolated forms; the former obtained whenever possible. Clear enunciation.— R 3.

115 Town of Falmouth (Teaticket), Barnstable Co.

Settled c. 1660 (inc. 1686), chiefly by Quakers from Barnstable (q.v., 116); some families from Sandwich. —Agriculture, fishing; formerly also whaling, shipbuilding and manufacture of salt and glass. Large summer colonies. Many Portuguese and Finnish farmers. Chief contacts with Wareham across Buzzards Bay.—Pop. 1764: 1125, '90: 1639, 1820: 2370, '50: 2621, '80: 2422, 1910: 3144, '30: 4821.—Celebration of the 200th anniversary of the town of Falmouth. . . . 153 p. Falmouth, 1887. Jenkins, C. W. Three lectures on the early history of Falmouth. . . . 113 p. Falmouth, 1889.

Retired dealer in notions, 93. For 50 years did business up and down the Cape, working out of New Bedford. Went to sea twice on whaling voyages around Cape Horn.—Family long settled on the upper Cape.—Grammar school. Reads religious books. —Oldest man in town. Formerly wide acquaintance; sees few people now.—Good representative of uncultivated old-fashioned speech.—Incomplete record: only pp. 2–11, 14–24, 26–57, short work sheets. —R 22.

116 Town of Barnstable (West Barnstable), Barnstable Co.

Settled 1637 (inc. 1639) largely from Scituate (see 110 Hanover); other families from Lynn, Plymouth and Sandwich.—Formerly coastwise and overseas trade. Salt works. Now summer resort. Shellfisheries. County seat.—Pop. 1764: 2138, '90: 2610, 1820: 3824, '50: 4901, '80: 4242, 1910: 4676, '30: 7271.— Otis, Amos. Genealogical notes of Barnstable families. . . . Revised by C. F. Swift. 2v. in 1. Barnstable, 1888–90.

1. Farmer, dairyman, 80. Aged 28 to 30, lived in Marshfield, Plymouth Co. (c. 40 m. northwest).— Old Cape Cod family.—Grammar school. Reads farm journals; eager student of agriculture and of geography.—Fairly well acquainted locally.—Likes to talk and tell stories.—High pitch. Some nasalization.—Auxiliary informant: wife.—R 12.

2. CULTURED INFORMANT. Town officer, 73. Formerly lecturer for the Grange.—F descended from sea-faring Cape family.—Left school at 14, but educated himself. Wide reading, especially on agricultural subjects. Has made three trips to the West and South with Grange leaders.—Known all over Cape Cod. Has had many contacts with agricultural authorities in Mass. Now occupies himself with town affairs and the visits of friends.—Mind works with great speed. Collaborated earnestly.—Tempo varies. Nasalization.—R 13.

117 Town of Harwich (Pleasant Lake), Barnstable Co.

Settled c. 1670 (inc. 1694) from Plymouth, Eastham and other places.—Formerly many of the inhabitants went to sea. Now summer trade and cranberry bogs. Pleasant Lake is a rural inland community in Harwich town.—Pop. 1764: 1772, '90: 2392, 1820: 1980*, '50: 3258, '80: 3265, 1910: 2115, '30: 2329.—Paine, Josiah. A history of Harwich. . . . 503 p. Rutland, Vt., 1937.

Cranberry farmer, 88; formerly went out with the Grand Banks fishing fleet. Taught 3 winters in a one-room schoolhouse. Between the ages of 11 and 25 traveled to the South on his father's ship.—Family came to Cape Cod from England in 17. cent.—Grammar school. Some reading. Interested in geology.—A few local contacts.—Mild, gentle. Suprisingly extensive vocabulary and interests.—Voice now somewhat feeble and asthmatic; articulation not always distinct.—R 14.

118 Town of Chatham, Barnstable Co.

Settled c. 1670 (inc. 1712), principally from Yarmouth; other early settlers from Eastham, Harwich and Nantucket.—Compact rural community. Much intermarriage. Fishing and clamming. Many summer guests. Formerly also whaling, shipbuilding, salt manufacture.—Pop. 1764: 678, '90: 1134, 1820: 1630, '50: 2439, '80: 2250, 1910: 1564, '30: 1931.— Smith, William C. A history of Chatham, Mass. . . . Hyannis, 1909–17.

1. Retired grocer and coal dealer, 76. Town officer. —F a sea captain. His ancestor bought land here

from the Indians in 1664.—Grammar school. Reads magazines.—Retired at 52. Many local contacts. Lately confined to his home much of the time.— Self-made man in good circumstances. Upright, unyielding, punctual.—Aware of his deviations from correctness; responses guarded at times.—R 15.

2. Builder of ship models, 50.—Descended from old local family.—Little education except for religious training at home.—Contacts with buyers of ship models and townspeople interested in ships.— Extremely rapid speech.—Incomplete record: only pp. 2–11, 14–24, 26–31, short work sheets.—R 21.

119 Town of Eastham (1 North Eastham; 2 Eastham), Barnstable Co.

Settled 1644 (inc. 1651), from the membership of the church at Plymouth (q.v., 112).—Scattered declining population. Truck farms. Formerly also shipping and fishing.—Pop. 1764: 1331, '90: 1834, 1820: 766*, '50: 845, '80: 692, 1910: 518, '30: 543.—Pratt, Enoch. A comprehensive history, ecclesiastical and civil, of Eastham, Wellfleet and Orleans, from 1644 to 1844. 180 p. Yarmouth, 1844.

1. Asparagus farmer and laborer, 80. Here until aged 20, except for 2 winter fishing trips; aged 20 to 35, worked in and near Boston.—F's ancestor settled in Chatham in 17. cent.—Left school at 12. Reads only farm and fishing news.—Practically no social contacts.—Feels he is a plain man; doubted his ability to provide information about local speech. Slow-moving; looks younger than his age.—Slight stammer with forced articulation for some initial consonants.—R 16.

2. Town officer, asparagus farmer, 48. Takes produce to Boston once a week. Born in Brewster (c. 10 m. southwest), came here aged 6. At 18 worked his passage to England and back. Several vacation trips to northern N.E.—Old local family. One grandmother born in Nova Scotia. M died when he was 8.—Did not finish high school. Cares little for reading.—Wide business contacts. Not much social life. —A hard worker.—Natural, unguarded, at times slovenly speech. Rapid tempo. Aware of certain local features in his speech, and of the influence of the schools.—R 17.

120 Town of Truro (1 North Truro; 2 Truro), Barnstable Co.

Settled c. 1700 (inc. 1709), probably from Barnstable (q.v., 116). Family names point to Cornwall, England.—Rural community. Many summer residents. Large Portuguese element. Formerly much fishing, whaling, salt making. Sharp drop in population since 1850.—Pop. 1764: 925, '90: 1193, 1820: 1241, '50: 2051, '80: 1017, 1910: 655, '30: 513.— Rich, Shebnah. Truro . . . or, Land marks and sea marks. 580 p. Boston, [1883].

1. Orchardman, gardener, handy man, 73. Formerly mate and captain on coastwise fishing vessels.

In North Carolina aged 24 to 26; in the Magdalen Islands (north of Nova Scotia) aged 29 to 30.—F and PGF sailed to Africa and Cuba; all his greatgrandfathers were sea captains. M, MGF born here; MGM born in England.—Not much education except what he gave himself. Reads the daily paper.—Not active socially.—Independent, ingenious. Lively, curious mind and dry sense of humor. Enjoys the radio. Likes to tell stories.—Entirely natural in conversation, sometimes over-careful in phrasing his replies to a direct question. Always fluent.—R 19.

2. Poultry farmer, real estate dealer, 60.—Parents born here, probably grandparents also.—High school. Never out of Mass. except for automobile trips to N.H. Not much reading.—Few social contacts.—Reticent.—Unaffected idiomatic speech. Has forgotten all rules of grammar and cares nothing for correctness. Vowels frequently long.—Short work sheets.—R 18.

122 Town of West Tisbury (Makonikey), Dukes Co. (Martha's Vineyard).

The island of Martha's Vineyard was discovered in 1602 by Bartholomew Gosnold, an English navigator, who was one of the founders of Jamestown, Virginia. It was permanently settled c. 1642. At first independent, though nominally under the Province of Maine; in 1664 made part of New York by royal grant; finally ceded to Mass. Natives of the north shore are reported to be different in speech and character from those of the south shore.—Whaling center in 18. and 19. cent. Now many summer residents.—West Tisbury settled c. 1670 as part of Tisbury; set off in 1892. (Tisbury, originally common land, was at first called Middletown.)—Rural community. Makonikey is near Lamberts Cove, which is on Vineyard Sound on the north shore of the island. Farming and fishing; formerly whaling and lumber trade. Population largely of native stock, descended from early settlers.—Pop. 1910: 437, '30: 270. (Pop. of Tisbury 1764: 838, '90: 1140, 1820: 1223, '50: 1803, '80: 1518.)—Banks, C. E. History of Martha's Vineyard. . . . 3v. Boston, 1911–25. Hough, Henry B. Martha's Vineyard, summer resort, 1835–1935. 276 p. Rutland, Vt., 1936.

1. Farmer, 61. Lived 20 years in Vineyard Haven, town of Tisbury; last 22 years back in his birthplace.—F, PGF and his F born here. PGM and her F born in Tisbury. M, MGF, MGM born in Chilmark (adjoining town).—School here until 16.—Cordial and fully coöperative. Good sense of humor. Quick, keen mind. Entirely honest about his speech.—Tempo rapid. Essex Co. (Mass.) type of stress and intonation. Vowels are short.—L 143.

122 Town of Chilmark, Dukes Co. (Martha's Vineyard).

See above. Originally common land, then est. as Manor of Tisbury, Chilmark was given all the pow-

ers of a town in 1714.—Rural community. Fishing. Population largely of native stock, descended from early settlers.—Pop. 1764: 851, '90: 771, 1820: 695, '50: 747, '80: 494*, 1910: 282, '30: 252.

2. CULTURED INFORMANT. Former schoolteacher, 56. Lived here (on the south shore) until 12, then 3 years at school in West Tisbury (adjoining town). Attended school and taught for 10 years in Woonsocket, Providence Co., R.I. Last 25 years in West Tisbury.—Parents and grandparents born here, of old native stock.—Well educated.—Congregational Church. Historical society. Many local contacts.—Energetic, cordial. Interested in history and genealogy.—Unaffected speech. Usually knows what forms are due to reading or school influence. Fairly rapid tempo. Essex Co. (Mass.) type of stress and intonation. Precise articulation. Rather short vowels.—L 144.

123 Town of Edgartown (1 Edgartown Plains section; 2 Edgartown), Dukes Co. (Martha's Vineyard).

Settled 1642 by 12 families bound for Virginia who were forced by storms to land here. They formed a church and engaged in agriculture and fishing. The town was inc. 1671, when its name was changed from Great Harbor.—Whaling port in 18. cent. Various home manufactured products in 19. cent.: candles, socks, mittens, etc.—County seat. Summer visitors.—Pop. 1764: 1030, '90: 1344, 1820: 1374, '50: 1990, '80: 1303*, 1910: 1191, '30: 1276.

1. Farmer, 77.—Descended from oldest island families. F, PGF, PGM born here; PGM of Scotch descent. M, MGF, MGM born in West Tisbury (adjoining town).—School until 15.—Congregational Church. Never goes to town.—Entirely rustic, friendly.—Leisurely type of speech. Tempo moderate. Vowels sometimes long.—L 146.

2. Piano tuner, 82. Born in Vineyard Haven, town of Tisbury; came here aged 3 or 4. Lived 3 years in Taunton, Bristol Co., aged 17 to 20. Spent 2 winters in New York City, aged 28 to 29.—Descended from old island families. F, PGF born here; PGM born in West Tisbury. M, MGF, MGM born in Vineyard Haven.—School here until 16.—Dry, reserved, but glad to answer the questions.—Speech like that of West Tisbury. Retroflection is weaker, however, and not always present.—L 145.

124 Town of Nantucket (1 Nantucket; 2 Siasconset; 3 Quase), Nantucket Co.

Like Martha's Vineyard, this island was discovered by Gosnold in 1602. Included in the royal grant to the Plymouth Company in 1621. Purchased by Thomas Mayhew of Watertown in 1641; most of it sold to nine others (chiefly from Salisbury) in 1659. Amesbury and Salisbury men, disliking the Puritan régime, came here in 1661; also Peter Folger of Martha's Vineyard.—Nantucket County was united with Dukes Co. (Martha's Vineyard; see 122) until 1695. Comprises only one town, Nantucket (town name changed from Sherburn in 1795).—Farming, fishing, sheep raising were the early settlers' chief occupations. Greatest of the whaling towns in the 18. cent.; c. 1820 outstripped by New Bedford. Shipbuilding and the manufacture of nails and woolen goods c. 1800.—Many of the pioneers were Baptists or Presbyterians, but in the 18. cent. the Quakers became the strongest religious sect, and remained so for c. 150 years.—During the whaling period Portuguese from the Azores sometimes joined a crew and eventually settled in Nantucket. Irish farm laborers came in the 1840's and 50's.—The usual sort of migration from old settlements took place here. Fishermen from Nantucket and Cape Cod moved to Nova Scotia in the 1750's. Quaker fishermen from Nantucket and Martha's Vineyard settled Hudson, N.Y., in 1783.—By c. 1850 society reached a high cultural level, with considerable prosperity, but about this time the population began to decrease.—Fishing now and some farming. Famous as a summer colony.—Siasconset, on the east shore, has been called the Newport of Nantucket; many summer people come to this region as well as to the centrally located village of Nantucket. Polpis and Quase are rural communities northwest of Siasconset.—Pop. 1764: 3526, '90: 4555, 1820: 7266, '50: 8452, '80: 3727, 1910: 2962, '30: 3678.—Douglas-Lithgow, R. A. Nantucket, a history. 389 p. New York, 1914. Godfrey, E. K. The island of Nantucket; what it was and what it is. . . . 365 p. Boston, 1882. Hinchman, L. S. Early settlers of Nantucket: their associates and descendants. [Ed. 2.] 347 p. Philadelphia, 1901. Macy, Obed. The history of Nantucket . . . with a concise statement of prominent events from 1835 to 1880 by W. C. Macy. Ed. 2. 313 p. Mansfield, 1880. Macy, William F. The Story of Old Nantucket, a brief history of the island and its people from its discovery down to the present day. Ed. 2. Boston and New York, 1928. Starbuck, Alexander. The history of Nantucket, county, island and town. 871 p. Boston, 1924.

1. Farmer, janitor of public buildings, bell ringer, 83. Aged 18 to 22, on whaling trips in the Atlantic and Indian Oceans. Then 4 years in Cambridge, Middlesex Co., as horsecar driver. Afterwards, until c. 50, lived in the farming section of the island around the villages of Siasconset (on the east shore) and Polpis. Back in Nantucket village for the last 30 years.—F born here; PGF, PGM in Sandwich, Barnstable Co.; both came here when young. M born in Sandwich, came here when young; MGF, MGM from Sandwich.—School until 16.—Companionable, merry, energetic. Quick, bright mind. Enjoyed every question.—Rapid tempo, with pauses for emphasis. Vowels moderately long, but may be greatly lengthened for emphasis.—L 141.

2. Farmer, 78. At 16 went to Middleborough,

Plymouth Co., for 7 years. Then to a lighthouse at Sankaty (bluff at east end of Nantucket Island). At 28 settled on a farm in Siasconset.—From island stock, partly Quaker. F descended from first settlers here.—School until 16. Writes humorous items for local paper.—Cordial, hospitable, intelligent. Likes to talk about whaling and old times on the island.—Tempo rapid. Vowels usually short, but may be long for emphasis.—L 142.

3. Housewife, 79. At 19 went to Quase, in the farming region, where she spent much of her life. Now in Siasconset.—Parents and grandparents born here of old local stock.—Educated by private teacher, a Quaker woman.—Methodist. Lives with her daughter.—Typical New England woman, cordial, yet reserved; not garrulous. Mind quick and keen.—Frank, unguarded responses. Frequently prolongs vowels, especially when already long, for emphasis.—L 140.

125. Town of Nantucket (1 Siasconset; 2 Polpis), Nantucket Co.

See 124.

1. Farmer, 85. Now living in the village of Nantucket.—Parents born here of old local stock.—Intelligent, precise. Easily bored.—Incomplete record: only pp. 7–11, 14–23, 26–27.—L 148.

2. Farmer, 85. Went to sea when young.—Parents born here of old local stock.—Very deaf. Mind failing.—Incomplete record: only pp. 7–10, 14–22.—L 147.

140 Town of Norfolk, Norfolk Co.

Set off from Wrentham (q.v., below), Franklin, Medway and Walpole in 1870. Like Wrentham, the three latter were settled from Dedham (c. 1660); they were not inc. as separate towns until the 18. cent.—Agricultural. Prison colony est. 1927.—Pop. 1880: 930, 1910: 960, '30: 1429.—Blake, Mortimer. A history of the town of Franklin. . . . 289 p. Franklin, 1879.—Jameson, E. O. The history of Medway. . . . 534 p. [Providence, R.I., 1886.]—Lewis, I. N. A history of Walpole. . . . 217 p. [Walpole,] 1905. De Lue, Willard. The story of Walpole, 1724–1924; a narrative history prepared under authority of the town. . . . Norwood, 1925.

1. Farmer's wife, 75. Lived in Foxborough (c. 8 m. southeast) for 5 years after her marriage. A few years ago moved to Franklin (c. 6 m. southwest).—Old local family.—Grammar school.—Congregational Church.—Small, wiry, old-fashioned. Shy at first, but she readily answered the questions. Often appealed for confirmation to her daughter, who was present and who gave some additional forms.—Pp. 10–13, 24–5, 27–8, 32, 40–3, 48–9, 51–103, also scattered items on other pages, supplied by this informant.

Supplementary informant: uneducated man, 87.—Lives with his son, his only companion.—Very poor.—Mind beginning to fail. Interviews discontinued.—

Pp. 1–9, 14–23, 26, 29–31, 33–9, 44–7, 50, and scattered items on other pages. These entries are not starred on the maps.—HS 40.

140 Town of Wrentham, Norfolk Co.

Settled c. 1670 (inc. 1673, set off from Dedham), by the sons and sons-in-law of Dedham families.—Agricultural. Woolen and cotton mills since early 19. cent. Summer colony in recent years.—Pop. 1764: 2030, '90: 1766*, 1820: 2801, '50: 3037, '80: 2481*, 1910: 1743*, '30: 3584.—*Dedham:* Mann, Herman. Historical annals of Dedham, from its settlement in 1635 to 1847. 136 p. Dedham, 1847. Smith, Frank. A history of Dedham, Mass. 543 p. Dedham, 1936. Worthington, Erastus. The history of Dedham. . . . 146 p. Boston, 1827.

2. Single woman, at home, 63.—F's family came from Needham (c. 20 m. northeast) 1737. Five generations have lived in same house. M born in Smithfield, Providence Co., R.I., of English family.—High school; 1 year at academy.—Lives with sister, 66, and brother, c. 70, in the old homestead. Attends to all their business affairs. Formerly also helped her sister, who was librarian 30 years.—Interest centers in her family and its heirlooms. Alert, intelligent.—Sure of her speech. Knew what was 'proper,' but kept to her normal forms. Decided nasalization.—HS 34.

141 Town of Foxborough, Norfolk Co.

Settled 1704; inc. 1778, set off from Stoughton (originally part of Dorchester), Sharon (q.v., 142), Wrentham (q.v., 140) and Walpole (see 140 Norfolk).—Industrialized early: foundry est. 1781; straw bonnet industry during 19. cent.; precision instruments.—Pop. 1790: 683, 1820: 1004, '50: 1880, '80: 2950, 1910: 3863, '30: 5347.—Carpenter, R. W. Brief history of Foxborough. 100 p. Needham, Mass., 1890.

Farmer, 87.—F, PGF born here. GGF a French Huguenot. M born in Wrentham (c. 5 m. west).—Public and private grammar schools. 1 term of high school.—Congregational Church. Formerly prominent in local affairs. Very well informed about his town.—Feeble, rather laconic, but much interested in the interviews.—Genuine old-fashioned local speech.—Auxiliary informant: wife.—HY 44.

142 Town of Sharon, Norfolk Co.

Settled c. 1700; inc. 1775, set off from Stoughton, of which it was the 'second parish.' Stoughton was originally part of Dorchester.—Rural; health resort.—Pop. 1790: 1034, 1820: 1010*, '50: 1128, '80: 1492, 1910: 2310, '30: 3351.—*Stoughton:* Huntoon, D. T. V. History of the town of Canton. 666 p. Cambridge, 1893. *Dorchester:* Dorchester antiquarian and historical society. The history of the town of Dorchester. By a committee of the . . . society. 672 p. Boston, 1859. Orcutt, W. D. Good old Dorchester: a

narrative history of the town, 1630–1893. 496 p. Cambridge, 1893.

Farmer, 56.—F, PGF born here. M, MGF born in Easton, Bristol Co. (c. 8 m. south); MGM born in Taunton, Bristol Co. (c. 16 m. south).—High school. Well read.—Masons and I.O.O.F. Highly respected. Has been selectman.—Intelligent, straightforward.—Speech clear, crisp, vigorous. His wife, a former Maine schoolteacher, tries unsuccessfully to correct him.—HY 45.

146 Town of Cohasset (Beechwood), Norfolk Co.

Settled c. 1635, originally part of Hingham (q.v., below). Set off in 1770; inc. 1775.—During 18. and 19. cent., fishing, farming and shipbuilding. Residential now, like Hingham; summer colony. Many Portuguese in the neighborhood. Beechwood is the most rural section of the town.—Pop. 1790: 817, 1820: 1099, '50: 1775, '80: 2182, 1910: 2585, '30: 3083.—Bigelow, E. V. A narrative history of the town of Cohasset. 561 p. [Boston,] 1898.

1. Market gardener, c. 70. Always here except for 2 short visits to Norwich, Conn.—F and paternal ancestors born here. M born in Watertown, Middlesex Co., worked in North Scituate, Plymouth Co.; married here.—Grammar school in Beechwood; 2 years of high school in Cohasset.—Congregational Church. 30 years in local bands.—Speech more purely local and less standardized than that of informant 2.—HY 34.

146 Town of Hingham, Plymouth Co.

Settled 1633 (inc. 1635) from Hingham and vicinity, Norfolk, England, 206 people arriving in the first 6 years.—Formerly fishing, now mostly residential; within commuting area of Boston.—Pop. 1764: 2506, '90: 2085*, 1820: 2857, '50: 3980, '80: 4485, 1910: 4965, '30: 6657.—History of the town of Hingham. 3v. in 4. [Hingham,] 1893. Lincoln, Solomon. History of the town of Hingham. 183 p. Hingham, 1827.

2. Sexton, 75. In Nova Scotia aged 7 to 10. Worked 20 years in upholstering factory here. Operated a 'bake house' 13 years.—F and M born here. F ran a sloop between here and Nova Scotia 'pickin' up lobsters.'—2 years of high school.—Meets many tourists.—Laconic, but will talk fluently about his church.—Speech influenced by contact with outsiders.—HY 33.

150 City of Boston, Suffolk Co.

Settled 1630 by the Puritans under the leadership of John Winthrop. Within four or five years several thousand Englishmen had come to Boston and its vicinity. Trade and shipbuilding, increasing rapidly after the Revolution.—Many industries in Boston and in the adjoining cities and towns in the Boston metropolitan area.—The present city (inc. 1822) includes the following annexations: Roxbury (1868),

Dorchester (1870); Brighton, Charlestown, West Roxbury (all in 1874); Hyde Park (1911).—Large foreign elements in the population, chiefly Irish (since c. 1840), French-Canadian, Italian.—Capital of Mass. Always a dominant cultural center.—Pop. of Boston (including annexations) 1764: 15,520, '90: 18,038, 1820: 42,536, '50: 136,881, '80: 362,839, 1910: 670,585, '30: 781,188.—Pop. in 1930 of cities and towns in the Boston metropolitan area: Cambridge 113,643, Chelsea 45,816, Everett 48,424, Malden 58,036, Medford 59,714, Newton 65,276, Revere 35,680, Somerville 103,908, Waltham 39,247; Arlington 36,094, Belmont 21,748, Brookline 47,490, Watertown 34,913, Winthrop 16,852.—Total pop. in 1930 of the Boston metropolitan area 1,508,029.— Boston Tercentenary Committee. Fifty years of Boston, a memorial volume. 799 p. Boston, 1932. Bushee, F. A. Ethnic factors in the population of Boston. 171 p. New York, 1903. (American economic assoc. publications, 3d series, v. 4, no. 2.) Cullen, J. B. The story of the Irish in Boston. 443 p. Boston, 1889. Gilman, Arthur. The story of Boston. A study of independency. 507 p. New York, 1889. (Great cities of the republic, v. 3.) Professional and industrial history of Suffolk Co. 3v. [Boston,] 1894. Quincy, Josiah, 3d. A municipal history of the town and city of Boston during two centuries, from Sept. 17, 1630, to Sept. 17, 1830. 444 p. Boston, 1852. Winsor, Justin. The memorial history of Boston, including Suffolk Co., 1630–1880. 4v. Boston, 1880–81.

1. Retired meat cutter (Faneuil Hall Market), 75. Has also lived in Roxbury; now at Home for Aged Men.—F born here, worked at same market. M born in Roxbury, of old local family.—Grammar school.— Universalist, as were his parents.—Active, vigorous, independent. Dislikes his enforced idleness.—Speech entirely natural.—HY 39.

2. Bookkeeper and picture framer, 86. Four years in New Jersey, aged 6 to 10, a short time in East Cambridge and 2 years in New York.—F and PGF born here; ancestors from England. M born in Athol, Worcester Co., came here when she married, died when he was 3. Stepmother from New Jersey.—Did not finish grammar school.—Belongs to no organizations.—Speech probably influenced by stepmother. —HY 43.

3. Club steward (for last 26 years), 61. Previously postal employee. When a young man, served 4 years as machinist's apprentice. Born in South Boston; lived in Newton, Middlesex Co. (part of the Boston metropolitan area), between the ages of 3 and 26; then always in the city.—Parents, grandparents, and their ancestors born in Newfoundland. F and M came here with their parents c. 1850.—Grammar school in Newton. Studied law 1 year at Boston Y.M.C.A. Wide reading. Has traveled extensively here and in Europe.—Social contacts: middle and upper middle class; also, as club steward, knows many persons of high social rank.—Likes to talk of old times. Unfamiliar with farm life.—Careful speech. Occasional malapropisms. Remembers many old Boston forms heard in his boyhood. Knows little of other dialects. Tempo medium to slow. Intonation rather monotonous. Articulation clear, sharp and forceful; marked nasalization.—B 87.

4. CULTURED INFORMANT. Married woman, at home, 74. Now lives in Cambridge, Middlesex Co. (c. 5 m. northwest).—F born here; PGF and his F born in Sudbury, Middlesex Co. (c. 20 m. west). M born here, as were her ancestors for 3 generations.— Public schools. 1½ years abroad. F a purist, of strict literary tastes, good representative of Boston culture in the mid-19. cent.—Accustomed to wealth and social position.—Careful pronunciation, entirely natural to her. Prominent secondary stresses. Her F considered the N.E. short o rustic, and corrected his family.—HY 25.

5. CULTURED INFORMANT. Married woman, 46. Lived 8 years, aged c. 23 to 30, in Beverly, Essex Co. (c. 20 m. northeast). Has spent summers in Me. and, more recently, in Essex Co.—Descended from several of the oldest families of the Bay Colony. F, PGF born in Boston. F of PGF came here from Salem, Essex Co. Family in Salem as early as 1629. M, MGF, MGM born in Boston. MGF's family came from Hingham, Plymouth Co., of Welsh stock. MGM's ancestors from Bedfordshire, England.—As a child, had German governess. Attended private school here until 18. Has traveled in Europe. Wide reading.—Extensive contacts in Boston and vicinity. —Unaffected, easy and gracious. Mentally wide-awake.—Uses certain expressions such as *between you and I, it's him*, which she knows to be contrary to grammatical rules, with complete unconcern. Medium tempo, with remarkably long vowels. Nasalization usually very strong, especially in unstressed vowels.—Auxiliary informant: husband, a lawyer, with background similar to hers. Harvard graduate. —B 86.

152 Town of Weston, Middlesex Co.

Settled c. 1630 (inc. 1713); originally the westerly precinct of Watertown, the most populous town in the early days of the Bay Colony.—Formerly agricultural and, until c. 1850, industrial; now chiefly residential. Weston College (Jesuit).—Pop. 1764: 768, '90: 1009, 1820: 1041, '50: 1205, '80: 1448, 1910: 2106, '30: 3332.—*Watertown:* Bond, Henry. Genealogies of the families and descendants of the early settlers of Watertown, including Waltham and Weston; to which is appended the early history of the town. Ed. 2. 2v. 1094 p. Boston, 1860. Francis, Convers. An historical sketch of Watertown, from the first settlement of the town to the close of its second century. 151 p. Cambridge, 1830.

1. Retired civil engineer, 71.—F born here, also his ancestors as far back as informant knows. M born in Roxbury, came here as a child.—High school.

Does not care to travel; rarely goes even to Boston. —Baptist, as were his parents. Associated in his profession c. 50 years with city of Newton (c. 6 m. east). —Non-local types of speech have influenced him very little.—HY 44.

2. Housewife, 60.—F born here; his family came here in 17. cent. M born in Milo, Piscataquis Co., Me., came here aged 16.—High school. (Daughter, Ph.D., teaches in a N.Y. college.)—Episcopalian. Parents were Baptists.—Vigorous, intelligent. Genuine local type of speech, somewhat influenced by conventions of correctness.

Auxiliary informant: husband, employee of electric company. Has always lived here, working in Wayland (c. 4 m. west), in other neighboring places and in Boston.—F born here, M in Boston.—High school.—Masons, Knights of Pythias, Grange.— Thoroughly representative local type of speech. Less concerned with 'correctness' than his wife.—HY 42.

154 Town of Sherborn (1 Sherborn Center; 2 Sherborn), Middlesex Co.

Settled c. 1652 (inc. 1674) from Dorchester. Dorchester, now part of Boston, was settled in 1630, the early settlers coming largely from the western counties of England.—Secluded, self-contained rural community. One of the earliest shoe manufacturing centers. Now almost entirely agricultural: dairies, orchards. Population largely of native stock; some Irish and Italian families.—Pop. 1764: 673, '90: 858, 1820: 811*, '50: 1043, '80: 1401, 1910: 1428, '30: 943*.—Biglow, William. History of Sherburne from its incorporation, 1674 . . . including that of Framingham and Holliston, so far as they were constituent parts of that town. 80 p. Milford, 1830. Morse, Abner. A genealogical register of the inhabitants and history of the towns of Sherborn and Holliston. 340 p. Boston, 1856.

1. Retired farmer, auctioneer's clerk, 80. Formerly in shoe factory and in shoe business.—GGF on F's side came here from Charlestown (now part of Boston) after the Revolution; F born here in 1802. Family noted for longevity. M born here; MGF, MGM from Needham, Norfolk Co. (c. 8 m. northeast).—Grammar school, aged 4 to 12. High school (open only 3 months a year), 12 to 16. Allen's Classical School in West Newton (c. 12 m. northeast) for 1 term. Has read widely and written articles for historical journals. Was a well known 'water witch' (rhabdomancer), traveling through eastern Mass. and southeastern N.H., to locate wells with a 'divining rod.'—Knows everybody in town; is well liked and respected. Was a member of the State Legislature and has held most of the town offices.—An intelligent observer with a receptive mind. Honest and straightforward.—Old-fashioned speech, often ungrammatical except when guarded. Feeling for local idiom, especially for that of an older generation, very sound. Slow tempo. Wide range of pitch. Articulation energetic but indistinct. Violent aspiration of stops, voiced as well as voiceless. Assimilation frequent, also across the word-boundary. Strong glottalization. Vowels long and diphthongal.—B 85.

2. Farmer, formerly lumberman, 72.—F born here of prominent old local family. M born in Oxford, Worcester Co., came here when a young woman.— School until 13. (F taught school when young. Wife a schoolteacher, later secretary to a minister. Son and daughter graduated from college.) Reads considerably.—Has held town offices and served in State Legislature. Member of I.O.O.F., 50-year Granger. Knows all the older people in town.—Hospitable, friendly, obliging. Dry sense of humor.—Sure of his own speech; influenced by educated members of his family. His speech is free of nearly all the obvious improprieties of grammar and of many old-fashioned pronunciations. Slow tempo. Pitch variations slight, with occasional sharp rises and falls. Slack, indistinct articulation. Weak sounds and final syllables obscured.

Auxiliary informant: daughter-in-law, born and brought up here.—School in Cambridge.—Furnished reliable check on informant's responses.—B 84.

156 Town of Concord, Middlesex Co.

Settled 1635 from Kent, Surrey, Bedfordshire and Yorkshire.—Historic community with distinguished cultural past. Largely residential; many families of the old stock. Foreign element recent.—Pop. 1764: 1564, '90: 1585, 1820: 1788, '50: 2249, '80: 3922, 1910: 6421, '30: 7477.—Bartlett, G. B. Concord: historic, literary and picturesque. Ed. 15, revised. 200 p. Boston, 1895. Hudson, A. S. The history of Concord. Concord, 1904. Walcott, C. H. Concord in the colonial period . . . 1635–89. 172 p. Boston, 1884.

1. Farmer, 73.—Old local stock. His farm in the family since town was settled. Parents and grandparents born here, except MGM, born in Houlton, Aroostook Co., Me.; she came here as a girl.—School until 17.—I.O.O.F., Grange.—Bluff, frank, loudvoiced, full of good cheer. Likes to talk.—Speech entirely unaffected by outside influences or local culture.—L 158.

2. Painter, 74. Police officer a few years. Lived in the rural section until 21.—Parents born here of old local stock.—Educated here. (A sister of Louisa M. Alcott was his teacher.)—Sells his drawings of the Minute Man statue at the battlefield. Has mingled to some extent with the old aristocratic families. Regarded here as a sage.—Mild in manner. Intelligent, somewhat eccentric. Old-fashioned, not urban. Likes to tell stories.—Speech a mixture, result of rustic childhood and later cultured associations. Moderate tempo. Vowels frequently lengthened, though not to excess.—L 153.

158 Town of Burlington, Middlesex Co.

Settled c. 1672 (inc. 1799); originally the northwestern part of Woburn. Woburn settled 1642 from

Charlestown, which in turn was settled in 1628 from England.—Rural community.—Pop. 1820: 508, '50: 545, '80: 711, 1910: 591, '30: 1722.—*Woburn:* Sewall, Samuel. The history of Woburn, from the grant of its territory to Charlestown, in 1640, to the year 1860. 657 p. Boston, 1868.

Farmer, fire chief, tree warden, 69.—F born here; PGF born in Charlestown (c. 12 m. southeast); PGM born in Truro, Barnstable Co. M, MGF, MGM born here.—School until 14. Education often interrupted by F's illness. (M had taught school.)—Middlesex Forest Association, Redmen.—Genuine countryman. Friendly, but reserved; honest and dependable. Quick thinker.—Reliable responses. Rapid tempo. Vowels rather short. Precise utterance with strong stress, except when careless or hurried.—L 152.

160 Town of Billerica (1 East Billerica; 2 Billerica Center), Middlesex Co.

Settled c. 1653 (inc. 1655), named for Billericay in Essex, England. Many directly from England, others from Cambridge. (Cambridge settled c. 1631.)—Rural community; some manufacturing.—Pop. 1764: 1234, '90: 1191*, 1820: 1380, '50: 1646, '80: 2000, 1910: 2789, '30: 5880.—Hazen, H. A. History of Billerica. 319 + 183 p. Boston, 1883.

1. Farmer, 77. Has spent last 30 years in Billerica Center.—F, PGF, PGM born here. M born in Reading (c. 10 m. southeast), died when he was 4.—School until 14.—Unitarian. I.O.O.F. Few social contacts.—Thinks slowly. Did not understand purpose of investigation.—Extremely conservative, fixed, local type of speech. Slow, monotonous drawl. Long vowels.—L 150.

2. CULTURED INFORMANT. Physician, psychiatrist, 48. Administrative officer of medical school.—Descended from first settlers here. F, PGF and his parents born here; PGM in Boston. M born here; MGF in Arlington; MGM in Bedford.—High school here; Tufts College 1 year, Tufts Medical School 4 years.—Eminent member of community. Often lectures in various parts of the state.—Brilliant mind. Keen insight. Interested in old local families and houses.—Tried always to answer spontaneously. As a child, spent much time with his grandfather; knows speech of older generation. Rapid tempo. Short vowels, occasionally lengthened. At home uses N.E. short *o* as in *coat*, *broken*, etc.; thinks he avoids it in public lecturing.—L 149.

180 Town of Marblehead, Essex Co.

Settled c. 1629 (inc. 1649) as a plantation of Salem by fishermen from the Channel Islands and Cornwall.—Highly independent and self-contained. Fishing and formerly also shipping. Now many summer estates; yachting.—Pop. 1764: 4954, '90: 5661, 1820: 5630, '50: 6167, '80: 7467, 1910: 7338, '30: 8668.—Roads, Samuel, Jr. The history and traditions of Marblehead. [Ed. 3.] 595 p. Marblehead, 1897.—*Salem:* Banks, Charles E. The 'west country' origin of Salem's settlement. Essex Institute historical collections, 66 (1930), 317–24. Osgood, C. S. and H. M. Batchelder. Historical sketch of Salem, 1626–1879. 280 p. Salem, 1879. Perley, Sidney. The history of Salem, Mass., 1626–1716. 3v. Salem, 1924–28. Phillips, James D. Salem in the seventeenth century. 420 p. Boston and New York, 1933. Phillips, James D. Salem in the eighteenth century. 533 p. Boston and New York, 1937.

1. Real estate dealer, 85. Formerly sold provisions. Army service in the South, aged 15 to 17, during the Civil War. Did business regularly in Cambridge and Boston. Lived in Cambridge 3 years, aged c. 60 to 63. Never went to sea.—F's ancestors came from England to Cape Cod, then went to Me., then came here. Parents born here. M's family from Salem. (Wife a native of Newfoundland.)—Grammar school.—Methodist. Officer of G.A.R.—Shrewd business man. Holds firmly to his opinions.—Genuine local type of speech. Final consonants often indistinct. Strong retroflection.—HY 40.

2. Accountant, 68. Worked in Boston 30 years, but always commuted.—F born here. 'We go back 6 generations.' M, MGF, MGM born here.—2 years of high school.—Congregational Church. Has held town office for years.—Highly intelligent. Interested in all that pertains to the community.—Like most people here, feels no desire to change his normal speech.—HY 41.

182 City of Beverly, Essex Co.

Settled c. 1629; set off from Salem 1668, inc. as a city 1894. Salem settled by the Puritans in 1629.—Urban community with old seafaring traditions. Houses of the old families have many heirlooms brought from all over the world. Summer estates.—Pop. 1764: 2171, '90: 3295, 1820: 4283, '50: 5376, '80: 8456, 1910: 18,650, '30: 25,086.—Lapham, Alice G. The old planters of Beverly in Mass. and the thousand acre grant of 1635. . . . 133 p. Cambridge, 1930. Lapham, Alice G. and Katherine P. Loring. Historic Beverly. 38 p. Beverly, 1937. Stone, E. M. History of Beverly . . . from its settlement in 1630 to 1842. 324 p. Boston, 1843.

1. Janitor of public buildings (for 20 years), 89. Formerly worked in shoe shop. In the South 5 or 6 months during the Civil War.—Parents born here of old local families. F went to sea.—Grammar school. —G.A.R. and I.O.O.F.—Genial, amiable.—Rather self-conscious about his speech. Has tried to remove what he considers illiteracies. In words like *car*, *barn*, older local people do not have the front vowel [a] common in Boston and used here by the younger generation.

Auxiliary informants: wife, aged 87; daughter, c. 55; and another relative, c. 84; all good representatives of local speech.—HY 37.

2. CULTURED INFORMANT. Single woman, 74.—
Parents and ancestors born here, descended from
early settlers. Genealogy published.—Public schools
here and Abbot Academy, Andover (c. 16 m. northwest).—Episcopal Church. Officer of historical society. Assured social position.—Natural, unaffected
speech. Clear, precise articulation. Has not paid
much attention to other types. (Teachers insisted
upon [hw] in *wheel*, etc.)—HY 38.

184 Town of Topsfield (South Topsfield), Essex Co.

Settled as part of Ipswich 1639 (est. as town 1650)
from Ipswich (settled 1633, population mixed) and
Salem (settled 1629).—Agricultural community with
many summer homes.—Pop. 1764: 719, '90: 781,
1820: 866, '50: 1170, '80: 1165, 1910: 1174, '30: 986.
—Webber, C. H. and W. S. Nevins. Old Naumkeag:
an historical sketch of the city of Salem and the
towns of Marblehead, Peabody, Beverly, Danvers,
Wenham, Manchester, Topsfield and Middleton.
312 p. Salem, 1877.—*Ipswich:* Waters, T. F. Ipswich in the Mass. Bay Colony. . . . Ipswich, 1905.

Farmer, auctioneer of antiques, 56.—F descended
from original settlers here. M born in Salem (c. 10 m.
south).—Friendly, kind-hearted, but rather stern.
Well-to-do.—Precise speech with vowels sharply cut
off.—Incomplete record: only pp. 26–51, 54–64.

Supplementary informant: housewife, 93. Born in
town of Boxford (c. 4 m. northwest).—Parents born
in Topsfield.—Old-fashioned cultivated speech. Precise articulation. Very strong stress at times.—Pp.
7–11, 14–23. These entries are not starred on the
maps.—L 151.

190 City of Haverhill (1 Ayers Village; 2, 3, 4 Haver-hill), Essex Co.

Settled 1640 (inc. 1645, as city 1869) from Newbury (q.v., 194) and from Haverhill, Suffolk,
England.—First a prosperous frontier town; then a
trade center, building its own ships; thereafter an
important shoe manufacturing center (since early 19.
cent.). Large foreign population: Irish, French-
Canadian, Italian, Polish.—Pop. 1764: 1992, '90:
2404, 1820: 3070, '50: 5877, '80: 18,472, 1910:
44,115, '30: 48,710.—Chase, G. W. The history of
Haverhill, from its first settlement in 1640 to the
year 1860. 638 p. Haverhill, 1861. Corliss, J. B. The
first era in the history of Haverhill. . . . 40 p. Haverhill, 1885.

1. Farmer and local librarian, 73. Has always
lived in Ayers Village, a rural section (with some shoe
factories introduced early from the city proper).—
Parents born here.—Grammar school.—Quiet, dignified, pleasant. Memory slower now than formerly.—
FW thought his use of retroflection in words like *girl*
might have been learned at school, perhaps a spelling
pronunciation.—L 1.

2. Housewife, 63.—F, PGF, PGM born here. M,
MGF, MGM born in Merrimac (c. 6 m. northeast).

—Grammar school.—First Baptist Church.—L 4.

3. Housewife, 85. Formerly worked in shoe factory.—F born in Alexandria, Grafton Co., N.H. M
born in Andover, Merrimack Co., N.H.—Grammar
school.—Baptist. Now in Old Ladies' Home.—
Friendly, pleasant, with old-school courtesy and reserve. Independent, still active. Memory beginning
to fail.—Rapid tempo and precise articulation. Very
short vowels. Strong lip action in diphthongs.—L 2.

4. Shoe worker, 36. Born in Irish section of the
city, moved to country district (within city limits)
when 7 or 8.—Parents and grandparents born in Co.
Limerick, Ireland.—2 years of high school. Sent by
labor organization on 3 months' visit to Europe.—
Roman Catholic.—Highly intelligent, frank, coöperative. Interested in the investigation.—Good feeling
for local usage and some familiarity with other dialects. Has never examined his own speech, which is
mainly a local type with only a few Irish traits. Voice
strong and powerful with slight rasp. Rapid tempo.
Clear utterance; strong articulation of final consonants. Rather short vowels.—L 11.

194 Town of Newbury (1, 2 Byfield; 3 Old Town), Essex Co.

Settled 1635 (inc. 1635), from Wiltshire, England.
—Agricultural and residential.—Newburyport, formerly part of Newbury (set off 1764), engaged in
shipbuilding and in foreign trade and later became
an industrial city (inc. 1851).—Pop. 1764: 2960, '90:
3970, 1820: 3671*, '50: 4426, '80: 1566*, 1910: 1482,
'30: 1530.—Coffin, Joshua. A sketch of the history
of Newbury, Newburyport and West Newbury, from
1635 to 1845. 416 p. Boston, 1845. Currier, J. J.
History of Newbury, 1635–1902. 755 p. Boston, 1902.
Ewell, J. L. The story of Byfield, a New England
parish. 344 p. Boston, 1904.— *Newburyport:* Currier,
J. J. History of Newburyport, 1764–1905. 766 p.
Newburyport, 1906.

1. Retired postal employee, 81. Worked as shoe
laster in Haverhill, aged 18 to 44, but lived here in
Byfield.—Descended from old Essex Co. families.
Parents born here.—Grammar school and Dummer
Academy.—Junior Order of American Mechanics.—
L 6.

2. Housewife, 53. Lived in city of Newburyport
(c. 5 m. northeast), aged 19 to 30; then 2 years in
Salisbury (c. 3 m. north of latter). Lives in rustic
section of Byfield, her birthplace, which forms a
rather close-knit community and has had considerable inbreeding.—Descended from old Essex Co.
families.—Grammar school until 13.—Evangelist
Mission (Gospel Meeting). Very popular in the community.—Hospitable, kind, earnest. Attentive to
form and details, to propriety and conduct. Emotional at times.—Fairly well able to compare her
speech with that of others. Brought up by GM and
GGM; remembers speech of older generation, and
still uses some archaisms. Rather clear utterance,

with weak final consonants. Vowels normally short, but lengthened in the pondering, hesitant style she sometimes uses.—L 16.

3. Single woman, at home, 55.—Descended from old local families. Lives on property in Newbury Old Town first settled by F's ancestor.—High school in Newburyport.—Belongs to several local societies. Usual contacts of a countrywoman of good family.—Pronunciation affected by her mother, a schoolteacher; attempts to distinguish such words as *cock*, *cork* and *caulk*, which are all alike in her natural speech.—L 8.

196 Town of Rowley, Essex Co.

Settled 1638 (inc. 1639), from Yorkshire, England.—Shipbuilding 1780–1850. Now a quiet country town traversed by the Shore Road. Recent foreign elements.—Pop. 1764: 1481, '90: 1772, 1820: 1825, '50: 1075*, '80: 1201, 1910: 1368, '30: 1356.—Gage, Thomas. The history of Rowley . . . from the year 1639 to the present time . . . 483 p. Boston, 1840.

1. Shoemaker, road commissioner, cemetery commissioner, 86. Native of the east end of the town.—Descended from old Rowley and Newbury families. F, PGF, PGM born here. M, MGF born in Byfield (c. 4 m. northwest); MGM born in Ipswich (c. 5 m. south).—School here until 14.—Apparently well thought of; never defeated when he ran for town office.—Genuine old Mass. type. Practical-minded.—Measured tempo. Extremely precise articulation. Usually very short vowels.—L 9.

2. Housewife, formerly bookkeeper, 61. Two years in Salem (c. 15 m. south), aged 14 to 15. One year in Everett, Middlesex Co., aged 19. 1½ years in Ipswich (c. 5 m. south), aged 20 to 21.—Descended from first settlers. F, PGF, PGM born here. M, MGF born here; MGM born in Ipswich.—8 years of school here, 2 years in Salem (including 1 year of high school), 8 months of business school in Boston.—Historical society and several other organizations.—Motherly, domestic, content with life.—Willing to report the older speech which, in unguarded moments, is entirely natural to her.—L 10.

198 Town of Essex, Essex Co.

Settled 1634 as part of Ipswich; set off in 1819. Ipswich settled 1633, population mixed.—Rural community; fishing and summer trade. Formerly shipbuilding.—Pop. 1820: 1107, '50: 1585, '80: 1670, 1910: 1621, '30: 1465.—Crowell, Robert. History of the town of Essex, from 1634 to 1868 . . . 488 p. Essex, 1868.

Farmer, 70.—Local stock.—Pleasant, somewhat dull. Rather self-conscious.—Slow tempo. Slight retroflection at times in words like *girl*.—Interviews discontinued because of informant's ill health. Incomplete record: only pp. 1–31.—L 19.

200 Town of Rockport, Essex Co.

Settled 1690 as part of Gloucester, set off in 1840.

Gloucester settled in the 1630's.—Has shared with Gloucester the seafaring traditions of Cape Ann. Now a conservative agricultural and fishing community with many summer residents and a prominent artists' colony.—Pop. 1850: 3274, '80: 3912, 1910: 4211, '30: 3630.—Rockport Committee on Town History. History of the town of Rockport. . . . 295 p. Rockport, 1888.—*Gloucester:* Babson, J. J. History of the town of Gloucester, Cape Ann, including the town of Rockport. 610 p. Gloucester, 1860. Babson, J. J. Notes and additions to the History of Gloucester. 94 p. Gloucester, 1876; 2d series: 187 p. [Salem,] 1891. Hawes, Charles B. Gloucester by land and sea. 226 p. Boston, 1923. Pringle, J. R. History of the town and city of Gloucester. 340 p. Gloucester, 1892.

1. Farmer, landscape gardener, 44.—F, PGF born here. M, MGF born in Gloucester (adjoining town).—School until 12. Ignorant of many aspects of life outside his own work.—Speech extremely old-fashioned, more so than that of the other two informants here. Frequent Malapropisms.—L 5.

2. Real estate dealer, c. 70. Used to go out with fishing fleet. Now spending his old age in Gloucester.—Direct descendant of first settler; entirely of old local stock.—Grammar school.—Respected citizen.—Interested in local antiquities. Genial, kindly, willing to talk. Did not understand purpose of the investigation.—Retroflection in words like *girl* varies greatly.—L 7.

3. Single woman, at home, 68.—F born here; PGF born in Eliot, York Co., Me.; PGM born here, descended from 2 original families. M born in Charlestown (now part of Boston; c. 30 m. southwest); MGF in Newburyport (c. 20 m. northwest); MGM in Boston.—Public school and 2 years of private school.—Congregational Church. D.A.R., Woman's Club, Garden Club. Lives alone.—Highly intelligent; active and enthusiastic in manner and speech. Distinctly of the older school in point of view.—Willing to be frank about her speech, and trustworthy in reporting it. Quick tempo. Precise, energetic articulation. Vowels short, lengthened for emphasis. Lip action rather strong in rounded vowels. Retroflection seems entirely fortuitous.—L 3.

201 Town of Uxbridge, Worcester Co.

Settled c. 1662 as part of Mendon (q.v., below); set off in 1727.—Formerly agricultural, now a mill town.—Pop. 1764: 1213, '90: 1308, 1820: 1551, '50: 2457, '80: 3111, 1910: 4671, '30: 6285.—Chapin, Henry. Address delivered at the Unitarian Church in Uxbridge, in 1864 . . . 214 p. Worcester, 1881. (Edited with . . . appendices relating to the history of Uxbridge, by R. D. Burr.) Sprague, Beatrice P., comp. Uxbridge year by year, 1727–1927. 126 p. Woonsocket, R.I., 1927.

1. Coal dealer, 83. Lived 3 years in Norwich, New London Co., Conn.—PGF, a Quaker, built oldest

house in town.—High school and private instruction. (Daughter a college graduate.) Has traveled in New England.—I.O.O.F. Once very active, now moves about with difficulty. (Was badly injured recently in an automobile accident.) Skilled chess player.— Looks much younger than his age. Alert and intelligent. Jovial.—Speech natural and unguarded.—HS 37.

201 Town of Mendon, Worcester Co.

Settled c. 1660 (inc. 1667) from Braintree and Weymouth. (Braintree and Weymouth had settlers by 1629; more extensive settlement of the latter in 1635, from Weymouth in Dorsetshire.)—Agricul-tural.—Pop. 1764: 1843, '90: 1556*, 1820: 2254, '50: 1300*, '80: 1094, 1910: 880, '30: 1107.—Metcalf, J. G. Annals of the town of Mendon, from 1659 to 1880. 723 p. Providence, R.I., 1880.

2. Housewife, 67. Taught school 1 year.—Local family.—High school.—Few social contacts.—Seems only middle-aged, rather than elderly. Reserved. Intelligent. Answered questions readily.—Gave honest responses, even when she thought they were not 'grammatical.' Speech clear and deliberate.—HS 36.

202 Town of Oxford, Worcester Co.

Settled 1686 (inc. 1693) by 30 French Protestant families, later driven out by Indians. Reoccupied after 1713 by families from Newton (Middlesex Co.), Roxbury (now part of Boston) and Salem.—Mill village in rural setting on Worcester-Putnam road.— Pop. 1764: 890, '90: 995, 1820:. 1562, '50: 2380, '80: 2604, 1910: 3361, '30: 3943.—Daniels, G. F. History of the town of Oxford, with genealogies and notes on persons and estates. 856 p. Oxford, 1892.

1. Shoemaker, 87. Town officer 30 years. Postmaster c. 26 years. Lived 7 years in Webster (c. 5 m. south).—Old local family.—High school. Has read widely and done much to educate himself.—Universalist Church.—Straightforward. Mind, sight and hearing extraordinarily keen for his age. Grew up in the town and knows little of farm life.—Grammar consciously 'correct,' though he says *ain't* regularly and prefers it. Said *them are* only once, and then hurriedly changed to *those are.* Much fluctuation in vowels and diphthongs.—HS 39.

202 Town of Charlton (Charlton Depot), Worcester Co.

Settled 1727 as part of Oxford (q.v., above); set off as a district in 1755 and made a town in 1775. Many of the first settlers from Salem; others from Sutton, Mendon, Bellingham, Marlborough, Newton and Stoneham; from Essex and Plymouth Counties; and from Thompson, Windham Co., Conn.—Chiefly agricultural.—Pop. 1764: 741, '90: 1963, 1820: 2134, '50: 2015, '80: 1900, 1910: 2032, '30: 2154.

2. Housewife, c. 60. Taught district school 8 years. Spent girlhood here; a few years in Worcester

(c. 14 m. northeast); now in Charlton Center.—Old local family.—Educated here and in Worcester.— Active in church and in Village Improvement Society. Her home a favorite meeting place for all her relatives.—Energetic, alert.—Natural speech. Knows the 'proper' grammatical forms, but is 'too busy' to think of them. Retroflection is evident, but not consistently used. Linking *r* is usual.—HS 41.

203 City of Marlborough, Middlesex Co.

Settled c. 1657 (inc. 1660, as city 1890) from Sudbury. Sudbury settled 1638 from England.—Industrial city in an agricultural region. Shoe manufacturing. Large Italian element.—Pop. 1764: 1287, '90: 1552, 1820: 1952, '50: 2941, '80: 10,127, 1910: 14,579, '30: 15,587.—Hudson, Charles. History of the town of Marlborough, from its first settlement in 1657 to 1861; with a brief sketch of the town of Northborough. 544 p. Boston, 1862. Pitman, J. A. Notes on the history of Marlborough. 12 p. Marlborough, 1905.

1. Farmer's wife, 74. Aged 19 to 34, taught grade school.—F born in Sudbury (c. 10 m. east), came here as a child. M born here.—Grammar school.— Grange. Rather limited contacts.—Showed extraordinary alertness and perception in her replies, but said the whole business was 'a mess of nonsense from beginnin' to end.'—Natural, unguarded responses. 'Correct' speech artificial to her, although she taught school for 15 years. Vigorous but not over-clear articulation.—B 30.

2. Florist, 50. Has farmed on a small scale, worked on a railroad, and made shoes. Lived in Brooklyn, N.Y., 6 months, aged 18.—F born in Boston (c. 30 m. east), came here when 20; PGF, PGM born in Boylston, Worcester Co. (c. 15 m. west). M born in Berlin, Worcester Co. (c. 6 m. west).—Grammar school. Has been as far west as Chicago, also south. Went through N.Y. State as pianist with a traveling show.—Belongs to no organizations. Knows the city well.—Understood purpose of interviews and coöperated enthusiastically.—Aware of 'ungrammatical' features of his speech, but does not avoid them. Rapid, sharp, jerky tempo. Clear articulation; no nasalization; frequent glottalization.—B 29.

204 Town of Shrewsbury, Worcester Co.

Settled 1717 (inc. 1720) from Marlborough (q.v., 203).—Rural community. Now a residential suburb of Worcester.—Pop. 1764: 1401, '90: 963*, 1820: 1458, '50: 1596, '80: 1500, 1910: 1946, '30: 6910.— Ward, A. H. History of the town of Shrewsbury from its settlement in 1717 to 1829. 508 p. Boston, 1847. Ward, Elizabeth. Old times in Shrewsbury. Gleanings from history and tradition. 187 p. [New York, 1892.]

1. Civil engineer, farmer, bank director, 80.—F's family settled in present homestead in 1725. M born in Marlboro, Windham Co., Vt., came here aged 20.

—Public schools. Learned engineering as apprentice in a Worcester office. Has traveled through the West on vacations.—Congregational Church, I.O.O.F., Grange, historical society. Has held every town office.—Vigorous, alert, intelligent, helpful.—Some acquaintance with, and interest in, other dialects; but always used his natural idiom. (His wife values 'correctness.') Rather rapid tempo. Slight nasalization. Clear but not painstaking enunciation. Greatly retracted articulation.—B 27.

2. Farmer, 26.—F born here of old local family, who bought present farm in 1796. M born in Yorkshire, England; came to New York City aged 10; here since 1901.—Public schools. Has been writing a history of the town.—Society for Preservation of N.E. Antiquities. Knows many people here of all ages.—Slow and quiet in movements and in speech. Rarely laughs. Kindly and courteous, but wary of strangers.—Speech definitely of the younger generation, with certain old-fashioned traits. 'Correct,' though colloquial; 'careless' forms avoided. Slow tempo, not exactly a drawl, but a low, even murmur. Vowels very long. Slight nasal twang. Initial *p, t, k* strongly aspirated.—Long work sheets pp. 1–26, short work sheets pp. 27–103.—B 28.

205 City of Worcester, Worcester Co.

First permanent settlement 1713, evidently from Marlborough (q.v., 203). In 1718 many Scotch-Irish arrived. Town privileges granted 1722, inc. as city 1848.—Manufacturing center: textiles since 1789; manufacture of paper, wire, tools and machinery, and other industries, since the Civil War. Many Irish since 1840, followed by French-Canadians, Swedes, Italians, Poles and Jews.—Clark University, Worcester Polytechnic Institute, Holy Cross College, American Antiquarian Society and other important cultural institutions.—Pop. 1764: 1478, '90: 2095, 1820: 2962, '50: 17,049, '80: 58,291, 1910: 145,986, '30: 195,311.—Cutler, U. Waldo. Jottings from Worcester's History. 142 p. Worcester Historical Society, 1932. Lincoln, William. History of Worcester. . . . 448 p. Worcester, 1862. Nichols, C. L. Bibliography of Worcester . . . 216 p. Worcester, 1899. Sutherland, J. H. The city of Worcester and vicinity and their resources. 124 p. Worcester, 1901. Wood, O. B. Worcester: its past and present. 247 p. folio. Worcester, 1888.

CULTURED INFORMANT. Retired manufacturer, 83. Spent his boyhood on a farm.—F born here; his family came here in 1770. M born here; her family came from Brookfield (c. 20 m. west) in 1810.—Public schools, Harvard University. Travel abroad.—A leading citizen. Officer for 20 years of American Antiquarian Society.—Fine example of N.E. aristocracy. Has kept his active interest in the world, his mental curiosity and his alertness. Intelligent, coöperative. Did not clearly remember his early farm life.—Knows no speech radically different from his

own except urban class-dialects. Amused by artificial diction, not afraid of colloquialisms. Speaks confidently, never slurs or mumbles. Tempo deliberate, unhurried. No nasalization.—B 26.

206 Town of Spencer, Worcester Co.

Originally part of Leicester (set off in 1753, inc. 1775). First permanent settlement 1717 by Nathaniel Wood of Ipswich. (Ipswich settled 1633 from England.) Leicester was settled shortly before 1720; some families came from Malden.—Manufacturing since early 19. cent., especially shoes. Considerable farming: dairy products, poultry. Many French Canadians.—Pop. 1764: 664, '90: 1321, 1820: 1548, '50: 2244, '80: 7466, 1910: 6740, '30: 6272.—Draper, James. History of Spencer from its earliest settlement to the year 1841, including a brief sketch of Leicester to the year 1753. Ed. 2. 276 p. Worcester [1860]. Tower, H. M. Historical sketches relating to Spencer. 3v. Spencer, 1901–03.—*Leicester:* Coolidge, A. H. A brief history of Leicester. 69 p. 1890. Washburn, Emory. Historical sketches of the town of Leicester during the first century from its settlement. 467 p. Boston, 1860.

1. Sexton, formerly milkman, 65.—Parents and grandparents born here. Ancestors came from Paxton (c. 6 m. northeast).—School until 15. Not much reading. Wife (born here, of old local families) a former schoolteacher.—Social life is centered in his church. Has never been outside the town longer than a week.—Typical old-fashioned Yankee. Alert, shrewd. Difficult to approach, but friendly and helpful when his confidence is won.—Genuine unguarded responses. Not familiar with other dialects, but knows what is old and what is modern in his own speech. Slow, halting tempo. High-pitched, slightly nasal voice. Fairly clear articulation.—B 7.

2. Dentist, 67. Spent much of his early life on a farm here. In Worcester (c. 12 m. east) during apprenticeship, aged 18 to 20; in West Brookfield (c. 10 m. west), aged 20 to 22.—F, PGF, PGM born here. F's ancestors came here from Watertown, Middlesex Co., c. 1720. M born in Leicester (c. 5 m. east).—Grammar school, 1 year of high school. School of Dentistry, U. of Maryland, aged 21 to 23.—Much interested in local history. Knows most of the townspeople. Regarded with affection and respect.—Kindly, courteous.—Speech habits firmly settled. Makes no effort to avoid ungrammatical forms. Tempo fairly slow. Articulation fairly clear.

Auxiliary informant: former schoolteacher, 74. Worked 25 years in a store. Business trips around Worcester for 5 years.—F, PGF born here, of prominent old local family. M born in Winchester, Cheshire Co., N.H.; moved to Boston as a girl; came here aged 28.—High school.—Reading club, church missionary work.—B 4.

3. Post office employee, 56. Worked on farm as a boy, then in shoe shop 15 years.—F born in East

Livermore, Androscoggin Co., Me., died when informant was 3. M born here, cousin of famous local family of inventors; descended from old settlers.—High school. Considerable reading. Has traveled a little recently.—Many friends in town, but appears to take no active part in social life.—Reserved, phlegmatic, intelligent; dry sense of humor.—Upper level of local speech. Usage rather fixed. Tempo moderate. Enunciation clear and fairly distinct, without much emphasis. No nasalization.—Long work sheets pp. 1–70, short work sheets pp. 71–103.—B 5.

207 Town of Sterling, Worcester Co.

Settled 1720 (inc. 1781) as part of Lancaster. Lancaster settled 1643–44 from Watertown.—Agricultural community. Small industries. Close contacts with Worcester (c. 15 m. south).—Pop. 1790: 1428: 1820: 1710, '50: 1805, '80: 1414, 1910: 1359, '30, 1502.—*Lancaster:* Marvin, A. P. History of the town of Lancaster, from the first settlement to the present time, 1643–1879. 798 p. Lancaster, 1879. Safford, Marion Fuller. The story of colonial Lancaster. 190 p. Rutland, Vt., 1937.

1. Retired R.R. station agent, 76.—F born here. M born in Troy, Cheshire Co., N.H. (c. 40 m. northwest); came here at 25.—High school; business school in Worcester 3 months. 'Reads up' on whatever catches his interest.—Masons, I.O.O.F., N.E. Ass'n. of R.R. Veterans. Public library trustee. Knows everyone in town.—Kindly, courteous; lively sense of humor. Intelligent, alert. Familiar with local customs and idioms.—Usually gave unguarded responses. Speech careless, though not slovenly; many weak sounds suppressed. Tempo a little more rapid than average. No nasalization.—B 22.

2. Farmer, 82. Taught district school 7 winters, aged 25 to 32.—F born here. M born in Lancaster (c. 5 m. east).—Grammar school; Allandale Institute here (1½ terms). Member of local school committee 11 years.—Belongs to the Grange. Used to know everyone in town.—Enfeebled but still active. Hard of hearing. Easy-going, good natured, coöperative.—Has little feeling for local usage, but is sure of his own. Tries to avoid such forms as *ain't, goin'*. Articulation slow, rather muffled and adenoidal, careful only when he is on guard.—Short work sheets.—B 25.

208 Town of Templeton, Worcester Co.

Laid out 1733, settled c. 1750 (inc. 1762). First proprietors' meeting held in Concord.—Agricultural hill town. Small industries. Rather isolated until recently.—Pop. 1764: 348, '90: 950, 1820: 1331, '50: 2173, '80: 2789, 1910: 3756, '30: 4159.—Adams, E. G. An historical discourse in commemoration of the 100th anniversary of the . . . First Congregational Church in Templeton . . . With an appendix embracing a survey of the municipal affairs of the town. 175 p. Boston, 1857.

Retired farmer, 86. Aged 20 to 23, worked in New Jersey flour mill. Aged 29 to 31, lived in Illinois; aged 56 to 58 in Springfield, Hampden Co. (Mass.).—F born in Royalston (c. 10 m. northwest), came here at 18. M born here of old local family.—Not much education.—Many friends in the community. Farmers went to him for advice.—Physically and mentally weakened. Kind, affable, glad to be of help.—Articulation weak and muffled. Lack of front upper teeth impaired his enunciation and made certain sounds difficult to distinguish.

When the informant died after completing 72 pages of the record, his wife offered to carry on the work: housewife, 72. Lived 2 years in Springfield, aged 42 to 44.—Both parents born in Barre (c. 10 m. south), came here after their marriage.—High school. —More alert than her husband.—Speech less archaic than his and more clearly articulated. Somewhat more careful in achieving 'correctness.' No nasalization.—Pp. 73–103, and scattered items on other pages.—B 14.

209 Town of Lunenburg, Worcester Co.

Settled in the 1720's (inc. 1728). Rapid growth in the 1730's. Many of the first settlers from Ireland and Scotland.—Still agricultural and residential. Many summer homes in the vicinity.—Pop. 1764: 821, '90: 1277, 1820: 1209, '50: 1249, '80: 1101, 1910: 1393, '30: 1923.—Torrey, R. C. History of the town of Fitchburg, comprising also a history of Lunenburg, from its first settlement to the year 1764. 128 p. Fitchburg, 1865.

1. Housekeeper on brother's farm, 62. Worked in a store in Leominster (c. 6 m. southwest) 2 years, aged 47 to 48.—F born here. M born in Shirley, Middlesex Co. (c. 5 m. southeast), came here when married.—Grammar school.—Grange. Has rather limited social contacts, but is acquainted with most of the townspeople.—Regarded the investigation with mingled curiosity, amusement and resignation. Rather strict.—Knows only the local dialect of her social level. Unaffected speech, not too painstakingly articulated, but fairly clear. Rather slow tempo. Slight nasalization. Tendency to assimilate one sound to another.—B 24.

2. Farmer, 55.—F born here. M born in Charlestown (now part of Boston), came here aged c. 20.—Grammar school. Reads mostly religious books. (Sent his children to college.)—Knows many townspeople.—Physically strong, mentally energetic; intelligent, though by no means intellectual. Interests are limited to his immediate concerns. Good-natured. Thoroughly understood purpose of investigation.—Feeling for local idiom almost infallible. Stated his fixed usage without hesitation. Rapid, clear speech, forcefully articulated, not nasalized. Retroflection varies.—B 23.

210 Town of Winchendon, Worcester Co.

Settled by 1760 (inc. 1764). Some early settlers from Ipswich (settled 1633).—Manufacture of toys and furniture since early 19. cent.—Pop. 1790: 945, 1820: 1263, '50: 2445, '80: 3722, 1910: 5678, '30: 6202.—Marvin, A. P. History of the town of Winchendon from the grant of Ipswich Canada, in 1735, to the present time. 528 p. Winchendon, 1868.

1. Farmer, 81. Used to do some carpentry. Lived in southern Kansas and Illinois aged 23 to 24.—F born here of old local family. M born in Westminster (c. 15 m. southeast), came here at 21.—High school here. Commercial school in Boston.—Grange, Ancient Order of United Workmen.—Physically well-preserved and still fairly alert mentally.—Slow speech, not nasalized. Slovenly, mumbling articulation made constant repetition necessary. Certain archaic constructions: *if you were engaging of a room; an open place where that they feed stock.*—B 20.

2. Painter and carpenter, 40. Worked 2 years on a farm.—Both parents born here of old local families.—Grammar school. Very little reading. Has traveled no farther than White River Junction, Vt.—Few acquaintances.—Tried to answer all questions honestly. Said he had never heard *stirrups, orphan, almonds, fertile,* etc. Speech perfectly natural, despite occasional concern with 'correctness.' Not nasalized. Typical in syntax and morphology of lower-class speech. Tempo average. Articulation rather sharp. Final consonants often suppressed; vowels generally rather short. Extreme variation in postvocalic *r*. Frequent intrusive *r*'s.—B 21.

211 Town of Groton, Middlesex Co.

Settled c. 1655 (inc. 1655); many of the early families from Reading (settled 1639 as part of Lynn, Essex Co.).—Agricultural: fruit and poultry. Two paper mills.—Two well-known college preparatory schools.—Pop. 1764: 1443, '90: 1840, 1820: 1897, '50: 2515, '80: 1862*, 1910: 2155, '30: 2434.—Butler, Caleb. History of the town of Groton, including Pepperell and Shirley, from the first grant of Groton plantation in 1655. 499 p. Boston, 1848. Green, S. A. An historical sketch of Groton, 1655–1890. 263 p. Groton, 1894.

1. Farmer, 91. Managed grist mill 15 years; also worked in lumber mill.—F born in Saugus, Essex Co. (c. 40 m. southeast), came here aged 28 when he married; died when informant was 12. M born in Danvers, Essex Co. (c. 40 m. east), came here aged 21 when she married.—Grammar school. Traveled to Wisconsin (3 months) when young.—Member of historical society. Used to know everyone in town.—Still works all day on his farm. Memory slightly clouded; slow of thought in his old age.—Many forms he characterized as old-fashioned are merely modern 'ungrammatical' colloquialisms. Slow tempo. Articulation fairly distinct. No nasalization.—Long

work sheets pp. 1–16, short work sheets pp. 17–103.—B 32.

2. Manager of grain company (for last 5 years), 52. 16 years in paper mill as clerk and department head. 8 years traveling as paper salesman. Always made his home here.—F born here; family one of the oldest here. M born in Bath, Sagadahoc Co., Me., came here aged 17.—High school. Boston Univ. 3 years. Has traveled throughout N.E. on business.—I.O.O.F. Knows most people in town, especially the farmers.—Mind quick but not keen. Understood purpose of investigation.—Tried to offer his true, unaffected speech. Often apologized for some 'incorrect' form which he had become accustomed to use. Voice slightly nasal. Tempo rather slow. Enunciates with a minimum of effort, just clearly enough to be easily understood. Stressed vowels tend to be overlong.—B 31.

212 Town of New Salem, Franklin Co.

Settled 1737 (est. as a district 1753, made a town 1775), chiefly from Middleborough, Plymouth Co.; some settlers from Danvers, Essex Co. Middleborough settled 1669 by the sons and grandsons of the Pilgrims. Danvers settled by expansion from Salem.—Agricultural community with decreasing population, on old stage coach route between Worcester and Brattleboro, Vt. Small summer colony.—Pop. 1764: 375, '90: 1543, 1820: 2146, '50: 1253*, '80: 869, 1910: 639, '30: 414.—The New Salem sesqui-centennial . . . Aug. 20th, 1903. 77 p. Athol, 1904. (Historical address by Eugene Bullard, p. 13–49.)

1. Farmer, 77.—F born here of old local family who settled in 1752.—M born in Wendell (adjoining town).—Grammar school. Attended the academy, but did not graduate.—Grange. Almost entirely occupied with his farming.—Still active. Intelligent and alert, with sense of humor. Somewhat deaf.—Sure of his factual information and of his personal usage. Speech slow and deliberate, characterized by deep throaty articulation. His respect for education may be responsible for a rather careful enunciation of final consonants, as it certainly is for his use of grammatically correct forms in preference to colloquialisms.—B 16.

2. Keeper of general store, postmaster, tax collector, 42.—F born in Shutesbury (adjoining town), came here aged 12. M born here.—High school. Reads widely.—Grange. Knows everybody in town.—Understood FW's purpose. Highly intelligent.—Has good ear for dialect and can usually tell what forms are current locally. Speech of average tempo, clearly articulated. Somewhat nasal.—B 15.

214 Town of Gill, Franklin Co.

Settled as part of Deerfield (q.v., 228), probably c. 1700; included in Greenfield, which was set off from Deerfield in 1753; set off from Greenfield in 1793. Many early settlers were descendants of the

Deerfield pioneers.—Rural community. Mt. Hermon School (for boys) founded in 1881.—Pop. 1820: 800, '50: 754, '80: 733, 1910: 942, '30: 983.—*Greenfield:* Thompson, F. M. History of Greenfield . . . [1682–1900.] 2v. Greenfield, 1904. Willard, David. Willard's history of Greenfield. 180 p. Greenfield, 1838.

1. Farmer, 63. Spent 3 winters in California, aged 22 and 53 to 54.—F and his ancestors for 8 generations born in Northfield. M born in Chesterfield, Cheshire Co., N.H. (c. 20 m. north), came here aged 23.—Grammar school and Mount Hermon.—Member of church society. Most of his friends live in Northfield and are somewhat younger. Lives alone in house where he was born.—Vigorous, active. Understood purpose of investigation.—Knows local usage. Speaks more consciously and carefully than the average farmer; responses often guarded, especially in syntax. Speech extremely staccato, almost spasmodic in its short, emphatic grouping of words and phrases. Articulation sharp. No nasalization.—B 17.

214 Town of Northfield, Franklin Co.

First permanent occupation c. 1714 (inc. by 1723) by settlers from towns further down the Conn. River.—Agricultural community. Many summer residents. Northfield Seminary (for girls) founded in 1879.—Pop. 1764: 415, '90: 868, 1820: 1584, '50: 1772, '80: 1603*, 1910: 1642, '30: 1888.—Parsons, Herbert Collins. A Puritan outpost: a history of the town and people of Northfield, Mass. 546 p. New York, 1937. Temple, J. H. and George Sheldon. A history of the town of Northfield, for 150 years. . . . 636 p. Albany, N.Y., 1875.

2. Storekeeper, 70. Has also farmed a little.—F born here; one ancestor came over with Governor Winthrop. (Genealogy published.) M born here; her ancestors were original settlers of the town.—Private and public grammar schools here, then full course in private high school. Has written articles for Springfield paper. (Wife formerly taught school.)—Officer of Masons. Knows town and people thoroughly.—Very well informed.—His literary interests may have influenced his usage to some extent. (Informant's wife thought some of his responses were stilted.) Speech slightly nasalized, but very clearly articulated. Slow tempo.—B 18.

218 Town of Hardwick (Hardwick Center), Worcester Co.

Settled in the 1730's (inc. 1739), largely from the Plymouth Colony: Dartmouth, Rochester, Sandwich, Harwich, Eastham. Others from Hatfield, Hampshire Co., and from Shrewsbury (204) and vicinity in Worcester Co.—Rural community with recently decreasing population, formerly a mill and mining center. Many old families. Newcomers chiefly Polish and French.—Pop. 1764: 1010, '90: 1722, 1820: 1836, '50: 1631*, '80: 2233, 1910: 3524, '30:

2460.—Paige, L. R. History of Hardwick. 555 p. Boston, 1883.

1. Poultry farmer, 63.—Most of his ancestors have been farmers. F born here; PGF born just outside the town, but lived here most of his life. M, MGF born here.—Primary school here. High school for a few months in Brimfield, Hampden Co. (c. 20 m. south). Visit to Chicago when c. 25. Reads a good deal.—Grange, I.O.O.F. Knows practically everyone in town, but has not many intimate friends.—Slow thinker. Unimaginative, yet interested in many events and problems outside the range of his immediate concerns. Undemonstrative and phlegmatic; 'I'm not specially given to talk,' he stated once.—Answered questions conscientiously. Some concern for 'correctness.' Keen feeling for local usage. Tempo exceedingly slow. Articulation usually careless and lax. No nasalization.—Auxiliary informant: wife.—B 3.

2. Single woman, at home, 64. Formerly a dressmaker. Occasionally 'tends the library.'—F born in Barre (adjoining town), moved here early, died when informant was c. 17. M born here of English or Scotch parents.—Public school until 15. Private high school 1 year. Some intellectual interests.—Knows few people now, and never had a wide circle of associates, but is a friend of all the children in the neighborhood.—Kind, pleasant, retiring.—Representative local idiom, despite attempts to speak 'correctly.' Feeling for local dialect reliable. Moderate tempo, changing to excessive rapidity in moments of emotional stress. Precise, clear articulation. Little nasalization.—B 2.

219 Town of Granby, Hampshire Co.

Settled 1727 as part of Hadley; set off from the district of South Hadley in 1768. Hadley settled 1659 from Windsor (see 45 East Windsor), Hartford (q.v., 40) and Wethersfield (see 1 Stamford) in Conn.—Agricultural and residential; formerly small industries. Mostly old stock. Business contacts with Holyoke, Hampden Co. (c. 6 m. southwest).—Pop. 1790: 596, 1820: 1066, '50: 1104, '80: 753, 1910: 761, '30: 891.—*Hadley:* Judd, Sylvester. History of Hadley, including the early history of Hatfield, South Hadley, Amherst and Granby. 43+504+205 p. [New ed.] Springfield, 1905. Walker, A. M. Historic Hadley: a story of the making of a famous Massachusetts town. 130 p. New York, [1906].

1. Retired farmer, 73.—F, PGF, PGM born here. Ancestors among first settlers. M, MGF, MGM born in South Hadley (adjoining town), decended from original settlers.—High school. (Sisters well educated.)—Grange. Knows many townspeople, but not the foreign-born.—Content with his status as dirt farmer.—His contempt for learning (moderated only by some natural pride in his sisters' achievements) may be partly responsible for his pure rustic dialect. Normal tempo. Slight nasalization.—B 11.

2. Cultured informant. Farmer, 77. Taught school 1 year in southern New Jersey, aged c. 28, and the following 3 years here.—F born in N.H., but lived here 50 years; PGF from Worcester. M born here, descended from original settlers of Hadley.—Elementary school here; 2 years at Monson Academy (c. 15 m. southeast). 1 year, aged c. 21, at Williams College (Williamstown); next 3 years at Amherst College (c. 10 m. north of here). Has recently interested himself in genealogy. (Wife went to Mount Holyoke College, South Hadley.)—Grange, church organizations. Formerly knew nearly everyone in town, now knows as friends only the older people.—Eager to help with the investigation.—Considers ungrammatical speech vulgar. Responses guarded and consciously correct. Theory of correctness somewhat compensated by informant's feeling for dialect and genuine sense of local idiom. Tempo rapid, spasmodic and staccato. Rather careful articulation, except when tired.—B 9.

220 Town of Palmer, Hampden Co.

Settled 1716 by Scotch-Irish, and from Springfield (q.v., 224) and vicinity; est. as district of Palmer 1752, town 1775.—Manufacturing town in agricultural region, with a compact Polish settlement.—Pop. 1764: 508, '90: 809, 1820: 1197, '50: 3974, '80: 5504, 1910: 8610, '30: 9577.—Temple, J. H. History of the town of Palmer . . . 1716–1889. . . . 602 p. [Springfield,] 1889.

Civil engineer, 80.—F born here; PGF settled here in 1780, after fighting in the Revolution. M born in Colrain, Franklin Co., but lived here 70 years.—High school here; 2 years in Leicester Academy (near Worcester). In Minnesota 1 year (aged 28) and in N. Y. State 1 summer (aged 55) on railroad surveying trips.—Until recently a leader in the community, holding town offices. Now spends most of his time at home. Highly respected.—Somewhat deaf. Quick intelligence. Memory of a long, active life is clear. Well-informed on all subjects treated in the investigation. Saw no sense in the questions, but submitted to them graciously and obviously enjoyed the interviews. An ideal informant.—Usage, except in a few minor respects, definitely fixed. Many items secured in conversation. Feeling for dialect extremely keen. Tempo rather slow. Little nasalization.—B 6.

221 Town of Monson, Hampden Co.

Settled as part of Brimfield c. 1717; est. as district 1760, town 1775. Brimfield settled from Springfield, Lexington and Woburn.—Manufacturing and farming community. Population largely indigenous.—Pop. 1764: 389, '90: 1331, 1820: 2126, '50: 2831, '80: 3758, 1910: 4758, '30: 4918.—Brimfield: Historical celebration of the town of Brimfield, Oct. 11, 1876; with the historical address of Rev. C. M. Hyde . . . 487 p. Springfield, 1879.

Retired farmer, 78. Sexton in local cemetery since 1886.—Both parents born here; 2 grandparents born here, and another brought up in the town. F's ancestors came in 1774 from Ashford, Windham Co., Conn.—Public schools and 1 year at Monson Academy.—Social and Literary Club of Universalist Church. Familiar with older people in town, but has not a very wide circle of friends.—Memory no longer altogether trustworthy.—Natural unguarded responses. Slow tempo. Muffled enunciation. No nasalizing or slurring. Postvocalic r extremely variable.—B 8.

222 Town of Holland, Hampden Co.

Settled in the 1730's as part of Brimfield (see 221 Monson) by Brimfield families. Other settlers from Woodstock (q.v., 49) and Union, Conn. (Union settled 1727 by Scotch-Irish from Worcester.) Holland est. as the East Parish of South Brimfield (now town of Wales) in 1766, as district 1783, as town 1835.—Rural community with sharply decreasing population; mostly old stock. Summer colony.—Pop. 1790: 428, 1820: 453, '50: 449, '80: 302, 1910: 145, '30: 137.—Lovering, Martin. History of the town of Holland, Mass. 749 p. Rutland, Vt., 1915.

Cattle dealer, also engaged in lumber business, 56. Lived in Worcester (c. 25 m. northeast) 10 years, aged 6 to 16.—F born in Worcester, but came here aged 3. M born in Brimfield (adjoining town). Family among earliest settlers of this region. All 4 grandparents born in neighboring towns.—Public school, including 3 months of high school, in Worcester. Although he reads more than most farmers do, his interests are restricted to affairs of family, farm and town.—Prominent in local politics.—Successful. Intelligent. Good informant.—Reproduced his natural idiom honestly, even when he realized it was at variance with 'correct' usage. Speech habits definitely fixed. Strong feeling for local dialect. Rather deliberate tempo. Articulation vigorous and clear. No nasalization.—Auxiliary informant: wife, a native of this town.—B 1.

224 City of Springfield, Hampden Co.

Settled 1636 (inc. 1641, as city 1852) by Englishmen who had stayed in the Mass. Bay Colony for a few years. Suffered severely in King Philip's War (1675).—Metal goods, rifles since Revol. War; U.S. Armory since 1794. Rapid industrial development in 19. cent., esp. metal products, electrical equipment and paper. Many skilled workmen. Large foreign element (c. ¼ of pop. foreign born): Irish, French-Canadians, Italians, Russians, Poles.—Pop. 1764: 2755, '90: 1574*, 1820: 3914, '50: 11,766, '80: 33,340, 1910: 88,926, '30: 149,900.—Burt, H. M. The first century of the history of Springfield; the official records from 1636 to 1736, with an historical review and biographical mention of the founders. 2v. Springfield, 1898–99. Green, M. A. Springfield, 1636–1886: History of town and city, including an account of the quartermillennial celebration at Springfield, May 25 and 26, 1886. 645 p. [Springfield,] 1888.

1. Housewife, 80. Born on Long Island, N.Y., came here when one year old. Spent 4 years in Conn. (Waterbury, Danbury, Stamford, Bridgeport), aged 58 to 62.—F born in Tolland, Tolland Co., Conn. (c. 25 m. southeast). M born in Somers, Tolland Co., Conn. (c. 15 m. southeast). Came here when they were married.—Private and public schools until 15. —Has many friends, old and middle-aged, but belongs to no organization. Formerly had wide acquaintance among shopkeepers and farmers.—Conscious of having seen better days. Intelligence fair, memory rather shaky.—Sometimes uncertain about her normal usage. Replies had to be carefully checked against her unguarded conversation because her anxiety to help often prompted her to say what she thought would be most pleasing. Speech perhaps not typical of lower middle class; gives impression of being less archaic and more conventionally 'correct' than might be expected. Moderate tempo. Articulation clear. Final consonants usually distinct. Weak syllables often disappear.—B 19.

2. Farmer, c. 71. Lives on outskirts of city.— Parents emigrated from County Kerry, Ireland; came here in 1858.—Elementary school (ungraded). —Belongs to no organizations. Limited circle of friends. Lives with unmarried sister.—Handsome, stalwart, not more than 50 in appearance. Good example of gentleman farmer, jovial, intelligent and alert. Not much interested in the 'old country.'— Excellent informant, giving prompt responses with the air of knowing his own usage thoroughly. Free from all timidity about 'correctness.' Voice unusually resonant and loud. Deliberate tempo. Sharp, clear articulation. Some Irishisms, mostly phonetic: [ɪ] in such words as *men, commenced;* [ə] in *garret,* etc.; strong retroflex [r] after vowels and in unstressed syllables, as in *horse, hammer.* Most obviously Irish feature of his speech is a peculiar intonation pattern.—Short work sheets.—B 10.

3. CULTURED INFORMANT. Single woman, 73. Used to do welfare work with blind people.—Ancestors came here nearly 100 years ago; became prominent in local affairs. F born in Bath, Grafton Co., N.H., came here aged 10. (Was landscape painter.) M born in Southwick (c. 10 m. southwest of here), came here aged 7.—Private schools. At fashionable school for girls she learned 'proper' pronunciation. (Cultured family: great-uncle a professor at Dartmouth College, MGF a distinguished lawyer.)—Member of several clubs. Friends include old and young.—An aristocrat, keenly intelligent. Much interested in the investigation. Knows little of rural life.—Rigidly disclaims all phrases verging on 'commonness'; rejects with ridicule any suggestion that she might use a form not impeccably proper. Her consciousness of differences between her speech and that of lower social levels is shown by the frequency of such responses as '[wɪdo], not [wɪdə].' Tempo somewhat slow. Articulation invariably clear and sharp. No nasalization.—B 13.

4. CULTURED INFORMANT. Married woman, 55. Spent childhood on a farm. Lived 5 months in Jackson, Mich., at age of 27.—F born in Cambridge, Middlesex Co., came here as infant; his parents from Vt. M born here; her parents born in Amherst and Belchertown, both in Hampshire Co., lived here after their marriage.—Public schools until 12; private schools, 12 to 17; then finishing school in Boston. At 18 and again at 40 traveled abroad for a few months. —Woman's Club. (Husband a prominent local historian.)—Intelligent. Much interested in the investigation.—Usually sure of her usage and frequently able to point out how it had changed. Aware that her speech represents transition from more rustic, colloquial type of her childhood to cultivated variety. Remembers GM's archaisms. Tempo rather slow. Articulation usually clear and careful, perhaps because of early efforts to cultivate polite speech. No habitual nasalization. Frequent glottal stops.— Short work sheets.—B 12.

225 Town of Southampton, Hampshire Co.

Settled c. 1730 from Northampton (q.v., 226), of which it was a part until est. as the district of Southampton in 1753.—Quiescent agricultural community; tobacco growing. Formerly sawmills and other small industries. Recent influx of Poles.—Pop. 1764: 437, '90: 829, 1820: 1160, '50: 1060*, '80: 1046, 1910: 870, '30: 931.

Farm housekeeper, 61. Lived one year as a child in Marlboro, Windham Co., Vt.—F born here of old local family, died when informant was a child. M born here, descendant of pioneer settler. (Stepfather born in Lincoln Co., Maine.)—School until 14.— Woman's Club. Formerly knew many people in town.—Cheerful and friendly. Rather intelligent, though information not in all respects adequate.— Has trained herself to substitute for certain 'vulgar' colloquialisms more 'elegant' forms acquired from books. Willing, when pressed, to give natural equivalents. Except for certain 'corrections,' her speech belongs to the local middle-aged uneducated type. Tempo normal. Nasalization weak, occasionally (before [m, n]) strong. Articulation clear; over-careful in guarded utterances.—B 58.

226 City of Northampton, Hampshire Co.

Settled 1653-54 (inc. as city 1883) from Hartford (q.v., 40) and Windsor, Conn. (see 45 East Windsor). —Residential and industrial city. Prosperous agricultural community in 18. cent. Scene of the 'Great Awakening' (in the 1740's) inspired by Jonathan Edwards.—Manufacture of silk hosiery, cutlery, brushes, etc.—Smith College, founded 1875, has had much influence on the community.—Pop. 1764: 1285, '90: 1628, 1820: 2854, '50: 5278, '80: 12,172,

1910: 19,431, '30: 24,381.—Trumbull, J. R. History of Northampton, from its settlement in 1654. . . . 2v. Northampton, 1898–1902.

1. Proprietor of an inn, c. 55. Always here except when at college.—Old local family.—2 years of college (in N.E.).—Social contacts are outside the local academic groups.—Educated type of local speech, less cultivated than that of informant 2. No affectations.—J 16.

2. CULTURED INFORMANT. Secretary (to college administrative officer), 51. Taught school in Perth Amboy, N.J., aged 24 to 26.—F, PGF, PGM born here. M born here; MGF, MGM born in Germany.—Graduated from Smith College.—Occupies good position in college society.—Capable, intelligent, coöperative.—Realizes confusing effect of speech-consciousness on usage. Always knew whether her forms were native or acquired; careless, normal or over-careful. Medium tempo. Clear enunciation. Pronunciation unusually stable.—J 10.

228 Town of Deerfield (1 Pine Nook section; 2 Old Deerfield), Franklin Co.

Settled c. 1672 from Dedham (settled 1635). Its pop. of 125 abandoned the town during King Philip's War (1675) and reoccupied it in 1683. Deerfield remained a frontier town until c. 1750.—Historic agricultural community. Several private schools.—Pop. 1764: 737, '90: 1328, 1820: 1868, '50: 2421, '80: 3543, 1910: 2209*, '30: 2882.—Sheldon, George. Pocumtuck, 1636–1886: A history of Deerfield. . . . 2v. Deerfield, 1895–96.

1. Farmer, 66. Has always lived in Pine Nook section.—F born here; M in Halifax, Windham Co., Vt. (c. 20 m. northwest). Came here when they were married.—Grammar school until 12.—Never married. Few social contacts.—Not particularly interested in the investigation, but willing to coöperate.—Rather slow of response. Speech natural. Fast tempo. Little nasalization.—J 7.

2. CULTURED INFORMANT. Insurance agent, newspaper correspondent, 66. Has always lived in the section known as Old Deerfield.—Old local families.—High school graduate. Reads considerably.—Extensive social contacts. Popular.—Carefree, unambitious. Courteous.—Local cultivated speech; fluent, accurate, without affectation. Loud, hearty voice. Diphthongs variable.—J 5.

230 Town of Colrain, Franklin Co.

Settled 1732 (inc. 1761). Most of the early settlers were Scotch-Irish from Londonderry, N.H. (q.v., 318), and from the Mass. towns of Pelham, Stow, Woburn and Roxbury.—Good farming country; a few small factories. Now losing population.—Pop. 1764: 297, '90: 1418, 1820: 1961, '50: 1785, '80: 1777, 1910: 1741, '30: 1391.

1. Farmer, formerly slater, 41.—F born in Halifax, Windham Co., Vt. (c. 8 m. north), came here

aged 28. M born here of old local family.—1 year of high school.—Intelligent, socially inclined, courteous. Attracted by the investigation as a new sort of test.—Makes some effort to appear to advantage, but does not conceal his natural idiom; his first response is sometimes guarded. Utterance clear, slow and even. Slight nasalization.—J 8.

2. Man of leisure, 75.—Both parents born here; all grandparents born here or near-by. Ancestors on both sides from Conn.—1½ years at Powers Institute, Bernardston (c. 8 m. east), equivalent to 2 years of high school. Reads a good deal.—Social contacts restricted. Accepted by the community as a gentleman of leisure.—Reserved. Generally liked because of his kindliness and courtesy.—Often uses forms of cultivated speech, but is sure of his local dialect. Clear articulation except when he is tired.—J 4.

232 Town of Cummington, Hampshire Co.

Settled c. 1770 (inc. 1779). Many of the early settlers from Abington and Bridgewater (q.v., 108), Plymouth Co.—Abington settled c. 1668 from surrounding towns: Weymouth, Hingham, Scituate; many families thought to be originally from Devonshire and Dorsetshire.—Agricultural and residential with declining population; formerly some manufacturing. Summer colony.—Pop. 1790: 873, 1820: 1060, '50: 1172, '80: 881, 1910: 637, '30: 531.—Miller, H. E. Sketches and directory of the town of Cummington. 46 p. West Cummington, 1881.

1. Housewife, 76. Born in Montague, Franklin Co. (c. 25 m. northeast), came here aged 3.—F born here of old local family. M born in Plainfield (adjoining town), of old local family.—High school in Springfield, Hampden Co. (c. 30 m. southeast). Reads considerably.—Is considered one of the 'best people' here, but has had no aspirations to social leadership.—Slightly deaf. Complains that her memory is failing. Courteous and obliging.—Has a tendency to give literary rather than colloquial words and phrases, but pronunciation is not affected. Consults the dictionary, but normally follows what she considers the best local usage. Utterance clear and precise. Voiceless stops strongly aspirated.—J 2.

2. Keeper of general store, 43. Taught school here a year, aged 17. Office work in Northampton (c. 17 m. southeast), aged 18 to 24.—Descended from first settlers.—Aged 14 to 17, at high school in Northampton.—Town officer. Knows everybody. Meets farmers frequently.—Very intelligent.—Excellent representative of modern local speech. Knows local usage of all classes, and half-consciously adapts his language to the company and situation. Made no effort to be correct, saying, 'I'd better see if I can't sort o' sneak up on myself unawares.' Tempo rather fast. Articulation clear, but not careful. Vowels in general short. Retroflection varies. Not much nasalization.—J 3.

3. Housewife, 80. Taught school in near-by towns c. 8 terms between ages of 17 and 30.—F born in Goshen (adjoining town); M born here. Both families in this region since 1780 or earlier.—School c. 6 months a year until 17.—Few social contacts. Lives on isolated farm.—Admires correct speech.—J 6.

233 Town of Middlefield, Hampshire Co.

First settled c. 1773 (inc. 1783), chiefly from Connecticut.—Farming community with decreasing population. Summer visitors. Formerly sheep raising and woolen mills.—Pop. 1790: 603, 1820: 755, '50: 737, '80: 648, 1910: 354, '30: 197.—Middlefield: A memorial of the 100th anniversary of the incorporation of the town, Aug. 15, 1883, containing the historical discourse by E. P. Smith. 96 p. Middlefield, 1883. Smith, Edward C. and Philip M. A history of the town of Middlefield, Mass. 662 p. [Menasha, Wis.,] 1924. (Privately printed.)

Farmer, 76.—F born here of old local family. M born in Ohio, went to Conn. when a child, then came here to marry.—2 years of high school.—Normal social contacts, occasionally with outsiders. —Courteous, intelligent, well informed. Thinks slowly and is somewhat affected by senility.—Tries to be 'well spoken,' but does not consult the dictionary. Slow, precise speech, even in conversation. Utterance clear, not nasal. Vowels short. Final consonants lax.—J 1.

234 Town of Blandford, Hampden Co.

Settled 1735 (inc. 1741) by Scotch-Irish from Hopkinton, Middlesex Co. Blandford orig. called Glasgow.—Declining population. Dairies and fruit farms. Formerly sheep raising. Many summer homes.—Pop. 1764: 406, '90: 1416, 1820: 1515, '50: 1418, '80: 979*, 1910: 717, '30: 545.—Gibbs, W. H. Address delivered before the Literary Association, Blandford, Sept. 21, 1850, upon the history of that town. 76 p. Springfield, 1850.

1. Farm housewife, 73.—F born in Stamford, Fairfield Co., Conn. (c. 85 m. south); M born in Barkhamsted, Litchfield Co., Conn. (c. 17 m. south). —High school and 2 years of normal school. Some travel since the age of 50; now spends winters in Brooklyn, N.Y., and in Cuba. Reads a great deal.— Sociable, popular.—Intelligent and observant.— Good representative of local educated type. Inclined to use literary words. Tempo rapid. Utterance clear. Pronunciation seldom careful even in guarded speech.—Auxiliary informant: farmer, 60.—Practically illiterate.—J 9.

2. Farm housekeeper, 45.—Descended from old local family.—Grammar school.—Usual social contacts.—Intelligent. Courteous and accommodating, but shy.—Does not put on airs, but is careful of her speech before strangers. Retains many pronunciations learned at school.—J 15.

235 Town of Granville, Hampden Co.

Settled in the 1730's (est. as district 1754, town 1775) from West Springfield. West Springfield, originally a part of Springfield (q.v., 224), settled c. 1655.—Rather isolated farming community with decreasing population. Small factory.—Pop. 1764: 682, '90: 1980, 1820: 1643*, '50: 1305, '80: 1205, 1910: 781, '30: 674.

1. Factory worker, 82. Farmed until he was 40. At 21, spent a year in New York State. Was in Collinsville, Hartford Co., Conn. (c. 25 m. south), a few years.—Parents and grandparents born here.— Grammar school here. High school in Westfield (c. 10 m. northeast). 1 year at academy.—Popular, sociable. Town officer.—Intelligent.—Has a good ear for strictly local idiom. Utterance clear and unhurried. Nasalization rare. Vowels tend to be centralized.— J 12.

2. Factory worker, formerly farmer, 49. Aged 20, spent a winter in Westfield.—Old local family.— Academy in Winchendon, Worcester Co. (c. 60 m. northeast), aged 12 to 17.—Town officer. Knows many people here.—Quiet, courteous.—Natural, ungarded speech, but not strictly local.—Incomplete record: lacking about 20 pages of scattered items.— J 14.

236 Town of New Marlborough (Mill River), Berkshire Co.

Settled in the 1740's (est. as district 1759, town 1775) by families from Marborough, Middlesex Co. (q.v., 203), and from Canterbury, Windham Co., Conn. (q.v., 48). Others came from Northampton (226), and from Suffield, Hartford Co., Conn.— Declining rural community: dairies; formerly gunpowder and paper manufacturing. The village of Mill River has general store, post office, library, school.—Pop. 1790: 1550, 1820: 1668, '50: 1847, '80: 1876, 1910: 1124, '30: 864.

1. Laborer, 76. Born here in section which was then part of town of Sheffield. At 13 worked a year in North Hillsdale, Columbia Co., N.Y. (just over Mass. state line). Has worked in N.Y. c. 5 years in all, in Columbia and Dutchess Counties; also from time to time, after he was 40, in Waterbury, New Haven Co., Conn. Here continually for the last 30 years.—Thinks F was born in New Lebanon or Lebanon Springs, Columbia Co., N.Y.—Grammar school.—Congregational Church.—Shrewd and hardworking. Not prosperous. Represents lower social level.—Speech slow, drawling, but quite distinct; prolonged vowels and glides. Rather melancholy intonation.—HY 12.

2. Housewife, 74. Aged 22, went to Minnesota; lived there c. 9 years.—F born here. M born in Egremont (c. 12 m. northwest); MGM's parents were Dutch.—Local schools. South Berkshire Inst., New Marlborough. 1 term at a school in Rochester,

Minn.—Congregational Church.—Small, neat; extremely precise in everything from her housekeeping to her speech. Represents upper social level.—Tries to speak 'correctly.' Utterance rapid and crisp. Vowels rather short.—Short work sheets.—HY 11.

238 Town of Egremont (South Egremont), Berkshire Co.

Settled c. 1730 (est. as district 1760, town 1775), several of the families coming from Rhinebeck, N.Y.—Formerly manufacturing and marble quarrying. Now chiefly agricultural, with decreasing population.—Pop. 1790: 759, 1820: 865, '50: 1013, '80: 875, 1910: 605, '30: 513.

Retired farm worker (woman), 89. Lived here until aged 51, except for a year of schoolteaching in Sheffield (c. 5 m. southeast) when she was 20. After middle age she moved about to Southfield (c. 12 m. southeast, town of Sandisfield), to Mill River (c. 10 m. southeast, town of New Marlborough), to Newark, N.J., and Stottville, N.Y. Has lived in Pittsfield (c. 22 m. north) for the last 6 years.—F born here, she thinks, of old local family. M born in Mt. Washington (c. 5 m. southwest).—Grammar school and academy here.—Failing physically and mentally.—Hard to interview because of clouded memory. Expressions often had to be suggested.—B 74. (56 pages in first part of record by J.)

239 Town of Alford, Berkshire Co.

Settled in the 1750's, mostly from Connecticut; set off from Great Barrington, with certain common lands, and est. as district 1773; made a town 1775.—Agricultural with sharply declining population. Marble quarrying recently given up.—Pop. 1790: 577, 1820: 570, '50: 502, '80: 348, 1910: 275, '30: 200.—Taylor, C. J. History of Great Barrington. 516 p. Great Barrington, 1882.

Farmer, dairyman, butcher, 67.—F, PGF born here; latter's F in Ireland. M, MGF born here; MGM in W. Stockbridge (c. 7 m. north).—School intermittently until 12, then each winter until 16.—Town officer 20 years. Knows practically everybody. Purely social contacts rather limited.—Hearty and pleasant, but very opinionated and sententious. Eager to voice his views on whatever subject is broached.—Except for a few elegancies, his speech is typical of his community in vocabulary and pronunciation. In grammatical features it is less representative, since he has educated himself to speak 'correctly.' Tempo very slow and deliberate. Articulation careful and distinct. Strong nasalization.—B 75. (Pp. 7–11, 14–23, 27–39 and a few others by J.)

240 Town of Stockbridge, Berkshire Co.

Indian mission established 1739. Settled in the 1750's from Northampton (226), Spencer (206), Worcester (205), Weston (152).—Many of the townspeople are prosperous farmers of the old stock. Summer colony. Good roads and schools. Formerly some manufacturing.—Pop. 1764: 465, '90: 1336, 1820: 1377, '50: 1941, '80: 2357, 1910: 1933, '30: 1762.—Jones, E. F. Stockbridge, past and present; or, Records of an old mission station. 275 p. Springfield, 1854.

Farmer, 86.—F's family here since 1804. M born in Warren, Litchfield Co., Conn. (c. 40 m. south).—Public school and academy until 17. One year of business school in Poughkeepsie, Dutchess Co., N.Y. Has read widely.—Held town offices for many years. Respected. Normal social contacts.—Kindly, ceremonious, well-to-do. Excessively proud of his family. Great respect for learning.—Has always been careful of his speech and is much influenced by the literary language in vocabulary and grammar. His pronunciation, however, is distinctly local. Avoids mentioning vulgar or profane words. Slow tempo. Fairly clear articulation.—J 11.

241 Town of Lenox, Berkshire Co.

Settled in the 1760's as part of Richmond (est. as district 1767, town 1775), chiefly from West Hartford (see 40 Hartford) and Wallingford (q.v., 36), Conn. Richmond settled 1760, the first families coming from Kent, Litchfield Co., Conn., and from Long Island.—Farming community; summer colony. Formerly an iron foundry, marble works, glass factory.—Pop. 1790: 1169, 1820: 1315, '50: 1599, '80: 2043, 1910: 3060, '30: 2742.—Mallary, R. D. Lenox and the Berkshire Highlands. 363 p. New York, 1902. Palmer, C. J. History of Lenox and Richmond. 48 p. Pittsfield, 1904.

Retired boardinghouse keeper (woman), 83.—F born in N.H.; M born in Constantia, N.Y. (near Syracuse); they married here.—High school.—Wide acquaintance.—Hard of hearing. Occasionally forgetful, but still intelligent.—Speech representative of the middle class, or a level somewhat lower, of the country about Pittsfield.—J 13.

242 City of Pittsfield, Berkshire Co.

Settled in the 1750's (inc. 1761, as city 1889) from Wethersfield, Conn. (see 41 Glastonbury), and from Westfield and Northampton (q.v., 226). Westfield settled in the 1660's from Springfield (224).—At first a thriving agricultural town, soon the trading center of the Berkshires. Shortly after 1800, manufacture of wool carding machines and looms. Woolen mills. Later manufacture of shoes, paper, metal products and electrical machinery.—Rapidly growing city. Summer colony and winter sports.—Pop. 1764: 428, '90: 1982, 1820: 2768, '50: 5872, '80: 13,364, 1910: 32,121, '30: 49,677.—Boltwood, Edward. The history of Pittsfield, Mass., 1876–1916. 387 p. Pittsfield, 1916. Field, D. D. A history of the town of Pittsfield. 80 p. Hartford, 1844. Smith, J. E. A. The history of Pittsfield. 2v. Boston, 1869–76.

1. Laborer, 63. Was motorman on a trolley car 5 years. At present janitor of tenement house in poor district. Born in Lebanon Springs, Columbia Co., N.Y. (c. 10 m. northwest). Family moved to Canaan, Litchfield Co., Conn. (c. 30 m. south of here), when he was a child; then settled here when he was c. 13.— F and M born in Lebanon Springs. (Wife born in Hannover, Germany, came here as a girl.)—Grammar school in Canaan 6 years. Practically illiterate. —Associates entirely with his own class.—Dull, slow-thinking. Remarkably good-natured and obliging.—Good example of the lowest social level in the city. Moderately fast tempo. Loud, very slightly modulated voice. Strong nasalization. Initial *p, t, k* strongly aspirated. Much glottalization.—B 76. (Pp. 1–11, 14–48 by J.)

2. CULTURED INFORMANT. Retired businessman (17 years in grocery store, etc.), 85. Brought up on a farm, lived there until he was 21.—F, PGF born here of prominent old family. M born in Monterey (c. 20 m. south).—High school here. Has a fairly large popular library. Traveled in N.Y. State, Nevada, Mexico and other places on business.—24 years deacon of First Congregational Church. Has held municipal offices. Knows many local people, but says he is 'a good deal of a home-body.'—Softspoken, stolid, undemonstrative. Passively friendly, on guard against strangers. Information adequate.— Old-fashioned cultivated speech. Occasional substandard forms in unguarded conversation. Slow tempo. Occasional nasalization. Fairly clear articulation.—B 77.

246 Town of Cheshire, Berkshire Co.

Settled 1767 (inc. 1793), principally from Rhode Island (Baptists). Some settlers from Connecticut.— Agricultural, with some manufacturing. Many Poles, Italians and French-Canadians.—Pop. 1820: 1202, '50: 1298, '80: 1537, 1910: 1508, '30: 1697.—Raynor, Mrs. E. M. and Mrs. E. L. Petitclerc. History of the town of Cheshire. 214 p. Holyoke, 1885.

1. Proprietor of general store (also in charge of town construction work), 84. Born in North Adams (c. 10 m. north), came here aged 6. Spent 1 summer in Shelburne Falls, Franklin Co.; 1 in Easthampton, Hampshire Co.; 1 in Hardwick, Worcester Co.; and 1 in Keene, Cheshire Co., N.H.—F born near Bennington, Bennington Co., Vt. M born in or near Greensboro, Orleans Co., Vt. Ancestors of informant were for several generations associated with the region around Cheshire.—Grammar school here. 2 terms at Fort Edwards Institute (on Hudson R. above Troy).—Mason. Has been town officer 3 years; was formerly too busy to hold office. Famous as an 'old-timer.'—Strong-minded; intelligent, but unimaginative. Thinks well of himself.—Has tried to improve his speech by eliminating some local features. Tempo slow. Nasalization slight. Articulation weak and rather slovenly. Voice deep and resonant, but somewhat muffled. Enunciation of final consonants and of unstressed syllables usually very weak.—B 65.

2. Master carpenter, formerly rural mail carrier, 40. In Springfield, Hampden Co. (c. 45 m. southeast), aged 15 to 16.—F and M born here. F's family one of those which settled the town from Providence, R.I.—Grammar school here. High school 1 year in Adams (c. 6 m. north). Reads a good deal. Traveled in Florida 3 winters on construction jobs; also in Texas.—Mason. Used to know everybody in town. Very little social life.—Pleasant, intelligent. Essentially a family man and householder.—Colloquial rustic speech. The informant was brought up by his GM and owes many of his archaisms to her. Because of his travels, he is aware of regional differences, but his own speech has remained genuinely local. Tempo very rapid, usually increasing in speed toward the end of a breath-group. Strong nasalization. Articulation so lax and careless as to be often entirely unintelligible. Postvocalic *r* extremely strong and retroflex; *l* usually very dark.—B 66.

248 Town of Williamstown (South Williamstown), Berkshire Co.

Settled after 1750 (inc. 1765). Many settlers from Colchester, New London Co., Conn., and some from Canaan, Litchfield (16) and New Milford (12) in Litchfield Co., Conn.; others from Warren, Worcester Co., and New Salem (212), Franklin Co., Mass.—Primarily a college town (Williams College). Many summer homes in the vicinity. South Williamstown entirely agricultural: dairy farming.— Pop. 1790: 1769, 1820: 2010, '50: 2626, '80: 3394, 1910: 3708, '30: 3900.—Perry, A. L. Origins in Williamstown. Ed. 2. 650 p. New York, 1896. Perry, A. L. Williamstown and Williams College. 847 p. [Norwood,] 1899.

1. Farmer, 66. Used to operate trucking business in Williamstown. Born in Pownal, Bennington Co. Vt. (short distance across state line), came here aged 2. When c. 50, spent 19 months in North Adams (adjoining city).—F born in New Ashford (c. 5 m. south). M born in Stamford, Bennington Co., Vt. (just across state line to the northeast).—Grammar school 3 years in New Ashford and 2 terms here.— Formerly belonged to Grange, Sons of Veterans, Foresters. Has been town officer 11 years. Knows almost everybody except the students.—At first considered the investigation foolish, but gradually became much interested.—Speech fairly natural, definitely archaic and rustic. Certain 'incorrect' constructions are consciously avoided, but occur in unguarded conversation. Dialectal differences between his own section of Mass. and the bordering region of N.Y. have impressed him. Tempo slow. Marked nasalization. Monotonous intonation. Weak articulation of unstressed syllables.—B 63.

2. Farmer, laborer, at present caretaker in ceme-

tery, 37. Spent 2 or 3 months in Bennington, Bennington Co., Vt. (c. 15 m. north). Aged 29 to 34 in Hancock (c. 10 m. south).—F born here; his family in same house for 5 generations. F's GGF came from northern Ireland. M born in southern Vt., came here when 14 or 15.—Grammar school and 1 year of high school in Williamstown; 2 months of business college in North Adams (adjoining city). Traveled to several European countries when c. 24 as fireman on ship.—Many contacts. Occupies low social position in community.—All bone and muscle; coarse in appearance. Surprisingly kindly and ready to help others. Quick-witted. Excellent informant.—Strikingly rustic speech of a purely local type. Tempo medium. Nasalization strong. Articulation fair to slovenly. Weak syllables very obscure.—B 64.

VERMONT

252 Town of Shaftsbury (South Shaftsbury), Bennington Co.

Settled c. 1763 from Providence (80), R.I., and from Hartford (40) and Norwich (33), Conn.; others from Worcester Co., Mass. In 1768 the first Baptist Church in Vt. was established here.—Agricultural town with some manufacturing.—Pop. 1790: 1990, 1830: 2142, '50: 1896, '80: 1887, 1910: 1650, '30: 1631.

1. Painter, formerly a farmer, 56. Born in Wisconsin, came to So. Shaftsbury aged 2. Lived 1 year in North Bennington village (c. 2 m. southwest).—F born in Glastenbury (adjoining town); M born here. They lived 10 years in Wis.—Grammar school until 12 or 13. 'I don't have nothin' but only a common school education, an' not much o' that.'—Limited social contacts.—Plain, undistinguished, hospitable, completely honest. Did not understand purpose of investigation. Responded bluntly and without affectation.—Perfectly natural, unguarded rustic speech. Rather low, monotonous voice. Articulates with a minimum of effort. Does not usually nasalize.—B 56.

252 Town of Bennington (Old Bennington village), Bennington Co.

Settled 1761 (granted by N.H. in 1749, claim disputed by N.Y.); some Dutch settlers from the Hudson Valley before the arrival of Mass. settlers from the Conn. Valley (Sunderland, Amherst, Westfield) and from Hardwick (218). Later others from Cambridge and Dedham, Mass., and from Norwich (33), Conn.—Trading center of sw. Vt. Site of an important engagement in the Revolutionary War. Paper and woolen mills since the Revolution.—Bennington College (for women) est. 1932. Many summer guests.—Pop. 1790: 2350, 1830: 3419, '50: 3923, '80: 6333, 1910: 8698, '30: 10,628 (Bennington village 7,390; North Bennington village 933; Old Bennington village 174).—Dodge, Stanley D. The Vermont valley: a chorographical study. Papers of the Michigan Academy of science, arts and letters 16 (1931), 241–74. (Contains information about the growth of Bennington.) Jennings, Isaac. Memorials of a century, embracing a record of individuals and events chiefly in the early history of Bennington, Vt., and its First Church. 408 p. Boston, 1869. Merrill, John V. and Caroline R. Merrill. Sketches of historic Bennington. 99 p. Cambridge, 1911.

2. Retired farmer, 75. Sells antiques.—F born here. F's GGF came from Hardwick, Mass., in 1761 as pioneer founder of this town; his son built the house in which the informant was born and has always lived. M born here.—Grammar school and 2 years at Mt. Anthony Seminary in Bennington.—Congregational Church. Sons of American Revolution. Chamber of Commerce. Town officer. Lives with his sister. His house, famous as a fine example of old N.E. architecture, draws many visitors.—Kindly and jovial. Fond of telling jokes and anecdotes, still fonder of relating his family's rôle in Vt. history. As a consequence of the dignity with which his house and his ancestral honors endow him, he has made an effort to rise above the status of a rustic 'old feller.'—Guards his speech carefully, tries to avoid archaisms and colloquialisms. Wavers in many cases between an old-fashioned turn of phrase, natural to him, and a more modern one which he has acquired. Speaks in slow drawl, frequently interrupted by sharp exclamations (never profane). No very distinct nasalization. Enunciates clearly, but not carefully.—B 57.

254 Town of Wilmington, Windham Co.

Settled shortly before the Revolution; org. by 1778. Settlers from Worcester Co., Mass., and the Conn. Valley; others from Cape Cod and the Boston area.—Largely agricultural (dairies); some manufacturing. Now many summer guests.—Pop. 1790: 645, 1830: 1367, '50: 1372, '80: 1130, 1910: 1229, '30: 1171.

1. Deputy sheriff, formerly contractor, teamster, horse-trader, 69. Lived on a farm until c. 25.—F born here. M born in Marlboro, adjoining town.—Grammar school. Reads considerably and has done much to educate himself.—Knows practically everyone in town, but withdrew at wife's death from social life. Now lives alone.—Grave, dignified, rather taciturn except with his grandchildren, who are extremely fond of him.—Has dropped from careful speech many rustic vulgarisms and grammatical improprieties, but admits that in casual conversation he still uses most of them. Has a good memory for archaisms, but otherwise no feeling for dialectal variations. Tempo painfully slow, one word at a time. Rather clear articulation.—B 67.

2. Former dairy farmer (now 'taking it easy'), 58.

—F born in Peru, Bennington Co. (c. 25 m. north). M born here.—Grammar school here. 2 years of high school in Hinsdale, Cheshire Co., N.H. (c. 22 m. east). Does not read much.—Belongs to Masons, Eastern Star, the Grange and the Chamber of Commerce. Has been town officer. Knows most of the townspeople and goes frequently to card parties, dances, etc.—Easy-going, kind, hospitable. Accustomed to physical labor, he finds work even in his retirement to keep him occupied.—Has some fear of committing grammatical blunders, but not enough to prevent him from using naturally what he would regard, on reflection, as improprieties. Slow tempo. Not much nasalization. Articulation clear, but not painstaking.—B 68.

256 Town of Brattleboro (West Brattleboro), Windham Co.

Granted by N.H. in 1753, settled soon afterward; org. c. 1768. Early settlers from all parts of Mass.; others from central Conn. and sw. N.H.—Modern manufacturing town in agricultural surroundings: cotton goods, paper, granite monuments, organs. Health report c. 1845–70 (mineral springs). Winter sports.—Pop. 1790: 1589, 1830: 2141, '50: 3816, '80: 5880, 1910: 7541, '30: 9816 (Brattleboro village 8709).—Burnham, Henry. Brattleboro, Windham Co., Vermont: Early history, with biographical sketches of some of its citizens. Ed. by Abby Maria Hemenway. 191 p. Brattleboro, 1880. Burt, Henry M. The attractions of Brattleboro: Glimpses of the past and present. 108 p. Brattleboro, 1866. Cabot, Mary R. Annals of Brattleboro, 1681–1895. 2v. 1104 p. Brattleboro, 1921–22.

Housewife, 85.—F, PGM born here; PGF settled here. M, MGF born here; MGM from N.Y. State or Canada.—Glenwood Ladies' Seminary here.—Has done Red Cross work.—Coöperative.—Rising inflection common. Considerable unvoicing.—Complete record except for pp. 16–31.1 inclusive.

Supplementary informant: housewife. Lived until aged 15 in Jacksonville, town of Whitingham (c. 12 m. southwest).—The vowels of *lot* and of *law* are separate phonemes in her speech.—Pp. 16–31.1 inclusive. These entries are not starred on the maps.—L 49.

257 Town of Newfane, Windham Co.

Settled c. 1766 (org. 1774) largely from Worcester Co., Mass. Other settlers from the Conn. Valley in Mass., s. Vt. and sw. N.H.—Historic shire town with decreasing population. Agricultural.—Pop. 1790: 660, 1830: 1441, '50: 1304, '80: 1031, 1910: 820, '30: 662.—Centennial proceedings and other historical facts and incidents relating to Newfane, the county seat of Windham Co., Vermont. 256 p. Brattleboro, 1877.

Farmer, 73. Between the ages of 41 and 68, traveled in eastern N.Y. and in N.E. working for

American Bridge Co. Aged 47 to 59, made his home in Brattleboro (c. 12 m. southeast).—F born here; PGF, PGM born in N.E., of English parentage. M born here; MGF, MGM born in Malden, Middlesex Co., Mass.—School until 17. In 1927 served in State Legislature.—Member of I.O.O.F., Grange, historical society. Town officer.—Mind not as quick as it used to be. Information reliable.—Rather rapid tempo. Precise utterance. Velar-pharyngeal voice quality. Dark *l* in all positions. Retroflection variable. Vowels tend to be short.—L 41.

258 Town of Rockingham, Windham Co.

Settled before 1760 (org. 1760), largely from eastern Mass. and southern N.H.—Agricultural town, including the manufacturing village of Bellows Falls (paper mill since 1802, farm machinery). First bridge across Conn. River 1784. Turnpike (Third New Hampshire, 1799) connecting Keene, N.H., and Rutland, Vt., passed over this bridge.—Pop. 1790: 1235, 1830: 2272, '50: 2837, '80: 3797, 1910: 6207, '30: 5302 (Bellows Falls village 3930).—Hayes, Lyman S. History of the town of Rockingham, Vermont. . . . 850 p. Bellows Falls, 1907.

Housewife, 81. When a girl, went to live in Chester, Windsor Co. (c. 8 m. northwest).—F born here. M born in Townshend (c. 15 m. southwest). Stepmother born in Walpole, Cheshire Co., N.H. (c. 10 m. southeast, just across state line), of Conn. ancestry.—School here until 10, then academy in Chester; Black River Academy in Ludlow, Windsor Co. (c. 20 m. northwest), until past 20.—Congregational Church.—Very active for her age. Friendly and coöperative. Comparatively well educated, but not highly intelligent.—Rather cultivated speech. Insisted she had never heard a number of common expressions, perhaps because she thought them not 'proper.' Quick tempo. Short vowels. Retroflection rare.—L 42. (Pp. 7–21, 32–48, 69–78 by C.)

259 Town of Andover (Simonsville), Windsor Co.

Settled c. 1761 from Enfield (see 44 Somers) and Lebanon, Conn.; some from N.H. and Mass. Lebanon (New London Co.) settled c. 1695; population mixed.—Rural community with decreasing population.—Pop. 1790: 275, 1830: 975, '50: 725, '80: 564, 1910: 284, '30: 258.

Farmer, 75. Has worked in cheese factory. Taught country school 3 years. Lived 4 years (some time after he was 21) in Mt. Holly, Rutland Co. (c. 15 m. northwest). Has spent the last 4 years in Chester (c. 6 m. east).—F born in Andover; PGF, PGM came from Foxborough, Norfolk Co., Mass. M born in Andover; MGF, MGM came from Wilton, Hillsborough Co., N.H.—School here until 20. Three years in State Legislature.—Has held most of the town offices.—Very keen, bright, honest, dependable. Always knew his own mind.—Tempo rather rapid, voice quality somewhat velar and pharyngeal (cf.

informant 257). Extremely dark *l* in all positions. Retroflection varies considerably. Vowels are short. —L 35.

260 Town of Pawlet, Rutland Co.

Settled 1761 (org. 1769), chiefly from e. Conn. (48 Canterbury, 33 Norwich), c. Conn. (Suffield, 41 Glastonbury, Woodbury), and Cape Cod (115 Falmouth). Many soldiers settled here after the Revolution.—Agricultural: cattle raising and dairying. In 1830 a busy mill town and a rival of Rutland.— Foreigners have been employed in the slate works of West Pawlet.—Pop. 1790: 1458, 1830: 1965, '50: 1843, '80: 1696, 1910: 1959, '30: 1476.—Hollister, Hiel. Pawlet for one hundred years. 272 p. Albany, 1867.

1. Farmer, deputy sheriff, 67.—F born here, died early; PGF from Canterbury, Windham Co., Conn., bought present farm c. 100 years ago. M born here; M's GF born in Danby (adjoining town); her GM born here.—School until 14. (His second wife used to teach school.) Reads newspapers thoroughly every day. State Legislature 1 winter. 4 short visits to Nebraska and 3 to Iowa. Traveled all through Vt., N.H. and part of Conn. for the Farm Bureau.— Known by his nickname to many N.E. farmers. Townspeople hold him in high esteem. Keeps up his wide circle of acquaintance in spite of serious lameness.—Intelligent, quick-witted, kind and helpful. Extensive knowledge and lively sense of humor.— Speech unaffectedly rustic. In several cases his unguarded conversation belied his more carefully considered statements (e.g., that he never says *ain't*). Deep voice. Slow tempo. Nasalization rather strong, especially before nasal consonants (which sometimes disappear). Articulation usually clear. Vowels short. —B 59.

3. Farmer's wife, 55.—F born in Danby (adjoining town); M born in Wallingford (c. 15 m. northeast). They lived in Danby 1 or 2 years after their marriage, then settled here.—Grammar school. 2 half-terms at Troy Conference Academy in Poultney (c. 15 m. northwest).—Contacts with prosperous farmers' wives, especially those who have received more than average education.—Proud of her standing in the community, her education and her knowledge of what is right and wrong in speech. Not very talkative, rather shy with strangers. Intelligent.— Not a very satisfactory informant. Her speech has a naturally rustic foundation overlaid with acquired, self-conscious gentility. Slow tempo. Rather careful articulation. Nasalization absent or very slight.—Incomplete record: long work sheets pp. 1–34, short work sheets pp. 35–45.—B 60.

260 Town of Dorset, Bennington Co.

Settled c. 1768 (org. 1774) from New York State, from c. Conn. (Suffield, Mansfield, Wethersfield) and from Stockbridge (240), Mass.; others from R.I.—

Formerly marble quarrying; now a quiet resort in agricultural surroundings. Many writers, painters and business men have homes here. Summer visitors. —Pop. 1790: 957, 1830: 1507, '50: 1700, '80: 2005, 1910: 1472, '30: 1120.—Humphrey, Zephine. The story of Dorset. 288 p. Rutland, 1924. (Anecdotes, character sketches, etc.)

2. Mail carrier, general handy man, 48.—F, PGF, PGM born in Rupert (adjoining town). F's family long here, with descendants throughout the county. M, MGM born here.—Grammar school. High respect for education. (Wife a former schoolteacher. They have encouraged their children to use polite speech. His F and several ancestors were physicians. Has sent 2 sons through medical school.)—Popular. Knows everyone in town. Carries the local news as he goes on his rounds.—Highly intelligent. Entered actively into the spirit of the work and tried to be natural.—Good example of idiom current among younger and middle-aged generation in this part of Vt. Keen feeling for local dialect; can give excellent imitations of speech more rustic or old-fashioned than his own. Contact with summer guests has smoothed out many of the more rustic features of his native usage. Rapid tempo. Slight nasalization. Rather sharp, almost precise enunciation. Fairly clear articulation of weak syllables.—B 61.

262 Town of West Rutland, Rutland Co.

Set off from Rutland in 1886. Rutland first settled in 1770 (granted in 1761 by N.H.) by families from the Hudson Valley; most settlers from Conn.: Simsbury (24), Middletown (38), Wallingford (36), Coventry; Pomfret (49); Salisbury, Stamford (1). Others from e. Mass. and from R.I.—Famous marble quarries, worked since c. 1845. Many Italians and Slavs in recent decades. Intimate contacts with the city of Rutland.—Pop. 1910: 3427, '30: 3421.—Pop. of Rutland Town: 1780: 1417, 1830: 2753, '50: 3715, '80: 12,149, 1910: 1311*, '30: 1387. Pop. of Rutland City (set off 1892): 1910: 13,546, '30: 17,315.—Centennial celebration of the settlement of Rutland, Vt., October 2–5, 1870, including the addresses, historical papers . . . etc. Comp. by Chauncy K. Williams. 122 p. Rutland, 1870.

1. Farmer, 71. Has worked in slate mill. Aged 30, went to live in Castleton (adjoining town).—F born in West Rutland. M born in Essex, Chittenden Co.— Grammar school. Reads only the newspapers.— Knows most of the farmers in the neighborhood.— Gruff to strangers, playful with his small grandchildren. Keen, shrewd, loquacious. One step removed from the rustic.—More old-fashioned in pronunciation than in vocabulary. Good feeling for old and modern expressions. Slow but uneven tempo. Slight nasalization. Careless utterance.

Auxiliary informant: housewife, 88. Says she 'dressmaked' 70 years. Married at 16 and left West Rutland for Castleton. (Husband was farmer, carpenter.)—F born in West Rutland. M born in Pittsford (c. 8 m. north).—School, very irregularly, until 15. Has visited a good deal in Rutland.—Belongs to lower middle and farming class. Proud of her contacts as a dressmaker with people of relatively greater wealth and culture.—Straight-backed and agile, as keen-witted and sharp as she ever was. Independent; lives alone.—Rather old-fashioned speech with some traces of acquired elegance.—Pp. 1–13 and scattered items.—B 50.

262 Town of Castleton, Rutland Co.

Settled c. 1770 (org. 1777); the principal proprietor came here from Salisbury, Conn. Settlers from c. and e. Conn.: Simsbury (24), West Hartford (40), Bethlehem; Norwich (33); others from Williamstown (248), Mass., and from Bennington Co.—Agricultural town (dairying) in slate quarrying region. Slate manufactures. Many people trade regularly in Rutland (c. 10 m. east).—Summer colony at Lake Bomoseen.—First medical college in Vt. (c. 1818 to 1854) est. here. State Normal School.—Pop. 1790: 809, 1830: 1783, '50: 3016, '80: 2605, 1910: 1885, '30: 1794.

2. Farmer, mail carrier for 23 years, 52. Lived in city of Rutland part of a year, aged 26; 1 year, aged 27, in Mechanicville, Saratoga Co., N.Y.—F, PGF, PGM born here. M born in Truthville, Washington Co., N.Y. (c. 20 m. west).—Local schools, including 1½ years of normal school. Reads a great deal.—Mason. Never held office, but knows most of the townspeople.—Well informed. Prompt in response.—Speech unguarded and unaffected. Somewhat removed from local rustic speech because of early training and extensive reading. Tempo medium to slow. No nasalization. Rather careful attention to weak sounds; articulation even of final stops usually distinct.—B 51.

264 Town of Wallingford (South Wallingford), Rutland Co.

Settled 1773 (org. 1778) from Conn.: Cornwall (18), Cheshire, Wallingford (36), Stonington (34); from Hancock, Mass., and N. Kingstown (58), R.I.—Agricultural: dairy farming, with some manufacturing (garden tools). South Wallingford was a small mill center c. 1850.—Pop. 1790: 538, 1830: 1741, '50: 1688, '80: 1846, 1910: 1719, '30: 1564.—Thorpe, Walter. History of Wallingford, Vermont. 222 p. Rutland, 1911.

Dairy farmer, 73. Aged 22 to 25, lived in Rutland (c. 15 m. north).—F born in Danby (adjoining town) of old Wallingford family, came here as a child. M born in Poultney (c. 15 m. northwest), came here as a child.—Grammar school and high school (for a short time) in Wallingford. (M a former teacher.)—Mason; belongs to the Grange. Former town officer. Used to know most people here, but has lost track of younger generation. Fair amount of social life.—

Lively mind, many interests. Sense of humor.—Speech rustic in most respects, but he uses technical and even learned words freely. Knows school precepts and the dictionary, but disregards them in practice. Good feeling for old-fashioned (versus modern) words and pronunciations. Extremely rapid tempo, which often leads to slurring of weak sounds or of whole syllables. Articulation careless, but not indistinct.—B 55.

265 Town of Mount Holly (Belmont), Rutland Co.

Settled 1781 (org. 1792); settlers came from w. Conn. (18 Cornwall), e. Conn. (Preston), R.I. and Mass. (Bedford, Middlesex Co.). Many were Quakers.—Isolated rural community. Dairying. Summer visitors.—Pop. 1830: 1318, '50: 1534, '80: 1390, 1910: 871, '30: 727.

Postmaster, 58. Works in general store. Brought up on a farm. Lived in Brooklyn, N.Y., 1 year, aged c. 27.—F born in N.H., came here aged c. 18. M born in Mt. Holly.—Grammar school. Not much formal education. Reads newspapers and light novels.—Member of I.O.O.F. Well liked. Contacts limited to the village. Meets summer visitors from Mass., Conn. and N.Y.—Intelligent and quick-witted. Kindly and obliging, for all his sharpness. Not talkative.—Pronunciation strikingly archaic in some respects, grammar less so. Vocabulary rather modern. Has good ear for dialect and reports reliably on local usage. Medium tempo. No nasalization. Articulation fairly careful. Postvocalic r exceedingly vacillating.

Auxiliary informant: former bookkeeper, 75. Born in Iowa, came here when 1½ years old. Lived 1 year in California and 7 years in Kansas, aged 48 to 56. Has also lived 6 years in Rutland (c. 15 m. northwest) and 23 years in Wallingford (adjoining town west).—F born in Canada, but came here when a child; PGF born here. M born here.—Grammar school (not for long) and 1 or 2 terms of high school, both in Ludlow, Windsor Co. (adjoining town east).—Pp. 1–10, starred forms.—B 54.

266 Town of Plymouth (1 Tyson; 2 Plymouth Union), Windsor Co.

Settled 1777, org. 1787. Large influx 1790–1800. Pop. from e. Worcester Co. (Mass.), e. Mass. and se. Vt.—Rural town with decreasing population. Many summer visitors.—Pop. 1830: 1240, '50: 1226, '80: 1075, 1910: 482, '30: 331.

1. Retired farmer and cattle dealer, 73. Was deputy sheriff and for several years ass't. judge.—F born in Cavendish (c. 10 m. southeast); PGF from Littleton, Middlesex Co., Mass., was in War of 1812; GGF from Littleton, was in Revolution. M born in Reading (adjoining town east); her family from Walpole, Cheshire Co., N.H. (c. 30 m. southeast).—Grammar school. Several years of high school in Ludlow (adjoining town south). Aged 32 to 35, traveled in mowing machine business. In

State Legislature 2 years. (F was only physician in town. Older brother professor of agriculture.) Has written articles for Vt. newspapers.—Knows many people throughout this part of the state. Rather high social standing here. Popular.—Very amiable and coöperative.—Speech lacks the harshness, loudness and nasality of that of his wife and of many people in the town. Slight tremor occasionally. Medium tempo, slower than the average here. Fairly clear utterance, never laborious, now and then indistinct. Short vowels. Final consonants weak.—HN 1.

2. Housewife, 48. Taught school 2 years, aged c. 17 to 19. Has been town clerk for the past 13 years. Lived 6 months in N.H.; 1½ years, aged 24 to 25, in Dedham, Norfolk Co., Mass.—F from Cornish, Sullivan Co., N.H. (c. 20 m. east). M born here, descended from first settlers. (Husband not a native.)—Grammar school here. High school less than 2 years in Ludlow.—Normal social contacts in and around the town.—Semicultured informant, rather on guard at first. Represents newer trend in local usage. Little influenced by other dialects. Tried to be 'correct' and precise, especially at the beginning. Rather rapid tempo. Harsh voice and nasalization. Vowels mostly short, often simple rather than diphthongal. Retroflection more frequent in replies to questions than in unguarded conversation.—HN 2.

268 Town of Windsor, Windsor Co.

Settled 1764 from Farmington, Conn. (q.v., 20)· Many settlers from e. Conn. and the lower Conn· Valley; others from e. Mass.—Important center in early Vt.: the constitution of Vt. adopted here; often a meeting-place of the General Assembly up to 1805. Sheep raising and woolen mills c. 1820; firearms after the 1830's; machine shops since c. 1890. By 1900 dairy farming had replaced sheep raising as the chief agricultural enterprise. Rather large foreign elements: French-Canadians, Poles, Russians.—Pop. 1790: 1542, 1830: 3134, '50: 1928*, '80: 2175, 1910: 2407, '30: 4359 (Windsor village 3689).—Dana, Richard T. The bridge at Windsor, Vt., and its economic implications. New York, 1926. Wardner, Henry Steele. The birthplace of Vermont: a history of Windsor to 1781. New York, 1927. Wilson, Harold Fisher. The roads of Windsor. The Geographical Review 21 (1931), 379–97.

1. Retired farmer, 76. For the last 26 years has built, rented and sold houses.—GF started present farm in 1788. (Wife born in Claremont, Sullivan Co., N.H.; her F in Bethel, Windsor Co., Vt.; her M here).—2 or 3 years of high school. Refused to go to Dartmouth College. (His brother attended the college and later taught there.) Has never been away except for short trips.—Has held town offices. Highly respected. Religious; generous to charities.—Pleasant, agreeable, rather slow. Refused to help with the investigation at first, but later enjoyed it.—Has

practically no affectations. (Wife, who was present at all interviews, leans toward 'correctness.') Speaks slowly, but in jerky spurts. Articulation not over-exact. Not much nasalization.—Auxiliary informant: wife.—HN 4.

2. Postmaster (for the last 10 years), 54. Previously a machinist, plumber, railroad man. Born on a farm. Lived for a time, aged c. 20, in Poughkeepsie, Dutchess Co., N.Y. Has spent short period in White River Junction (c. 12 m. north) and 6 months in Springfield, Mass.—F, PGF born here. M from Mich.—1 year of high school. Later 4 or 5 months at business college in Poughkeepsie. Has done a small amount of traveling.—Belongs to several organizations. Calls most of the people here by their first names.—Sociable, friendly; helpful, but busy and inclined to begrudge the time given. Absent-minded. Likes to tell stories.—Speaks naturally and carelessly, though he tries to be 'correct' in guarded speech. In conversation regularly uses such forms as *I give, we done* (preterites), etc. Tempo somewhat slow. Not much nasalization. Final consonants tend to be dropped.—HN 3.

271 Town of Stockbridge, Windsor Co.

Settled 1784–85 (org. 1792) from e. Conn.: Hampton, Pomfret (49); and from Gardner, Mass., and Hillsborough, N.H.—Agricultural town, deep in the mountains east of the main ridge. Decreasing population, mostly old stock.—Pop. 1790: 100, 1830: 1333, '50: 1327, '80: 1124, 1910: 737, '30: 460.

1. Farmer, 67.—F born here. M born in Royalton (c. 10 m. east), came here at 28 when she married.—Grammar school until 16. Went on visits of six weeks each, long ago, to Bethel (adjoining town) and to Keene, Cheshire Co., N.H.—Has held town office. Friends are mostly 'old-timers.'—Runs his big farm almost single-handed. Good-humored; kind and gentle. Alert, with memory unimpaired.—Speech definitely archaic and radically different from the speech of northwestern Vt. Slow, muffled, careless articulation.—Auxiliary informant: brother.—B 49.

2. Farmer, laborer, 64. Spent 2½ years in Randolph, Orange Co. (c. 10 m. northeast). As a boy lived 2½ years in Pittsfield, Rutland Co. (adjoining town west of here), and 2½ years in Barnet, Caledonia Co. Aged c. 27 to 38, lived in Hudson, Middlesex Co., Mass. Aged c. 47 to 50, lived in Franklin Park, N.J. Aged c. 50 to 63, lived in Rochester (adjoining town north of here).—F born here. M born in Canada, came here as a child; MGF, MGM born here or nearby.—Grammar school here and for a short time in Barnet.—Lives alone. Not much social life. Knows townspeople pretty well.—Extremely poor. Kind, hospitable and friendly. Keen-minded and quizzically humorous. Thoroughly pleasant to work with.—Definitely rustic and fairly old-fashioned local dialect. Although he lived in eastern Mass. for 10 years, he appears to be representative

of the community in which he grew up, and in (or near) which he has spent the greater part of his life. Can point out certain features in which his speech differs from that of other sections. Tempo very slow. Nasalization weak, but perceptible. Articulation often indistinct. Lack of upper front teeth makes him occasionally pronounce *v* bilabially.—B 62.

272 Town of Northfield (1 West Hill district; 2 Northfield village), Washington Co.

Settled c. 1785, many of the early settlers coming from Conn.—Granite works, also textiles. Since 1867 seat of Norwich University (military, founded in 1819 at Norwich).—West Hill district is mostly woods.—Pop. 1790: 40, 1830: 1411, '50: 2922, '80: 2836, 1910: 3226, '30: 3438 (Northfield village 2075).—Gregory, John. 1776–1876: Centennial proceedings and historical incidents of the early settlers of Northfield, Vt. . . . 319 p. Montpelier, 1878.

1. Farmer's wife, 69. Has hardly been out of town, or off her own back hill, more than 3 or 4 times.—F born here. M born in Claremont, Sullivan Co., N.H., came here when a child.—Grammar school in this section.—Secluded life. Sees few people except a dozen families on the hill.—Fairly intelligent. Lively sense of humor.—Rustic speech, not much influenced by her respect for correctness. Remembers old-fashioned pronunciations and words used in childhood. Her pronunciation is extremely unstable, perhaps affected by that of her M (born in southwestern N.H.). Rapid tempo. Strong nasalization. Vowels rather long and very open. Postvocalic *r* rare in natural conversation, but introduced when a word is pronounced in isolation or with great emphasis.—B 73.

2. Retired mail carrier (22 years), 70. When a young man, worked for a while on the railroad.—F born in Pepperell, Middlesex Co., Mass. M born in Underhill, Chittenden Co. (c. 30 m. northwest).—Grammar school.—Mason. Not a sociable man, but knows townspeople fairly well.—Sententious. Excellent memory.—Extensive familiarity with rustic and archaic speech. His own is rather modern. Like many Vermonters, he can point out with amusement words peculiar to natives of N.Y. or N.H. Speaks slowly—as it were, grudgingly. Nasalizes markedly.—B 72.

274 Town of Cornwall, Addison Co.

Settlement begun 1774; abandoned during Revol. War. In 1784 c. 30 families came from Conn. (esp. Cornwall, q.v., 18).—Prosperous agricultural town, chiefly dairying; formerly sheep-raising and horse-breeding. Decreasing population.—Pop. 1790: 825, 1830: 1264, '50: 1155, '80: 1070, 1910: 789, '30: 640.—Matthews, Lyman. History of the town of Cornwall, Vermont. 356 p. Middlebury, 1862.

1. Retired carpenter (cabinet maker, wagoner, etc.), 88. At age of 12 moved to Weybridge (c. 6 m.

north), lived there 10 years. Aged 22 to 29, in business in Saratoga Springs, Saratoga Co., N.Y. In Boston aged c. 29 to 37; then returned here.—Parents and grandparents born here. (His late wife born here, of old local family.)—School in Cornwall and Weybridge until 16; then learned his trade. Has read a good deal and still reads daily newspaper. Radio helps him to keep abreast of the times. Information extensive.—A good churchman (Congregationalist), fairly liberal. Formerly member of the Grange.—Kindly, eager to make friends, courteous and considerate. Memory excellent, now and then somewhat slow in functioning.—Old-fashioned rustic speech with a considerable addition of book language. Able to distinguish between his literary and his homelier vocabulary. Speaks slowly and clearly, but with very weak articulation of unstressed syllables and final consonants, and with a rather noticeable nasal twang.—B 52.

2. Farmer, carpenter, 54.—F born here; PGF, who wrote a history of this town, born in Braintree, Orange Co. (c. 22 m. east); PGF's F lived on farm where informant now lives; PGM born near Boston. M, MGF, MGM born here.—Began his education at home. Grammar school in Middlebury (c. 4 m. north). Then 3½ months at Vt. Academy, Saxtons River, Windham Co.—Formerly a member of the Grange. Has held town office for last 20 years. Knows nearly everybody here. Lives with his mother.—Reserved, taciturn. Every word had to be wrung from him by explicit questions. Extremely slow thinker.—Responses, especially in the matter of morphology, usually guarded and consciously 'correct.' Lack of natural conversation on his part made it difficult to check artificial forms. He commented on specific instances in which N.Y. or eastern Vt. speech differed from what he felt to be 'correct.' Low-pitched, almost lifeless voice. Tempo very slow. Intonation monotonous. Enunciation, in general, over-careful. Phonemes fairly stable.—B 53.

276 Town of Ferrisburg (1 North Ferrisburg; 2 Ferrisburg), Addison Co.

Settled 1784–5 from Bennington (q.v., 252) and from Conn.—Entirely agricultural; no center or village proper, except for the 'Four Corners' with the general store. Formerly many Quakers.—Pop. 1790: 481, 1830: 1822, '50: 2075, '80: 1684, 1910: 1433, '30: 1285.

1. Farmer, carpenter, 69. Used to run a garage. Has many brief visits to Florida and Canada, but dislikes being away from Vt.—F born in Bristol (c. 10 m. southeast); PGF from Conn. M born in Hinesburg, Chittenden Co. (c. 8 m. northeast).—Grammar school in Ferrisburg; 3 years at Green Mountain Seminary, Waterbury, Washington Co. (c. 25 m. east).—Belongs to Masons and the Grange. Active in town politics.—Difficult of approach, but all kindness and hospitality on nearer acquaintance. Short-

spoken, independent. All his loyalties center in his town and state, but he is awake also to the affairs of the world outside. Alert, quick-minded, with keen sense of humor. Loves the woods and mountains around him with almost poetic passion.—His one trait not typical of rural Vt. is his contempt for school education. Speech perfectly unguarded and unaffected. Contemptuous of 'modern' or 'citified' expressions. Speaks rapidly when sure of his ground; otherwise in grudging monosyllables. Monotonous intonation with long sequences of unstressed syllables. Rather strong nasalization. Initial *p, t, k* often unaspirated. Final consonants weak.—B 45.

2. Farmer's wife, seamstress, 81. Assistant postmistress (as a girl) and storekeeper. Born in Fond du Lac, Wis., came here aged 3.—F born in Canada, died when informant was 3. M, MGM born here; Scotch ancestry on MGF's side. Husband born in Middlebury (c. 14 m. south).—Private school here 'off and on' until 14; public school, aged 14 to 15; then a year at boarding school in Newbury, Orange Co. (c. 60 m. east). Lately has become a great reader of the Bible and of novels, including dialect stories.—Many contacts in the town. Influential in town politics. 'I'm a Republican, a Protestant and a Prohibitionist.'—Independent. Sentimental, kindhearted. Sense of humor and *joie de vivre.*—Speech genuinely local. Has some consciousness of a 'correct' standard, and avoids expressions such as *ain't* and *to home,* which, nevertheless, crop up in her conservation. Has command of vocabulary and imagery (largely Biblical) that comes only from wide reading. Her fear of giving offense made her refuse to utter words like 'fool' and 'miser.' Very rapid tempo. Length of vowels and clearness of final syllables vary considerably with relative emphasis. Initial voiceless stops frequently unaspirated. No nasalization.—B 44.

278 Town of Huntington, Chittenden Co.

Settled 1786 from Manchester and Sunderland, Bennington Co.; some of the other early settlers from Conn., and from Dutchess and Westchester Counties in N.Y. Settlement of Manchester was begun in 1764 from Dutchess Co. First settlers of Sunderland came c. 1766 from Guilford, Conn. (q.v., 28).—Small, self-contained, isolated upland valley town. Scattered farms; dairies, sawmills.—Pop. 1830: 923, '50: 885, '80: 808, 1910: 760, '30: 621.—*Manchester:* Munson, Loveland. The early history of Manchester, an address delivered . . . December 27, 1875. 63 p. Manchester, 1876.

1. Farmer, 77.—F born in Buels Gore 'just over the line' (unorganized township or division, with population of 18 in 1840, of 4 in 1930). M born here. All grandparents born here or in neighboring towns. (Wife born in a neighboring town.)—Grammar school. Not much education. (Wife formerly taught in local ungraded school 4 or 5 years.) No travel; even

visits to near-by towns have been rare.—Has been town officer. Knows everybody here.—Good-natured. A hard worker. Mentally slow, unimaginative. Somewhat deaf.—Speech fairly archaic, though he has weeded out some specific archaisms (probably at his wife's insistence). On the whole, his responses were natural and unguarded. Speaks slowly and with a mimimum of muscular effort. Does not nasalize.—Auxiliary informant: retired farmer, 75.—B 46.

2. Farmer, 54.—F, PGF, PGM born here. M born in Enosburg Center, Franklin Co. (c. 45 m. north), came here to teach and soon married.—Grammar school.—Too busy to accept town office. Social contacts center about his farm.—Taciturn. Cheerful, alert, intelligent.—Saw little sense in the questions, but answered them quickly and well. Responses always natural. Speech strongly nasalized, but articulated with a fair amount of precision and energy. Many phonemes are of an archaic type.—Auxiliary informant: wife.—B 47.

280 City of Burlington, Chittenden Co.

Settled 1774–75 (granted 1763 by N.H.); abandoned during Revolution; reoccupied 1783 (org. 1797, inc. as city 1865). Many early settlers from Conn.—Lumber trade with Canada throughout the 19. cent. Steamships introduced 1809. The Champlain Canal (1823), connecting Lake Champlain with the Hudson River, opened the New York market; the railroads established connections with New York and Boston. Cotton mills and other industries now. —French-Canadians since c. 1860; Irish and Italians. —Seat of the University of Vermont (chartered 1791).—Pop. 1790: 330, 1830: 3525, '50: 7585, '80: 11,365, 1910: 20,468, '30: 24,789.—Benedict, Robert Dewey. Charter history of the University of Vt., an address delivered . . . June 24, 1891. 46 p. Free Press Ass'n., Burlington, 1892.—Burlington, Vt., as a manufacturing . . . and commercial center, with sketches of its history . . . and institutions. Published for the Board of Trade. 152 p. Glens Falls, New York, 1889.

1. Retired farmer, 81. Has also 'rustled freight' at the railroad station. Born in Shelburne (c. 8 m. south), came here as an infant. Spent most of his life on a farm to the south of the city proper, his later years in a kind of slum district.—F born in or near Shelburne (informant is very uncertain). M probably born in Shelburne, died when he was 14.—Grammar school in South Burlington. 'I've got a *fair* education: I can read and write and spell, and figger some.' —Restricted contacts, on low social level.—Feeble, sickly, indigent. Loquacious on a variety of irrelevant subjects. No understanding of the investigation.—Speech basically archaic, noticeably altered by conscious efforts. Affects a grandiloquent style, even in casual conversation.—Incomplete record: long work sheets pp. 1–10, short work sheets pp. 11–43, and scattered items.—B 41.

2. Fireman, 50. Used to work in a lumber yard.— F, PGM born in Shelburne; PGF from Ireland. M born here; MGF, MGM from Ireland. (Wife a French-Canadian.)—Grammar school until 12.— Knows people all over the city. His circle definitely of the lower class, urban in type. Though he knows many French-Canadians, he has never learned a word of French.—Wide-awake, intelligent. Courteous and eager to oblige. Information on farm life acquired from hearsay.—Perfect representative, linguistically and in other respects, of lower-class urban society. All responses natural and unguarded. Speaks in moderate tempo, without nasalization, and with fairly clear articulation. No definitely Irish speech habits.—B 42.

280 Town of Charlotte, Chittenden Co.

Settled 1784. Many from Conn.; some from Lanesborough, Berkshire Co., Mass. (settled c. 1761, also from Conn.).—Rural community c. 12 m. south of Burlington. Orchards. Summer colonies. Ferry to N.Y. established 1790.—Pop. 1790: 635, 1830: 1702, '50: 1634, '80: 1342, 1910: 1163, '30: 1089.

3. CULTURED INFORMANT. University professor of Classical languages, 40. Aged 18, left Charlotte for college, but has lived here a good deal from time to time. Last 11 years in Burlington.—F's family in Conn., near New Haven, from 1654 to the 1780's; then moved here. M's family came here from Williston (c. 12 m. northeast) c. 1850. All his relatives derive from old Vt. settlers.—Grammar school here. High school 2 years in Shelburne (adjoining town north), 1 year in Bakersfield, Franklin Co. (c. 40 m. northeast). U. of Vt., Harvard: A.M. 1916, Ph.D. 1921. At Harvard aged 23 to 27. Aged 27 to 29 in Italy and Greece.—Up to the age of 18 his contacts were limited; since then they have included chiefly academic circles in this country and abroad.— Thoroughly cultivated man with rustic background. —In morphology and syntax he conforms to the written language; in pronunciation he retains a good many local peculiarities. His speech is natural—free from affectations and the influence of other dialects. Though he was not brought up in Burlington, he may be taken to represent cultivated usage in the city. Feeling for his native idiom is very keen. Remembers many old-fashioned forms heard from parents and grandparents. Speaks slowly; articulates very distinctly, with slight nasalization. Most striking personal peculiarity is a strongly labialized and velarized r.—B 43.

281 Town of South Burlington, Chittenden Co.

Set off from Burlington (q.v., 280) in 1865.— Agricultural.—Pop. 1880: 664, 1910: 927, '30: 1203.

Retired farmer, 76. Lived 7 years in Burlington (c. 30 years ago).—Represents the 5th generation of his family in the town.—Local grammar school and 2 terms at Shelburne Academy (adjoining town south). Feels his lack of education rather keenly. Reads a great deal since he gave up managing his farm.—Has held a number of town offices. Used to know everybody here.—Laconic, quiet, kindly. Alert and intelligent.—Usage firmly fixed. Answered the questions rapidly and surely. Often would remark, 'That ain't proper, but that's the way we say it around here.' Speech slow, un-nasalized, articulated without much energy or clearness. Diphthongs waver between archaic and newer types. Postvocalic r also wavers.—B 48.

282 Town of Calais (1 North Calais; 2 East Calais), Washington Co.

Settled 1787 from Charlestown, Mass. (now part of Boston), and vicinity.—Granite quarries.—North Calais is an isolated farming community; East Calais a rural village with a sawmill and considerable dairying.—Barre (c. 12 m. south) is the shopping center.—Pop. 1790: 45, 1830: 1539, '50: 1410, '80: 1253, 1910: 1042, '30: 811.

1. Farmer, storekeeper for the past 10 years, 73. As a boy, lived 1 year in East Montpelier (c. 8 m. south) and less than a year in Cabot (c. 10 m. east). —F born in East Montpelier in 1819. M born in Calais.—Grammar school, winters only.—Belongs to Modern Woodmen. Has held several town offices, but retired from politics 12 years ago.—A cherubic old man with a kindly face. Noted among his townsmen for his memory. Intelligence now a little fogged. —Speech habits firmly set. His information proved more than adequate, but his memory of an older type of speech was disappointing. Tempo slow. Nasalization not very strong. The instability of phonemes, characteristic of Calais speech, made recording difficult.—B 71.

2. Retired farmer, 85. Kept general store 25 years. Town clerk 26 years.—Parents born in Calais. 2 grandparents born in Montpelier (c. 10 m. southwest); 1 elsewhere in Vt.; 1 in N.H.—Calais Grammar school. 3 years at Barre Academy, Barre. Reads a great deal of magazine fiction.—Mason. Has held several town offices. Used to know everyone here. Enjoys visiting with his neighbors at the general store.—Good-natured, frankly enjoying the ease and freedom of his retirement from active life. Confronted by a stranger, he showed the caution typical of a rustic dignitary; but was affable and friendly when his suspicions were allayed.—Speech in some respects fairly old-fashioned. In grammar especially, and in the pronunciation of certain words, he has consciously modernized his usage. Slow tempo. Some nasality.

Auxiliary informant: his cousin and housekeeper, who has had much the same training and heritage. Her speech is more old-fashioned than his, both in vocabulary and phonology.—B 70.

284 Town of Johnson, Lamoille Co.

Settled 1784 from N.H.: New Boston (322), Amherst (320); others from Belchertown and elsewhere in Mass.—Agricultural: cattle raising and dairying. Johnson village is industrial: woolen mill, sawmills, talc manufacturing, woodworking.—Normal School since 1866.—Pop. 1790: 93, 1830: 1079, '50: 1381, '80: 1495, 1910: 1526, '30: 1378.—Baker, Mattie W. History of the town of Johnson, Vt., 1784–1907. 83 p. Burlington, 1907.

1. Farmer, 64. Until recently he lived on the big hill farm where he was born; when forced to sell it, he moved into the village, where he still farms on a reduced scale.—F born in Bakersfield, Franklin Co. (c. 13 m. northwest), came here as a young man. M born here; MGF came from Ireland as a young man.—Attended grammar school very irregularly until c. 18.—No clubs or organizations. Has held town office. Used to know everybody in town, but is not acquainted with the newcomers.—His whole existence has centered in his farm. His information in this field is authoritative; of other subjects he knows little.—Very archaic type of speech. No knowledge of any other dialect. Rather strong nasalization. Slow, deliberate drawl. Vowels very long, sometimes almost dissyllabic, and often followed by an off-glide. Articulation extremely lax; assimilation common.

Auxiliary informant: wife, 57. Born in West Fairlee, Orange Co. (c. 55 m. southeast); at the age of 2, moved to Hyde Park (c. 5 m. southeast), where she lived for 18 years. Came here at 20.—F born here. M born in Hyde Park.—Grammar school in Hyde Park.—Speech quite as natural and unaffected as her husband's. She too nasalizes, and her drawl is even more marked than his. (As a child she had to speak very slowly to overcome stammering.) Articulates clearly and carefully, almost painstakingly.—B 39.

2. Farmer, 77. Born in what was then the town of Sterling, later annexed to Johnson.—F born here of old local family. M born in Morristown (c. 8 m. south).—Grammar school here. A few terms at high school in Morrisville (in the town of Morristown).—Formerly belonged to the Grange. Well known to all the townsmen and rather highly regarded.—Courteous and obliging. Intelligence above average. Sense of humor evident in his vast fund of entertaining anecdotes.—Although he is older than informant 1, his speech is much less archaic, partly because of his superior education. He has a sure feeling for local usage, and in his anecdotes consciously changed his own level of grammar and pronunciation to that of less literate speakers. Speech slightly nasalized, slow in tempo, enunciated with clearness but not with precision.—B 40.

3. Farmer, 56.—Both parents born here of old local families.—School until 16. (Wife was a school-teacher c. 30 years ago.)—Has a wide circle of friends and is apparently well liked.—Vigorous, hard-working, fairly prosperous. Not gifted with much imagination, but intelligent in a practical, hard-headed way.—Fairly natural speech, though on guard at times. Usage unsettled on certain points, as reflected in hesitating responses. Appears to have some feeling for local idiom. Moderate tempo. Monotonous intonation. Some nasalization. Fairly clear articulation.—Incomplete record: long work sheets pp. 1–12, short work sheets pp. 13–53, and scattered items.—B 38.

286 Town of Enosburg, Franklin Co.

Granted to General R. Enos by Vt. in 1780. Settled 1797, largely from se. Vt. (Marlboro, Royalton, Sharon, Strafford); others from Pownal and Charlotte, Vt., and from Conn.—Agricultural town with business and social center at village of Enosburg Falls. In the 19. cent. the village was noted for patent medicines; now a shopping center.—Pop. 1830: 1560, '50: 2009, '80: 2213, 1910: 2212, '30: 2093 (Enosburg Falls village 1195).

1. Farmer's wife, 81. Taught district school 2 years, aged 22 to 24.—F born here; PGF came here from Bennington, Bennington Co., at the age of 21. M born in Bakersfield (adjoining town south).—Local grammar school and academy in Barre, Washington Co. (c. 50 m. south). 2 years at normal school in Johnson, Lamoille Co. (c. 20 m. south). Has made 2 western trips of a couple of weeks each.—Member of Farm Bureau. Associates mostly with farmers of the community.—Information about rural life deficient despite many years on the farm. Little interest in the interviews.—Has shaken off the more obviously old-fashioned traits of her speech. Responses often guarded; conversation restrained. Rapid but spasmodic tempo: a sort of hasty ejaculation of disjointed phrases. Fairly clear enunciation. Nasalization rare. Frequent glottalization.—B 33.

2. Farmer, 47.—Both parents born here of old local families.—Grammar school. (M was a school-teacher here and carefully instructed her children in 'correct' grammar.)—Mason; belongs to the Grange. Has held town office. Well acquainted here.—His whole life bound up in his farm and in local affairs.—Pronunciation local. Grammatical forms and syntax largely standardized through M's influence. Rapid, spasmodic tempo. Glottalization extremely frequent. Great fluctuation in the first element of diphthongs. —B 34.

3. Proprietor of gasoline filling station, 32. Worked 1½ years in automobile plant in Burlington; 5 months in Bristol, Hartford Co., Conn.; 5 months in Detroit, Mich.; and 2 months in Flint, Mich.—F born in Enosburg of old local family. M born in Berkshire (adjoining town north).—Grammar school.— I.O.O.F. Prominent in local affairs.—Local speech with some admixture resulting from outside con-

tacts. Informant is keenly aware of certain differences between his natural speech and what he calls city speech, but has no desire to modify his own. He reported many changes in local speech that have recently occurred.—Short work sheets.—B 35.

288 Town of Troy, Orleans Co.

Settled c. 1800 (org. 1802) from Peacham, Caledonia Co., and other towns on the upper Conn. River in Vt. and N.H.—Rather isolated hill town, c. 10 m. west of Newport. Formerly lumbering, now dairy farming.—North Troy village is industrial: formerly iron mine and blast furnace, now manufacturing of plywood and veneer products.—Pop. 1830: 608, '50: 1008, '80: 1522, 1910: 1686, '30: 1898 (N. Troy village 1045).

1. Farmer, now school janitor, 76. Born in Westfield (adjoining town west), came here aged 18. Lived 1½ years in Wisconsin.—F born in Bath, Grafton Co., N.H., came here as a young man. M born in Westfield (or possibly in Troy).—Grammar school in Westfield. 'I ain't got no education.'—Many cronies among the old men. Universally liked; called by his first name by old and young.—Radiates good humor, kindliness and sly wit. Interests are all local and present: the outside world hardly concerns him, and his memories are not nearly so important to him as the day's latest news.—First-rate informant. Usage fixed. Knows nothing of grammatical distinctions. Loquacious, racy in his idioms, full of anecdote and proverbial wisdom. Articulation careless but clear, free from nasalization and glottalization.—B 36.

2. Farmer, 38. Also shoe repairer, tinker, carpenter, etc. (Practically everything that needs repairing is brought to his shop.)—F born in Georgia, Franklin Co. (c. 40 m. west), came here aged 15. M born here.—10 years of school.—Mason. Respected as a craftsman and generally liked. His shop is a gathering place for the men of the town.—Handsome, swarthy young giant, rather taciturn except among his friends; a great worker. Intelligence and quick imagination.—Good feeling for differences between his own speech and that of the older generation. Responses for the most part natural. Many items observed in conversation. Tempo rapid. Articulation fairly clear, not meticulous. No nasalization. Vowels rather short.—B 37.

290 Town of Lemington, Essex Co.

Settled from Conn. c. 1781.—Isolated rural community.—Pop. 1790: 31, 1830: 183, '50: 187, '80: 222, 1910: 138 '30: 133.

Farmer and photo-retoucher, 57.—F born here; PGF born in Vt. or N.H., of eastern Mass. ancestry; PGM born here of Conn. ancestry. M born in Dixville, Prov. of Quebec (a few miles across the Canadian border); MGF born in northern N.H.; MGM born in N.H. of Plymouth ancestry.—School until

18.—Genial, fairly modern in point of view though living in such a remote community. Brother more old-fashioned.—Rather drawling speech. All vowels and diphthongs somewhat centralized. Confusing variation from one style of speech to another.— L 108.

292 Town of St. Johnsbury (St. Johnsbury Center), Caledonia Co.

Settled c. 1786 from Providence, R.I. (q.v., 80), by Jonathan Arnold and associates; others from Petersham, Mass., and from Winchester and Fitzwilliam, N.H.—In 1856 the county seat was moved here from Danville (adjoining town west).—Industrial prosperity began c. 1830, when Thaddeus Fairbanks patented his lever scale. At present St. Johnsbury is the most important town in ne. Vt. Famous for its manufacture of scales, shipped all over the world, and for its maple sugar industry.—St. Johnsbury Academy founded 1842.—St. Johnsbury Center is a quiet residential suburb, c. 3 m. north of the village proper.—Pop. 1790: 143, 1830: 1592, '50: 2758, '80: 5800, 1910: 8098, '30: 9696 (St. Johnsbury village 7920).—Fairbanks, Edward T. The town of St. Johnsbury, Vt., a review of 125 years to the anniversary pageant, 1912. 592 p. St. Johnsbury, 1914.

1. Retired farmer, 81. When a young man, worked 15 years in scales factory here. Until recently lived always on a farm.—F, PGF, PGM born here. M, MGF born here.—Went to log schoolhouse in the country intermittently until 15 or 16.—Formerly belonged to the Grange.—Typical local farmer of older uneducated school, with reserved, formal outlook. Keen-minded. Much interested in his ancestors.—Good informant. Reported many old-fashioned words he used as a boy. Vowels rather long. —L 110.

292 Town of Lyndon (East Lyndon section), Caledonia Co.

Chartered 1780 to Jonathan Arnold of Providence, R.I. (q.v., 80). Settled 1788. Most of the early settlers came from R.I. and from Rehoboth (104) and Seekonk, Mass.; others from the interior of Mass. and the Conn. Valley.—Semi-mountainous country. The village of Lyndon Center has long been known for its academy, Lyndon Institute. The village of Lyndonville was for some time after 1866 the headquarters of a division of the B.&M.R.R., and flourished as a railroad center.—East Lyndon is rural.—Pop. 1790: 59, 1830: 1822, '50: 1752, '80: 2434, 1910: 3204, '30: 3285 (Lyndonville village 1559).—Greenleaf, Jonathan. A sketch of the settlement of the town of Lyndon. . . . 24 p. Middlebury, 1852.

2. Farmer, 68. When c. 21, spent 1½ years in Scituate, Plymouth Co., Mass.—F born here; PGF born in Danville (c. 12 m. southwest); PGM born in

Mass.; GGF born in R.I. M, MGF born in St. Johnsbury (c. 7 m. south).—Lyndon Institute and St. Johnsbury Academy until 18.—Obliging, friendly, democratic. Intelligent and quick to respond. Not inclined to express his emotions.—Casual, succinct manner of speaking: not rapid or precise. Vowels tend to be very short in most positions. The diphthong as in *cow* varies from [ɛʊ] to [aʊ] and is short, as in the speech of many people in northern Vt. and northern N.H. *b* and *d* tend to be velarized.— L 109.

294 Town of Ryegate (1 North Ryegate section; 2 Ryegate), Caledonia Co.

Founded 1773 (org. 1776) by a colony of Scotchmen from Glasgow led by James Whitelaw and David Allen, who purchased the territory from Dr. Witherspoon, president of Princeton.—The town developed as a dairying community.—The Scotch here are democratic, but clannish and proud of their race. The surrounding towns, Barnet, Peacham and Groton in this county, and Topsham and Newbury in Orange Co. (q.v., 296), also have many Scotch inhabitants.—North Ryegate is rural, remote, hilly and wooded. East Ryegate has a paper mill; South Ryegate has granite works.—Pop. 1790: 187, 1830: 1119, '50: 1606, '80: 1046, 1910: 1194, '30: 1216.— Miller, E. and F. P. Wells. History of Ryegate, Vermont. . . . 608 p. St. Johnsbury, 1913.—*Barnet:* Wells, F. P. History of Barnet, Vermont. Burlington, 1923.

1. Farmer, 63. Lived 6 years in Boston, aged 22 to 28.—F, PGF born here; PGM born in Scotland. Parents of PGF from Scotland. M, MGM born here; MGF born in Scotland. Parents of MGM were Irish Presbyterians.—Educated here until 21.—By nature an antiquarian. Was easily persuaded to answer the questions, but did not entirely understand the purpose of the investigation. Hardworking and industrious.—Considerable Yankee influence, probably, on both his character and his speech. (Informant's wife, from Topsham, whom he recently married, has a more Scotch type of speech with regard to intonation, stress and shortness of vowels.) Pronunciation not affected by notions of correctness, though his wife and stepdaughter laughed at some of his forms. Tempo deliberate. Vowels fairly short. *r* varies extremely, as with most Ryegate people.— L 112.

2. Former nurse, 71. Has also been teacher, milliner, housekeeper. At 27 began nursing here and in Barnet. Now lives in Barnet.—F born here; PGF (Scotch) born in northern Ireland; PGM of Plaistow, Rockingham Co., N.H., ancestry. M born here; MGF born in N.Y. State in 1800, while his parents (both Scotch from northern Ireland) were on a journey to Ryegate; MGM born in Antrim, northern Ireland.—Early education here. At 19 graduated from high school in Newbury (adjoining town south),

Orange Co.—Presbyterian, W.C.T.U.—Pleasant, agreeable. Glad of an opportunity to talk about the Scotch, in whom she is much interested. Fairly literate and modern.—Moderate tempo. Vowels and diphthongs short, occasionally lengthened. *r* stronger than is usual here, and always present in all positions. —L 111.

296 Town of Topsham, Orange Co.

Settled c. 1781 (org. 1790) from Francestown (q.v., 322) and other N.H. towns, and from Newbury, Mass. (q.v., 194).—Small secluded community with declining population; orchards and dairies.— Pop. 1790: 162, 1830: 1384, '50: 1668, '80: 1365, 1910: 918, '30: 720.—Craig, Frank H. Sketches of the town of Topsham, Orange Co., Vt. 198 p. Printed in Bradford, Vt., 1929.

1. Cattle dealer and farmer, 86.—Parents born here. PGF and latter's F born in England. Many families here have this informant's surname.—'I went to school half a day; the teacher didn't come, so I went home.' Never learned to write anything but his name. When about 40, learned to spell out easy passages in the newspaper.—Became local political boss by force of character and power of oratory. Has held various town offices. 'I wa'n't never learned enough to be town clerk, and I wouldn't be selectman even after they'd elected me to it!' Served in the State Legislature; was notorious for his vigorous and often profane speeches.—Tremendous self-confidence and personal magnetism. Keen intelligence. Exhaustive information on all familiar subjects. Now blind and crippled by 'rheumatiz.'—Most of the record was jotted down from his incessant flow of conversation, reminiscence and anecdote. He retains many extremely archaic traits, and probably speaks very much as his father did in the early 19. cent. No school or book influence. When he said that a certain form was wrong or 'incorrect,' he meant only that it did not sound natural to him. Rapid tempo. No nasalization except when fatigued. Phonemes fairly stable.—B 69.

296 Town of Newbury (Jefferson Hill section), Orange Co.

Settled 1762, largely from se. N.H. and from Newbury, Mass. (q.v., 194); the first settlement on the Conn. River north of Charlestown, N.H., and for a long time an isolated outpost. Some Scotch settlers.—Rural community. Wells River is the industrial village of the town, manufacturing paper for over a century.—Pop. 1790: 872, 1830: 2252, '50: 2984, '80: 2316, 1910: 2035, '30: 1744 (Wells River village 553).—Wells, F. P. History of Newbury, Vermont. 779 p. St. Johnsbury, 1902.

2. Housewife, 77. Taught school 8 years in neighboring towns: Corinth, Topsham, Groton.—F, PGF, PGM born here. M born here; MGF born in Marblehead, Essex Co., Mass.; MGM born here or

in Marblehead.—High school.—Congregationalist. President of Temperance Union.—A rustic type. Mind much less keen now than formerly.—Old-fashioned speech background. Very quick, nervous

tempo. Vowels and diphthongs tend to be short. Her *r* varies considerably, but is never as strong as it is among the Scotch.—FW thinks it may be of Marblehead origin.—L 107.

NEW HAMPSHIRE

302 Town of Seabrook (South Seabrook), Rockingham Co.

Settled c. 1638 (as part of Hampton, settled 1636 from 194 Newbury, Mass.) from 112 Plymouth and Ipswich, Mass.; originally under Mass. jurisdiction. Quaker meeting house built 1701. Seabrook inc. 1768 from Hampton Falls, which had been set off from Hampton.—Whaling in early 19. cent. Shoemaking, first in homes, then in factory.—The inhabitants of South Seabrook preserve many old local customs. Suspicious of strangers. Much inbreeding. Seabrook Beach is an unpretentious summer community.— Pop. 1775: 607, '90: 715, 1820: 885, '50: 1296, '80: 1745, 1910: 1425, '30: 1666.—*Hampton*: Dow, Joseph. History of the town of Hampton. . . . 2v. 1104 p. Salem, 1893. Sanborn, Victor C. Grantees and Settlement. 24 p. Salem, 1917.—*Hampton Falls*: Brown, Warren. History of the town of Hampton Falls, N.H. 2v. 637+448 p. Manchester and Concord, 1900–1918.

1. Shoe factory employee, 63. In Newburyport, Essex Co., Mass. (c. 6 m. south), aged 22 to 30.— Old local families. Parents and 3 grandparents born here.—Grammar school, 2 years of private school. Speaks French and Spanish fairly fluently and knows something of German and Italian.—Town officer; delegate to political conventions. Junior Order of United American Mechanics.—Good mind. Interested in neighbors and local affairs.—Speaks the local dialect, although he knows the literary forms. Tempo fairly rapid, articulation rather precise. Initial adverbial conjunctions and auxiliary verbs have high pitch and stress, as in British English.— L 23.

2. Grocer, formerly shoemaker, 39. Lived in Newburyport, Mass., until 16.—Old local families. Parents and grandparents born here.—Grammar school in Newburyport.—Junior Order of United American Mechanics. Makes many contacts at his store.—Frank and child-like, but also nervous and suspicious.—Vowels rather long, articulation slurred. Glottalization rather sharp and fairly strong. Intonation as in 304.1.—L 15.

304 Town of Rye, Rockingham Co.

Settled c. 1635, inc. 1726. Originally part of Portsmouth (settled c. 1623) and Hampton (see 302 Seabrook). Some of the early settlers from Rye in Sussex, England; others from Mass.—Isolated rural community; many old families. Summer guests.— Pop. 1775: 870, '90: 865, 1820: 1127, '50: 1295, '80: 1111, 1910: 1014, '30: 1081.—Parsons, Langdon B.

History of the town of Rye. 675 p. Concord, 1905.— *Portsmouth:* May, Ralph. Early Portsmouth history. 285 p. Boston, 1926.

1. Farmer, 69.—Old local families. Parents and grandparents born here.—School until 17.—Many friends among the farmers and tradesmen. Seldom goes out of town.—Loquacious and jolly.—Very rapid speech, not always precise, with much slurring and elision. Final consonants rather well articulated. Nasalization fairly prominent. Vowels tend to be short, but may be lengthened. In questions and emotional statements, intonation falls gradually without reaching the lowest level of the voice, giving the impression of a gentle quaver.—L 14.

2. Farmer, 68. Sailed to China and back when he was 16, and made a few fishing trips. Was a coast guard 5 winters. Since he left the sea, has farmed in East Rye.—F, PGF born here; PGM born in Newcastle (c. 5 m. north), descended from an Italian or Greek who was put off a ship there c. 200 years ago. Many Newcastle people bear his name.—M, MGF born in North Hampton (c. 4 m. southwest); MGM born in Hampton (c. 6 m. southwest).—School intermittently until 14.—Few social contacts. Takes summer boarders.—Quiet, slow. Leads a rather monotonous life. Wanted to stay at sea, but came home to take care of his mother; after her death he remained a farmer.—Speech entirely natural. Slow, weak utterance with some nasalization. Almost complete absence of glottal stops. (Glottal action very weak in N.H. coastal communities north of Seabrook.) Phonetic system different from that of informant 1. Lip action strong, leading to overrounded vowels. No extremely short vowels. Velar stops often represented by fricatives.—L 12.

306 Town of Lee (North Lee), Strafford Co.

Settled c. 1666, set off from Durham in 1766. Durham in turn was set off from Dover in 1732. Dover settled 1623. Many settlers from Plymouth in Devonshire and from various points along the Bristol Channel.—The northern part of the town has small farms and woods. Formerly lumbering. Decreasing population.—Pop. 1775: 954, '90: 1036, 1820: 1224, '50: 862, '80: 715, 1910: 479, '30: 376.— *Durham:* Stackpole, Everett S., Lucien Thompson and Winthrop S. Meserve. History of the town of Durham. 2v. 436+502 p. N.p., 1913.—*Dover:* Ham, John R. Bibliography of Dover. 74 p. Concord, 1892. Nye, A. E. G., comp. Dover, New Hampshire, its history and industries. 154 p. Dover, 1898. Scales, John. History of the town of Dover, v. 1. 516 p.

Manchester, 1923. Wadleigh, George. Notable events in the history of Dover. 334 p. Dover, 1913.

1. Farmer, 89. When younger, traveled 15 years through neighboring towns as butcher. Was in Civil War 3 years, aged 19 to 22, in Penn., Va. and Ga.—F born in South Lee, M in Madbury (c. 5 m. northeast).—School until 13.—G.A.R. Has been town road surveyor.—Pleasant and genial; opinionated, but never cantankerous. Still physically strong. Proud of being old-fashioned.—Genuinely rustic, archaic speech, with some modern locutions when on guard. Aside from a few recollections of the Civil War, knows only the local idiom. Remembers forms heard in childhood from elderly people. Rather slow tempo with vowels somewhat long. Articulation fairly precise, except for some medial *t*'s and *n*'s and final consonants. Frequent use of secondary stress makes his speech rhythm different from that of Essex Co., Mass. Glottalization weak, generally confined to very emphatic speech. Considerable nasalization near nasal consonants.—L 17.

2. Road contractor, lumberman, 66. Aged 21 to 31, peddled meat through country towns. Has spent last 23 years in Dover. Street Commissioner of Dover 9 years.—From old N.H. families, PGF and GGF born in Lee; latter's F born in northern Ireland, came to Durham. PGM born in Barrington (c. 6 m. north of Lee). M born in Nottingham; MGF born in Northwood; MGM born in Newmarket (Rockingham Co. towns surrounding Lee).—School in Lee until 16 or 17; 2 terms at Franklin Academy in Dover and 2 years at Northwood Seminary.—Generous, hospitable. Inspires confidence and knows how to deal with people. Slow thinker.—Has heard many dialects similar to his own and, especially during his 10 years as traveling butcher, much old-fashioned language. Does not call expressions to mind readily, but recognizes them at once when they are suggested. Slow tempo without much drawl. Vowels tend to be long. Fairly clear articulation. Nasalization rather pronounced.—Short work sheets. —L 21.

307 Town of Barrington (East Barrington), Strafford Co.

Settled c. 1732–40 from Portsmouth (see 304 Rye) and Dover (see 306 Lee); also some Scotch-Irish settlers.—Sparsely settled; much forest land. Until about 1900 there was a backward inbreeding community in the southern part of the town, known as Leathers City, to which our informant attributes a particularly archaic dialect.—Pop. 1775: 1655, '90: 2481, 1820: 1610*, '50: 1752, '80: 1497, 1910: 900, '30: 613. ·

Farmer, blacksmith, 88. Was in Civil War, stationed in Penn. For the past 12 years has lived in Lee.—F, PGF, PGM born in Barrington. M, MGF born in Barrington; MGM born in Portsmouth, Rockingham Co. (c. 16 m. southeast).—School in East Barrington until 17.—Has held local offices. Respected citizen.—Fairly good memory for older forms. Recalls Pennsylvania dialect heard during Civil War. Somewhat nasal speech, rather measured in tempo.—Long work sheets pp. 1–12, short work sheets pp. 13–103.—L 22.

308 Town of Kingston, Rockingham Co.

Set off from Hampton (see 302 Seabrook) in 1694. Settled from Hampton; others from Ipswich, Newbury, Salisbury, Lynn, Watertown, Mass.—Good farm land. Truck gardening and poultry raising. Small woodworking plant.—Pop. 1775: 961, '90: 905, 1820: 847, '50: 1192, '80: 1080, 1910: 1015, '30: 1017.— *Hampton:* Dow, Joseph. History of the town of Hampton. . . . 2v. 1104 p. Salem, 1893. Sanborn, Victor C. Grantees and Settlement. 24 p. Salem, 1917.

1. Farmer's wife, 75.—F, PGF born in North Danville (just over Kingston line); GGF and his F born in 'Hawk' (old name for Danville). M born in East Kingston (c. 3 m. east); MGF and his parents born in Brentwood (adjoining town north); MGM, her F and her PGF born in West Kingston.—School until 18. Reads magazines.—Lives on remote farm, but is often visited by friends and relatives. Eager for social contacts.—Extremely kind and hospitable. —Speech definitely N.H. in type. Tempo not as rapid as in northeastern Mass. Vowels tend to be half-long; final stressed syllables and words in isolation are very long.—L 47.

2. Farmer, 77.—Old local stock, originally settled in Hampton (c. 12 m. east).—Local schools.—Incomplete record: only pp. 7–31.—L 34.

310 Town of Loudon (Loudon Ridge), Merrimack Co.

Settled c. 1760 as part of Canterbury (settled 1727); inc. 1773. Settlers came from earlier N.H. towns, esp. Hampton (see 302 Seabrook) and Epping. (Epping had been part of the old town of Exeter until 1741. Exeter settled 1638 by Rev. John Wheelwright and other exiles from Mass.)—Rather secluded good farming district with decreasing population.—Pop. 1775: 349, '90: 1074, 1820: 1694, '50: 1552, '80: 1221, 1910: 838, '30: 801.—*Canterbury:* Lyford, James O. History of the town of Canterbury. 2v. 498 +449 p. Concord, 1912. Robinson, Charles E. Concise history of the united society of believers called Shakers. 134 p. East Canterbury, 1893.

1. Farmer, 79.—F, descended from old N.H. family, born in Rochester, Strafford Co. (c. 25 m. east), came here when 21; PGF, PGM (first cousins) born in Rochester. M born in Greenland, Rockingham Co. (c. 35 m. southeast), came here after her marriage; her F's family originally from Ireland.—Until 20 went to school in Loudon a few weeks each year.—Congregationalist. Lives on isolated farm

with his children and grandchildren; has few contacts outside his family.—Gentle, dignified, independent, reserved. Whole life centered in his religion and his farm.—Family speaks old-fashioned dialect. His speech slow and precise, with extremely monotonous intonation. Never uses glottal stops and seldom nasalizes. Final consonants usually clear. Vowels rather short, though when a word of one syllable is pronounced in isolation, the vowel is generally fully long.—C 5.

310 Town of Belmont, Belknap Co.

Settled 1761 as part of Gilmanton; inc. 1859. Settlers from older N.H. towns of Exeter, Epping (see Loudon, above), Londonderry (q.v., 318); and from Haverhill, Mass. (q.v., 190).—Agricultural.— Pop. 1880: 1226, 1910: 1390, '30: 1299.—Badger, Francis A. Historical sketch. Unpaged. Belmont, 1905.—*Gilmanton:* Lancaster, Daniel. History of the town of Gilmanton. 304 p. Gilmanton, 1845.— *Exeter:* Bell, Charles H. History of the town of Exeter. 469+88 p. Exeter, 1888.

2. Farmer and trader, 88. Born here when Belmont was part of Gilmanton. 2 years in Me., aged c. 30 to 32. Lived in Concord, Merrimack Co. (c. 18 m. south), aged 33 to 58.—F born here; PGF born in Gilmanton, his F in Exeter, Rockingham Co., and his M in Gilmanton; PGM born in Candia, Rockingham Co. (c. 30 m. south). M born in Northfield, Merrimack Co. (c. 8 m. southwest); MGF, a seafarer, went there from Me.; MGM born in Northfield, her M in Canterbury, Merrimack Co. (c. 10 m. southwest), her F believed to be of Russian descent (but name sounds Danish).—School in Belmont. Later attended a private school. Educated himself in law sufficiently to manage his own affairs.—Member of Christian Church (branch of Free Will Baptist).— Talkative and jolly, but with the reserved politeness of the old school.—Quick tempo. Strong, fairly even syllable stress. Short vowels. Speech very different from that of informant 1 from Loudon. (Speech varies greatly by families in this section.)—L 40.

312 Town of Gilford (Gunstock Hill section), Belknap Co.

Settled c. 1778 as part of Gilmanton (settled 1761); inc. 1812. Settlers from older N.H. towns of Exeter (see 310 Loudon), Portsmouth (see 304 Rye), and Loudon (q.v., 310); and from Newbury, Mass. (q.v., 194).—Rural community. Winter sports center. Summer visitors.—Pop. 1820: 1816, '50: 2425, '80: 2821, 1910: 744*, '30: 783.—100th anniversary of the incorporation of the town, 1912. 75 p. Lakeport, 1918.—*Gilmanton:* Lancaster, Daniel. History of the town of Gilmanton. 304 p. Gilmanton, 1845.

1. Retired farmer, 84. For the past 11 years has lived in Laconia (c. 6 m. southwest).—F born here; PGF born in Lee, Strafford Co., came here in 1798;

PGM born in Portsmouth, Rockingham Co. (c. 50 m. southeast), her F in Braintree, Norfolk Co., Mass., and her M in Portsmouth. M born here; MGF born in Londonderry, Rockingham Co. (c. 45 m. south); MGM born in Methuen, Essex Co., Mass. —Gilford public schools and 3 or 4 terms at Laconia Academy.—A bachelor living with his sister, aged 81. Answered the questions mechanically; did not fully understand purpose of investigation.—Very quick speech, not precise, with frequent stumbling. Unstressed syllables rather heavy. Vowels short. No trace of glottalization.—Short work sheets.—L 39.

312 City of Laconia (farming suburb), Belknap Co.

Settled c. 1748 as part of Meredith; inc. 1855, as city 1893. Settlers from older N.H. towns: Hampton (see 302 Seabrook), Kingston (q.v., 308), Exeter (see 310 Loudon); and from Lowell, Mass.—Vigorous industrial community and shopping center surrounded by farmlands and lakes. Sawmills, car shops (since 1850); manufacture of knitting machines and hosiery. Summer and winter sports.—Many French-Canadians since the last decades of the 19. cent.— Pop. 1880: 3790, 1910: 10,183, '30: 12,471. (Pop. of Meredith: 1775: 259, '90: 882, 1820: 2416, '50: 3521.)—Whittier, Horace G. Historical sketches of Lakeport. 103 p. Lakeport, 1915. (Lakeport adjoins the city proper.) Wilcomb, Edgar H. Ancient Aquadoctan, the Weirs. 56 p. Worcester, Mass., 1923.

2. Farmer, 70. Lives in sparsely populated section.—F, PGF, PGM born in Gilford (c. 6 m. northeast). M born in Meredith (in section now in Laconia); MGF born in Moultonboro, Carroll Co. (north of Laconia across Lake Winnepesaukee); MGM born in Meredith of old family there.—School until 18.—Dignified and rather pompous. Reserved. —Vocabulary not large and seemingly uninfluenced by modern tendencies. Speech and motions slow, deliberate. Monotonous intonation. No nasalization. Glottal stops rare. Consonants vigorous, even in final position. Vowels relatively long. No retroflex vowels.—C 2.

314 Town of Webster, Merrimack Co.

Settled c. 1763 as part of Boscawen (settled 1734); inc. 1860. Many early settlers from Essex Co., Mass.: Newbury (194), Amesbury, Bradford; others from Concord, Mass. (q.v., 156), and from New Boston, N.H. (q.v., 322).—Rural community.—Pop. 1880: 647, 1910: 445, '30: 360.—Coffin, Charles Carleton. History of Boscawen and Webster, 1733–1878. 666 p. Concord, 1878.

1. Farmer's wife, 96.—Both parents born here. At least 2 grandparents came from Newburyport, Essex Co., Mass.—Grammar school. Does not read much.—Lives on lonely farm in sparsely populated district. Spends her time indoors, knitting and sew-

ing, occasionally visited by her grandchildren and great-grandchildren.—Independent, reserved, always dignified, respected by her family and friends. Good sense of humor. Dislikes gossip.—Speech very quick, vigorous and staccato. No marked difference in force between stressed and unstressed syllables. No nasalization or glottal stops.—C 3.

2. Dairy farmer, 76. Has always lived in Courser Hill section of the town, except for 1 year on a farm in Illinois when he was 16.—F born here; PGF settled here from Newburyport, Mass.; PGM born in Boscawen. M, MGF born here; MGM born in West Concord, descended from first settlers of Concord (c. 12 m. southeast).—School until 16.—Social contacts through the Grange.—Pleasant and agreeable. Not highly intelligent.—Perhaps not entirely trustworthy as an informant.—L 38.

315 City of Concord, Merrimack Co.

Settled 1727 as part of Penacook plantation (granted to Mass. men by Mass. in 1725, part of N.H. since 1740). Of the 100 original settlers, 36 were from Haverhill, Mass. (q.v., 190), and 29 from Salem, N.H. (then in Mass.). Concord was incorporated in 1733 as Rumford, Mass., in 1765 as Concord, N.H. (inc. as city 1853). Many of the early settlers were from Essex Co. (194 Newbury, Bradford, Andover, Salisbury), others from Middlesex (Chelmsford, 160 Billerica, Woburn), others from the older towns in N.H.—Industries developed with the opening of the Middlesex Canal (1815) and the coming of the railroad (1842). Wagons, carriages, stage coaches built here; granite quarries. Capital of N.H.—In the village of Penacook (partly in Concord and partly in the town of Boscawen) there are woolen mills and woodworking plants employing many French-Canadians.—Pop. 1775: 1052, '90: 1738, 1820: 2838, '50: 8576, '80: 13,843, 1910: 21,497, '30: 25,228.—Bouton, Nathaniel. History of Concord. . . . 786 p. Concord, 1856. Lyford, James O., ed. History of Concord. . . . 2v. 1477 p. Concord, 1903. —*Penacook:* Brown, David Arthur. The history of Penacook, N.H., from its first settlement in 1734 up to 1900. 570 p. Concord, 1902.

CULTURED INFORMANT. Single woman, 70.—F, PGF, PGM born here. M born in Exeter, Rockingham Co. (c. 33 m. southeast).—Grammar school; then Bradford Academy in Haverhill, Mass. Reads a great deal. One trip to Europe.—Congregational Church, D.A.R., Woman's Club, Music Club.—Rather reserved, calm, dignified. Kind-hearted and hospitable. Old-fashioned in ideas and tastes. Not an original thinker.—Admires all that is English, particularly English speech. Small vocabulary. Not much familiarity with country dialects. Slow, deliberate tempo. No nasalization. Final consonants generally clear. Greater difference in force of stressed and unstressed syllables than in local folk speech.—Short work sheets.—C 4.

316 Town of Deerfield (South Deerfield), Rockingham Co.

Settled 1756–58 as part of Nottingham (settled c. 1727); inc. 1766. Settlers came from older N.H. towns (Hampton, Kingston, Epping), from northern Essex Co. (Newbury, Salisbury, Amesbury, Andover, Boxford), and from other parts of Mass. Bay (Boston, Woburn, Billerica).—Rural community with sharply decreasing population.—Pop. 1775: 929, '90: 1613, 1820: 2133, '50: 2022, '80: 1569, 1910: 917, '30: 635.—Cogswell, Elliott C. History of Nottingham, Deerfield and Northwood. 790 p. Manchester, 1878.

1. Farmer, 79.—F's family perhaps originally from Newburyport, Mass. F, PGM born here; PGF born in Candia (adjoining town southwest). M, MGF, MGM born in Candia.—School in Candia until 18. 2 terms at academy in New Hampton, Belknap Co. (c. 40 m. northwest).—Lives on remote back road and spends most of his time at home.—Sociable, warm-hearted, old-fashioned countryman. Keen sense of humor. Thought the questions were foolish, but was willing to answer them.—Uses naturally a great many archaic expressions. Speech mostly of the N.H. coast type; resembles that of 308.1. Tempo rather quick, with considerable vowel lengthening for emphasis and in final drawls.—L 46.

316 Town of Candia, Rockingham Co.

Settled 1743–48 as part of Chester (settled 1722); inc. 1763. Early settlers from older N.H. towns (Portsmouth, Hampton, Rye, Derry), from Essex Co., Mass. (Haverhill, Bradford, Newbury, Andover, Ipswich), and also from Ulster, Ireland.—Mostly agricultural. Some manufacture: shoes, hosiery. Decreasing population. Summer guests.—Pop. 1775: 744, '90: 1040, 1820: 1273, '50: 1482, '80: 1340, 1910: 993, '30: 812.—Moore, J. Bailey. History of the town of Candia . . . 528 p. Manchester, 1893.—*Chester:* Chase, Benjamin. History of the town of Chester. 702 p. Auburn, 1869. Chase, John Carroll, comp. History of Chester, . . . a supplement to the History . . . published in 1869. 535 p. Derry, 1926.

2. Farmer's wife, 61.—F, PGF, PGM born here. M, MGF, MGM born in Hooksett, Merrimack Co. (c. 10 m. northwest).—School until 17. Likes reading, chiefly travel books, but has little time to indulge herself.—Congregational Church. Social contacts limited to an occasional visit with local farm people.—Works hard looking after her family. Matter-of-fact. Rather stern and forbidding, except when something amuses her. Likes to tell anecdotes, but is uncommunicative about her own affairs, and never commits herself by giving personal opinions.—Old-fashioned speech, similar to that of informants 316.1 and 308.1. Tempo moderate; vowels fairly short.—C 10.

318 Town of Derry (East Derry), Rockingham Co.

Settled 1719 as part of Londonderry (q.v., below); inc. 1827.—Industrial village in rural surroundings. Until early 19. cent. linen weaving, introduced from Ireland, was the basic industry; then the manufacture of shoes. Pinkerton Academy est. 1814.—Pop. 1850: 1850, '80: 2140, 1910: 5123, '30: 5131.—For bibliography see Londonderry, below.

1. Farmer, 77.—F, PGF born in Derry; PGM born in Salem (c. 10 m. southeast). M, MGF, MGM born in Sandown (c. 8 m. northeast).—Incomplete record: only pp. 7–62.—L 32.

318 Town of Londonderry (Londonderry Center), Rockingham Co.

Settled 1719 by Scotch-Irish who had arrived in Boston in 1718; inc. 1722. Presbyterian Church est. 1719.—Flax culture and linen weaving introduced from Ireland. Agricultural: dairy farming, vegetables, poultry. Farms being taken up by recent immigrants.—Pop. 1775: 2590, '90: 2604, 1820: 3127, '50: 1731*, '80: 1363, 1910: 1533, '30: 1373.—Browne, George Waldo, ed. Early records of Londonderry, Windham and Derry, 1719–1762. 2v. 416+384 p. Manchester, 1908–11. (Manchester Historical Association collections, v. 5–6.) Parker, Edward L. History of Londonderry, comprising the towns of Derry and Londonderry. 358 p. Boston, 1851. Willey, George F. Book of Nutfield: a history. 367 p. Derry Depot, 1895.

2. Farmer, fruit grower, 68.—F, PGF born here; GGF born here (wife was Scotch); GGF's F Scotch (wife, daughter of an Irish lord, came from Ireland in 1719); PGM Scotch, from New Boston, Hillsborough Co. (c. 16 m. west). M born in Danvers, Essex Co., Mass.; MGF, MGM from Danvers, came here in 1861.—School here and Pinkerton Academy in Derry (c. 5 m. southeast). Fond of reading and good music. Trip to Europe.—Christian Scientist. Has held local office and served in the State Legislature.—Intelligent, level-headed, prosperous. Genial and friendly, but rather reserved.—No definitely Scotch traits in his speech. Vowels usually short.—L 48.

320 Town of Bedford, Hillsborough Co.

Settled 1737, most of the early settlers coming from northern Ireland and the Scotch-Irish town of Londonderry (q.v., 318); inc. 1750.—Rural community.—Pop. 1775: 495, '90: 897, 1820: 1375, '50: 1905, '80: 1204*, 1910: 1110, '30: 1326.—Town History Committee. History of the town of Bedford. 1132 p. Concord, 1903.

1. Farmer, 74. Born in Amherst (c. 8 m. southwest), came here aged 7 and lived here 54 years. Aged 61, returned to Amherst.—F born here; PGF, PGM born in Chelmsford, Middlesex Co., Mass. (c. 27 m. southeast). M born in Bradford, Merrimack Co. (c. 32 m. northwest).—School in Amherst and here until 13 or 14. Reads newspapers and farm magazines.—Few social contacts. All his energy concentrated on his farming.—Strong and vigorous, upright, extremely independent.—Speech is rather slow, as if he were unaccustomed to much talking, but very vigorous. Nasalization infrequent. Final consonants generally clearly articulated.—C 6.

320 Town of Amherst, Hillsborough Co.

Settled c. 1735 (inc. 1760) from eastern Mass.: Salem and vicinity, Reading, Woburn and Cambridge. Also some Scotch-Irish.—Rural community of conservative old families. Seat of the state government for a brief period and county seat for many years. Local industries perished when the railroad avoided the village. Lately some Nova Scotians, Swedes and Irish.—Pop. 1775: 1428, '90: 2369, 1820: 1622*, '50: 1613, '80: 1255*, 1910: 1060, '30: 1115.—Secomb, Daniel F. History of the town of Amherst, 1728–1882. 978 p. Concord, 1883.

2. Single woman, 86.—F, PGF, PGM born in Chelmsford, Mass. (c. 25 m. southeast). M, MGF born in Old Dunstable, now Nashua (c. 12 m. southeast).—High school until 16. Reads a good deal, especially religious books and biographies.—Congregationalist. Much interested in church work. Regarded as a leading citizen.—Erect and dignified; loquacious, but quiet in manner. Pious, strict in her ideas. Well developed sense of humor and remarkable memory.—Speech like that of informant 1, but her voice and manner of speaking, in spite of her lack of formal education, suggest the cultivated type.—C 12.

322 Town of Francestown, Hillsborough Co.

Settled 1760 by Scotch-Irish from Londonderry (q.v., 318); inc. 1772.—Remote rural community with sharply decreasing population.—Pop. 1775: 200, '90: 983, 1820: 1479, '50: 1114*, '80: 937, 1910: 602, '30: 363.—Cochrane, Warren R. and George K. Wood. History of Francestown, N.H., 1758–1891. 1016 p. Nashua, 1895.

1. Housewife, 70.—Partly of Scotch-Irish descent.—Grammar school.—Unsatisfactory informant. Afraid to commit herself on any point for fear she might be wrong.—Incomplete record: long work sheets pp. 7–29, short work sheets pp. 30–53.—L 45.

322 Town of New Boston, Hillsborough Co.

Settled 1742–8 by Scotch-Irish from Londonderry (q.v., 318); inc. 1763.—Remote rural community: dairying, poultry raising. Decreasing population. A few summer residents.—Pop. 1775: 569, '90: 1204, 1820: 1686, '50: 1477*, '80: 1414, 1910: 982, '30: 693.—Cogswell, Elliott C. History of the town of New Boston. 469 p. Boston, 1864.

2. Minister's housekeeper, 78.—Of pure Scotch-Irish ancestry, descended from early settlers.—Apparently well educated and well read.—Very

quick and intelligent. No interests apart from the church and the minister's household. Decided that answering the questions was not worth her time.—Incomplete record: only pp. 7–11, 14–24.—C 7.

324 Town of Antrim (1 North Branch section; 2 Antrim), Hillsborough Co.

Settled c. 1768 (inc. 1777) from northern Ireland and from the Scotch-Irish towns of Londonderry (q.v., 318) and New Boston (q.v., 322).—Agricultural. Some manufactures: cutlery and paper.—North Branch used to be a Scotch community, but many of its inhabitants have moved away.—Pop. 1790: 526, 1820: 1330, '50: 1143*, '80: 1172, 1910: 1235, '30: 1254.—Cochrane, Warren R. History of the town of Antrim. 791 p. Manchester, 1880.

1. Farmer, lumberman, 66. Aged 29 to 31, worked in a bakery in Hinsdale, Cheshire Co. (c. 34 m. southwest).—Local parentage.—School in Antrim until 12 or 14. Though his education has been slight, its influence is evident.—Belongs to the Grange. Lives on a back road and seldom leaves home.—Excellent naïve informant. Hearty type of old-time farmer. Understood purpose of investigation. Was much interested in comparing words and recollecting old expressions, enjoying the interviews as a kind of game.—Certain traits of speech reminded FW of informant in 356 Biddeford Pool, York Co., Me.: strong velarization, strongly retroflex r before vowels, and marked backing of vowels. Strongly retroflex, but usually weak, r is nearly always present after vowels, though it is variable.—L 44.

2. Manufacturer, mechanic, 67. Lately has been engaged in construction work.—F born here; PGF born elsewhere in N.H. of Dedham, Norfolk Co., Mass., ancestry; PGM born here of Scotch-Irish descent. M, MGF born here; latter's F from Framingham, Middlesex Co., Mass.; MGM born in Pittsfield, Merrimack Co. (c. 35 m. northeast).—Grammar school here. Academy in Francestown (c. 6 m. southeast) and in Ashburnham, Worcester Co., Mass.—Mason, I.O.O.F.—Good-natured. Gave intelligent assistance. Memory slightly failing.—Speech reminded FW of Essex (198) and Rockport (200) in Essex Co., Mass. Pleasant drawl, with a kind of caressing intonation. High vowels. Variable retroflection.—L 43. (Pp. 17–24, 26–37, 46–48 by C.)

328 City of Keene, Cheshire Co.

Permanently settled c. 1750; inc. 1753, as city 1873. Most of the early settlers came from eastern Mass. (140 Wrentham, Norton, 184 Topsfield), and from Worcester Co. (201 Uxbridge, 205 Worcester, 209 Lunenburg, Lancaster, Fitchburg, etc.); later Keene attracted people from many of the rural towns of sw. N.H.—Industries developed rapidly with the coming of the Boston and Maine R.R. in 1849: pottery, glass, textiles, furniture. Many Irish since 1840, French-Canadian mill workers since c.

1870. Old families keep to themselves.—State normal school.—Pop. 1775: 756, '90: 1307, 1820: 1895, '50: 3392, '80: 6784, 1910: 10,068, '30: 13,794.—Griffin, Simon G. History of Keene. 792 p. Keene, 1904.

1. Housewife, former schoolteacher (7 years), 74.—Welsh and English ancestry. F, PGM born here; PGF born in Fitzwilliam (c. 14 m. southeast). M, MGF born in Roxbury, Mass.; MGM born in Rutland, Worcester Co., Mass.—High school here; later normal school. A voracious reader.—Congregationalist. Women's Auxiliary of American Legion.—Vivacious, much interested in everything around her. Quick mind, excellent memory.—Originally old-fashioned speech, evidently much influenced by education. Quick tempo, each syllable staccato. Very careful articulation. Vowels relatively short.—C 13.

3. CULTURED INFORMANT. Housewife, 77. Before her marriage was assistant in the public library. Taught school for a short time. Has always lived in the heart of the city.—F born in Franklin, Norfolk Co., Mass., of Scotch-Irish ancestry. M born in Wrentham, Norfolk Co., Mass., of English ancestry. Her GF was an officer in the Revolutionary War.—High school. Afterwards studied French. Spends much time reading. Very little travel.—Congregationalist. Active in church work until recent ill health. Now visited by many friends.—Seems only middle-aged in speech, manner and appearance. Enjoys entertaining, likes to impress people, knows how to make conversation.—Speech has the rather short staccato vowels (unless words are pronounced in isolation) typical of Keene. Has heard a number of old-fashioned words and phrases, but seldom uses them herself. Soft, sweet voice. Voiceless stops in stressed syllables strongly aspirated.—Short work sheets.—C 8.

328 Town of Marlow, Cheshire Co.

Settled 1764–67 from eastern and central Mass. (Watertown, Dorchester, Framingham; Harvard) and from older N.H. towns.—Rural community (c. 15 m. north of Keene) with decreasing population. Farming, sawmills.—Pop. 1775: 207, '90: 319, 1820: 597, '50: 708, '80: 701, 1910: 425, '30: 330.

2. Surveyor, civil engineer, banker, 80. In Keene for the past 21 years.—F born here; PGF born in Dublin (c. 18 m. southeast); latter's F in Framingham, Middlesex Co., Mass. M, MGF born in Stoddard (adjoining town east); latter's F in New Ipswich, Hillsborough Co. (c. 32 m. southeast).—Academy here; McCallum Institute, Mont Vernon, Hillsborough Co. (c. 30 m. southeast), for a year; Dartmouth College, Hanover, Grafton Co. (c. 40 m. north), degree in electrical engineering. Has spent vacations in California and Florida.—Congregational Church. Apart from gardening and reading the newspapers, has little interest in anything except his work.—Prosperous, hard-headed business man,

extremely methodical in his habits. At first much interested in the investigation, but became impatient.—Rather slow and careful staccato speech. Vowels usually short. Voiced stops fully voiced. Voiceless stops entirely unaspirated.—C 9.

330 Town of Charlestown, Sullivan Co.

Settled in the 1740's, inc. 1753. Settlers came from eastern Mass. (Pepperell, 211 Groton, Shirley), from Worcester Co. (209 Lunenburg, Rutland), and from the Connecticut Valley in Mass. (228 Deerfield, 214 Northfield, Hadley, 226 Northampton) and in Conn. (Mansfield, Enfield).—Prosperous rural community. Woolen mill. Many old families, few foreigners.—Pop. 1775: 594, '90: 1094, 1820: 1702, '50: 1644, '80: 1587, 1910: 1496, '30: 1644.—Saunderson, Henry H. History of Charlestown, N.H. 726 p. Claremont, 1876.

1. Housewife, 66.—F, PGF born here. M, MGF born in Conn. M died when informant was 15.—School until 16.—Unitarian Church.—Extremely set in her ways.—Much interested in recalling old words. Often no retroflection after vowels or in unstressed position.—L 36.

2. Housewife, 56.—F born in Walpole, Cheshire Co. (c. 12 m. south); PGF born here; latter's F fought in the Revolutionary War. M born in Unity (c. 10 m. northeast); MGF, MGM born probably in Unity.—Grammar school irregularly until 14, then part of a year at high school. Does not care for reading.—Episcopal Church and church societies. Knows everybody in town and every detail of local news. Well liked.—Cheerful, kindly. Much interested in the investigation. Does not have the reserve and independence characteristic of many N.E. farm people. Likes to talk and to entertain friends.—Old-fashioned speech. Very rapid tempo. Staccato utterance. Considerable aspiration. Occasional nasalization. Vowels sometimes long and sometimes very short. Some vowel phonemes vary greatly.—C 11.

331 Town of Goshen (Mill Village), Sullivan Co.

Formed c. 1800 from parts of Newport (q.v., 332) and several other surrounding towns. Settled c. 1770.—Rural community with decreasing population. Mill Village is noted for maple sugar and syrup. Some of the mill workers from Newport (just across the town line) live here.—Pop. 1820: 687, '50: 659, '80: 511, 1910: 329, '30: 255.

Manager of tourist hotel, farmer, 56. Formerly blacksmith and carpenter. For the past 17 years has operated small store and gasoline station. Worked out of town a little, but never lived anywhere else.—F born in Unity (c. 7 m. west), came here 60 years ago; his family from Lempster (c. 6 m. southwest); ancestors from Conn. M born in Acworth (c. 10 m. southwest), came here 70 years ago.—School until 18. Reads a great deal.—Does not belong to clubs or lodges, but is apparently very popular.—Gener-

ous, kindly, coöperative, rather dignified.—Recognizes his lack of learning, but knows that many people are much more 'ignorant.' Some ideas of correctness. Says he varies his speech for different types of hearers, but he is absolutely unaffected. Rather slow tempo. Nasalization less than is common in this locality. Fairly clear utterance always.—HN 8.

332 Town of Newport, Sullivan Co.

Settled c. 1766 from Killingworth, Conn. (q.v., 29); others from Groton and Enfield, Conn., from Amesbury and 214 Northfield, Mass., and from Alstead and Hillsborough, N.H.—County seat. Shopping center surrounded by farms. Shoe manufacturing, woolen mills.—Polish and other foreign groups.—Pop. 1775: 157, '90: 779, 1820: 1679, '50: 2020, '80: 2612, 1910: 3765, '30: 4659.—Wheeler, Edmund. History of the town of Newport, 1766–1878. 600 p. Concord, 1879.

Merchant, 75. Aged 40 to 60, spent some time in city of Rochester, Strafford Co. (c. 60 m. east), and in Boston, Mass.—Ancestor on F's side was an early settler in Dedham, Norfolk Co., Mass. In 1840 PGF bought farm here and came to live; F was then 10 years old. M born in Acworth (c. 12 m. south). (Wife from Lebanon, Grafton Co.)—'Darn little' education. Grammar and private schools.—Congregationalist, active in church affairs. Associates with upper level of society. (Father was important in local politics and served in State Legislature.)—Good example of uneducated, successful business man, but a reluctant informant. Thought that a more learned man should answer the questions.—Deliberate responses, perhaps not entirely trustworthy because of his desire to be correct. Daughter, a schoolteacher, had told him that many of his expressions were wrong. Vocabulary and pronunciation too well fixed, however, to be much modified. Speech generally unhurried, but often uttered in spurts. Somewhat throaty voice. Slight pervading nasalization. In general, informant in 331 is probably a better example of the speech of this region.—HN 7.

333 Town of Wilmot (Wilmot Flat), Merrimack Co.

Inc. 1807, consisting of Kearsarge Gore and the northern part of New London. New London settled 1775; many settlers from eastern Mass. (Attleboro, Dedham; Amesbury, Bradford), others from surrounding N.H. towns.—Rural community on Concord-Hanover turnpike (1800). Sharply decreasing population. Many summer residents.—Pop. 1820: 670, '50: 1272, '80: 1080*, 1910: 614, '30: 495.—
New London: [Lord, Myra B.] History of the town of New London. 774 p. Concord, 1899.

1. Farmer's wife, 89. Born in Bridgewater, Grafton Co. (c. 17 m. northeast of Wilmot Flat), came here aged 23.—F, PGF (?) born in Bridgewater; PGM born perhaps in Pembroke, Merrimack Co. (c. 28 m. southeast of Wilmot Flat). M, MGF, MGM

born in Bridgewater. M used to be village nurse.—
School until 15.—Has been crippled for some years.
Few contacts outside her family. Keeps informed,
nevertheless, about the neighborhood news.—Pleasant, good-natured, talkative.—Old-fashioned local
speech. Very rapid tempo. Vigorous articulation of
all sounds. No nasalization or glottal stops. Vowels
relatively short and clear. Sometimes—but not
usually—the vowel in words such as *corn* and *girl*
is retroflex; whether because of affectation or not,
it is impossible to say.—C 1.

333 Town of Sutton (Sutton Mills section), Merrimack Co.

Settled 1767 (inc. 1784) from the lower Merrimack R.: Haverhill (190), Bradford, Newbury (194)
in Mass. and Atkinson, Hampstead in N.H.—Rural
community with sharply decreasing population.
Summer visitors.—Pop. 1775: 130, '90: 520, 1820:
1573, '50: 1387, '80: 993, 1910: 698, '30: 512.—
Worthen, Augusta H. History of the town of Sutton. 2v. 1110 p. Concord, 1890.

2. Farmer, 84. Born in Newbury (adjoining town
west), came here aged 3. Worked 3 summers, aged
22 to 25, as stone mason in city of Manchester,
Hillsborough Co. (c. 35 m. southeast).—F, PGF,
PGM born in Goffstown, Hillsborough Co. (c. 28 m.
southeast). F came to Sutton when 4 years old. F of
PGF from Mass. M, MGF born in Newbury;
MGM born in Bradford (c. 5 m. south). F of MGF
born in Kennebunkport, York Co., Me.—School in
Sutton.—Unordained preacher in nearby towns for
many years.—Very loquacious.—Slight retroflection,
due perhaps to Scotch-Irish influence.—L 37.

334 Town of Canaan, Grafton Co.

Chartered 1761 to 62 Conn. proprietors and
settled 1766 from Conn.; after 1780, others came
from Haverhill (190) and Amesbury, Mass., and
from Hampstead, Plaistow and Newmarket in se.
N.H.—Always agricultural. Now a tourist center.
Winter sports.—Pop. 1775: 67, '90: 483, 1820: 1198,
'50: 1682, '80: 1762, 1910: 1408, '30: 1301.—Wal-
lace, William A. History of the town of Canaan.
748 p. Concord, 1910.

1. Farmer, blacksmith, 77.—F, PGF born here.
Latter's F, of Irish origin, lived here. M born here;
MGF from Princeton, Worcester Co., Mass., came
here to live; MGM from Princeton.—School until
15.—Belongs to the Grange.—Good-natured, sociable, willing to talk.—Tempo moderate. Vowels tend
to be somewhat long.—L 117.

2. Farmer, 75.—F born in Pembroke, Merrimack
Co. (c. 42 m. southeast), came here as a boy; PGF
born in Pembroke; PGM born in city of Concord,
Merrimack Co. (c. 38 m. southeast). M probably
born here; MGF born in Billerica, Middlesex Co.,
Mass.—Grammar school; academy in New Hampton, Belknap Co. (c. 18 m. east).—Knights of

Pythias, Grange.—Intelligent. Likes to talk of old
times. Well-to-do.—L 118.

335 Town of Hanover, Grafton Co.

Chartered 1761, settled 1765 from Mansfield and
Lebanon in Conn.—Site of Dartmouth College
(chartered 1769; Rev. Eleazar Wheelock of Lebanon
the first president). New Hampshire College of Agriculture and the Mechanic Arts (now University of
New Hampshire) here from 1866 to 1893, when it
was moved to Durham. Pottery making and weaving
in the early days.—Pop. 1775: 434, '90: 1379, 1820:
2222, '50: 2350, '80: 2147, 1910: 2075, '30: 3043.—
Chase, Frederick and John K. Lord. History of
Dartmouth College and Hanover. 2v. 682+785 p.
Cambridge and Concord, 1891–1913.

1. Native farmer. Biographical information not
available.—Incomplete record: only pp. 1–32, and
scattered items.—HN 9.

2. Native farmer.—PGF came from Scotland to
Canada. M's immediate ancestors were New Eng-
landers.—Incomplete record: only pp. 1–7.—HN 10.
(Simultaneously recorded by K.)

336 Town of Lyme (Lyme Plain), Grafton Co.

Settled 1764 from eastern Conn. (Mansfield, Tolland, Ellington, Bolton, Lyme); others from e.
Mass. (Bridgewater). More recently people from
Clinton and Franklin Counties in northern N.Y.
have come here; they are locally known as 'Cha-
teaugese' (for Chateaugay, Franklin Co., N.Y.).—
Rural community with declining population.—Pop.
1775: 252, '90: 816, 1820: 1824, '50: 1617, '80: 1313,
1910: 1007, '30: 830.—Goldthwait, J. W. A town
that has gone downhill. Geographical review, 17
(1927), 527–52.

1. Farmer, 75. Except for 2 years, has constantly
held town offices since 1890. Spent 3 or 4 winters in
Concord, Merrimack Co. (c. 52 m. southeast), coming home every weekend.—Ancestor of F was an
early settler in the 18. cent.; Gen. U. S. Grant supposed to be descended from this man's brother.
M's family also old residents of Lyme.—Grammar
school. 5 fall terms at academy in Thetford, Orange
Co., Vt. (adjoining town across state line). Served
twice in State Legislature.—Congregational Church.
—Pleasant, opinionated, inclined to give short
answers.—Normally unaffected speech. Frequently,
however, points out difference between what is
'right' and what is usual, trying to give preference
in his own usage to the former. Speaks in spurts,
uttering groups of clipped sounds very fast and not
always distinctly. Tempo not rapid throughout.
Some nasalization regularly.—HN 5.

2. Farmer, painter and decorator, 47. Has done
'about everything except teach school and preach.'—
Ancestor of F came here in the 18. cent. from Middleborough, Plymouth Co., Mass. M from Dorchester
(next town east of Lyme).—Grammar school.—

Well known locally. Has held town and state offices.
—Easy-going, but a steady worker. Not inclined to
waste words.—Local unaffected speech. Probably
too ready to agree to any suggestions made about
his usage. Responses short and rather clipped, anecdotes slightly drawled. Leisurely tempo, except for
occasional spurts. Articulation not entirely clear.
Slight nasalization. Vowels rather short.—HN 6.

337 Town of Orford (Orfordville), Grafton Co.

Chartered 1761, settled 1765 from eastern Conn.
(Lebanon and 42 Hebron).—Rural community with
good farm land. Declining population.—Pop. 1775:
222, '90: 540, 1820: 1568, '50: 1406*, '80: 1050,
1910: 799, '30: 636.—Centennial celebration of the
town of Orford, N.H., . . . September 7, 1865, with
some additional matters relating to the history of
the place. Printed at Manchester, N.H.

Native farmer.—No biographical information.—
Incomplete record: only pp. 2–10, and scattered
items.—HN 11.

338 Town of Plymouth, Grafton Co.

Chartered 1763, settled 1764 from Hollis in
southern N.H. Hollis settled as part of Dunstable
(now city of Nashua) in the 1730's, many coming
from Middlesex Co., Mass.: Concord (156), Billerica
(160), Groton (211), etc.; some from Essex Co.,
Mass.—Rural community with many old families.
Small industries. Shopping center. Site of normal
school. Many summer residents; winter sports.—
Pop. 1775: 382, '90: 625, 1820: 983, '50: 1290, '80:
1719, 1910: 2200, '30: 2470.—Stearns, Ezra S. History of the town of Plymouth. 2v. 632+801 p. Cambridge, 1906.— *Hollis:* Worcester, Samuel T. History of the town of Hollis, N.H. 394 p. Nashua,
1879.— *Nashua:* Parker, Edward E. History of the
city of Nashua. 622 p. Nashua, 1897. Stearns, Ezra S.
Early generations of the founders of Old Dunstable.
103 p. Boston, 1911.

1. Housewife, 52. Born in Bridgewater (c. 10 m.
south), came here aged 6.—F, PGF born in Bridgewater; PGM born here. M born here; MGF born in
Bridgewater, was partly Irish; MGM born in New
Hampton, Belknap Co. (c. 12 m. south); some of
latter's ancestors from France.—School here until
c. 14.—Old-fashioned, uneducated, naïve.—Usually
responded promptly, though hesitant when confronted with an alternative. Moderate tempo.
Vowels and diphthongs rather short. The diphthongs
[aɪ] and [aʊ] have a high second element, as in
southern N.H. and northeastern Mass.—L 116.

2. Glove manufacturer, 56.—F born in Groton (c.
8 m. southwest), came here when young; PGF and
his F born in Bridgewater (c. 10 m. south); PGM
born here. M, MGF, MGM born here.—School until
15.—I.O.O.F.—Quick, bright, modern, with little of
the country type about him. Coöperative.—Rather
quick tempo. High second element in the diphthongs [aɪ]and [aʊ].—L 115.

340 Town of Haverhill, Grafton Co.

Granted 1763 to residents of Haverhill, Mass.
(q.v., 190). Settled about that time from Haverhill
and from Northfield, Mass. (q.v., 214); others from
lower Merrimack Valley (194 Newbury, Mass.;
Hampstead, Hampton, N.H.).—County seat. Shopping center in agricultural area.—Pop. 1775: 365,
'90: 552, 1820: 1609, '50: 2405, '80: 2455, 1910: 3498,
'30: 3665.—Bittinger, John Q. History of the town
of Haverhill. 442 p. Haverhill, 1888. Whitcher, W. F.
History of the town of Haverhill. 781 p. N.p., 1919.

1. Farmer, 83.—Parents born here. One GF from
Mason, Hillsborough Co., the other from Sandwich,
Carroll Co. (of Exeter, Rockingham Co., ancestry).
—School until 14.—Rustic, eccentric. Refused to
finish the interviews.—Rather precise speech, with
short vowels. Moderate tempo.—Incomplete record:
only pp. 7–11, 14–23, 26–86.—L 106.

2. Merchant, 75.—F, PGF born here; F of PGF
born in Lunenburg, Worcester Co., Mass. (of Groton, Middlesex Co., Mass., ancestry), went to live
in Rindge, Cheshire Co., N.H.; M of PGF from
Landaff (c. 12 m. northeast of Haverhill); PGM of
Newburyport, Essex Co., Mass., ancestry. M born
in Orford (c. 10 m. south); MGF born in Atkinson,
Rockingham Co.; MGM born in Candia, Rockingham Co.—School here and academy in St. Johnsbury, Caledonia Co., Vt. (c. 26 m. north). (Son a
graduate of Columbia Univ.)—Congregational
Church.—Glad to help with the investigation.—
Very precise in thought and speech. Quick tempo.
Vowels fairly short.—L 105.

342 Town of Lancaster, Coos Co.

Settled 1764 from Worcester Co., Mass. (Lancaster, 209 Lunenburg, Petersham).—County seat.
Shopping center in good agricultural area: dairy
farms. Some manufacturing since 1830. Trade connections with Portland, Me. (R.R. since 1870), and
with Boston. French-Canadians and Irish in recent
years.—Pop. 1775: 61, '90: 161, 1820: 844, '50: 1559,
'80: 2721, 1910: 3054, '30: 2887.—Somers, Amos N.
History of the town of Lancaster. 652 p. Concord,
1899. Whittlesey, Derwent. Coast land and interior
mountain valley: a geographical study of two typical localities in northern New England [Lancaster
and Ellsworth, Me.]. New England's prospect: 1933,
ed. by John K. Wright. American Geographical
Society, special publication no. 16, 446–58. New
York, 1933.

1. Farmer, 80.—F, PGF, PGM born in Middletown, Middlesex Co., Conn. F came here with his
parents when he was a boy. M, MGF, MGM
born in Dalton (c. 6 m. southwest of Lancaster).
—School until 15.—Methodist. Grange.—Old-fashioned, rugged pioneer type. Lived in a log house until
he was 13. Shows the impulsiveness and wandering
attention of a primitive mind. Somewhat reserved
and taciturn. Saw little sense in the investigation,

but thought it his duty to serve.—Old-fashioned speech. Deep, powerful voice. Moderate tempo. Vowels tend to be centered.—L 113.

2. CULTURED INFORMANT. Single woman, formerly railroad office clerk, 71.—F born in village of Fabyan House, town of Carroll (c. 18 m. south); PGF, PGM born in Guildhall, Essex Co., Vt. (c. 7 m. north). F of PGF was of Scotch-Irish descent, his M of Conn. stock. F and M of PGM were of Mass. ancestry (Marlborough, Middlesex Co., for the former; Grafton, Worcester Co., and Brimfield, Hampden Co., for the latter). M born in Montville, Waldo Co., Me.—School until 16. Often goes to Boston, and travels South and to Europe. Has read considerably. (PGM wrote a history of the White Mts.)—Episcopalian. Many social contacts.—Talkative, adept at conversation.—Glad to contribute her knowledge of the local idiom; believes in speaking naturally. Very quick, nervous, precise speech, showing the cultural influence of her associations, but preserving the phonetic features of this region.—L 104.

344 Town of Columbia (East Columbia), Coos Co.

Settled c. 1786 from Connecticut.—Rural community with decreasing population.—Pop. 1820: 281, '50: 762, '80: 762, 1910: 619, '30: 524.

Farmer, lumberman, 73. Last 9 years in Colebrook (c. 5 m. north).—F born here; PGF, PGM from Northfield, Merrimack Co. M born in Stewartstown (c. 10 m. north); MGF, MGM from Campton, Grafton Co. (c. 68 m. south).—School irregularly until 17.—Grange.—Difficult to approach. —Old-fashioned speech.—L 114.

346 Town of Shelburne (northern section), Coos Co.

Settled c. 1775 from Maine and Mass.; inc. 1820.— Rural community in the White Mts. Forest land, sparsely settled. Tourists.—Pop. 1790: 35, 1820: 295, '50: 480, '80: 252, 1910: 305, '30: 196.—Peabody, Mrs. R. P. History of the town of Shelburne. 127 p. Gorham, 1882.

1. Farmer, formerly engineer and carpenter, 80.— F born in Gorham (adjoining town west); PGF born in northern Ireland, went to Dracut, Middlesex Co., Mass., where he married, later settled in Gorham; PGM of Scotch and Welsh ancestry. M born here; MGF of Scotch ancestry; MGM from Mass. (sister of PGM).—School during the fall and early winter only. (F was a teacher.)—Kind, neighborly. Has

practical intelligence. Gave definite, accurate information about specific objects and facts, but was slow to respond when dealing with abstractions or questions of syntax.—Fairly slow tempo. Clear articulation. Rather long vowels.—L 55.

2. Farmer (supervising a number of men who work for him), 77. Lives c. 1½ m. from Me. line on old farm estate.—F, PGM born in Gilead, Oxford Co., Me. (just across state line); PGF born in Wakefield, Middlesex Co., Mass. M born in Gilead. MGF, MGM probably born Isle of Wight, England.— School here, then academy in Bethel, Oxford Co., Me.—Mason, Rotarian.—Cultivated gentleman of the older N.E. school. Primarily a farmer, however, and a local type. Good-humored, energetic, efficient. Keen, precise intellect.—Rather precise speech. Slight nasalization. Vowels somewhat long.—L 54.

348 Town of Conway (1 Center Conway; 2 Conway), Carroll Co.

Settled 1764–66 from older N.H. towns (306 Lee, Portsmouth; 315 Concord).—The village of Conway is the shopping center of Carroll Co. Small manufactures. North Conway is a center of the tourist trade; art colony since c. 1850.—Pop. 1775: 273, '90: 574, 1820: 1365, '50: 1767, '80: 2094, 1910: 3413, '30: 3217.—FW believes there is a definite dialect boundary between Conway, N.H., and 368 Denmark, Oxford Co., Me. (c. 15 m. east).

1. Farmer, 81.—F born here; PGF born in Wells, York Co., Me. (c. 50 m. southeast), came here when young; PGM born in Limington, York Co., Me. (c. 25 m. southeast), came here when young. M, MGF, MGM born in Waterboro, York Co., Me. (c. 35 m. southeast). M came here early with her parents.—School until 18. Likes to read.—Fine character, with old-fashioned reserve and good manners. Intelligent.—Slow, careful speech. Clear articulation. At times slight nasalization.—L 51.

2. Merchant, 81. Born in Eaton (adjoining town south).—F born in Bartlett (c. 11 m. northwest); PGF born in Lyman, Grafton Co. (c. 46 m. northwest); PGM born in Virginia. M, MGF born in Lyman.—School in Eaton until 16. At c. 30, began to take long trips to Kansas and the West.— Methodist Church.—Moderate ability; staunch, firm character.—Had often noticed differences in the speech of various communities and was interested in making comparisons. Tempo not rapid. Some nasalization. Vowels rather short.—L 50.

MAINE

352 Town of York (Cape Neddick), York Co.

Settled in the 1620's, inc. 1641. Originally Episcopalian, later tending to be Puritan. Settlers from London, from the counties of Kent, Norfolk, Gloucester, Dorset, Devon and Durham in England, and from Scotland; also from the N.H. coast towns

and Essex Co., Mass.—Rural community. York was the shire town until 1832.—Cape Neddick is a small coast settlement on a main road. Many old families. York Beach, a village c. 2 m. south, has a large group of summer residents.—(The town of Wells, home of the auxiliary informant, was settled in the 1640's from Exeter, N.H.)—Pop. 1764: 2298, '90: 2898, 1820: 3224, '50: 2980, '80: 2463, 1910: 2802, '30: 2532.—Banks, Charles E. History of York, Me. . . . 2v. Boston, 1931–35. Emery, G. A. Ancient city of Gorgeana and modern town of York (Maine) from its earliest settlement to the present time . . . 256 p. Boston, 1874. Moody, Edward C. Handbook history of the town of York, Maine, from early times to the present. 251 p. Augusta, [1914.]

1. Farmer, woodsman, landscape gardener, 42. Lives on backwoods road off the coast.—F born here; PGF, a sea captain; PGM born in Somersworth, Strafford Co., N.H. (c. 15 m. west). M, MGF, MGM born in York. M was brought up by a Welshwoman. —Little education.—Illiterate type of speech. Extreme drawl with undulating intonation.—Incomplete record: pp. 1–87.3.

Supplementary informant: brother, 54, with same background and similar mentality.—Much quicker tempo.—Pp. 87.4–103, forms not starred.

Auxiliary informant: farmer, 82, living in Wells (adjoining town north).—Pp. 1–20, starred forms.— L 33.

2. Plasterer, bricklayer, riveter, fisherman, 55. Has been rural mail carrier for the past 12 years.— All his ancestors from York and Wells. F born in Wells, came here when 5 years old; PGF born in Wells; PGM born here. M, MGF, MGM born in York Village (c. 5 m. south).—Grammar and high schools in York.—Mason. Has met many summer visitors lately.—Sturdy, independent, sensible. Offered many valuable suggestions. Knows this region well.—Rather imitative, but a trustworthy informant. Reported his native dialect, into which he falls easily, despite a fair amount of education. Has some acquaintance with other dialects. Very quick tempo. Choppy, slurred utterance. Lax articulation, especially of final consonants. Extreme nasalization near nasal consonants, but also elsewhere. Not much glottalization. Vowels tend to be short.—L 13.

354 Town of Kennebunkport, York Co.

First settled as Cape Porpoise c. 1630, inc. (under Mass.) 1653; abandoned during the Indian Wars. Resettled c. 1714; name changed in 1718 to Arundel, in 1820 to Kennebunkport. Some settlers came to this region from England; others from Essex Co., Mass. (Amesbury, Salisbury, 184 Topsfield, Ipswich, Salem), from the N.H. coast towns (Greenland, Exeter), and from York (q.v., 352).—Coast town. Fishing, agriculture. Formerly the chief shipbuilding port of York Co.—Summer residents.—Pop. 1764: 837, '90: 1461, 1820: 2478, '50: 2706, '80: 2405, 1910: 2130, '30: 1284*.—Bradbury, Charles. History of Kennebunkport from its first discovery by Gosnold, May 14, 1602, to 1837. 301 p. Kennebunk, 1837. Brooks, Annie Peabody. Ropes' Ends: traditions, legends, and sketches of old Kennebunkport and vicinity. Kennebunkport, 1901.

Farmer's wife, c. 70. When young, worked a few years in a department store in Haverhill, Essex Co., Mass.—Good family, long settled here.—Grammar school.—Average social contacts.—Old-fashioned speech, less local than that of most natives; probably some Mass. influence. Rapid tempo. Clear utterance.—Incomplete record: only pp. 7–49.—L 30.

356 City of Biddeford (Biddeford Pool), York Co.

First settled c. 1630 as Saco, inc. (under Mass.) 1653; abandoned 1690 during the Indian Wars. Inhabitants began to return c. 1714. Town was settled largely from Devonshire (renamed 1718 for Bideford in Devon); others from southern York Co., the N.H. coast towns and Essex Co., Mass. (Amesbury Salisbury, 190 Haverhill).—Mill city (chiefly textiles and textile machinery) with large French-Canadian population. (City of Saco across the Saco River, originally part of Biddeford, is residential rather than industrial.)—Biddeford Pool is a quiet coast village (c. 8 m. southeast of Biddeford proper). Fishing; formerly shipbuilding. Old native stock. Many summer people.—Pop. 1764: 753, '90: 1018, 1820: 1738, '50: 6095, '80: 12,651, 1910: 17,079, '30: 17,633.—Folsom, George. History of Saco and Biddeford. . . . 331 p. Saco, 1830. Locke, J. S. Shores of Saco Bay; a historical guide to Biddeford Pool. . . . 105 p. Boston, 1880. Ridlon, G. T., Sr. Saco Valley settlements and families. 1250 p. Portland, 1895.

Merchant, formerly fisherman, 78. Lifeguard 10 years, when young.—F born in Biddeford; PGF a coast guard in England, came here from Canterbury, Kent. M born here; MGF born in Nantucket, Mass., came here early with his F; MGM born in Biddeford. (Wife German, from St. Louis, Mo.)—Attended school irregularly until 13 or 14. (Had his daughters educated in Brooklyn, N.Y.) Values education, but is not ashamed of his own lack of it.—Knights of Pythias. Seems popular.—Kind, tolerant, unassuming. Not talkative.—Can distinguish between local words and those used by outsiders. Slow tempo. Dull, deep, hollow resonance (common here). Rather lax utterance, with weak final consonants. Nasalization fairly prominent. Glottalization rare. Extremely retroflex r rather long, as in Haverhill (190) and Rowley (196), Essex Co., Mass. Vowels tend to be long.—L 25.

357 Town of Acton, York Co.

Settled 1772 as part of Shapleigh (q.v., 358); inc. 1830.—Remote, sparsely settled country town in the mountains. Poor roads. Some of the inhabitants leave their homes only once a year when they go to the Acton Fair.—Decreasing population.—Pop. 1850: 1359, '80: 1050, 1910: 603, '30: 449.—Fullonton, Joseph. History of Acton, Me. 36 p. Dover, 1847.

Farmer, 75.—F, PGF born here. Latter's F born

in Brentwood, Rockingham Co., N.H. (c. 40 m. south), came here in 1780. M born in Wakefield, Carroll Co., N.H. (c. 7 m. northwest); MGF born here; MGM born in Milton, Strafford Co., N.H. (c. 10 m. southwest).—School until 18, usually for short periods.—Knights of Pythias. Former town officer.—Simple, friendly, with restrained emotions. A certain ease of manner and detachment from practical affairs.—Uses few old-fashioned expressions and finds it hard to recall them. Gentle, quavering voice. Slow, undulating drawl. Utterance clear, though not precise. Nasalization fairly frequent. All vowels tend to be long.—L 20.

358 Town of Shapleigh, York Co.

Land purchased from Indians in the 1660's; settled much later, c. 1770 (inc. 1785), from Berwick and Kittery and from adjoining N.H. towns (chiefly Dover).—Rural community in hilly, agricultural region with sharply declining population.—Sanford (c. 8 m. southeast) and Springvale (c. 5 m. southeast) in the town of Sanford have become mill centers with immigrants from Canada and the north of England.—Pop. 1790: 1319, 1820: 2815, '50: 1348*, '80: 1128, 1910: 691, '30: 530—Loring, Amasa. History of Shapleigh. 40 p. Portland, 1854.

Farmer, carpenter, cooper, 78—Ancestors on F's side born here. M born in Springvale (c. 5 m. southeast).—School here until 12, then in Sanford until 15.—Few social contacts. Likes to talk with his neighbors in the local store.—Quizzical, humorous, never really serious. Makes absurd puns and will engage in endless repartee. Not particularly interested in the investigation and difficult to work with. —Fairly rapid tempo. Some nasalization. Vowels rather long.—Short work sheets.—L 18.

359 Town of Cape Elizabeth, Cumberland Co.

Settled in the 1630's as part of Falmouth (see 360 Portland). Original settlement abandoned; resettled 1719–20 (inc. 1765).—Farming town on the coast, c. 5 m. south of Portland; now a fashionable residential district. Lobster fishing.—Pop. 1790: 1356, 1820: 1688, '50: 2082, '80: 5302, 1910: 1857*, '30: 2376.—Baxter, J. P., ed. The Trelawney papers with historical notes and an appendix. 520 p. Portland, 1884. (Trelawney held a patent of Cape Elizabeth.)

Farmer, 72.—F born here, descended from original settlers. M, MGF born here; MGM born in Deering, then part of town of Falmouth.—Finished high school.—Grange. Highly respected.—Well bred and intelligent. Obviously feels superior to inland dwellers of the back country.—Able to report older speech. Moderate tempo. Clear utterance. Stress not very strong, rather even, giving the impression occasionally of a slight drawl (more marked in the speech of his sister). Vowels at times rather long. High

vowels, mid vowels and diphthongs have a high tongue position, in strong contrast to the speech of northern Essex Co., Mass.—L 66.

360 City of Portland, Cumberland Co.

Settled 1716 as part of Falmouth, under authority of Mass. (Original settlement in the 1630's destroyed during the Indian Wars.)—Falmouth prospered through trade and shipbuilding until the Revolution: it was burned by the British in 1775. (Only c. 700 people said to be here in 1777.)—Portland set off in 1786, inc. as city 1832. New industries, as well as shipping, in 19. cent. Great fire of 1866 followed by rebuilding and further commercial activity.—Although shipping declined after the World War, Portland still exports wood-pulp products, fish, potatoes, paper, etc., and remains the chief fishing port of Me.—County seat. Many educational institutions. —Population largely native stock. Foreign groups: Irishmen, Italians, Jews, Scandinavians; a small number of negroes. Many tourists.—Pop 1790: 2239, 1820: 8581, '50: 20,815, '80: 33,810, 1910: 58,571, '30: 70,810.—Baxter, J. P. Christopher Levett of York, the pioneer colonist in Casco Bay. 166 p. Portland, 1893. Day, Clarence P. and William E. Meyer. The port of Portland and its hinterland. Portland, 1923. Goold, William. Portland in the past, with historical notes of Old Falmouth. 543 p. Portland, 1886. Moulton, Augustus F. Portland by the sea, an historical treatise. 243 p. Augusta, 1926. Willis, William. History of Portland from its first settlement, with notices of the neighboring towns, and of the changes of government in Maine. Ed. 2, enlarged. 928 p. Portland, 1865.

1. Leather worker, 63. Has made trunks and leather goods for 45 years. Also for 16 years janitor of church. Lives in the suburbs.—F, PGF born here; PGM born in Bridgton (c. 35 m. northwest). M born here; MGF, MGM born in England.—Grammar school.—Unitarian. I.O.O.F. Has met many Irish and Maine French people.—Typical middle-class city workman of old native stock. Outlook entirely different from that of the country people. Lacks the stability and canny thinking of the old N.E. rustic. Simple, good, affable. Rather talkative. Very prompt responses.—Drawling speech. Vowels rather long. Greater rise and fall in pitch than in the speech of the surrounding country; secondary stresses and glottalization more common. Rather clear articulation. Some nasality. Portland pronunciation seems to resemble the speech of eastern Mass. rather than that of the rural districts around Portland.—L 24.

2. Barber, negro, 77. Began his trade at 17, working for his father.—F born here; his parents from Conn. M born here; MGF born in Gorham (c. 10 m. west); latter's ancestors were negro slaves here in Colonial days. (Wife a Nova Scotian negress.)—

Grammar school and 2 years of high school.— Through his work, has known many Portland people and many fishermen and sea captains.—Manner and speech typical of N.E. Has dignity, reserve, and a cool, unemotional attitude toward the world.— Knows city speech, and the way it differs from that of the country. Measured tempo. Because of his falling intonation, all his statements have an air of finality. In spite of a careful manner of speaking, articulation tends to be lax. Some nasalization, lengthening of vowels and weakening of final consonants.—L 26.

3. Cultured informant. Music teacher, 67.— F born in Standish (c. 17 m. west); PGF and PGM of old Standish families. M born here in 1817; MGF, MGM born in Standish, descended from old families there.—High school. Studied music in Boston at the N.E. Conservatory; also in New York, Berlin and Oslo. Has been to Europe 8 times. Learned Norwegian and French. Interested in dramatics. On the stage, when he was younger, in Boston, Portland and Augusta.—Swedenborgian Church. I.O.O.F., Knights of Pythias, musical club.—Aristocratic. Adept at conversation. (Often begins a series of long, interesting digressions, returning with ease after 15 or 20 minutes to the original topic.)— Much inclined to imitate unconsciously the speech of others. His own speech never guarded. Frequently uses old-fashioned pronunciations and ungrammatical constructions. Rapid tempo. Precise articulation. Strong lip action. Vowels tend to be shorter than is usual here.—Long work sheets pp. 1–38, short work sheets pp. 39–103.—L 29.

362 Town of Standish, Cumberland Co.

Settled 1763 (inc. 1785) from Hampton, N.H. (see 302 Seabrook). Rural community, largely of native stock. Rather poor farm land; many orchards.— Pop. 1790: 705, 1820: 1619, '50: 2290, '80: 2035, 1910: 1637, '30: 1317.—Ridlon, G. T., Sr. Saco Valley settlements and families. 1250 p. Portland, 1895.

Farmer, formerly lumberman, 75.—PGF born in 359 Cape Elizabeth; PGM was Irish, from 360 Portland; they settled here. PGF's F was a Scotch sea captain. MGF born here; MGM from Winterport, Waldo Co. MGF's F from England.—Left school before he was 12. Never studied grammar. Sings old country songs very well.—A friend to all boys, always glad to 'help a young feller out.'— Likes gaiety and merry talk. Was generous to his sons, establishing them on farms of their own, which they failed to manage successfully. Once well-to-do, now very poor.—Rustic, old-fashioned, uncultivated speech. Slow drawl. Fairly precise articulation. Vowels tend to be long and nasal. The younger generation here shows more clearly than the older a tendency to use velarized sounds and retracted vowels.—L 27.

363 Town of Limington (North Limington), York Co.

Settled c. 1773 (inc. 1792), chiefly from Scarboro, Cumberland Co.; others from Saco, Buxton, Biddeford (356), York (352); some from Harvard and Charlestown, Mass., and from Scotland and Ireland. —Rural community in forest land, with sharply declining population.—Pop. 1820: 2122, '50: 2116, '80: 1431, 1910: 980, '30: 747.—Ridlon, G. T., Sr. Saco Valley settlements and families. 1250 p. Portland, 1895.

Railroad trackman, 43. Has lived in Steep Falls, town of Standish, Cumberland Co. (just across county line), since he was 30. Farmed when a young man.—PGF born in Limington; PGM born in Porter, Oxford Co. (c. 14 m. west). Farmer's GF came from Scarboro, Cumberland Co. (c. 22 m. southeast), descended from original Me. settlers who came in the 17. cent. from the Isle of Jersey. MGF, MGM born in Limington; MGM descended from prominent old family.—Limington Academy 4 years.—Has held town offices. Belongs to several fraternal organizations and lodges. Likes dances and visiting. The life of the party wherever he goes.—Intense, enthusiastic. Thoroughly modern in point of view. Mind remarkably quick and fertile, though somewhat erratic. The investigation roused his curiosity at once.—Remembers his great-grandparents; has always been interested in old-fashioned speech and in odd sayings. Could give numerous synonyms for many of the items in the record. Extremely rapid tempo. Fairly precise articulation. Vowels tend to be rather long and slightly nasal.—L 31.

364 Town of Yarmouth (1 Yarmouth; 2 Yarmouthville), Cumberland Co.

Settled c. 1721 (earlier settlement had been destroyed by Indians), set off from North Yarmouth in 1849. Many of the early settlers from the Plymouth Colony.—Once a busy port and shipbuilding center. Fishing. Close contacts with Portland. Site of North Yarmouth Academy, est. 1810.—Pop. 1850: 2144, '80: 2021, 1910: 2358, '30: 2125. (Pop. of North Yarmouth: 1764: 1079, '90: 1923, 1820: 3679.)— Rowe, W. H. Ancient North Yarmouth and Yarmouth, Maine, 1636–1936; a history. 427 p. Yarmouth, 1937.

1. Railroad man (in Me., N.H., and Vt.), 84. Blacksmith 4 years in his youth.—Parents and grandparents born in North Yarmouth (adjoining town).—Grammar school and 2 years at academy here. Has traveled to Montreal.—I.O.O.F.—Reserved, but interested in all humanity. Patiently answered the questions out of pure kindness; saw little sense in them. (His daughter, who lives in Portland, was much interested.)—Prompt responses. Though Yarmouth is a fairly modern community, his speech is somewhat archaic. Deliberate tempo.

Fairly precise articulation. Not much lengthening of vowels.—L 68.

2. Retired sea captain, 80. Went to sea when he was c. 18, first as mate; at 24 became master of a ship. Home only a few months at a time until he retired at the age of 50. Made voyages to China.— Descended from old families. F and M were distant cousins. F, PGF born in Yarmouth; family originally from Mass. M, MGF born in Cumberland (adjoining town southwest).—Yarmouth Academy, of which he is now a trustee. Then for a short time at school in Norridgewock, Somerset Co. (c. 65 m. north), until c. 16. A few months at business college in N.Y. City. Traveled to England when he was 17.—Mason, officer of Portland Marine Society. Enjoys company. —Quick, nervous manner. Memory rapidly slipping. Thinks only of old times.—Rapid tempo. Clear utterance.—Short work sheets.—L 28.

366 Town of Casco (1 Webbs Mills; 2 South Casco), Cumberland Co.

Settled as part of Raymond c. 1770 from Plymouth Colony (Duxbury); inc. 1841.—Rural community. Casco speech differs noticeably from that of 368 Denmark, Oxford Co. (c. 15 m. west).—Pop. 1850: 1046, '80: 908, 1910: 688, '30: 713.

1. Merchant and postmaster, 64.—F born here. PGF born in Westbrook near Portland, settled here. M born in Vermont, came here as a child.—School until 18.—Rather intelligent, but uncommunicative and passive.—Rapid tempo. Utterance not very clear, and yet precise, reminiscent of the speech of eastern Mass. Vowels tend to be short. The [a] is much fronted and the [æ] fronted and raised.— L 59.

2. Housewife and clerk in store, 49. Born and brought up in Casco; lived in Mechanic Falls, Androscoggin Co. (c. 15 m. northeast), for 24 years; recently came back to Casco.—Parents and paternal grandparents born here. PGF's parents from Mass. MGF born in Rome, Kennebec Co.; MGM in Naples (adjoining town west of Casco).—School until 17.— Not very clear-minded, but possesses a good feeling for local usage and recalls many old-fashioned expressions.—Slow, drawling speech, with long vowels and diphthongs. Caressingly childlike intonation. [a] as in car is apt to be rather front. The diphthongs as in way and no have an open beginning.—L 58.

368 Town of Denmark (1 East Denmark; 2 South Road), Oxford Co.

Settled c. 1778, several of the early settlers coming from Andover, Mass.; inc. 1807, formed from part of the town of Brownfield (settled 1765, inc. 1802) and from several State grants of land.—Rural community with sharply declining population.—Pop. 1820: 792, '50: 1203, '80: 904, 1910: 596, '30: 474.— Ridlon, G. T., Sr. Saco Valley settlements and families. 1250 p. Portland, 1895.

1. Cattle farmer, 71. Has lived in Bridgton, Cumberland Co. (c. 10 m. northeast of Denmark), for the past 20 years.—F, seaman, and PGF, farmer and sailor, born in Cumberland, Cumberland Co. (c. 35 m. southeast). Slight strain of Indian blood. M born in North Kennebunkport, York Co. (c. 38 m. south), of Scotch descent.—School until 15.—Full of life and energy; hard-working and skillful in managing his affairs. Clear, sharp, quick mind.—Speech natural, old-fashioned. Rapid tempo, but rather long vowels. The intonation of connected narrative is characterized by successive up-glides or down-glides.—L 56.

2. Farmer, 68. Born in Hiram (c. 6 m. south), but came to Denmark aged 6 months; moved to Sandy Creek, town of Bridgton (c. 8 m. northeast of Denmark), 14 years ago.—F born in Hiram; PGF born in Waterboro, York Co. (c. 30 m. south); GGF, an officer, came to Maine to fight Indians; PGM born in Ireland, emigrated to Cornish, York Co. (c. 10 m. south). M born in Denmark; MGF born in Stow, Middlesex Co., Mass.; MGM born in Australia; both grandparents of Scotch descent.— School in Denmark until 18.—Pleasant and genial; somewhat slow mentally. Inveterate story teller.— Slow tempo and even stress. Vowels rather long.— L 57.

370 Town of Woodstock (Bryant Pond), Oxford Co.

Settled c. 1798 (inc. 1815). Most of the families seem to have come from Plymouth Co., Mass.— Rural community.—Pop. 1820: 392, '50: 1012, '80: 952, 1910: 808, '30: 848.—Lapham, W. B. History of Woodstock, Me., with family sketches and an appendix. 315 p. Portland, 1882.

1. Farmer and laborer, 77. Born in Paris (c. 11 m. southeast), but came to Bryant Pond aged 3.— Parents born in Paris. PGM born in Welchville (c. 9 m. south of Paris). MGF born in Oakham, Worcester Co., Mass.; MGM born in Paris.—Bryant Pond school until 16.—Still strong and active. Rather talkative. Did not understand purpose of investigation.—Even stress and long vowels. The vowels as in *three, shoe, no, way,* are but slightly diphthongal, approaching [iˑ, uˑ, oˑ, eˑ].—L 52.

2. Mill worker, previously blacksmith, 74.—F born here; grandparents born in Dover, Strafford Co., N.H., came here in 1805. M born in Hebron (c. 18 m. southeast).—Bryant Pond school until 17. —Conservative, of limited interests, rather slow mentally. Direct and plain-spoken in the New England manner. Enjoys making good-natured fun of people.—Slow tempo, long vowels. Some nasalization. Sentences end in a drawled falling-rising inflection.—L 53.

372 Town of Hanover, Oxford Co.

Settled c. 1780 as part of Bethel; set off and (with the addition of Howard's Gore) inc. 1843. (First settler came to Bethel c. 1774 from Newton, Mass.) —Small rural community.—Pop. 1850: 266, '80: 203, 1910: 196, '30: 170.—Lapham, W. B., comp. History of Bethel, formerly Sudbury Canada, Oxford Co., Maine, 1768–1890, with a brief sketch of Hanover and family statistics. 688 p. Augusta, 1891.

Mechanical engineer, 71. Aged 26, went to Providence, R.I., and then to the Pacific coast. Taught in school of science in Pullman, Washington, and for 4 years in So. Dakota Agricultural College. Aged c. 38, went to live in Lawrence, Essex Co., Mass. Returned to Hanover when he was 65.—F, PGF, PGM born here. PGF's F born in Haverhill, Essex Co., Mass., went to work in Derry, Rockingham Co., N.H., and came here at 20. M born in Bethel (c. 8 m. southwest); MGF born in Londonderry, Rockingham Co., N.H., went to Bethel when young; MGM born in Gilead (c. 16 m. southwest), daughter of early settlers there.—Public school here. Academy at North Bridgton, Cumberland Co. (c. 26 m. south). B.M.E. degree from U. of Me. (Orono, Penobscot Co.).—Belongs to Masons, local clubs, engineering societies.—Pleasant, agreeable, intelligent.—Speech not precise. Vowels rather long.—The FW felt that the informant was representative of his birthplace, despite his long absence. However, his long stay in Lawrence, Mass., must have had some influence on his speech. The record is therefore not representative of Hanover in every respect.—L 61.

373 Town of Newry (North Newry), Oxford Co.

Settled 1781 (inc. 1805), some of the first settlers coming from Essex Co. (Methuen), Mass., and from Cape Elizabeth (q.v., 359).—Rural community with sharply decreasing population. Summer residents and tourists.—Pop. 1820: 304, '50: 459, '80: 337, 1910: 271, '30: 188.

Housewife, 83. Born in Grafton township (c. 9 m. northwest), a small rural community now depopulated. (Population reduced from 64 in 1910 to 5 in 1930.) Aged 7, went to Bethel (c. 10 m. south of North Newry). Married at 20 and came here to live. —F, PGF, PGM born in Dixfield (c. 20 m. east). M born in Londonderry, Windham Co., Vt., went to Grafton when she was a child.—Bethel Academy 2 years.—Methodist Church, Grange. Popular.— Kindly, intelligent, well informed.—'Better spoken' than the average, but willing to offer old-fashioned sayings she recalled. Moderate tempo. Speech not very precise. Slight nasalization. Vowels rather long. —L 60.

374 Town of New Portland, Somerset Co.

Granted to town of Falmouth (see 360 Portland). Settled c. 1785 (inc. 1808), some of the early settlers coming from ne. Mass. (Chelmsford, 211 Groton).— Rural community.—Pop. 1820: 817, '50: 1460, '80: 1271, 1910: 882, '30: 818.

Dry goods merchant, 63. Now lives in Kingfield, Franklin Co. (c. 7 m. northwest).—F, PGF born in Dead River plantation (c. 24 m. north of New Portland); latter's F born in Woburn, Middlesex Co., Mass. M born in Brooks, Waldo Co. (c. 55 m. southeast); parents moved here when she was young.—School until 17.—Masons, Lions Club, I.O.O.F.—Good-natured man of somewhat limited understanding.—Intonation characterized by short groups of falling tone.—L 135.

376 Town of Farmington (1 West Farmington; 2 Farmington), Franklin Co.

Settled c. 1781 (inc. 1794) from Dunstable, Middlesex Co., Mass. (Many of the first settlers of Dunstable were from 150 Boston.)—Farmington is the trading center of a fertile valley. Apple orchards.— County seat. Air of culture and of pride in family traditions. State normal school, est. 1863 (previously Farmington Academy, inc. 1807).—West Farmington is rural.—Pop. 1820: 1938, '50: 2725, '80: 3353, 1910: 3210, '30: 3600 (F. village 1737).— Butler, F. G. History of Farmington, Franklin Co., Maine, from the earliest explorations to the present time, 1776–1885. 683 p. Farmington, 1885.

1. Farmer, 67.—PGF born in Farmington; PGF's F born in Damariscotta, Lincoln Co. (c. 55 m. southeast). Family of the latter was of French descent, the original settler landing at Newburyport, Essex Co., Mass. PGF's M from Nobleboro (next town north of Damariscotta). PGM born in Damariscotta. MGF born in Farmington; MGF's F born in Truro, Barnstable Co., Mass.; MGM's F born in Farmington, of Truro ancestry; her M born in Farmington.— School here until 22, including normal school. Interested in all educational projects.—Kindly, very hospitable. Somewhat pompous.—Quick, nervous speech. Short vowels.—L 97.

2. CULTURED INFORMANT. College student, 22.—F (lawyer) born in Stonington, Hancock Co., of Nova Scotian ancestry. M born here, descended from old local families.—Academy at Hebron, Oxford Co. (c. 35 m. southwest), for 1 year, aged 18. Now in his 3rd year at Colby College, Waterville, Kennebec Co. (c. 28 m. east).—Fraternity man.—Much interested in the investigation.—Eager to answer the questions and thoroughly honest about his speech. Ignorant of many words natural to older people in this region, but uses unconsciously a number of local expressions. Articulation not quite as precise as that of most older people of his social station. Vowels tend to be long in syllables which are final or stressed for emphasis; otherwise short.—L 122.

377 Town of Turner, Androscoggin Co.

Settled 1775 (inc. 1786). Many families from Plymouth Colony.—Rural community. Small preparatory school.—Pop. 1790: 349, 1820: 1726, '50: 2536, '80: 2285, 1910: 1708, '30: 1362.—French,

W. R. History of Turner, Maine, from its settlement to 1886. 312 p. Portland, 1887.

1. Farmer, 73.—F born here; PGF born in Standish, Cumberland Co. (c. 40 m. southwest), of Cape Cod ancestry, partly Indian; PGM born in Buckfield, Oxford Co. (adjoining town west); her F was from Cape Cod. M born in Jay, Franklin Co. (c. 18 m. north), came here as a girl; MGF born in Auburn (c. 13 m. south).—Informant is a cousin of 2. Their uncle was once a presidential candidate and a favorite of the frontiersmen.—School here.—Hard of hearing. Becoming obtuse.—Archaic speech.—L 129.

2. Farmer, retired postal clerk, 72. Aged c. 29 to 39 was in California.—F born in Buckfield (see informant 1); PGF born in Gorham, Cumberland Co. (c. 43 m. southwest); PGM born in Hebron, Oxford Co. (c. 8 m. southwest). M born here; MGF born in Standish (see 1); MGM born in Buckfield. MGF and MGM were cousins, of Cape Cod ancestry, with some Indian blood.—School until 18. Rather well educated.—Universalist.—Intelligent, with a sense of humor. Fully understood purpose of investigation.—Does not employ certain old-fashioned pronunciations which are natural to informant 1, his cousin. Utterance a trifle slurred. Slight nasalization.—L 101.

378 Town of Webster (Sabattus), Androscoggin Co.

First settler in 1774 from Brunswick (q.v., 380). Set off from Lisbon and inc. 1840.—Factory village in rural area.—Pop. 1850: 1110, '80: 980, 1910: 1213, '30: 1134.

1. Factory worker, 83. Born in Greene (next town northwest).—Parents born here, had same surname; PGF born in Greene; PGM born on Cape Cod, lived in Greene.—School until 16, including 2 terms at a private high school.—Mason.—Rather typical of aged N.E. natives. Intelligent.—Old-fashioned speech. Numerous archaic features which he attributes to others actually appear in his unguarded conversation. Moderate tempo.—L 102.

2. Business man (real estate and wood), 42.—F, PGF born here, descended from original settlers; PGM born in Greene (adjoining town). M born in Lancashire, England, came here aged 10.—School here. 1 year of business college in city of Lewiston (c. 7 m. west).—Masons, Knights of Pythias.—Placid, mild-mannered, simple. Much interested in the questions.—Tempo often retarded. Slight nasalization. Vowels usually of moderate length.—L 103.

380 Town of Brunswick, Cumberland Co.

Settled c. 1730, inc. 1738 (earlier settlements had been destroyed). According to the names in the census of 1790, the pioneer families were largely Scotch-Irish.—One of the oldest lumbering regions in the state; center of the industry in early 19. cent. Cotton mills est. c. 1810. Shipbuilding in early 19. cent.—Trade center for a large section of the coast, including a number of summer resorts. Manufacturing: textiles, paper, boxes.—Nearly 60 percent of the population is of French-Canadian stock.—Bowdoin College (chartered 1794) forms a separate community with considerable prestige throughout the state.—Pop. 1764: 504, '90: 1387, 1820: 2931, '50: 4977, '80: 5384, 1910: 6621, '30: 7604 (B. village 6144).—Cleaveland, Nehemiah and A. S. Packard. History of Bowdoin College, with biographical sketches of its graduates from 1806 to 1879 inclusive. 905 p. Boston, 1882. Wheeler, G. A. and H. W. Wheeler. History of Brunswick, Topsham and Harpswell, Maine, including the ancient territory known as Pejepscot. 959 p. Boston, 1878.

1. Housewife, 81. Born in the village, moved west into the rural section at 3 or 4, then at 20 returned to the village again.—F, PGF born here; PGF's F born in Falmouth (c. 20 m. southwest), came here in 1760. Latter's F and M born in Gloucester, Essex Co., Mass.; his PGF came from the Isle of Jersey; his PGM's parents were from Freeport (c. 8 m. southwest). PGM born here; PGM's F born here of Scotch parents; her M born here. M born in Harpswell (c. 8 m. south); MGF born in Harpswell, of family originally from Mass.; MGM born in Boxford, Essex Co., Mass.—School here until 16.—Congregational Church. Informant enjoys good position in local society.—Old Me. type of speech, entirely different from the speech of the informant in 382 Harpswell (her mother's birthplace). Pinched, complacent, nasal voice. Unhurried tempo. Fairly precise articulation. Vowels and diphthongs have high tongue position and tend to be lengthened.—L 93.

380 Town of Topsham, Sagadahoc Co.

Settled 1717–22; settlement renewed 1730 (inc. 1764), largely Scotch-Irish. By 1749 hostility of the Indians had reduced the population to 25.—Residential town just across the Androscoggin R. from Brunswick (q.v., above), with which its development is bound up. Wood pulp first produced here in 1868.—Pop. 1764: 327, '90: 826, 1820: 1429, '50: 2010, '80: 1544, 1910: 2016, '30: 2111.—Wheeler, G. A. and H. W. Wheeler. History of Brunswick, Topsham and Harpswell, Maine. . . . 959 p. Boston, 1878.

2. Housewife, 74. Has done some farming and kept a restaurant and boarding house. Born in Bath (c. 6 m. east), came to Topsham aged 9, now lives in Brunswick. (Topsham and Brunswick are really parts of the same urban community.)—F born in the state, lived in Bath; his parents from Freeport, Cumberland Co. (c. 10 m. southwest). M, MGF, MGM born in Freeport. MGF's family originally from Nantucket, Mass.—School in Topsham until 16. (Son a well-known poet.)—Congregational Church.—Quick in manner and speech; alert and

cheerful.—Quick tempo. Articulation precise, but gentle. Vowels tend to be short.—L 94.

382 Town of Harpswell (Bailey Island), Cumberland Co.

Settled, c. 1720; set off from North Yarmouth (see 364 Yarmouth) and made a precinct in 1750; inc. 1758. Family names in U. S. census of 1790 point to Essex Co., Mass.—Bailey Island (locally Bailey's Island) was formerly a fishing community; many summer residents now. A bridge leads to Orr's Island, which is connected by bridges with the mainland. Previously the inhabitants communicated by boat with the other islands of Casco Bay and with Portland (c. 15 m. southwest).—Pop. 1764: 836, '90: 1071, 1820: 1253, '50: 1534, '80: 1773, 1910: 1650, '30: 1364.—Wheeler, G. A. and H. W. Wheeler. History of Brunswick, Topsham and Harpswell, Maine. . . . 959 p. Boston, 1878.

Postmaster, storekeeper, fisherman, 69.—F, PGF born here; PGF's F born on Orr's Island in 1765; latter's F born in Co. Wexford, Ireland; his M from Hingham, Plymouth Co., Mass. PGF's M born in Harpswell, daughter of Scotch-Irish pioneers. PGM born on Orr's Island. M, MGM born in Harpswell; MGF born in Monmouth, Kennebec Co. (c. 35 m. north), of Kittery, York Co., ancestry.—School here until 20.—Has many local contacts and is engaged in a good deal of town business.—Easy-going. Much interested in the investigation.—The diphthongs as in *way* and *no* sometimes have a very open beginning.—L 95.

384 Town of Waldoboro, Lincoln Co.

Settled between 1733 and 1740 by Germans who were invited to come here by General Samuel Waldo, proprietor of the Waldo Patent, a large tract of land including this town. (Waldoboro originally known as the plantation of Broadbay.) Also Scotch-Irish settlers. Laid waste by Indian attack in 1746. More German settlers c. 1752 (town inc. 1773).—Most of the people are descended from the original German colony. A number of families here spoke German until c. 1850, and a Lutheran church was maintained until after 1860.—Formerly some shipbuilding. Now fishing and summer tourist trade. Button factory.— The informant lives in the North Waldoboro section, a rural community.—Pop. 1790: 1720, 1820: 2449, '50: 4199, '80: 3758, 1910: 2656, '30: 2311.—Eaton, Cyrus. Annals of the town of Warren, with the early history of Broadbay. Ed. 2. Hallowell, 1877. Jordan, J. W. Sketch of the Moravian settlement at Broadbay, Maine, 1760–1770. 12 p. Bethlehem, Pa., 1891. (=Transactions of the Moravian Historical Society, v. 4, pt. 1.) Miller, Samuel. History of Waldoboro. 281 p. Wiscasset, 1910.

1. Farmer and miller, 99. Lived 10 years in R.I. when he was young, working as a cooper; then for a time in West Townsend, Middlesex Co., Mass. Was in the army. Returned home after the Civil War.— F, PGF born in Warren, Knox Co. (c. 5 m. east); PGF's F from Scotland, settled in Warren; his M from Ireland. PGM probably German. M born here; her parents of German descent.—School in North Waldoboro. 2 years at academy in Warren.— Mason.—Well-preserved, but very deaf. Mind quite clear.—Speech not markedly rustic or provincial. Pleasant, genial voice. Tempo not rapid. Clear articulation. Rather long vowels. His *r* is a weak, harsh, semi-fricative, retroflex sound. According to his granddaughter, he has always used it. Younger people here do not pronounce postvocalic *r*.—Short work sheets (lacking pp. 12–13, 24–25).—L 63.

384 Town of Nobleboro (Damariscotta Mills), Lincoln Co.

Part of the old Pemaquid Patent, a 17. cent. grant. Permanently settled c. 1730 (inc. 1788). Many Germans (see Waldoboro above) and Scotch-Irish.—Damariscotta Mills (a village partly in Nobleboro, partly in the adjoining town of Newcastle) was formerly a wealthy, aristocratic community.—Sharply declining population.—Pop. 1790: 1310, 1820: 1583, '50: 1408*, '80: 1142, 1910: 775, '30: 599.—Cushman, D. Q. History of ancient Sheepscot and Newcastle, including early Pemaquid, Damariscotta and other contiguous places, from the earliest discovery to the present time. . . . 458 p. Bath, 1882. Johnston, John. History of the towns of Bristol and Bremen in the state of Maine, including the Pemaquid settlement. 524 p. Albany, 1873.

2. Cultured informant. Single woman, at home, 50.—F, PGF, PGM born here; both PGF and PGM from old families of English ancestry. M, MGF, MGM born in Newcastle (adjoining town); MGF's parents born in Boston; MGF's GF, a prominent sea captain, came from Ireland.—School here. 3 or 4 years at Lincoln Academy in Newcastle. 2 years at a Catholic academy in Portland. (Mother formerly taught school.) Aged 20 to 40, spent winters in Cambridge, Middlesex Co., Mass.—Roman Catholic. D.A.R. Several local clubs.—Very intelligent. Much interested in the investigation.—A modern type of N.E. speech, reflecting her own family background rather than the usage of the community. Rapid tempo. Articulation moderately precise. Vowels inclined to be long.—L 64.

386 Town of Pittston, Kennebec Co.

Settled 1760 (inc. 1779) from Falmouth, Cumberland Co. (cf. Farmingdale below).—Rural community on the Kennebec R.—In the latter half of the 19. cent. quantities of ice were cut and stored here each winter. Much of the ice was shipped south by boat.—Pop. 1790: 603, 1820: 1337, '50: 2823, '80: 2458, 1910: 954*, '30: 893.—Hanson, J. W. History of Gardiner, Pittston and West Gardiner . . . from

1602 to 1852, with genealogical sketches. 343 p. Gardiner, 1852.

1. Farmer, 76. In winter cuts ice on the river. Aged 27, spent 4 months in N.Y. City.—F, PGF born here; latter's parents were Scotch; PGM (probably English) came from Bath, Sagadahoc Co. (c. 20 m. south). M born here; MGF born in Georgetown, Sagadahoc Co. (c. 30 m. south), of Irish parentage; MGM born in N.H.—School until 17.—Kindly, fond of children.—Local, uneducated type of speech, entirely unguarded. In sententious utterance his voice becomes solemn and resonant, and he speaks with homely eloquence and moral fervor. Deliberate tempo. Clear articulation usually. Some nasalization at times.—L 65.

386 Town of Farmingdale, Kennebec Co.

Settled c. 1787; org. 1852, including parts of Gardiner, West Gardiner and Hallowell. Gardiner settled as part of Pittston (q.v., above) c. 1760 from Falmouth, Cumberland Co.; some from New Hampshire and from Essex Co., Mass. Hallowell settled c. 1762, largely from Essex Co., Mass.—Farmingdale is practically a suburb of the city of Gardiner.— Pop. 1880: 789, 1910: 823, '30: 1044.— *Hallowell*: Nason, E. H. Old Hallowell. 359 p. Augusta, 1909. North, J. W. History of Augusta from the earliest settlement . . . with notices of the Plymouth company and settlements on the Kennebec. . . . 990 p. Augusta, 1870. (Contains information about Hallowell.)

2. Housewife, 62. Lived in Portland, Cumberland Co. (c. 48 m. southwest), aged 20 to 22. Then married and settled in Gardiner.—F born here; PGF, PGM born in Gardiner; PGF's GF born in Ireland, came to Mass., settled in Gardiner in 1760. M born in Gardiner; MGF born in Scarboro, Cumberland Co. (c. 55 m. southwest); MGM was of Scotch descent.—School until 18.—Methodist Church. Belongs to several organizations.—Rustic type. Slow thinker.—Slow, drawling speech. Fairly clear utterance. Some nasalization, some glottalization. The diphthongs as in *three, shoe, way, no* have an open beginning, which is greatly exaggerated in final position. Vowels normally short are long in her pronunciation and have an off-glide. Voiceless stops are strongly aspirated.—L 67.

388 Town of China (1 South China; 2 China), Kennebec Co.

Settled 1774; inc. 1796 as Harlem. Many of the early families appear to have come from Cape Cod and 124 Nantucket. (The adjoining town of Vassalboro was settled largely from Cape Cod.) Quaker and Baptist meeting houses in the town when it was finally inc. as China, including parts of Albion and Winslow, 1818-22. Albion had only six families in 1790; many of the early settlers were from York Co. Winslow had settlers in 1754 at Fort Halifax; a

number of Plymouth Colony families in the 1760's.— Declining rural community, with summer homes.— Pop. 1820: 894, '50: 2769, '80: 1769, 1910: 1297, '30: 1163.

1. Farmer, 76.—F born here; PGF in Brunswick, Cumberland Co. (c. 38 m. southwest), or in Durham, Androscoggin Co. (c. 40 m. southwest); PGM in Brooks, Waldo Co. (c. 25 m. northeast). M born here; MGF in Brunswick; MGM in Berwick, York Co.—School until 17.—Speaks at Quaker meetings here.—Intelligent.—Measured tempo. Clear utterance. Rather long vowels.—L 62.

2. Housewife, 55.—F, PGF, PGM born here. PGF's family originally from Cape Cod. M, MGF, MGM born here. MGF's family from Berwick, York Co.—School until 16. Likes reading better than housekeeping. People here consider her educated, capable and progressive.—Used to go to Friends' Church. Belongs to the Grange. Husband died 5 years after their marriage. Lives with her son and her mother, aged 99, in a remote farmhouse on a back road.—Energetic, obliging, fairly intelligent. Dislikes to make definite statements; frequently undecided.—Fairly trustworthy informant. Moderate tempo. Clear articulation.—L 69.

390 Town of Norridgewock, Somerset Co.

Settled c. 1783 (inc. 1788) from Middlesex Co., Mass. (156 Concord, 211 Groton).—When Somerset County was est. in 1809, Norridgewock became for a while the county seat.—The informant lives outside the center of town in a rural section to the south.— Pop. 1790: 332, 1820: 1454, '50: 1848, '80: 1491, 1910: 1608, '30: 1481.—Allen, William. History of Norridgewock, comprising memorials of the aboriginal inhabitants and Jesuit missionaries . . . 252 p. Norridgewock, 1849. Hanson, J. W. History of the old towns of Norridgewock and Canaan. . . . 371 p. Boston, 1849.

1. Farmer, 53.—F born in Mercer (c. 7 m. west); PGF of Cape Cod ancestry; PGM born in Windham, Cumberland Co. M, MGF born here; latter's F born in Canaan (c. 13 m. northeast), son of an original settler from Chelmsford, Middlesex Co., Mass.; MGM born in Vt.—School until 17.—Grange. Knights of Pythias.—An old bachelor. Interested in the history of the early settlers. Likes to talk.— Naturally uses old-fashioned speech. Slow tempo.— L 127.

390 Town of Skowhegan, Somerset Co.

Settled as part of Canaan in 1792 (inc. 1823), largely from Middlesex Co., Mass. (The first families came from 156 Concord.)—Skowhegan, now the county seat, is the shopping center of a good agricultural section.—Pop. 1850: 1756, '80: 3860, 1910: 5341, '30: 6433.—Hanson, J. W. History of the old towns of Norridgewock and Canaan, comprising . . . Skowhegan. . . . 371 p. Boston, 1849.

2. Osteopath (woman), 71. Was born in a rather primitive rural section of the town, now lives in central part.—F born in Palmyra (c. 20 m. east); PGF in Raymond, Rockingham Co., N.H.; latter's F from Hampton, Rockingham Co., N.H., of family from the Isle of Jersey; his M from Hampton. PGM and her F born in Gorham, Cumberland Co.; her parents were of Barnstable Co., Mass., ancestry (town of Barnstable). M, MGM born in Athens (c. 11 m. north); MGF in Limington, York Co.; MGM's parents in Exeter, Rockingham Co., N.H.—Rural school. 3 years in American School of Osteopathy, Kirksville, Mo.—Very agreeable and coöperative.—Speech fairly modern, probably because of her numerous contacts. *p, t, k* strikingly unaspirated.—L 121.

391 Town of Newport, Penobscot Co.

Settled c. 1808 (inc. 1814) from older Me. towns.—A rather modern town. The population is extremely varied. During the last 25 years people from Aroostook Co. have been coming here.—Pop. 1820: 510, '50: 1210, '80: 1451, 1910: 1747, '30: 1731.—A brief history of Newport, Maine. Centennial souvenir, 1814–1914. 58 p. Newport, 1914.

¹ Farmer's wife, 91. Used to visit Mass. in her youth, a few months at a time. For the last 20 years has lived in Bangor (c. 25 m. east).—F born in Hallowell, Kennebec Co. (c. 50 m. southwest), moved to Mercer, Somerset Co. (c. 33 m. west); PGF from Hallowell, formerly of Turner, Androscoggin Co. (c. 65 m. southwest), of Scotch descent; PGM from Readfield, Kennebec Co. (c. 45 m. southwest). M, MGF born in Augusta, Kennebec Co. MGF fought in the Revolution.—School until 14. Reads considerably.—Baptist. Does church work.—Tall, strong healthy. Appears much younger than her age. Has the reserved good manners of the older generation, but is by no means old-fashioned in her interests and associations. Keen-minded, quick, friendly, natural.—Speech suggests western Me. More leisurely and quiet than Penobscot Co. speech, with longer vowels and less painfully sharp enunciation.—L 71.

2. Automobile mechanic and assistant postmaster, formerly store clerk, 64.—F born in Howland (c. 43 m. northeast); PGF in St. Stephen, New Brunswick, Canada; PGM in Milford (c. 33 m. east); PGF's F born in Epsom, Merrimack Co., N.H.; his M in Gouldsboro, Hancock Co. (c. 65 m. southeast). M born in Greenbush (c. 35 m. northeast); MGF in The Forks plantation, Somerset Co., at the junction of Dead R. and the Kennebec R. (c. 50 m. northwest); MGM in Argyle (c. 35 m. northeast).—School until 16. Reads a great deal, especially books of science and natural history. Has many interests.—Mason; Grange.—Modern in point of view.—Very quick, nervous speech. Precise enunciation. Short vowels. Represents the Penobscot Co. element in the town, whereas informant 1 represents the western Me. element.—L 72.

392 Town of Dover-Foxcroft (Dover), Piscataquis Co.

The towns of Dover and Foxcroft were joined in 1922. Dover org. as a plantation in 1812 (inc. 1822); first settler from Temple, N.H. Foxcroft was one of several towns granted by the state c. 1795 to Bowdoin College; settled 1805 (inc. 1812).—County seat. Modern shopping center of a good agricultural region. Rather isolated. Inhabitants largely of native stock.—Pop. 1820: 211 (Foxcroft only), '50: 2972, '80: 2950, 1910: 3958, '30: 3750.—Lowell, Mary C., comp. Old Foxcroft, Maine, traditions and memories with family records. 262 p. Concord, N.H., 1935.

1. Housewife, 84. Born in Dover; moved to Garland, Penobscot Co. (c. 10 m. south), when she married; lived there 40 years. For the last 13 years has been back in town, in Foxcroft section.—F born in Dover, PGF, PGM from Dover, latter of Cape Cod ancestry. M born in Readfield, Kennebec Co. (c. 65 m. southwest); MGF, a Quaker, born on Cape Cod; MGM from Readfield.—School in Dover. Academy, aged 16 to 18. Correspondent for newspaper 28 years. Interested in genealogy and history.—Quick, alert.—Rapid, precise speech suggests possible Cape Cod influence.—L 98.

2. Housewife, 68.—F born in Dover; PGF in Pembroke, Plymouth Co., Mass.; PGM born in 1796 in Norridgewock, Somerset Co. (c. 43 m. southwest), came here aged 9; PGM's F in Pepperell, Middlesex Co., Mass.; her M, PGF and PGM in Groton, Middlesex Co., Mass. M born in Dover; MGF in Thomaston, Knox Co. (c. 77 m. south); MGM (supposed to be Dutch) in Rockland, Knox Co. (c. 75 m. south).—School in Dover until 14. (Has made many sacrifices to educate her children.)—Baptist. Belongs to several organizations.—Kind, motherly.—Drawling, pleasant voice. Long vowels.—L 99.

394 Town of Owls Head, Knox Co.

Settled 1776 by three men from Harpswell (q.v., 382), from Plainfield, Conn., and from Middleton, Mass. Set off from South Thomaston in 1921. South Thomaston set off from Thomaston in 1848. Thomaston permanently settled 1763 (inc. 1777) from eastern Mass. (Bradford, Gloucester; Walpole, Stoughton; Attleboro).—Owls Head is a maritime town, with a summer colony, on a small cape south of Rockland (q.v., below).—Thomaston formerly built ships.—Pop. 1930: 574. (Pop. of South Thomaston: 1850: 1420, '80: 1771, 1910: 1438, '30: 579*.)—Eaton, Cyrus. History of Thomaston, Rockland and South Thomaston, Maine, from their first exploration. . . . 2v. Hallowell, 1865.

1. Housewife, 90. Has done tailoring. Lived for 23 years in the lighthouse here. Used to go to sea with her male relatives.—F born here; PGF in Kittery, York Co.; PGM near Bangor, Penobscot Co.

M born here; MGF, MGM in Rockland.—School until 16.—Active social contacts.—Very lively for her years; slightly forgetful.—Extremely quick speech with very short vowels. Articulation would be precise if it were not so rapid. Stress fairly even, nowhere actually strong. Weak retroflection is characteristic of the older people here, although some younger speakers in Owls Head have it.—L 75.

394 City of Rockland, Knox Co.

Settled c. 1769. Set off from Thomaston in 1848, became a city 1854. (For Thomaston see Owls Head, above.)—County seat, on the west shore of Penobscot Bay. Formerly a busy fishing and sailing port, with shipbuilding and limestone quarrying. Tourist trade now. Excellent lobster fishing. The lime industry, which was at its height c. 1900, is again becoming active.—Pop. 1850: 5052, '80: 7599, 1910: 8174, '30: 9075.

2. Town officer, formerly bookseller, 60.—F born in Rockport (c. 7 m. north); PGF in Frankfort, Waldo Co. (c. 37 m. northeast); PGM in Searsmont, Waldo Co. (c. 20 m. north). M, MGF, MGM born here; MGGM of original German stock here.—School until 18.—Mason. Highly respected.—Intelligent and accurate.—Rapid tempo. Naturally precise and clear-cut articulation. Usually very short vowels.—L 92.

396 Town of Frankfort, Waldo Co.

Settled as early as 1770 (inc. 1789), largely from Cape Cod.—Several towns, including Winterport, and parts of towns have been taken from Frankfort. —A country town on the Penobscot R., near enough to Penobscot Bay to have known something of seafaring life.—Pop. 1790: 891, 1820: 2129, '50: 4233, '80: 1157*, 1910: 1157, '30: 468.—Jones, Erasmus. History of Frankfort. 57 p. Winterport, 1897.— *Winterport:* Littlefield, Ada Douglas. An old river town: a history of Winterport. 249 p. New York, 1907.

1. Retired stone worker and farmer, 78. For the past 20 years has lived in Belfast (c. 15 m. south).— F, PGF born here. M born in Prospect (adjoining town south); MGF, MGM in Bucksport, Hancock Co. (just across the river).—School until 12 or 14. Semi-illiterate.—Very poor. Not in good health. Open and approachable, simple, guileless. Apart from his own practical experience, his knowledge is limited.—His rapid and precise enunciation, short vowels and strong, equal stress suggest Cape Cod or other eastern Mass. ancestry. Occasionally uses weak retroflection (cf. 394.1), which is not found in the speech of the younger generation (cf. the rather modern speech of informant 2.—L 70.

396 Town of Searsport, Waldo Co.

Originally part of Belfast and Prospect; inc. 1845. Belfast settled c. 1770 by Scotch-Irish from London-

derry, N.H. (q.v., 318). Many of the Prospect settlers were from Cape Cod.—Searsport (c. 10 m. south of Frankfort), formerly a shipbuilding port, is now a quiet town. Shipping of potatoes which come by rail from Aroostook Co.—Summer residents.— Pop. 1850: 2208, '80: 2322, 1910: 1444, '30: 1414·— *Belfast:* Williamson, Joseph. History of the city of Belfast in the state of Maine from its earliest settlement in 1770 to 1875. 956 p. Portland, 1877. Second volume, 1875–1900. Completed and edited by Alfred Johnson. Boston, 1913.

2. Postmaster, official of a bank and of an electric company, formerly shipmaster, 72. Aged 18 to 40, went on voyages all over the world with only occasional visits home. Then settled in the eastern section of the town.—F, PGF born here; PGM born here, of English descent. GGF from Londonderry, Rockingham Co., N.H., of Scotch ancestry. M, MGF, MGM born in Thomaston, Knox Co. (c. 30 m. southwest). M came here when she was 10.— School here until 14. Academy in Hallowell, Kennebec Co. (c. 45 m. west), until 17. Never learned much about foreign life except in the ports to which he voyaged.—Intelligent. Respected by the townspeople.—Friendly, but rather dignified and reserved. Somewhat nervous in manner. Power of word-association neither good nor quick.—Rather modern type of speech.—L 74.

398 Town of Bluehill, Hancock Co.

Settled 1762 (inc. 1789), largely from Essex Co., Mass. (Andover, 182 Beverly, 194 Newburyport).— Several small mills and much shipbuilding by c. 1800. Busy seaport c. 1850. Copper was formerly an important product, but has not been mined for 20 years.—Now a quiet town, its chief activities bound up with its summer colony.—Pop. 1790: 274, 1820: 957, '50: 1939, '80: 2213, 1910: 1462, '30: 1439.— Candage, R. G. F. Settlement and progress of the town of Bluehill, Maine. 43 p. Bluehill, 1886. Candage, R. G. F. Historical Sketches. 83 p. Ellsworth, 1905.

1. Farmer, road commissioner, fence viewer, 81. Lives in rural section, 3 miles out of village.—F born here; PGF, one of the early settlers here, born either in Boston, Mass., or in southwestern Me.; PGM born here (1st child born in Bluehill Falls). M born here; MGF, MGM were fairly early settlers.—School until 14, but practically uneducated.—Member of Grange for 49 years.—Highly intelligent, old-fashioned farmer, purely local in type.—Rapid tempo. Good articulation.—The FW heard no retroflex vowels in Bluehill. In Brooklin (c. 10 m. south), where many people settled from Gloucester, Essex Co., Mass., the FW heard a strong r-vowel from one man and a weaker one from several speakers.— L 78.

2. Housewife, 58.—F, PGF born here; PGM in Sedgwick (c. 8 m. south). PGF's PGF was an origi-

nal settler from Beverly, Mass. M born here; MGF, MGM in Bucksport (c. 15 m. northwest).—Academy here.—Well acquainted in the town.—Modern, up-to-date. Intelligent, quick, coöperative.—Rapid tempo. Good articulation.—L 79.

400 Town of Tremont (Bayside), Hancock Co.

Originally part of town of Mount Desert (inc. 1789) on Mount Desert Island; set off and inc. in 1848 as town of Mansel; name changed to Tremont the same year.—The island had been settled c. 1763 from Gloucester, Cape Cod and other parts of Mass., and from the older Maine towns. During the 19. cent. fish and lumber industries, later granite quarrying. By c. 1875 the important summer tourist business had begun.—Pop. 1850: 1425, '80: 2011, 1910: 1116*, '30: 954. (Pop. of Mount Desert town: 1790: 744, 1820: 1349, '50: 782*.)—Cousins, E. M. 1792–1895: the Mount Desert Congregational Church, Tremont, Maine; historical sermon and notes. N.p., n.d. De Costa, B. F. Hand-book of Mount Desert, coast of Maine, with the routes thither, . . . sketches of the history. . . . 161 p. New York, 1878. Street, George E. Mount Desert, a history. Ed. by S. A. Eliot. 370 p. Boston, 1905.

1. Housewife, 79.—PGF born here, of family from Boothbay, Lincoln Co., of Highland Scotch descent; PGM born here. MGF, MGM born here (possibly of German ancestry).—School until 16. Few educational advantages.—No contacts with tourists.—Depressed, in rather poor health. Extremely rapid association of ideas. Either knows an expression at once or else has to have it suggested to her.—Unguarded, effortless speech. Very quick tempo. Short vowels. Retroflection variable; of the Gloucester, Mass., type like that found west of Mt. Desert Island across the channel in Brooklin (see remarks under 398.1). Younger generation has no retroflection.—L 80.

400 Town of Southwest Harbor, Hancock Co.

Set off 1905 from Tremont (q.v., above).—Resort town on Mt. Desert Island. Many people come to this region in summer.—Pop. 1910: 888, '30: 888.

2. Housewife, 74. Aged c. 31, went to live in Northeast Harbor, Mt. Desert town (in the eastern part of the island, with summer colony).—F born in Ireland, settled here. M, MGM born here; MGF born in northern Ireland; MGM's F from Gloucester Mass., descendant of a Jew from Archangel in Russia, who settled there c. 1700; her M from Newbury, Essex Co., Mass.—School until 16.—Has some social distinction here.—She and the supplementary informant have been lifelong friends and insisted on answering the questions together.—Speech of these two women very similar. Retroflection inconsistent: sometimes absent, sometimes very strong, usually fairly mild; the type may have originated with the Gloucester settlers who came to Brooklin on the mainland. Scotch-Irish influence, however, cannot be overlooked. (Younger speakers do not use retroflection.)

Supplementary informant: housewife, 80. Aged 28, went to live in Northeast Harbor.—F born in Bar Harbor (in the eastern part of the island), of Irish descent. M, MGF born here; MGM of English descent. MGF's ancestor who first settled here was from Castine (on the eastern shore of Penobscot Bay).—School until 12. Then lived in lighthouse 4 years. Attended school again, aged 16 to 18.—The contributions of this supplementary informant are not identified.—L 96.

402 Town of Penobscot, Hancock Co.

Settled 1760 (inc. 1787), probably from Cape Cod. (Castine, set off 1796, had an early Plymouth Colony trading post, later a French fort. French occupation lasted through the 17. cent. Baron Castine settled here in the 1660's.)—Small town on Penobscot Bay. Summer visitors.—Pop. 1790: 1040, 1820: 1009*, '50: 1556, '80: 1341, 1910: 985, '30: 708*.—Wheeler, G. A. History of Castine, Penobscot and Brooksville, Maine, including the ancient settlement of Pentagoët. 401 p. Bangor, 1875.—*Castine:* Wheeler, G. A. Castine, past and present; the ancient settlement of Pentagoët and the modern town. 112 p. Boston, 1896.

1. School janitor (retired 4 years ago), 90. Born on a farm in the northern part of the town. Aged 18, went to live in Ellsworth (c. 15 m. east), where he worked in a mill; later was janitor there for 36 years.—F, PGF born in Castine (c. 8 m. southwest); PGM a Scotch Presbyterian, lived in Castine. PGF's F, an Irishman, was an early settler there. M born in Brooksville (c. 10 m. south); MGF from Brooksville, of English descent.—School here until 18.—Very active for his age. Inveterate talker. Glad to give all the information he could.—Deliberate tempo. Often rather long vowels. The diphthong as in *way* has a close beginning.—L 76.

402 City of Ellsworth, Hancock Co.

Settled 1763 (inc. 1800, as city 1869), mostly from Saco, York Co. (see 356 Biddeford).—County seat. Small, wealthy, aristocratic city, which used to be prominent in lumbering, manufacturing and shipping. Now attracts tourists.—Pop. 1820: 892, '50: 4009, '80: 5052, 1910: 3549, '30: 3557.—Davis, Albert. History of Ellsworth, Me. 244 p. Lewiston, 1927. Whittlesey, Derwent. Coast land and interior mountain valley: a geographical study of two typical localities in northern New England [Ellsworth and Lancaster, N.H.]. New England's prospect: 1933, ed. by John K. Wright. American Geographical Society, special publication no. 16, 446–58. New York, 1933.

2. Housewife, 83.—F born here; PGF, from London, England, was a land agent here; PGM born in

Taunton, Bristol Co., Mass., daughter of an officer in the Revolution. M born here; MGF born in Rutland, Rutland Co., Vt.; MGM born in Castine (c. 25 m. southwest); latter's parents from Castine.—Private school until 16.—Well-to-do. Has quiet, friendly air of good breeding.—Rapid tempo. Precise articulation. Short vowels. Very clear *l* in most positions.—L 77.

403 Town of Holden (East Holden), Penobscot Co.

Set off from Brewer (q.v., 404) in 1850. Brewer settled 1786 from southeastern Mass. (140 Wrentham, Mansfield, Norton).—Rural community.—Pop. 1880: 717, 1910: 609, '30: 543.

Farmer, deputy sheriff, 73. When he was younger, spent much time trapping in the woods. 1 year in Colorado, aged 22.—F born in Eddington (c. 7 m. north); PGF settled in 1811 in Dedham, Hancock Co. (c. 3 m. south); he and his wife were probably from Wrentham, Norfolk Co., Mass. M, MGF born in China, Kennebec Co. (c. 47 m. southwest).—School until 19.—Congregational Church. I.O.O.F.—Genuine, open, companionable nature. Answered the questions because he believed his type of speech should be preserved for the younger generation.—Very quick tempo. Precise articulation. Very short vowels. Stress not strong, and more or less even.—L 73.

404 City of Brewer, Penobscot Co.

Settled as part of Orrington in 1786 (inc. 1812, as city 1889), from se. Mass. (140 Wrentham, Mansfield, Norton). John Brewer had come to Orrington from Worcester (205) in 1770, but settlement was checked by the Revolution.—Part of the urban area of the city of Bangor (just across the Penobscot R.).—Used to build ships, now manufactures pulp and paper.—Pop. 1820: 744, '50: 2628, '80: 3170, 1910: 5667, '30: 6329.—Paine, A. W. The territorial history of Bangor and vicinity. Maine Historical Society collections 9 (1887), 221–34. Portland.

CULTURED INFORMANT. Housewife, 68. Has lived for short periods in Chicago and other places.—F born in Hampden (c. 7 m. southwest); PGF in Pelham, Hillsborough Co., N.H., of Essex Co., Mass., ancestry; PGM in Frankfort, Waldo Co. (c. 15 m. south), of Cape Cod ancestry. M born in Hampden; MGF in Hampden, of Durham, Strafford Co., N.H., ancestry; MGM in Fairfield, Somerset Co. (c. 43 m. southwest), of Cape Cod ancestry. MGF's M also of Cape Cod ancestry.—Academy in Andover, Essex Co., Mass., and Smith College, Northampton, Mass. Has done research in Maine ballads and local history.—Knows speech of Maine woodsmen. Has observed local dialects carefully, without being conscious of slight differences in pronunciation. Reported her own usage objectively: the natural speech of a cultivated person of democratic background from an urban community. Moderate tempo. Rather precise articulation. Short vowels.—L 100.

406 Town of Gouldsboro (1 Gouldsboro; 2 West Gouldsboro), Hancock Co.

Settled 1764 (inc. 1789) from Saco, York Co. (see 356 Biddeford) and vicinity. Many of the settlers were lumbermen.—Rural town on the coast. Summer residents.—West Gouldsboro, on Frenchman Bay, is a small community which considers itself more progressive than the rest of the town.—Pop. 1790: 267, 1820: 560, '50: 1400, '80: 1825, 1910: 1349*, '30: 1115.—Clarke, Grace Wood. Historical researches of Gouldsboro. 108 p. West Gouldsboro, 1904.

1. Housewife, 59.—Descended from early settlers here. F, PGF, PGM, PGF's F born here; PGF's M from Cherryfield, Washington Co. (c. 12 m. northeast); PGF's PGF born in South Berwick, York Co., in 1726; PGF's PGM born in Berwick, York Co., in 1749, came here when she was c. 15; PGF's GGF came to America in 1700, married in Portsmouth, Rockingham Co., N.H. M, MGF born here; MGM born in West Gouldsboro.—School here until 21.—Methodist. Active member of the Grange. Keeps house for her brother, a bachelor.—Good-hearted, buxom country woman. Trustworthy informant.—Although she is younger, her speech is more old-fashioned than that of 2. Unvoicing of final stops and fricatives reminded FW of York Co. and of coastal N.H. speech (this characteristic continues to the east). As an individual feature, consonants at the end of breath groups are followed by [ə].—L 81.

2. Housewife, former schoolteacher, 77. Aged 13, lived 1 year in Woburn, Middlesex Co., Mass.—F born in Sorrento (a short distance west on a peninsula jutting into the bay); PGF born in Hollis, Hillsborough Co., N.H.; PGM born in Steuben, Washington Co. (c. 8 m. east). M, MGM born in Fredericton, New Brunswick; MGF born in York, York Co. M came here as a child.—School until 18. Used to travel by boat twice a year to Boston.—Quiet, effortless speech with precise articulation and short vowels.—L 82.

407 Town of Jonesport, Washington Co.

Probably settled by the Cumberland Co. families who first came to Jonesboro in the 1760's (see Roque Bluffs, 408); inc. 1832.—Fishing community. Sardine packing.—Jonesport people are amiable, trusting, inclined to be superstitious. (Life on the islands to the south is more primitive than on the mainland.)—Many summer visitors in this region.—Pop. 1850: 826, '80: 1563, 1910: 2074, '30: 1641*.—Drisko, G. W. (anon.) The revolution: life of Hannah Weston with a brief record of her ancestry, also a condensed history of the first settlement of Jonesborough, Machias and other neighboring towns, by a citizen. 163 p. Machias, 1857

1. Worker in fish factory, former fisherman, 90. Born on Head Harbor Island. Spent last 40 years on the mainland.—F born in Frankfort, Waldo Co., came here to Great Wass Island when a boy; PGF, PGM born in Frankfort. M, MGF born on Beals Island, descendants of original settler from York Co. (Beals town was organized from part of Jonesport in 1925).—Was 12 years old when a school was established on the island; went for a few years. Practically illiterate. Limited experience.—A noted local story teller, entertaining his friends night after night with long narratives.—Still walks to his work and sometimes stands nearly all day.—[æ] in many words of the type of *pass*. The diphthong as in *nine* has a low and backish beginning, as in the speech of some other island people; this type is not heard on the mainland. His post-vocalic *r* is consonantal and very retroflex; sometimes it is absent (depending on the style of speech). The *r* also is characteristic of some of the island people and not of the mainland, but it is nowhere common.—The inhabitants of Jonesport have very melodious voices and a peculiar rising and falling intonation.—L 83.

2. Housewife and hotel manager, 61. Born in Monsapec, formerly called Mason's Bay.—F born in Machias (to the northeast). M, MGF, MGM born here. MGM's family from Gardiner, Kennebec Co.—School until 18.—Surrounds herself with young people.—A motherly woman of some taste and refinement. Rather modern, but essentially of her community. Somewhat lacking in critical faculty.—Her speech belongs to the mainland type, not to that of the islands. Local type of intonation. Rapid tempo. Vowels often prolonged.—L 84.

408 Town of Roque Bluffs, Washington Co.

Settled as part of Jonesboro; set off and inc. 1891. Jonesboro settled 1763–64 (inc. 1809) from Cumberland Co.: Falmouth (see 360 Portland), Scarborough. (Scarborough permanently settled c. 1715.)—Small farming town on the peninsula to the east of Englishman Bay (east of 407 Jonesport and 7 m. south of Machias). Its people are noted for being simple and easy-going and for having a drawling speech.—Pop. 1910: 105, '30: 108. (Pop. of Jonesboro: 1820: 675, '50: 466*, '80: 555.)

1. Fisherman, ship carpenter, farmer, 50.—F born here; PGF in Jonesboro; PGM and PGF's M from Jonesport. M, MGF, MGM born here; MGF's F born here in 1793, son of a Hessian soldier who married a woman from Quincy, Norfolk Co., Mass.; MGF's M from Jefferson, Lincoln Co.—School until 15.—Well acquainted locally.—Dislikes hurry and bother. Will discuss anything.—Very drawling speech with vowels often much prolonged. All vowels rather open. Some nasalization. Uses retroflex tap *r*, which reminded the FW of York and Cumberland Counties.—L 86.

408 Town of Machias, Washington Co.

Settled 1763 (inc. 1784) from Scarborough, Cumberland Co. Plymouth Colony trading post here as early as 1633. (The 17. cent. settlement in Scarborough had been destroyed; town resettled c. 1715.)—County seat. Aristocratic little town with something of the rough, democratic character of the frontier; built up by lumbering and shipping.—Pop. 1790: 818, 1820: 2033, '50: 1590*, '80: 2203, 1910: 2089, '30: 1856.—Drisko, George W. History of Machias. 589 p. Machias, 1904.

2. CULTURED INFORMANT. Lumberman, 66.—F born in East Machias; PGF's family from St. George, Knox Co.; PGM from St. George, partly of Scotch-Irish descent. M born in East Machias; MGF in Machiasport (both neighboring towns) MGF's F from Northampton, Hampshire Co., Mass.; MGM's F from Cumberland Co., Nova Scotia; MGM's MGM from Newport, R.I., of Mass. ancestry.—School here and for 2 years in Providence, R.I.—32nd degree Mason. Interested in state politics.—Well-to-do, prominent here. Has spent much of his life in the woods to the north, roughing it with his men.—Cultivated speech. Deliberate tempo. Uses retroflex tap *r*, as does informant 1.—L 85.

410 Town of Lubec (North Lubec), Washington Co.

Settled c. 1776 from Cumberland Co., Nova Scotia, by fugitives forced by the Revolution to leave British territory; inc. 1811, set off from Eastport. (Eastport settled during the same period; fishermen from Newburyport, Mass., seem to have come in 1772, and later some of the Lubec men left the mainland to settle in what is now the island town of Eastport.)—Quiet coast town; fishing, canning of fish. A number of people from Campobello Island (Canada) have come here; also some Irishmen from St. Andrews, New Brunswick.—Pop. 1820: 1430, '50: 2814, '80: 2109, 1910: 3363, '30: 2994.—Kilby, W. H., ed. Eastport and Passamaquoddy, a collection of historical and biographical sketches. 505 p. Eastport, 1888.

Housewife, former teacher, married, 68. Now living in Lubec. (Left North Lubec at 14.)—F, PGF, PGM born here. PGF's family of Mass. origin. PGM's family from Gouldsboro, Hancock Co., originally from South Berwick, York Co. (family from which 406.1 is descended). M born in Perry (c. 10 m. north across the bay); MGF born near Augusta, Kennebec Co., of Scotch-Irish origin; MGM from same place.—Taught by her M (former schoolteacher). High school in Pembroke (c. 10 m. northwest across the bay). Later went to school for a year in Salem, Essex Co., Mass. Taught in Lubec c. 5 years.—Appears interested in everything about her; conventional mind, which catalogs each matter in its proper place.—Thin, high-pitched, nasal voice that cuts each word off sharply, and yet has a certain grace and delicacy. Some lengthening of vowels and slurring of consonants.—L 87.

411 Town of Perry, Washington Co.

Settled c. 1790 (grant made 1786; inc. 1818).—Rural town on Passamaquoddy Bay.—Pop. 1820: 407, '50: 1324, '80: 1047, 1910: 1153, '30: 992.

Fisherman, farmer, town officer, 70. Went to sea 15 years, aged 23 to 38.—F, PGF born here of American ancestry; PGM born in northern Ireland (Protestant). M born in Robbinston (c. 8 m. north); MGF |from Robbinston, of American ancestry; MGM born in Ireland (Catholic).—School until 20. 1 year of high school in Dennysville (c. 10 m. southwest).—Baptist Church, Grange.—Never troubled to inquire about the purpose of the investigation.—Gave quick responses. Speech very rustic and old-fashioned, with rather long vowels and somewhat precise articulation. Some nasalization.—L 88.

412 City of Calais (1 Bog Brook neighborhood; 2 Red Beach), Washington Co.

Settled in the 1780's (inc. as town 1809, as city 1850).—Small backwoods town until after 1820. Lumbering, shipbuilding. Many people from New Brunswick.—Red Beach is a fishing and farming community c. 7 m. east of the city proper (a ward of the city).—Pop. 1820: 418, '50: 4749, '80: 6173, 1910: 6116, '30: 5470.—Knowlton, I. C. Annals of Calais, Maine, and St. Stephen, New Brunswick. . . . 208 p. Calais, 1875.

1. Civil engineer and land surveyor, 64. Lives in a rural section of Calais.—Some Scotch-Irish ancestry on both isdes. F born here; PGF born in China, Kennebec Co., in 1801; PGF's F of family from Nantucket, Mass.; PGF's M from China, Kennebec Co.; PGM and her M (of Dutch descent) born in New Brunswick, just across the St. Croix R.; PGM's F born in Troy, Rensselaer Co., N.Y. M, MGF born here; MGF's F born in Machias (c. 35m. south); MGF's M from Eastport (c. 25 m. southeast); MGF's PGM from Machias, of family from Scarborough, Cumberland Co.; MGM born in Steuben (c. 60 m. southwest); MGM's F born in Scarborough; MGM's M from Cherryfield (c. 50 m. southwest); MGM's PGM from Portland, Cumberland Co., was first woman physician in Me.—School until 19.—Rather well educated and intelligent.—Somewhat self-conscious about his speech. Rapid tempo. Short vowels usually. His slight retroflection, in the FW's opinion, is probably not due to Canadian influence.—L 89.

2. Musician, 53. Lived 15 years in Boston but spent every summer here.—F born on Dochet Island (U.S.A.) in the St. Croix R.; PGF born in Milltown, Calais; PGF's F from Randolph, Norfolk Co., Mass.; PGM lived here, born probably in Scotland. M born in Pictou, Nova Scotia, of Irish

descent, came here aged 2.—2 years of high school in Calais; graduated from high school in Boston; 2 years at Classical Institute in Houlton, Aroostook Co.—Masons, I.O.O.F., Knights of Pythias, Rotary Club, etc.—Pleasant, coöperative. Artistic in temperament, not intellectual.—In personality and speech rather like 408.1. Mild-mannered drawl, slow tempo, vowels overlong.—L 90.

416 Town of Lincoln, Penobscot Co.

Settled c. 1825 (inc. 1829).—Country town on the Penobscot R., in wooded region. Agriculture. Woolen manufacturing.—Pop. 1850: 1356, '80: 1659, 1910: 1988, '30: 2970 (L. village 2161).

1. Housewife, 90.—F born in Amesbury, Essex Co., Mass., came here when young. M born in (?) Charleston (c. 35 m. southwest).—Physically in good condition for her years, but tires easily. Did not understand purpose of investigation.—Old-fashioned local speech.—Incomplete record: only pp. 7–11, 14–23, 26–42, 44–47, 50–51, 54–56, 58–84.—L 133.

416 Town of Lee, Penobscot Co.

Granted by Mass. to Williams College (in 248 Williamstown) and sold to Cumberland Co. men. Two of the first few settlers, who came in 1824, were from Howland and Lowell in Penobscot Co. Town inc. 1832.—Small country town in wooded region, c. 10 m. east of Lincoln.—Pop. 1850: 917, '80: 894, 1910: 748, '30: 669.

2. Company storekeeper for manufacturing firm, 62. Timekeeper 15 years. Formerly taught school. Born in Lee, but has lived in Lincoln since he was 30.—F born in Williamsburg, Piscataquis Co., came here when a child; PGF born in Brunswick, Cumberland Co., of Scotch-Irish descent; PGM born in Brunswick. M born here; MGF, MGM born in Otis, Hancock Co.—Graduated from academy here. 6 months of business college in Augusta, Kennebec Co.—I.O.O.F.—Kindly, coöperative, intelligent.—L 128.

418 Town of Waite, Washington Co.

Settled 1832; inc. 1876. A number of people from Charlotte Co., New Brunswick, were among the early settlers.—Rural community in wooded section.—Pop. 1880: 204, 1910: 162, '30: 165.

Housewife, 61. Since she was 20, has lived in Princeton (c. 8 m. southeast).—F born in South Princeton, came here when a year old; PGF born in Gorham, Cumberland Co.; PGM in St. Stephen, New Brunswick. M born in Alexander (c. 18 m. southeast); MGF in St. Stephen, New Brunswick; MGM in Princeton; MGM's M in Scarborough, Cumberland Co., of Irish descent.—School until 15.—Rugged, hardy country woman. Kindly, glad to coöperate. Very honest.—L 136.

420 Town of Houlton, Aroostook Co.

Settled c. 1805 (inc. 1831), by a few men from 212 New Salem, Franklin Co., Mass.—The southern part of Houlton had been granted to New Salem; the northern to Williams College (in 248 Williamstown, Mass.).—Lumbering, then growing of potatoes. U.S. military post here from 1828 to 1847.—County seat. Trading and railroad shipping center for a large agricultural area. Many Canadians and Irish.—Pop. 1820: 115, '50: 1453, '80: 3228, 1910: 5845, '30: 6865.—Barnes, Francis (anon.). The story of Houlton from the public records, and from the experiences of its founders, their descendants and associates to the present time. . . . Houlton, 1889. Gilman, G. H. (anon.). History of the town of Houlton, Maine, from 1804 to 1883, by an old pioneer. 64 p. Haverhill, Mass., 1884.

1. Merchant, bank president, 85.—F born in Roxbury (Boston), Mass., of old stock. M born in New Salem, Franklin Co., Mass., of family originally from Salem, Essex Co., Mass.—School until 14.—Prominent in the town.—Very intelligent. Undertook the interviews from a strict sense of duty.—In FW's opinion, essentially a Mass. type of speech. Voice now somewhat weak and mumbling.—Incomplete record: lacks pp. 1–6, 12–13, 24–25, 42–43, 49, 52–53, 57, 102–103 and scattered items.—L 125.

2. Housewife, 47.—F born here; PGF of Scotch-Irish descent. M born in New Limerick (c. 5 m. west); MGF born in Limerick, York Co. (Informant is descended from the early settlers of New Limerick, which was settled from Limerick, York Co.)—School until 15. Not well educated, but would like to be.—Christian Scientist. Woman's Club.—Has always lived in town and knows nothing of the country.—Speech shows Canadian and Irish influence. Retroflection varies. (Her daughter, aged 10, uses weak retroflection in all positions.) Rather slow tempo.—Incomplete record: only pp. 1–6, 38–41, 45–48, 50–51, 54–56, 59–103.

Supplementary informant: housewife.—Like 2, descended from the early settlers of New Limerick. —Very talkative and friendly. Lapses of memory caused by motor accident.—Archaic type of speech. —Pp. 7–11, 14–23, 26–37. These entries are not starred on the maps.—L 124.

422 Town of Fort Fairfield, Aroostook Co.

Settled 1816 (inc. 1858) from the St. John River Valley in New Brunswick. People here call themselves Americans, not Yankees, and the majority are of New Brunswick origin, of Irish and English descent. The first Yankees came considerably later; they are a separate element in the population.—Agricultural community. Many potato farmers.—Pop. 1850: 401, '80: 2807, 1910: 4381, '30: 5393 (F.F. village 2616).—Ellis, C. H. History of Fort Fairfield and biographical sketches. . . . 382 p. Fort Fairfield, 1894.

1. Farmer, 71.—F born here; PGF born in England, of Irish descent, was an early settler here in 1816; PGM born in England. (PGF had been given land in New Brunswick after the War of 1812.) M born here; MGF probably an Englishman from the St. John Valley.—School until 18.—Church of England. Mason.—Well-to-do. Genial, coöperative. —Old-fashioned speech, rather like that of the Irish in New Brunswick, e.g., strong r. (After the War of 1812 many Irish and English immigrants settled north of Woodstock, N.B., which is c. 45 m. south of here.) [ə] regularly appears in the unstressed syllables of houses, bucket, etc.—L 120.

2. Housewife, 71.—F, a Protestant, born in Dublin, Ireland, was an early settler here. M born here; MGF, a Catholic, born in Ireland, was also an early settler; MGM, of Dutch descent, born in New Brunswick, east of the St. John Valley.—School until 15.—Baptist Church. Grange.—Prosperous, amiable farm woman.—Modern speech. Retroflection variable.—L 119.

423 Town of Ashland, Aroostook Co.

Settled c. 1837 (inc. 1862) from older parts of Me., chiefly the Kennebec Valley.—Trading center of a sparsely settled section. Lumber and potatoes.—Sheridan Plantation annexed in 1901.—Pop. 1880: 505, 1910: 2173, '30: 2198.

Blacksmith, 70. Aged 24, spent 1 year in states of Minnesota and Washington.—F born in Charleston, Penobscot Co.; PGF and PGM moved here from Charleston. M born in Lisbon, Androscoggin Co.; MGF moved here from Lisbon; MGM born there of Scotch descent.—School until 18.—Mason.—Intelligent, agreeable. Typical descendant of American settlers from within the state.—Very little New Brunswick influence in his speech.—L 123.

424 Town of Fort Kent, Aroostook Co.

Settled by French families (Acadians) driven from Canada; inc. 1869. There are comparatively few English-speaking families here; some are of Kennebec Co. origin, some of New Brunswick. The French territory extends south almost to 423 Ashland. (The fort built in 1841 was named for Gov. Kent of Me.)—Lumbering and farming. Bangor and Aroostook R.R. reached here in 1902. Training school for teachers of French schools est. 1878.—Pop. 1880: 1512, 1910: 3710, '30: 4726 (F.K. village 2245).

Merchant, 43.—Entirely of Me. Yankee stock. F born in Lincoln, Penobscot Co.; PGF, PGM born in the state. M born here; MGF, MGM born in the state.—School until 18. Speaks both French and English, but only English at home. (M also bilingual, F spoke English only.)—Mason. Respected by everyone.—Good local type. Quick, intelligent, coöperative.—Rapid tempo. Short vowels, often very short. At times there is something definitely French about his speech, notably in his handling of stress and intonation.—L 126.

New Brunswick, Canada

[The historical notes on the New Brunswick communities are based entirely on **Ganong, W. F.** A Monograph of the Origins of Settlements in the Province of New Brunswick (Proceedings and Transactions of the Royal Society of Canada, series 2, v. 10, section II, 3–185; Ottawa and Toronto, 1905). This study contains also a brief bibliography and maps showing the history of the settlement and the recent distribution of population. It is one of several monographs on New Brunswick by Ganong published in the Proceedings and Transactions of the Royal Society. The Collections of the New Brunswick Historical Society should also be consulted.

The Canadian government has published a number of valuable studies of the resources of this region; see, for example, **Canada, Department of the Interior** (Natural Resources Intelligence Branch). The Province of New Brunswick, its Natural Resources Developed and Undeveloped (92 p. 1921). For local writings, see **McFarlane, W. G.** New Brunswick Bibliography, the Books and Writers of the Province (98 p. St. John, 1895).

The history of the Loyalists is treated in **Sabine, Lorenzo.** The American Loyalists (Ed. 2. 2v. Boston, 1864), and in **Van Tyne, C. H.** The Loyalists in the American Revolution (New York, 1902).

Lowman, who investigated this area for the Atlas, makes the following observations regarding the people of western New Brunswick and their speech:

The majority of the Loyalists came from New York, New Jersey and western Connecticut, but there were some from Pennsylvania and Maryland, and from various parts of New England as well. The speech of this mixed population is much like midwestern American, except that the vowel as in *father, calm, lot, bother* is fully back. The New England 'short o' is exceedingly rare in the St. John Valley.

In both the St. John and the St. Croix regions immigrants who came from Great Britain during the 19. cent. have affected New Brunswick speech. For instance, many Irish settlers occupied the region between 431 Woodstock and 422 Fort Fairfield, Me.; and Harvey in York-Sunbury Co. was settled in 1837 by families from the border country between England and Scotland.

Many people in Charlotte Co. have a strong aversion to English, Scotch and Irish types of speech and prefer what they regard as their own Canadian speech, i.e., the speech of the old Loyalist families. The speech of 412 Calais, Me., they regard as affected.]

426 Parish of St. Stephen, Charlotte Co., N.B.

Parish est. 1786, comprising the New England settlement of Scoodic (on the present site of St. Stephen) and the site of the small French settlement Chartier (est. c. 1695). Scoodic, settled c. 1770, had 9 families in 1779. The present town of St. Stephen was settled chiefly by the Port Matoon Ass'n. of Loyalists, whereas Milltown, adjoining, was settled in 1785 by soldiers of a disbanded Scotch regiment.—St. Stephen was inc. 1871. Located at the head of navigation on the St. Croix R., it developed at first through its lumber trade; now it is a manufacturing center. Close connections with the city of Calais, Maine, (q.v., 412) just across the St. Croix. A number of old British families.—Charlotte Co. (notably St. Stephen, St. Andrews and St. George) is regarded by people living in the St. John Valley as very different from their own region. In the opinion of the FW, it resembles New England, but has strong Scotch and northern Irish elements.—Pop. 1824: 1673, '71: c. 3000, '81: 2338, 1911: 2836, '31: 3437.

Housewife, 87. Taught school for a short time.—F born here; PGF, of Scotch descent, born in northern Ireland. Brought by his mother to N.Y. and bound out to a potter. Enlisted in the British Army during the Revolution. Finally settled here. PGM born in Oak Bay (c. 5 m. east). M born here; MGF in New Boston, Hillsborough Co., N.H., of Scotch-Irish descent. He was a Loyalist and settled here. MGM born in Oak Bay.—School here until 16. Normal school for 3 months in St. John (c. 60 m. east).—Church of England.—Vigorous, intelligent. Thoroughly loyal to the British Isles, though they seem to her as far away and as foreign as they would to a New Englander. Accurate informant.—Deep voice; somewhat fuller, more resonant and friendlier in quality than the usual N.E. voice. Precise articulation. Speech obviously mixed: r in all positions, [ə] in unstressed syllables, but [ɑ] in words like *half*, and the 'New England short o.'—L 91.

427 Parish of St. Croix (Bay Side), Charlotte Co., N.B.

St. Croix was part of St. Andrews parish (est. 1786) until 1874, when it was est. as an independent parish. It was settled 1784–85 by the Penobscot Ass'n. of Loyalists, whose descendants have expanded somewhat to the interior.—Rural, agricultural, sparsely settled.—Pop. 1891: 674, 1911: 462.

Farmer, 77.—F born here; PGF born here in 1789; PGF's F went from Boston, Mass., to Castine, Hancock Co., Me., then came here; PGF's M came here from Castine with the Penobscot Loyalists. M of Scotch descent; MGM born here; MGM's parents from northern Ireland.—Beginning to be affected by old age. Bitter feeling toward England: thinks that the Loyalists backed the wrong cause.—Moderate tempo. Short vowels.—The r sound is distinctly weaker here than in the St. John Valley, though it occurs in all positions.—L 139.

428 Parish of Kingston (White Head), Royal Co., N.B.

Kingston settled 1783 (org. as a parish 1786) by Loyalists from Long Island and from western Conn. —County seat until 1871.—White Head had many Scotch and Irish settlers.—Pop. 1891: 1811, 1911: 1494.

1. Janitor in museum, 53. Worked 24 years for a hardware firm. Has lived in St. John for the last 32 years.—F born here; PGF born in Kingston, of Loyalist stock; PGM from old Loyalist family. M, MGM born in Bayswater; MGF born there, of Scotch descent.—School until 15.—Serious, earnest informant. Not accustomed to do much talking. Sometimes a little slow in grasping what was meant. —Vowels usually short. The vowel as in *hot* tends to be slightly raised and fronted, more so than with most speakers. His retroflex tap *r*, which is very striking in emphatic speech, is probably (according to the FW) of Scotch origin. His *r*-vowel is stronger than that of 2.—L 137.

428 City of St. John, St. John-Albert Co., N.B.

Loyalist city, laid out in 1783 (as the town of Parr) on the then unoccupied peninsula, and settled at once by several thousand Loyalists, chiefly from New York and its vicinity. Later many Irish and some Scotch and English, recently also French-Canadians. (Economic conditions in Ireland sent many people to N.B. during the early 19. cent. The N.B. government encouraged immigrants from Great Britain, often paying their passage and granting them land on easy terms. Ships carrying lumber to England brought many new settlers on their return voyages.)—Inc. as city 1785, when extended to include Carleton. Carleton a Loyalist town founded 1783 on the site of two older settlements: Menagoueche, which had been occupied by the French; and Conway, which had been granted to a company in 1765 and partially settled.—In 1889 the city of Portland was united with St. John. Portland was an early trading village formed at the mouth of the river in 1762 by several men from Newburyport, Essex Co., Mass. It grew slowly until the Loyalists came. Many later immigrants. Est. as parish 1786, as town 1871, as city 1883.—St. John became the seaport for half New Brunswick and grew steadily into an important commercial center. County seat.— Pop. 1824: 8488, '71: 41,325, '91: 39,179, 1911: 42,511, '31: 47,514.

2. CULTURED INFORMANT. Housewife, 52.—F born here; PGF born here, of N.Y. Loyalist family; PGM born in West St. John; PGM's F born there, of N.Y. Loyalist family. M born in Petite Rivière, Nova Scotia, came here when young; MGF in Trois Rivières, Quebec, of English descent; MGM in Louth, Lincolnshire, England.—School (including high school) until 17.—Church of England.—Talkative, friendly, coöperative.—Cultivated local speech. Rather quiet, gentle way of speaking. Vowels not lengthened. Use of low central [ɑ] in *father, calm*, instead of the low-back vowel which the FW found usual here among all classes, may be due to her English ancestry or may be an affectation. Her low-back vowel, as in *hot*, tends to be weakly rounded. The *r*-vowel is neither strong nor long. Her use of retroflex tap *r* medially is not universal here (probably of Scotch or northern Irish origin).—L 138.

429 Parish of Hampstead (Elm Hill), Royal Co., N.B.

Parish est. 1786; settled by Loyalists in 1784–85 along the St. John R. Later immigrants went to the interior.—Negro settlement at Otnabog (Elm Hill), a small rural community. According to local tradition, the settlers were former slaves from Virginia and came c. 1812, presumably with the Loyalists. (FW thinks some of the people may be descended from the slaves of the N.Y. Loyalists.) The Otnabog grants were made in 1830.—Pop. 1891: 1130, 1911: 985.

Housewife, negress, 79. Aged 9 to 15, lived in Woodsville near Lower Hampstead; then returned here.—F born here; PGF born in N.Y., came here as a freeman with the Loyalists. M, MGF, MGM born in this region near Grand Lake; MGF's F born in N.Y., came here as a freeman.—Went to school here, but not in Woodsville.—Local contacts entirely.—Kind, obliging, poor. Very religious. Has quiet spiritual fervor and is naturally devout.— Moderate tempo. Vowels of moderate length. The vowel as in *hot* is low-back and slightly rounded; the vowel as in *father* either low-back or low-central. —Incomplete record: only pp. 7–11, 14–23, 26–69.— L 134.

430 Parish of Southampton (Lower Southampton), York-Sunbury Co., N.B.

Parish est. 1833. Settled by a disbanded Loyalist regiment from Pennsylvania and by other Loyalist families. From the St. John R. the settlement gradually expanded into the back country.—Rural community.—Pop. 1891: 2310, 1911: 2194.

Farmer, 72.—Loyalist ancestry on both sides. F, PGF born here; PGF's F born in New Brunswick; latter's parents born in England or Holland; PGM born here; PGM's F born in Kennebunk, York Co., Me.; PGM's GGF born in Nash Co., No. Carolina. Latter's F from Devonshire, England, said to be a descendant of Sir Francis Drake. M born here; MGF in St. John; MGM in Southampton.—School here.— Baptist. Has occasionally preached in this region.— Simple, kindly, religious. Mind beginning to fail.— Slow, soft, gentle utterance. Remembers having heard 'short o' in words like *coat*.—Incomplete record: only pp. 7–11, 14–23, 26–48, and scattered items.—L 132.

431 Parish of Brighton (Hartland), Victoria-Carleton Co., N.B.

Settled mostly between 1800 and 1812, by expansion from the lower St. John Valley. Parish est. 1830.—Rural community.—Pop. 1891: 2382, 1911: 2605.

1. Manufacturer, 76. A miller for 29 years.—F born in York-Sunbury Co., New Brunswick; PGF of German origin, PGM of English origin, both born in Bronx Co., N.Y.; M born in Fredericton (c. 50 m. southeast); MGF from England.—School until 20.—Baptist. Town officer. Belongs to Canadian Order of Foresters.—Glad to assist in anything he considered educational.—Loud, hearty voice. Slow tempo. Long vowels and diphthongs.—L 130.

431 Parish of Woodstock, Victoria-Carleton Co., N.B.

Parish est. 1786. Settled first along the St. John in 1784 by disbanded Loyalist regiments: the King's American Regiment below Meductic, and Delancey's Brigade above it. The interior was settled by expansion from these and other Loyalist settlements on the St. John. (Meductic, located at what is now Lower Woodstock, was the most important Indian village of the St. John R. in the late 17. and early 18. cent. Excellent fishing. Grantees allowed the Indians to remain there until a reservation was bought for them in 1851.)—The town of Woodstock grew up with the lumber industry on the Meduxnekeag after 1817 (inc. 1856). Prosperous farming center.—Pop. 1824: 816, '71: c. 2000, '91: 3288, 1911: 3856, '31: 3259.

2. Farmer, 57. Aged 23 to 24, spent 1½ years in Yukon region, Alaska. Lives 2 or 3 m. out of Woodstock on a farm which accommodates tourists.—F, PGF born here; PGF's F born on Staten Island, N.Y.; latter's F born in Essex, England; his M of a French Huguenot family on Staten Island; PGF's M, of English descent, born in Stamford, Fairfield Co., Conn.; PGM born in St. John; PGM's F born in New Rochelle, Westchester Co., N.Y., of Huguenot descent. M, MGF born in York-Sunbury Co., New Brunswick; MGF's F born in Stamford. Conn., descendant of first settlers there; MGF's M born in N.Y. state, went to live in St. John; MGM born in Kingston; MGM's F born in Norwalk, Fairfield Co., Conn.; MGM's M born in St. John; latter's F born in Conn.; her M born in Stamford, Conn.—School here until 14; then 1 year of high school in Fredericton (c. 50 m. southeast). Reads considerably. Much interested in history.—Church of England. Proud of his Loyalist ancestry.—Very intelligent and coöperative.—L 131.

NAMES OF THE COMMUNITIES

Connecticut

1 Stamford-Greenwich
3 Bridgeport-Westport
4 Weston
6 Milford
8 Danbury-Bethel
10 Southbury
11 New Fairfield
12 New Milford
14 Wolcott
16 Litchfield
18 Cornwall
19 Sharon
20 Farmington
21 Hartland
22 Winchester
23 Granby
24 Simsbury
26 New Haven
28 Guilford-Madison
29 Killingworth
30 Old Saybrook
31 East Lyme
32 New London
33 Norwich-Bozrah
34 Stonington
36 Wallingford
38 Middletown
40 Hartford
41 Glastonbury
42 Hebron
43 Windham
44 Somers
45 East Windsor
46 Tolland
48 Canterbury
49 Woodstock-Pomfret

Long Island

50 Southold
51 Easthampton-
   Southampton

Rhode Island

52 New Shoreham
   (Block Island)
54 Richmond
56 Narragansett - South
   Kingstown
57 South Kingstown
58 East Greenwich -
   North Kingstown
60 Newport
62 Middletown
64 Portsmouth
80 Providence
81 East Providence
82 Foster

Massachusetts

102 Westport
103 Fall River
104 Rehoboth

106 Taunton-Raynham
108 Bridgewater
110 Hanover
112 Plymouth
113 Wareham
114 Rochester
115 Falmouth
116 Barnstable
117 Harwich
118 Chatham
119 Eastham
120 Truro
122 West Tisbury -
    Chilmark
123 Edgartown
124 Nantucket
125 Nantucket
140 Wrentham-Norfolk
141 Foxborough
142 Sharon
146 Hingham-Cohasset
150 Boston
152 Weston
154 Sherborn
156 Concord
158 Burlington
160 Billerica
180 Marblehead
182 Beverly
184 Topsfield
190 Haverhill
194 Newbury
196 Rowley
198 Essex
200 Rockport
201 Uxbridge - Mendon
202 Oxford - Charlton
203 Marlborough
204 Shrewsbury
205 Worcester
206 Spencer
207 Sterling
208 Templeton
209 Lunenburg
210 Winchendon
211 Groton
212 New Salem
214 Northfield-Gill
218 Hardwick
219 Granby
220 Palmer
221 Monson
222 Holland
224 Springfield
225 Southampton
226 Northampton
228 Deerfield
230 Colrain
232 Cummington
233 Middlefield
234 Blandford
235 Granville
236 New Marlborough
238 Egremont
239 Alford

240 Stockbridge
241 Lenox
242 Pittsfield
246 Cheshire
248 Williamstown

Vermont

252 Bennington-
    Shaftsbury
254 Wilmington
256 Brattleboro
257 Newfane
258 Rockingham
259 Andover
260 Pawlet-Dorset
262 West Rutland -
    Castleton
264 Wallingford
265 Mount Holly
266 Plymouth
268 Windsor
271 Stockbridge
272 Northfield
274 Cornwall
276 Ferrisburg
278 Huntington
280 Burlington-Charlotte
281 South Burlington
282 Calais
284 Johnson
286 Enosburg
288 Troy
290 Lemington
292 St. Johnsbury -
    Lyndon
294 Ryegate
296 Newbury-Topsham

New Hampshire

302 Seabrook
304 Rye
306 Lee
307 Barrington
308 Kingston
310 Belmont-Loudon
312 Laconia-Gilford
314 Webster
315 Concord
316 Candia-Deerfield
318 Derry-Londonderry
320 Bedford-Amherst
322 Francestown - New
    Boston
324 Antrim
328 Keene-Marlow
330 Charlestown
331 Goshen
332 Newport
333 Wilmot-Sutton
334 Canaan
335 Hanover
336 Lyme
337 Orford
338 Plymouth

340 Haverhill
342 Lancaster
344 Columbia
346 Shelburne
348 Conway

Maine

352 York
354 Kennebunkport
356 Biddeford
357 Acton
358 Shapleigh
359 Cape Elizabeth
360 Portland
362 Standish
363 Limington
364 Yarmouth
366 Casco
368 Denmark
370 Woodstock
372 Hanover
373 Newry
374 New Portland
376 Farmington
377 Turner
378 Webster
380 Brunswick-Topsham
382 Harpswell
384 Waldoboro-Nobleboro
386 Farmingdale-Pittston
388 China
390 Skowhegan-
    Norridgewock
391 Newport
392 Dover-Foxcroft
394 Rockland - Owls
    Head
396 Searsport-Frankfort
398 Bluehill
400 Tremont - Southwest
    Harbor
402 Ellsworth-Penobscot
403 Holden
404 Brewer
406 Gouldsboro
407 Jonesport
408 Machias - Roque
    Bluffs
410 Lubec
411 Perry
412 Calais
416 Lincoln-Lee
418 Waite
420 Houlton
422 Fort Fairfield
423 Ashland
424 Fort Kent

New Brunswick

426 St. Stephen
427 St. Croix
428 St. John - Kingston
429 Hampstead
430 Southampton
431 Woodstock-Brighton

PLATE 1

Red arrows: lines of expansion from the early eastern settlements

Green arrows: lines of expansion from the early western settlements

Red shading: infusion of eastern population in the western area

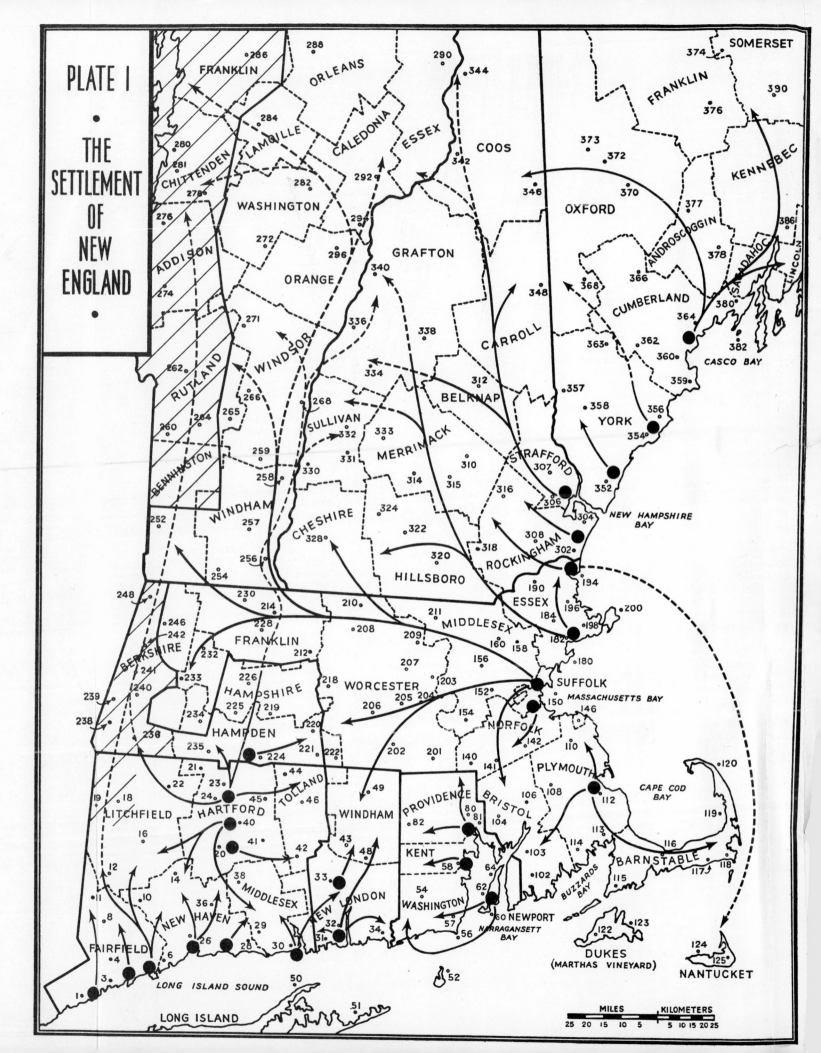

PLATE 1

THE SETTLEMENT OF NEW ENGLAND

NAMES OF THE COMMUNITIES

Connecticut

1 Stamford-Greenwich
3 Bridgeport-Westport
4 Weston
6 Milford
8 Danbury-Bethel
10 Southbury
11 New Fairfield
12 New Milford
14 Wolcott
16 Litchfield
18 Cornwall
19 Sharon
20 Farmington
21 Hartland
22 Winchester
23 Granby
24 Simsbury
26 New Haven
28 Guilford-Madison
29 Killingworth
30 Old Saybrook
31 East Lyme
32 New London
33 Norwich-Bozrah
34 Stonington
36 Wallingford
38 Middletown
40 Hartford
41 Glastonbury
42 Hebron
43 Windham
44 Somers
45 East Windsor
46 Tolland
48 Canterbury
49 Woodstock-Pomfret

Long Island

50 Southold
51 Easthampton-
    Southampton

Rhode Island

52 New Shoreham
    (Block Island)
54 Richmond
56 Narragansett - South
    Kingstown
57 South Kingstown
58 East Greenwich -
    North Kingstown
60 Newport
62 Middletown
64 Portsmouth
80 Providence
81 East Providence
82 Foster

Massachusetts

102 Westport
103 Fall River
104 Rehoboth
106 Taunton-Raynham
108 Bridgewater
110 Hanover
112 Plymouth
113 Wareham
114 Rochester
115 Falmouth
116 Barnstable
117 Harwich
118 Chatham
119 Eastham
120 Truro
122 West Tisbury -
    Chilmark
123 Edgartown
124 Nantucket
125 Nantucket
140 Wrentham-Norfolk
141 Foxborough
142 Sharon
146 Hingham-Cohasset
150 Boston
152 Weston
154 Sherborn
156 Concord
158 Burlington
160 Billerica
180 Marblehead
182 Beverly
184 Topsfield
190 Haverhill
194 Newbury
196 Rowley
198 Essex
200 Rockport
201 Uxbridge - Mendon
202 Oxford - Charlton
203 Marlborough
204 Shrewsbury
205 Worcester
206 Spencer
207 Sterling
208 Templeton
209 Lunenburg
210 Winchendon
211 Groton
212 New Salem
214 Northfield-Gill
218 Hardwick
219 Granby
220 Palmer
221 Monson
222 Holland
224 Springfield
225 Southampton
226 Northampton
228 Deerfield
230 Colrain
232 Cummington
233 Middlefield
234 Blandford
235 Granville
236 New Marlborough
238 Egremont
239 Alford

240 Stockbridge
241 Lenox
242 Pittsfield
246 Cheshire
248 Williamstown

Vermont

252 Bennington-
    Shaftsbury
254 Wilmington
256 Brattleboro
257 Newfane
258 Rockingham
259 Andover
260 Pawlet-Dorset
262 West Rutland -
    Castleton
264 Wallingford
265 Mount Holly
266 Plymouth
268 Windsor
271 Stockbridge
272 Northfield
274 Cornwall
276 Ferrisburg
278 Huntington
280 Burlington-Charlotte
281 South Burlington
282 Calais
284 Johnson
286 Enosburg
288 Troy
290 Lemington
292 St. Johnsbury -
    Lyndon
294 Ryegate
296 Newbury-Topsham

New Hampshire

302 Seabrook
304 Rye
306 Lee
307 Barrington
308 Kingston
310 Belmont-Loudon
312 Laconia-Gilford
314 Webster
315 Concord
316 Candia-Deerfield
318 Derry-Londonderry
320 Bedford-Amherst
322 Francestown - New
    Boston
324 Antrim
328 Keene-Marlow
330 Charlestown
331 Goshen
332 Newport
333 Wilmot-Sutton
334 Canaan
335 Hanover
336 Lyme
337 Orford
338 Plymouth

340 Haverhill
342 Lancaster
344 Columbia
346 Shelburne
348 Conway

Maine

352 York
354 Kennebunkport
356 Biddeford
357 Acton
358 Shapleigh
359 Cape Elizabeth
360 Portland
362 Standish
363 Limington
364 Yarmouth
366 Casco
368 Denmark
370 Woodstock
372 Hanover
373 Newry
374 New Portland
376 Farmington
377 Turner
378 Webster
380 Brunswick-Topsham
382 Harpswell
384 Waldoboro-Nobleboro
386 Farmingdale-Pittston
388 China
390 Skowhegan-
    Norridgewock
391 Newport
392 Dover-Foxcroft
394 Rockland - Owls
    Head
396 Searsport-Frankfort
398 Bluehill
400 Tremont - Southwest
    Harbor
402 Ellsworth-Penobscot
403 Holden
404 Brewer
406 Gouldsboro
407 Jonesport
408 Machias - Roque
    Bluffs
410 Lubec
411 Perry
412 Calais
416 Lincoln-Lee
418 Waite
420 Houlton
422 Fort Fairfield
423 Ashland
424 Fort Kent

New Brunswick

426 St. Stephen
427 St. Croix
428 St. John - Kingston
429 Hampstead
430 Southampton
431 Woodstock-Brighton

PLATE 2

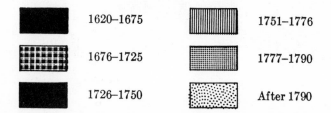

1620–1675
1676–1725
1726–1750
1751–1776
1777–1790
After 1790

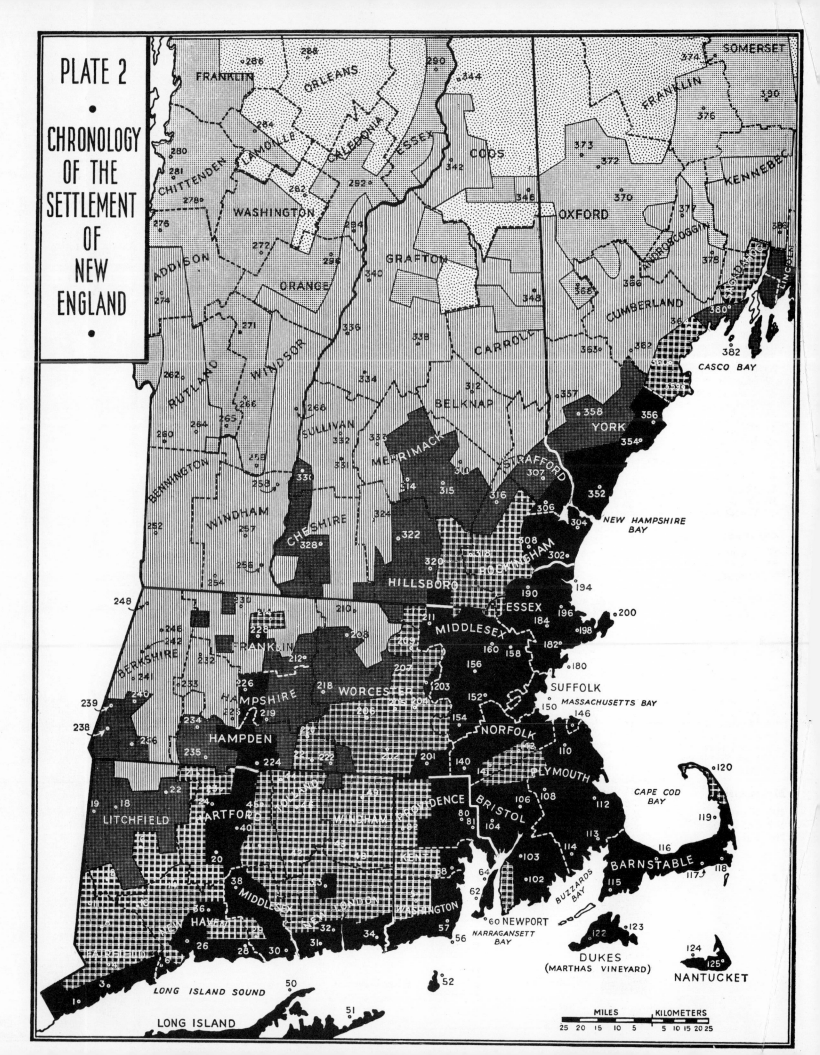

PLATE 2

CHRONOLOGY OF THE SETTLEMENT OF NEW ENGLAND